READINGS IN AMERICAN NAVAL

HISTORY

SEVENTH EDITION

EDITED BY HISTORY DEPARTMENT

UNITED STATES NAVAL ACADEMY

Readings in American Naval History, Seventh Edition

Permissions Department
Academx Publishing Services, Inc.
P.O. Box 56527
Virginia Beach, VA 23456

Printed in the United States of America

ISBN-10: 1-60036-384-9
ISBN-13: 978-1-60036-384-9

Contents

C H A P T E R O N E

Life in the Age of Sail

Ernest Prothero

FOCUS QUESTIONS

1. Describe the types of guns aboard a ship-of-the-line and purposes for each of the munitions they fired.
2. How was life as a midshipman during the Age of Sail different from today?
3. What were the medical challenges for a ship's surgeon?
4. What types of men joined the naval service?
5. What were some of the disciplinary measures available during the Age of Sail?

The chief royal shipbuilding yards were at Chatham, Deptford, Woolwich, Plymouth, and Devonport. The first-rates and other big vessels were built in dry dock and floated out, while the smaller ones were built on slips that sloped down to the water's edge. Reference has been made to the effect open-air building had on the timbers of ships. In later times they were constructed under cover, which gave vessels much longer lives; the modern warship is built in the open, but as wood forms no part of the hull, the weather effects are practically *nil*.

"Hearts of Oak," indeed, were our wooden walls, for to build even a 74-gun ship, the third-rate, of which our Navy contained so many, from 1500 to 2000 oak trees were needed. There was no wonder that British oak grew scarcer and more costly, and we had to requisition oak of foreign growth, that was less lasting than our native variety. The sheathing of vessels below the waterline was one of the greatest problems of the shipbuilder; and he tried various expedients to defeat the ravages of the teredo worm that was a special enemy of oak. Sheathing with lead was a device even of the ancients, but our builders found it too heavy, and in any case it was not very effective. A common and fairly efficacious method was to put on a layer of pitch, upon which was plastered brown paper, short hair and tar, which was then covered with a thin planking of deal, which wood was least to the liking of the teredo. About the middle of the eighteenth century a 32-gun frigate was given a sheathing of thin sheets of copper. This not only repelled the teredo worm, but the ship's bottom was less subject to the accumulation of barnacles, etc., that often impeded the speed of a ship with a wooden bottom by several knots an hour. But copper sheathing was found to have its disadvantages, for it corroded the heads of all the iron bolts with which it came in contact. This was avoided by first using a thin sheathing of wood to prevent the direct contact of the copper with the bolts. Later, copper bolts were employed instead of iron, and copper sheathing became general, not only in the Navy, but also in the merchant service.

At one time masts were made from single trees, but now they generally were built up of two or more pieces of fir, secured together with iron hoops. At the royal yards were kept immense stocks of masts, spars, sails, etc., suitable for all rates, which were built as like as possible; and thus a mast or spar of any one 74, for example, would fit any other 74 in the service. Theoretically the idea was quite sound, but it broke down largely in practice; for the simple reason that many of our really best ships had been captured from enemies, and taken into our own service, and for these our stock sizes of gear were useless. The French ships, as a rule, were bigger and faster than our own; they possessed larger batteries; and their lowest tier of guns was higher in order to fight them in rough weather; whereas in most English ships, the lower deck-ports could not be opened in a rough sea without danger of swamping the ship. Fortunately for us, the French did not pay equal attention to the effectiveness of their guns, or many of our battles with them would have ended far differently.

An English first-rate line-of-battle ship measured from 2000 to 2600 tons; length of lower gun-deck about 180 feet; armament, 100 or more guns, with a broadside capacity of about 2500 lbs.; crew, about 900 men; cost of ship, exclusive of guns, from £70,000 to £100,000. Second-rates mounted 90 to 98 guns; tonnage about 2000; crew 750. Third-rates mounted 64, 74 or 80 guns, with broadsides of from 1200 to about 2000 lbs., but not exceeding the last-named figure; the displacement varied from 1300 to 2000 tons; and the crews ranged from 500 to 750 men. Fourth-rates mounted 50 guns; fifth-rates from 32 to 44 guns; and sixth-rates from 20 to 28 guns.

The external painting of our warships varied, but generally the chief features were somewhat as follows. Just above the copper sheathing a wide black line ran right round the ship, and above this the sides were yellow or brownish, the port lids being of the same colour; the upper works above the gun-decks mainly showed a vivid red or blue; but Nelson adopted a different style, changing the brown or yellow of the sides and outer port-lids to black, with streaks of yellow to mark each gun-deck. This style became known as the "Nelson Chequer." Round the forecastle there was a scarlet or pale blue band with an edging of gold, and this was continued down the beak to the figure-head. The stern generally presented a most ornate appearance, there being a wealth of elaborately-gilded carving, in which cherubs and the like found a prominent place, together with red and blue and green and gold devices, such as the royal arms, wreaths, cornocupias, etc. The ship's figure-head was sometimes suggested by the name of the ship, although often as not it was a ramping red lion, not necessarily very true to nature, or an allegorical figure, more or less difficult to trace. The seamen generally took a great pride in the figure-head, keeping it in good repair, and its paint and gilt constantly fresh.

The interiors of ships were painted largely according to the fancy of the captain, but the sides of the gun decks were almost invariably of a blood-red colour, so that during an action gruesome splashes would not show more than could be avoided. As the inner port-lids were of this colour, when they were thrown open, the scarlet squares well diversified the sides of the ship. Guns and gun-carriages were red or chocolate. Top masts and upper spars generally showed dark brown, with the yards and gaffs black. English masts were often painted white before an engagement, in order not to confound them, in the battle smoke, with the French, who usually painted their masts black.

The terms three-decker and two-decker referred only to complete gun-decks, and in both types of ship guns were carried also on the forecastle and quarter-deck. Dealing with a three-decker and commencing at the bottom, we will take the several decks in order. The orlop deck, which was a non-fighting deck immediately above the hold, was several feet below the water line. It was a gloomy hole lighted only by a few scuttles in the sides of the ship, and by miserable rush-lights in tin sconces or lanterns, which served for little more than to make the darkness visible. The senior midshipmen, master's and surgeon's mates slung their hammocks in the after-cockpit, which was of considerable size; for it was in this part of the ship that the wounded received attention during and after an action. The table which was fixed in the middle of the berth was not only for mess purposes, but was the surgeon's operating table. Near by the after-cockpit were cabins for the junior lieutenants, surgeon's, purser's and captain's stewards. In the fore-cockpit were the cabins and store-rooms of the boatswain and carpenter. The greater part of the ship's carpentering was done in the daylight on the upper deck, but in the carpenter's quarters were tools and materials for stopping shot holes, etc. The boatswain's storeroom contained everything necessary for refitting and repairing rigging, etc. On the orlop deck, too, were racks in which the seamen stowed their bags, and the marines their chests. Amidships was the sail-room, and also great racks where the cables were coiled, when the ship weighed anchor. The spirit room was sometimes near the after-cockpit, but as often as not it was in the after-hold.

Below the orlop deck were the powder magazines, one fore and one aft, in the hold. These were far below the water line. In the bulkheads of the magazines were built small chambers with windows in which were placed lanterns; thus the magazine was lighted safely from without. The floors and sides of the magazines were covered with thick felt, and anyone entering these rooms had to wear felt slippers; and also had to see that his pockets contained no metal of any kind that could strike and give rise to a spark. The fore-magazine was the larger of the two. Casks of powder were stowed in rows one above the other. Here the cartridges were filled with loose powder, and here were kept the hand grenades, musket cartridges, as well as the cartridges for the 32-pounders on the lower gun-deck.

In most-ships there was a hoist from this magazine to the orlop, and thus the boys ("powder monkeys"), who carried the explosives to where they were needed, did not have to go into the magazine. The after-magazine was a storeroom used for the cartridges for the 18- and 24-pounders on the upper deck, as well as for the guns or carronades on the forecastle and quarter-deck. The hatches leading from the orlop to the magazines were always guarded by a marine sentry, and during an engagement by a guard with fixed bayonets, or by midshipmen armed with pistols.

Between the two magazines was the hold, which contained the ballast, provision casks, water casks, etc. The ballast generally was gravel, through which water would drain into the well from which it could be pumped out. Even the best of ships made a lot of water by way of the lower ports, which seldom were quite water-tight. But not infrequently the seams sprung, and, in fact, sometimes a ship was in such a rickety state, that a stout cable was wound round her for six or seven turns in order to hold her timbers together. Very often this state of affairs was due to dry rot, to which some of the foreign timber, which we used when our native supplies commenced to run short, was very subject. When Anson was rounding Cape Horn in the "Centurion" the vessel grew loose in her upper works, leaking at every seam, so that even the officers seldom slept in a dry bed. The "Portland" a 50-gun ship in Hawke's squadron, did not possess a dry sleeping place for anybody when it rained. This vessel was dismasted during a storm, and when the stumps of the mast were removed they crumbled into powder. Yet the ship was not broken up; she was repaired, and took part in Hawke's famous action with the French off Ushant.

The insanitary conditions on board ship were terrible, and the men had to put up with "undrinkable beer; bad beef, putrid pork, maggoty biscuit and indescribable water." Even as late as the year 1800, Vice-Admiral Lovell complained that "the bread was full of maggots and weevils, the flour musty and swarming with insects, the water so putrid, thick and stinking, that often I held my nose with my hand, while I drank it strained through my pocket-handkerchief."

From the time of the Armada, every man and boy in the Navy was allowed a gallon of beer a day, a quart for the morning, a quart at dinner, a quart in the afternoon, and a quart in the evening. Even for men who required plenty of sustaining food and drink, this might seem a very liberal allowance of liquid, but if it were bad, it would have been better had there been less of it. During a protracted voyage in the days when preservatives were practically unknown, even with the best of care it would be difficult to keep eatables and drinkables in good condition, but when it was a fact that the fish, flesh, biscuit, peas, meal, etc. were generally kept in the hold, nearest to the poisonous, fever-breeding vapours that arose from the bilge water, one ceases to wonder that the food and drink took to themselves highly undesirable qualities. And this without taking into account that rascally contractors dumped aboard the ship provisions of doubtful quality, even before the voyage commenced.

Above the orlop was the first, or lower gun-deck. On this deck, in the "Victory" for example, were thirty 32-pounders. This deck was the strongest and most roomy; and as it was the scene of the fiercest fighting, it was the principal deck of the ship. The gun-room, the quarters of the gunner and his mess, was right aft; the gun-room was also the armoury, where were stored the muskets, pistols and cutlasses. The chief gunner was supposed to keep an eye on the younger midshipmen, who generally slung their hammocks in the gun-room. If the vessel carried cattle, sheep or pigs, they were usually penned amidships on this lower deck, which did not add to the comfort of the large number of men who ate and slept on the same deck. It was almost as dark here as on the orlop deck below, for even when the weather was only moderately bad, the port-lids had to be closed. Amidships were the racks containing the 32 lb. shot for the guns.

Next above the lower-deck was the middle-deck, carrying twenty-eight 24-pounders; and above that, the upper deck carrying thirty 18-pounders. In a two-decker, there was no middle-deck, but the names of the others were the same as in a three-decker. The upper-deck was upper only between the fore- and the mainmasts; for before the foremast it carried the forecastle; and abaft the main-mast it carried the quarter-deck, above which was the poop, reached by short ladders from the quarter-deck. The quarter-deck and forecastle nominally carried twelve 12-pounders to make up the complement of a hundred guns, but in actual practice, carronades of large calibre often were substituted for the 12-pounders.

The guns were classified according to the weight of the balls they threw; the old names such as are given on page 101 were no longer employed. For a long time we had used a gun that threw a 42-pound shot, but the discharge of a gun so ponderous shocked and strained the timbers of a vessel, and it had to be abolished. From 1790, our biggest gun was the 32-pounder. It was from 8 to 9½ feet long and weighed from 50 to 55 cwts. The powder charge was 10 or 11 lbs. in weight. The point blank range was less than 400 yards; and the extreme range, at about 10° elevation, was nearly 3000 yards. The 24-pounder varied in length from 6 feet to 9½ feet and the weight from 31 cwts. to 50 cwt. The powder charge was from 6 to 8 lbs. The point blank range was from 220 to 300 yards, and extreme range 2870 yards. The 18-pounder varied from 51 to 8½ feet in length; weight from 27 to 42 cwts.; and the powder charge and the range were about the same as the 24-pounder. The 9- and 12-pounders, which were as light as 25 cwts., and not heavier than 34 cwts., threw their shots 300 yards at point blank range, or 1800 yards at a 6° elevation.

Carronades, so called because they were first made at Carron, came into use about 1780. They were short and squat, from 2 to 5 feet long, and throwing balls from 6 to 12 lbs. in weight. Being light guns, they were particularly suited to the forecastle and quarter-deck, and the biggest of them could be worked by four men. Owing to their shortness, the point blank range of carronade guns was small. At a 4° elevation a 32-pounder gun had a range of about a mile, but a 32-pounder carronade not much more than half that distance. But the latter was infinitely more destructive, so much so, that it was known as the "devil gun." Swivel guns, that were so often used in the tops, threw a ½-pound shot.

The missiles fired by guns and carronades were cast-iron round-shot; leaden shot was perhaps more effective, but too expensive. Being stored in the hold, the shot were subject to rust and they had to be scraped, or they would not enter the muzzles of the guns. Grape shot consisted of a bag of 2-lb. shot, a bag containing sixteen for a 32-pounder, and fewer for the smaller guns. These discharges were very effective against rigging and did much towards bringing down masts. Case, or canister, shot consisted of musket balls, or ½-pound shot packed in tin cylinders. At short range it was murderous, but at a greater distance it spread out and lost its effectiveness. Chain-shot was designed specially against masts and sails; it consisted of two shots joined together with a piece of iron chain. Langridge was a cylinder made up of scraps of old iron, chain, nuts, bolts, etc. For dismantling sails, etc., iron bars of about 2 feet long were bound together. When vessels were engaged alongside each other, or in close action generally, the powder charge was reduced, for a shot fired thus would only just penetrate a hull, but would have a more splintering effect than one which passed clean through the timber at greater velocity.

In loading a gun, the powder cartridge was inserted by way of the muzzle, by means of a long-handled shovel, the head of which was something like a cylindrical spoon. When the cartridge was thrust into its place, the shovel needed but to be turned over to be free for withdrawal. A wad of rope yarn was then rammed home upon the charge. The shot followed, and was rammed home with a wad of wood wrapped round with yarn. The captain of the gun then thrust his priming-iron, which was a kind of corkscrew apparatus, down the touch-hole, and cut through the cartridge. From his priming-box he took a priming-tube, which contained mealed powder mixed with spirits of wine, and placed it in the touch-hole with its sharp end entering into the cartridge. In place of the priming-tube, sometimes mealed powder was poured from a powder horn into the touch-hole, some of the powder being laid in a little train in a channel cut in the gun. The charge was fired by means of a match, which consisted of twisted cotton wicks soaked in lye, that would keep alight for hours. The wicks, twisted about a short staff, made what was commonly called a linstock. When the match was applied to the train, the gunner had to spring back smartly to avoid the spurt of flame that came from the vent. Towards the end of the eighteenth century guns were fitted with flint locks, and the gun fired by a spark struck from a flint on to the train containing the priming powder. Although the flint-lock arrangement was safer, easier and quicker than the old match style, for a long time sailors disliked the innovation. It was not until a ship using flint-locks made remarkably good practice at the battle of the Nile that the seamen were convinced of their superiority. The recoil of the guns was very violent, sometimes being lifted up to the beams above; and in action many men were killed or maimed from this cause.

The small arms in use in the Navy were much handier than in former times. The marines used the musket, with a smooth-bore barrel of 1-inch diameter. It was a flint-lock, muzzle-loader with a sure range of little more than 100 yards, although it might kill at twice that distance. The seamen were trained to use this weapon, too. The musketoon was a big bore with a bell mouth, something like a blunderbuss. The ball weighed from 5 to 7½ ozs. This weapon kicked forcibly and was little used except against boarders. The pistols were cumbrous, especially if they had more than one barrel. Boarders usually carried two of the weapons, throwing them down as soon as emptied, for there was no time to reload, and then going for the enemy with cutlass, boarding-axe, or boarding-pike. The last named was a stout ash staff ending in a metal spike; the whole pike, or halberd, about 8 feet long, with a metal head, half axe, half spear, was still carried by the sergeant of marines.

During action, a gundeck was "a most infernal scene of slaughter, fire, smoke, and uproar." If the ship were engaged on both sides, as was often the case, there would be thirty-two guns in two rows flashing, thundering and recoiling. In a first- or second-rate, only a few feet above, was another deck with its similar pandemonium. Add to these the roar of the carronades on the upper works; the marines firing their muskets, and the swivels at work in the tops. Nor was this all. At rapid intervals, if the enemy were doing good work, there would be the thunderous smashes of their shot as they came home. Men stripped to the waist, working and fighting like demons, wounded men screaming, blocks and spars and rigging, if not masts, coming down with crashes all combined to make a frightful racket. The foul smoke from the black powder came up the hatches, as if from factory chimneys; in some places or other the ship was on fire, happily only to be extinguished before it made headway. In the thick of the fight the cock-pit men were picking up and carrying off the wounded, heaving dead or dying men overboard out of the way. The decks literally ran with blood and had to be sanded to afford foothold for those who still maintained the fight. All told, a ship in action, burning perhaps 1000 lbs. of powder a minute, was like some nether pit with the furies run mad; a demoniacal scene that no pen can adequately describe.

It has been mentioned already that the seamen were berthed on the lower deck: the marines occupied the middle deck in a first-rate, but in a two-decker they joined the seamen on the lower deck. On each of the decks above the lower gun-deck the after-parts were partitioned off to provide living rooms for the officers. The principal cabin was in the after-part of the living deck, and on a flagship this was set apart for the admiral, while the captain's cabin was under the poop, where the first lieutenant, master, and the admiral's secretary also had their cabins. When there was no admiral on board, the captain occupied the better accommodation in the top part of the upper deck. This principal cabin was divided into the fore-cabin and the after-cabin, the latter being the private apartment of the admiral or captain. The fore-cabin was a meeting room for councils of war, court-martials, etc. The after-part of a middle deck in a three-decker, or the after-part of the upper deck in a two-decker, contained the ward-room, which was the general cabin and mess of the lieutenants, marine officers, master, surgeon, chaplain and purser. In some cases the chaplain messed with the captain, but not at all infrequently neither the captain, nor the occupants of the ward-room, would have anything to do with him, in which case the "sky-pilot" had to mess alone in his own cabin.

It must be remembered that the officers' quarters were portions of the gun-decks and in even the sleeping cabins the occupants had grim guns for company. When a ship was cleared for action, the bulkheads on the gun-decks were taken down and stowed below, and thither went all furniture and everything movable. Each deck thus became an unobstructed gun platform, with nothing to incommode the gunners, or which could be struck into splinters to the danger of the men. When a ship was taken by surprise, and all too little time to prepare for the enemy, everything movable would be thrown overboard through the ports. More than once the French suffered for failing to clear their decks completely. At the battle of Dominica they stowed their mess gear, and even cattle, on the offside of the deck. But when Rodney broke through their line, it was the offside guns that the French needed, and they could not be worked on account of the *impedimenta.* Rodney was enabled to pound the enemy with shot to which they could not reply; and as the English missiles smashed up the bulkheads, tables, stools, etc., the decks were filled with flying splinters, that carried wounds, if not death, with them. To add to the horrors of the scene were the mutilated and stampeding cattle. Such a lesson should have been unforgettable, yet at the battle of the Nile, many of the French ships had failed to clear their decks, although this was probably due to the fact that they did not expect the attack to commence until the morrow. They had no cattle aboard upon that occasion. The British ships had brought a few animals with them from Syracuse, but they were promptly dropped over the sides out of the way.

It was nothing uncommon for war vessels in these days to carry quite a large number of cattle and sheep in order to supply fresh meat for the crew. For health's sake it was necessary to pay the greatest attention to the cleanliness of the stalls and pens. This was not a very difficult matter in the case of poultry, which were frequently kept aboard for the use of the principal officers. It is related that a second lieutenant, who was a great stickler for cleanliness gave a goose a coating of whitewash, and coal-tarred its beak and legs. Years afterwards, when the young officer had risen to senior captain, he had an unexpected reminder of the incident. He was taking his seat in a stall at the opera house,

Valetta, when a breezy voice from amongst the gods inquired, "Who white-washed the goose?"

Sometimes a goat was shipped to supply the admiral with milk. Needless to say the animal speedily became the ship's pet, and the sailors would devote infinite pains to teach the creature to drink rum and chew tobacco. Into the men's grog tub would be put an extra pint of water, so that the four-legged debauchee could have an allowance, and none of its two-legged friends go short of a spot of their regulation *quantum.* It would be interesting to learn whether the addiction to rum and tobacco had a good or ill effect upon the milk supplied.

Now for a glance at the personnel of a line-of-battle ship. The captain was responsible for his ship and all who served on her. He possessed almost absolute power. He could not sentence a man to death, except by confirmation of other captains, but he could flog a seaman and cut flesh off his back with a cat-o'-nine-tails until the poor wretch was senseless. He could degrade some of his officers and send them forward. He lived alone, taking his meals by himself, except when he unbent sufficiently to invite the lieutenants and midshipmen to his table. Whenever he came on deck he was guarded by a red-coat with a drawn sword. But he did not interfere with the ordinary working of the ship, unless matters were going wrong, and called for rectification. Naturally captains differed in disposition, some being the most tyrannical fiends ever permitted to curse their fellow men, while others were afflicted with streaks of mildness and forgiveness. It may be said that of the two extremes, the seamen almost preferred the man who made their lives a misery. Of course, there were ideal captains who, while martinets in discipline, gained the love and affection of their men by their well-tried courage, their abilities, and their solicitude for the comfort of those who served under them. Of this last type was Nelson, who frequently fought the authorities in order to get redress for the grievances of the seamen. Of the many duties laid down by the Admiralty regulations for the captain, the three outstanding were to defend and maintain the honour of his country, to guard the secret of the private signals, and "to burn, sink, and destroy" the enemy, whenever and wherever he could.

On a ship-of-the-line there were from three to eight lieutenants. The first-lieutenant worked the ship according to the captain's orders. He was the captain's proxy in all respects. He spent his days here and there about the ship; but he shared no night watch, although if danger were afoot, he would be found on deck. A lieutenant of the watch had a host of duties, in the performance of which he would not find time hanging idly on his hands. He saw that the helmsman kept the ship strictly to her assigned course, that the log was hove hourly, and that the rate of sailing was duly recorded. His eyes were on the men to see that they were smart and alert, and in readiness for any sudden emergency. The midshipmen and master's mates had their duties allotted, but it was the lieutenant who saw that they stuck to their tasks. In the night watch, it was necessary for him to keep the look-out men awake, and not to post them too long at their trying stations. If a sail were sighted at night in war time, the officer at once sent a midshipman to apprise the captain, who would give necessary instructions. While the captain was dressing, the lieutenant would be getting the ship ready for action, but taking care to keep out of gunshot of the strange sail until her identity was disclosed.

The lieutenant was responsible for the master-at-arms going his rounds regularly. Twice during each watch the carpenter's mates had to be sent to sound the ship's well, and to note that the lower-deck ports were quite secured. He also had to send the gunner's mates to examine the lashings of the guns and ease them, if straining. Every morning the boatswain reported to the lieutenant the state of the rigging, and the carpenter the same concerning the masts and yards. The admiral's signals had to be answered and recorded. At night too, there was the lighting of the lanterns and the loading of certain guns, in case they were required for night signals. In time of fog there were arrangements to be made for the firing of guns, beating of a drum, or the striking of the ship's bell. In action, a lieutenant commanded a battery of guns, keeping the men at their posts; endeavouring to infuse spirit into them, if it were needed; and urging them to take careful aim. It was the lieutenant's duty to see that the men kept themselves clean by frequent washing, and that hammocks were scrubbed and clothing washed. Junior lieutenants were in charge of the ship's muskets, and they exercised and trained the seamen in the use of the weapon. If the captain were absent from duty for any length of time on leave or owing to sickness, etc., the first-lieutenant took his place. An important duty that fell to the lieutenant was to see that no boat either left the ship or came alongside without his express permission. In setting forth the foregoing multifarious duties, it is not meant that they all fell to one lieutenant, but they were all within the duties prescribed for the office. These were the ordinary daily and nightly tasks. What lieutenants could do upon special occasions is placed upon record many times in these pages, in brilliant boat actions, and in dashing attacks upon the enemy on land. There was considerable variety in the dress worn by the captains, many of whom adopted whatever uniform they pleased. In the Royal United Service Institution there are preserved some interesting uniforms of captains and lieutenants, which date back to 1748, in which year they were first appointed for wear in the Navy. The three-cornered hats are trimmed with lace, and are adorned with cockades, which George I introduced. The coats of thick blue cloth have the lapels buttoned back; in the captain's coats the cuffs are white. Lace was also often worn at the neck and wrists. The costume of an admiral was very similar, but with a profusion of elaborate lace and rich embroidery. A long white kerseymere waistcoat, white knee-breeches and silk stockings made up a striking attire. The lieutenant's uniform was marked by blue slashed cuffs. At the time of Trafalgar, the captain's lapels were white and the cuffs were striped with gold. Epaulettes came into use only towards the end of the eighteenth century; a captain of three years' standing wore them on both shoulders. With these alterations in the captain's uniform, that of the lieutenant now showed white cuffs.

The master was next in rank to the lieutenant, and in former times was his superior. His chief duty was to control the sailing of the ship, including the trimming and setting of sails, and the manoeuvring during an action. The stowage of the hold devolved upon him. He was responsible for the cabin tiers and the spirit room. He examined provisions when they came aboard, and he had to see that old provisions were eaten before inroads were made upon new stock. He examined all beer and water casks every evening. He was responsible for the spare sails in the sail rooms. Ascertaining the ship's position was a daily duty, and in this operation he was assisted by his mates and some of the midshipmen, who thus were taught their business. Whenever a ship was in foreign waters, the master had to survey inlets and carefully record soundings etc., in order to check those marked on the printed charts with which the Admiralty supplied him. If rope were needed, this officer attended the rope-walk in order to prevent the rope-maker wasting any yarns. A master's uniform differed very little from that of a captain, except that the lapels and cuffs of the coat were blue instead of white; the knee breeches and waistcoat were the usual white.

On first-, second- and third-rate ships the master was assisted by a second master, while on ships of all rates there were master's mates, who engaged in the rougher parts of the master's duties. In the day-time one of these mates kept order on the lower-deck, while it was the duty of another to see that the main-deck was kept as clear as possible. A master's mate was employed in various other duties, such as booking the number of messes for the information of the first lieutenant; the numbering and fixing of the hammocks; the opening or closing of the port-lids according to the state of the weather. Dinner was ordinarily at noon, but the helmsman, sentries and lookout men went on duty at that time, and consequently took their meal half an hour earlier. It was the duty of the master's mate to attend this earlier meal and see the food served out. The master's mate wore a plain blue frock coat with gold anchor buttons. Like his superior he was supposed to wear a white waistcoat and breeches, but not infrequently he was too poor to obtain them, and wore what clothes he could get.

Next in grade to the master's mate came the midshipman, who usually entered the service through interest. If he had passed two years at Gosport Naval Academy, he was a midshipman from the moment he joined the ship; if not, he entered as a "first class volunteer," and served two years before he was classed as a full midshipman. First-, second-, and third-rate ships carried from twelve to twenty-four midshipmen. In the time of Nelson a middy could enter the service even before eleven years of age, but later only the sons of officers could enter so young. From nine to twelve each day the midshipman studied under the schoolmaster, who also was expected to pay some attention to the morals of his charges. Often the schoolmaster was the chaplain, to whom the midshipman paid £5 for the instruction he received. In small vessels that did not carry a chaplain or schoolmaster, the education of the youngsters was undertaken by the captain, who in most cases took at least some interest in his youngest officers.

So far as duties were concerned, the chief occupation of the midshipmen was to be at the beck and call of the first lieutenant. When in port they were sent to and fro in the ship's boats. At sea they mixed much with the men in order to learn their duty. In the morning they had to see the hammocks stowed. On some ships they were sent aloft with the men to learn how to furl and reef sails, etc. At the age of fifteen, the middy became an "oldster," and was freed from the schoolmaster, which the budding admiral in most cases viewed as an unmixed blessing. At the same time he received an addition in pay and also attained the dignity of a grog allowance. It was at this stage that the midshipman transferred his quarters to the orlop deck to pass under the charge of the chief gunner. Two years' further service entitled him to be examined for master's mate, a knowledge of seamanship and navigation being the chief qualifications for promotion. Having attained the age of nineteen, and with six years service at his back, he could take the examination for the post of lieutenant. A midshipman could step up direct to the last-named post. It was not compulsory to qualify for master's mate first, but most enthusiastic midshipmen took the intermediate post, if only because it sometimes gave an opportunity of navigating a prize into port.

A midshipman's pay on a first-rate was less than £3 a month, and consequently it was necessary for him to possess private means, if he were to live and dress decently. The regulation uniform was a blue cloth tailcoat lined with silk, ornamented with small gold anchor buttons, and bearing a white patch on the collar; breeches and waistcoat of white nankeen or jean; hat, three-cornered, with a gold loop and cockade. After a long cruise or a protracted stay on a foreign station, the boy often would present a very different appearance, and be garbed in "togs" got from the slop-chest, or even be absolutely in rags. When his wardrobe was at a low ebb and the captain invited him to dine, the youngster would have to borrow from all around, in order to appear with befitting neatness.

In the midshipmen's mess, in the after-cockpit on the orlop deck, a lantern was necessary even in daytime. The dingy hole was not sufficiently high for a middy to wear his hat. It was far from an ideal spot wherein to take a meal, for they were no wafts of Araby that came up from the noisome bilge, to say nothing of the mixed odours from the rancid butter and rotten cheese in the purser's store-room hard by, or the tarry and musty smell of old rope that was ever present. As some of the midshipmen were grown men of from thirty to forty, and master's mates were sometimes quite veteran, the berth was not a particularly choice abode for boys, especially when the grog was flowing at night. It may however, be placed to the credit of the older men, that before they settled down to a carousal, the younger members of the mess were packed off to their hammocks.

These small-fry officers indulged in considerable horse-play among themselves, and the weakest got bullied and robbed of a portion of their food. Spare time was occupied chiefly in fighting or fooling, varied by foraging expeditions against the purser's stores for extra food or drink. The middy's berth was generally the most uproarious in the ship, and some of the reprobates were seldom out of hot water. Punishment of these young gentlemen usually took the form of mastheading, sometimes for as long as twenty-four hours. Generally the delinquent could look for no food being sent up from his berth, his absence from mess meaning a trifle more for some of his mates. In such a case some of the topmen would provide the midshipman with food and drink. For sleeping on watch an irascible lieutenant would sometimes have an offending midshipman lashed in the weather rigging; and with his arms and legs stretched out and his face exposed windward, the delinquent found the punishment fairly severe. Some captains ordered particularly wild midshipmen a dozen with a knotted rope's end; but one captain was courtmartialled and reprimanded for what was considered undue severity, and every middy in the fleet rose up and called the court blessed.

Although a midshipman might be a mere child in years, and younger still in experience, he was an officer; and so far as the lower ranks were concerned, he was armed with an officer's powers. A malicious youngster could curse or even strike a seaman, however strong and capable, and the man would have to endure it, for resentment would be construed into mutiny, for which the lieutenant would have him flogged at the gangway. In most cases an appeal to the captain would lead to no redress. It is related that an admiral upon one occasion said to his seamen: "By the god of war, I'll make you touch your hats to a midshipman's coat, even though it's only hung on a broomstick to dry."

The surgeon was responsible for the health of all aboard. The ordinary sick-bay was in the forecastle, but in war-time it was advisable to remove it to the orlop deck, out of reach of the enemy's shot. The commonest complaint from which the crew suffered was ulcers. Gaol fever was brought aboard newly commissioned ships by the scouring of the prisons, and every year large numbers of sailors died from this disease. Another dread complaint, against which the surgeon had to guard, was scurvy. Even the best of ships were subject to foul smells, liable to breed epidemics amongst men, who were packed together in cramped spaces that were dark, damp, and dismal. At intervals the surgeon would superintend the fumigation of the ship. This was done by burning a preparation of gunpowder and vinegar in pans about the decks, or pans of tobacco and brimstone were used. Fire-buckets were lowered into the hold and then sprinkled with vinegar and brimstone.

In those days medical science included no knowledge of antiseptics. Lint was expensive, and wounds were washed with sponges. As even the sponges were limited in number, one would be used to dress a dozen wounds, with the result that blood-poisoning was often conveyed to a man who was suffering from only a slight injury. During an action a ship's cock-pit was a scene of indescribable horror. As the wounded were brought from above, they were laid down in rows. The rule was, first come, first served; officer or seaman, it made no difference. Serving all alike at first strikes one as perfectly equitable, but in practice it meant that while some were being treated for comparatively light wounds, other terribly-mangled sufferers were bleeding to death. The chaplain, purser, stewards, and other non-combatants rendered what aid they could to the sufferers, in giving them drink and applying tourniquets, etc. While the guns boomed overhead, leaping and banging and shaking the ship throughout her timbers, the surgeon and his assistants were busy at the operating table, amputating limbs, etc., by the light of snuffy tallow candles. An operation was performed with remarkable expedition. There were no anaesthetics. The patient took a swig of rum; into his mouth was thrust a leathern pad upon which his teeth could vent his agony, while the surgeon carved and sawed. During a fight nobody worked harder than the surgeons. Everything was done at express speed. A glance at an injury told the practised eye whether it was mortal, or whether there was hope in an operation, and if the latter, it was performed, there and then, in full view of the other sufferers, who were awaiting their turn.

The chaplain ranked and messed with the wardroom officers, as already stated, and sometimes he would add the duties of schoolmaster to his sacred office. The ship's company was expected to attend divine service on Sunday morning, unless the weather, or the presence of an enemy, prevented it. The captain was enjoined by the regulations to support the chaplain in repressing bad language, gambling, drunkenness, quarrelling, etc. Officers and men who died at sea at ordinary times were committed to the deep at the gangway, with a funeral service, in the presence of all aboard. Men killed in action were generally flung overboard without ceremony. Sometimes a ship's company mustered for prayers before a battle; and a thanksgiving service often took place after a victory. The chaplain was supposed to fortify the men with prayers and Christian precepts, when a ship was on fire or foundering; but it is on record that the chaplain at such stressful times generally helped to pass the water buckets or took a hand at the pumps.

The boatswain, or warrant officer, ranked with the master's mates and midshipmen, although not "on the quarter-deck." He was in charge of the boats, sails, rigging, cables, anchors, cordage, colours, etc. Usually he was an old sailor, who had his business at his fingers' ends. Everyday he inspected the rigging thoroughly, and before going into action he saw that everything was in readiness to repair it, if the enemy caused damage. His badge of office was a silver whistle. When an officer issued an order, the "bosun" sounded the known call belonging to such order, and then shouted it down the hatchway, where the boatswain's mates took up the cry, till the order reached those whom it concerned. And if the crew did not carry out the order with alacrity it would not be the fault of the boatswain and his mates, who used their rattans, or colts, on laggards without mercy. Malingerers were the boatswain's pet aversion, and he picked them out almost unerringly. Says one writer: "This small stick of his seems little inferior to the rod of Moses; it has made many a poor cripple take up his bed and walk; and sometimes it makes the lame to skip and run up the shrouds like a monkey." It was the work of the boatswain and his mates to see the hammocks lashed and stowed, when the men turned out in the morning. The sluggard who failed to turn out smartly stood a good chance of forfeiting his hammock for a month, during which time he had to sleep under a gun, or in any corner that would afford shelter. The boatswain wore a blue cloth coat with blue lapels and collar, gold anchor buttons on the cuffs and pockets. The trousers were blue or white, whichever the wearer fancied. His top-hat was low, glazed, and with a cockade on one side. On a first-rate the pay of a boatswain was about £4, 16s. a month. His mates received about half as much. They wore no distinctive uniform, but their pay enabled them to dress better than the seamen. These mates were really the pick of the seamen, who had been selected to act as drivers of the crew. One unpleasant duty that fell to them was the flogging of men at the gangway, who often were sentenced to that dreadful punishment for quite trivial offences.

The purser ranked with the boatswain and drew the same pay; but the pay was only a small portion of the money that he could put into his pockets. He was in charge of the ship's provisions. Before commencing duty on a first-rate he had to provide security for £1200, and a smaller sum on the lower-rate ships. Very often merchants, supplying the ship's goods, were the purser's guarantors, and the merchants and purser between them robbed the seamen of a portion of their allowances of food and drink, sometimes by giving out less than the regulations provided, or by foisting on them food of inferior quality. Very often the purser and captain stood in together in these nefarious practices, in which case complaints were little likely to have any effect. In addition to the proceeds of barefaced robbery, the purser received £25 on his accounts being passed; 5 per cent. on the sale price of slops; 5 per cent. on the sale of dead men's clothes; 10 per cent. on the tobacco issued; as well as a number of other perquisites that soon helped to build up a comfortable fortune.

The carpenter held a most responsible post, as shown by his pay of £5, 16s. a month. He was responsible for the good order of the ship's timbers and the pumps; and after rough weather he would carefully examine the masts and yards. During action he and his mates were stationed on the orlop deck, in readiness to stop shot-holes as fast as they were made. One of his under hands was a caulker, ever on the look-out for a defective seam or a faulty port-lid; and it was most important that the flooring of the decks should be kept in good trim to prevent water dripping below to the discomfort of those berthed there.

The quartermaster's duties did not call for great activity, and consequently this officer was usually an old, but trusted, seaman. His chief work was to superintend the helmsman, to watch the weighing out of provisions by the purser, and to keep the time, which was struck every half hour on the ship's bell. The sailmaker drew the same pay as the quartermaster, viz., £2, 5s. 6d. a month. He kept the sails in good order, repairing old ones, and seeing that new ones were ready, when required.

The master-at-arms was the ship's chief policeman, working under the first lieutenant. He spent most of his time in looking for petty breaches of the peace, for which he placed the delinquent in irons until the captain could deal with him, which usually resulted in a flogging. Naturally the quartermaster was by no means a popular person with those who had to thank him for punishment; and as he made his rounds during the dark night watches, he was ever in danger of being paid back by some vindictive sufferer. At one time the master-at-arms, as implied by his name, instructed the seamen in the use of the musket, which duty now fell generally to the junior lieutenant. Another very important duty was to take precautions against fire, seeing that no naked candles were used below decks, and that no unauthorised lights were in use at any time. He also watched that there was no smoking except in the galley, which meant that only a few seamen at any time could enjoy a pipe; but most of the men preferred to chew their tobacco, "like Christians." The master-at-arms had to post all sentinels; and he saw to it that no intoxicants were smuggled aboard from any boat that came alongside. His couple of assistants were known as ship's corporals. They were armed with rattans, like their superior, and did not hesitate to use them on wrongdoers.

The cook was usually an old Greenwich pensioner, and was often minus a limb. He did not cook for the captain, who required a better *chef* than one whose culinary knowledge was almost limited to the boiling of junk and the making of pea-soup. This worthy got only about 35 shillings a month to add to his pension. Half the fat or slush skimmed from the coppers was used for the ship's grease; the other half was the perquisite of the cook, and realised a decent sum annually. He could have made more, if the regulations had allowed him to sell it to the seamen, who would have used it in making puddings, etc., notwithstanding its unwholesomeness and its liability to breed scurvy.

In past chapters there have been many incidental references to the ordinary seamen; and in the present chapter there have been numerous additions to our knowledge of those who, more or less cheerfully, shed their blood and gave their lives, that those who followed after might live pleasant days. "They passed, those mighty ones, in the blackness of the cock-pit, in the roaring hell of the gun-deck, that we might hear no noise of battle."

In our sea-loving nation there have always been volunteers for the fleet, but when men were required in large numbers, and when, apart from the ordinary wear and tear of a dangerous calling, incessant fighting made frightful gaps in the crews, the volunteer system alone could not provide sufficient men to man the ships. The Royal Navy was a minotaur that simply devoured men, and fresh supplies were got by hook or crook, generally the latter. Boys joined the Navy to become man-of-war's men, and remained so as long as they were fit for service, chiefly because they were never allowed to escape, and also because, after a time, there was no other calling open to them. A good many men joined the service from patriotic motives, speedily to learn that patriotism afloat was a very different thing from singing a song or wagging a flag ashore, when the people at home went mad over a victory. Specious placards, and glib recruiting agents, who spoke glowingly of prize money and endless grog, drew a certain proportion into the net, as did the premiums and bounties that were constantly offered to volunteers.

But the vast majority of our seamen were dragged neck and crop into the service by the press-gangs, who knew a likely man the moment they set eyes on him. Merchant ships were the happy hunting-grounds of the press-gangs, who would often denude a ship of her officers and crew and leave the captain with insufficient men to work his ship. When a warship had got a good nucleus of men, already accustomed to sea life, the vacancies were filled up with any men, who could be seized, anyhow and anywhere. No matter what the landsman's occupation, business or professional man, married or single, they were knocked on the head if they showed fight, and were carried aboard, and remained there till the ship was paid off, or a war was at an end. Another source of supply was the criminal courts, where prisoners were allowed to escape punishment for their crimes by going to sea; in many cases they found out, when it was too late, that they would have been infinitely better off in gaol.

Towards the end of the eighteenth century neither bounties nor the utmost efforts of the press-gangs could provide sufficient men for the Navy's hungry maw; and laws were passed compelling each county to furnish its quota of men. This was an excellent chance for the sheriffs to ship off gipsies, poachers, and rogues and vagabonds of every description. "In a man-of-war," said Edward Thompson in his "Sailor's Letters," "you have the collected filths of jails: condemned criminals have the alternative of hanging or entering on board, where the scenes of horror and infamy are so many and so great."

Men thus raked together could not all prove good material, else would all have been moulded in the heroic form. The fighting crew necessarily were picked men with their heart in their work; the forecastle men and the top-men were among the smartest of the tars. But in a ship there was endless work that could be done by anybody with a pair of hands, and the brutal discipline ensured the work being done, whether those put to it liked it or not. The men of the after-guard and the great company in the ship's waist performed duties that were despised by the real sailors. The scavenging, swabbing, pumping and dirty work generally fell to the landsmen; there was work to do in the hold, painting, etc. In 1797 an able seaman received 33 shillings a month, but before that time he got a great deal less; an ordinary seaman's pay was 25s. 6d. a month, and the raw landsman received several shillings less. In the seaman's ordinary working dress there was great variety, the main features being white duck or blue cloth trousers, and serge, duck or flannel frocks of blue, red, or green. In Nelson's time the going ashore dress consisted of a blue jacket with brass buttons, often with strips of canvas stitched down the seams; duck trousers, either white or striped; a red waistcoat, although not a few men preferred canary-yellow; a checked shirt; and a low-crowned tarpaulin hat, from which the sailor got the name "tar." On the front of the hat was painted the ship's name. Most men wore a well-greased pigtail down the back. A sheath-knife belt, white silk stockings, an open unstarched collar with a black silk neckerchief, completed a fairly distinctive and picturesque attire.

Something has been said already concerning the quality of the food. The weekly rations for a man consisted as a rule of: biscuit, 7 lbs.; beer, 7 gallons; beef, 4 lbs.; pork, 2 lbs.; pease, 2 pints; oatmeal, 1½ pints; sugar, 6 ozs.; butter, 6 ozs.; and cheese, 12 ozs. The meat, even when not bad, was dark, gristly and hard as a stone. It might have been rendered fairly eatable by long soaking; but the meat was only put in the steep tub for twenty-four hours, which did little more than dissolve the salt crystals. The pork was a shade better, but even that was so hard that sometimes sailors would carve it into fancy articles instead of eating it. Old tars used to tell the boys awesome stories of the discovery of horse shoes in the meat casks, and of weird barkings and neighings that had been heard down in the holds where the casks were kept; and many an urchin quite believed that any negro who ventured near a naval victualling yard would disappear and be seen no more, until he showed up on board a ship as junk. The biscuit was often in such a condition that it could almost walk, and it had to be rebaked in the ship's oven. Many of the men, however, would save their "bread" until night, and then darkness would hide, not its deficiencies, but its unwelcome additions. The peasoup usually was fairly good, but the oatmeal gruel was generally unspeakably bad, and most of it was consigned to the pigs. Many men would not draw this ration at all, choosing to take money instead at the end of a cruise.

Probably the tars were of opinion that there was no such thing as bad beer; some might be better than other, but never bad. In any case even bad beer was better than the atrocious water that was carried in none too clean wooden casks. When the beer was exhausted, wines or spirits were dealt out, one pint of wine, or a half pint of rum or brandy, taking the place of a gallon of beer. Christmas day was a great festal occasion aboard ship, and the officers left the men to carouse to their heart's content. For a month they would save up a portion of the daily grog; and on Christmas night practically the whole crew would be in a state of most awful intoxication, and it was no unusual thing for several men to be found dead next morning. The grog allowance at this time was too large, and there was scarcely a seaman who would not have preferred to take a flogging rather than waste good liquor. Captain Hall says that in ships on hot foreign stations, "one-third of every ship's company were more or less intoxicated every evening." It was an anomaly to punish men with the cat for getting drunk, and yet at the same time offer every encouragement to excess by a too liberal allowance of intoxicants.

The punishments on board ship were terribly drastic. Flogging was considered the only effective way of maintaining discipline; and yet, as Lord Charles Beresford has said, "In those days we had the cat and no discipline; now we have discipline and no cat." Some captains flogged almost the whole ship's company, until sometimes the men scarcely knew whether to kill themselves; or the fiend who made their lives a hell. We shall learn what happened aboard the "Hermione" in 1797, and there were many ships in which similar tragedies easily might have happened.

Flogging had a degrading effect all round; it broke the heart of a good man; it rendered a bad one only callous. That there was no need for undue flogging was proved in many cases. Lord Collingwood insisted upon perfect discipline, and his whole ship's company worked with the precision of a machine; yet he rarely flogged more than one man per month, fairly serious offenders only getting from six to a dozen lashes. Unless his crime was theft, a man sentenced to be flogged could always count upon the sympathy of his mess-mates. They would save up some portion of their previous night's grog allowance for him, and thus he was partly, if not wholly, stupefied before the punishment commenced.

The most terrible form of flogging was being "flogged through the fleet," which was the punishment for striking a lieutenant or any officer upwards. In this case the offender was put in a boat, and received so many strokes from a boatswain's mate of his own ship. He was then rowed to each ship of the squadron in turn, and at each vessel he received additional stripes. Even if he died under the punishment, the corpse received the lashes still due; and then it would be buried in the mud on the shore, without any funeral rites. If a man lived through such an ordeal, he would be unfit for service when he was able to leave the sickbay; and usually he died within a short time.

Among some of the other punishments was "running the gauntlet" for thieving. The culprit, however, was not allowed to run. First he was flogged by a boatswain's mate with the thieves' cat, and then had to walk slowly between a double line of men who were armed with knotted ropes with which they struck him, even on the head. The victim's pace was ordered by the master-at-arms, who pointed a drawn sword at his breast, while a couple of ship's corporals held similar weapons behind his back. A too hasty advance or a step to the rear entailed a prick from the swords. When the poor wretch had gone through his punishment, his wounds were rubbed with brine, and he lay in hospital until he was healed. Having thus expiated his offence, he was supposed to have "no stain on his character"; and his shipmates would never make reference to the incident.

The boatswain and his mates, the master-at-arms and his corporals, were often requested by the lieutenant to punish a man on the spot for some breach of regulations. In these cases the rattans, or sometimes "colts" of 3-in. rope, were laid unmercifully about a man's head and shoulders, and his arms, with which he endeavoured to protect himself. Ducking in the sea was a punishment in the fleet from very early times, that afterwards developed into keel-hauling, which meant that a man was dropped overboard on one side of the ship, and was then dragged under the keel and pulled up on the other side. In the eighteenth century this punishment had been discontinued. Although the majority of the men were confirmed chewers, spitting on the decks called forth instant punishment, more inconvenient than painful. The offender had to walk about with a bucket suspended round his neck, until it was considered the necessity for better manners had been impressed upon him sufficiently.

CHAPTER TWO

JOHN PAUL JONES, THE *RANGER* AND THE VALUE OF THE CONTINENTAL NAVY

DENNIS CONRAD, PH.D.

FOCUS QUESTIONS

1. What were some of the detractors and "indirect" costs of establishing a Continental Navy?
2. What new naval strategy did John Paul Jones advocate and why?
3. How did the *Ranger* help to validate the existence of the Continental Navy?

In the early months of the American Revolution, the need for a professional navy was not universally recognized, despite the American colonies' reliance on seafaring industries and their intimate knowledge of the capabilities of Great Britain's navy. While John Paul Jones's early years as a Continental Navy officer, and especially his tenure as captain of the sloop of war *Ranger*, were marked by many of the complaints and controversies that made some revolutionaries reluctant to create the new service, in the end, the contribution of Jones goes far to prove the good value the new nation received from its navy.

Certain members of the Continental Congress feared that creating a navy would turn the full might of the Royal Navy against the colonies and end the possibility of reconciliation. Some Southerners also perceived a navy as a New

England concern, as the southern economy did not rely so heavily as the North on sea-going trade. Those critics and some later historians further contended that the resources needed to establish and maintain a navy could be better spent elsewhere. Historian Jonathan Dull has argued that the role assigned to the new Continental Navy by Congress could have been performed equally well by a combination of state navies, the Continental Army, privateers, and chartered vessels—these latter to execute such tasks as carrying messages, diplomats, and supplies.

Once Congress officially authorized the development of a navy, the embryonic service was plagued by sectional conflict, internal divisiveness, political maneuvering, accusations of preferment, recruiting difficulties, a shortage of ships, and inactivity. These problems have led some scholars to comment on the "indirect costs" associated with the new Continental Navy. Included among these non-material costs were the drain on the attention and energy of American diplomats, Congressional delegates and other civil servants, and the "bad feeling" created among the officers of the service and their supporters in Congress by the shortage of vessels.

Jones received his commission as a lieutenant in the new Navy on 7 December 1775, less than six weeks after the service had been authorized by Congress. Moreover, it appears that Jones had been working for the Naval Committee of Congress for nearly a month before the date of his commission, fitting out the armed ship *Alfred.* As the senior first lieutenant in the Navy, Jones, who stood sixth in order of seniority, could have had his own command, but chose instead to serve in *Alfred*, a 30-gun ship of war, under the direct command of Captain Dudley Saltonstall and the overall command of Esek Hopkins, the "Commander in Chief" of the Navy. He did so, Jones later explained, because he believed he could be more immediately useful in that position and learn more about ship handling and fleet maneuvering serving under a flag captain. It was a decision he was later to regret.

While serving in *Alfred*, Jones participated in the raid on New Providence in the Bahama Islands and the squadron's engagement with HMS *Glasgow*, near Block Island, Rhode Island. The mishandling of the latter engagement by Hopkins convinced Jones that he had nothing to learn from either Saltonstall, whose style of command Jones had already come to despise, or Hopkins and prompted him to criticize both of these New England officers—but particularly Saltonstall—in letters to Joseph Hewes, a delegate to Congress from North Carolina and Jones's friend and benefactor. Given another chance at an independent command, Jones eagerly accepted *Providence*, a "lightly armed" sloop.

With *Providence,* Jones—who shortly after taking command received a captain's commission in the Continental Navy—made a cruise to the Grand Banks in September 1776. During that cruise, which lasted "Six weeks and five days," Jones captured sixteen British merchant vessels and destroyed the local fishing fleets at Canso and Isle Madame, Nova Scotia. In November, he made a second cruise to the Grand Banks, this time as captain of the larger *Alfred.*

Accompanying Jones was *Providence,* commanded by Hoysteed Hacker. During this cruise, Jones took seven more prizes, including the armed transport *Melish* and its cargo of winter uniforms, which were distributed to the then near-naked Continental Army.

While on the cruise, *Providence* began taking on water and her officers agitated to return to Rhode Island. Jones, whose own ship had a pump going continuously, believed the agitation to be "Unaccountable murmuring" and tried to persuade the crew to continue and complete the squadron's mission, which was to "relieve a number of our Citizens from Slavery in the Coal mines" of Cape Breton. But the following night, during a "slight Snow Squall," Hacker gave Jones "the Slip" and sailed back to Rhode Island.[1] Despite the desertion of *Providence* and discontent among his own crew, Jones continued the mission and, though unable to "relieve" the American prisoners who had enlisted in the Royal Navy, captured or destroyed six additional British vessels.

Imagine Jones's reaction when he learned a short time after returning from this voyage that, despite his notable successes, he had been ranked eighteenth on the list of Continental Navy captains set by Congress in October 1776 and that ranked above him, at sixteenth on the list, was Hoysteed Hacker. This ranking caused Jones to launch a letter-writing campaign aimed at advancing himself and discrediting several of the captains ranked above him, particularly Hacker. Obviously Congress, in constructing the seniority list, was more driven by political considerations and the ability of officers to attract seamen recruits than with proven command ability, and Jones's belief that he must sully the reputations of others to advance his own chances of command jibes with critics' accusations of preferment.

It is important to note, however, that Jones was included on the list and did get a command. Jones was a recent immigrant to America, having arrived in this country in 1773 after fleeing Tobago under threat of prosecution for having killed an alleged mutineer on a merchant ship he commanded. Once in America, Jones changed his name from John Paul, his birth name, to John Paul Jones. Given these circumstances and his lack of political connections and influence in any one colony, Jones may not have had a command at all had there been no Continental Navy. Without a national navy, therefore, it is possible that the finest fighting commander the United States produced during the Revolution would never have had a chance to demonstrate that ability.

Imagination, Initiative, and Audacity

In 1777, while pressing his case for advancement, Jones advocated a new strategy for the Navy that demonstrated imagination, initiative, and audacity. It was also a strategy that neither state navies nor privateers, the alternatives to a Continental Navy, could have executed. Understanding that the small American navy was not strong enough to protect the country's coasts—something that the state navies attempted unsuccessfully to do—and that there was minimal strategic advantage in naval ships acting as privateers and preying on

British commercial shipping, he and Robert Morris, a delegate to Congress, member of the Marine Committee, and a Jones patron, advocated a different role for the Continental Navy. As stated by Morris in a letter to Jones, they believed that the Navy's mission should be to "attack the Enemies defenceless places & thereby oblige them to Station more of their Ships in their own Countries or to keep them employed in following ours and either way we are relieved so far as they do it."[3] In other words, the Navy should attack the British where they least expected it and were most vulnerable.

Jones first suggested executing this strategy by his leading a flotilla to Africa to prey on the "English African Trade which would not soon be recovered by not leaving them a Mast Standing on that Coast."[4] Morris, speaking for Congress, endorsed the main outlines of Jones's plan but ordered that the attack be against British posts in the Caribbean, West Florida, and near the mouth of the Mississippi River. This expedition never took place, however. Jones blamed the jealousy and backwardness of the commander of the Continental Navy, Esek Hopkins; Hopkins cited the inability of the Navy to man the ships needed for the proposed expedition. Instead, Jones was given command of *Ranger,* a sloop of war then under construction at Portsmouth, New Hampshire, and was ordered to Europe. As it turned out, this assignment gave Jones the perfect opportunity to execute his plan of attacking the British where they least expected it.

Before that could happen, however, Jones had to spend several months readying *Ranger* for sea. His experience validates what the critics contended, that the Continental Navy was a significant financial burden to the new American government, which lacked the power to tax. Because building ships was so expensive, construction of naval vessels such as *Ranger* were marked by economies that delayed completion, affected vessel performance, and forced officers to beg and cajole for the materials needed. Jones later wrote that completing and outfitting this "small ship" was "more trouble" and cost him "more anxiety and uneasiness than all the other duty" that he "performed in the service."[5]

Even when the vessel was completed, Jones was dissatisfied with it. He decided that it was too lightly built to carry twenty cannon and reduced its armament to eighteen. Also, in order to save money, secondhand materials had been used, including spars intended for a larger vessel. As a result, the ship was over-sparred, a judgment that was confirmed by the voyage to France, during which *Ranger*, according to Jones, sailed "very Crank."[6]

To correct this defect, Jones, while anchored in the River Loire in December and January, ordered the spars shortened, added thirty tons of lead to the ballast, and had the sails recut. He then, as a test voyage, took *Ranger* into the rough winds and waters between Quiberon Bay and Brest, after which, in April and May 1778, Jones ordered further alterations to the vessel hoping to improve its ability to sail to windward. He set the masts farther aft, shortened the sails on the lower spars, and repositioned the ballast. He also had his crew scrape and clean the vessel's bottom, maximizing its speed. With all of these alterations, *Ranger* was as ready as Jones could make her to fulfill his strategic plans.

In the midst of these preparations, *Ranger* had the honor to be the first vessel flying the Stars and Stripes to receive formal recognition. On 13 February, Jones anchored at Quiberon Bay where a squadron of line-of-battle ships and three frigates under the command of Admiral La Motte-Picquet of France were at anchor, giving Jones the opportunity he had long coveted to exchange salutes with a French flag officer. Jones informed La Motte-Picquet that he was prepared to discharge a thirteen-gun salute if the French admiral would "return Gun for Gun." Jones was insulted when La Motte-Picquet responded that he would reply with a salute of nine guns, but was mollified on learning that nine guns was the same salute that was offered to "an Admiral of Holland or of any other Republic." Jones also saw it as an important symbolic moment because the salute was the first time the flag of America was "recognized in the fullest and amplest manner by the Flag of France" and it was "an Acknowledgement of American Independence."[7] In this exchange, the Continental Navy was playing a role—representative of the new republic—that could not have been performed nearly as well by non-Navy vessels.

At about the same time, Jones received orders concerning his mission from Benjamin Franklin, Silas Deane, and Arthur Lee, the American commissioners in France. Jones had sailed to Europe anticipating that he would receive a frigate, *L'Indien,* which the American government had arranged to have built in a Dutch shipyard. The British learned of these plans, however, and persuaded the Dutch not to deliver *L'Indien* into American hands. The American commissioners, who were then in the midst of delicate negotiations with the French, decided not to press the matter. As a result, Jones was denied a new frigate and ordered to remain in *Ranger* and, in that vessel, to attack the enemy.

The strategy Jones had advocated is to be found in the orders given him by the commissioners, vague though their directive was. He was to distress the enemy "by Sea, or otherwise." Jones had spelled out his intentions in an earlier letter to the commissioners: "I have always since we have had Ships of War been persuaded that small Squadrons could be employed to far better Advantage on private expeditions and would distress the Enemy infinitely more than the same force could do by cruising either Jointly or Seperately—were strict Secrecy Observed on our part the Enemy have many important Places in such a defenceless Situation that they might be effectually Surprised and Attacked with no considerable Force."[8]

In a letter to the Marine Committee of Congress in February 1778, Jones reiterated his ideas, adding: "I have in contemplation several enterprizes of some importance—the Commissioners do not even promise to Justify me should I fail in any bold attempt—I will not however, under this discouragement, alter my designs.—When an Enemy think a design against them improbable they can always be Surprised and Attacked with Advantage.—it is true I must run great risque—but no Gallant action was ever performed without danger—therefore, tho' I cannot insure Success I will endeavour to deserve it."[9]

As seen in these two letters, Jones understood that Americans must fight a kind of guerilla war at sea. They could not engage the enemy fleet against fleet, nor was commerce raiding the answer. While the latter might be profitable for the captains and crews involved, it did not, in the end, significantly help the nation's interest. Striking the enemy where least expected would keep the British dispersed and force them to redeploy some of their squadrons away from the American coast. Jones's ideas reflected a patriotism that was willing to sacrifice personal gain and advancement for a greater good, something privateers rarely did. It was not, however, a strategy that appealed to his crew, who saw commerce raiding and the attendant prize money as their best chance to supplement meager wages. In *Ranger* and subsequent commands, Jones had problems with dissatisfied crews because of his reputation as a risk taker and hard fighter who eschewed commerce raiding for more perilous missions.

The cruise of *Ranger*, which began in April 1778, was truly remarkable. It lasted 28 days, and in that time, according to Jones biographer Samuel Eliot Morison, Jones and his crew "performed one of the most brilliant exploits of the naval war."[10] In addition to taking two merchantmen—Jones was not against capturing merchant ships when it did not detract from the overall strategic goal—and destroying several others, *Ranger* captured a British man-of-war, took some 200 prisoners, and, most notably, executed a land raid. It was the latter that caught the attention of the public in both England and America.

Jones had planned to destroy a British coastal city as retaliation for English raids against towns on the Connecticut coast. On the night of 22 April, Jones and his crew raided Whitehaven, the third largest port city in England. They successfully spiked the guns of the fort protecting Whitehaven harbor and set fire to colliers anchored nearby. The damage inflicted was minimal, but the alarm that the raid created was significant. Not since 1667 had an enemy successfully raided a British seaport, and, in the weeks and months following this raid, the citizenry demanded and received a redeployment of British naval resources to protect them.

On the day following the raid on Whitehaven, Jones led a party ashore on St. Mary's Island in Kirkcudbright Bay. This raid was intended to seize an "important" prisoner who might force a change in the British policy concerning American naval prisoners. The British government was willing to exchange captured American army officers and soldiers, but insisted on treating American naval prisoners as pirates who had no rights as belligerents. Thus, many American seamen languished in British jails. The British could pursue such a policy because American privateers captured few British prisoners and kept even fewer. Concerned about the fate of these American naval prisoners, Jones hoped that by taking an English nobleman captive, he would force the British ministry to authorize "a general and fair Eschange of Prisoners, as well in Europe as in America."[11]

Jones's miscalculation was in supposing that Lord Selkirk, his intended target, was a great lord whose capture would force the British to alter their policy. Selkirk was, in fact, an unimportant Scottish peer. Moreover, he was away from home when the raiding party arrived so Jones—at the insistence of his crew—did nothing more than authorize his men to loot the Selkirk household silver, which they did. Jones refused to accompany his men on their plundering expedition and later purchased the silver from his men and returned it to the Selkirks.

These raids roused the countryside and caused the Admiralty to send warships in pursuit of *Ranger*. Jones, unaware that he was being chased, decided to attack the 20-gun British ship *Drake*, though "both officers & men discovr'd great unwillingness to make the attempt."[12] It was an even match. *Ranger* had more and heavier armament but *Drake* had more men, which led Jones to fight an action designed to disable *Drake* with cannon fire while preventing the British warship from closing with *Ranger* and boarding it. In a battle that lasted just over an hour and was "warm close and obstinate," *Ranger* forced *Drake* to surrender. It was also a testament of Jones's ability as a captain. In the battle, Jones lost only three killed and five wounded, while the British suffered forty-two casualties.[13] Morison contends that Jones was able to "take the lee gauge so that *Ranger*'s angle of heel would elevate her guns and enable grape and chain-shot to tear through sails, spars, and rigging; while *Drake*, her guns depressed, could only hit *Ranger*'s hull near the waterline with her light six-pound cannon balls."[14] Because of this advantage, *Ranger* suffered little damage and few casualties.

Jones, understanding the publicity value of bringing a British warship into a French port after having executed his daring land raid, decided to take *Drake*, whose rigging was in tatters, with him to France. For almost twenty-four hours, therefore, he remained off Whitehaven, England, jury rigging the damaged *Drake*. Jones then sailed for France via the northern tip of Ireland, which was an inspired choice because British pursuers had taken up positions south and east of Whitehaven on the more direct route to the continent. With him, Jones took 200 prisoners, including the surviving members of *Drake*'s crew. These prisoners were later exchanged for Americans held in England, so one of Jones's goals was at least partially met.[15]

The end of *Ranger*'s remarkable voyage was marked by controversy. Jones put his first lieutenant, Thomas Simpson, in charge of the captured *Drake*, which was under tow by *Ranger*. On 4 May, as the two vessels were approaching the French coast, Jones saw a ship in the distance that he believed might be a potential prize. Casting off the towline, he called to Simpson to follow him as he took *Ranger* to investigate. Simpson either deliberately disobeyed orders (Jones's version) or misunderstood the orders (Simpson's contention) and continued on a course for Brest. When Jones overtook *Drake* two days later, he relieved Simpson of his command and had him arrested.

The situation was complicated by the fact that Simpson was the brother-in-law of the builder of *Ranger*, John Langdon, and knew and was liked by most of the crew, the majority of whom came from the area around Portsmouth, New Hampshire, where the vessel had been built. Recall also that Jones had been expected to command *Ranger* only until it first arrived in France, when he would leave the ship to take command of *L'Indien.* At that point, *Ranger* was to pass to Simpson. Finally, the crew and Simpson wanted *Ranger* to act more like a privateer and were not interested in the dangerous, less lucrative, though strategically more valuable, mission that Jones executed. All of these factors, combined with Jones's tendency to act in "a very high handed and presumptions" manner led many of the crew and officers to support Simpson against Jones.[16] In the end, Jones dropped his demand that Simpson be court-martialed, and Simpson and *Ranger* returned to America while Jones remained in France and began to assemble the flotilla that he took into English waters in 1779.

Reaction to the raid in England is interesting. In some publications, Jones was characterized as a bloodthirsty pirate interested only in murder and mayhem. These newspaper accounts described Jones, who was approximately 5'6", had light brown hair, fair skin, and hazel eyes, as big, dark and swarthy—just how a buccaneer is supposed to appear. Despite the attempt to demonize Jones, many among the English lower classes came to see him as a Robin Hood figure, who took from the upper classes but was considerate of the English workingman. This impression was solidified when, on his return voyage to France, Jones set ashore fishermen he had earlier captured to gain knowledge of the local waters and reportedly gave them money to replace their ships.

While the Simpson affair dimmed the luster of the voyage among the American commissioners in France, in America Jones was lionized. It was thought that he had repaid the British in kind for their attacks on American coastal towns. John Banister, an American delegate to Congress from Virginia, wrote that Jones's raid gave the British "a small specimen of that Conflagration & distress, we have so often experienced." Another delegate, James Lovell, appreciated the strategic value of the attack writing that it would "make England keep her ships at home." Even Abigail Adams was smitten, writing her husband John: "John Paul Jones is at present the subject of conversation and admiration. I wish to know the History of this adventurous Hero."[17]

Jones's raid calls into question the contention that the American Continental Navy had no value. While the raid did not profoundly alter the course of the war, it did have an impact. As can be seen from the reaction in America and England, it boosted the morale of Americans and brought home the war to the British. It also validated the strategic ideas of Jones and Robert Morris, as the raid caused the British Admiralty to station five ships, a sloop of war, and many other smaller vessels—ships that otherwise might have been used against the Americans—in the Irish Sea and on the West Scottish coast to protect against future incursions.

Jones's activity also gave the Americans a forward presence. Operating out of European ports, Jones and other American naval captains, such as Lambert Wickes and Gustavus Conyngham, helped to make the American conflict with Britain more visible in Europe and to "persuade friendly European powers that the United States was capable of collective effort on the high seas."[18] Their actions also served to introduce irritants in the relations between England and these European countries, which in turn helped to bring the latter into the war as American allies.

Finally, Jones captured some 200 British prisoners, which led to an exchange of British and American seamen and forced the British to at least temporarily alter their policy of treating American seamen as pirates and not exchanging them. As none of the alternatives to the Continental Navy—the state navies, privateers, or leased vessels—would have, or probably could have, executed such a raid, it is clear that the Continental Navy, in the person of John Paul Jones, did "earn its keep" for the fledgling United States. And beyond that, Jones established a level of professionalism and purpose that gave the new Navy a firm foundation and a legacy for the future.

Dr. Conrad is with the Early History Branch of the Naval Historical Center. He was formerly editor and project director of The Papers of General Nathanael Greene.

Sources

Dudley, William S. and Michael A. Palmer, "No Mistake About It: A Response to Jonathan R. Dull," *The American Neptune*, vol. XLV (1985)

Dull, Jonathan R., "Was the Continental Navy a Mistake?" *The American Neptune*, vol. XLIV (1984).

Fowler, William M., Jr., *Rebels Under Sail: The American Navy during the Revolution* (New York NY: Charles Scribner's Sons, 1976)

John Paul Jones and the Ranger, edited by Joseph G. Sawtelle (Portsmouth NH: Portsmouth Marine Society, 1994)

Jones, John Paul, *John Paul Jones' Memoir of the American Revolution*, ed. and trans. by Gerard W. Gawalt (Washington DC: Library of Congress, 1979)

Journals of the Continental Congress, 1774–1789. 34 vols, ed. by Worthington C. Ford, et al (Washington DC: Government Printing Office, 1904–37)

Morison, Samuel Eliot, *John Paul Jones: A Sailor's Biography.* Reprint (Boston MA: Northeastern University Press, 1985)

Naval Documents of the American Revolution, edited by William Bell Clarke, et al. (Washington DC: US Government Printing Office, 1964–)

Papers of the Continental Congress, National Archives, Washington DC

Notes

1. Jones to the Continental Marine Committee, 16 November 1776 and 12 January 1777, William Bell Clark, et al., eds. *Naval Documents of the American Revolution*, 10 vols. to date (Washington DC: US Government Printing Office, 1964), 7: 183, 935. Hereafter NDAR; John Paul Jones to the

President of Congress, 7 December 1779, Papers of the Continental Congress, item 168, vol. 2: 107, National Archives, Washington DC. Hereafter PCC and DNA.

3. Robert Morris to Jones, 5 Feb. 1777, NDAR, 7: 1109.

4. Jones to Robert Morris, 17 0ct. 1776, NDAR 6: 1302.

5. Jones to John Brown, 31 Oct. 1777, NDAR, 10:362.

6. Jones to the Continental Marine Committee, 10 December 1777, item 58, p. 137, DNA.

7. Jones to William Carmichael, 13 Feberuary 1778, (Henry Huntington Library, San Marino CA) and 14 February 1778, DNA; Jones to the Continental Marine Committee, 22 February 1778, PCC, item 58, p. 143, DNA.

8. American Commissioners to Jones, 16 January 1778, PCC, DNA; Jones to the American Commissioners in France, 5 December 1777, DNA.

9. Jones to the Continental Marine Committee, 22 February 1778, DNA.

10. Morison, Jones, p. 162.

11. Jones to the Countess of Selkirk, 8 May 1778, PCC, item 168, vol. 1: 75, DNA.

12. Ezra Green, "Diary of Dr. Ezra Green," entry of 24 April, *JPJ and the Ranger*. (Portsmouth, N.H., Portsmouth Marine Society, 1994), p. 205. Hereafter, Green, "Diary."

13. Jones to the American Commissioners, 27 May 1778, Library of Congress, Washington, D.C. Hereafter DLC. *Ibid* The British set their official losses at four killed and twenty-three wounded (Public Record Office, Admiralty Papers, 1–3972).

14. Morison, Jones, p. 158.

15. Jones to the American Commissioners, 9 May 1778, DNA; there is some discrepancy about the number of prisoners from the *Drake.* Two lists of them exist at Historical Society of Pennsylvania; one gives the number as 133, the other 145.

16. Lyman H. Butterfield, ed., *Diary and Autobiography of John Adams*, 4 vols. (Cambridge MA: Harvard University Press, 1961) 4: 165; Crew of the Ranger to the American Commissioners, [3] June 1778, PPAmP; Warrant and Petty Officers of the Ranger to the American Commissioners, 15 June 1778, PPAmP.

17. James Lovell to William Whipple, 14 July 1778, John Banister to Theodorick Bland, Jr., 31 July 1778, Paul H. Smith, ed., Letter to the Delegates of Congress, 26 vols. (Washington DC: Library of Congress, 1976–200) 10: 278, 376). Abigail Adams to John Adams, 18 January 1780, Lyman H. Butterfield, et.al., eds., Adams Family Correspondence. 4 vols. (Cambridge MA: Harvard University Press, 1963–1973), 3: 262.

18. William S. Dudley and Michael A. Palmer, "No Mistake About It: A Response to Jonathan R. Dull" *The American Neptune,* vol. XLV (1985), p248.

CHAPTER THREE

The Anti-Navalists

The Opponents of Naval Expansion in the Early National Period

Craig L. Symonds

FOCUS QUESTIONS

1. What is the purpose for which Symonds wrote this article? What is his thesis?
2. What were the major arguments put forward by the navalists and anti-navalists to support their vision of how the U.S. Navy should look? Given the political, economic, and social context of late-18th century America, which argument made the most sense?
3. If, as Symonds suggests, military organizations should reflect the societies that create them, is the U.S. Navy of today an accurate reflection of contemporary America and its priorities?
4. Is the navalists/anti-navalists debate relevant today?

The naval policy debate in the United States which began almost immediately after the nation had secured its independence in the Treaty of Paris in 1783, pitted the proponents of a regular professional navy on the European model against those who favored reliance on a militia navy founded on the Minuteman concept. Almost without exception, the history books have sided with the advocates of a professional navy. A composite of their collective viewpoints would reflect the following generalizations:

1. Americans have always been a seagoing people. The availability of the tall pines of Maine and the strong oaks of the southern forests as well as the hemp and tar of the Carolinas made the thirteen colonies a natural factory for ships. From the earliest days of nationhood, Americans drew wealth from the sea as fishermen, whalers, and carriers of marketable goods. Given all this, it would seem natural that the United States would also devote a healthy percentage of its national wealth to the construction, maintenance, and operation of a sea force to guard such riches—that is, to a navy.
2. Moreover, a navy serves a larger purpose than simply patrolling the seas. A navy 'in being' (as Admiral Mahan would phrase it) could serve as a clear warning to potential aggressors that American 'rights' are not to be interfered with thoughtlessly. A navy serves a diplomatic function as well as a military function in that it 'shows the flag' in foreign ports; it can be moved to potential trouble spots in time of danger where it can either be on hand to fight if necessary, or better yet, prevent a fight from taking place at all. In short, a navy can be an instrument of peace as well as war.
3. The opponents of naval expansion were irresponsible ideologues who openly rejected the principle of preparedness for the most petty of reasons: economy. Their leader and spokesman, Thomas Jefferson, was prejudiced against a national navy because of his heritage as a planter. A Physiocrat, Jefferson exalted agriculture over commerce, and this parochial view led him to look upon naval forces as unimportant at best, and possibly even dangerous to American liberties. Along with a pack of equally shortsighted followers—the penny-pinching Albert Gallatin and the venomous old John Rhea of Tennessee, for example—Jefferson fought hard to prevent the United States from achieving its true destiny as a naval power. In the long run, of course, he could only postpone it.

This traditional view has had hearty support from naval historians. Quite aside from the obvious institutional loyalties of Admiral Mahan, the earliest and still one of the most vociferous attacks on Jefferson's naval policy can be found in the pages of Henry Adams' lyrical *History* (1891). Though reviewers were quick to note that his anti-Jeffersonianism was perhaps to be expected considering his pedigree, few took the trouble to challenge his conclusions regarding Jefferson's 'short-sighted' naval policy. Writing two decades later, Charles O. Paullin concluded that 'Jefferson was loath to learn that his versatile mind was not competent to master naval problems, whose solution belonged to men versed in the naval profession.' Fully in this tradition, Harold and Margaret Sprout published their *Rise of American Naval Power* in 1939 which remains the most widely quoted treatment of American naval policy. In it their lack of sympathy for the opponents of naval expansion, and Jefferson in particular, is a consistent theme.[1]

Although Jefferson has attracted his share of defenders,[2] few have analyzed the opponents of naval expansion to determine if, in fact, they were mere obstructionists, or if they had a positive naval policy of their own. Were they impelled to their opposition by selfish interests or a parochial view? Were they pennywise and pound-foolish in their pleas for government economy? The answer in both cases is no.

The real cleavage between the advocates of a large seagoing navy (the Navalists) and their opponents (the Anti-navalists) was not based exclusively on economy after all. The single most important issue in the naval policy debate throughout the Early National Period was the question of the proposed *mission* of the navy, and this, more than any other factor; marked the intellectual schism between Navalist and Anti-navalist.

Navalists saw the navy as a tool for raising American prestige, as an adjunct to diplomacy, and as a means of entry into that exclusive club of European powers who determined the world power balance. With visions of national greatness dancing before their eyes, American Navalists argued that the construction of a large and powerful national naval force would ensure future American participation in that determination. In other words, the prescription for national greatness through sea power which made Alfred Thayer Mahan famous a century later was already being forwarded by American Navalists in the 1790s. But what *was* different in the late-eighteenth century was that the political climate would not support a navy designed to secure for America its 'place in the sun.' A majority of Americans, not just a willful minority, stood unalterably opposed to a premeditated program of national assertiveness by bluff and bluster. Navies were seen as instruments of national defense, not auxiliaries to successful diplomacy.

Anti-navalists did not disagree that a large navy would lead to closer ties with Europe and American participation in a world power balance, but they argued that those ends were not desirable. The respect of others, for example, was of no value in and of itself. It was only when a lack of respect led to some overt action that threatened American *interests* that the United States ought to consider the use of naval power to assert its rights. To create a naval force expressly to assure *respect* was more likely to serve as a temptation to violence than a deterrent. The fact is that most of the 'Anti-navalists' were not anti-naval at all; their guiding concern was that the size and configuration of the navy be fully dependent on the national needs, or, to use a nautical metaphor, they preferred to trim the country's sails to the winds how and when they blew, rather than set storm canvas for a gale that might not come.[3] What they did oppose was the construction of a powerful peacetime naval fleet whose major function would be to serve as an instrument of political influence. That is, they opposed a navy whose mission it would be to impress other nations with America's potential strength and vitality and thereby to act as a deterrent to war or a means of exercising leverage on the policies of other nations. They recognized that the possession of naval power carries with it political risks as well as opportunities and that frequently the risks could seriously outweigh the advantages. Naval expansion, they warned, could provoke potential adversaries or even potential allies into hostility. A peacetime navy could serve as a vehicle for unwanted involvement in European affairs, and its fiscal cost was likely to exceed even the most extravagant estimates. Therefore, they consistently argued that the costs, both fiscal and political, be weighed carefully before making a commitment to a peacetime navy.[4]

Would a United States Navy act as a deterrent or a catalyst? Disagreement over the answer to this question stemmed from differing views about America's proper relationship to Europe. Navalists admired Europe (and England in particular) and believed that United States participation in the general European system of states would boost American prestige and bring numerous intangible benefits to America. But Anti-navalists wanted to know what tangible good would result from closer ties with Europe. John Williams of New York argued that no fair comparison could be made between the powers of Europe and the situation of America. 'It was necessary there,' he said, 'to keep up the balance of power; but we were three or four thousand miles distant from them.' So far as he was concerned, 'we were sufficient to manage our own concerns without European support.' A few even went as far as to state, as John Nicholas of Virginia did, that the United States 'ought to have no political connection with Europe.'[5]

This basic disagreement is apparent in the arguments presented by both sides during congressional debates of naval policy. Whereas Fisher Ames argued that 'the possession of force is the only way of gaining respect,' skeptical Anti-navalists feared that an American fleet would provide Britain with 'an excellent opportunity to pick a quarrel with the United States'; and while Josiah Masters claimed that the construction of ships of the line 'would command more respect among foreign nations and thereby aid and assist our negotiations,' William Branch Giles argued that such a fleet would be 'hostage to its full value for our good behavior to the great powers.' Far from bringing America greater flexibility, he warned, naval expansion would lead to unnecessary and unwanted conflict.[6]

Navalists denied that an American navy would be 'hostage' to the great powers. Even a small American navy, they claimed, would be sufficient to 'hold the balance' between Britain and France and thus both sides would be compelled to seek our friendship. Alexander Hamilton clearly expressed this view in the *Federalist Papers:*

> A few ships of the line, sent opportunely to the reinforcement of either side, would often be sufficient to decide the fate of a campaign on the event of which the interests of the greatest magnitude were suspended. . . . A price would be set not only on our friendship but upon our neutrality. By a steady adherence to the union, we may hope, erelong, to become the arbitur of Europe in America, and to be able to incline the balance of European competitions in this part of the world as our interest may dictate.[7]

The arguments of John Nicholas of Virginia were representative of the Anti-navalist response:

> If our situation, as gentlemen say will make a small force so operative in our hands in time of European wars, will not our possessing it be sufficient to produce war with Great Britain when it is always a sufficient cause for war in the opinion of Great Britain, for any other maritime power to put a few more ships in commission than their ordinary establishment?[8]

This argument was dramatically underscored in the first decade of the nineteenth century when England twice attacked neutral Denmark solely to ensure that its naval forces would not be used against them.

It is important to realize that most Anti-navalists did not oppose the construction of naval vessels out of dogma or unalterable prejudice, but they insisted that the size of the United States Navy should be determined on the basis of national *need* rather than national *pretensions.* As Albert Gallatin said, 'We might have two or three frigates indeed, but . . . we could not support a navy such as could claim respect, in the sense which those gentlemen spoke of it; such as being an object of terror to foreign nations.' It was Gallatin who put his finger directly on the question at issue between these two groups of advocates when he said that 'The question is, whether it be proper; at the present time, to lay the foundation of a navy of a fleet that might be able, hereafter, to give us a certain weight in relation to European nations.'[9]

In fact, the Anti-navalists often voted in favor of naval expansion when they perceived a clear danger to American interests. In 1794, when the attacks of the Barbary pirates threatened to drive American commerce from the Mediterranean, those who had opposed Hamilton's grandiose schemes for American participation in a new balance of power came out strongly for the construction of a squadron of frigates to meet the threat. Years before, when the Continental Congress struggled with this same issue, it had been Thomas Jefferson who had argued in favor of meeting the threat with force and in 1794 his followers in Congress did the same. In 1801, when the issue again arose, so staunch an opponent of Navalism as William Branch Giles stated on the floor of the House that he would support a motion to expand the fleet and send it against the Barbary powers even though he was still opposed to any 'improper' augmentation of the navy. He went on to say that 'with respect to the Navy, he was friendly to it as it now stood, or to any augmentation of it to meet any particular emergency.'[10] The critical point here is that Anti-navalists favored any naval augmentation aimed at meeting specific emergencies while Navalists believed the value of a navy was as great in peace time as it was in war and that the nation ought therefore to devote itself to a permanent system. As Josiah Quincy argued: 'The duty is permanent and ought to be fulfilled by a permanent system.'[11]

Like most Anti-navalists, Jefferson was a realistic statesman. More so than the ambitious Navalists in Congress, he carefully calculated the possible gains against the probable costs before advocating a naval program. The careful calculation of object and cost which went into Jefferson's decision to send a squadron to the Mediterranean in 1801 also went into his decision not to support the construction of a battle fleet during the crisis with Britain in 1806-1807. The cost not only in terms of money but in terms of the ill will of Britain, was greater than any possible advantages that he could foresee. His biographer has asserted that 'Jefferson's opinion, especially after Trafalgar, that a strong seagoing navy would have been an utter waste was not as silly as certain later enthusiasts for seapower were to claim.[12]

Though the Anti-navalist philosophy is clearly inappropriate for the United States in the twentieth century this should not automatically condemn the advocates of Anti-navalism in the nineteenth century. It was Karl von Clausewitz who first emphasized the importance of matching national means to political objective. But in the first decade of the nineteenth century, when Clausewitz was still piecing together his views on war; Anti-navalists in America were already acting in accordance with his future dictum. Indeed, it was the Navalists, driven as they were by visions of national greatness and international power, who were promoting an irresponsible naval policy at a time when the United States was hard pressed to keep hostile Indians under control.

Notes

[1]Henry Adams, *History of the United States of America* (New York, 1891); Charles O. Paullin, *Paullin's History of Naval Administration* (Annapolis, 1968), p. 135; Harold and Margaret Sprout, *The Rise of American Naval Power* (Princeton, 1939).

[2]See, for example, Julia Macleod, "Jefferson and the Navy: A Defense," *Huntington Library Quarterly* (February 1945), pp. 153–84.

[3]The metaphor is borrowed from J.E. Neale, *Elizabeth I* (London, 1934), p. 229.

[4]See Ken Booth, "Foreign Policies at Risk: Some Problems of Managing Naval Power;" *Naval War College Review* (Summer 1976), pp. 3–15.

[5]*Annals of Congress,* 4th Congress, 1st session, p. 873; Page Smith, John Adams (Garden City, 1962), p. 949.

[6]*Annals of Congress,* 4th Congress, 1st session, pp. 882–83; 3rd Congress, 1st session, p. 433; 4th Congress, 1st session, p. 844; 3rd Congress, 1st session, p. 491.

[7]Alexander Hamilton et al., *The Federalist* (New York, 1961), p. 77.

[8]*Annals of Congress,* 5th Congress, 3rd session, p. 2853.

[9]*Ibid.,* 4th Congress, 1st session, p. 2129; 5th Congress, 3rd session, p. 2824.

[10]*Ibid.,* 7th Congress, 1st session, p. 327.

[11]*Ibid.,* 9th Congress, 1st session, p. 1031.

[12]Dumas Malone, *Jefferson and His Time* (Boston, 1948–70), V, xx.

C H A P T E R   F O U R

Six Ships That Shook the World

THEIR SECRET technology turned the young United States into the globe's most advanced naval power

Roger Archibald

FOCUS QUESTIONS

1. What were the arguments made for and against a permanent, standing Navy in the years immediately following the American Revolution? How did it affect the construction of the Humphrey's frigates?
2. What role did frigates play in navies of the late eighteenth century?
3. What technical improvements were introduced in the Humphrey's frigates, and what tactical advantages did they yield?
4. How effective were the super-frigates in the War of 1812?

"America certainly can not pretend to wage war with us," a London newspaper declared on June 10, 1812. "She has no navy to do it with." Such was the disdain for American sea power on the eve of the War of 1812 that the British politician George Canning dismissed the infant U.S. Navy as "a few firbuilt frigates with hits of hunting at the top."

Yet within a year the British Admiralty would order its captains to avoid individual contact with the enemy's formidable new vessels and to attack only when in squadron strength. In reporting the loss of HMS *Guerriére* to "a new enemy, an enemy unaccustomed to such triumphs and likely to be rendered insolent and confident by them," the *Times* of London concluded that, "never before in the history of the world did an English frigate strike [its colors] to an American."

ONE RECENT CAPTAIN of the *Constitution* referred to the ship's system of diagonal riders as "the stealth technology of its day."

The progression of the United States from a country with an odd assortment of warships in 1783 and with no navy at all in 1794 to a world sea power in 1815 constitutes one of the most impressive examples of strategic power growth in history. At the focal point of this accomplishment was the creation of a handful of warships that put a distinct American stamp on naval warfare around the world. Their influence is still being felt. One of these ships—the USS *Constitution*—survives as the world's oldest commissioned naval vessel, maintained by the Navy at the decommissioned Charlestown Navy Yard not far from the site on the old Boston waterfront where she was launched almost two centuries ago on October 21, 1797.

Today we take for granted the United States' role as the pre-eminent world power. But two hundred years ago in post-Revolutionary America, debate about the new nation's place in the world was wide open.

During the war for American Independence, the Continental Navy, despite several well-publicized triumphs, had not contributed substantially to the final victory. A varied collection of vessels that were either bought or hurriedly built, it was never a match for the Royal Navy and usually resorted to raiding Britain's merchantmen rather than taking on her capital ships. The naval balance of power did not tip in America's favor until the French navy entered the conflict following the Franco-American Alliance of 1778.

OF FISCAL NECESSITY, WHAT remained of the Continental Navy following the war had been sold off by 1785, and when all the sailors were discharged, the country was left with no seagoing armed forces whatsoever. The Jeffersonian Republicans (not to be confused with today's party) identified with the agrarian South and the frontier. They distrusted large, centralized government with its high taxes and believed that a standing navy, through its efforts to protect American merchant shipping, would lead the country into the wars still raging abroad. The breadth of the Atlantic Ocean and the preoccupation of European navies with troubles at home were defense enough, they reasoned. As early as 1781 Thomas Jefferson had commented, "They can attack us by detachment only, and it will suffice to make ourselves equal to what they may detach." More than a century later the naval historian Alfred Thayer Mahan described distance as "a factor equal to a certain number of ships."

Of the opposite belief were merchants, traders, financiers, and people from

New England and seaport cities associated with maritime interests. They embraced the Federalist views expounded by Alexander Hamilton. They believed that the only way the United States—and especially its merchant ships trading abroad—would be respected in the world was as if the nation demonstrated its power, symbolized by warships flying the American flag. "A nation despicable by its weakness," Hamilton exclaimed in 1787, "forfeits even the privilege of being neutral."

As with many great issues in American history, both sides had their strong points. And in what has come to be a pattern in American politics, resolution was reached not so much through debate as through the influence of subsequent events. When Britain seriously dishonored the treaty ending the Revolutionary War by ignoring American sovereignty on the high seas, the framers of the U.S. Constitution in 1787 granted the new government the power and taxing authority "to provide and maintain a Navy."

During the next seven years, American merchant ships not only were harassed and interdicted by the warring powers of Europe—principally Britain and France—but were also plundered and confiscated, their crews held for ransom by North African pirates from the Barbary States of the Mediterranean. Political pressure to build a navy grew steadily in Congress. It culminated with passage of the Naval Act of 1794, which provided for the construction of six warships. President George Washington signed the bill into law on March 27, and the United States Navy was created.

Although the opponents of a standing navy had failed to block the legislation, they had succeeded in attaching an amendment providing that should the United States reach "peace" with the Barbary States before construction of the new ships was complete, there would be "no farther proceeding . . . under this act." This provision would prove to be problematical.

FOR MORE THAN A YEAR BEFORE the passage of the Naval Act, a Philadelphia ship designer and builder of some note had been quietly but persistently lobbying the new federal government to expedite warship construction (conveniently for him, Philadelphia was the national capital at the time). Joshua Humphreys wrote to his influential friend Robert Morris, a senator from Pennsylvania, that the United States "should take the lead in a class of ships not in use in Europe, which would be the only means of making our little navy of any importance. It would oblige other Powers to follow us intact, instead of our following them."

On the eve of the nineteenth century, the great navies of the era—the British, French, Spanish, and Dutch—had evolved a number of different vessel classes, similar to weight classes in boxing. On top were the ships of the line, the heavy hitters in any naval encounter. Packing somewhere around seventy-four guns on three different decks, they would simply get in line opposite one another and battle it out until one side or the other prevailed. They could fire a broadside capable of stopping any lesser vessel in its tracks but were sluggish under sail, averaging perhaps five knots.

Next came the frigate, perhaps the most versatile of all sailing warships. It usually carried thirty to forty somewhat lighter guns on two decks and was faster, reaching speeds of eight to ten knots, with greater maneuverability than ships of the line. Frigates were more likely to be used for patrol, blockade, convoy duty, and harassment of enemy merchant shipping rather than major fleet encounters. If involved in the latter, they would usually duel with one another.

At the bottom of the hierarchy was everything else mounting guns on only one deck: sloops of war (which, like ships of the line and frigates, were three-masted) and brigs, schooners, gunboats, and other auxiliaries, all of which had no more than two masts and considerably lighter armament. While slower than a frigate, they were significantly more maneuverable. Nevertheless, they rarely played a decisive role in any fleet action unless they were sacrificed in some way, as a decoy or a fire ship.

THE SHIPS COULD excel in both speed and firepower because of Humphreys's brilliant solution to a formerly intractable dilemma.

Joshua Humphreys was soberly aware of what could happen when a lighter vessel went up against one of a heavier class. During the Revolutionary War the *Randolph,* a frigate he had designed and built, was blown out of the water with a loss of all but four hands in action against a British ship of the line off Barbados in 1778.

STILL, FRIGATES WERE Humphreys's first choice for the new U.S. Navy, but not the standard type. What he envisioned became known as super-frigates. "None ought to be built less than 150 feet keel," he continued in his letter to Robert Morris, and they should "carry twenty-eight 32-pounders or thirty 24-pounders on the gun deck. . . . These ships should have scantlings [measurements] equal to 74's [seventy-four-gun ships of the line], and . . . may be built of red cedar and live oak."

Humphreys's conclusions about what these vessels could achieve have proved prescient. At the time, however, they sounded farfetched: "Ships built on these principles will render those of an enemy in a degree useless, or require a greater number before they dare attack our ships. . . . Their great length gives them the advantage of sailing. . . . They are superior to any European frigate, and . . . [will] never be obliged to go into action, but on their own terms."

What Humphreys was proposing, on the basis of the prevailing knowledge of naval architecture at the time, simply couldn't be done. The warship designer of that period was faced with an intractable dilemma: You could have speed, or you could have firepower, but you couldn't have that much of both.

For a ship to remain afloat, a force equal to her weight has to be exerted up against the entire submerged portion of the hull. Over a long time a vessel built of wood, with its characteristic flexibility, will experience a natural bowing up of its keel amidships as a result of the constant hydrostatic pressure on its bottom. The phenomenon is known as "hogging," since the resulting curvature in the keel resembles the arch of a hog's back.

The upward pressure of buoyancy is constantly at work on a ship afloat, year in, year out. It is greatest at the deepest part of the vessel, the keel. And the keel is weakest where the ship is widest, generally in the midsection. Left unchecked, a vessel will hog until her timbers can flex no more; then they will break, and the ship will sink.

Long before it reaches this dire state, however, hogging produces a detrimental effect on a ship's performance. An upward concavity in the bottom of a vessel interferes with the flow of water past it, trapping some, slowing the ship down. The greater the hog, the greater the amount of water trapped, and the more slowly the vessel will go.

The greater a ship's displacement (weight), the greater the hogging pressure. And the one thing that can make a light vessel very heavy is the installation of a large gun battery like those aboard eighteenth-century warships. Not only did the guns' immense weight (two to three tons each) exacerbate a vessel's hogging, but their location did as well.

Unlike a heavy cargo, which would be stowed deep in the hold and directly over the keel (and thus help alleviate hogging), a ship's armaments were of necessity placed on the periphery of the vessel and high enough above the water line so as to be of use even when rolling in high seas. This location gave their weight an added leverage that worked to hog the vessel all the more.

The other factor affecting hogging is a ship's length. Just like the limb of a tree, the longer it is, the easier it is to bend. But any tendency to design shorter ships was more than offset by a simple fact of naval architecture well know even in the eighteenth century: The maximum hull speed of any vessel (whether it's an eight-oared racing shell or an aircraft carrier) is directly proportional to its length.

Throughout the era of wooden ships, hogging was the bane of shipbuilders. The longer a vessel was, the faster it could theoretically go. But very quickly the added hogging generated by the extra length and weight of additional armament would cancel out any speed benefits.

For all these reasons Joshua Humphreys's 1794 superfrigate proposal, with its provisions for both great length and heavy armament, should have been dismissed outright. Had he submitted it to a competent naval authority (like the U.S. Navy's current Bureau of Ships), it probably would have been. But to his great good fortune—as well as the Navy's and the country's—his plan landed on the desk of Secretary of War Henry Knox.

As a former Revolutionary War general, Knox was not particularly knowledgeable about marine science. Since there was no Navy Department at the time, he referred the matter to a committee. It found Humphreys's ideas appealing and asked him to submit a detailed design. Up to this point apparently no one reviewing the proposal knew it couldn't be done.

After Humphreys provided the War Department with his frigate design, Henry Knox wanted to make sure it was reviewed by a competent authority, and as luck would have it, such a person had recently arrived from England. Following a long apprenticeship in the shipwright and shipbuilding trades, Josiah Fox had traveled extensively throughout Europe studying various ship designs. Independently wealthy, he had come to America to learn about shipbuilding woods and subsequently met Secretary Knox in Philadelphia, where Fox had relatives.

KNOX ASKED FOX, WHO HAD become a War Department employee and submitted a frigate design of his own, to comment on the Humphreys design. Fox met Humphreys, and the two men entered into a collaboration that largely remains a mystery to this day. Historians differ somewhat about the extent of Fox's contribution to the final design. But if the fruit of their combined labors—the *Constitution*-class frigates—is any indication of the success of their partnership, it was a whole far greater than the sum of its parts. Their accomplishment in creating some of the most successful sailing warships that ever went to sea is all the more ironic since both these men were Quakers.

The final design they achieved delivered on every promise Humphreys had made in his original proposal. At 175 feet on the water line, and capable of setting almost an acre of sail, the superfrigate had the speed to outrun any other man-of-war in the world, up to thirteen knots. With a main battery of long twenty-four-pound guns that could fire broadsides more than seven hundred pounds to distances of up to 800 yards, it could easily overpower other frigates, which customarily carried only eighteen-pounders.

What made this all possible, what gave the design both speed and firepower, was the brilliant way Humphreys overcame shipbuilding's most intractable dilemma of the eighteenth century. He solved the hogging problem with an innovative system of internal structural supports that significantly reduced hull distortion by effectively transferring the weight of the guns on the upper decks down to the ship's keel.

LIVE OAK WAS the most prized wood in the world for building warships, and it grew only in America.

THE PRINCIPAL COMPONENT OF this system was a set of diagonal riders, massive live oak beams two feet wide and as much as a foot thick, deep in the vessel's interior. Parallel neither to the ship's backbone (her keel) nor to the ribs (her frames), which ascend perpendicularly from the keel to curve up and give the hull its shape (just like a human rib cage), these timbers rise along the internal curvature of the hull but at a forty-five-degree angle forward or aft, from the area of the keel amidships toward either far end of the deck above. There are eight of them on each side of the vessel, three sloping forward, five aft. Radiating upward and outward from the point in the hull most prone to hogging, the diagonal riders act like the buttresses of a great cathedral—only upside down. Instead of holding the roof of a building up, they keep the bottom of a ship down.

In addition to this revolutionary innovation, which one recent *Constitution* captain called "the stealth technology of its day," the Humphreys design included several other unique features intended to prevent the hull from distorting under the tremendous weights and forces exerted on it. One was a series of "locked strakes," two pairs of special deck planks on either side of both the gun and berthing decks (located immediately beneath the ship's uppermost, or spar, deck). They run the full length of the vessel and tie into structures at either end. Rather than being just fastened down like regular planks, these are cut to lock in with one another and with each deck beam they cross. There was also a system of twelve pairs of "knees" (support timbers that bend at a ninety-degree angle), located along each side of the berth deck, that transfer the load of the main gun battery on the gun deck above down to the diagonal riders below.

Humphreys's innovations did not stop with preventing hull distortion. For protection against enemy fire, the design called for a three-layered hull. At the center were the frames (ribs) curving up vertically from the keel. Over these, thick planks were laid horizontally on both the inside and outside. Unlike merchant ships, where frames only six inches wide might be separated by a foot or more, Humphreys's frigates had twelve-inch-wide frames that were "sistered" together in pairs to result in a combination that was two feet wide. The separation between each pair was on average less than two inches. The enemy was thus presented with a virtually solid wall of wooden armor up to twenty-five inches thick in places.

And not just any wood. The design specified live oak. With that choice the resulting ships (and Navy) were doubly blessed. Not only was live oak the most prized wood in the world for building warships, but it was also to be found only in America.

Growing in coastal areas of the southeastern United States between Virginia and Texas (a little also grows in western Cuba), live oak (*Quereus virginiana*) gets its name from the fact that it does not lose its leaves in winter. Known for its slow growth, massive gnarled trunk, and long, expansive limbs that can reach out horizontally forty feet or more, the tree produces one of the densest and hardest woods in the world. Unless dried in a kiln, it is heavier than water and will sink. Most important for shipbuilding, milled live oak lumber gets even harder when left out in the weather.

Humphreys's original plan called for live oak in the keel, the frames, the diagonal riders, and many other structures throughout the vessel, while the planks on either side of the frames were to be made of only slightly less dense white oak. (This combination would prove so protective for the *Constitution* that in forty-two actions throughout her fighting life, her hull was never once penetrated by enemy fire. After seeing cannonballs bounce harmlessly off the frigate's topsides during the first of her four major victories in the War of 1812, a sailor is reported to have exclaimed, "Huzzah! Her sides are made of iron!" Thus was born her nickname, "Old Ironsides.")

ONCE THE WAR DEPARTMENT accepted the design, contracts were awarded to construct the six frigates. Rather than build them all at the same yard, which might have better assured quality control and kept the price down by eliminating unnecessary duplication, the government chose the politically expedient alternative. To benefit as many local communities as possible from public spending, and to encourage popular support for the Navy as well, the work was spread among six port cities along the East Coast.

The *Constitution* was to be built in Boston; the *Constellation*, in Baltimore. New York got the *President*; Norfolk, Virginia, the *Chesapeake*; and Portsmouth, New Hampshire, the *Congress*. Joshua Humphreys himself was chosen to build the *United States* in Philadelphia. (The ships were named as they neared completion. At the start they were designated with the letters A through F.)

Obtaining materials—specifically live oak—was the first priority. All told, it took the wood of more than 1,500 trees of various species to build one of these ships. A party of more than eighty New England shipwrights and woodcutters headed for the islands off the Georgia coast in the fall of 1794, but by the following spring, after a hard winter of foul weather and disease, only four remained. John Morgan, their leader, wrote Humphreys, "If I am to stay herfe] till all the timber is cut I shall be dead. . . . If you was here you would curse live Oak."

IN 1795 THE U.S. signed a peace agreement with the Barbary States. By law, this meant that work on the vessels had to stop.

MORGAN WASN'T ABLE TO get the timber-cutting operation going satisfactorily until he turned to local planters who rented him slaves. Accustomed to the climate and working conditions, they were able to make good headway, and shortly after their arrival, oak shipments started to arrive at shipyards in the North. So in yet another irony surrounding the *Constitution* and her sister ships, the most important materials needed to build these vessels destined to defend American freedom could be successfully obtained only through slave labor.

By early 1796 work on the six frigates was again stymied, this time by political events. Word had been received of a peace agreement with the Barbary States in North Africa. According to law, this meant that all work on the vessels should cease. And it did, for a time. But the momentum of the new Navy had already built up too far for it to end so abruptly. President George Washington appealed to Congress to let the vessels' construction continue, and eventually a compromise was reached: Work would continue, but only on the three frigates nearest completion.

The U.S. Navy was finally launched in 1797. The first of the three frigates to slide down the ways was the *United States* in Philadelphia on May 10. The *Constellation,* somewhat smaller than the others, came next in Baltimore on September 7. Then finally came the *Constitution* on October 21 in Boston.

Initially the men of the new Navy were not up to its ships. Starting from scratch in 1794, the service was fast becoming just another Federalist bureaucracy by the time tangible evidence of its purpose finally arrived: the superfrigates. Without any professional traditions, it lacked focus. Its highest offices had been filled by either political appointees or experienced captains from the old Continental Navy, each of whom had his own ideas about how it should be run.

Embarrassments were more often the norm than achievements. The first captain appointed to command a U.S. Navy vessel abruptly went on furlough so he could sail a merchant ship to China. The first captain of the *Constitution*, a political appointee, had to be relieved of command after several errors of judgment during the vessel's inaugural voyages. And the *Constellation* drifted aground while anchored in the Delaware River, then rolled over on her side when the tide went out.

But in time the new Navy finally shook down into a professional fighting armed service worthy of its ships. It ordered more frigates and completed the three left unfinished in 1797. It responded to the crises that initially had led to its creation. It took the fight and the flag to the doorstep of the tormentors of American merchant ships, first in the Caribbean during the Quasi-War with France, then to the Mediterranean against the Barbary pirates.

Command of one of the squadrons sent to accomplish this first major projection of American power overseas went to a captain far down on the seniority list, Edward Preble of Maine. In the same way that the *Constitution* is now symbolically viewed as the flagship of the entire U.S. Navy, Edward Preble is revered as the founding father of the naval officer corps. It was around him that all of the modern Navy's traditions of service, duty, and professionalism coalesced shortly after the turn of the nineteenth century, as he commanded the *Constitution* off the Barbary Coast.

Preble had a reputation as a disciplinarian with a short temper. He demanded perfection from his crews, which at first led to a fair degree of dislike for him. But opinion started to change after an incident aboard the *Constitution* while en route to Gibraltar one night in September 1803. Threatening to open fire, Preble faced down a menacing British warship that in the dark claimed to be a more powerful ship of the line, but which was actually much lighter. Recognizing his courage and spirit during that confrontation, the young officers he had been assigned—whom he initially called "nothing but a pack of boys"—started to show him more respect.

DURING THE YEAR THAT followed, the Mediterranean squadron labored under harsh conditions at sea, political pressure from home, and the decline of Preble's health in the effort to force the Barbary States to cease attacking American merchant ships. The squadron suffered some ignominious defeats but also enjoyed some spectacular successes, like the boarding and burning of a captured American frigate right under the enemy's guns, which Britain's Lord Nelson later called "the most bold and daring act of the age."

Through it all Preble set an example of leadership for his cadre of young officers, who solidified into the nucleus of the Navy's future professional career officer corps. Known as Preble's Boys, these officers—almost to a man—went on to great achievements in the next decade during the War of 1812. Stephen Decatur, the best-known hero of the Barbary campaign, commanded three of the Navy's first six superfrigates, the *Congress, United States*, and *President.* The *Constitution* was commanded in her three major battle encounters of the War of 1812, all victorious, by three alumni of the Preble's Boys fraternity: Isaac Hull, William Bainbridge, and Charles Stewart.

En route back home in late 1804 after his squadron had been relieved, Preble called at Gibraltar before heading out across the Atlantic. Witnessing the *Constitution*'s arrival from the quarterdeck of HMS *Victory*, flagship of the Royal Navy, Lord Nelson is said to have remarked, "In the handling of those trans-Atlantic ships there is a nucleus of trouble for the Navy of Great Britain."

That trouble was less than ten years in coming. The *Constitution* first proved her worth during the War of 1812 not by defeating a British warship but by masterfully evading five of them that had trapped her off the New Jersey coast during a calm. A month later, however, when she encountered one of her pursuers alone en route to Nova Scotia for repairs, Capt. Isaac Hull's only desire was to demonstrate his vessel's superior armament.

APPROACHING FROM THE advantageous windward side, he held fire until within "half a pistol's shot," then let loose a double-shotted broadside from which the HMS *Guerrière* never recovered. Within fifteen minutes her mizzen mast had toppled, and the other two masts soon followed.

Aboard the *United States*, Capt. Steven Decatur achieved a similarly brilliant victory when he engaged HMS *Macedonian* off the Azores in October 1812. Taking advantage of the superior range of his twenty-four-pound guns over the enemy's eighteen-pounders, he managed to cripple his opponent's rigging before his vessel was in effective range of their guns.

Even when stalemated, the superfrigates still managed to play a role in the war. Despite being bottled up in Norfolk for the entire duration by an effective British blockade, the *Constellation* nevertheless managed to take up station in Hampton Roads and prevented the British from destroying harbor fortifications defending the port.

But credit for the greatest tactical victory of the War of 1812 must go to the *Constitution*, which in the closing days of the conflict managed to defeat two attacking vessels, HMS *Cyane* and HMS *Levant*, simultaneously. When the *Cyane* attempted to maneuver behind *Constitution* and expose her to deadly raking fire (a broadside fired the length of an opponent's deck), Capt. Charles Stewart put his sails aback and threw the *Constitution* into reverse—no small feat for a 3,000-ton sailing vessel—and cut the *Cyane* off. She had no option but to break away, exposing herself to the *Constitution*'s own raking fire.

AS LEWIS AND CLARK opened the frontier, the new ships opened Old World ports to American commerce.

Time rather than any enemy was what eventually destroyed most of the Navy's first six frigates. The *Chesapeake* and the *President* were captured by the British, taken to England, and broken up (scrapped) between 1817 and

1820. On the basis of the lines taken off the latter—a common practice—the British constructed HMS *President.* In 1820 the *Congress* became the first American warship to visit China, the highlight of a career that was otherwise singularly uneventful. She was broken up at Norfolk in 1836.

THE *CONSTELLATION* WAS once thought to have been preserved. A sloop of war of that name that has been on display since 1955 on Baltimore's Inner Harbor was formerly believed to have been converted from the 1797 superfrigate. However, research revealed that this present *Constellation*, currently undergoing restoration, is actually the last full-fledged sailing warship built for the Navy. She was launched in 1855 at Norfolk, two years after the original *Constellation* was broken up there.

The *United States* lasted until the Civil War. Falling into Confederate hands with the loss of Norfolk in 1861, the by-then relic was dubbed the *Confederate States* and outfitted as a floating gun platform for harbor defense. A year later, when Union forces were again threatening, the Confederates ordered her sunk in a river channel to obstruct enemy vessels. The story goes that her live oak timbers were still so sound that workers ruined a boxful of axes in their attempt to scuttle her. They finally had to bore a hole from the inside to get her to sink. Refloated by Union forces, she was broken up in 1866.

The *Constitution* alone survives intact. In anticipation of the vessel's bicentennial (being celebrated throughout 1997), the Navy has been carrying on a three-year, $12 million restoration and refit that has left the *Constitution* in the best condition she has been in since she was built.

The success of the restoration comes in no small part from an exhaustive research effort that was mounted in advance of any actual work on the ship. It reached as far afield as the National Maritime Museum in Greenwich, England, and as far back in time as the era of the vessel's construction. Researchers had to rediscover the diagonal riders, which had been removed from the *Constitution* sometime between 1820 and 1850 and never replaced. Since no original records remained of this revolutionary innovation, researchers had to turn first to the plans the English had taken from the captured *President*, which included short diagonal riders of iron (a British variation on the original design due to the shortage in England of timber of suitable size). Close examination of the *Constitution*'s hull once out of water revealed the pattern of where the original timbers had once been installed. Tests on a laboratory model proved their utility, and the Navy decided to reinstall them aboard the ship, where they have now successfully reversed the fourteen inches of hog that had developed in the vessel's keel since her last major restoration sixty-five years ago.

As a result, plans were set in motion to put the ship under sail once again. This happened in July 1997 in Massachusetts Bay off Boston. Before then, the *Constitution* had last sailed in 1881.

CMDR. MICHAEL BECK, THE Constitution's sixty-fourth commanding officer, leads the way below from the vessel's topside, down to the gun deck, then the berth deck, and finally the bilge. Here at a point about twelve feet below the water line he steps over a massive timber that rests atop the planks—one of the diagonal riders.

"This is the technological key that unlocked America's access to the world," he says.

At the vertex where two of the beams meet above the keel, he continues. "We went from an isolationist country composed of disparate states to an assertive union of people determined to take a leadership role in the world. Diagonal riders provided the technological breakthrough to achieve that. These ships enabled the United States to gain a reputation in the world as a power to be reckoned with. And that allowed American interests to eventually become global in scope."

It is perhaps no coincidence that at the same time as Lewis and Clark were taking the American flag westward across the continent to reach the sea beyond, the *Constitution* and Capt. Edward Preble were carrying the American flag across the Atlantic to be seen on those continents beyond. In the same way that Lewis and Clark opened the frontier to the onslaught of American civilization, the *Constitution* and the other superfrigates of the early U.S. Navy opened the ports of the Old World to American commerce.

"It was manifest destiny to the east," says Michael Beck. "A manifest destiny for world trade."

Roger Archibald, who served with the Navy in Vietnam, writes often on maritime subjects.

CHAPTER FIVE

The Role of the United States Navy in the Suppression of the African Slave Trade

George M. Brooke, Jr.

FOCUS QUESTIONS

1. Why did the U.S. leadership act as it did in its decisions about stationing a squadron off the coast of Africa? What were the motivations of the American government?
2. What was the United States' relationship with the other sea powers of the time? What limitations did the U.S. Navy face?
3. Considering its relative naval power, were American naval policies and operations effective at accomplishing national goals?

One hundred years ago the expanding United States had half a dozen naval squadrons stationed in various parts of the world. One of these, the African Squadron, had a special function, that of suppressing the foreign slave trade.

But attempts by the young republic to close the foreign slave trade long antedated the organization of the African Squadron. In 1807 Congress outlawed the importation into the United States 'from any foreign kingdom, place, or country, any negro, mulatto, or person of colour, as a slave, or to be held to service or labour.'[1] The President was empowered to use warships along the coasts of the United States to enforce the act, but the results were disappointing.[2]

Subsequent legislation in 1819 authorized the President to send cruisers to the coast of Africa to suppress the slave trade.[3] The act of 1819 was materially strengthened the following year by a law which branded the slave trade as piracy; the law carried the death penalty.[4] Enforcement rested entirely with the United States Navy, however, because the act gave no permission to foreign warships to seize American slavers. The first American cruiser detailed for the west coast of Africa under the new legislation was the sloop of war *Cyane.* Arriving in March 1820, the sloop cruised along the coast for several weeks and captured four slavers.[5]

Between 1820 and 1839 the efforts of the United States to suppress the slave traffic on the west coast of Africa were spasmodic and ineffective. Occasionally a single cruiser from the Gulf Squadron was dispatched to Africa to return by the route of the slavers.[6] Quite often, however, when a cruiser did overhaul a suspected slaver, the latter won immunity by running up a foreign flag or displaying double sets of papers. And when American naval commanders caught slavers redhanded, the courts were inclined to be lenient. Frequently a convicted slave trader suffered no more than the loss of his slaves; less often he lost his ship as well.[7] It is worth remembering that no slave trader suffered the death penalty in the United States until President Lincoln's administration.[8]

Under such conditions the foreign slave trade flourished. Some 'get rich quick' capitalists risked all on one venture by using very large vessels. So great were the profits in the illicit traffic that one successful round trip by a big ship would pay all the costs of the operation many times over, even should it be necessary to burn the vessel as evidence upon completion of the voyage. One of the finest of the large vessels was the Baltimore-built *Venus* of 460 tons. It is recorded that this ship was so fast that when pursued by naval cruisers she, on occasion, even shortened sail to tease her outdistanced pursuers. On her first voyage she landed over eight hundred slaves at a net profit of approximately three hundred dollars per head; she had cost but $30,000.[9] Other slave traders with a healthy respect for British cruisers—if not of American—used small schooners with a low silhouette and plenty of speed. These traders, usually unable to afford a large vessel, were the ones who lived with the trade, found it congenial, and derived a steady income from it. They knew all the tricks to evade capture. To escape detection some small schooners were constructed so that the masts could be dismantled and oars substituted should a cruiser loom over the horizon. Schooners as small as ten tons were used, and it is reported that boats 'no more than twenty-four feet-long' carried as many as thirty-five children across the narrow waist of the Atlantic from west Africa to Brazil.[10] Steamers were soon introduced by the hard-headed traders and became increasingly popular.

Before 1830, the dealers in human flesh generally sought refuge under the flags of Spain, Portugal, and France, but around 1830 the United States' flag began to find favor. By 1839 the situation had become so bad that Governor Thomas B. Buchanan of Monrovia felt impelled to declare that 'The chief obstacle to the very active measures pursued by the British government for the suppression of the slave-trade on the coast, is the American flag.'[11]

Such statements shook the United States from its lethargy, though the government seemed more concerned about the fraudulent use of the American flag than by the steady growth of the slave trade. In 1839, at the direction of President Martin Van Buren, two fast-sailing vessels were dispatched to the coast of Africa to protect the flag.[12] In his annual message that year the President referred to the matter at some length and urged Congress to revise the laws pertaining to the sale and transfer of American vessels outside the limits of the United States. The defects in existing laws enabled foreign-owned vessels to feign American ownership so completely 'as to afford them comparative security in prosecuting the slave trade.'[13] But the recommendation was ignored by Congress.

At the close of 1840 the secretary of the navy reported that the two ships detailed to the African coast had remained on that station constantly except for the sickly season. Yet, the commanders of the two vessels observed that the slave trade appeared larger than it had ever been, and the laws seemed to serve 'no other purpose than to excite the cupidity of unprincipled adventurers, by increasing the value of slaves.'[14] The slave trader's chance of evading the cruisers was good, for the slaves were collected by native chiefs at stations or barracoons along the coast, where under cover of night they were transferred to slavers standing off shore. At the end of the second year of cruising by the two American warships the slave trade was still very extensive, and Secretary of the Navy Abel P. Upshur foresaw the need of a larger squadron.[15]

The suppression of the slave trade was a complex problem which could be solved effectively only through international cooperation. Great Britain had been the leader in this campaign ever since she had abolished the traffic in 1807. She had long felt that the only practical solution was mutual right of search and she had directed her diplomacy to that end.[16] As the United States, Spain, Portugal, and Brazil were the great slave trading countries, Great Britain concentrated her efforts on them especially. As early as 1820 Spain and Portugal granted Britain a limited right of search and joined in the establishment of mixed courts. But Brazil, though she promised in 1826 to abolish the slave trade in three years, remained a great offender until 1853. In her efforts to wipe out the traffic, Britain was aided by the great powers. In 1831, France agreed to a mutual right of search within a limited geographical area, and in December 1841 Britain signed a treaty with Russia, Prussia, and Austria which branded the slave trade as piracy and provided for a mutual right of search.[17] Moreover, the zealous British concluded many treaties with native African tribes, for without their help it was believed the white traders would wither on the vine.[18]

Surely the British were vigorous in their efforts to suppress the slave trade, yet, as more and more slavers took refuge under the American flag, it was clear by 1842 that in large measure British efforts had been thwarted. The United

States was the offender. After the War of 1812 Britain had sought the adherence of the United States to an agreement for mutual right of search.[19] But the United States had refused because, so long as Great Britain controlled the seas, the United States stood to lose far more by the abuse of the privilege than did the British. The impressment of American seamen was still fresh in the public's mind. A fruitless attempt in 1824 to negotiate a treaty granting reciprocal right of search apparently closed the matter.[20] In fact, the United States, while forbidding foreign warships to search suspected slavers flying the American flag, failed to maintain an adequate force off the coast of Africa to do the job itself.

To solve the dilemma posed by the fraudulent use of the American flag, Great Britain devised the principle of the right of visit as distinguished from the right of search. She recognized that the right of search could be obtained only by treaty, but she defended the right of visit as a natural right.[21] According to this doctrine, England insisted that if a British cruiser came upon a ship flying American colors and the British commander had reason to suspect the colors were false, he could board the ship and determine its nationality by an inspection of the ship's papers. The United States did not accept this doctrine.

Between 1837 and 1841 the stopping of several American ships—some of them slavers—by British cruisers provoked considerable friction between the two governments, and the American minister to Great Britain stated categorically that the United States would never consent to a right of search 'under any form, however limited or modified."[22] Finally, in 1841, President John Tyler, in a message to Congress, declared that he recognized no technical distinction between the right of visit and the right of search, and if the British detained or seized a ship which turned out to be bona fide American, they would be liable for damages.[23] The legitimate American trade in Africa was growing, and Tyler wished to spare American merchant ships the inconvenience of visit or search by British cruisers.

The growing tension was eased in 1842 when the British government dispatched a special envoy to the United States empowered to settle all differences between the two governments. Of these differences, President Tyler regarded the Maine boundary dispute and the suppression of the slave trade the most pressing.[24] For this important mission the British Foreign Office selected Alexander Baring, first Lord Ashburton, who, during the hot summer of 1842, negotiated with the able American secretary of state, Daniel Webster. The product of their labors was the Treaty of Washington, or Webster-Ashburton Treaty signed 9 August 1842. The eighth article of the treaty stipulated that the two nations would each 'maintain in service, on the coast of Africa, a sufficient and adequate squadron, or naval force of vessels, of suitable numbers and descriptions, to carry in all not less than eighty guns, to enforce separately and respectively, the laws, rights, and obligations, of each of the two countries, for the suppression of the slave trade.[25]

In this manner was born the African Squadron. Initially, its cruising range extended 'from the Madeira and Canary Islands to the Gulf of Biafra, and from the coast of Africa to the 30th degree of west longitude."[26] The entire area lay north of the equator, but a few years later the southern limit was extended to Cape Frio, about eighteen degrees south of the line.

Although independent, the British and American squadrons were supposed to cooperate when possible. With the inauguration of this so-called joint cruising, the United States inferred Great Britain had given up her claim to the right of visit as it was not mentioned in the treaty. But Lord Aberdeen, British Foreign Secretary, soon informed the United States that his government had not changed its position on the right of visit at all.[27] British commanders were reminded 'that most assuredly Great Britain never will allow vessels of other nations to escape visit or examination by merely hoisting a United States flag.'[28] As a result, British cruisers continued to seize ships displaying the American flag, though the presence of a permanent American squadron reduced the number of such seizures.

The first commander of the African Squadron was Commodore Matthew Calbraith Perry. His long and detailed letter of instructions assigned him two primary duties: the protection of American commerce, and the suppression of the slave trade carried on by American citizens or under the American flag. The instructions left no doubt that the protection of American commerce was regarded as the more important duty. Perry was warned that 'The rights of our citizens engaged in lawful commerce are under the protection of our flag, and it is the chief purpose, as well as the chief duty of our naval power, to see that these rights are not improperly abridged or invaded.'[29] The most valuable commodity obtained in legitimate trade was probably palm oil, widely used as a lubricant. For purposes of barter American traders used cotton and tobacco. With regard to the slave trade, Perry was advised 'that while the United States sincerely desires the suppression of the slave trade, and design to exert their power in good faith for the accomplishment of that object, they do not regard the success of their efforts as their paramount interest nor as their paramount duty.'[30] Great Britain, on the other hand, although she was the greatest trading country in the world, put chief emphasis upon the suppression of the slave trade.[31]

The Navy Department's instructions pertaining to the right of visit were explicit.[32] Perry was directed to have his vessels cruise jointly with British warships, when feasible, so that the British would have no excuse to board suspected slavers flaunting the Stars and Stripes. Should a British officer board a ship that proved to be a bona fide American, he was to be held to strict accountability. On the other hand, American officers were enjoined to be very careful in their detention of suspected slavers, with the implication that should they unnecessarily detain a vessel they could be held personally liable.[33] To help detect slavers more readily Perry was advised that they usually carried double sets of papers, an unusually large number of water casks, and huge stores of provisions.

The United States was slow to dispatch a squadron to the coast of Africa in compliance with the treaty. In December 1842 the secretary of the navy reported that the United States had no squadron off Africa because the naval appropriations for the year were scarcely sufficient for more important stations.[34] Not until August 1843, twelve months after the treaty was signed, did Commodore Perry reach Monrovia; his command consisted of one frigate, two sloops of war, and one brig, totaling ninety-three guns.[35] Commodore Perry and his successors, in line with their instructions spent most of their time attempting to protect and stimulate legitimate American trade. Much of this work would normally have been handled by consuls or commercial agents, but as there were none of these officials upon the coast, it devolved upon the navy.[36]

The harassed commander of the African Squadron wore many hats. In addition to the basic duties already mentioned, he was charged with many others, such as: to give aid to the settlements at Cape Palmas and Monrovia when necessary; to cultivate friendly relations with the native tribes; to survey the coast; and to provide experience and training in practical seamanship.[37] There was no important change in duties assigned the African Squadron from Perry's time until the American Civil War.

To assist in the accomplishment of their multifarious duties cruisers on the African station were permitted to hire Kroomen, coast Negroes who by intercourse with vessels had acquired some knowledge of duties aboard ship. The Kroomen, who were excellent swimmers, were used 'as messengers, interpreters, boatmen, and in communicating with the shore, in bringing off provisions, wood, water, etc., and in all those services of exposure to the climate which the constitution of the white man is incapable of bearing.'[38] The number employed ranged from six for small vessels to as many as thirty for frigates. Many Kroomen had colorful names such as Frying Pan, Flying Jib, Wash Woman, Pea Soup, Upside Down, and Prince Albert.[39]

Ships of the African Squadron after loading provisions at Porto Praya in the Cape Verde Islands, the supply base for the squadron, generally cruised along the west coast of the Dark Continent making an appearance at the various ports within the assigned cruising range.[40] Vessels ordered to cruise in the northern division sailed principally about the Bights of Benin and Biafra, and usually did not penetrate south of the equator. Vessels assigned to the southern division covered that part of the cruising ground south of the line.

Until the Civil War the African Squadron remained the approximate size of the first squadron under Perry.[41] The small size of the squadron, in conjunction with its diverse responsibilities, required that the vessels be almost constantly on the move. Commodore Perry, who set the pattern for his successors, reported that he had 'never known vessels of war kept in more constant motion.'[42] For example, his flagship on one cruise of seventy-three days anchored fifty times and was in port only sixty-six of the first 224 days she was on the coast. Perry boasted that 'during a period of four months, almost every known trade or slave mart from Cape Verde to the equator will have been visited at least once by an American vessel of war, and many of them several times.[43]

Much of the cruising of the African Squadron was lost motion under the faulty supply arrangements made by the Navy Department. For many years

Porto Praya was the only supply base for the squadron, though it lay more than a thousand miles from the slave trading area, and even farther in sailing time in a zone where calms prevailed. Commodore Francis H. Gregory in 1850 complained that ships in the southern division lost two thirds of their time in returning to Porto Praya for supplies.[44] And some years later Secretary of the Navy Isaac Toucey remarked that the vessels—and they were only sailing vessels for many years—were most of the time employed in making the voyage from the proper cruising ground to Porto Praya for supplies, and back again to the cruising ground, and the voyage was scarcely performed before it was necessary to repeat it.'[45] This unsatisfactory arrangement was continued despite repeated recommendations by various squadron commanders that either the base be moved further south or a storeship be utilized.

The supply problem was the crux of the squadron's difficulties. It was the intention of the Navy Department to keep Porto Praya stocked with provisions shipped from the United States. But at times the supply lines broke down and the squadron was placed in a predicament, for the sterile Cape Verde Islands offered little of value.[46] The extension of the cruising range south of the equator aggravated an already bad condition.

Another major problem confronting the African Squadron was that of health. Africa coast fever in particular was much dreaded and took a heavy toll. For example, the brig *Preble* on one occasion returned to Porto Praya from a mission to the coast with forty-five officers and men down with the disease.[47] Because the high temperature and excessive humidity were believed 'productive of permanent or long-standing injury to health; the tour of duty on the African station was eventually limited to two years, instead of the usual three.[48] To safeguard health the Navy Department prescribed comprehensive regulations for the African station which reduced the death rate to less than one percent.[49]

The suppression of the slave trade would have been a full-time job for a large squadron of fast steamers freed from other responsibilities. It was completely beyond the capabilities of the insignificant American squadron, composed as it was of sailing vessels dependent upon the wind, and saddled with a host of other duties. The handful of slow-moving ships was wholly inadequate to police the long coastline from the Cape Verde Islands to Benguela, Angola, a distance of five thousand miles. Moreover, the hard-pressed American commanders were forbidden to seize slavers unless slaves were actually aboard.[50] The hopelessness of the task with the tools afforded is suggested in official correspondence. A British officer in 1850 reported that the American squadron was so small in proportion to the length of the slave coast that unless it were enlarged, or the British squadron were granted the right of search, the slave trade would never be suppressed.[51] The same year the American squadron commander wrote that the large English force of twenty-four vessels had made several captures, including some ships displaying the American flag.[52] The efficient British force was composed principally of steamers and fast, small sloops. Though the American squadron was at nearly peak strength in the early fifties, an American passed midshipman confided in his journal that the efforts of the United States to suppress the slave trade were 'a perfect farce.'[53] The young officer came to the heart of the matter when he wrote: 'The Government will not support its officers if the prize gets off through false witness, they must pay the damage if they can.'[54]

Rising slave prices in the years before the Civil War attracted ever more Americans to the iniquitous traffic, American activity reaching an all-time high between 1840 and 1860. An authority on the subject states that by 1845, a large part of the trade was under the stars and stripes, by 1850 fully one-half the trade, and in the decade 1850–1860 nearly all the traffic, found this flag its best protection .[55] An American consul admitted that American ships were preferred by slave traders because no other flag provided the same immunities.[56] Moreover, American-built merchant ships were good sailors and could often outrun naval cruisers. In 1845 it was reported that slave dealers got all their good ships from the United States.[57] The American minister to Brazil, Henry Alexander Wise, urged that ship owners in the United States and their American agents abroad be made to pay the price for their willing connivance in the slave traffic, and deplored directing all of the punishment at the officers and crew who were often ignorant dupes.[58] About the same time, an American consul in Brazil suggested that the best way to break up the slave trade was to prohibit American ships from sailing to Africa from foreign ports.[59] To the pleas of minister and consul alike the United States government turned a deaf ear. The result was that despite the Webster-Ashburton Treaty, the slave trade finally came to be carried on principally by United States capital, in United States ships, officered by United States citizens, and under the United States flag.[60] Small wonder that British officers and missionaries complained that practices tolerated by the United States government nullified the efforts of British cruisers to suppress the slave trade.

With the passage of the years the slave traders improved their techniques and shifted their bases of operation. Relying more and more upon small, swift vessels with light draft, they established dummy slave stations to act as decoys while they carried on their activities elsewhere.[61] Over the years the trade shifted steadily to the region south of the equator.[62] But even there it could not be pinpointed. As the slave traders became more furtive they frequently changed their base; one year it would be Ambriz, the next, Cabinda, etc.

Attempts to wipe out the slave trade during the two decades the African Squadron was in service were unsuccessful. It is estimated that by 1837 the number of slaves brought to the New World approached two hundred thousand annually.[63] The annual total had declined by 1842 to thirty thousand because of the abolition of the slave trade by various Latin American countries. But by 1847 the number had climbed to one hundred thousand annually and during the decade of the fifties the traffic reached 'very high proportions.' The ultimate destination of many slaves was the United States. It is estimated that for every four slaves landed in the New World one died in the middle passage.

How zealous was the United States in living up to its treaty obligations?

The records disclose that after ratification of the Webster-Ashburton Treaty the United States maintained a far weaker squadron on the coast of Africa than did Great Britain.[64] The United States in seven different years had fewer guns than the treaty limit, and throughout the period it averaged fewer than its quota. Great Britain, on the other hand, only fell below the treaty limit twice and maintained an average far in excess of the minimum requirement. The American cruisers varied in size from ten gun brigs to forty-four gun frigates, though few frigates were used.[65] The average for the period was roughly sixteen guns per vessel—the size of a small sloop of war. The basic reason for the failure for the navy to maintain an adequate force on the African station was the small size of the fleet.[66] For example, in 1844 there were only forty-eight ships in commission, and in 1857, only thirty-two; of these, about twenty percent were ships of the line or frigates not suited for catching slavers. And this small fleet had to be divided between six farflung squadrons. The cost of the African Squadron from 1843 through 1858 was $5,767,500—about $384,500 per year.[67]

During the period, 1843–1857, the African Squadron captured only nineteen vessels, of which six were condemned and four were released by the court.[68] The fate of the others was not known to the Navy Department. Contrast these unimpressive figures with the 594 seizures and 556 condemnations secured by the British during the shorter nine-year period, 1840–1848.[69] Of course, the American Squadron was empowered to seize American ships only, whereas the British could seize not only British ships, but those of countries with whom Britain had treaties granting mutual right of search.

Who was responsible? Why did the government pursue such a pusillanimous policy in honoring the antislave trade provision of the Webster-Ashhurton Treaty? One explanation is that prior to 1861 the Cabinet usually included a powerful Southern element which strongly influenced the President. During this period the South stopped defending slavery as a necessary evil and began to proclaim it a positive good. As cotton culture spread to the Gulf States the demand for more slaves mounted and the pressure on the executive branch mounted with it.

The year 1858 marked a turning point in the attitude of the United States government towards the suppression of the slave trade. The government began to spend more money on the African Squadron—the annual average between 1858 and 1866 being $500,000.[70] In 1858 the Navy Department dispatched four steamers to the west coast of Africa to cooperate with the sailing vessels already on station, and transferred the supply base from Porto Praya to St. Paul de Loanda, eight degrees south of the equator;[71] both of these changes had been recommended fifteen years earlier by Commodore Perry. Finally, in 1860 the northern limit of the cruising range was fixed at twenty degrees north latitude instead of at Madeira, twelve degrees further north.[72] This meant the squadron had a smaller area to cover.

Why did the government adopt a more vigorous and forthright policy in 1858? The explanation would seem to be that by that date the slave traffic had reached such monstrous proportions under cover of the American flag that the United States was forced to take decisive action to preclude England from doing so.[73]

The results of these progressive steps were soon apparent. In 1860 seven slavers were seized by the African Squadron—mainly off Cabinda and the Congo River—including the ship *Erie* loaded with 897 slaves and the brig *Storm King* with 619.[74] During the same period five slavers were caught by ships of the Home Squadron off Cuba, which island Secretary of the Navy Isaac Toucey called the only wide open slave market in the world, despite an Anglo-Spanish treaty of mutual search.[75] The twelve slavers seized by United States cruisers in 1860 had a total of 3,119 slaves aboard. During the first six months of 1861 three more slavers were apprehended by the African Squadron, including the bark *Cora* with a cargo of 705 Africans and the brig *Bonita* with a cargo of 750.[76]

Meanwhile the Civil War had supervened. Needing every available vessel to enforce President Lincoln's blockade of the Confederacy, all but one of the vessels comprising the African Squadron were recalled. Only the sloop *Saratoga,* mounting eighteen guns, remained to uphold the Webster-Ashburton Treaty. But with the war public passion was much aroused against the foreign slave trade. Indicative of changed attitudes was the hanging of Nathaniel Gordon of Portland, Maine, a convicted slave trader. This execution in 1862 was the first under the ancient law of 1820 which branded the foreign slave trade as piracy.

Finally, as part of a plan to attract greater European sympathy to the Northern cause, Secretary of State Seward on 7 April 1862, signed a treaty with Great Britain granting a limited right of search.[77] Now zealous British captains, backed by the full power of Her Majesty's government, could seize vessels hiding under the Stars and Stripes. This treaty ended an era in United States naval history.

George M. Brooke, Jr, graduated from Virginia Military Institute where he is presently a Professor of History. He received his M.A. from Washington and Lee University, and his Ph.D. from the University of North Carolina. His dissertation related to American naval history of the mid-nineteenth century. He has maintained a keen interest in that field and has written numerous scholarly and popular articles.

Notes

[1]Henry Steele Commager (ed.), *Documents of American History,* third edition (New York: F.S. Crofts & Co., 1946), p.197.

[2]William Edward Burghardt DuBois, *The Suppression of the African Slave-Trade to the United States of America, 1638–1870* (New York: Longman, Green, and Co., 1904), p. 107.

[3]*The United States Statutes at Large, III,* 532–533.

[4]*Ibid.*, pp. 600–601.
[5]United States 17 Cong., 1 Sess., *House Reports,* II, No. 92, pp. 1–2.
[6]United States 19 Cong., 2 Sess., *Senate Documents,* No. 1, p. 10.
[7]DuBois, op. cit., p. 128.
[8]*Ibid.*, p. 123.
[9]John Randolph Spears, *The American Slave-Trade, an Account of its Origin, Growth, and Suppression* (New York: Charles Scribner's Sons, 1900), pp. 38–39. Spears also wrote a five-volume history of the United States Navy.
[10]*Ibid.*, p. 38.
[11]Andrew H. Foote, *Africa and the American Flag* (New York: D. Appleton & Co., 1854), p. 152.
[12]United States 26 Cong., 1 Sess., *House Documents,* I, No. 2, p. 534.
[13]United States 26 Cong., 1 Sess., *House Journal,* pp. 117–118.
[14]United States 26 Cong., 2 Sess., *House Documents,* I, No. 2, p. 405.
[15]United States 27 Cong., 2 Sess., *House Documents,* I, No. 2, p. 349.
[16]DuBois, op. cit., pp. 133–140.
[17]*Ibid.*, p. 146.
[18]*An Exposition of the African Slave Trade, from the Year 1840, to 1850, Inclusive,* published by direction of the representatives of the Religious Society of Friends, in Pennsylvania, New Jersey, and Delaware (Philadelphia: J. Rakestraw, printer, 1851), pp. 48–49. (Hereinafter cited as *Exposition of the African Slave Trade.*)
[19]DuBois, op. cit., pp. 136–137.
[20]*Ibid.*, pp. 138–140.
[21]William Law Mathieson, *Great Britain and the Slave Trade, 1839–1865* (New York: Longmans, Green and Co., 1929), p. 69.
[22]United States 27 Cong., I Sess., *House Documents,* No. 34, p. 12.
[23] United States 27 Cong., 2 Sess., *House Journal,* pp. 14–15.
[24]United States 27 Cong., 3 Sess., *House Reports,* III, No. 283, p. 764.
[25]Commager, op. cit., p. 300.
[26]United States 35 Cong., 2 Sess., *House Executive Documents,* IX, No. 104, p. 6.
[27]United States 27 Cong., 3 Sess., *House Documents,* v, No. 192, pp. 1–4.
[28]United States 35 Cong., 2 Sess., *House Executive Documents,* IX, No. 104, p. 24.
[29]*Ibid.*, p. 3
[30]*Ibid.,* p. 6
[31]*Ibid.,* pp. 22–25.
[32]*Ibid.,* p. 6
[33]*Exposition the African Slave Trade,* p. 157; John Mercer Brooke, *Porpoise,* to Lizzie Brooke, 2 August 1850, in Brooke Papers in author's possession.
[34]United States 27 Cong., 3 Sess., *House Documents,* I, No. 2, p. 532.
[35]United States 31 Cong., I Sess., *House Executive Documents,* IX, No. 73, p. 3.

[36]United States 28 Cong., 2 Sess., *Senate Documents,* IX, No. 150, p. 101.
[37]United States 35 Cong., 2 Sess., *House Executive Documents,* IX, No. 104, p. 395.
[38]United States 28 Cong., 2 Sess., *Senate Documents,* IX, No. 150, pp. 3–4.
[39]*Porpoise* Log, 8 August 1850, in Records of the Bureau of Naval Personnel, National Archives.
[40]United States, 28 Cong., 2 Sess., *Senate Documents,* IX, No. 150, p. 50 and passim; John Mercer Brooke, *Porpoise* Journal, 9 June 1850-18 May 1851 in Brooke Papers in author's possession.
[41]United States 35 Cong., 1 Sess., *Senate Documents,* XII, No .49, pp. 28–29; *Navy Register United States,* 1843–1861.
[42]United States 28 Cong, 2 Sess., *Senate Documents,* IX, No. 150, p. 50.
[43]*Ibid.,* p. 51.
[44]United States 31 Cong., 1 Sess., *Senate Executive Documents,* XIV, No. 66, p. 2.
[45]*lbid.*
[46]United States 28 Cong., 2 Sess., *Senate Documents,* IX, No. 150, p. 64; Mercer Brooke, *Porpoise* Journal, 9 June 1850, 18 May 1851, in Brooke Papers in author's possession.
[47]United States 28 Cong., 2 Sess., *Senate Documents,* IX, No. 150, pp. 147–148.
[48]United States 31 Cong., 1 Sess., *Senate Documents,* X, No. 40, pp. 1–3. United States 32 Cong., 2 Sess., *House Executive Documents,* I, No. 1, p. 291.
[49]United States 31 Cong., 1 Sess., *Senate Documents,* X, No. 40, p. 2; United States 31 Cong., 1 Sess., *House Executive Documents,* IX, No. 73, pp. 1–2.
[50]DuBois, op. cit., p.160.
[51]United States 31 Cong., 1 Sess., *Senate Executive Documents,* XIV, No .66, p. 8.
[52]Commodore Francis H. Gregory, Commanding African Squadron, to Secretary of Navy, 30 August 1850, in Letters from Officers Commanding Squadrons, 1841–1886, Office of the Secretary of the Navy, Naval Records Collection of the Office of Naval Records and Library, National Archives.
[53]John Mercer Brooke, *Porpoise,* to *Lizzie Brooke,* 3 August 1850, in Brooke Papers in author's possession.
[54]*Ibid.*
[55]DuBois, op. cit., p. 143.
[56]United States 28 Cong., 1 Sess., *Senate Documents,* IV, No. 217, p. 28.
[57]*Exposition of the African Slave Trade,* p.78.
[58]United States 28 Cong., 2 Sess., *House Documents,* IV No. 148, p. 54.
[59]United States 28 Cong., 1 Sess., *Senate Documents,* IV No. 217, pp. 3-5.
[60]DuBois, op. cit., p. 162.
[61]*Exposition of the African Slave Trade,* pp. 50, 79.
[62]United States 32 Cong., 1 Sess., *House Executive Documents,* II, No. 2, p. 4.
[63]DuBois, op. cit., p. 143.
[64]United States 35 Cong., 1 Sess., *Senate Documents,* XII, No. 49, pp. 28–29.
[65]*Navy Register of the United States,* 1843–1861.

[66]*Ibid.*
[67]United States 31 Cong., 1 Sess., *House Executive Documents,* IX, No. 73, pp. 1–2.
[68]United States 35 Cong., 2 Sess., *House Executive Documents,* IX, No. 104, pp. 31–2.
[69]*The African Repository,* XXVII (May, 1851), 148.
[70]DuBois, op. cit., p. 122.
[71]United States 36 Cong., 1 Sess., *Senate Executive Documents,* III, No. 2, pp. 1138–1139.
[72]United States 36 Cong., 2 Sess., *Senate Executive Documents,* III, No. 1, pp. 13–14.
[73]Richard W. Van Alstyne, "The British Right of Search and the African Slave Trade," *Journal of Modern History,* 11 (March, 1930), 39.
[74]United States 36 Cong., 2 Sess., *Senate Executive Documents,* III, No. 1, pp. 8–9.
[75]*Ibid.,* p. 9.
[76]United States 37 Cong., 1 Sess., *Senate Executive Documents,* No. 1, p. 97.
[77]Van Alstyne, op. cit.

CHAPTER SIX

THE *SOMERS* MUTINY

SAMUEL ELIOT MORISON

FOCUS QUESTIONS

1. What was the mission and crew composition of the *Somers*?
2. What were Commander MacKenzie's options for dealing with the "mutineers?" According to Morison, did he make the right decision?
3. How might political and social factors have influenced these events?

During the summer of 1842 Commodore Perry concerned himself with finishing, equipping and manning a smart new man-o'-war brig, *USS Somers.* Designed by Samuel Humphreys and built under his and the commodore's supervision at the Brooklyn Navy Yard, she was an exquisite example of marine architecture. One hundred and three feet long on deck and 25-foot abeam, she was no bigger than many sailing yachts of today or fishing schooners of yesterday; but she carried a press of square sail. Four yards crossed each of her two tall, raking masts. In addition to her square sails, three or four jibs could be set on her monstrous long bowspirit; spencer and spanker were bent on foremast and mainmast, and there were ample light sails. She carried a complement of 120 officers and men, and ten guns peered out of square ports on her spar deck. Together with her sister ship *Bainbridge* and the three slightly larger brigs *Truxtun, Lawrence* and *Perry,* built almost simultaneously, she was designed along Baltimore clipper lines—wineglass-shaped cross-section and sharp ends—primarily for speed. These were the fastest ships in the United States or perhaps in any navy, but badly over-rigged; two of the four capsized in squalls, with heavy loss of life. With the sloops-of-war built about the same time, they were the last of our war vessels designed with no other view than wind power, and the brigs were the first to be named after naval heroes.

Commodore Perry had *Somers* assigned for an experimental schoolship cruise by naval apprentices. He took particular pains in selecting the officers. To command her, he chose his brother-in-law Master Commandant Alexander Slidell Mackenzie, whom we have frequently encountered since the building of USS *Chippewa.* At the age of thirty-nine Mackenzie, already an old hand in the navy, had managed to educate himself and establish a literary reputation. When pursuing pirates in the West Indies Squadron, he suffered two attacks of yellow fever, obtained a furlough to recover his health, traveled in Europe, and wrote *A Year in Spain.* This book earned him the friendship of Longfellow and Washington Irving, for whose *Life of Columbus* he plotted the discoverer's courses. In 1830–1832 he was attached to *Brandywine,* Commander Biddle's flagship in the Mediterranean. After that he took a two-year furlough, traveled in Europe, published three more books, and in 1835 married Catherine Robinson. Returning to active duty in 1837, he visited Russia and Brazil as First Lieutenant of USS *Independence,* and in Brazil was made commanding officer of the new man-o'-war brig *Dolphin.* After a year or two in her, chasing slavers along "the Brazils," he took another furlough to repair his health, bought an estate at Tarrytown, wrote a biography of John Paul Jones, and the *Life of Oliver Hazard Perry* that stirred up J. Fenimore Cooper. Returning again to active duty in 1841, he was assigned to the new war steamer *Missouri,* and from her transferred to the command of brig *Somers.* As Commodore Perry's shipmate since 1816, close collaborator at the Brooklyn Navy Yard, and sharer in his ideas for naval improvement, he was the natural choice.

Despite the navy's congenital suspicion of officers who write books, Mackenzie had won golden opinions from the captains and commodores under whom he served, and his attractive personality made friends for him elsewhere. "Mackenzie is one of the . . . kindest, plainest men I know," wrote Francis Lieber, the publicist; "very quiet, yet so kind and mild, so true and unaffected, that one cannot help liking, nay, cherishing him." Professor Felton, a Greek scholar who later became president of Harvard College, remarked on Mackenzie's "calmness, gentleness and refinement." Such was the man whose resolute action to preserve the lives of his men and the honor of his flag has been presented by the malignant and the sentimental as that of a savage martinet, a sadist, or a coward who preferred hanging innocent men to taking risks.

Four other members of the Perry-Rodgers clan were on board *Somers.* Lieutenant Matthew C. Perry Jr., twenty-one years old but already eight years in the navy, served as acting master, officer next junior to first lieutenant. Calbraith, as the family called him, was a rather stolid young man, brave and loyal like all the Perrys, but relatively undistinguished during a long naval career. Oliver H. Perry II, the commodore's seventeen-year-old son, was on the roll as captain's clerk. His father had failed to get him a midshipman's billet, since the navy then had a superfluity of reefers, but once the cruise started, Mackenzie created him acting midshipman. Young Oliver, too, showed that he had the guts to help quell a mutiny, but the experience left him somewhat shaken. Henry Rodgers, younger son of the old commodore, was another *Somers* midshipman, and Adrien Deslonde of Louisiana, a brother of Mrs. John Slidell, who had lived in the Perry household as a young lad and been recommended for a midshipman's warrant by his uncle Calbraith, was also on board. All four proved towers of strength to Mackenzie in time of trouble, as did the first lieutenant, Guert Gansevoort. That member of an old Knickerbocker family, thirty years old, had already served nineteen years in the navy.

Perry and Mackenzie hoped that the prospect of a foreign cruise in a smart new brig would persuade respectable parents in country towns to send their best; but the reputation of naval ratings was such that the commander could not procure many boys of that class. Even so, he selected 74 out of the 166 apprentices on the receiving ship and got rid of some of the worst after the shakedown cruise. Whether the Navy Department or Mackenzie selected the able seamen and petty officers to season *Somers's* crew and teach raw boys the ropes is uncertain, but someone made two very bad choices. Samuel Cromwell, a great brute of a man about thirty-five years old, bearded and whiskered, became boatswain's mate and senior petty officer; Elisha Small, of about thirty, a shifty little fellow but an excellent sailor, was captain of the main top. Both had served in slavers before entering the navy, and Cromwell, if not at one time a pirate, had acquired an intimate knowledge of piratical procedure. But the worst assignment, the fatal one, came from the Navy Department and Commodore Matthew C. Perry. That was the appointment of Midshipman Philip Spencer, aged nineteen.

This youth belonged to one of the first families of New York. His grandfather Ambrose Spencer had been chief justice of the state supreme court. His father John Canfield Spencer, one of the ablest lawyers of the Albany bar, was secretary of war in President Tyler's cabinet. Philip was young in years but old in vice. At Hobart College, whence he had been dropped or expelled, he was chiefly remembered for his favorite reading, *The Pirate's Own Book,* and for having boasted that he would become a pirate. He spent a few months at Union College and dropped out there. Now obtaining an acting midshipman's warrant through his father's influence, he was first assigned to USS *North Carolina,* receiving ship for the Brooklyn Navy Yard. Passed Midshipman William Craney to whose cabin and care he was assigned, could do nothing with Spencer and was twice struck by him-a serious offense which, when reported to the Navy Department and Commodore Perry, was ignored. The Commodore then assigned Spencer to USS *John Adams,* bound for Brazil. At Rio where she spent a month, Spencer (as one of his shipmates recalled) passed most of his shore liberty in "the reeky bagnios" of the *Rua Saboa,* and on one occasion became so obstreperously drunk as to be reported to Commodore Charles Morris of the Brazil Squadron. The Commodore, like Perry, evidently fearing that proper punishment of the lad would get him in wrong with the administration, had Spencer transferred to frigate *Potomac* for return to the United States, "there to receive the decision of the Secretary of the Navy." On board both her and *John Adams* (so he later confessed to Lieutenant Gansevoort) he had plotted mutiny. Secretary Upshur, after perusing "with pain" the correspondence transmitted by Commodore Morris, and too easily believing in Spencer's penitence, ordered him in August 1842 to report to Commodore Perry for duty in USS *Somers,* then fitting out at Brooklyn.

Commander Mackenzie, who knew Spencer's record, refused to accept him but offered to transfer him to another ship. Spencer then went over Mackenzie's head to Commodore Perry, who made the fatal mistake of having him reinstated as a midshipman in *Somers*—his second intervention in the young rascal's favor. One can only guess at the commodore's reasons. Among other arguments for the apprentice system, he claimed that it would cure juvenile delinquency; here was a chance to prove it. And, one may surmise, Perry wished to please the Tyler administration, since he and his kin had been conspicuous in the Jackson camp. However you look at Spencer, he was a prototype of what nowadays is called a "young punk," and Commodore Perry's giving him another chance was a singular instance of very bad judgment.

One striking thing about this cruise of the *Somers* was the youthfulness of her crew—70 percent of them under the age of nineteen. Commander Mackenzie at thirty-nine was the oldest man on board, and only three others—Quartermaster Charles Rogers, boatswain's mate Cromwell and carpenter's mate Thomas Dickerson—were over thirty. She had five senior officers, including the commander, the purser and the surgeon, and seven midshipmen. Three of the middies were twenty years old and up, the other four between sixteen and nineteen years of age. She had eight petty officers, nineteen enlisted seamen (only five of whom were aged twenty or up), and eight cooks and stewards, mostly American Negroes. All 74 apprentice boys were minors, 22 of them under sixteen years of age. Most of them had never been to sea before. With a total of 121 on board, *Somers* was badly overcrowded; her sister ship *Bainbridge* carried only 100 officers and men including 16 marines; and when sunk in the Mexican War, *Somers* had a total complement of 76.

In June—July 1842, prior to Spencer's assignment, *Somers* made a shakedown cruise under Commander Mackenzie to Puerto Rico and back in which everything went well. She now made a gala departure from New York on 13 September 1842, officers' and apprentices' relatives flocking to see her off as if she had been a flash packet ship on a pleasure cruise. In order to give her a mission, she carried dispatches for USS *Vandalia,* then cruising on the West African coast looking for slavers. Prosperous winds attended *Somers* on the outward passage. As far as Madeira, where she arrived 5 October, she was a happy ship. Since naval mutinies fresh in the public mind, such as the one on HMS *Bounty* and those at the Nore and Spithead, had been caused by "cruel hard treatment of every degree" as the old chanty puts it, there was an effort at the subsequent inquiry and court-martial to prove that Commander Mackenzie had been another Captain Bligh. Every one of the enlisted men and boys interrogated testified that they had enjoyed good usage; that Mackenzie showed unusual interest in their welfare, sending delicacies to seasick boys from his own table, buying fresh fruit and vegetables for them in the islands, giving plenty of liberty, and never losing his temper. Only a few of the boys had to be punished, and they with the comparatively mild colt rather than the cat. Boatswain's Mate Cromwell, however, cuffed the boys so frequently that Mackenzie had to reprove him more than once and even threaten that if he continued he would lose his rating, to which Cromwell made an insolent reply. The only odd feature of the outward passage was the conduct of Midshipman Spencer, who neglected his duties, shunned his messmates, but chatted endlessly with the boys and enlisted men on deck, gave them cigars and tobacco, and even put up a steward to filch brandy from the wardroom to distribute among his cronies. There was no grog ration in the *Somers,* and the boys were not supposed to use tobacco, but Spencer got around that with his gifts.

After calling at Tenerife (8 October) and Porto Praja (21 October), she sailed to Monrovia in search of *Vandalia,* arriving 10 November. The frigate having already sailed for home, Mackenzie decided, as his orders allowed, to follow. He departed next day, shaping a course for St. Thomas, where he hoped to encounter *Vandalia,* intending to reach New York before Christmas.

On this return passage, and especially after departing from Africa, the atmosphere of the ship changed. Orders were obeyed grumblingly, or after repetition, rather than cheerfully and with alacrity. "The elder portion of the crew," testified Matthew C. Perry Jr., "were surly and morose in their manner." And this manner "daily grew worse until the execution." Spencer was observed holding extended conversations with Cromwell and redoubling his efforts to curry favor with the crew, whilst the big boatswain's mate laid off cuffing the apprentices, became playful and palsy with the older boys, and threw coins on the deck to be scrambled for by the young ones. There was nothing you could put a finger on, as Mackenzie later admitted, hardly anything you could express in words; but the sum total of attitudes told any man who knew sailors that something sinister was cooking.

On 25 November things began to happen. Spencer took James W. Wales, the purser's steward, to the booms. That was the place amidships where the brig's boats were lashed down and the spare yards and studdingsail booms were stored. Here, partly in the presence of Small, the renegade midshipman unfolded a plan startling for ingenuity as well as its utter criminality. He would kill the officers, capture the *Somers,* and turn her into a pirate ship. The key members of this conspiracy were Spencer himself, Cromwell, Small, and Wales if willing. Spencer had a list of the "certain," and "doubtful," and those "to be kept *nolens volens,* concealed in his neckerchief. The rest, unwilling sailors and useless boys, the majority of the crew, were to be "disposed of." The mutiny would be sparked off before reaching St. Thomas, during the midwatch when the captain was below, Spencer on duty, Midshipman Rodgers officer of the deck, McKinley (one of the "certain" conspirators) at the arms chest, and McKee (one of the "doubtful") at the wheel. Cromwell and Small would start a mock fight with some of their pals on the forecastle head. Rodgers, on Spencer's appeal, would come forward to stop the fight and, when he reached the gangway, be overpowered and pitched overboard. McKinley would distribute firearms (Spencer having given him the key to the chest), Spencer would dive into Mackenzie's cabin and murder the sleeping captain "with the least noise possible," and then, with Cromwell and Small assisting, penetrate wardroom and steerage and cut the throats of Lieutenant Gansevoort, Master Perry, Purser Heiskell, and a few midshipmen for good measure. Spencer would then call all hands on deck, select "such as would suit his purposes," and cause the rest to be tossed overboard. The brig, now in possession of mutineers, would proceed to Cape St. Antonio or the Isle of Pines off Cuba, where Cromwell had friends among the pirate fraternity. With professional cutthroats added to her complement, she would scour the North Atlantic trade routes as a pirate ship, plundering and sinking defenseless merchantmen and murdering all hands, except that any "females" on board would be taken to the brig "for the use of the officers and men, using them as long as they saw fit; after that, to make way with them." The pirates, after gorging themselves with lust and plunder, would put in at a Cuban port, sell the brig, and live in luxury.

Fantastic as this scheme may now appear, it was practicable. *Somers* could outsail anything afloat except her sister ships, overhaul any merchantman, and overpower any vessel smaller than a frigate. And she would have been far more difficult to catch than CSS *Alabama* in the Civil War or the German raiders of the two world wars.

Spencer picked on Wales to join the gang because he had had an altercation with Commander Mackenzie on the shakedown cruise and, Spencer assumed, cherished resentment. Wales, however, was a loyal man and decided at first opportunity to get word of the plot to his captain. That was easier said than done.

At this point we must glance at the deck and cabin arrangements of *Somers* to appreciate what Mackenzie was up against. A flush-decker, her quarterdeck was merely that part of the gun or spar deck abaft the mainmast, not raised above it as on sloops, frigates and 74's, so not easily defensible against mutineers. Along the midships fore- and aft-section of the quarterdeck rose a rectangular house, like the cabin trunk of a modern yacht, affording light and air to the captain's cabin, the wards room, and the steerage. At the after end of the cabin trunk, and only two feet four inches forward of the binnacles, a booby hatch led down to the captain's cabin; and at the forward end of the trunk a companionway and ladder led to the steerage where the midshipmen slung their hammocks and ate their meals. Sole access to the tiny wardroom (eight by ten feet) where four officers slept, ate, and worked out their navigational problems, was by a door from the steerage, a compartment only eight feet long and fourteen wide. Forward of the steerage, separated from it by a flimsy bulkhead and sliding door, lay the berth deck where the seamen, petty officers and apprentices lived. Its headroom measured only four feet ten inches. Normal access to berth deck from spar deck was through a hatch just abaft the galley, which snuggled close to the foremast. The brig could not have been better planned for a surprise attack. Even if the afterguard managed to rally they would find it almost impossible to defend quarterdeck and three cabins from determined mutineers.

It took some time for Wales to get his startling news into the right ears, for in a crowded vessel like the *Somers* privacy was a rare commodity. Not until next day, Saturday 26 November, was he able to confide the portentous secret to Purser Heiskell, who carried it to Lieutenant Gansevoort, who told the captain. Mackenzie at first refused to believe the story; he did not want to believe it. But Lieutenant Gansevoort did, and made it his business to find evidence. He was told about Spencer's lengthy conferences with Cromwell and Small, and that he had been seen examining a chart of the Isle of Pines. At evening quarters, acting on Gansevoort's advice, Commander Mackenzie summoned Spencer to the quarterdeck, ordered Master Perry to take the wheel, and confronted the midshipman with Wales's story. Spencer admitted that the steward had reported him correctly, but insisted it was all a joke. "This, sir, is joking on a forbidden subject," said Mackenzie. "This joke may cost you your life. . . . You must have been aware that you could only have compassed your design by passing over my dead body and, after that, the bodies of all the officers; it will be necessary for me to confine you, sir."

At the captain's command, Gansevoort arrested Spencer, took away his sword, seated him on the starboard arms chest close to the wheel, chained him to the bulwarks and handcuffed him as an additional precaution. Each successive officer of the deck was ordered to put Spencer to death immediately if he tried to communicate with the crew, but in the meantime to see that he was properly fed and that his other necessities were taken care of. Gansevoort covered him with his own cloak during rainsqualls.

Shortly after this arrest Midshipman Rodgers, searching Spencer's sea chest in the steerage, found in his razor case the paper of which he had spoken to Wales, listing five "certain," ten "doubtful" and eighteen "to be kept *nolens volens,"* and assigning posts at wheel, arms chest, cabin, wardroom and steerage during the mutiny. Spencer, thinking to conceal his sinister design, had used the transparent schoolboy device of writing names and directions in Greek letters. The forms of many letters were wrong, but it was not difficult for Rodgers, who knew some Greek, to translate them. He brought the result to the captain. There were only thirty-three names on the list, leaving more than eighty to be murdered or thrown to the sharks. Spencer did not even contemplate the humanity of the *Bounty* mutineers, who allowed officers and loyal men to depart in a well-provisioned boat.

Armed with this evidence of who was or might be in the plot, and pondering his next move, Mackenzie decided, largely on the basis of an incident that happened next afternoon (Sunday the 27th), to arrest Cromwell and Small. The tradewind had moderated; *Somers* was making only 7.5 knots (she was capable of 12). The captain, eager to make best speed, ordered main skysail and royal studdingsails to be set, and sent a boy to the main royal yard to help. Cromwell, Wilson, and others high on Spencer's Greek list went to the main top, which was not their proper station but, owing to the rake of the mainmast, lay directly over the quarterdeck. Midshipman Hays, officer of the deck, ordered the weather royal yard brace to be let go. Small, who was at that station, instead of obeying the order, hauled in the brace "very violently" with the aid of a boy, and belayed it "very hard."[1] Consequently the topgallant and royal yard with the sails bent onto them came tumbling down on deck, and the boy on the yard narrowly escaped going overboard by grabbing the lee royal shrouds. It looked as if this was a plan by Cromwell and his cronies to rescue Spencer by taking advantage of the confusion, especially if a boat had to be lowered to pick up the boy. Fortunately Lieutenant Gansevoort rushed on deck and efficiently took charge of clearing up the mess of spars, sails and lines. After dark the same day, when the topgallant mast was about to be swayed up into place, and Rodgers ordered four or five men to help on the quarterdeck, some twenty men and boys rushed aft, stamping their feet in a way unusual and unallowable on a man-of-war. Gansevoort jumped onto the cabin trunk and, pointing his pistol at the tallest man, threatened to shoot anyone who put his foot on the quarterdeck. This, again, looked very much like a rescue attempt.

Mackenzie now decided to arrest Cromwell and Small. The boatswain's mate was seated on the port arms chest of the quarterdeck, facing Spencer and ironed to the rail; Small forward of him next to the after gun.

Somers was rolling along, sailing large with the tradewind on her starboard quarter; but the wind appeared to be diminishing, an additional anxiety to Mackenzie. Unless he encountered *Vandalia* at St. Thomas and turned the prisoners over to her, he would have to go on to New York and have them tried there. But could he safely make even St. Thomas, at least a week's sail distant? Discipline was disintegrating. *Somers* had no brig where prisoners could be confined, and no marines to guard them. After the event, shoreside critics of Mackenzie asked why he could not have confined them to the hold or chained them to pad-eyes in his own cabin—a trapezoidal-shaped cubbyhole eight feet long, eight feet broad forward and two feet broad aft. The bulkheads between captain's cabin and wardroom, as between wardroom and steerage, were so flimsy that a strong push could have breached them. The hold was full of ballast, water casks and stores to within a few inches of the berth deck; anyone confined there would have suffocated. What was Mackenzie to do, with this sinister plot simmering, and no possible help from anyone outside the ship? What might not happen in a sudden squall at night? Mackenzie knew perfectly well a stern fact which Admiral Nimitz recalled to the Pacific Fleet a century later:—"The time for taking all measures for a ship's safety is while still able to do so. Nothing is more dangerous than for a seaman to be grudging in taking precautions lest they turn out to have been unnecessary. Safety at sea for a thousand years has depended on exactly the opposite philosophy."

Let us pause a moment to consider the dramatic contrast between the brightly illuminated setting, the dark designs of the plotters, and the dismal apprehensions of the intended victims. Sailing west to "the Indies" in the winter northeast trades is perhaps the most beautiful sailing in any ocean; and *Somers,* rolling and dipping in the long swells, had the wind just where she wanted it, on the quarter, to make best time over a sapphire ocean flecked with whitecaps. Flying fish flashed silver past the foam at her bow. Puffy tradewind clouds raced her overhead, and occasionally one lashed her with rain. No throb of engines assaulted the ear; there were no sounds but the striking of the ship's bell, the creaking of spars and timbers, lines slatting against the sails, and the rush and gurgle of great waters. Every few hours the square sails changed color: golden gossamer when the last-quarter moon rose, polished silver just before dawn, ruddy at sunrise, and cream-white at high noon. But the fatigued, harassed and anxious officers, and the conspirators guessing whether or not they were found out, had neither taste nor time for aesthetic appreciation. Sailors collected in knots to exchange gossip. Officers, divided "watch and watch" (eight hours on and eight off), armed themselves with two pistols and a cutlass each, and even in their watch below kept continually moving about the vessel, to break up any attempt at rescue. Thus Monday passed, and Tuesday, with increasing tension and fatigue on the part of the loyal officers and increasing insubordination on the part of the crew. Orders were obeyed sullenly after repetition; the men "would go growling along as though they did not care," said Wales. Knives and other lethal weapons were discovered in handy spots. Four suspects failed to appear at muster, and it was always they who brought food to the prisoners, hoping perhaps to communicate with them. On the night of the 29th there was another ominous rush aft when the spanker boom preventer tackle carried away, and young Calbraith Perry had some difficulty chasing unwanted hands off the quarterdeck.

On Wednesday morning, 30 November, Mackenzie arrested four suspects whose names were high on Spencer's Greek list: sailmaker's mate Wilson, landsman Daniel McKinley, and apprentices McKee and Green. Seven prisoners were now chained to the bulwarks of the quarterdeck, their presence interfering with the proper handling of the ship.

The commander's next action was to order the four wardroom officers (Lieutenant Gansevoort, Purser Heiskell, Surgeon Leacock and Master Perry) and the three senior midshipmen (Rodgers, Thompson and Hays) to deliberate, take evidence, and give him their collective advice. They met in the little wardroom the rest of that day and most of the night, thirteen to fourteen hours in all, discussing the affair and questioning several older members of the crew. All oral evidence strengthened the case against Spencer, Cromwell and Small. The witnesses agreed that Cromwell was the most dangerous man on board, the brains of the conspiracy. Spencer's piratical ambitions might have remained the mere fantasies of a depraved youngster's mind had not Cromwell showed him how to make the dream come true. But Cromwell, who was very "cagey"—

using an alias on Spencer's Greek list—would hardly have conspired without Spencer, the son of a cabinet member whose influence could be counted on to get them off if anything slipped.

At nine in the morning of Thursday 1 December, five days since Wales had communicated the mutiny plot to Mackenzie, the seven officers reported in writing that they had "come to a cool, decided, and unanimous opinion" that Spencer, Cromwell and Small were "guilty of a full and determined intention to commit a mutiny," and that the uncertainty as to who was in their gang, and "the impossibility of guarding against the contingencies which 'a day or an hour may bring forth,' " had convinced them "that it would be impossible to carry them to the United States; and that the safety of the public property, the lives of ourselves and of those committed to our charge, require that . . . they should be put to death, in a manner best calculated . . . to make a beneficial impression upon the disaffected."

Mackenzie had already reached the same conclusion—that the three ringleaders be put to death. His authority he found in an Act of Congress passed in 1800: "If any person in the navy shall make or attempt to make any mutinous assembly he shall on conviction thereof by a Court Martial, suffer death." The council of officers was not a court-martial, and Mackenzie had no authority to call one; but it was the best substitute at hand. He felt that since Spencer, Cromwell and Small were the only three men, other than the loyal officers, capable of navigating a ship, their removal would discourage any attempt to carry out Spencer's diabolical plan. But could not Mackenzie have waited until his ship reached Danish St. Thomas, which she did on 5 December, or squared away for a nearer island? There the prisoners could have been incarcerated ashore, to await safe transportation to New York for trial. Mackenzie, however, considered "that a naval commander can never be justified in invoking foreign aid in reducing an insubordinate crew to obedience." He had hoped to encounter USS *Vandalia* in St. Thomas and turn over the prisoners to her; but, owing to "the daily and hourly increasing insubordination of the crew," he dared no longer delay the execution of the ringleaders.

Once the decision was made, Mackenzie proceeded to the execution. All three men were informed that they were about to die, and had better make their peace with God. Spencer, who hitherto had been sneeringly confident, counting no doubt on a big public trial in New York and his father engaging the best legal talent to get him off, now fell on his knees, blubbering, and confessed his guilt. But he exonerated Cromwell. The boatswain's mate also knelt and begged for mercy, but protested his innocence. Small kept a stiff upper lip but freely confessed his guilt.

Three whips, as the tackles used for hoisting in stores were called, were now rigged to the main yardarm, two on the starboard arm for Cromwell and Small, one on the port arm for Spencer. The condemned men were given time to read the Bible and pray. Spencer said, "There are few crimes that I have not committed; I feel sincerely penitent." All three asked the loyal officers and men to forgive them; Cromwell begging Lieutenant Gansevoort to forgive him was the nearest he came to confession, and he tried to shake off his guard and jump overboard. Little Elisha Small died a manly death. He admitted that the captain was doing his duty, told him, "I honor you for it; God bless that flag!" He made a dying speech to the ship's company, warning them against mutinous intendments and against slaving. "Twas going in a Guineaman that brought me to this." He concluded, "Now, fellow topmen, give me a quick death." The nooses were put in place, one around Spencer's neck as he stood on the quarterdeck under the port yardarm, one around each of the others as they stood on the bulwarks under the starboard yardarm. Spencer's face was covered with a black handkerchief, those of Cromwell and Small by sailors' blouses. Two men were detailed to haul on each whip, and officers were stationed beside them, with cutlasses drawn and orders to cut down anyone who faltered. Spencer was offered the privilege of giving the word for the execution signal gun to be fired, but his nerve failed him and he asked the captain to do so. Mackenzie called, "Stand by, fire!" A boy applied a live coal from the galley to a touch-hole, the cannon roared, the men at the whips hauled away, and within a minute three dead men were dangling from the main yard.

Mackenzie now called the crew aft and delivered a sermon on truth, honor and fidelity. He concluded by calling for three cheers for the flag. "They gave three hearty ones," and this seemed to relieve the minds of all from the prevailing gloom. The crew were now piped to dinner. Mackenzie was shocked that some of the boys, as they went below, pointed at the dead bodies and laughed. But was that not natural? They were now safe from mutineers who had planned to throw them to the sharks.

Dinner is eaten. The bodies are lowered and prepared for proper burial at sea. Mackenzie, a stickler for doing everything properly, orders Spencer, as an officer, to be buried in uniform in a coffin, and "Chips" claps together two sea chests to make one, weighted and bored with holes for a quick sinking. The enlisted men are sewed up by messmates in their own hammocks, the last stitch being taken, according to ancient sea custom, through the nose, and a cannonball placed at each man's head and feet for quick sinking. During these preparations a black squall passes over *Somers,* as if a last salute by the powers of darkness. There is a delay while the three bodies, laid out in order of rank, are decently covered with tarpaulins.

By the time the squall is over, the short tropical twilight has faded, the new moon has set, and battle lanterns are broken out to light a solemn scene on the spar deck. Prayer books are handed around. While *Somers* sails slowly through the velvety tropical night under the star-studded firmament of heaven, with no other music than the swish of parting waters, Captain Mackenzie reads from the Book of Common Prayer the office for burial of the dead at sea. Bearded men and smooth-faced boys, gathering on the booms and in the gangways, speak the responses reverently, and the four men in irons whisper what they can remember of the service.

> *We therefore commit their bodies to the deep, to be turned into corruption, Looking for the resurrection of the body (when the Sea shall give up her dead), and the life of the world to come, through our Lord Jesus Christ.*

There are three loud splashes as the corpses drop into a three-thousand-fathom deep. Ensign and pendant, half-masted for the burial, are now two-blocked and *Somers* continues on her course—west and by north—from which she had never deviated during these five days of fear and tension.

There was no further trouble about discipline on board. The arrested men were kept below deck most of the passage to New York, and took their meals with the others. The crew obeyed orders cheerfully, apparently greatly relieved, although the presence of four enlisted men in irons reminded them that justice was not yet satisfied. After calling a few hours at St. Thomas on 5 December, the brig proceeded to New York. She had a quick passage, nine days later anchoring off Brooklyn Navy Yard. No visitors were allowed on board, and nobody was granted leave or liberty. Mackenzie dispatched Acting Midshipman O. H. Perry II to Washington with his report, then took his entire crew ashore and marched them to the nearest church to give thanks for the preservation of ship and company from capture and murder. The officers were so fagged out with their extra duties and lack of sleep that, when they crossed the lawn to the Commandant's quarters, they reeled and staggered like drunken men.

Notes

[1]Much of the discussion turns on whether this was accidental or not. Every yachtsman knows that if you tauten a vang and let out the mainsheet you risk breaking the gaff, and that shrouds too taut may break a wooden mast. It is inconceivable that an old seaman like Small could have hauled in and belayed the weather brace accidentally, especially when ordered to do the contrary and when the ship was rolling to leeward.

CHAPTER SEVEN

MUTINY?

EDWARD L. BEACH

FOCUS QUESTIONS

1. What was the mission and crew composition of the *Somers*?
2. What were Commander MacKenzie's options for dealing with the "mutineers?" According to Beach, did he make the right decision?
3. How did the *Somers* incident affect discipline and training in the U. S. Navy?
4. After reading both articles concerning the *Somers* incident, do you believe that MacKenzie's actions were justified? Is one account more credible than the other?
5. Why is one account more believable than the other? Does one article use source material more effectively than the other?

In 1842, there occurred another incident that is consistently deemphasized but that nevertheless had important long-range effects. This was the so-called mutiny aboard the brig *Somers*. The *Somers,* named for Richard Somers, who died when our converted bomb-ketch *Intrepid* exploded prematurely in Tripoli harbor, was a tiny 290-ton training ship. Her crew during the voyage in which the "mutiny" occurred consisted almost entirely of young trainees: apprentice sailors and midshipmen. She also carried a small leavening of experienced officers and enlisted hands, and her captain was a sanctimonious prig by the name of

Alexander Slidell Mackenzie, whose wife was a member of the famous Perry family.

An article of faith among followers of the maritime professions is contained in the old saying, "The best place for a young man is at sea." It followed that the environment of a ship at sea was where navy midshipmen and apprentice seamen should receive their training, and the system in vogue until 1842 amounted simply to assigning them to cruising ships where they would be exposed to what they were expected to learn. The popular term for this, still in use, was "the school of the ship." Training at sea has unquestioned merit, honored by annual cruises of some kind by nearly all maritime training institutions. In 1842, the idea that all instruction of midshipmen or apprentice seamen, even in academic subjects like mathematics or physics, should take place aboard ship and preferably under way, was virtually a form of religion. Nevertheless, it had drawbacks.

Aboard ship, officers and petty officers often could not or did not give adequate time to instructing their charges. Although there were outstanding exceptions, they were frequently poor teachers with neither interest nor training in the role. In an attempt to improve the education of the navy's future officers, schoolmasters were assigned to the bigger ships and shore installations, and regular study times were prescribed for the midshipmen or young officers preparing for their examinations. Subjects taught were usually left entirely to the particular inclinations of a ship's schoolmaster, sometimes with her commander's overview and approval. Conscientious schoolmasters generally tried to teach navigation, astronomy, and mathematics, with occasionally something more frivolous, such as English or literature, thrown in. The cramped conditions on board ship were not conducive to study, but even had they been, a single schoolmaster could not effectively cover all the possible subjects, nor, aboard ship, was he usually accorded the rank and prestige necessary to command the serious attention of his students. Invariably he found himself competing with the ship's own needs, which were always more immediate and usually more interesting. Many otherwise motivated schoolmasters were unequal to the special challenges of instructing in an active ship; almost uniformly, whenever they are mentioned in accounts of service in those times, the reference is disparaging.

When a ship was in port was the most difficult of all, for the midshipmen, boys of high school age for the most part, were hard to handle at best. If a ship were to be in harbor for a lengthy period, her crew and officers were frequently reduced and there was neither anything for the midshipmen to do nor anyone to supervise them. The school-master's authority derived from that of the captain; unless he were an exceptional individual and had his captain's full support, he might lose his young charges entirely. There was, fortunately, one such exceptional teacher. William Chauvenet, a graduate of Yale, entered the schoolmaster system in 1841 and quickly impressed everyone who encountered him. In 1842, aged only twenty-two, he took over a school to help senior midshipmen prepare for the examinations for lieutenant. Schools of this type were originally informal—set up aboard ship or ashore, anywhere they were needed.

Buildings ashore were far better suited to such use, and over the years some of them took on a form of permanence. The one run by Chauvenet was in the Philadelphia Naval Asylum, an institution for old and indigent sailors. From this it became known as "the asylum school." Chauvenet began immediately to agitate for a real naval school, with a curriculum, faculty, and regular classes. By good fortune, Commodore James Biddle, of the same Philadelphia family that had produced Nicholas thirty-three years earlier, was then serving as governor of the asylum. Biddle, recognizing the importance of Chauvenet's proposals, supported him enthusiastically.

For enlisted men, training in basic shipboard skills was expected to be automatic through their daily duties. Midshipmen were required to learn these skills as well. But all shipboard functions required supervision by someone skilled in doing them. Danger was always present in a sailing ship, for yards and sails were massive, forever in movement, and continually in need of attention; ground tackle—anchors and their associated cables, chains, and hoisting gear—was likewise cumbersome and generally slippery with slime; lines in running and standing rigging were in constant use and often under heavy tension—an unnoticed weakness could, and often did, cause an accident. Yet speed of execution was nearly always necessary, or at any rate demanded by impatient officers intent upon demonstrating efficiency. To a busy ship and crew, the presence of raw recruits was often a hindrance, seldom a help.

There were many criticisms of the system, both from those who begrudged the resulting loss of efficiency and from those who felt the trainees, both midshipmen and enlisted apprentices, were not receiving the attention they should. There was growing pressure for establishment of a true naval academy for future officers (the army had established such a school at West Point years before) and a preliminary training school for enlisted men, where recruits could be better indoctrinated with basic skills before they went aboard ship. Nevertheless, the adherents of the school of the ship continued to win the day in Congress, where new ideas always stumbled over the additional expense invariably accompanying them. In 1841, however, a small experiment had been authorized. In addition to the schools in regular ships, there would be a training ship, a small one of course, expressly designed for and assigned to the initial training of newly recruited sailors and midshipmen. The *Somers* was the result. She was built for that purpose, but in addition, since she was not intended to engage in battle, her designer, Samuel Humphreys (son of Joshua), apparently felt he could indulge his fancy for low and racy lines and make her very fast, almost like a yacht. She was fitted with guns, since they would be needed for training, but her thin sides were not expected to encounter serious gunfire. *Somers,* in truth, could have been described as a large toy. She was launched in 1842, and Commander Mackenzie, the navy's most literarily inclined officer and also something of a preacher and moralist, was assigned to command.

He seemed an obvious choice. The brig was too small to harbor a schoolmaster, logical though it might have been to include one aboard. There was no spare space in her to use for schooling in any case. However, Mackenzie could be trusted to give much attention to improvement of the minds of his young charges. As a writer of books, he would be sure to insist that midshipmen study tomes devoted to navigation, seamanship, and gunnery, and also that they improve their minds by reading some of the classics he would select for them. His known pedantry would be usefully employed supervising the practical training of the teenage boys, many fresh from the farm and recruited as apprentice seamen, in marlinspike seamanship (splicing and reeving ropes, called "line") operating ground tackle, handling small boats, working the sails, and operating the ship's small broadside guns. With nearly everyone aboard new to naval service, his evangelistic streak would also be put to good use: he could be expected to see to their proper moral uplifting. This last point was considered very important.

The *Somers's* tiny hull, 103 feet between perpendiculars and 25 feet extreme beam, could not have been designed with much thought to what a school ship should be. The "tween decks" dimension (floor to overhead) of her one covered deck, the berth deck, was only 4 feet 10 inches. Her crew would have to stoop lower than in any other ship of our navy, except in the *Somers's* near identical sister, *Bainbridge.* She had been built for the large complement, considering her small size, of ninety-eight persons, in keeping with her mission as a school ship. Of these, the two commissioned officers in her planned complement (one of them the captain), the three warrant officers, and fourteen seaman billets could be counted as experienced. There were also to be seventy-two apprentices cooped up in her, sleeping in hammocks from closely spaced hooks in a part of the berth deck, and seven midshipmen. The midshipmen's berth, also graced by the 4-foot 10-inch overhead, measured 8 by 14 feet. Here the seven youths were to sleep, take their meals, and keep all their equipment.

Almost immediately there was a complication. A ship exclusively devoted to training would relieve the cruising ships of much of the nuisance of instructing ignorant sailors and stupid midshipmen, and give the ships more space for other purposes. Nearly all seized the opportunity to divest themselves of an unpopular duty. Recruits and midshipmen were assigned to the *Somers* with no apparent regard for her extremely limited space, so that before setting forth on his first cruise, Mackenzie protested at the excessive number of persons detailed to his tiny craft. No one paid attention. When the *Somers* finally got under way, she was literally bulging with more than 120 men aboard, most of them young trainees.

No vessel could have been less appropriate for training new navy men, whether destined for the quarterdeck or "before the mast." She was too heavily sparred, too shallow of draft, too slender of hull. She was fast, but also very tender, easily listed over by a strong breeze. She had no reserve for awkwardness in handling sail, or in trimming ship, or any other of the many functions in which an unhandy crew of apprentices might be less than expert. Skill was required to sail her, and continual vigilance against sudden disaster. Many a better-found ship had foundered, sometimes even despite adequate warning of bad weather. Mackenzie was concerned about this, and he was right to be so.

Four years later she did indeed capsize and sink, with heavy loss of life, and in 1863 so did her sister, *Bainbridge.*

In 1842, Mackenzie had already celebrated his thirty-ninth birthday and had served twenty-five years in the navy. At that age, Stephen Decatur's career had been nearing its end; he was twenty-four when he leaped to fame from the burning *Philadelphia,* and thirty-three when his big *United States* captured the *Macedonian.* Oliver Perry, Mackenzie's brother-in-law, commanding a squadron, had won the Battle of Lake Eric when he was only twenty-eight. At thirty-one, John Rodgers had commanded all U.S. naval forces in the Mediterranean. In contrast, Mackenzie, at thirty-nine, commanded only a small school ship.

Mackenzie was a friend and occasional visitor of Washington Irving, by whom he was much influenced, and who had assisted him in the promotion of his first book, written after a lengthy furlough in Europe, *A Year in Spain.* By 1842 he had published six books, three of them biographies (of John Paul Jones, Stephen Decatur, and Oliver Hazard Perry). None of his writings was enduringly important, but to a navy composed of persons not noted for literary accomplishment and easily awed by a bound book and the speaking acquaintance of Washington Irving, they were uncritically accepted as brilliant. As it happened, the last month of 1842 and the first half of 1843 became the period of Mackenzie's greatest output, consisting entirely of self-justification for hanging three members of his crew because he believed they were plotting to convert their swift little school ship into a pirate corsair.

It was, in fact, simple murder, an act of panic by an unstable man who had no business being autocrat of his own little kingdom in a ship of the U.S. Navy. Yet such was his ability at presenting the facts to his own advantage that even though one of his victims was the son of Secretary of War John Canfield Spencer, and even though Spencer vowed to avenge his son's death by seeing to it that Mackenzie was tried in civilian court for first-degree murder, the guilty captain got off scotfree, acquitted by a navy general court-martial of all charges. No official notice was taken of the eleven more "mutineers" he brought back under arrest in the *Somers,* some in irons. Despite the fact that their "confederates" had been hanged for the crime of mutiny, or planning to mutiny, not one was even brought to trial. In dribs and drabs, they were all simply released and allowed to return home, the obligated time remaining on their enlistments forgotten. The charges under which they had been manacled for weeks and jailed for months in New York were never vacated, nor any lesser ones brought. In today's more legally sophisticated society, they could have sued for false arrest.

There was, however, an unlooked for result. Everyone in the naval service—and to a greater extent yet, the body politic of the country—was uneasily aware there was something radically wrong with an organization that could justify high-handed action like Mackenzie's. The new school-ship program, barely begun, came under intense scrutiny, as did the older system of sending midshipmen and recruits to sea to learn by doing. As discussed later in this chapter, a radical change was indicated, and the upshot was the founding in 1845 of the United States Naval Academy.

The sordid details: Philip Spencer, the eighteen-year-old son of the New York politician who was Tyler's secretary of war, had long been in rebellion against his father. He did poorly in school, was slovenly in his person, was almost never without a cigar in his mouth, and hated constructive activity or authority of any kind. He drank to excess (though evidently he could hold liquor well) and insulted his elders whenever he thought he might do so without punitive consequences. He was either cross-eyed or walleyed, a physical affliction that may have been one of the root causes of his personality disorder.

With little understanding or sympathy for his troubled son, his father thought to straighten him out by procuring him an appointment as midshipman in the navy. This was less than successful; Midshipman Spencer had already been turned out of two ships as unsuitable for naval service when Secretary of the Navy Abel P. Upshur, acting on the personal request of his colleague, reversed the most recent dismissal and sent young Philip to the new school ship. No doubt both cabinet officers believed that if anyone could wean him from his debauched habits, the *Somers's* schoolmaster-preacher-skipper, over a period of time, would be able to do so.

But the concatenation of circumstances worked exactly in the opposite direction. Spencer's last-minute arrival crowded the tiny midshipmen's quarters unbearably. Spurned by his messmates because of his antisocial appearance and behavior, the young misfit found companionship among the enlisted men of the crew, thus breaking another taboo. The apprentices were flattered that an officer, even an unprepossessing one, should find them interesting, the older hands gave him lip service in return for surreptitious handouts of food, tobacco, and liquor—some from the midshipmen's mess, some that the well-heeled lad purchased ashore. Philip Spencer might have become a writer of adventure stories had he lived, for he apparently had a good imagination and evidently indulged himself and his audiences with fantasies about turning pirate. Unfortunately for him, one crew member reported what he had heard. Mackenzie had Spencer seized and searched. A paper with Greek characters in his handwriting was found concealed in his neckerchief, supposedly listing those to be killed and those who would join him in his piratical adventure.

The *Somers* was homeward bound. She hard crossed the Atlantic twice, touching first at Madeira and then at Monrovia, capital of the newly created Free Liberia, and now she was within a week of reaching her next port, St. Thomas, Virgin Islands, still one of the avenues for the illegal importation of slaves to the New World. The last known case of piracy on the high seas had occurred ten years before, but the illegal slave trade still existed and, by international agreement, all ships in the slave trade were defined as pirates.

The accusation by a crew member trying to curry favor, when added to Spencer's Greek paper, was enough for the humorless and credulous Mackenzie. Deciding that he and his loyal crew members were in mortal danger, he clapped the hapless midshipman in hand and leg irons and put him under guard on the quarterdeck. (There was nowhere he could be confined in the packed spaces below.) Soon Mackenzie had two other unpopular crew members in irons also, and within a couple of days a number of others; four more at first, finally a total of eleven, were added. During the next four days, as the *Somers* steadily approached St. Thomas, Mackenzie directed his executive officer and the others in the wardroom to consider the situation and give their opinion as to the action he should take. After a number of recommendations that did not satisfy him, he received what he subconsciously must have wanted to hear: Spencer and the other ringleaders constituted a danger to the ship and should be put to death. They were hanged immediately.

Two days later the rakish training brig entered the lovely harbor of St. Thomas, then a Danish dependency. Tarrying only long enough to take aboard fresh provisions and water, she got under way as quickly as possible, bound for New York.

Historian Samuel Eliot Morison has given as his opinion that Mackenzie was justified in directing the executions, but this conclusion cannot stand inspection. By naval regulation (and tradition too), only the highest naval court, a general court-martial, has power to award the death penalty, and even then it cannot be carried out until approved at the highest level. This was the rule in 1842, and it is the rule today. After a half century, our code of naval law was thoroughly established. A mere captain of a ship could not (in 1842, any more than now) order a general court-martial. He could—and may still—order lesser courts-martial, each rigidly limited as to offenses that may be tried and punishments that can be awarded. In 1842, as today, only flag officers were empowered to order general courts-martial. (Nowadays, the proceedings and verdicts must be reviewed by the officer ordering the court, who may not be a member, and forwarded for review up the chain of command until they arrive before the judge advocate of the navy, its highest-ranking law officer.) Mackenzie, only a commander in rank, ordered no court of any kind. He directed his officers to "advise" him, sent them back repeatedly until they said what he wanted to hear, permitted the accused men no opportunity to defend themselves, and after rendering the fatal judgment allowed them only ten minutes, later extended to an hour, to make their peace with God.

Summary executions have taken place during war, particularly in the case of spies and traitors, but whenever possible due form of trial has always been carried out. Even pirates were brought in for trial if at all possible.*

In the *Somers* case there was no war, and no lack of facilities at her captain's disposal. There was an American consul in St. Thomas, with the customary consular powers. The prisoners, still in irons if the captain felt it necessary, could have been turned over to him for further transport, under charges, to New York or any other port. In his defense, Mackenzie made much of his fears that his disaffected crew would rise and take the ship during those last two days, but this is in fact a measure of the hysteria that gripped him. The charge of planned mutiny was never proved, nor was it ever tried, either aboard the *Somers* or

* piracy is generally considered to have ended in 1834 with the execution of one Captain Gibert, but his sentence was preceded by a full trial in Boston.

later, when the remaining eleven unexecuted accused could have been brought before a court in New York City. To this day there are only the suspicions of a paranoid captain, based on garrulous talk by a lonely misfit as reported by a favor-currying member of the crew, that a mutinous plot existed.

Even had there been, it seems hardly credible that the officers and loyal members of the crew, with access to the ship's arms chest, could not have held control against many times their number of fearful and demoralized youths, up to 14 of whom were already in chains. The far more likely scenario is that the whole crew was terrified, and had good reason to be.

Whatever rationale may be offered for Mackenzie's conduct, the fact remains that Midshipman Spencer, Boatswain's Mate Samuel Cromwell, and Seaman Small were hanged in contravention of their rights under the laws and Constitution of their country, without due process, without the knowledge that their execution was being debated or that a "trial" was being held—without an opportunity to speak even as witnesses in their own defense. And once the decision had been taken, they were killed with cruel speed.

The *Somers* continued to New York with eleven prisoners manacled on deck, and on arrival her skipper sent off the first of several reports to Secretary of the Navy Upshur. When news of the executions came out, initial reaction was favorable to Mackenzie; but as reporters pried more deeply it began to shift against him. From here on it is difficult to assess exactly what took place, and why. Much was kept secret, passed only by word of mouth, with no records kept. Secretary of War Spencer was of course outraged. He had never understood Philip, nor made much of an effort to help him; but his being hanged for mutiny was a different matter. What occurred in Washington in the private councils that must have taken place between the two cabinet members can only be guessed at. What is clear is that Upshur defended his skipper and the navy, that a dispute of grand proportions erupted between the two politicians, that the skipper of the *Somers* never admitted there was ever any question whatever of the absolute probity and rightfulness of his action nor of the compassionate feelings with which, as he described the moment, he painfully gave the dreadfully difficult orders. And after official investigation by a court of inquiry and trial by general court-martial, all of which lasted dreary months, Mackenzie was exonerated of all wrongdoing.

The press behaved as might have been expected, eagerly following the story and developments in the court-martial so long as there was public interest. A short time after the initially favorable press reports, a spirited defense of the three unfortunates had appeared in a Washington newspaper, signed only by the letter S., which stated their side of the case and generated a great deal of interest. The popular guess of the time was that its author could only have been Philip Spencer's father. Though conclusive proof does not exist, the intimate knowledge the writer had of the case, and of Philip Spencer personally, could hardly have been possessed by anyone else. As the press began to delve more deeply into the matter, James Gordon Bennett of the *New York Herald* wrote scathing editorials. James Fenimore Cooper angrily denounced Mackenzie in letters and articles. And Commander Mackenzie, as soon as the chill began to descend, asked for an official court of inquiry.

This court, acting in much the same way as a civilian grand jury, after examination of all the evidence and circumstances gave as its verdict that there was no cause for further action against Mackenzie.

In the meantime, Cromwell's young widow, Margaret, had become associated with Secretary Spencer in an effort to bring Mackenzie before a civilian judge on charges of murder. Charges were actually preferred, but, citing the possibility of double jeopardy, the judge before whom they were placed refused to admit them while the court of inquiry was still in session. Several weeks later, however, once the naval court of inquiry had found no basis for prosecution, there were four days during which civilian charges could again have been filed. None was.

On the fourth day, in disregard of the verdict of the court of inquiry, Navy Secretary Upshur nevertheless ordered a general court-martial and directed that charges be preferred. With his signature to this order, the rule against double jeopardy stood again between Mackenzie and civilian justice.

A few editorialists, chief among them Bennett and Cooper, publicly excoriated Mackenzie before and during his trial and denounced the results of the courtmartial when they were given out. The verdict rendered was perhaps what one might have predicted, given the composition of the court and the high-level advice it may have received—although it is only speculation that such advice was ever given, or that the members of the court would so have betrayed their sworn oaths. But it is not guessing to state that the navy's top officials wished to sweep everything under the rug for fear of public reaction, that the members of the court shared this desire, and that all of them had the wit not to do this hurriedly. Strangely, in the face of these circumstances, nowhere was a rationale found for the indecisive action of the new principals in the affair: the secretary of war, John Spencer, and Mrs. Margaret Cromwell, a recent bride and now suddenly a widow.

In fact, Margaret Cromwell and Secretary Spencer had had several meetings. A former judge experienced in military legal procedures through his service as the army's chief, Spencer well knew how and when to bring charges before a civil court. Without question, he was well aware of the four-day hiatus during which he could have re-filed the charges of murder. What is inexplicable is why he—and the widow—neglected this opportunity and so precipitously abandoned their campaign to clear his son's and her husband's names (not to mention that of Seaman Small, who seems to have had no one taking his part). Speculation suggests a plausible answer, but, not surprisingly, there is no hard evidence.

That the two bereaved persons did not pursue the matter, while an opportunity they could not have failed to recognize lay before them, can lead to but a single conclusion. Not only must they have felt there was nothing to be gained, no rehabilitation of the dead or vengeance upon their killer, but not improbably there was something more that might yet be lost. There are only two possibilities, both of which could have been operative at the same time. One can imagine Secretary Spencer reviewing all he could find out about his son's last days. He was well aware that his son was a troubled youth, that at times he behaved strangely. He would have found out that his son consorted more with the enlisted men than with his fellow midshipmen and superiors, that he patronized them with gifts and hard drink, and perhaps with something more: strange drugs. There comes down to us the account of an excursion on shore in Liberia, from which young Spencer returned in a very different mood, approaching euphoria, from that in which he began it. Secretary Spencer would have found out that his son had varying moods on board as well.

Not much was known of mind-altering drugs in 1842, beyond the fact that they existed. Typically, there was much misinformation as to their effects, but one thing had already changed greatly. They no longer had their earlier social acceptance. They were becoming viewed as responsible for aberrant behavior, as addictive, and as responsible for many awful permanent effects. The case against drugs had only begun to be compiled, but social reaction was already severe. Drug users were held in utmost scorn, fear, and condemnation: lost souls whose families bent every effort to keep the dread affliction secret and whose friends avoided them. To John Spencer, even the unsubstantiated suggestion of drug abuse by his son would have been personally devastating, politically very damaging, and at the same time awfully believable. Drugs could explain all of Philip's abandoned behavior, but the cost to his family, in particular to his father, would have been very high.

The secretary of war would also have discovered that his son was disliked, distrusted, and—I speculate—he may have been suspected of being "queer." There may well have been a suggestion of perversion, an accusation extremely easy to make and, by the clandestine nature of both accusation and alleged behavior, extremely hard to defend against. The merest whisper of it was enough to make one a pariah. Society was adamantly unforgiving. Reaction, even to mere rumor, was horrified and spontaneous. Neither wife nor father could wish such accusations to become public property.

Today, historians and psychologists alike accept—given the conditions that were known to have existed in ships of the time—that sexual deviation must have been far more common than anywhere admitted. Philip Spencer's continued association with members of the crew, to the exclusion of his own peers, might easily have brought this suspicion, justified or not, upon him. The merest hint of such a calamitous accusation would have been sufficient to demolish utterly both the father and the wife, and nothing else could have had such extraordinary effect. But there had to be a credible, powerful source for the suggestion, one whose hinted concern could not be ignored. There was but one man who could fill these qualifications, only one man to whom Spencer would have to listen: his colleague in President Tyler's cabinet, Abel Upshur, the secretary of the navy. It is not generally known that he was the older brother of one of Mackenzie's close friends—thus establishing a perfect conduit for informal communication. It is only speculation to infer that the dread insinuation was made. But something obviously happened to cause Spencer to stay his obvious move. In the meantime, to ensure that the case would remain within naval jurisdiction in case of a later stiffening of his colleague's will, Upshur hastened nevertheless to hale Mackenzie before the most powerful naval court, where he would be subject to legal jurisdiction but, through the double jeopardy rule, safe from civilian processes of law.

He may even have assured Secretary Spencer that the navy court would prosecute Mackenzie to the full extent of naval law, certainly as stringent as applicable civilian statutes, but if so, Upshur then came close to actually breaking his word. The man he ordered as president of the court-martial was Matthew Perry, Mackenzie's other brother-in-law. Perry permitted the accused the widest latitude in conducting his defense, which he dramatically did, in uniform, while the prosecutor was hindered at nearly every turn. The voluminous proceedings took months. The court's final verdict on each of the several charges preferred was not guilty. Three days later, in the tiny wardroom of the *Somers,* the brig's doctor, who had reluctantly gone along with Mackenzie's demand for a death sentence, committed suicide. No doubt he was in despair, but no explanation has ever been offered.

Noteworthy in naval court-martial proceedings is that they can adjudge a higher level of acquittal than civilian courts are allowed: over and above a verdict of not guilty, they can "most fully and most honorably acquit." This higher degree of innocence was, and is still, sometimes adjudged when the court feels it necessary totally to absolve the accused of any suspicion whatsoever. But Alexander Mackenzie's court-martial, despite the pressures upon it, could not bring itself to approve his action to this degree. It had done enough for him. The navy's dirty linen would not be further exposed to public view. The embattled skipper was simply found not guilty. Nothing was said about being "most fully and most honorably acquitted." All the same, it was enough.

Many of the facts about the "mutiny" in the *Somers* must forever remain in the realm of speculation. Historians whose training permits them only to record what is provable often rail at their inability to state more than what they can prove by reference to some established fact. Persons desirous of concealing something, or controlling history's later reports on events within their interest, know this well. The *Somers* is a case in point.

With Mackenzie's less-than-full acquittal he was nonetheless protected from further legal action. He was safe from all but the slow verdict of the society and the service to which he had caused such devastating damage. Secretary Spencer came to realize he had been tricked and was so angry with Secretary Upshur that they nearly came to blows at a cabinet meeting and had to be separated by other members. Mackenzie continued writing, remained always totally convinced of the rightness of his decision aboard the *Somers,* but had no further impact on the navy.*

In the quiet recesses of thoughtful consideration there can sometimes be the ground swell of what might be called a psychic reaction. The nation, and more to the point the navy, knew that three men had been summarily hanged without any of the protections guaranteed by the Constitution and by law. The man who killed them had been judicially protected by two successive naval courts, which seemed partisan, to say the least. Murderer or not, he had been held above the law.

In public opinion the navy had already suffered a great deal from the support it gave James Barron after his murder by duel of the popular Stephen Decatur—support that extended to keeping him in service in positions of responsibility and trust. Barron was now the senior officer on active duty, in charge of a naval station. There, judging by the *Somers* case, he could inflict death upon anyone he chose, and would be defended and even exonerated by the navy. His friend, Jesse Elliott, whose intent to kill the navy's other young hero, Oliver Hazard Perry, was well known, was also still responsible for the well-being of hundreds of young officers and sailors. Nor was it lost to public perception that despite the high rank and honor given to both, neither Barron nor Elliott had behaved admirably during the War of 1812, and, according to well-substantiated reports (but passed clandestinely, for fear of Elliott's revenge), Elliott had cravenly run away from the fatal dueling ground at Bladensburg.

The navy was fast gaining the reputation of being a law unto itself, in which the officer class lived and acted by tradition and rules foreign to the rest of the population.

Things seemingly could not have gotten much worse, but the ultimate apostasy took place only a year later, when the great gun on the *Princeton*'s forecastle killed two members of the cabinet, one of them Abel Upshur, now elevated to the State Department portfolio. Others were Upshur's successor as secretary of the navy; the father of President Tyler's fiancée (and possible future United States senator); a promising diplomat; and four other persons—and came close to taking the life of the President. In 1815, the navy was one of the objects of the nation's greatest pride. Only thirty years later it had sunk to a nadir of national regard. It was clearly headed for the most precarious of times, but by great good fortune there were some farsighted men in positions of authority.

James K. Polk became president in 1845, succeeding John Tyler, who had not been nominated for a second term. His secretary of the navy was George Bancroft, who was already much concerned over what he had been hearing about the service now under his charge. For forty years the army had had an

* Our destroyers numbers 17, 175, and 614 have been christened Mackenzie, but they were named after his son, Lieutenant CommanderAlexander Slidell Mackenzie, Jr., who was born in 1842 and was killed in action in Formosa in 1867. The official Dictionary of American Fighting Ships, contrary to usual custom in such cases and despite the identical name, does not list the senior Mackenzie as one of those whom the ship honors.

academy for its cadets located at West Point, site of a famous Hudson River fort. There, among other things inculcated into impressionable minds, high and idealistic principles of probity and honor were fostered. Proposals for a similar navy establishment had always been overturned because of the cost, on the grounds that in any case the school of the ship produced the best training for young men of the navy, whether officers or enlisted.

The *Somers* had demonstrated, however, nearly all the bad features of such a system of training and none of the possible good ones. Principal among its faults was that the ship would be at sea, out of touch with the land, or the country, for long periods during which it would be entirely subject to a man over whom there could be no supervision whatsoever. Whether he was a good teacher and schoolmaster or a poor one, while the ship was at sea there was no way his absolute control over his little school could be monitored. Even under the best of circumstances, operation of the ship must always take precedence over simple schooling. In a sense this was endemic to all ships at sea, any of which might by misfortune have a poor or stupid captain, or one who became so under stress. But a naval ethic that would support capital punishment on suspicion alone was unsupportable under any rationalization. Naval officers had to have a better understanding of their duties and responsibilities than this.

Bancroft came into office with determination to set up a naval academy on the lines of the one at West Point. With the willing acquiescence of Secretary of War William L. Marcy—whose son (schoolmaster William Chauvenet's enthusiastic assistant at the Philadelphia Naval Asylum) was a "passed midshipman" in the navy—Bancroft took over old Fort Severn at Annapolis, Maryland, for the site and quietly moved the residue of all the various schools and schoolmasters into it.* Chauvenet, who had ceaselessly campaigned for a better edu-

*Mindful of the difficulty in getting Congress to fund the establishment of a naval academy (several previous proposals had been defeated), Bancroft resolved to set it up in a series of small steps, each carefully planned to be within his statutory authority. Initially, for example, no new faculty was appointed; the old schoolmaster system was simply changed, the schoolmasters ordered to Annapolis instead of to various ships and stations. All the shore-based schools, including the Asylum School, were terminated, and any midshipmen in attendance were ordered to Annapolis. The academy was in place before anyone except Bancroft's advisers (many of them prominent officers) was aware it existed.

During this period there were several strong moral reform movements in American society as a whole, some of them quite militant, such as the abolitionist wing of the antislavery movement. Prohibition of alcoholic beverages was another popular reform movement. As a moral evangelist, Mackenzie had much company, probably most among the abolitionists. One of the basic purposes behind foundation of the Naval Academy was to get midshipmen away from grog, then routinely served aboard ship (it was abolished in the U.S. Navy in 1862), and all the other "bad influences" reputed to exist in men-of-war. Franklin Buchanan, its first superintendent, was noted for his moral rectitude, and this was one of the reasons for his selection.

Another story about the founding of the Naval Academy relates that Bancroft himself, as acting secretary of war, officially signed over Fort Severn to the navy on a day when Marcy was temporarily absent. The deal had nevertheless been made, and Marcy was in full accord. One might even speculate that the signing detail was deliberately set up.

cational system and was noted already for his energy and brilliance as a teacher, was appointed to head its faculty. The establishment of the "Naval School" was announced in 1845. Its first class graduated the following year.

Today, at the Naval Academy at Annapolis, the spot where old Fort Severn stood can be found only on old maps of the grounds. It is well removed from the water now, for much heavy fill has been placed around it during succeeding years. The fort itself, a nondescript round structure, is long gone. In its place stands a looming granite building of great size and sprawl: Bancroft Hall, the midshipmen's dormitory, largest in the world, housing more than four thousand young men and women. Not far away is a new academic building named Chauvenet Hall.

To start developing continuity, tradition, patriotism, honor, and idealism, Bancroft needed the right superintendent. For this post he picked the most outstanding man he could find, Commander Franklin Buchanan, a well-known and highly thought of officer from Maryland.

Buchanan was not, however, to make his mark on naval history through supervising a school, even one as important as the U.S. Naval Academy. Fate had a much more dramatic role, on a much broader and more highly colored tapestry, destined for him. But he would have to wait some fifteen years longer.

CHAPTER EIGHT

The Naval Sieve: The Union Blockade in the Civil War

William N. Still, Jr.

FOCUS QUESTIONS

1. What is the thesis of Still's essay?
2. What evidence does Still offer to support his argument? Is the evidence convincing?
3. How could you use Still's evidence against his thesis? What evidence is missing from the essay that might also complicate Still's argument?

A navy imposes a blockade in order to isolate the enemy, or some part of his territory, from the rest of the world. In most wars the side with the stronger fleet tries to blockade the other side. Thus the British Navy has blockaded, among others, France, the United States, Germany, and most recently the Argentine forces in the Falkland Islands. The United States Navy has blockaded Mexico, the Confederacy, the Spanish forces in Cuba, Japan, and, briefly, North Vietnam.

Blockade has been hailed by those who have used it, or wish to employ it anew for some current conflict, and has been reviled by its victims. When we look at its results we find that it has been useful. However, it has not always had the influence with which it is often credited. The American Civil War in 1861–1865 is a good example.

Historians generally agree that the Union navy's major task in the Civil War was the establishment and maintenance of the blockade. This was determined on 19 April 1861, when Lincoln proclaimed a naval blockade against the seceded states. His navy's secondary tasks included the protection of American foreign commerce and the support of land operations. Both the blockade and support of land operations would necessitate combined operations, including amphibious operations, against the Confederate states. In his first annual report, for 1861, the Union Secretary of the Navy, Gideon Welles, listed these tasks:

1. The closing of all the insurgent ports along a coast of nearly three thousand miles, in the form and under the exacting regulations of an international blockade, including the naval occupation and defense of the Potomac River. . . .
2. The organization of combined naval and military expeditions to operate in force against various points of the southern coast, rendering efficient naval cooperation with the position and movements of such expeditions when landed, and including also all needful naval aid to the army in cutting intercommunication with the rebels and in its operations on the Mississippi and its tributaries; and
3. The active pursuit of the piratical cruisers which might escape the vigilance of the blockading force. . . .

These tasks determined Union naval strategy for the war.

Although this strategy is obvious, the results of it are not so clear. In fact, historians continue to debate the Union navy's effectiveness in the war. This has been particularly true of the blockade. What makes this issue highly significant is the emphasis placed on the blockade. An impressive number of historians consider it a major factor in the Confederacy's ultimate collapse. They hold that the ever-tightening blockade strangled both the import of vital war material and essential necessities of life from Europe, and the export of cotton, the Confederacy's most acceptable collateral to European ports; that is, the blockade was instrumental in stimulating the economic chaos that ultimately shattered the Confederacy's will to fight as well as its means. For example, E. Merton Coulter in *The Confederate States of America 1861–1865* wrote, "Without a doubt the blockade was one of the outstanding causes of the strangulation and ultimate collapse of the Confederacy," and Rear Admiral Bern Anderson in what is probably the best one-volume naval history of the war, stated, "Without the relentless pressure of Union sea power economic disintegration could not have been achieved. The blockade was the active instrument of that sea power, and it was one of the major factors that brought about the ultimate collapse and defeat of the South."[1]

Charles F. Roland wrote that "The silent grip of the Federal navy grew tighter and the number of captures among blockade-runners steadily mounted. Still more significant, Southern ports were avoided altogether by the major cargo vessels of the world. By 1864 the blockade was strangling the Southern economy."[2]

Roland's statement implied that the Union navy expanded until it was powerful enough to close the inlets and river mouths scattered along the more than 3,000 miles of Southern coastline as well as to provide support for operations on the Mississippi River and its tributaries. From approximately ninety warships in 1861, the navy expanded to more than 700 by April 1865.

James R. Soley, one of the first writers to accentuate the Union navy's role in defeating the Confederacy through the blockade, wrote that "The number of prizes brought in during the war was 1,149 of which 210 were steamers. There were also 355 vessels burned, sunk, driven on shore, or otherwise destroyed, of which 85 were steamers; making a total of 1,504 vessels of all classes. . . . Of the property afloat, destroyed or captured during the Civil War, the larger part suffered in consequence of the blockade."[3]

There can be no question concerning the economic exhaustion within the Confederate states. A host of writers have graphically described it; the sufferings and hardships of civilians and soldiers; the impact it had on both the means and the will to continue the struggle. Students of the war overwhelmingly agree that this economic collapse was a major factor in Confederate defeat. The question is, however, the role that the Union blockade played in the collapse. Was it a principal reason as Anderson, Coulter, Soley, and others have suggested? There is considerable evidence that it was not. If the blockade was not a major factor in the Confederacy's economic exhaustion, why not? This certainly was the objective of the blockade. Was it because the blockade was ineffective and, as Frank L. Owsley wrote, a "leaky and ramshackled affair?"

Some fifty years ago, Owsley's monumental study *King Cotton Diplomacy* was published. In a chapter entitled, "The Effectiveness of the Blockade," Owsley evaluated the Union blockade in terms of numbers of violations along with the increase in Confederate cotton exports and the successful delivery of huge amounts of cargoes to the South. For example, in the last four months of 1864, more than 90 percent of the cotton shipped out of the Confederacy managed to get through the blockade. More than 80 percent of the ships carrying munitions to the Confederacy in 1862–1864 reached their destinations.[4]

Owsley's conclusions concerning the blockade were not generally accepted by historians, but in later years other studies appeared that substantiated his work. By far Marcus W. Price's series of articles published in *American Neptune* have been the most important. In an article entitled "Ships that Tested the Blockade of the Carolina Ports, 1861–1865," he estimated that out of 2,054 attempts to run past the blockading vessels off Wilmington, North Carolina, 1,735 succeeded. They amounted to an average of 1.5 attempts per day with 84 percent of them getting through. In a second article he analyzed the blockade off the Gulf ports. Between 20 April 1861, and 4 June 1865, according to his calculations, 2,960 vessels attempted to slip through the blockade, a daily average of two. As with the Carolina ports, in 1861 very few vessels were taken. But in 1862 and 1863, the blockade was tightened. During that period the percentage of successful runs into and out of these ports was 65 percent and 62 percent respectively. He attributes the lower percentage of successful runs to the larger number of sailing vessels used in the Gulf. In 1864 and 1865, however, the picture changed dramatically, particularly in steam-propelled vessels challenging the blockade. Eighty-seven percent of vessels in 1864 and ninety-four percent in 1865 that challenged the Gulf blockade got through. Although there is reason to believe that Price exaggerated his statistics on successful runs by including so-called violations that were not, he nevertheless clearly suggests that the blockade was quite porous.[5] It certainly was off Wilmington, North Carolina, which became the most important port in the Confederacy for blockade running. One recent study estimates that 230 runners entered the port in 1863–64, and 15 more slipped in before the port was taken early in 1865.[6]

In several of his books, Frank Vandiver recognized the ineffectiveness of the blockade. In a study of blockade running through Bermuda, published in 1947, he wrote, "It must be apparent that the blockade was, from the Union point of view, far from a completely effective measure . . . it is not too much to say . . . that the amount of supplies which did arrive through the blockade enabled the Confederate armies and people to carry on appreciably longer than would otherwise have been possible."

Over thirty years later he remained convinced of this: "The task of sealing off the South with its vast coastline was super-human; not even the Federal navy could meet the challenge."[7] A recently published study by Richard L. Lester, a British historian, agrees substantially with Vandiver.[8]

Because the blockade was the major Union naval strategy, it has been assumed by many historians that the major strategy of the Confederate navy was to destroy the blockade. As Anderson wrote, the Union blockade "automatically made attempts to thwart that blockade the primary task of the Confederate Navy."[9] This was not true. From the beginning Stephen Mallory, the Confederate secretary of the navy, viewed defending the harbors and rivers as his navy's major responsibility. This, of course, fits in well with Jefferson Davis' overall strategy of defense.

It is true that Mallory wanted to challenge the blockade. A principal reason for the assault on Union shipping by cruisers such as the *Alabama* and *Florida* was to force the Federal navy to weaken the blockade by drawing off ships to protect Northern shipping. Also, early in the war, the secretary ordered the construction of armored vessels both at home and abroad to attack blockaders.

Neither idea was successful. The Union navy did not weaken its blockade despite losses among Union merchant ships, and only one of the armored ships built in Europe, the *Stonewall,* actually reached Confederate hands. She was too late to have even challenged the blockade. Mallory also tried to build five large ironclads within the Confederacy capable of going to sea, but of these only the *Arkansas* and the *Virginia* were completed, and they were not seaworthy.[10]

Historians in general consider the Confederate naval effort a failure. This is particularly true of the ironclad program. They base this on the erroneous assumption that the ironclads were built to challenge the blockade and that only a few were commissioned. Out of approximately fifty armored vessels laid down within the Confederate states, twenty-two were completed and placed in operation. With the exception of the five initial vessels, the ironclads were built as harbor and river defense vessels.[11]

Confederate officials wrote surprisingly little about the blockade in their official correspondence. Much of what was written concerned the international implications of the blockade rather than the blockade itself or its effects. President Davis had little interest in naval affairs and generally left them in the capable hands of Secretary Mallory. His few references to the blockade indicate concern from an international point of view; that it was a paper blockade, clearly illegal and should be ignored by other nations.[12]

In January 1865, Davis issued one of his few directives concerning naval operations when he ordered the Confederate naval squadron at Charleston to attack Union forces off the harbor; not, however, because of the blockade, but in order to prevent if possible a linkup between the warships and the approaching army of Major General William T. Sherman.[13] Even Mallory in his reports and correspondence rarely mentions the blockade. This suggests that many Confederate officials did not consider the blockade to be very effective or a serious threat to the Confederacy. This does not mean to say that they ignored the existence of the blockade, but from their vantage point it was never damaging enough to require a change in strategy. It is often asserted that Confederate officials ignored it during the early months of the war, but as its effectiveness increased they became more concerned. In fact the blockade was being broken more frequently in 1864–65 than at any time previously and Confederate officials were aware of this.[14]

A major factor in explaining their attitude was the industrial revolution experienced by the Confederate states. In order to have a chance to win, the Confederacy had to industrialize. This transformation from an agrarian to an industrial economy has never been completely told, but in recent years several writers have examined aspects of it. Vandiver in his biography of Josiah Gorgas, Confederate ordnance chief, recounts his success in developing an arms industry. Goff does the same with the quartermaster stores, while Still tells of the creation of a naval shipbuilding industry. Although self-sufficiency was not obtained, the Confederacy made extraordinary progress. As Raimondo Luraghi wrote, "Never before in history had anything like this been seen. A backward agricultural country, with only small pre-industrial plants, had created a gigantic industry, investing millions of dollars, arming and supplying one of the largest armies in the world. . . ."[15]

This does not mean to say that supplies from abroad were not vital—they were. What it does say, however, is that the economic collapse of the Confederacy cannot be blamed on the blockade, but on its internal problems, primarily the breakdown in transportation and inadequate manpower resources.

Although the Confederate government would nationalize industry, it generally allowed blockade running free rein until early 1864. Even when it finally established trade regulations on blockade running it only required ships to reserve one-half of their cargo for government shipments. During the first years of the war the evidence strongly suggests that, to those involved in the blockade running business, what sold well was far more important than the needs of the war effort. As late as November 1864, only a few months before the final collapse, a Wilmington, North Carolina, firm was writing to its agent in Nassau not to send any more chloroform as it was too hard to sell. The firm requested perfume, "Essence of Cognac," as it would sell "quite high."[16] Cargo manifests found in port newspapers and elsewhere suggest that this was not an isolated incident.

In describing efforts by the Union navy to enforce the blockade, historians usually emphasize the numerical increase in warships on blockade duty during the course of the war, suggesting that at some point there were enough ships on station in Southern waters to retard blockade running significantly The evidence does not substantiate this. One recent study points out that although the number of blockaders on the Wilmington station steadily increased, the number of blockade runners captured or destroyed remained approximately the same.[17] Squadron commanders were constantly appealing for additional vessels. Because of the shortage of vessels for both blockade duty and combined operations, vessels had to be shifted from one point to another. Although this was a normal naval procedure, it did affect the blockade's efficiency. This would frequently result in a noticeable increase in shipping activities at the port from which blockaders were withdrawn.[18]

Union squadron commanders encountered extremely difficult logistical problems in their efforts to enforce a tight blockade. The use of steam-powered vessels theoretically helped the efficiency of a blockade, but this was largely offset by problems of maintenance and supply. As early as 1862 the four blockade squadrons required approximately 3,000 tons of coal per week, and the amount needed grew as the number of blockaders increased.[19]

Robert Browning's recent study of the blockade off Wilmington, North Carolina, clearly demonstrates that the naval force on that station, by 1863 considered the most important, was frequently and seriously weakened by the inefficiency of the vessels deployed there. Many of them were too slow or were poor sea boats. A large number were converted vessels, without the qualities necessary to operate at sea for long periods. Carrying heavy guns, for which they were not designed, in numerous cases had a detrimental effect on their performance. Breakdowns in machinery were all too often normal occurrences resulting in vessels having to leave their station for repairs without being replaced. Browning suggests that repairs kept from one-third to two-fifths of the vessels constantly away from the station. At one time ten vessels from the Wilmington station were in the yards undergoing repairs.[20]

Although the blockaders replenished some provisions and supplies while on station, coal and ordnance stores usually could be obtained only by leaving the station. Beaufort, North Carolina; Port Royal, South Carolina; and Pensacola, Florida, became the most important supply depots for the various squadrons in the Atlantic and the Gulf. Even the depots were frequently short of coal, resulting in delays for vessels returning to their station. The coal shortage also affected their readiness while on station. In September 1863, Rear Admiral Samuel P. Lee, in command of the North Atlantic Blockading Squadron, wrote to the force commander off Wilmington: "You may find it expedient not to keep more than one of the little vessels moving about at a time, even at night."[21] If logistical problems and vessel inefficiency were the same throughout all the blockading squadrons, and they probably were, the effectiveness of the blockade was seriously affected.

How effective was the Union blockade? It would be an oversimplification to say that it was either effective or not effective. It was both. In general, its effectiveness increased as the war progressed. Nevertheless, no Confederate port was completely closed until it was captured by Union forces.

Perhaps a more important question would be what effect did the blockade have on the war's ultimate outcome? Was it an important factor, as various writers say, in Confederate defeat? In this case, the answer is no. It was not a major factor in the collapse of the Confederacy.

Obviously, imports could at best provide the Confederates with only a small percentage of the material they needed to fight the war. In fact, a substantial percentage of the imports consisted not of war materials, but of clothes, liquors, and other items that would bring high profits. In order to fight, the Confederacy had to industrialize and did so. There was never a serious shortage of guns, munitions, and other war material. In fact, no Confederate army lost a major engagement because of the lack of essential supplies and arms.

The Union navy might well have contributed more to victory by concentrating more on combined operations along the seaboard and the inland rivers. The blockade absorbed hundreds of ships and thousands of men, and generally had little effect on the war's outcome.

Notes

[1]F. Merton Coulter; *The Confederate States of America 1861–1865* (Baton Rouge: Louisiana State University Press, 1950), p. 294; Bern Anderson, *By Sea and By River* (New York: Knopf, 1962), p. 232.

[2]Charles P. Roland, *The Confederacy* (Chicago: University of Chicago Press, 1960), p. 137.

[3]J. Russell Soley, *The Blockade and the Cruisers* (New York: Scribner, 1890), pp. 44–45.

[4]Frank L. Owsley and Harriet C. Owsley, *King Cotton Diplomacy: Foreign Relations of the Confederate States of America* (Chicago: University of Chicago Press, 2nd ed., 1959), pp. 229–267, 392.

[5]Marcus W. Price, "Ships that tested the Blockade of the Carolina Ports, 1864–1865," *America Neptune,* July 1948, pp. 196–241; "Ships that tested the Blockade of the Gulf Ports, 1861–1865," *ibid.,* October 1951, pp. 262–297; "Ships that tested the Blockade of the Georgia and East Florida Ports, 1861–1865," *ibid.,* April 1955, pp. 97–132.

[6]Richard F. Wood, "Port Town at War: Wilmington, North Carolina 1860–1865," PhD dissertation, Florida State University, 1976, pp. 183–194.

[7]Frank F. Vandiver, ed., *Confederate Blockade-Running through Bermuda, 1861–1865: Letters and Cargo Manifests* (Austin: University of Texas Press, 1947), p. xli; Vandiver, *Their Tattered Flags: The Epic of the Confederacy* (New York: Harper and Row, 1970), pp. 233–234.

[8]Both Lester and Richard Goff say, however, that the war might have been won by the Confederacy if the blockade had been destroyed. They imply that the Confederates were unable to create a naval force powerful enough to challenge Union sea power and break the blockade. In fact, the Confederate government never gave priority to challenging the Union blockade. Richard I. Lester, *Confederate Finance and Purchasing in Great Britain* (Charlottesville: University Press of Virginia, 1976), pp. 49, 165, 168, 177, 197, 199; Richard D. Goff, *Confederate Supply* (Durham, N.C.: Duke University Press, 1969), p. 139.

[9]Anderson, p. 288.

[10]William N. Still, Jr., *Iron Afloat: The Story of the Confederate Armorclads* (Nashville: Vanderbilt University Press, 1971), passim.

[11]For the Confederate ironclad program see *ibid.*

[12]Dunbar Rowland, ed., *Jefferson Davis, Constitutionalist: His Letters, Papers, and Speeches* (10 vols., Jackson, Miss.: Little & Ives Company, 1923), vol. V, p. 405.

[13]Davis to Tucker, 15 January 1865, *Official Records of the Union and Confederate Navies in the War of the Rebellion* (31 vols., Washington: US Govt. Print. Off., 1894–1927), Series I, Vol. XLVII, Pt. 2, p. 1014.

[14]Raimondo Luraghi, *The Rise and Fall of the Plantation South* (New York: New Viewpoints, 1978), p. 136; Goff, pp. 145, 247.

[15]Luraghi, p. 128.

[16]Wood, p.178.

[17]Robert Browning, "The Blockade of Wilmington, North Carolina: 1861–1865," MA thesis, East Carolina University, 1980, pp. 176–177.

[18]Goff, p. 141.

[19]Robert E. Johnson, "Investment by Sea: The Civil War Blockade," *American Neptune,* January 1972, pp. 53–54.

[20]Browning, pp. 58–59.

[21]Lee to Ludlow Case, 4 September 1863, *Official Records of the Union and Confederate Navies in the War of the Rebellion,* Series I, Vol. IX, p. 191.

CHAPTER NINE

The Origins and Persistence of Mahanian Doctrine

CAPTAIN C. C. FELKER, USN

FOCUS QUESTIONS

1. In what ways did Alfred Thayer Mahan distinguish sea power from sea control? How, to Mahan, did the study of history contribute to an understanding of both concepts? Why did he dismiss technology as the most important factor to understanding naval warfare?
2. Why did Mahan's ideas have so much international appeal? How did they fit into the organizational, technological, and professional changes affecting the U.S. Navy in the late-nineteenth century?
3. What were the chief weaknesses in Mahan's ideas? In what ways does the U.S. Navy of today reflect those ideas? In what ways has the Navy moved away from Mahan?

Henry L Stimson, recalling his tenure as secretary of war during World War II, remarked on the "peculiar psychology of the Navy Department, which frequently seemed to retire from the realm of logic into a dim religious world in which Neptune was God, Mahan his prophet, and the United States Navy the only true church."[1]

Stimson's comments were correct in one sense. Much of the strategic thinking of interwar naval officers was informed by lectures and books written by Capt. Alfred Thayer Mahan in the late nineteenth century. But to consign his ideas to the realm of the metaphysical suggests an incomplete understanding of his work. Mahan was not a prophet. His conception of the navy's role in national policy was not spiritually divined but rather the product of experience and intellectual pursuit. At sea he experienced firsthand the navy's transition from sail to steam. Through books he came to a disturbing revelation on the prospects of successful modernization. Without a firm doctrinal foundation, the future of the navy was uncertain. He discovered that foundation in history. In a late nineteenth-century navy of practical sailors, Mahan became the service's first intellectual and America's first naval strategist. He looked to the past to serve both the popular and professional dimensions of military transformation. From history came a theory that Mahan believed justified America's need for a modern navy. And to his less theoretically inclined colleagues, history was the tool from which theory could serve the practical purposes of naval warfare.

HISTORY AND SEA POWER

One would be hard-pressed to find the makings of a prophet in Mahan's biography. His parents were Mary Helena and Dennis Hart Mahan, and his father was a professor of civil and military engineering at West Point. At an early age Alfred was sent off to boarding school in Hagerstown, Maryland, and in 1854 enrolled in Columbia College in New York City. Against the advice of his father, Mahan left Columbia and entered the U.S. Naval Academy, graduating in 1859. Though Mahan graduated second in his Naval Academy class, he gained the reputation as something of a misfit and loner. His early naval career provided no clear indication of future greatness. His sea duty service was particularly uneventful. He began his career on the sailing frigate *Congress*. During the Civil War he served in several steam sloops on blockade duty off the Gulf coast and on the staff of Rear Adm. James Dahlgren, the commander of the South Atlantic Blockading Squadron.[2]

Mahan survived the postwar contraction of the navy, and his life settled into the peacetime routine of alternating duty at sea and ashore. Were it not for the intervention of Rear Adm. Stephen Luce, the founder and first president of the Naval War College, Mahan's naval career probably would have ended as inconspicuously as it began. Luce, who had served with Mahan at sea and at the Naval Academy, invited him to join the faculty at the new Naval War College as a lecturer in history and strategy. Mahan arrived at Newport, Rhode Island, in 1885. He relieved the sea-duty-bound Luce the following year and served two tours as president of the war college.[3]

Mahan's lectures on naval history and strategy found their way to broad audiences as a series of historical narratives. In 1890 Mahan published his first work, *The Influence of Sea Power upon History, 1660-1783*. Two years later a two-volume history, *The Influence of Sea Power upon the French Revolution and Empire, 1793–1812,* was released. Command of the armored cruiser *Chicago* delayed Mahan's next effort, a biography of Horatio Nelson, until his return from sea duty. *The Lfe of Nelson, the Embodiment of the Sea Power of Great Britain,* was finally completed in 1897. Mahan's last work in his sea power series, *Sea Power in Its Relations to the War of 1812,* was written in retirement and published in 1905.[4]

Mahan's writing career was relatively short but prolific. Over a twenty-three-year period he published twenty monographs, as well as numerous essays and articles for periodicals and professional journals. But Mahan's *Influence of Sea Power* series is of singular importance. In these volumes he synthesized disparate notions on the use of the sea and the purpose of navies into a coherent, historically based argument that formally linked "sea power" to national greatness.

Perhaps his most recognized work, *The Infuence of Sea Power upon History* laid the foundation for his subsequent efforts by establishing the theory of sea power. To Mahan the term was multidimensional. States that possessed certain geographical, political, and societal characteristics were more likely to become sea powers than nations deficient in one or more qualities. Britain, for example, was an island nation populated by a sea-going, industrious people and lying athwart the access points to the Mediterranean and North Seas. It embodied Mahan's image of a sea power. Most of the other maritime states in the North Atlantic were considered sea powers as well. But in nearly all cases save Britain, Mahan was quick to point out significant deficiencies, such as Holland's political divisiveness, France's continental aspirations, or the United States's lack of a seafaring population.[5]

Sea powers to Mahan, however, were not just born. They were also made. To Mahan the world was a global system of producers and consumers. He conceived the oceans as great highways of international commerce. But for a state to enjoy the benefits of overseas commerce required an investment in what Mahan also called sea power. As a policy, sea power consisted of three components. The first was access to overseas markets. In the late nineteenth century the most dependable market to Mahan was a colonial possession. The colony provided raw materials to the mother country. In return, it was the principal purchaser of finished products. Second, nations that sought to become sea powers needed a sufficient merchant marine to move articles of trade. Third, since Mahan believed that increased competition for overseas markets might lead to war, a sea power needed some form of armed naval force to protect its shipping.[6]

Mahan envisioned prosperity as the key to national greatness, international commerce as the means to achieve prosperity, and sea power as the policy best suited to harness the world's commercial resources. Such a theory might in itself inspire popular and political support for a large navy. But Mahan understood that his colleagues would receive such intellectually based notions with skepticism. So Mahan made the theoretical appear practical. As a nation's prosperity was dependent upon overseas commerce, it seemed logical that whoever controlled the "well-worn paths" across the "wide commons" of the sea controlled their own destiny. Diplomacy and resourcefulness ensured a nation access to the sea in peacetime. In war, though, a nation required a navy to protect its commerce. "Sea control," the policy in which the navy guaranteed access to the great highways for its own nation's shipping, while denying it to an enemy, made the theoretical practical.[7]

Mahan was convinced that history revealed the relationship between sea power and national greatness. He also believed that studying the past provided practical principles of naval warfare, from which naval strategy could be derived. But exactly how was a navy to achieve sea control? And when sea control was attained, how was it to be exercised? The conflicts within the newly established European state system offered answers that Mahan believed were relevant to modern times. In 1660 there was relative equality amongst the maritime states of Britain, France, the Netherlands, and Spain. Yet by 1763 Britain stood alone as Europe's preeminent power. To Mahan, the predominant reason lay in the island nation's concerted national policy to use and control the seas. The years between 1660 and 1763 represented a blueprint for the application of sea power. In the course of a century, Britain eliminated its European maritime competitors through a variety of policies, all of which were related to Mahan's trilogy of sea power.

Spain was already in a deteriorating state at the outset of the narrative. In Mahan's opinion, the Spanish Navy made no substantive contribution to the course of events. Dutch maritime strength, on the other hand, did pose a challenge to Britain. Dutch sea power was reduced both diplomatically and militarily by Great Britain. In 1651 Parliament enacted a series of Navigation Acts that restricted the trade between Britain and its colonies to ships manned predominantly by English crews. The policy was an act of economic warfare. A series of Anglo-Dutch naval wars ensued, which finished Holland as a competitor on the high seas. Mahan observed that the difference lay in the Royal Navy's overpowering strength in ships of the line. They were used against the Dutch fleet in two significant naval engagements, and thereafter "shut the Dutch merchantmen in their ports and caused grass to grow in the streets of Amsterdam."[8]

The removal of the Spanish and Dutch from the ranks of sea powers left Mahan to concentrate on the rivalry that he believed best exemplified his ideas. Among the European states, France enjoyed almost as many of Mahan's elements of sea power as did Britain. It had a stable government under the ambitious Louis XIV, good ports, and a navy growing in efficiency under the capable administration of Colbert. Conditions on the other side of the English Channel appeared to tip the balance of power further in France's favor. The ascension of William of Orange to the English throne in 1688 formally ended Anglo-Dutch rivalry. But the years of war left the Royal Navy in a declining condition. And the union with Holland only drew the island nation more deeply into affairs on the continent.[9]

The stage appeared set for an apocalyptic struggle between rival sea powers. What ensued was a series of wars that in Mahan's mind demonstrated how sea power shaped events on land. During the War of the League of Augsburg (1688–97), a single naval victory over the French at the Battle of Beachy Head in July 1690 forced the French navy back into port. Britain and Holland, having gained control of the sea, imposed a naval blockade on French ports. The blockade, Mahan concluded, checked Louis's advance into Spain. France ceded the sea altogether in its second war with England five years later. Of the four wars fought between 1688 apd 1763, however, the Seven Years War was the crowning demonstration of British sea power in the eighteenth century. The French, Mahan noted, used their navy principally to support land operations. Britain, by contrast, used its navy independently to shape events ashore. Gibraltar was reinforced, blocking any chance for French fleets in the Mediterranean and Atlantic to unite. The Royal Navy took advantage of a divided French Navy and defeated the French Brest fleet at the Battle of Quiberon Bay in November 1759.[10]

Mahan characterized Quiberon Bay as the "Trafalgar" of the war, because the aftermath so clearly illustrated the advantages offered by controlling the sea. French ports were blockaded. British warships eliminated French privateering in the West Indies. Mahan pointed out that much of what the British gained during the war was used to dictate the conditions of peace during the conference in Paris in 1763. While much of the territory acquired through arms was returned, Britain nevertheless emerged as the world's preeminent sea power. And "at the end of seven years," Mahan concluded, "the Kingdom of Great Britain had become the British Empire."[11]

Mahan could point with some confidence to events between 1660 and 1763 as clearly demonstrating the ability of sea power to affect events ashore. The period was less clear, though, when it came to fully explaining the concept of sea control. The principal reason, he contended, was due to the flawed policies of the French. Rather than using their navy to directly challenge Britain, the Bourbon kings instead emphasized military operations on the continent.[12] Such asymmetry complicated Mahan's argument. From the British perspective, the evidence pointed to a general notion that the objective in a contest for sea control was the enemy's navy. Ships of the line appeared the most effective platform to be used. Decisive battle seemed to be the most efficient means of using the great ships. Yet in many cases, diplomatic initiatives had also contributed to the attainment of sea control. In others, sea control was achieved by default. Finally, there was the problem of explaining the American War for Independence. Britain was the world's preeminent sea power in 1776. Yet one could hardly point to naval operations as the determining factor in the war.[13]

Though the early history of the age of sail only intimated what sea control was, Mahan was convinced that it firmly established what sea control was not. After he had lost control of the sea during the War of the League of Augsburg, Louis XIV shifted naval operations away from attacking warships to British and Dutch merchant shipping. The Sun King embarked on *guerre de course,* a naval policy in which an enemy's merchant ships became the principal objective.[14]

Mahan was not blind to the notion that an enemy's merchant fleet was an appropriate objective in war. What concerned him was efficiency. Using warships to roam the seas for enemy merchant ships would undoubtedly be painful for the victimized nation's economy. And for a nation with little or no naval capacity, such a strategy was the only option available. But for true sea powers, *guerre de course* was an inefficient form of naval warfare. It was a piecemeal strategy that would spread a navy thin and could not guarantee complete success against a nation with global trade links. Better first to free the seas of an enemy's warships, Mahan argued. With the naval threat removed, blockades could be established off the enemy's ports, while those merchants who found themselves stranded at sea could be hunted down leisurely.[15]

Mahan's vehement criticism of *guerre de course* had contemporary relevance. In the 1880s a group of French naval officers, known as Jeune Ecole, or "New School," argued that modern technology had made commerce warfare a viable naval policy. Led by a progressive minister of marine named Hyacinthe-Laurent-Théophile Aube, the policy they crafted applied new weapons to close the gap between France and her principal naval rivals. The technological innovation upon which their confidence rested was the torpedo, mounted on a small, fast, and highly maneuverable boat. Swarms of these boats, they believed, would drive off a blockading British fleet, freeing cruisers to attack merchant ships at will. The ensuing effects of a weakened economy and plummeting civilian morale, the Jeune Ecole predicted, would force the British to sue for peace. Aube's policy was no less applicable to France's rival in the Mediterranean. Italy's economic centers lay beyond the reach of Aube's torpedoes. But her civilians, living in weakly defended coastal towns, were well within range of bombardment from gunboats.[16]

The Jeune Ecole posed a significant challenge to Mahan's argument. For centuries the prospects of sinking a capital ship had been the principal motivation of early efforts to develop underwater weapons.[17] Aube and his colleagues took the strategy of the weak to a dimension unforeseen by the early pioneers of underwater warfare. The merging of new weapons and strategy in French naval policy appeared to dramatically alter the complexion of war at sea. With the advent of a torpedo-carrying commerce raider, *jus ad bellum* ("justice in war") was subordinated to military practicality. The torpedo boat would not conform to Prize Law, the internationally recognized agreement that prohibited sinking unarmed merchants before an inspection of the cargo and the safe removal of the crew. The great tactical advantage of the torpedo boat was its ability to attack from a great distance at night. Proceeding to its target virtually unseen, the new weapon enhanced the psychological effects of the Jeune Ecole's policy.[18]

Mahan addressed the challenge of the Jeune Ecole by attacking the torpedo boat from operational and historical perspectives. He questioned its seaworthiness, contending that in heavy seas the small boats would impede the speed of a fleet that they were accompanying. The boats might have some utility closer to shore. But as the fire ships of the seventeenth century had been rendered obsolete by the invention of incendiary projectiles, Mahan was confident that simply adding torpedoes to larger ships would obviate the need for the smaller vessels.[19]

To Mahan, *guerre de course* and the torpedo boat constituted the antithesis of a prudent naval policy. The Jeune Ecole had adopted the torpedo and developed a naval policy from it. They had in effect replaced history with technology as the determinant of naval strategy. Mahan was not averse to technology. What did concern him, though, were the implications of technological change. He assumed that the appearance of new weapons would require a navy to adopt necessary tactical countermeasures. But Mahan believed that effective naval strategy should not be deduced from such an erratic and unpredictable environment. The proper foundation for conceptualizing strategy, he believed, lay in timeless principles, which could be deduced only through the study of history.[20] Mahan was convinced that history had shown that sea control was accomplished not by chasing individual merchant ships but by "the possession of that overbearing power on the sea which drives the enemy's flag from it." It was a power that could only be satisfied by "great navies," whose primary objective was the enemy's navy. Once the seas were cleared of hostile warships, the victorious fleet would be free to act as it pleased to destroy the opponent's merchant shipping.[21]

SEA CONTROL

While Mahan's first book offered the historical justification for a national investment in sea power, *The Influence of Sea Power upon the French Revolution and Empire* was the apotheosis of Mahan's sea-control model. The period was marked by great naval battles, fought between concentrated fleets of the most powerful ships of the day. On Valentines Day in 1797 Adm. Sir John Jervis crushed a Spanish fleet off Cape St. Vincent. To Mahan the victory demonstrated the "worthlessness of the Spanish navy." It won for Jervis advancement to the peerage as the Earl St. Vincent. And to a rising young captain named Horatio Nelson, who had distinguished himself in the battle, came promotion to rear admiral. The following year Nelson, in command of his own fleet in the Mediterranean, attacked a French fleet anchored in Aboukir Bay. Mahan hailed the ensuing Battle of the Nile as "the most complete" and "most decisive" of naval battles. In his mind Nelson's victory secured control of the Mediterranean, left the French army trapped in Egypt, and thwarted Napoleon's grand strategic vision of loosening Britain's hold on India.[22]

With control of the Mediterranean attained, Britain next moved to secure its northern European reaches. Prime Minister William Pitt decided on a naval expedition to deter an alliance between the Baltic naval powers and France. The subsequent attack on Copenhagen in April 1801 did not exactly fit the Mahanian paradigm. The Danish fleet did not sail. Nelson, in command of the attacking naval force, directed his efforts against the city's fixed defenses, ignoring a signal from his apprehensive commander-in-chief to withdraw. Mahan nevertheless proclaimed the victory as "second in importance to none that Nelson ever gained" and "the most critical of all in which he was engaged."[23]

His tendencies towards insubordination aside, if there was one offficer in the Royal Navy who Mahan thought embodied British sea power, it was Horatio Nelson. And if Mahan could point to one event during Britain's naval history to embody his vision of sea control, it was Trafalgar. The battle was Nelson's crowning achievement. It was also in Mahan's mind an incontrovertible demonstration of sea control. Having chased the French Toulon fleet across the Atlantic for most of the summer of 1805, Nelson eventually cornered the French in Cadiz. On September 29, his birthday, Nelson met with his commanders and issued his famous plan of attack. "The business of an English Commander-in-Chief," the order began, being "to bring an Enemy's Fleet to Battle," his objective was "a close and decisive Battle." Nelson's intention was clear to his captains. The objective of the battle was the annihilation of the French and Spanish fleets.[24]

On October 21, 1805, two great fleets totaling sixty ships of the line converged for battle. Nelson cut a combined French-Spanish line in two and concentrated his efforts on the center and rear of the enemy's line. When the battle was over, Pierre de Villeneuve, commanding the combined fleet, had lost twenty-two of his thirty-three ships of the line. Nelson was killed in the battle, which in Mahan's mind was a fitting end for England's greatest naval hero. "Finis coronat opus," Mahan wrote at the conclusion of *The Life of Nelson,* "has of no man been more true than of Nelson. He needed, and left, no successor."[25]

As Nelson was "the embodiment of the sea power of Great Britain," Trafalgar embodied the professional dimension of Mahanian sea-power theory. A concentrated force of Britain's most powerful warships had annihilated a similar force in a decisive engagement. Mahan was convinced that the battle completely altered the strategic environment. Napoleon's designs for an invasion of England evaporated in a single day. The general did not immediately abandon the sea. But his attempt to wrest sea control from Britain by resurrecting *guerre de course* proved futile. The Royal Navy countered by blockading French ports, convoying merchants, and patrolling the approaches to England. French merchant ships were trapped in port. British merchants roamed the sea with relative freedom. And Parliament, recognizing the diplomatic advantages of sea control, dictated more forcefully to neutrals that wished to trade with France.[26]

Britain's control of the sea remained unchallenged for the remainder of the war. But to Mahan the victory at Trafalgar had far-reaching implications. In his first book he had posited the critical relationship between sea power and commerce. Commerce fueled a nation's economy in peacetime. But Mahan also believed that international commerce was the principal means of sustaining war.

A nation that controlled the sea in wartime was ensured an external source of revenue. A nation denied the sea would be forced to pay for war from within. The increasing demands of war on a national economy, Mahan believed, would act like a cancer. Without an external source of nourishment, war would eventually exhaust a nation.

During the dynastic wars the Bourbon kings consistently found themselves on the wrong side of the sea-control paradigm. Yet they were never completely isolated from their colonial possessions. In 1805, however, Napoleon was virtually cut off from the sea. British sea control, Mahan maintained, turned Napoleon inward. The general was forced to pay for war by extending French control over the continent. While crushing military victories consolidated most of Europe's resources under French control, Napoleon attempted to counter British sea control with his famous Milan and Berlin Decrees, which imposed a continent-wide trade embargo with England. England responded in kind with Orders in Council, which essentially prohibited all neutral merchant ships from landing in French-controlled ports.[27]

Between 1805 and 1812 the struggle between England and France resembled an encounter between a tiger and a shark. Each was dominant in its own environment yet unable to directly attack the other. The deciding factor, Mahan argued, was sea power. British merchants might be cut off from Europe, but they continued to trade with the rest of the world. As for France, the Royal Navy's ability to restrict its commerce exceeded Napoleon's ability to eke sustenance from his continental tributaries. The cancer of war, Mahan concluded, consumed the French treasury, drove Napoleon into a misguided invasion of Russia, and fomented revolution in Spain. Mahan acknowledged that Napoleon's genius had carried the war far beyond what the French Directorate could have imagined. But Napoleon was no match for British sea power, which "shut him off from the world, and by the same token prolonged her own powers of endurance beyond his powers of aggression."[28]

To Mahan the past was prologue. He viewed his country and navy as possessing potential but lacking clear direction. America enjoyed many of the geographic, political, and social conditions necessary to become a sea power. Even before Mahan published his first book, the United States had embarked on a modest naval construction program that included battleships. It was not necessarily the present, though, that worried Mahan. America's future concerned him. Would the United States adopt a maritime policy that ensured national greatness, as the British model so clearly illustrated? Or was the country to become another France?

Mahan was no less concerned with members of his own profession. The U.S. Navy had a rich tradition of capable mariners. Practical seamanship and gunnery had served a navy of frigates well. But unlike its wooden predecessors, steel battleships were national assets. They were too few and expensive to be used for purposes other than contesting the sea. If the United States was going to become a true sea power, Mahan argued, then its naval officers had to broaden their professional development to include strategic study. The stakes for a nation in a contest for control of the sea, he believed, were too high to delay strategic preparation until a war broke out.[29]

Mahan turned to history to accommodate both constituencies. The past provided the intellectual justification for a national policy of naval expansion. History also provided the means from which timeless principles of naval warfare could be deduced. Britain had prospered because of her colonial markets, her merchant fleet, and the Royal Navy. The navy was comprised of the most powerful ships of the day. Royal Navy squadrons might be dispersed at the outset of war but only to the extent that they could concentrate against an enemy fleet in a decisive battle. During the Napoleonic Wars decisive battles revealed the weakness of Spain, left Napoleon stranded in Egypt, and eventually shut France off from the outside world. In Nelson, Mahan had not only the embodiment of British sea power but also the model for the modern U.S. commander-in-chief. "Nelsonian boldness" was not impulse but courage and action tempered by intellectual insight. His "genius for war" was recognizing the importance of study prior to battle, which in Mahan's mind demonstrated the advantages of intellectually based risk taking.[30]

THE PERSISTENCE OF MAHANIAN SEA-CONTROL DOCTRINE

Alfred Thayer Mahan was not the father of the modern U.S. Navy. Nor was he the sole instigator of the new navalism emerging in the late nineteenth century. As Peter Karsten observed, it was the generation preceding Mahan that initiated institutional reforms such as the Naval War College, the Naval Institute, and the Office of Naval Intelligence. Robert Seager II noted that political and business leaders were fashioning the ideological, commercial, and geographical arguments for a new navy well before *The Influence of Sea Power upon History* was published. The first ships of all-steel construction were authorized in 1882. By 1886 the navy had its first two battleships, *Texas* and *Maine*. By the end of the decade U.S. ship builders were producing warships of more modern design, prompting Secretary of the Navy Benjamin Tracy to call for the construction of twenty battleships, eight for the Pacific and twelve for the Atlantic.[31]

The naval officer corps understood that their future demanded broader professional horizons. Congress was authorizing a navy of capital ships. Americans were coming to understand that geography was no longer an impediment to expansion nor a guarantee of security. The only missing piece was a coherent message that brought all these forces together. Mahan provided that message, and the navy enthusiastically adopted it. In an address in Boston on April 15, 1894, Assistant Secretary of the Navy William McAdoo carried the message of sea power to the general public. McAdoo downplayed the navy's meager early accomplishments as the consequence of early U.S. history. The nation was too focused on filling its territorial borders, he explained, and had yet.to fully exploit its vast resources. More importantly, McAdoo pointed out that "the great lesson that sea-power goes hand in hand with the right to rule on land was then little understood in the world." Even the greatest nations on earth had not recognized the connection between sea power and national greatness until Mahan wrote "his now universally accepted doctrine of the influence of sea-power on history." But now that the secret was out, McAdoo wanted his audience to understand that America's late entry into the world did not necessarily mean greatness was out of reach. "Our vast resources, our tremendous power, our advancing civilization," he exhorted, "make us a factor in the affairs of our neighbors." McAdoo's message was clear, and it was Mahanian. America was on the precipice of an explosion in commercial power. If Americans wanted to nurture this "doctrine of ascendancy," they needed more than presidential messages or congressional resolutions. America needed a strong navy.[32]

Responding to the Naval Institute's request to publish his Boston speech, McAdoo apologized in advance for the reception it might receive from professional officers. He reminded the secretary of the Naval Institute that his message was intended for the general public. Discussion of specific aspects of naval operations was never intended.[33] McAdoo clearly understood the multidimensional nature of Mahan's message. Sea-power theory was meant to reach out to the public. It was a grand vision intended to convince Americans of the connection between national greatness, prosperity, and a large fleet of battleships. Yet McAdoo also recognized that Mahan intended operational issues to be sorted out by naval professionals. Sea control, the professional dimension of sea-power theory, was vested to naval officers. And Mahan's colleagues in uniform proved as capable of sustaining his operational doctrine as McAdoo was of spreading the gospel of sea power.

The Mahanian canon was more than a balm to soothe professional anxiety. Naval officers perceived sea control as the means to redefine national defense in predominantly naval terms. Lt. Cdr. Richard Wainwright argued on the eve of the Spanish-American War that the navy's traditional role in coastal defense had become obsolete. Coastal fortifications, he contended, were not only expensive but also inefficient. Additionally, fixed coastal defenses failed to address America's increasing international responsibilities in the Western Hemisphere and Asia. Wainwright envisioned national defense in terms of a battle fleet, employed against an enemy's fleet near its own coast. Once the enemy fleet had been defeated, and "command of the sea" attained, then the navy would be free to operate in any way it saw fit to bring the war to a conclusion. Wainwright did not completely dismiss the relevance of fixed defenses. Forts might still be useful to defend important ports. But he viewed them as the last line of defense. The United States's "main coast defense" was a mobile battle fleet.[34]

Wainwright viewed sea control as the perfect fit for a modern navy of battleships. Critics of his position, he pointed out, had only to look at France. While Wainwright acknowledged that "Admiral Aube has a large following," he also noted the schizophrenic nature of French naval construction policy. The "ruling idea that appears to permeate those from the new school is that there is one type suitable for the strong naval power and another for the weak." But Wainwright also observed that Aube's ideas had not constrained France from continuing to build battleships. France's dilemma was its "misconception of the uses of sea power and the history of sea-fights." The Jeune Ecole offered an example of a naval policy the United States should avoid. Sea control, Wainwright concluded, would put the United States on the right side of history.[35]

Wainwright received an "honorable mention" award for his article, an indication that his recitation of Mahan was well received by his colleagues. One month after Wainwright's article was published, the navy found itself with an opportunity to put ideas to action. The war with Spain had not been completely unanticipated. Students and faculty at the Naval War College had provided the Navy Department with a plan in 1896 that proposed a joint army-navy assault on Havana in the event of war.[36] But the war college scheme was rejected in favor of a competing plan from the Office of Naval Intelligence, which wound up also being ignored. Strategy for the war with Spain regressed to the realm of ad hoc decision making. Admiral Dewey's orders for action against the Spanish in Manila came from assistant navy secretary Theodore Roosevelt. Public pressure to protect the east coast was the driving force behind the decision to divide warships between the Atlantic and Caribbean, which in Mahan's view resulted in a missed opportunity to catch the Spanish fleet before it entered Santiago.[37] Army and navy cooperation in Cuba deteriorated into a battle of personalities between Adm. William T. Sampson and his counterpart, Maj. Gen. William Shafter. American naval victories at Manila Bay and Santiago were due more to the Spanish navy's obsolete ships and incompetent leadership than to any strategic acumen within the Navy Department.

The war with Spain demonstrated that the practical application of Mahan's ideas was more complicated than his narratives had suggested. Yet the vitality of his sea-control doctrine was not diminished. Cdr. Bradley Fiske, in a March 1905 prize-winning article for *Proceedings,* showed how resolute the sea-control camp was. The navy's destiny, he argued, still lay in the battle fleet. The destructive power of the battleship outweighed arguments for any type of doctrine other than one that focused on the destruction of the enemy's battle fleet. The only technological advance that concerned Fiske was the torpedo. But as long as all ships in the fleet were outfitted with them, he did not envision technology significantly changing doctrine.[38]

Fiske's acknowledgement of a technological development unrelated to the battleship is noteworthy. Still, from the perspective of Fiske and most of his colleagues, the gun dominated naval warfare. Expectations were naturally muted, therefore, when weapons appeared that seemed to challenge the status quo. John Holland's submarine was introduced to naval officers by 1900, yet their enthusiasm for the new weapon was initially lukewarm. In one of the first articles on submarines to the *Proceedings,* Cdr. W. W. Kimball observed that they would pose a credible threat to surface ships that attempted to blockade U.S. coastal cities. But he also argued that limitations in speed and range, as well as the difficulty involved with underwater navigation, would diminish a submarine's effectiveness beyond the coast. Naval architect Lawrence Spear echoed Kimball's assessment. While he acknowledged great technical strides had been made in submarine development, Spear saw "no immediate prospect of the development of the large *submersible* into an *offensive* weapon." And in a 1905 article to the *Proceedings,* Lt. A. B. Hoff characterized submarines as slow, heavy, and "sluggish in all movements." Like Kimball and Spear, Hoff tempered his skepticism by suggesting that ships conduct maneuvering exercises to determine the best ways to chase down the boats. But the tone of the article reflected the emerging attitude of cautious optimism when it came to submarines. They might be useful but would not replace capital ships.[39]

Another potential challenge to Mahan was an even newer technological innovation, the airplane. The navy did not completely dismiss the potential of aviation. But it approached aviation with a caution that reflected the tenuous nature of the new technology. While European militaries were rapidly incorporating aviation in the early twentieth century, the first naval aviators were taking their flight training at Glenn Curtiss's cottage aircraft factory in Hammondsport, New York. In 1912, while the British were establishing the Royal Flying Corps, the four aviators in America's naval air force were training on a small air station on a spit of land across from the U.S. Naval Academy.[40]

The first naval war of the twentieth century appeared to validate a cautious approach. Naval officers might have been surprised that the first modern sea fights would occur in the western Pacific, but they did not seem surprised that a European power had been decisively defeated by an upstart Asian nation. Mahan provided a thoughtful interpretation of the war, arguing that the Russian naval disasters at Port Arthur and in the Tsushima Straits were object lessons in the improper application of sea control. Port Arthur fell because the Russian fleet had been mismanaged. The fleet, Mahan argued, had become nothing more than an extension of the land defenses, which in effect surrendered sea control to the Japanese. The naval battle in the Tsushima Straits additionally demonstrated the consequences of misidentifying the true strategic objective in a naval war. To Mahan, the Russian objective of getting their fleet safely to Vladivostok was ill fated from the start. Admiral Togo's decisive victory was due to his understanding that the fundamental objective of his fleet was to attain sea control, from which he devised a coherent strategy that defeated the Russian fleet in a decisive battle. Agreement with Mahan's interpretation is noted by the lack of commentary to the contrary. Officers did not challenge Mahan's assertion that the war illustrated the relevance of sea control.[41]

Still, it would be mistaken to infer that naval officers were simply enamored by the allure of the glorious victories implied in Mahan's work. The comments of Commodore W. H. Beehler in June 1909 exemplified the thoughtful attention given to the canon. Beehler wrote that the mere possession of battleships, cruisers, destroyers, auxiliaries, and bases was not sufficient to deter a potential enemy. What the navy had to demonstrate with its ships, he argued, was "efficiency." "They must be handled efficiently," Beehler wrote, "and foreigners, who might become possible enemies, must be convinced that our navy is handled efficiently." Beehler went on to define efficiency in the form of a battle fleet, free to operate on the high seas against an enemy's fleet in order to gain control of the sea. He pointed out that the war between Russia and Japan demonstrated that "the coast of Japan needed no protection against the formidable Russian fleet, because the Japanese first sought complete command of the sea." The destruction of the Russian fleet, Beehler observed, "rendered Japanese coast defences unnecessary."[42]

Naval officers often conflated the phrases "sea control" and "command of the sea" in their professional correspondence. But though they might confuse the semantics, they clearly understood the concept. That is, they understood what Mahan wanted them to. Sea control, the employment of concentrated firepower from battleships in a decisive naval engagement against an enemy fleet, was not just the most prudent use of the navy. It was, as Commodore Beehler repeatedly emphasized, the most *efficient* use of naval power. Mahan looked back to naval warfare in the age of sail and from the success of the Royal Navy crafted a positivist doctrine for a modern navy of steel ships. Sea control brought order to naval warfare. A line of battleships, in close formation, would converge on its opposite line. The doctrine additionally demonstrated the advantages of using the most powerful weapons available. Britain's unyielding faith in the ship of the line more than compensated for unorthodox ships such as commerce raiders. Finally, sea control was economical. Decisive battle eliminated the threat in a single event.

Scholars benefiting from the lens of history have identified the many deficiencies of Mahan's theory of sea power and doctrine of sea control. To take offense to my rather one-sided view of Mahan, though, ignores the historian's principal duty to explain the past within the context of the people who saw it as their present. The evidence suggests that most naval officers unconditionally accepted Mahan's sea-control doctrine well after the architect left active service. And at least for the foreseeable future, sea control would reign supreme in the U.S. Navy. Unlike the age of sail, however, naval technology in the late nineteenth and early twentieth centuries did not remain static. By the turn of the century the diesel-electric submarine was rapidly assuming its modern form. The torpedo was evolving into a more effective weapon. And aviation, although in its infancy, was beginning to show signs of a military application. For officers trying to come to grips with the transformation from wood and sail to steel and steam, sea control offered efficiency, order, and control. New weapons, at least for the time being, could be conformed to fit existing expectations. U.S. naval officers could only assume that they were prepared to fight a modern naval war, if presented with the opportunity.

THE NAVY PLANS FOR A MODERN WAR

As the 1896 Naval War College plan for war with Spain showed, naval officers had begun to think about and articulate war plans before the turn of the century. A navy of capital ships, fueled by commercial optimism and newly acquired possessions in the Caribbean and western Pacific following the Spanish war, made the United States a maritime empire. New imperial responsibilities intensified the need for coherence and consistency when it came to naval policy. The years prior to the U.S. entry into World War I were spent creating an administrative infrastructure capable of shaping naval policies to support the country's new global responsibilities. The Navy General Board was formed in 1900. Comprised of senior naval officers, the board was the principal medium through which the secretary of the navy received policy advice on issues ranging from ship construction to strategy. Two years later, a Joint Army-Navy Board was organized to coordinate planning and enhance interservice cooperation. The war-planning process became more formal in 1911, when Secretary George Meyer directed the General Board to designate the countries for which naval war plans were to be prepared. The Office of Naval Intelligence was assigned to provide the necessary background information on the specified country. The war college contribution was demoted to providing assistance, "as requested."[43]

The resulting plans, or "portfolios," were assigned a color representing the country the navy planned to fight. Although the imaginations of naval officers would lead them to develop twenty-three color-coded plans, efforts were predominantly focused on wars with the world's major naval powers. And with few direct experiences from which to draw, and little familiarity with emerging new weapons, planners shaped future wars using the doctrine that made sense to them.

Justification for the development of a "Red" portfolio against the British, for example, was made along historical, geopolitical, and economic lines. England was viewed as a historical thorn in America's side. British warships had blockaded the U.S. coast during the War for Independence and again during the War of 1812. No less egregious was Britain's apparent sympathy with the Confederate cause during the Civil War, reflected by the apparent ease with which southern naval agents were able to purchase English-built ships and turn them into commerce raiders.[44] The empire's geographic proximity to the United States also posed a potential strategic problem. Canada loomed to the north, while Britain's Caribbean holdings posed a potential challenge for control of the Panama Canal. Finally, Britain was a global commercial competitor. To officers educated in Mahanian sea-power theory, competition for overseas markets, the lifeblood of a nation, could certainly lead to war.[45]

Not unexpectedly, early versions of War Plan Red reflected a vision more in line with the eighteenth century than the reality of the twentieth. The first plan anticipated a massive reinforcement of Canada by the British, followed by a blockade of New England ports as a prelude for an invasion of New York. The U.S. fleet, outnumbered and outgunned by the Royal Navy, would be forced to abandon the east coast. Michael Vlahos has characterized the early versions of War Plan Red as nothing more than a "pernicious inheritance of arrested evolution." The logistic constraint of transporting thousands of British troops to

Canada alone was an issue, which if seriously considered, would have diminished the gravity of the British threat. Nor did Mahan seem to believe that a war with Britain was likely, viewing instead transnational cooperation as the key to keeping the United States relevant in world affairs. Perceptions of an Anglo-American war seem to have been more useful to generating some sense of self and mission within the U.S. naval officer corps than anticipating the reality of modern war.[46]

Similarly, the navy's 1913 plan for a war against Germany ("Black") was a model of Mahan's sea-control thinking. Navy planners envisioned the Kaiser's imperial designs in the western hemisphere as the most probable cause of the war. Upon learning of the German fleet movement, the navy would assemble in the lower Chesapeake Bay, then head to the Caribbean, the predicted destination of the enemy. Once concentrated in the Caribbean, the U.S. fleet would intercept the German Navy and destroy it in a climactic naval battle that would end the war.[47] The plan certainly remained loyal to Mahan. But it failed to address the salient question of why the German fleet would steam en masse to the Caribbean, leaving Germany vulnerable to its more proximate British rival. Nor did U.S. naval officers seem to consider the problem the Germans would face by moving a fleet across an ocean and fighting a major naval engagement without some sort of forward base.

In spite of some obvious deficiencies, plans for a future war with either Britain or Germany were crafted to fit nicely within the Mahanian paradigm. Between the United States and its possible European adversaries lay nothing but water, an ideal setting to choreograph the climactic sea battle. Even if the Germans made it to the Caribbean, the presence of the U.S. fleet would necessitate a naval engagement before the Kaiser could attempt to acquire an advanced base. But Japan, third on the list of most probable adversaries, was different. U.S. interests in the western Pacific were supported by a thin line of possessions taken from Spain following the war in 1898. The line was made even more tenuous by a mutual assistance treaty signed by Britain and Japan in 1902. Finally, just getting the fleet to the western reaches of the Pacific was problematic. Although the path from the west coast to the most western Hawaiian Islands was clear, the presence of numerous atoll chains between Hawaii and the Philippines seemed to imply that geography mattered a great deal.

Although the idea of war with Japan began germinating in the late nineteenth century, formal planning did not begin until 1906. By 1911, naval officers had what they believed to be a coherent vision of an "Orange" war. They predicted that Japan's increasing desire for hegemony in the western Pacific would increase diplomatic tensions between the two nations and threaten U.S. economic interests in China. Emboldened by its previous success against the Russians, Japan would eventually shift its activities from economic encroachment to outright aggression. The Japanese would initially attempt to drive the United States ("Blue") out of the region by seizing the Philippines and Guam and possibly threatening the Hawaiian Islands. In response, a U.S. fleet would assemble either off west coast ports or Hawaii and proceed en masse to the western Pacific. The Philippines, viewed as essential for sustaining fleet operations in the region, would either be relieved or retaken. Once the Philippines were secured, the U.S. fleet would then seek out and destroy the Japanese navy in a decisive battle. Having lost control of the western Pacific, Japan would either immediately sue for peace or be subject to a naval blockade.[48]

The sticking point in early versions of the plan was what to do about the islands. Planners dismissed geography, but not necessarily because they suffered from strategic myopia. Most of the intervening island chains were in the possession of European powers. The fleet would simply outrun any attempts by the Japanese to secure advanced bases in Pacific atolls. Still, unlike war plans with England and Germany, War Plan Orange added the problem of having to relieve or possibly retake islands in the western Pacific. The answer pointed to the U.S. Marine Corps. By the end of the nineteenth century, many of the Corps's traditional missions had been overtaken by the advent of modern warships. Marines had performed overseas expeditionary missions on several occasions in the nineteenth century and seemed the logical means of supporting Pacific contingencies.

Some naval officers even used the pretext of future amphibious requirements to push an agenda for the removal of marines from warships. Lt. William Fullam argued that the efficiency of the navy demanded bold personnel policies, chief of which was the removal of marines from warships. There was no responsibility given to them, he believed, that naval officers could not perform with equal competency. "A simple drill-book and a simple guard manual," he observed, "are needed—that is all." Fullam also believed that the presence of marines on board ships was "humiliating" to sailors, implying that they were untrustworthy. A more efficient use for the marines, Fullam believed, would be for them to be organized into shore-based battalions stationed at navy yards on the east and west coasts. A transport ship should also be assigned to each coast to facilitate their expeditionary responsibilities.[49] But in 1900 the Corps numbered only 174 officers and 5,200 enlisted men. Worse yet, the organizational culture of the "Old Corps" was lurching from waning missions, stagnant promotions, rivalry with the navy, and alcoholism amongst its officers.[50]

Nevertheless, it was to the marines that the Navy General Board looked to address the problem of seizing and defending advanced bases. The marines accepted their new mission enthusiastically. By the outbreak of World War I, a battalion-sized component had been formed and a rudimentary training school established to develop amphibious warfare techniques. But just as naval officers were intent on conforming the geography of the Pacific to fit their vision of a future war, the contribution of the Marine Corps was made so as not to conflict with established assumptions. The few exercises conducted by the navy and marines were extremely modest in scope and predominantly defensive in nature. Implied was the confidence that in a war with Japan the fleet would get to the Philippines before they fell. The offensive dimension of the amphibious-warfare mission was not fully explored.[51]

Soon after the war in Europe began, Pres. Woodrow Wilson suspended the war-planning process. The president feared that over-exuberant officers might compromise U.S. neutrality.[52] When the United States did enter the war in April 1917, it turned out that all parties had been grossly in error. Wilson's own exuberance to transform the international order more than made up for any possible embarrassment that the navy's war plans might have created. The navy's expectations proved no less accurate. The United States allied itself with two of the navy's three envisioned adversaries. And while planners could at least point with some satisfaction to Germany, the naval war in the Atlantic hardly matched the assumptions in War Plan Black.

SEA CONTROL IN THE CRUCIBLE OF WAR

Mahan's death in December 1914 was not particularly extraordinary. He had lived to the ripe age of seventy-four. The Naval Institute proclaimed in a memoriam that he "had used history as a tool with which to forge a philosophy whose effects, stupendous, titanic, are visible to this day."[53] But Mahan's passing was ill-timed in one respect. Naval officers were left to interpret World War I, with all of its technological nuances, without the calming influence of his observations. To complicate matters further, the U.S. Navy would spend the majority of the war not fighting but watching. By the time the United States entered, sea control had been transformed from seeking decisive battle to the unglamorous mission of protecting merchant convoys and troop transports from German U-boats.

There was little about the war's early progress that upset the navy's comfort level with its doctrine. Six months prior to the great naval battle at Jutland, Cdr. Dudley Knox offered a recitation of the sea-control canon. In true Mahanian fashion, Knox emphasized the principal objective of the navy as "the floating forces of the enemy." He characterized missions such as coastal raids and commerce warfare as "eccentric" and not justified until the enemy fleet had been decisively defeated. Knox then choreographed his vision of the modern sea battle. It would begin with converted merchants acting as distant scouts for the fleet. Once the enemy was located, cruisers, destroyers, and submarines would provide the commander-in-chief refined intelligence to help him shape the upcoming battle. Knox admitted that during this stage it would be natural to expect minor skirmishes to break out between the outer forces of the two fleets. Knox was nonetheless convinced that victory would be determined by the annihilation of the enemy in a decisive engagement between battleships.[54]

Even the German adoption of restricted and then unrestricted submarine warfare against Allied commerce following Jutland did not immediately lead to a wholesale change of attitudes. Prior to the war Ens. Holloway Frost observed that the torpedo, though dangerous, was no more immune from error than any other naval weapon.[55] Capt. Lyman Cotton viewed German U-boats with equal skepticism. He criticized *guerre de course* as a shortcut, an attempt to achieve "success in war without fighting" Cotton went on to use much of Mahan's historical evidence to reinforce the point that commerce warfare had always been an unproductive naval policy. As to the present, Cotton viewed the German employment of U-boats as a desperate measure resulting from the failure of their battle fleet to achieve sea control. He was confident that the U-boats would make only a tactical difference in naval warfare. Whereas the commerce raider of the nineteenth century captured its prizes, the U-boat simply destroyed its prey. Cotton was certain that technology had not elevated the strategic importance of commerce warfare.[56]

U.S. operational experiences appeared to reinforce the notion that the submarine threat was somewhat exaggerated. The few U.S. submarines that made it into the war failed to sink one ship. And operations against German submarines proved a dangerous yet manageable affair. Technological countermeasures such as underwater listening devices seemed to give surface ships an advantage over submerged submarines. Aircraft were demonstrating themselves as a useful antisubmarine search platform, though their success in attacking U-boats was mixed. Naval officers accepted their role as convoy escorts and testified to the Navy General Board that convoy operations were both an expedient and effective way to deter German submarines.[57]

What evidence naval officers could muster, either through observation or experiences, seemed to show that new weapons of naval warfare either suffered inherent limitations or could be minimized by countermeasures. Mahan's dictum that technology did not drive strategy seemed sound. Some officers, however, were less sure that the war offered no new lessons. Cdr. Yates Stirling was not convinced that the submarine had no strategic value. He did not disagree that the object of sea control was to ensure the use of the sea while denying its use to an enemy. But Stirling took issue with the notion that submarines played no role in the doctrine. The submarine was the natural tool for a weaker belligerent to challenge a stronger naval power. And should a navy fail to implement sufficient antisubmarine countermeasures, Stirling argued that submarines could achieve at least half of the sea-control mission by making the sea dangerous to a stronger belligerent. Bradley Fiske, who attained flag rank during the war, made a similar argument for aviation. He cautioned that it might be prudent to expand the term "naval power" to what he termed "mechanical power" and include aircraft along with the naval gun. Though Fiske admitted he was unsure how far aviation technology would advance, he was confident that aircraft would develop into a "major weapon of warfare" and predicted that a book might someday be written and entitled, "The Influence of Air Power on History."[58]

Even Jutland did not escape scrutiny. A more senior and wiser Cdr. Holloway H. Frost showed considerable professional courage by questioning the strategic relevance of the battle, which indirectly challenged the relevance of sea control to modern naval warfare. Frost was not impressed by the fact that the Royal Navy had achieved control of the North Sea following the battle. The Germans, he pointed out, still retained unfettered access to the Baltic. And as the U-boat campaign demonstrated, Jutland had not denied the Germans access to the sea. Frost then compared the alleged British victory with the accomplishments of the U-boats. The initial success of the submarine campaign had boosted the morale of the Central Powers. U-boats at one point reduced the flow of fuel oil to Britain to an eight-week reserve. Mounting merchant losses compelled the Allies to divert resources for the war to the construction of merchant ships. Finally, Frost pointed out an achievement that Mahan was convinced technology could not do. The U-boats had altered naval policy. Though the Allies controlled the surface of the sea, submarines compelled them to adopt a defensive strategy emphasizing convoys.[59]

CONCLUSION

Writing in the April 1921 edition of *The World's Work,* Navy Lt. Cdr. Lee P. Warren, who worked in Chief of Naval Operations Adm. Robert Coontz's office, reflected the resiliency of Mahan. In Warren's opinion nothing that occurred in the last war compromised the notion that the battleship was "the backbone of the fleet." He admitted that submarines had sunk great numbers of merchantmen. But they had not sunk one "modern" capital ship and had failed to keep British battleships from cruising the North Sea and keeping the German fleet in its bases. The airplane appeared no closer to replacing the battleship than the submarine, suffering from limitations of range, weather, and bomb load. The "control of the air," he pointed out, "depends on control of the sea." Warren concluded that the United States was still best served by battleships, which represented "the maximum concentrated power" that could be put into one vessel. No other vessels could adequately support a national defense, which he interpreted might extend to an enemy's coast.[60]

Henry Stimson's characterization of Mahan as "prophet" implied the existence of a following of true believers. Looking back to the turn of the century, it is not difficult to understand the appeal of Mahan's ideas to imperialists, naval officers, and civilian naval enthusiasts. He advocated an internationalist policy for the United States and made the navy central to supporting it. He additionally provided a clear message that the only proper navy was one comprised of battleships. The national investment required for these ships would ensure the navy's organizational survival. Finally, sea control was a tonic for the self-esteem of the naval officer corps. Running down unarmed merchants paled in comparison to the promise of great sea battles between massive fleets.

And yet, while they found Mahan's ideas sensible enough, officers of the new navy had to face an emerging reality that Mahan's narratives had dismissed. Mahan's gaze was fixed on a period of limited technological innovation. Many of the ships that fought during the Seven Years War had seen service in the Napoleonic Wars. The age of sail was a time that suited Mahan's intellectual needs. The period left him unprepared, though, to fully appreciate the role that technology was playing in the transformation of naval warfare to three dimensions. Twentieth-century naval officers were caught in a paradox. Their strategic conceptions were based upon principles deduced from the age of sail. Yet their limited experiences in World War I implied that they could not ignore the relationship between new weapons and doctrine. What appeared so clear to Mahan through the lens of history was murkier when it came to actually dealing with submarines and airplanes. Even Lieutenant Commander Warren proved incapable of completely ignoring submarines and airplanes, admitting that the new weapons inhibited the battleships' ability to achieve or exercise "command of the sea" without sufficient escort.[61] Somehow history and the present had to be reconciled. The medium naval officers turned to was warfare simulation.

Notes

[1]Henry L. Stimson, *On Active Service in Peace and War,* 506.

[2]Philip A. Crowl, "Alfred Thayer Mahan: The Naval Historian," in *Makers of Modern Strategy,* ed. Peter Paret, 446–47; Allan Westcott, ed., *Mahan on Naval Warfare,* 360–61.

[3]Crowl, "Alfred Thayer Mahan," 446–48.

[4]Alfred Thayer Mahan, *The Influence of Sea Power upon History, 1660–1783.* The Dover edition is a slightly altered republication of the 1894 edition of the work, originally published by Little, Brown, and Company, Boston, in 1890; Alfred Thayer Mahan, *The Influence of Sea Power upon the French Revolution and Empire;* Alfred Thayer Mahan, *The Life of Nelson, the Embodiment of the Sea Power of Great Britain;* Alfred Thayer Mahan, *Sea Power in Its Relations to the War of 1812.*

5Mahan, *Influence of Sea Power upon History,* 25–90.

[6]Ibid., 13–28.

[7]Ibid., 25–27; Westcott, ed., *Mahan on Naval Warfare,* 1–15.

[8]Mahan, *Influence of Sea Power upon History,* 107–33; E. B. Potter, ed., *Sea Power,* 18; Joseph Allen, *Battles of the British Navy,* vol. 1, 384–85; Sir Julian Corbett, ed., *Fighting Instructions, 1530–1816.* During the age of sail a warship was "rated," or classified, according to the number of guns it carried. Ship ratings therefore indirectly determined the ship's principal mission. First-, second-, and third-rate ships, for example, carried between seventy and one hundred guns. These were the ships identified to fight major naval battles. Potter uses the phrase "fit to be tied in the line" to demonstrate the derivation of the term "ships of the line" but fails to specifically cite the originator of the phrase. (A close reading of Sir Julian Corbett's collection of the Royal Navy's Fighting Instructions also failed to turn up the phrase.) Potter also makes the point that while Britain built a number of sixty-four-gun ships, which technically could be considered a ship of the line, he argues that they proved to be too small and saw little service in the line. Joseph Allen's collection of Royal Navy battles offers supporting evidence. During the Battle of the First of June 1794 (discussed in chapter 8), the ships of the line under Adm. Richard Howe of the Royal Navy included three of one hundred guns, four of ninety-eight, two eighty-gunned ships, and sixteen carrying seventy-four guns.

Fourth-rate ships, which carried around fifty guns, were principally used as flagships, as well as offering an economical means of providing presence during peacetime, when it was often necessary to "lay up" the larger warships. The fifth- and six-rate ships, the last in the system, were more commonly known as frigates. Carrying between thirty-two and thirty-eight guns, these were the most versatile of the rated warships. They served a multitude of functions, such as scouting, carrying messages to and from the flagship, enforcing blockades, and commerce raiding. Below the rated ships were naval vessels of smaller size, known as sloops, brigs, and schooners. These ships were limited by their size to a single gun deck and were used primarily as commerce raiders and for operations close to shore.

[9]Mahan, *Influence of Sea Power upon History,* 173–78.

[10]Ibid., 286–90, 302–07.

[11]Ibid., 314–24.

[12]Ibid., 105, 173–78, 286–88.

[13]Ibid., 505–40. Mahan resolved the paradox by ignoring events on land. He instead emphasized the conflict as "purely a maritime war" in which Britain had failed to decisively defeat the French navy.

[14]Ibid., 193–98.

[15]Ibid., 132–38.

[16]Ropp, *Development of a Modern Navy,* v–vii, 3–5, 157–65.

[17]Alex Roland, *Underwater Warfare in the Age of Sail,* 1–16, 156–82.

[18]Ropp, *Development of a Modem Navy,* 157–66.

[19]Mahan, *Influence of Sea Power upon History,* 111.

[20]Ibid., 9–10.

[21]Ibid., 132–38, 193–97.

[22]Mahan, *Influence of Sea Power upon the French Revolution and Empire,* 1 :220–29, 256–86.

[23]Mahan, *Life of Nelson,* 2 :90–99; Mahan, *Influence of Sea Power upon the French Revolution and Empire*, 2:44–52. While it is clear whom Mahan was praising, it is less clear exactly what he was praising. Nelson had argued against the enterprise. In his mind the Russian Baltic fleet should have been the objective. During the battle Nelson also disregarded an order from Sir Hyde-Parker, his commander-in-chief. Parker, who was well distant from the fighting, became increasingly anxious about Nelson's progress. A signal was sent to discontinue the attack. It is alleged that upon being informed of the signal, Nelson placed his glass to his blind eye (he had been blinded in the right eye during a landing on the Corsican town of Calvi in 1794) and replied to his flag captain, "You know, Foley, I have only one eye. I have a right to be blind, sometimes. I do not see the signal."

Mahan's interpretation of events is instructive. He judged the attack on Copenhagen as overly conservative and an imprudent use of naval force. Mahan was convinced that Nelson, whose genius provided a "clear discernment of the decisive features of a military situation," was right. Nelson, therefore, could be absolved from his apparent disobedience, for in Mahan's view his only fault was that he "had lifted and carried on his shoulders the dead weight of his superior," which in Mahan's mind had prevented the British fleet from demonstrating the true nature of sea control. And yet, it appears that attacking Copenhagen was successful. Hyde-Parker's conservative plan succeeded in securing a promise from the Danes not to interfere with British commerce in the Baltic. The Russian fleet likewise showed no inclination after the attack on Copenhagen to challenge the Royal Navy at sea. Sea control was attained, it appears, not by naval battle, but by projecting power ashore.

[24]Mahan, *Influence of Sea Power upon the French Revolution and Empire,* 2: 119–90; Mahan, *Life of Nelson,* 2:339–46.

[25]Mahan, *Life of Nelson,* 2:369–98; Mahan, *Influence of Sea Power upon the French Revolution and Empire,* 2:119–26, 184–96.

[26]Mahan, *Influence of Sea Power upon the French Revolution and Empire,* 2:199–203, 221–34.

[27]Ibid., 199–218, 272–91, 402–11.

[28]Ibid., 406–11.

[29]Westcott, ed., *Mahan on Naval Warfare,* 8–15. Mahan's belief that command decision-making skills could be developed through intellectual pursuits is a major theme in Jon Sumida's *Inventing Grand Strategy and Teaching Command.*

[30]Mahan, *Life of Nelson,* 1:312, 2:323–24.

[31]Potter, *Sea Power,* 160–61; Peter Karsten, *The Naval Aristocracy;* Robert Seager II, "Ten Years before Mahan: The Unofficial Case for the New Navy, 1889–1890," *The Mississippi Valley Historical Review* 40, no. 3 (Dec. 1953): 491–93.

[32]William McAdoo, "The Navy and the Nation," U.S. Naval Institute *Proceedings* 20, no. 2 (1894): 401–22.

[33]Ibid., 401.

[34]Richard Wainwright (lieutenant commander, USN), "Our Naval Power," U.S. Naval Institute *Proceedings* 24, no. 1 (Mar. 1898): 39–87.

[35]Ibid.

[36]Spector, *Professors of War,* 71–102.

[37]Alfred Thayer Mahan, *Lessons of the War with Spain,* 47–59.

38 Bradley A. Fiske (commander, USN), "American Naval Policy," U.S. Naval Institute *Proceedings* 31, no. 1 (Mar. 1905): 2–34.

[39]W. W. Kimball (commander, USN), "Submarine Boats," U.S. Naval Institute *Proceedings* 27, no. 4 (Dec. 1901): 739–46; Lawrence Spear, "Submarine Torpedo Boats: Past, Present and Future," U.S. Naval Institute *Proceedings* 28, no. 4 (Dec. 1902): 1000–13; A. B. Hoff (lieutenant, USN), "The Submarine as an Enemy," U.S. Naval Institute *Proceedings* 31, no. 2 (June 1905): 384–99.

[40]Clark Reynolds, *Admiral John H. Towers.*

[41]Westcott, ed., *Mahan on Naval Warfare,* 258–75; Alfred Thayer Mahan, "Reflections, Historic and Other, Suggested by the Battle of the Sea of Japan," U.S. Naval Institute *Proceedings* 32, no. 7 (June 1906): 447–63; Richard Wainwright (captain, USN), "The Battle of the Sea of Japan," U.S. Naval Institute *Proceedings* 31, no. 4 (Dec. 1905): 779–805; Bradley A. Fiske (commander, USN, "Why Togo Won," U.S. Naval Institute *Proceedings* 31, no. 4 (Dec.

1905): 807–809. Wainwright pointed to the superiority of Japanese ships and criticized the Russians for their lack of training. Fiske emphasized the advantage of experience. Togo's superiority in maneuvering and gunnery, he concluded, was the result of a fleet that had spent a great deal of time operating together.

42W. H. Beehler (commodore, USN), "The Navy and Coast Defense," U.S. Naval Institute *Proceedings* 35, no. 2 June 1909): 343–81.

43Spector, *Professors of War,* 102.

44Frank J. Merli, *The* Alabama, *British Neutrality, and the American Civil War,* ed. David M. Fahey. Queen Victoria's Neutrality Proclamation of 1861 prohibited the sale or transfer of military equipment to either belligerent during the war. Yet Confederate naval agent James Bulloch was successful in purchasing an English-built merchant ship that became CSS *Alabama,* the Confederacy's most successful commerce raider. Merli's excellent work softens previously held notions of conspiracy by senior British officials. Yet he does not succeed in completely exonerating London from responsibility for obvious violations of the neutrality law.

45Michael Vlahos, *The Blue Sword,* 99–102.

46Ibid; Sumida, *Inventing Grand Strategy and Teaching Command,* 82–92.

47Vincent Davis, *The Admirals' Lobby,* 129.

48Edward S. Miller, *War Plan Orange,* 21–36.

49William F. Fullam (lieutenant, USN), "The Organization, Training and Discipline of the Navy Personnel as Viewed from the Ship," U.S. Naval Institute *Proceedings* 22, no. 1 (1896): 83–116.

50Dirk A. Ballendorf and Merrill L. Bartlett, *Pete Ellis,* 25–27.

51Graham A. Cosmas and Jack Shulimson, "The Culebra Maneuver and the Creation of the U.S. Marine Corps' Advanced Base Force," in *Assault from the Sea,* ed. Merrill L. Bartlett, 121–41; Kenneth J. Clifford, *Progress and Purpose,* 7–11; Alan R. Millett, *Semper Fidelis,* 273; Raymond G. O'Connor, "The U.S. Marines in the 20th Century: Amphibious Warfare and Doctrinal Debates," *Military Affairs* 38, no. 3 (Oct. 1974): 97–98; Eli K. Cole (lieutenant colonel, USMC), "The Necessity to the Naval Service of an Adequate Marine Corps," U.S. Naval Institute *Proceedings* 40, no. 5 (Sept.–Oct. 1914): 1395–1401. Exercises were first held on the Puerto Rican island of Culebra in 1903. During the exercise, naval officers pressed marines into performing shipboard duties and interfered with their work on the island. The following year Gen. Leonard Wood, governor general of the Philippines, complained that marine exercises in Subic Bay were an intrusion on the army's mission and a conspiracy by the navy to take over the defense of America's western Pacific holdings. In 1914 the marines returned to Culebra for one final exercise before World War I. The exercise was designed to simulate the defense of an advanced base from a possible German incursion in the Caribbean. Marines from the newly established Advanced Base Force went ashore January 9 and commenced defensive preparations. An assaulting force, composed of sailors and marines from Atlantic

fleet warships, attacked on the January 21. Navy umpires judged that the defensive measures taken by the marines successfully thwarted the landing.
[52]Robert G. Albion, *Makers of Naval Policy,* 1798–1947, ed. Rowena Reed, 354–56.
[53]"Alfred Thayer Mahan, in Memoriam," U.S. Naval Institute *Proceedings* 41, no. 1 (Jan.–Feb. 1915): 1–9.
[54]Dudley W. Knox (commander, USN), "The General Problem of Naval Warfare," U.S. Naval Institute *Proceedings* 42, no. 1 (Jan.–Feb. 1916): 23–47.
[55]Holloway H. Frost (ensign, USN), "The Problem of Firing at a Fleet Under Way with Long Range Torpedoes," U.S. Naval Institute *Proceedings* 39, no. 2 (June 1913): 681.
[56]Lyman A. Cotton (captain, USN), "Commerce Destroying in War," U.S. Naval Institute *Proceedings* 45, no. 9 (Sept. 1919): 1495–1517. Cotton placed a motto under the title of the article that read, "Easy methods; inconsiderable results"; Cotton, "Unrestricted Commerce Destroying," U.S. Naval Institute *Proceedings* 45, no. 9 (Sept. 1919): 1517–1527.
[57]Richard Compton-Hall, *Submarines and the War at Sea,* 277; C. S. McDowell (captain, USN), "Anti-submarine Work during the World War," Washington, D.C.: National Archives and Records Service, 1977, 17–32. McDowell's report is an unpublished typescript, originally produced in December 1919; report of Capt. Frank W. Schofield, USN, Oct. 12, 1917, "Sound Detection," *Hearings before the General Board of the US. Navy, 1917–1950,* roll 1, frames 390–97; report of Maj. R. A. Milliken, U.S. Army, Jan. 18, 1918, untitled, *Hearings before the General Board,* roll 1, frames 83–93; Archibald Douglas Turnbull, *History of United States Naval Aviation,* 81–150; Kenneth Whiting (lieutenant, USN), "Aeronautics, January 16, 1918," *Hearings before the General Board,* roll 1, frames 61–75; report of Commanders A. W. Johnson and J. K. Taussig the General Board, Dec. 4, 1917, "Anti-submarine Warfare," *Hearings before the General Board,* roll 1, frames 685–705
[58]Yates Stirling (commander, USN), "The Submarine," U.S. Naval Institute *Proceedings* 43, no. 7 (July 1917): 1371–90; Bradley A. Fiske (rear admiral, USN), "Air Power," U.S. Naval Institute *Proceedings* 43, no. 8 (Aug. 1917): 1701–1705.
[59]Holloway H. Frost (lieutenant commander, USN), "The Results and Effects of the Battle of Jutland," U.S. Naval Institute *Proceedings* 47, no. 9 (Sept. 1921): 1335–54.
[60]Lee P Warren (lieutenant commander, USN), "The Battleship Still Supreme," *The World's Work* (Apr. 1921): 556–60.
[61]Ibid., 559.

CHAPTER TEN

Life of a Sailor

FREDERICK S. HARROD

FOCUS QUESTIONS

1. What roles did officers play in framing the nature of shipboard life?
2. How and why did the nature of the enlisted force change as the Navy moved into the twentieth century?
3. How did sailors relate to civilians within the US as well as those abroad?

A ship at sea becomes a world unto itself, isolated and self-sufficient. The Navy Department often remained a remote and mysterious force to men afloat. For a sailor, the navy was his vessel. To understand more fully enlisted men and their role in the navy, it is necessary to shift the focus of study to individual units. Here changes were more subtle than at a higher level, and they were blurred in the variety of men, ships, and places.

SHIPBOARD ORGANIZATION

Perhaps the most important factor determining the bluejacket's life was his position at the bottom of the naval hierarchy. The men implemented policy that was formed on high. One sailor neatly captured the reality of his existence in doggerel:

The Captain tells the Exec,
When he wants something done;

The Exec then tells the O.O.D.
And gets him on the run.
The O.O.D. looks wondrous wise
And strokes his downy jaw
Then he calls his trusty bosun's mate
And to him lays down the law.
The bosun's mate calls the coxswain
To see what he can see;
The coxswain gets a seaman
And that poor seaman is me.[1]

The heirarchy of rank was only part of the ordering of a naval vessel. As in the era of sail, in the modern navy every man had a place to be and a task to perform. Upon reporting for duty, a sailor was assigned to one of two watches, either port or starboard. He was simultaneously placed in one of six divisions; this assignment determined his actual duties. There were four "gun divisions," composed of men of the deck ratings, with each division responsible for maintaining a quadrant of the ship. A "powder division" consisted of electricians, shipwrights, carpenters, and men of other specialized ratings who performed their particular trades and cleaned their storerooms and work areas, and an "engineers' division" operated and cared for the fireroom and engine room. If the ship carried a marine detachment, it formed a seventh division.[2]

Most activities aboard ship required smaller units than watches and divisions. For such work, every ship had a watch, quarter, and station bill. Each man on a ship had a number. The bill was a catalog listing the duty station for various drills of the number holder and designating where the sailor ate, slept, and stowed his hammock.[3]

While the bill determined where on the ship the bluejacket performed his tasks, a daily schedule specified when the work was to be done. Table 13 of the Appendix outlines a typical daily schedule. A similar pattern of activity existed on all ships throughout the navy. Although special duty such as coaling ship or target practice disrupted the routine temporarily, at most times and in most places bluejackets lived under this timetable.

An enlisted man's precise duties, of course, depended upon his rating. The deck force—which consisted of seamen and ordinary seamen and such ratings as boatswain's mate, quartermaster, and gunner's mate—supplied lookouts, helmsmen, and messengers. These men also did the daily scrubbing, sweeping, and polishing that a ship needed. Under the watchful eyes of their petty officers, seamen quickly learned that housekeeping required special efforts to meet navy standards. On his first day after completing a training program, Charles Blackford twice failed to sweep the deck to his chief's satisfaction. On the third try, with the chief's assistance, Blackford discovered dirt under lines, inside gun mounts, and in other nooks and crannies he had overlooked.[4]

Seamen in the deck force also scraped and painted the ship inside and out. Many men shared John Kendig's experience, squeezing through narrow manholes to clean and paint the space between the double bottom of a battleship.[5] At such times, no doubt, more than a few sailors ironically recalled navy recruiting posters.

In the engine room, the sixth division—which was composed primarily of coal passers and firemen but also included machinists, oilers, and water tenders—cleaned the area and worked the machinery of the ship. Men in the engine room received a higher starting pay than did seamen entering the deck force. The bonus was well earned; the work of feeding boilers on a coal-burning ship was the most arduous task in the navy. In addition, the men worked in close quarters and in extreme heat. In 1924 during a voyage in the Persian Gulf, for example, the temperature on the cruiser *Trenton* reached 105 degrees in the shade on the top decks and 110 degrees below; men in the fireroom, in contrast, broiled in 145-degree heat. Only men in the galley had to endure similar temperatures.[6]

The laborious engine-room work required individuals of considerable stamina, but in times of expansion the navy assigned this duty to some recruits who were physically unsuited. The surgeon general, recognizing the health hazard to all men, reported his objections to these conditions. In 1907 he wrote that the engineers' force

> is often short-handed and even if not and the individual members are all physically qualified for such duty, which is not always the case, the demands of the Department in and out of port keep the men too long employed below decks and away from the sun and fresh air which they need so badly as an aid in recuperating from their arduous duties.[7]

In spite of the Bureau of Medicine and Surgery's warning, those practices persisted.[8] Apparently only the conversion from coal- to oil-burning ships improved conditions in the engine room.

DRILL

Duty on a man-of-war entailed more than operating and maintaining the ship. Because a naval vessel was supposed to be constantly ready to wage war, a large amount of time was devoted to drilling to prepare for an emergency or for combat.

The most common exercises were general quarters, clearing the ship for action, and fire, battalion, collision, and gunnery drills. General quarters required manning battle stations. Clearing the ship for action, less common than general quarters, involved manning battle stations plus removing anything that would interfere with the sweep of the guns—stanchions, davits, and awnings—or which would impede shelling—chests, mess tables, and benches.

The navy also regarded coaling ship as a drill, partly because in time of war rapid refueling was necessary. In elevating coaling to a drill, however, the navy may also have been attempting to lend some prestige to a tiresome and difficult job. Coaling ship required the efforts of all hands. After lighters had brought the coal alongside, gangs of men shoveled the coal into large bags, which were hoisted aboard. The coal was then sent into the holds through canvas chutes. From there, other gangs transferred it into the bunkers. Fine coal dust pervaded the vessel; after the ship was coaled—a task often consuming most of a day—the crew had to clean first the ship and then themselves.

Coaling, however, did offer some compensations. Old, nonregulation clothing was permitted. The ship's band, if there was one, serenaded the workers. And rival gangs or ships competed in emptying their lighters. In general, though, coaling was a job best viewed in retrospect: old hands might look back nostalgically from oil-burners to the exploits of true sailors in the days of coal, but while they were actually carrying out the assignment, most men considered it unpleasant. During World War I a sailor-poet on the *Plattsburg* expressed his sentiments, complete with ethnic slurs:

I'll face Hun submarines
Davy Jones' fierce Jyreens,
I'll stay for a cruise to Khan-kee,
But loading soft coal,
In a coal-burner's hold,
Is a job for spicks—coolies—Not me[9]

DANGER IN THE SAILOR'S LIFE

Military Action

The purpose of drill and training is obviously to prepare for a military encounter. In the four decades following the Spanish-American War, the major military experience was, of course, World War I. Because by April 1917 the war was being fought primarily on land, the navy received less attention than the army. Nevertheless, the navy contributed to the Allied war effort in various ways. American vessels helped lay the North Sea mine barrage, and American torpedo boats participated in the attack on the Austrian base at Durrazzo in September 1918. On shore, naval gun crews operated large railway guns in France. In the air, naval aviators flew numerous missions in both heavier-than-air and lighter-than-air craft.[10]

Even though the navy had varied assigments, its major tasks were antisubmarine patrol and convoy duty; most naval personnel engaged in these duties. On May 4, 1917, six American destroyers under the command of Lieutenant Commander J. K. Taussig reached Queenstown, Ireland, the first Americans to operate in European waters. These vessels and later arrivals spent long, difficult hours at sea but seldom saw the enemy. An occasional encounter did produce a hero—as when Gunner's Mate Osmond K. Ingram of the *Cassin* died trying to disarm depth charges before a torpedo struck his destroyer.[11] But most men seldom engaged in battle. Chief Torpedoman Harry S. Morris, as an example, served on board the destroyer *Downs* and never fired a torpedo during the whole war. In his case, no action may have been a blessing, since he recalled that "the storms were so heavy in the war years that there was a time I couldn't even get the torpedoes out of the tubes. They were rusted in."[12]

The number of navy casualties reflects the routine nature of the service's role in the war. From a force of almost a half million, the navy lost a total of 6,929 men and 438 officers. Of the enlisted deaths, 5,352 were attributed to disease, 1,193 to accidents, and 384 to enemy action. Thirty-eight officers died in battle, 284 of disease, and 116 through accidents. Thus, only 422—or 0.8 percent—of the 53,402 Americans who died in battle during World War I were in the navy.[13]

Even if postwar tabulations showed naval casualties to be negligible, the danger was real. The nature of submarine warfare made it impossible to anticipate an attack, and this uncertainty heightened tension for crews in the war zone. Searching too hard for U-boats, sailors spotted them where none existed. Wreckage, porpoises, waves, the evening star, and nonbelligerent craft were reported as the enemy. Men on duty in dangerous areas for the first time were particularly prone to making false reports. When the gunboat *Yankton* first crossed the Atlantic at the beginning of American entry into the war, the lookouts spotted what they thought was a submarine. The ship lobbed shells at the object; a lookout, mistaking the splashes of these shells for enemy fire, reported that the submarine was returning fire. With that report, the *Yankton* increased its firing, and the enemy hoisted sail and fled. The "submarine" proved to be native fishing boats from the Azores.[14]

In addition to its role in World War I, between 1899 and 1939 the navy engaged in frequent smaller operations. After the Spanish-American War, the service was immediately involved in the Philippine Insurrection from 1899 to 1902. During that same period, it joined a combined English and American landing force in Samoa in 1899 and cooperated with other nations in suppressing the Boxer Rebellion (1900-1901). The service was particularly active in Latin America. It was used in Cuba from 1906 to 1908 and in 1912; in Nicaragua in 1912 and 1925 and from 1926 to 1928; in Mexico in 1914; in Haiti in 1915; in Panama in 1921; and in Honduras in 1924 and 1925. In 1924 the navy again fought in the Philippines as a result of the Moro uprisings; in the same year it formed the Cavite Provisional Company of two officers and 100 enlisted men for service in China.[15]

In addition to these military operations, the Caribbean Special Services quadron, the Yangtze River Patrol, and the South China Patrol operated in perennially troubled areas. The men on these assignments were involved in frequent military encounters. In a fairly typical experience for 1922 to 1925, the gunboat *Asheville* of the South China Patrol landed nine patrols—four that included navy men and five that were composed solely of marines. The 1937 bombing of the *Panay* by the Japanese, in which two sailors and one civilian were killed and eleven officers and men were wounded, attests to the dangers of operating in a war zone even if one is nonbelligerent.[16]

Reports of the sailors' performances ashore were generally good. After a

1906 landing in Cienfuegos, Cuba, Commander William F. Fullam expressed satisfaction with pride in his men, boasting that the managers of two Cuban sugar estates had requested that the marines rather than the sailors be withdrawn.[17] Because Fullam had long advocated training sailors for duty ashore and championed removing marines from ships, his men might have been better prepared than others, and his evaluation may have been overly generous.[18] Nevertheless, comments on enlisted men's performances in other actions were also favorable. In April 1914 bluejackets landed at Veracruz, Mexico. While securing the city, they received fire from snipers, from regular troops, and because of the confusion, from their own comrades. During the landing, American naval forces sustained casualties of seventeen dead and sixty-seven wounded—compared to estimated Mexican casualties of 125 killed and 200 wounded. Rear Admiral Charles J. Badger, commander in chief of the Atlantic Fleet, wrote proudly to Secretary Daniels that the "restraint of our men under the terrible punishment being dealt among them by individuals hidden on housetops or on balconies or where any cover could be obtained was very remarkable."[19]

Official reports, of course, presented an incomplete account of actions ashore. Danger was often slight or over quickly, and the men then proceeded to perform their military duties with good humor. In 1926 Dom Albert Pagano, a sailor from the cruiser *Galveston*, landed in Bluefields, Nicaragua, where he was placed in charge of a patrol to keep peace in the town. After enforcing an eight o'clock curfew, his men spent the rest of their watch chasing pigs down the streets and switching the flags that merchants flew in front of their shops. A Chinese merchant might have awakened to discover that he was displaying the Union Jack. Later, when Pagano served as a sentry on a boat going up river for bananas, he passed the time by firing at alligators and other wildlife.[20] Although it is not surprising that official accounts omitted such skylarking, to the men it was a memorable part of military encounters.

Because relatively few sailors saw military action, even of the lighthearted variety, accidents were far more lethal to enlisted men than was enemy fire. Most mishaps that befell the bluejacket were only indirectly connected with the navy. Falls and injuries sustained during athletic contests and in automobile accidents consistently occupied top positions in statistics the surgeon general collected. These two categories alone comprised almost 70 percent of all accidents. Usually grouped under headings such as "industrial and miscellaneous hazards," most accidents could have happened to civilian workers. Drowning—which accounted for only 0.1 percent of all accidents—was a hazard unique to service on the water, but not unique to the navy. Other accidents, however, arose from the specialized nature of the navy's work. Submarines and airplanes, for example, were experimental and dangerous vehicles that a civilian was unlikely to operate.[21]

Although most naval accidents involved only a few men each, disasters that emphasized the underlying danger of naval service did sometimes occur. A brief examination of a few of these incidents illustrates these hazards. A boiler explosion in 1905 on the gunboat *Bennington* claimed sixty-six lives. In 1923 twenty-three enlisted men died when seven destroyers grounded at Honda, California, during a fog. The world of underseas craft presented a constant risk—a risk recognized in the pay schedule. The first American submarine disaster took place March 25, 1915, when the *F-4* sank off Honolulu, losing the entire crew of one officer and nineteen enlisted men. On September 25, 1925, the *S-51* was struck by the coastal steamer *City of Rome*; of the forty officers and men board, only three enlisted men escaped. In 1927 the submarine *S-4* collided with a Coast Guard cutter in Cape Cod Bay, and when it sank, eighteen men died.[22]

The presence of high explosives on board naval ships meant continuing danger. In 1904 a flashback in the *Missouri's* twelve-inch turret ignited powder in the handling room, killing eighteen men in the turret and twelve in the handling room and magazines. Two years later on the *Kearsarge*, three bags of powder were accidentally set off during gun drill, and two officers and eight men died. In 1924, powder bags were ignited in a turret of the *Mississippi*, and forty-eight officers and men were killed. An exploding gun on the *Wyoming* in 1937 left seven dead and twelve injured.[23]

Early air travel was also hazardous, but crashes usually involved only one or two enlisted men. Only lighter-than-air craft carried a large enough crew to capture national headlines. On September 2, 1925, for example, the *Shenandoah* broke up in a storm near Byesville, Ohio, leaving eighteen dead. On April 3, 1933, the airship *Akron* crashed into the Atlantic. Among the eighteen officers and fifty-five men who died in this accident was Rear Admiral Willaim A. Moffett, then chief of the Bureau of Aeronautics and previously commandant of the Great Lakes Naval Training Station. And the *Macon*, the *Akron*'s sister ship, crashed February 12, 1935, with a loss of two.[24]

THE SHIP

In any account of the activity of enlisted men, it is important to consider the ships to which men were assigned. Although a standard pattern of daily activity and the rating structure tended to impose a rough unity throughout the navy, the size, age, and location of the bluejacket's ship produced some diversity and profoundly influenced the nature of his service.

Size directly affected comfort and discipline. As a general rule, small ships such as destroyers and submarines offered few amenities. Aboard these vessels, men vied with machinery for space. Because of their size, these ships never felt the full impact of the boom in shipboard recreational facilities that occurred on cruisers and battleships in the forty years after the Spanish-American War. There was no room for a gymnasium, a piano, or much of a library. Even motion pictures were ordinarily shown only when the ships were in port, where the crews of several vessels could be assembled for the screening.

Small vessels also behaved differently in heavy seas from their larger sisters. On destroyers, notorious for their violent pitching in storms, the movements of the ship interfered with sleep, inflicted bumps and bruises, and often prevented the serving of hot meals. Although submarines were less likely than destroyers to be at sea in rough weather, submarine service entailed discomforts in the form of cramped space, noxious fumes, and bad air. Describing his home, one submariner wrote:

Born in the shops of the devil,
Designed by the brains of a fiend;
Filled with acid and crude oil,
And christened "A Submarine."

We eat where'er we can find it,
And sleep hanging up on hooks;
Conditions under which we're existing
Are never published in books.

Life in these boats is obnoxious
And this is using mild terms;
We are never bothered by sickness,
There isn't any room for germs.[25]

In spite of such complaints, men were devoted to the small boats; many who served on them vowed they would never return to the battleship navy. Indeed, there were enough men of this sentiment that both destroyers and submarines were usually manned solely by volunteers.

A prime attraction of the smaller vessels was the freedom the crews enjoyed from the spit and polish of the larger men-of-war. The ships were "just small enough to make a home for the crew," as one destroyerman explained. He continued:

> Going aboard the black boats in port one is struck with the absence of—of—well, everything which one sees on a white ship. You might stay about for a week and you would never hear a bugle blowing quarters or see the men doing "monkey drill," setting up exercises or standing stiffly at attention.[26]

In a small crew men knew each other better and had closer contact than was possible with the crew as a whole on a battleship or cruiser. On both destroyers and submarines the comradeship of officers and crew was greater than usual in the navy. One enlisted man's magazine said of the submarine service: "Men love the life. With the officers they are as one family, sharing everything equally."[27]

In addition to relaxed discipline, the smaller units permitted the men greater responsibility. With few officers to supervise them, enlisted men on small craft handled their work independently. On a patrol boat, a petty officer might be the senior engineering officer, whereas on a battleship he would have had warrant officers and commissioned officers overseeing him.

Larger ships, on the other hand, offered their own advantages. As the tonnage of navy vessels increased to accommodate the new guns, space became available for barbershops, libraries, and recreation rooms. Furthermore since the larger vessels rolled less in heavy seas, the men suffered less from seasickness.[29]

As living conditions aboard ship improved steadily after the Spanish-American war, the battleships and cruisers were usually the first to acquire modern comforts. For example, dishwashing machines first came into use on the battleship *Missouri* in 1904. Similarly, laundries, which freed sailors from scrubbing their own clothing, were introduced on battleships during World War I. Of greater importance, the larger ships generally had superior lighting, ventilation, and heating—problems whose satisfactory solution had eluded the navy throughout its history.[30]

Another benefit the new battleships made possible was improved food storage and preparation. Refrigerated compartments and ice machines, which were installed aboard some warshisp as early as 1893, increased the likelihood that the men would be served fresh rather than dried or canned meat and vegetables. Mechanical cooling equipment also permitted the introduction of electrical ice-cream makers. These devices enjoyed great popularity among the men. Writing in 1906 of such a machine aboard the *Missouri*, Paymaster George P. Dyer admitted that "some may smile at the association of sailors and ice-cream" but insisted that "the day of the salt-horse, rough-living tar has passed. His place has been taken by clear-eyed, intelligent, American youths who are of the metal to endure hardship if necessary, but who know what clean living and good fare are; and they have the usual American notion of the festive nature of ice-cream."[31]

In addition to acquiring cooling equipment for the fleet, the modern navy also began to centralize meal preparation for the entire crew. The old navy had considered each mess a virtually autonomous unit. The mess (composed of approximately twenty men) took charge of its own supplies, cared for its own equipment, prepared much of its own food, and assessed its members small amounts to purchase items not a part of the navy ration. This system had serious shortcomings. Messes often accused one another of theft of stores; mess treasurers sometimes deserted with their shipmates' money; and the food was often poorly prepared since the mess cooks, who frequently had little interest in their task, generally simply boiled the food. To an extent, the cramped quarters and limited storage of the wooden sailing ships had necessitated this type of dispersed mess arrangement. With the commissioning of the larger, modern ships, it was possible to try new methods. In 1896 the battleship *Indiana* experimented with centralizing all food preparation in a single galley under the supervision of a permanent staff of cooks. The quality of meals improved, and economies of scale made it possible to eliminate special assessments within the messes.[32]

After food preparation became centralized, the men continued to eat in berthing areas. Because food was issued to representatives of the mess six minutes before meal call, hot meals were rare. In 1916 the *New York* experimented with serving men in cafeteria style, but this idea apparently was soon dropped. The cafeteria method of serving and eating was apparently not adopted for another twenty years.[33]

The bigger ships were also first to introduce lockers and bunks for the men. Traditionally sailors kept their clothing in seabags, which were stored away; the men were allowed to get items from their bags only at specified times during the day, and at these times what they needed was invariably at the bottom. In the 1890s the navy began testing lockers aboard the *Philadelphia* but abandoned the experiment. The idea, however, was not dead. Shortly before World War I the men began agitating through their publications for such equipment. Nevertheless, it was apparently not until 1920, when the navy built lockers on the battleship *Tennessee*, that the service conducted another experiment on the feasibility of equipping ships with lockers.[34]

Shortly after this trial, the navy tested both lockers and bunks aboard the *California* and *Oklahoma* in 1924.[35] Previously men had slept in hammocks, which were slung at night and stored in the daytime. With some practice, a sailor could sleep satisfactorily in a hammock but never as comfortably as on a bed. Moreover, it was easy to slip from a hammock to the deck several feet below. In 1926 the surgeon general reported that ninety-four men were injured in such falls that year and that, as a result of these accidents, 1,787 days were lost.[36]

After placing bunks and lockers on the two battleships, the department solicited reactions. Officers reported that both innovations were popular with the crews. Furthermore, because bunks were not removed during the day, crew members could rest on them when they were not on duty—a welcome feature for the men. Despite the men's enthusiasm, the Bureau of Navigation was reluctant to accept service-wide use of bunks. It argued that bunks would be unsuitable during combat since wooden frames splintered when hit by a shell and thus presented a hazard not posed by hammocks; in addition, it said that because ship complements were increased in wartime, bunks permanently occupied space that would be needed for other purposes. The bureau concluded that during peacetime men should sleep in the hammocks they would have to use during wartime. It also considered it not "good practice to have men loafing in their bunks during the day" and suggested that off-duty men sleep on the open deck, as was customary. By 1927, however, the bureau had overcome its reservations and recommended that bunks be installed on all ships where possible. Yet complete conversion did not occur rapidly; it was not until 1946 that the *Bluejacket's Manual* omitted the section on the care of hammocks.[37]

An adequate amount of fresh water contributed greatly to a sailor's contentment; in this area, too, the large ships usually enjoyed an advantage. Because vessels under sail had had to carry and store fresh water, the stock was limited and carefully rationed. The introduction of steam engines meant that ships maintained equipment to distill water for the boilers and that the crew received any surplus. As steam engines grew more efficient and required less water, the distillation equipment increasingly could be used to provide water for the men. Bluejackets transferring from sailing ships to steamships were impressed both by the amount of fresh water available and by the presence of hot water.[38]

Water was more plentiful in the modern navy, but its supply was not unlimited. Some small ships, such as the *Machias*, barely distilled enough water for their boilers; the crews of these ships sometimes were rationed as little as one quart of water per day.[39] More commonly, water rations were small because captains decided to seek the red "E" awarded for engineering efficiency. Since purifying water required fuel, commanding officers often imposed rationing to reduce fuel consumption. In World War I, the *Texas* rationed fresh water to six quarts per man per day. The water supply was also sometimes shut off or the distillation process was sometimes accelerated, producing water that tasted salty. Because excessive control over water created discontent among the crew, some officers pointedly refused to strain for engineering efficiency, feeling that good morale resulted in proficiency in nonengineering areas.[40]

Size alone did not determine the habitability of a ship. The ship's age also influenced the degree of comfort a bluejacket could expect. While living conditions afloat steadily improved, older vessels remained in commission, and the navy could not or would not install all the new features on them. Among the most infamous of the older vessels were the gunboats acquired from the Spanish in 1898, which remained in service in Asia far into the new century. Concerning one such ship, the *Pampanga*, launched in 1888, a 1924 issue of the magazine *Orient* complained:

> The coolie-quarters on a slaver would be cabin space in comparison with the crew quarters on the *Pampanga*. If men sleep aboard they must sleep on the top side.
>
> And there is no lifeline, railing, bulkhead or bulwark sufficient to prevent anyone who might toss in his sleep, from rolling over the side.[41]

Vessels permanently assigned to distant patrol were not the only ships to show signs of age. In 1930 four enlisted men deplored conditions on the *Galveston*, which had been completed in 1903:

> Just why she is kept in commission nobody knows. There is a lot of talk about cleanliness, and clean and sanitary surroundings, but these things did not exist in the Navy of 25 or 30 years ago, that is compared to the modern battleships of today with a nice work room, clean bunks, and big recreation centres. . . . She loses a good percentage of her crew

> at every United States port she hits. The majority of the crew would rather face a court-martial or worse rather than make a 10-month cruise on the *Gally*.[42]

As new ships were built, older ones obviously suffered from comparison.

For the men, probably few improvements equalled the introduction of oil as fuel. Oil freed the entire crew from the ordeal of coaling ship and the engine-room force from stoking boilers. As was the case with other innovations, conversion to oil also proved slow. The navy first studied the use of fuel oil in 1904 aboard the torpedo boat *Rodgers*. Another experiment was conducted in 1909 aboard the *Cheyenne*. The chief of the Bureau of Steam Engineering pronounced the results of the *Cheyenne* tests satisfactory. As a consequence, the department began providing every new battleship and many new destroyers and submarines with oil-burning engines. Also in 1909 the Bureau of Navigation established fuel-oil storage facilities. Yet during World War I most of the battleships and many of the destroyers were still fired by coal, and after every maneuver the ships had to recoal in preparation for the next sortie.[43]

In addition to the ship's size and age, its duty station also affected the lives of the men. Different locales had decidedly different advantages and drawbacks.[44] The question of what was the best assignment was the subject of long debate. Men with families preferred vessels that spent much of their time in a United States home port. While family men tried to avoid being assigned to distant stations that required prolonged separation, other sailors had enlisted for travel, and they were determined to see the world. Europe offered both antique charm and, for many, a chance to visit relatives. Service in these waters consisted of cruises from city to city with formal visits at each stop between officers of the various fleets in port. Although this duty put the greatest demand on the officers, the men too experienced an increased attention to spit and polish and to formal ceremony. The Caribbean provided sunny islands and blue seas, but boredom plagued men cruising in the area for any length of time.

Farthest from the United States in both distance and culture was East Asia, which offered a suitably exotic setting. Even in the Orient, though, not every assignment was equally attractive. Some vessels remained all year in Philippine waters, while others escaped the torrid months of southern Asia by taking leisurely voyages to China or Japan. Other ships faced long calls in Chinese ports to protect American interests, even though the men were yearning to travel. Patrol boats on the Upper Yangtze were isolated at all times. During the months of low water when they were trapped up river, it took mail or supplies three months to arrive from the coast by junk.

OFFICERS

A major factor that influenced the quality of service was the type of officer under whom the enlisted man served. Although in some respects many officers were becoming interested in improving the treatment of the men, at the same time they retained a paternalistic attitude toward the enlisted force.

An officer was always aware of his superior and separate status at the top of the ship hierarchy, never imagining the seamen to be his equals. He fulfilled his obligations toward the men, but only rarely did he allow them to penetrate his consciousness as individuals. The lack of references to enlisted men in officers' letters and diaries suggests this impersonal attitude toward the men. Midshipman Hollis T. Winston, for example, kept a log from 1900 to 1903, carefully describing the three ships on which he served, but never mentioning a sailor. Amidst descriptions of armor, engines, and armament, not even a notation of the ship's complement is to be found.[45]

The few enlisted men who did rate a line in the officers' memoirs, moreover, appeared only in a limited and stereotyped way. Many were petty officers with long service, often much of it spent in the smaller navy of the years before the Spanish-American War. They were gruff old salts, relics of a bygone era, relating with bewilderment and regret the changes that had taken place since the old days. Some officers were also fond of relating drunken-sailor anecdotes. Usually competent seamen when sober, then men in these stories possessed a weakness for liquor that repeatedly undermined gains they had made. Because the drunken sailor accepted his fate with good humor or as a repentant child, officers wrote of him with fondness.[46]

Enlisted men's absence or appearance only as stereotypes in officers' narratives demonstrates the difficulty seamen encountered in achieving individual recognition. Frequent transfers of both officers and men exacerbated the situation. Furthermore, as officers achieved higher rank, they had little association with enlisted personnel. The contacts that did remain were with men performing direct services for them: i.e., yeomen, officers' stewards and cooks, and messmen.[47] The rest of the force dissolved into a uniformed blur.

The gulf between rank and rate also obscured sailors' perceptions of their superiors. In many cases, frequent transfers clouded seamen's memories of individual officers. Yet, because the seamen were in a subordinate position and dependent on their superiors for promotion, leave, and special favors, it was essential for them to know their officers. With so much of their lives determined by the men over them, sailors studied, recognized, and appreciated differences in officers' behavior.

Good officers made a ship a "home," the highest praise an enlisted man could bestow.[48] Such superiors were not lenient or soft, but fair, open, and as ready to praise as to censure. Under their leadership, sailors performed well and with reasonable contentment. They sometimes expressed their appreciation of a favorite officer by presenting a gift to his wife.[49] Many sailors, furthermore, remembered good superiors long after their service together had ended. One seaman, for example, wrote to the magazine *Bostonian* to commend Commander S. S. Robinson, who had "won the admiration and respect of all the crew" during tours as executive officer of the *Pennsylvania* and navigator of the *Tennessee*.[50] Upon receiving advancement to chief petty officer, R. A. Emery wrote Captain Rufus Johnston to thank him for acting leniently when Emery had been before the mast for fraudulent enlistment five years earlier. Rear Admiral Andrew T. Long received a letter of appreciation from a former crewman of the *Nevada* eleven years after he had commanded it.[51] Cumulatively, testimonials such as these demonstrate the ability of an officer to make a lasting and favorable impression on enlisted men.

Conversely, ships on which officers abused their power were called "madhouses." In one such case, a captain brought a "mad" destroyer around the Horn to the Pacific in 1908. When he transferred to another vessel, it too went mad. Eventually, the Bureau of Navigation removed him from command, but only after many enlisted men had had their rcords blemished or their ratings reduced.[52]

Overall there were probably more homes than madhouses, and most ships never attained either extreme. Yet a ship need not have degenerated to madness for the bluejackets to experience frustration and bitterness when confronted with the arrogance of rank. In most cases officers, secure on their side of the barrier, were oblivious to the sailors' feelings. Sometimes an officer, perhaps unknowingly, conducted his routine duties in a way that unnecessarily antagonized the men. John Kendig, an electrician on the *Kearsarge*, protested the behavior of his "beloved first luf," who often required extra work and refused small favors such as sleeping topside in hot weather. Because of the *Kearsarge*'s officers, Kendig ominously predicted that "a large percentage of the men will desert when we reach the States."[53]

Sometimes the sailors also resented officers' special privileges. In 1915 a veteran chief petty officer complained of not being allowed to take visitors below decks even though "an officer who has not been on the ship two months can take girls below whom he never saw before." And sometimes, discontent was directed against general assignments. Typical of such feelings were the charges by a sailor in 1904 that at Guantanamo the men were "driven like brutes and treated worse than the most deprived slaves."[54]

By themselves enlisted men's complaints about officers reveal little about the treatment of the men. Sailors have always been, and probably always will be, certain that their officers were personally responsible for all shortcomings in food, work, and weather. Yet, as has been seen, in the decades following the Spanish-American War, both the desertion and reenlistment rates improved. By deserting less often and reenlisting more often, sailors demonstrated their contentment with the service as a whole. Their treatment by officers probably contributed greatly to this overall regard for the service.

Even with the amelioration of many of the conditions under which enlisted men lived, sailors still occupied a clearly inferior position in the naval hierarchy. Their low status prevented even the most sympathetic officers from completely understanding the bluejackets' position, and enlisted frustrations remained unarticulated.

The resourceful sailor, however, was not completely blocked from releasing the tension created by his powerless position. Sometimes through good-natured skylarking he sparred with the system that dictated his impotence. Mark Murnane, a hospital corpsman in World War I, relished sauntering up Sands Street near the Brooklyn navy yard with other enlisted men and saluting officers who were returning from shopping. Forgetting in the surprise of the moment that regulations did not require returning a salute if it was inconvenient to do so, the officer fumbled with packages in an effort to free an arm. To increase the fun, the seamen sometimes separated, and the group passed in intervals of several feet. This sport was especially pleasurable when the officers were young and overly concerned about always being saluted.[55] At other times, sailors took more direct action, though in such a way as to avoid retaliation. Seamen, for example, might drop an unpopular officer's trunk into the sea, leaving the man to guess whether it was an accident or not.[56]

SHIPBOARD DIVERSIONS

Because sailors were too young and too lively to let the work unfold without interruption, the daily schedule presents only an incomplete picture of the lives of enlisted men. Sometimes the men were content with officially sponsored recreational activities; at other times they created their own opportunities to escape the monotony of the shipboard routine.

Officers occasionally permitted certain festivities that relaxed the lines of rank. During New Year's celebrations, for example, costumed bluejackets collected instruments and paraded around the ship. Usually forbidden areas in officers' territory were open to the procession. Some horseplay was tolerated; if an occasional officer was doused, he took it in the good humor of the evening.[57] Probably few men in command formulated detailed theories of behavior concerning these diversions, but most recognized that they improved ship morale because they allowed a brief respite from the restrictions of the usual discipline.

Crossing the equator called for the initiation of men passing over the line for the first time—a ceremony that was one of the most famous breaks from the routine. Celebration of the event on European ships can be traced to 1529.[58] Although American seamen did not invent the ritual, they adopted it enthusiastically. Furthermore, officers supported the undertaking to bolster morale; indeed, should a crew have been reluctant to prepare a proper ceremony, the officers would most likely have ordered it done.

Even though the officers supported the project, the crew themselves staged the event.[59] Spinning elaborate yarns about the coming ordeal, old hands set the mood from the time the ship left port. The day before a ship was to cross the equator, Davy Jones hailed her, requested permission to come aboard—which was immediately granted—climbed from the hawsehole, and made his way to the bridge. Here he greeted the captain and presented a summons. Written in suitably flowery language, this document demanded the presence in Neptune's court of all men entering the domain for the first time. The next day, as their ship reached the equator, she was boarded by Neptune's party, and the bridge was turned over to a member of the court during the stay of his majesty Neptunus Rex. Besides the king, his queen, and Davy Jones, the entourage usually included a royal navigator, a royal officer of the deck, a royal judge, a royal prosecuting attorney, a royal scribe, a royal barber, a royal dentist, and the royal police. If the sponsors of the show were sufficiently numerous and energetic, also in attendance were a royal baby—usually one of the largest men on the ship—a royal electrician, royal handmaidens, and miscellaneous pirates and naval heroes.

While the court made its way to the portion of the deck set aside for the ceremony, the royal police assembled the initiates. All officers and men who had not crossed the line before were required to appear before the assemblage to explain why they dared trespass on Neptune's domain when they were not certified "shellbacks." At each hearing the court quickly tried and convicted the accused. The prisoner was thereupon examined by the royal dentist and shaved by a royal barber, who used a large paint brush and a wooden razor. The royal doctor administered a foul-tasting pill. The chair in which the convicted man sat was then flipped backward, catapulting the victim into a canvas pool, where the royal bears playfully dunked him a few times. Although the pool was lined with several layers of canvas to cushion the deck and the bears tried to break the fall, this finale often produced sprains and broken bones. Assuming he survived unharmed, the new shellback could join the police searching for any men who were hiding.

Although all first-timers were called to the court, not all received the same treatment. Officers were permitted to purchase exemption from the rites, though most of the younger ones apparently did not. Before Secretary Daniels abolished the officers' "wine mess" in 1914, payment had been in beer; after that sad day cigars were substituted.[60] Generally, the first men received greater attention than the others, especially on a large ship which might have had to process several hundred men. Unpopular men or men who tried to hide were generally honored with a more elaborate initiation than the average sailor.

While the sailors welcomed a semiofficial event such as the crossing ceremony, they were not wholly dependent on special occasions for their amusements. Even in the regulated life of a man-of-war, the men had some time to call their own. Freed from both work and organized recreation, they used their ingenuity to pursue a surprisingly wide variety of pastimes. Some men filled their leisure profitably—caring for their outfits, studying for advancement, or earning extra money by doing sewing, laundry, and similar tasks for their shipmates. Others occupied themselves in more frivolous ways with games of chance and skill. Acey-deucey (a form of backgammon), cards, and dice were found on every ship. Although the *Regulations* forbade gambling, that prohibition never deterred the bluejackets. In storerooms or in other secluded spots, they gathered to try their luck. Some small vessels in the Phillipines early in the century also permitted cockfighting, but this spot rarely reached the bigger ships.[61]

Games were not the only source of recreation. A ship also prevented numerous opportunities for pranks. A recruit arriving on his first ship was sent in search of nonexistent but plausible pieces of equipment: hammock ladders, anchor covers, starboard scythes, starboard monkey wrenches, or red and green oil for running lights.[62] While a sailor fresh from training camp offered ideal prey, other men were not immune. John Kendig was victimized in a typical trick when someone placed an eight-inch shell in his hammock. Determined not to be the only dupe, he transferred it to a friend's hammock. Then, pretending to be asleep, Kendig was able to relish his shipmate's reaction. At another time, Kendig demonstrated the sailor's ability to seize every opportunity for a joke. One night he was awakened when a bear, the ship's mascot, climbed into his hammock. Recognizing a situation too good to let pass, he shifted the animal onto the man in the next hammock. His friend awoke swearing. Also realizing the possibilities of the incident, he in turn transferred the bear to yet another victim, who also awoke enraged, to the amusement of those watching.[63]

In addition to these pastimes, some enlisted men felt that proper relaxation required liquor. The navy, however, did not share this conviction. The grog ration for enlisted men had been discontinued in 1862. On February 3, 1899, Secretary John D. Long issued General Order 508 prohibiting the sale of beer to men on board ships or within the limits of naval stations. Long's order made drinking on board difficult, but not impossible. Using the time-honored tricks of the sea, some sailors resorted to smuggling. They taped flasks inside their trouser legs, hid bottles in ship supplies, and purchased liquor in baskets of fruit from bumboat men. A few bluejackets also smuggled for profit. B. J. Ducret of the cruiser *Princeton* sold liquor at five dollars a bottle—much of it to men in the brig—before a court-martial conviction in 1907 put him out of business. Other men relied on alcohol in supplies aboard ship. The dispensary stocked alcohol, to which the hospital corps had access. Additional spirits were aboard in the form of alcohol for torpedoes and shellac. Drinking shellac, however, was a measure of desperation, because it left an odious taste.[64]

LIBERTY

However enjoyable the pastimes aboard ship, the bluejacket received greatest respite from his duties during liberty. Going ashore released him from the rigid discipline of naval life and made it easier to endure the routine when he returned. Most officers recognized the relation between liberty and morale and tried to grant their men as much liberty as possible.[65]

Although enlisted men were always eager to touch land, not all ports were equally attractive. American cities such as New York and San Francisco were interesting, but they lacked the glamour of foreign climes. European ports were generally considered good liberty; Copenhagen was a favorite. In the Far East, Japanese cities reputedly ranked among the best in the world for the sailor on liberty. Sailors in China favored larger metropolitan areas, such as Shanghai or

Tsingtao, because in smaller ports facilities were limited. In smaller cities the men found only "two types of recreation constantly open to the dashing man-of-war's man . . . the gin mill and the dive." The Army-Navy YMCA offered facilities in Manila, Shanghai, Hankow, Tientsin, and Peking, but in other cities the sailor had to operate from his ship. In the Caribbean, Panama was a popular stop, as were some islands in the West Indies.[66]

Sailors also knew which ports were undesirable. In 1909 a sailor on the *Tennessee*, recounting a stop at Chatham Island in the Galápagos, dismissed the islands as "a lemon, not even a native, let alone a village." Guantánamo, which the fleet frequently visited for target practice, was considered dull. Without question, though, the leading contenders for the distinction of worst liberty were Guam and Samoa. Small, isolated, and under navy control, these islands were almost legendary. In describing the relative merits of various cities, one author asserted, "When good sailors die their souls go to Japan—the bad 'uns go to—well say Guam or Tutuila."[67]

Whatever the merits of the city, enlisted men disembarked determined to enjoy themselves. Having joined up to see the world, they set off to investigate new lands with the enthusiasm of compulsive tourists. In each new port seamen took in all the attractions. They gaped at New York skyscrapers, investigated Egyptian pyramids, examined Roman ruins, and roamed through the Vatican. In Japan, or even Tsingtao, bluejackets sought out geisha houses, changed into kimonos, and enjoyed an evening of oriental food and entertainment. Enlisted men were such inveterate sightseers that after Japan's invasion of China, the Japanese army organized tours of the war zone for curious Americans.[68]

Like all travelers, sailors collected mementos of their visits. George Eastman had begun marketing a simple hand camera in 1888, and modern enlisted men recorded their travels on film. Every invading liberty party was armed with Kodaks, which were fired indiscriminately in all directions. The camera captured smiling bluejackets riding in rickshaws in China and camels in Egypt. The men also returned from their adventures with trinkets of widely varying worth. On the 1907-9 world cruise, all hands received cloisonné cups from the Empress Dowager of China, but normally sailors purchased cheap souvenirs, which were stuffed into seabags and ditty boxes.[69]

Since sailors were free spenders, merchants made special arrangements for their visits. Often storekeepers raised prices "to untold heights" in honor of the American tourists.[70] The crews' patronage sometimes took precedence over local problems. When skirmishes of contesting revolutionary factions in Lisbon in 1918 prevented liberty, businessmen arranged an afternoon ceasefire so that the men from the visiting American ships could come ashore.[71] Special provisions of this nature were rarely necessary, but the incident reflects both the desire of the sailor to make purchases and the willingness of those ashore to assist him.

Not all relations between sailors and civilians were as cordial as in Lisbon. In fact, enlisted men entered the twentieth century with an image that made them outcasts in many strata of society and targets of discrimination, especially in the United States. As the composition of the enlisted force changed after the Spanish-American War, sailors began to challenge their status in the civilian world. Although the navy participated in some efforts to improve sailor-civilian relations, for the most part the department ignored aspects of enlisted men's lives outside naval jurisdiction. The major impetus for change in the treatment of sailors by civilians came not from the Navy Department as such, but from individual officers and from the men themselves.

RELATIONS WITH CIVILIANS AT HOME

In the nineteenth century, enlisted men usually experienced a cool reception when they went ashore on liberty. Because sailors bore a reputation for drinking and fighting, many neighborhoods of coastal cities tried to exclude them. Consequently, bluejackets restricted their activities to waterfront bars and boardinghouses. Here, while their money lasted, they were honored guests and among friends.[72]

The new enlisted force upset this equilibrium. Sailors became more and more unwilling to confine their leisure time to these traditional areas. Furthermore, their increased numbers could no longer be accommodated in the old facilities even if they had been content to remain there. Not only were individual ships larger, but the vessels now maneuvered as fleets.[73] Because more men were in port at one time than there had been in the nineteenth century, sailors overflowed their old haunts. In 1906, 500 seamen presented Norfolk with an unprecedented number of men on leave at one time. A newspaper observed that the bluejackets "fairly swarmed on the streets."[74] Soon cities faced several times that many young men invading from visiting warships.

Such a deluge of fun-seeking sailors easily overwhelmed existing amusement facilities in all parts of cities, and the men found themselves unwelcome. Regarding sailors as potential troublemakers who would drive away local patronage, proprietors banned them from their establishments. Sailors, for their part, resented exclusion based not on an individual's misconduct but on the uniform of national service.

The mushrooming in the numbers of sailors in the years following the Spanish-American War intensified friction between seamen and civilians. Not only did the new sailor abandon his traditional locales, but he also protested discriminatory treatment. In one of the first legal actions, Fred J. Buenzle lodged a suit in 1906 against the Newport Amusement Company. Buenzle, a chief yeoman at the Newport Naval Training Station and editor of *Bluejacket*, had purchased a ticket to a dance while he was dressed in civilian clothes. Changing into his uniform, he returned to the hall but was denied admission. He refused to accept a refund and sued the company. Although Buenzle appealed his case to the Rhode Island Supreme Court, he was unable to collect damages beyond the price of the ticket. Nevertheless, the suit attracted national attention when President Theodore Roosevelt contributed $100 in support of

Buenzle. The publicity attending *Buenzle v. Newport Amusement Company* no doubt encouraged the passage of a 1908 act in Rhode Island prohibiting discrimination against men in uniform.[75]

The practices that led to Buenzle's case were not restricted to Newport. Problems arose whenever enlisted men were present in large numbers. In 1911 the management of the Mammoth Skating Rink in Seattle refused admission to enlisted men.[76] In the same year, Commander George F. Cooper, commanding officer of the *Marietta*, protested to the mayor of Portsmouth, New Hampshire, that bluejackets were forbidden use of the dance floor at the Freeman's Hall. In January 1917 the proprietor of the Olympic Theater in Brooklyn was fined $250 for barring sailors.[77]

In addition to finding themselves unwanted in many public places, enlisted men discovered they were the prey of land sharks. Sailors encountered artificially inflated prices in waterfront areas close to the yards. Furthermore, in any kind of emergency a seaman found himself exceptionally vulnerable. In a particularly flagrant example in 1910, a San Francisco boatman increased the fare tenfold for a man hurrying to his ship. Sailors wishing to return to the camp at Pelham Bay Park in 1918 found the transportation rate had doubled.[78]

Even if he escaped such overt overcharging, the bluejacket had ample evidence that many citizens valued only his money. In 1910 Portsmouth, New Hampshire, complained that the transfer of the cruiser *Tacoma,* scheduled to be dry-docked for overhauling, to another yard deprived Portsmouth of the $5,000 the men would have spent. Decrying Portsmouth's excessive commercialism, *Our Navy* noted that Vallejo, California, and Bremerton, Washington, welcomed the men as well as their money.[79]

The hypocrisy of some civilians also irritated sailors. The same town that either rejected the men or appreciated only their cash value felt, at the same time, a perfect right to courtesies from the navy. In 1911 Portsmouth, New Hampshire, barred men in uniform from many public places and then felt aggrieved when the sailors were not ordered to march in the Memorial Day parade.[80]

Frequently the police also reflected a city's hostility toward enlisted men. In 1905 the secretary of the naval YMCA in Norfolk charged that enlisted men were deliberately harassed by some policemen who were trying to detect deserters and collect the reward money. A year later, Rear Admiral Evans accused the Portland, Maine, police of an unprovoked assault upon an orderly party of men returning from leave.[81]

Although incidents of discrimination were never completely eradicated, the situation improved during the first years of the twentieth century. Sailors were more likely to receive small kindnesses from civilians, even if only in the form of comfort bags sent by women's clubs.[82] Furthermore, cities began to prepare festivals for visiting fleets. At these celebrations, which began on a large scale with the voyage of the fleet in 1908, the bluejacket was lavished with food, lodging, and entertainment—either free or at minimal cost. Though an element of self-preservation motivated communities faced with an invasion of several thousand young men, the festivals demonstrated an interest in the men that helped counteract the effects of the exploitation the sailors so often experienced.[83]

A factor that undoubtedly contributed to improved relations between sailors and civilians at home was the fact that the type of good times most sailors pursued seems to have changed from earlier days. Observers both inside and outside the service noted sailors' improved behavior. An officer visiting New York's Metropolitan Museum in 1906 saw at least a hundred uniformed navy men touring the exhibits:

> Clean, clear cut, picturesquely dressed, they wandered through the rooms studying the catalogues which nearly every one of them had bought; absolutely unconscious of the attention they attracted and of the fact that they were doing something that sailors were not expected to do.[84]

In 1913 the secretary of the Brooklyn Naval YMCA reported to Rear Admiral Hugo Osterhaus, the commander in chief of the Atlantic Fleet, that it had been over a month since a drunken sailor had entered the Y. The admiral responded that he had not seen a drunken sailor for so long that he had "forgotten what one looks like."[85] After a visit of the fleet to San Diego in 1925, the mayor of the city expressed his appreciation for the conduct of the enlisted men. Although 20,000 young persons had descended on the city, "there was nothing but good reported of them from all quarters."[86] In 1929 Admiral Henry A. Wiley, commander in chief of the United States Fleet, was pleased, though perhaps also surprised, at the men's good behavior in Panama. The concentration of the fleet there doubled the population of Panama City, but only scattered incidents of drunkennes were reported.[87]

All of these evaluations of behavior, of course, were largely subjective; indeed, the whole question of deportment ashore defies statistical analysis. Nevertheless, these observations and many similar ones seem to reflect a noticeable change in enlisted conduct.

Every encounter between sailors and civilians was not happy. Some friction between the two groups continued, and the twentieth century saw its share of disturbances involving enlisted men. Sailors reacted to an overcharging of two members of a liberty party in 1908 by stoning the offending restaurant; two years later bluejackets drove an orator from his outdoor podium after he characterized "most of the men who man our warships" as "bums, derelicts and pikers."[88]

During World War I soldiers and sailors became the heroes of the hour. A smothering hospitality replaced the former discrimination. Shortly after war was declared, Mrs. Joseph M. Gazzam, wife of a prominent Philadelphia lawyer, announced that she was inviting fifty sailors to her home for tea to demonstrate that men in uniform would no longer be ostracized. As social leaders in other cities emulated Mrs. Gazzam, the bluejacket found himself no longer a pariah but besieged with invitations. The Winter Club at Lake Forest, Illinois, was among the many private facilities that welcomed enlisted men. The uniform also commanded benefits such as low-cost or free entertainment, meals, and lodging, all provided by charitable and fraternal organizations. Furthermore, sailors received spontaneous gestures of goodwill, including admission to fashionable parties.[89]

Not all the solicitude followed a course the men appreciated, for the war was used as an excuse to create a dry zone around camps and stations. A federal law passed in 1917 prohibited the sale of liquor to men in uniform.[90] Although the sailors in the twentieth century did not make drinking their sole occupation ashore, they still enjoyed imbibing when on liberty. Despite the hopes of the prohibition forces of the country, however, the new law did not eradicate the vice among enlisted men but merely changed the locale of drinking. Now the men had to patronize back rooms, thoughtfully provided by proprietors of bars near military installations.[91]

War brought recognition to enlisted men; peace ended it. After the armistice, civilians quickly reverted to normal relations, and sailors were plummeted from the social heights they had enjoyed. Symbolic of this reversal was the transfer in 1919 of weekly dances for sailors from the Cranston Country Club to Patten Gymnasium of Northwestern University.[92] Downtown commercial interests, too, no longer welcomed enlisted men. Early in January 1919 the Morrison Hotel of Chicago barred sailors. Although offended bluejackets quickly retorted that it was not the kind of hotel any self-respecting sailor wanted to patronize, it was obvious that times had changed. By late 1929, of the numerous New York City facilities that had catered to servicemen during the war, only the National Navy Club survived.[93]

Although the conclusion of the war ended special consideration from civilians, sailors nevertheless found their position more satisfactory than it had been in the nineteenth century or even earlier in the twentieth century. Wartime had improved their public image; their enhanced prestige doubtedly was carried over to the postwar era. In addition, bluejackets had gained a legal protection that had not existed for sailors of the old navy. A survey by the Bureau of Navigation revealed that by 1920 Rhode Island, New York, Massachusetts, Maine, Connecticut, and California had passed statutes prohibiting discrimination against men in uniform.[94] Because these six states contained the majority of ports and bases the navy used, they were the areas in which the concentration of enlisted men was large enough to arouse civilian hostility.

Discrimination against sailors became rarer in the 1920s and 1930s, even though some, of course, still existed. In 1932 the officer in charge of the Los Angeles recruiting station reported an alleged false arrest of a shipfitter, first class, for drunken driving, commenting that police in small communities around Los Angeles "are not as lenient with enlisted men as they are with civilians." He also believed that some police ran a racket on arrests of naval personnel.[95] And, of course, enlisted men still found prices raised in their honor. Nevertheless, during these two decades, the relationship between civilians at home and sailors attained a new level of cordiality. Each group could exist without overly offending the other.

RELATIONS WITH CIVILIANS ABROAD

Unlike their counterparts in the army, enlisted men of the navy frequently visited foreign countries and had continuing contact with civilians of other nations. Surprisingly, sailor-civilian relations abroad were free of much of the friction that existed in the United States. Indeed, the men often lamented that the uniform was better received abroad than at home.[96]

One factor in the absence of hostility was that the Americans rarely overwhelmed foreign seaports. The larger warships generally visited only major harbors, and merchants and guides in these cities were expert in handling foreign seamen. If American enlisted men were willing to accept some over-charging, they encountered little trouble. Advance planning for cities to accommodate any unusually large number of men who were to visit also helped reduce tension.[97]

Not all the behavior of enlisted men in foreign ports, of course, was admirable. Sailors had a reputation for brawling that was not totally underserved, and Americans saw their share of action even in the twentieth century. In 1908, for example, a disturbance occurred in Rio de Janeiro between "drunken native negroes and a few of the sailors from the American fleet." Five years later, citizens of Naples complained of the bluejackets' conduct.[98] Trouble was most common, however, in Asian ports. Contact with a radically different culture and the ineffective law enforcement in many cities freed the men from their normal restraints. In addition, seamen from various national fleets competed for female companionship. Here, as in other parts of the world, the free-spending Americans offended sailors from other fleets, who received less pay, and fights resulted.[99] Yet, although disruptions were common, they were usually confined to areas near the waterfront that were accustomed to the ways of sailors. The population there accepted the frays as a normal part of business.

During World War I many sailors were stationed in England and, in lesser numbers, in other Allied nations. No longer did they stay for just liberty; rather, they formed permanent garrisons. Their large numbers also increased chances for misunderstanding. Never before had the American navy stationed so many men in another country.

Initial developments augured well for smooth relations between the Americans and their hosts. A large, enthusiastic crowd greeted the first destroyers to arrive in Queenstown, Ireland, in May 1917, despite official secrecy about the arrival time. Going ashore, the men found the townspeople open and friendly. As the American presence grew, the men reached other cities—London, Paris, and Edinburgh. Here, too, they often received a warmhearted, spontaneous welcome.[100]

Although a widespread cordiality often existed, the potential for hostility was also present. Consequently, the navy counseled the men about their conduct. Before the end of 1917 the enlisted force was cautioned not to make inflammatory statements such as "We have come over here to finish the War for you because you cannot do it yourselves." Some months later, Vice Admiral Henry B. Wilson also found it necessary to instruct his men to act as befitted guests in someone's home.[101]

At times the undercurrent of hostility that some segments of the civilian population felt toward Americans erupted. In late 1917 mobs in the town of Cork attacked sailors who were with Irish girls, and the navy was forced to place Cork off-limits to men on leave.[102] Although incidents rarely provoked such extreme official reaction, in many cities some residents engaged in sporadic harassment of Americans. As Allied prospects in the war improved and the American presence grew, the comradeship that had been felt during less hopeful days faded. Confrontations involving American bluejackets and their hosts increased. Newcastle ruffians, for example, battled sailors from several ships; in 1918 the crew of the battleship *Texas* escalated the skirmishes to open war. After a series of attacks that the Americans felt were particularly unjustified, the bluejackets went ashore to deal with the Newcastle rowdies. During the night small bands of sailors engaged gangs of Englishmen, withdrew when the police arrived, only to re-form and attack again. The men dubbed the encounter the "Battle of Newcastle," considering it "the biggest, the bloodiest and the best battle of the entire war."[103]

The problem of relations during the war was further complicated by white Americans' hostility toward racially mixed couples. In November 1917 the chief of police of Newport, Monmouthshire, reported incidents involving the crew of the *Benham*, which was in port for repair from early September to November 1917. After a period of good relations, "a collision took place between a number of the crew and some coloured men, and so far as can be acsertained the origin of the trouble was the dislike of the American Seaman to coloured men cohabiting and associating with white women." After the trouble the local populace showed "signs of unfriendliness" toward the Americans.[104] Similarly, an enlisted man from the *Texas* witnessed a near riot caused by the reaction of sailors to a black enlisted man's arriving at a train station with two white women.[105]

In many ways, of course, the incidents of wartime resembled the brawls of peacetime. What makes them different was that they were more common, if only because there were more Americans spending more time abroad. Furthermore, since they detracted from Allied unity in the crusade against the Hun, they embarrassed the war effort. The navy never found the key to smoothing all contacts between enlisted men and Allied civilians. Only the withdrawal of the men after the armistice ended the difficulty.

Whether at home or abroad, an enlisted man found that his uniform identified him as a member of a particular group and that he was treated on the basis of this membership rather than as an individual. A bluejacket could protest discrimination, but his lot was determined by the reputation of the enlisted force as a whole. Improvements in the relationships between sailors and civilians could result only from a change in the enlisted force. In the twentieth century the enlisted force became more skilled and, of greater significance, more representative of the country it served. As civilians began to accord seamen greater respect, sailors gradually shed their status as outcasts.

Many ingredients, then, went into shaping enlisted men's lives. The large ships of the new navy increasingly offered facilities and comforts sailors had never before enjoyed: barbershops, reading rooms, recreation areas, dishwashers, laundries, improved heating, lighting, and ventilation, lockers and bunks, and greater supplies of fresh water. Larger ships also meant less seasickness, and the introduction of oil as a fuel relieved the men of the unpleasant task of coaling the ship. Yet the navy was never quite the same for any two men. The kind of ship on which they served, when and where they served, what their specialties were, the officers under whom they served, the reputation of the force as a whole, and their own characters all influenced the final experience. Nevertheless in the years between the Spanish-American War and World War II, the lives of most sailors were not unpleasant. Reminiscing in 1970, Chief Morris offered what may have been a typical attitude:

> Some of the experiences were good and some not. I don't regret any of it; I enjoyed it. In the old days in the Navy it was a little hard, but we didn't know any better. We enjoyed it: what did we know about it? Whether we got $9 a month or $90, it didn't mean anything to us.[106]

The action of D. N. Burke, boilermaker, first class, offers evidence that Morris' opinion was commonly held. Taking a substantial cut in pay, Burke returned to the navy in 1920 after working in the merchant marine, because, he said, there were "no good shipmates" there as in the navy.[107] The sentiments Morris and Burke expressed seem to have applied to most men, including those who did not make the navy a career. Sailors enjoyed the excitement of the sea, the adventure of travel, and the pleasure of good shipmates.

Notes

1 "Passing the Buck a la Navy," *Typhoon* 1 (September 14, 1921): 2.

2 For ship routine, see Thomas Beyer, *The American Battleship and Life in the Navy* (Chicago: Laird & Lee, 1908), pp. 34–50; Charles A. Gove, *An Aid for Executive and Division Officers* (Annapolis, Md.: U.S. Naval Institute, 1899), pp. 7–10; C. Aloysious Stumpf, *On a Cruise with the U.S. Pacific Fleet to the Orient: An Account of the American Bluejacket Afloat and Ashore* (Boston: Roxburgh Publishing Co., 1915), pp. 15–16.

3 See Gove, *Aid*, for a printed form of watch, quarter, and station bills. A. Bainbridge Hoff, *A Battle Ship's Order Book* (Annapolis, Md.: U.S. Naval Institute, 1908) also discusses bills. RG 24 has a collection of bills from a few ships.

4 Charles Minor Blackford, *Torpedoboat Sailor* (Annapolis, Md.: U.S. Naval Institute, 1968), pp. 9–10.

[5] John L. Kendig, Log, January 22, 1907, 1:8, Logs, Journals, and Diaries of Officers of the United States Navy at Sea (hereafter cited as Logs and Diaries), RG 45, NA.

[6] Alfred Young, *The Cruise of the U.S.S. "Trenton": A True Story of the Events Happening to and on Board the U.S.S. "Trenton" during Her Shakedown Cruise, from Saturday, 24 May 1924, to Monday, 29 September 1924* (n.p., n.d.), p. 107.

[7] *Annual Report of the Surgeon General, 1907,* p. 1249.

[8] See *Annual Report of the Surgeon General, 1908,* p. 947. C. F. Stokes, Surgeon General, to Department, May 10, 1911, No. 1159–406, GC, RG 24, NA. CNO to Chief Bureau of Medicine and Surgery, May 22, 1925, No. 125135-0, GC, Box 376, RG 52, NA.

[9] "On Coaling Ship." *U.S.S. "Plattsburg" in the Great War,* p. 23, Subject 338, "Ships Papers," GC, Sixthe Division, RG 24, NA. For further comments on coaling see Kendig, Log, December 27, 1907, p. 30; Clarence O'C. McDonagh, Sr., "Log, April 8, 1917, to August 12, 1919" (typescript), September 26, 1917, p. 6; Paul Schubert, *Come on "Texas"* (New York: Jonathan Cape & Harrison Smith, 1930), p. 15; "Coaling Ship," *Our Navy* 4 (June 1910): 18–19; Robert D. Jones, *With the American Fleet from the Atlantic to the Pacific* (Seattle: Harrison Publishing Co., 1908), p. 91.

[10] For the participation of the American navy in the war see Thomas G. Frothingham, *The Naval History of the World War: The United States in the War, 1917–1918* (Cambridge: Harvard University Press, 1926), and Willian S. Sims, *The Victory at Sea* (Garden City, N.Y.: Doubleday, Page & Co., 1920). Also useful are Willis J. Abbot, *Bluejackets of 1918* (New York: Dodd, Mead & Co., 1921), and Josephus Daniels, *Our Navy at War* (Washington: Pictorial Bureau, 1922).

[11] Abbot, *Bluejackets of 1918,* pp. 133–38; Daniels, *Our Navy at War,* pp. 54–55, 63.

[12] Harry S. Morris, Interview Conducted by Etta Belle Kitchen, January 31, 1970, Oral History Project, United States Naval Institute, Annapolis, Md., p. 35.

[13] U.S., Department of Commerce, Bureau of the Census, *Historical Statistics of the United States, Colonial Times to 1957* (Washington: GPO, 1960), p. 735.

[14] Malcolm F. Willoughby, *"Yankton": Yacht and Man-of-War* (Cambridge, Mass.: Crimson Printing Co., 1935), pp. 190–92. For other false alarms, see Ray Millholland, *The Splinter Fleet of the Otranto Barrage* (New York: Bobbs-Merrill Co., 1936), pp. 61–62, and George M. Battey, Jr., *70,000 Miles on a Submarine Destroyer* (Atlanta: Webb & Vary Co., 1919), pp. 33, 45.

[15] Compiled from *Annual Report of the SECNAV* for the years 1899 to 1939. U.S., Veterans' Administration, *List of Wars, Military Expeditions, Campaigns, and Other Disturbances in Which the United States Army, Navy, and Marine Corps Have Participated* (Washington: GPO, 1922).

[16] B. F. Dixon, "Excerpts from a Gunboat Cruise," *Hospital Corps Quarterly*

11 (January 1927): 1–28. Thaddeus V. Tuleja, *Statesmen and Admirals: Quest for a Far Eastern Naval Policy* (New York: W. W. Norton & Co., 1963), p. 172.
[17] Fullam to CAPT. Richard Wainwright, October 9, 1906, "Correspondence October-November 1906," William F. Fullam Papers, LC.
[18] Fullam, "The System of Naval Training and Discipline Required to Promote Efficiency and Attract Americans," *USNIP* 16 (1890): 475–78; idem, "The Organization, Training and Discipline of the Navy Personnel as Viewed from the Ship," *USNIP* 22 (1896): 109–14.
[19] Jack Sweetman, *The Landing at Veracruz, 1914* (Annapolis, Md.: U.S. Naval Institute, 1968), pp. 93–123; Badger to Daniels, April 29, 1914, in folder "Badger, Rear Admiral," Navy Period Correspondence, 1913–21, Box 35, Josephus Daniels Papers, LC.
[20] Dom Albert Pagano, *Bluejackets* (Boston: Meador Publishing Co., 1932), pp. 29, 44.
[21] Thomas Jerrell Carter, "Injury Statistics, Enlisted Personnel, United States Navy, 1935–1936," (Ph.D. diss., John Hopkins University, 1940), pp. 39–40. Accident statistics can also be found in most annual reports of the surgeon general.
[22] For the Bennington, see Holden A. Evans, *One Man's Fight for a Better Navy* (New York: Dodd, Mead & Co., 1940), pp. 161–78; and *Annual Report of the Surgeon General, 1906,* pp. 1048–49. For the Honda accident, Charles A. Lockwood and Hans Christian Adamson, *Tragedy at Honda* (Philadelphia: Chilton Co., 1960). For the *F-4, Annual Report of the SECNAV, 1915,* pp. 66–67. For the *S-51, Annual Report of the Chief of Naval Operations, 1926,* p. 68. For the *S-4, Annual Report of the Surgeon General, 1928,* p. 377.
[23] For the *Missouri,* see *Annual Report of the Chief of the Bureau of Ordnance, 1904,* p. 576; and Elting E. Morison, *Admiral Sims and the Modern American Navy* (Boston: Houghton Mifflin Co., 1942), pp. 138–41. For the *Kearsarge, Annual Report of the Surgeon General, 1906,* p. 1049. For the *Mississippi, Annual Report of the SECNAV, 1924,* pp. 26–27. For the *Wyoming, Annual Report of the SECNAV, 1938,* p. 17.
[24] For the *Shenandoah,* see Archibald D. Turnbull and Clifford L. Lord, *History of United States Naval Aviation* (New Haven: Yale University Press, 1949), pp. 249–51. For the *Akron,* ibid., pp. 282–83; Richard K. Smith, *The Airships "Akron" and "Macon": Flying Aircraft Carriers of the United States Navy* (Annapolis, Md.: U.S. Naval Institute, 1965), pp. 77–84; and *Bureau of Aeronautics News Letter,* No. 302, April 15, 1933. For the *Macon,* Smith, *Airships "Akron" and "Macon,"* pp. 153–57.
[25] "A Submarine," in Henry B. Beston, *Full Speed Ahead: Tales from the Log of a Correspondent with Our Navy* (Garden City, N.Y.: Doubleday, Page & Co., 1919), pp. 42–43.
[26] Alfred E. Bennett, "The Dungaree Navy," *Our Navy* 3 (July 1909): 6.
[27] "Life on a Submarine," *Man-o'-Warsman* 2 (November 1909): 714.
[28] Jones, *With the American Fleet,* pp. 224–25. John Stapler, "Gunboats,"

USNIP 42 (1916): 861–72. Herbert Corey, "Across the Equator with the American Navy," *National Geographic Magazine* 39 (June 1921): 581, 583, 587. B. F. Dixon, "The Romance of the Enlisted Doctors," *Hospital Corps Quarterly* 9 (July and October 1925): 23–24.

[29] Samuel Harvard Barboo, "A Historical Review of the Hygiene of Shipboard Food Service in the United States Navy, 1775–1965" (Ph.D. diss., University of California, Los Angeles, 1966), pp. 96–97. Hugh Rodman, *Yarns of a Kentucky Admiral* (Indianapolis: Bobbs-Merrill Co., 1928), p. 68.

[30] For dishwashing machines, see, Barboo, "Shipboard Food Service," p. 66, and Fleet Surgeon Battle Fleet to Chief BUMED, May 25, 1925, submitting "Annual Report of Fleet Surgeon, 1924," No. 125135–0, Box 376, GC, RG 52, NA; for laundries. *Fleet Review* 11 (August 1920): 3; and for lighting, ventilation, and heating, *Annual Report of the Surgeon General, 1908,* pp. 930–32, and *1927,* pp. 342–43.

[31] Dyer, "The Modern General Mess," USNIP 32 (1906): 636. For the introduction of refrigerated storage and ice machines, see Barboo, "Shipboard Food Service," pp. 58–61.

[32] For centralized meal preparation see Barboo, "Shipboard Food Service," pp. 61–66; Benton C. Decker, "The Consolidated Mess of the Crew of the U.S.S. *Indiana,*" *USNIP* 23 (1897): 463–67; and Daniel Delehanty, "A Proposed System of Messing the Crews of Our Men-of-War," *USNIP* 14 (1888): 739–49. The navy felt that the ration itself was generous and compared favorably with other navies. See Albert Leary Gihon, "Practical Suggestions in Naval Hygiene," in U.S., Navy Department, Bureau of Medicine and Surgery, *Medical Essays* (Washington: GPO, 1873) pp. 68–69; and J. H. Skillman, "The Evolution of the Navy Ration," USNIP 60 (1934): 1678–79. Barboo, "Shipboard Food Service" gives a history of the navy ration from 1775 to 1965.

[33] Barboo, "Shipboard Food Service," pp. 93–94. E. D. Foster, "Cafeteria Afloat," *USNIP* 63 (1937): 19–24.

[34] Fred J. Buenzle, with A. Grove Day, *Bluejacket: An Autobiography* (New York: W. W. Norton & Co., 1939), p. 177, contains an account of the experiment on the *Philadelphia.* For enlisted support of lockers see M. C. S., on *Minnesota,* Letter to Editor, *Fleet Review* 4 (May 1913): 57; unsigned, Letter to Editor, *Our Navy* 7 (February 1914): 25; and W. W. MacDonald, Chief Electrician, Letter to Editor, *Fleet Review* 5 (May 1914): 64. *Fleet Review* 11 (August 1920): 3, describes lockers on the *Tennessee.*

[35] D. L. Hasbrouk, CO *California,* to Bureau of Construction and Repair, November 26, 1924, No. 8956–101, GC, RG 24, NA. W. Pitt Scott, CO *Oklahoma,* to Commander Battleship Division, Battle Fleet, November 20, 1924, No. 8956-101, GC, RG 24, NA.

[36] *Annual Report of the Surgeon General, 1926,* p. 481. Most hammock-related injuries occurred early in a sailor's enlistment. In 1935 and 1936, hammocks caused only 1.7 percent of injuries for the entire navy but 31 percent for men who had been in the service less than amonth. Carter, "Injury Statistics," p. 42.

[37] D. L. Hasbrouk to Bureau of Construction and Repair, November 26, 1924,

No. 8956–101, GC, RG 24, NA. H. A. Wiley, Commander Battleship Divisions, Battle Fleet, to Commander in Chief Battle Fleet, November 29, 1924, No. 8956–101, GC, RG 24, NA. W. R. Shoemaker, Chief BUNAV, to Bureau of Construction and Repair, February 14, 1925, No. CV2(7), GC, RG 24, NA. Fleet Surgeon, Battle Fleet, to Chief BUMED, "Annual Sanitary Report of Fleet Surgeon," May 25, 1925, No. 125135–0, Box 376, GC, RG 52, NA. Correspondence to and by BUNAV on bunks, 1925–27, No. S33(8), GC, RG 24, NA: see especially CO *California* to CO Battleship Division, Battle Fleet, July 30, 1926; BUNAV to Bureau of Construction and Repair, February 14, 1925; Chief BUNAV to SECNAV, May 20, 1927. *Annual Report of the Surgeon General, 1926,* p. 315.

[38] Buenzle, *Bluejacket,* pp. 176–77.

[39] Murry Wolffe, *Memoirs of a Gob* (New York: Exposition Press, 1949), p. 13.

[40] Mark Raymond Murnane, *Ground Swells: Of Sailors, Ships, and Shellac* (New York: Exposition Press, 1949), p. 77. Daniel V. Gallery, *Eight Bells and All's Well* (New York: W. W. Norton & Co., 1965), p.64.

[41] "Heirlooms," *Orient* 1 (September 1924): 10. See also *Annual Report of the Surgeon General, 1922,* p. 284.

[42] "Four Future Admirals," Letter to Editor, *Our Navy* 23 (Mid-January 1930): 10.

[43] *Annual Report of the SECNAV, 1904,* pp. 16–17. *Annual Report of the Chief BUNAV, 1909,* p. 311. *Annual Report of the Chief, Bureau of Steam Engineering, 1909,* p. 714.

[44] Ralph Clifford Luks, "With the Navy in the Yangtze Kiang Valley, China," *Our Navy* 18 (May 1, 1924): 4–7. Wolffe, *Memoirs,* p. 33. Crew of the *Galveston,* Letter to Editor, *Our Navy* 10 (May 1916): 74. "Song Sung at Christmas Dinner, 1902," Hollis Taylor Winston Book, p. 185, George T. Winston Papers, SHC.

[45] Hollis Taylor Winston Book, George T. Winston Papers, SHC. Similar journals from Richard Wainwright and Charles E. Courtney are in Logs and Diaries, RG 45, NA.

[46] See, for example, Andrew T. Long, "Around the World in Sixty Years" (typed memoirs), pp. 78, 199, Box 2, Andrew T. Long Papers, SHC. Edward Simpson, *Yarnlets: The Human Side of the Navy* (New York: G. P. Putnam's Sons, 1934), pp. 31–34.

[47] Officers' papers contain numerous letters relating to filling such billets. See, for example, Andrew T. Long to RADM Philip Andrews, May 16, 1923, Folder 25, Box 2, Andrew T. Long Papers, SHC; William Sims to Rufus Z. Johnston, August 21, 1917, Scrapbook, Box 1, Rufus Z. Jonston Papers, SHC; Osborne B. Hardison to LCDR D. E. Wilson, March 14, 1939, Folder 9, Osborne Bennet Hardison Papers, SHC.

[48] Richard McKenna, *The Sand Pebbles* (New York: Harper & Row, 1962), pp. 23–25.

[49] Albert Gleaves, ed., *The Life of an American Sailor: Rear Admiral William Hemsley Emory, United States Navy* (New York: George H. Doran Co., 1923),

pp. 273–74. The gift was made to the wife because regulations forbade presents to a superior. U.S., Navy Department, *Regulations for the Government of the Navy, 1909* (Washington: GPO, 1909), p. 65.
[50] "A Sailor," Letter to Editor, *Bostonian* 4 (July 1910): 489.
[51] Emery to Johnston, February 12, 1926, Scrapbook, Box 1, Rufus Johnston Papers, SHC. Also Roderick J. Johnson to Johnston, June 22, 1930, Folder 2, Rufus Johnston Papers, SHC; Frank R. Olin to Long, November 28, 1929, Folder 28, Box 2, Andrew T. Long Papers, SHC.
[52] "Madhouse," *Our Navy* 7 (October 1913): 18–19.
[53] John Kendig, Log, February 12, 14, and 26, and March 2, 1908, 2:159, Logs and Diaries, RG 45, NA.
[54] "A C.P.O. with Three Cruises," Letter to Editor, *Our Navy* 8 (April 1915): 14. Anonymous letter to William Moody, n.d., received by BUNAV December 14, 1904, No. 3328–38, GC, RG 24, NA.
[55] Murnane, *Ground Swells,* pp. 108–9.
[56] Robert E. Coontz, *True Anecdotes of an Admiral* (Philadelphia: Dorrance & Co., 1935), pp. 24–25.
[57] James B. Connolly, *Navy Men* (New York: John Day Co., 1939), pp. 272–73.
[58] Henning Henningsen, *Crossing the Equator: Sailors' Baptism and Other Initiation Rites* (Copenhagen, Denmark: Munksgaard, 1961), p. 15
[59] For accounts of crossing the equator, see Stumpf, *On a Cruise with the U.S. Pacific Fleet,* pp. 66–79; Young, *Cruise of the U.S.S. "Trenton,"* pp. 26–28; Corey, "Across the Equator," pp. 610–11; Lyman A. Cotten, Diary, July 5 and 6, 1925, Lyman A. Cotten Papers, SHC; "Crossing the Line," *Fleet Review* 1 (August 1910): 37–38.
[60] The use of intoxicants was banned by General Order 99. See also Josephus Daniels, *The Wilson Era: Years of Peace, 1910–1917* (Chapel Hill: University of North Carolina Press, 1944), p. 386.
[61] Navy Department, *Regulations for the Government of the Navy, 1909,* pp. 168, 471. Frederick L. Sawyer, *Sons of Gunboats* (Annapolis, Md.: U.S. Naval Institute, 1946), pp. 82, 85–86.
[62] See, for example, Murnane, *Ground Swells,* p. 57.
[63] John L. Kendig, Log, October 22, 1907, and June 6, 1908, 1:80, 3:191–93, Logs and Diaries, RG 45, NA.
[64] Harold D. Langley, *Social Reform in the United States Navy, 1798–1862* (Urbana: University of Illinois Press, 1967), pp. 211–12. Murnane, *Ground Swells,* pp. 287, 292. Stanton H. King, *Dog-Watches at Sea* (Boston: Houghton, Mifflin & Co., 1901), pp. 236, 253. *San Francisco Examiner,* June 10, 1907, p. 2.
[65] *Regulations for the Government of the Navy* permitted a commanding officer to give liberty to half the crew at a time or to three-quarters if the ship was secured to a wharf in a navy yard. The regulations denied liberty only to men under punishment or in debt to the government. Navy Department, *Regulations for the Government of the Navy, 1913,* pp. 255–56, 264.
[66] "Welcome to Lil'l ol' New York," *Our Navy* 24 (May 1, 1930): 14–15. L. F. Veit, "With the Destroyers in Europe," Our Navy 19 (November 1, 1925): 21.

RADM W. C. Cowles to SECNAV, May 20, 1914, File: "Admiral Cowles," Correspondence, 1913–21, Box 38, Josephus Daniels Papers, LC. Charles Herget, "Dear Shipmate" (Xeroxed memoir of naval service, Turnersville, New Jersey, 1967), pp. 21, 26. Dixon, "Excerpts from a Gunboat Cruise," p. 5.

[67] J. M. Acuff, "Tennessee Notes," *Our Navy* 3 (May 1909): 20. W. S. Pierce, "The American Sailor in Japan," *Our Navy* 8 (November 1914): 9–13—the same article was republished in *Our Navy* 19 (Mid-June 1926): 6–8. Tutuila is the major island of American Samoa and contains the harbor of Pago Pago.

[68] Young, *Cruise of the U.S.S. "Trenton,"* p. 85. Millholland, *Splinter Fleet,* pp. 287–88. C. J. B., Letter to Editor, *Bluejacket* 5 (March 1906): 224–25. "U.S. Asiatic Fleet at Chefoo," *Orient* 1(August 1924): 7–8. F. P. Baird, " 'Beefing' in the Asiatics," *Our Navy* 32 (April 1, 1938): 8–9.

[69] Stumpf, *On a Cruise with the U.S. Pacific Fleet,* pp. 181–82. Willoughby, *"Yankton,"* pp. 92, 125. Franklin Matthews, *Back to Hampton Roads* (New York: B. W. Huebsch, 1909), p. 225.

[70] Young, *Cruise of the U.S.S. "Trenton,"* p. 84.

[71] Millholland, *Splinter Fleet,* pp. 287–88.

[72] William H. Rideing, "Jack Ashore," *Harper's New Monthly Magazine* 47 (July 1873): 161–63.

[73] A comparison of the two battleships called the *Texas* illustrates the increasing number of men on naval vessels. The first *Texas,* commissioned in 1895, had a designed complement of 362 men. The second, commissioned in 1914, carried 984 men. U.S., Navy Department, Office of the Chief of Naval Operations, Naval History Division, *Dictionary of American Naval Fighting Ships,* 6 vols. to date (Washington: GPO, 1959–), 1:189, 195.

[74] *Norfolk Virginian-Pilot,* December 26, 1906.

[75] *Fred J. Buenzle v. Newport Amusement Association,* in *Reports of Cases Argued and Determined in the Supreme Court of Rhode Island* (Providence: E. L. Freeman Co., 1909), 19:23–33. For Buenzle's account, see Buenzle, *Bluejacket,* pp. 316–18. Roosevelt's contribution is also noted in "President Aids Tar's Suit," *New York Times,* September 25, 1906, p. 8. The Rhode Island act is given in General Order 70 of June 15, 1908.

[76] "Sailorphobia in Seattle," *Our Navy* 4 (April 1911): 20–21.

[77] Cooper to Mayor of Portsmouth, March 8, 1911, No. 3328–93, GC, RG 24, NA. *New York Times,* January 13, 1917, p.15.

[78] "Shore-Boats and Boatmen," *Our Navy* 4 (June 1910): 24. *New York Times,* February 12, 1918, p. 12. See also "Navy Men Overcharged," *Fleet Review* 14 (February 1923): 14.

[79] *Our Navy* 4 (May 1910): 14–15.

[80] R. K. Crank, "The Navy as a Career," *Forum 56* (November 1916): 630.

[81] *Norfolk Virginian-Pilot,* December 27, 1905, p. 4. *New York Times,* September 14, 1906, p. 3.

[82] See, for example, Mrs. I. M. Keepers to Josephus Daniels, October 26, 1915, No. 1651–30, GC, RG 24, NA.

[83] For one man's reaction to a 1908 celebration, see John L. Kendig, Log, May 1 and 12, 1908, Logs and Diaries, RG 45, NA.
[84] Marbury Johnston, "Discipline in the Navy," *USNIP* 38 (1912): 852.
[85] Frank Hunter Potter, "A School for Bluejackets," *Army and Navy Journal of the Philippines* 1 (October 4, 1913): 11.
[86] United States Fleet Letter 32–25, April 4, 1925, No. 125135(41), File "Fleet, United States Serial, 1925," GC, RG 52, NA.
[87] Henry A. Wiley, *An Admiral from Texas* (Garden City, N.Y.: Doubleday, Doran & Co., 1934), pp. 300–301.
[88] *Baltimore Afro-American,* May 2, 1908, p. 2. *Enlisted Man* 1 (November 1910): 3.
[89] *New York Times,* May 28, 1917, p. 4. *Great Lakes Bulletin,* July 1, 1918, p. 2. Schubert, *Come On "Texas,"* p. 88.
[90] Act of October 6, 1917, in U.S., *Statutes at Large,* 40:393. This act extended to the navy provisions of the May 1917 Selective Service Act that prohibited the sale of intoxicants to army personnel in uniform and banned bars and bawdyhouses near army camps.
[91] Murnane, *Ground Swells,* p. 94.
[92] *Great Lakes Bulletin,* June 17, 1919, p. 2.
[93] "Morrison Hotel Bars Sailors," *Chicago Tribune,* January 17, 1919, in Scrapbook, V. A. H. Scales Papers, SHC. "Concerning the Morrison," *Great Lakes Bulletin,* January 13, 1919, p.4. Milton MacKaye, "The Modern Bluejacket," *Outlook and Independent* 152 (July 31, 1929): 558.
[94] "State Laws Protecting Men in Uniform from Discrimination," a tabulation of answers from inquiries sent to all states by the Sixth Division, Box 5, GC, Morale and Recreation Section, 1920–24, RG 24, NA. Arkansas, Delaware, Georgia, Nevada, New Mexico, Ohio, and Oklahoma did not respond. The remaining states reported no such legislation. Discrimination against men in uniform by theaters or public places of amusement in the District of Columbia, Alaska, and the insular possessions of the United States was prohibited by a March 1, 1911, act of Congress, in U.S., *Statutes at Large,* 36:963–64.
[95] G. W. D. Dashell to Chief BUNAV, December 21, 1932, No. A17–4(7), GC, RG 24, NA.
[96] Young, *Cruise of the U.S.S. "Trenton,"* p. 48.
[97] Samuel Wheeler Beach, *The Great Cruise of 1925* (San Francisco: International Printing Co., 1925), pp. 179–82.
[98] *New York Times,* January 15, 1908, p. 4, and November 17, 1913, p. 3.
[99] Herget, "Dear Shipmate," pp. 26–27. Sidney Knock, *"Clear Lower Decks": An Intimate Study of the Men of the Royal Navy* (London: Philip Allan, 1932), pp. 34–36.
[100] Daniels, *Our Navy at War,* pp. 54–55. *New York Times,* May 17, 1917, pp. 1–2. Blackford, *Torpedoboat Sailor,* p.76.
[101] Force Commander to Commander U.S. Patrol Squadron Based on Gibraltar, December 8, 1917, L4-a, "Discipline General—1917," Logistics File, 1911-27, RG 45, NA. *New York Times,* October 14, 1918, p. 17.

[102] *New York Times,* September 5, 1917, p. 6. Blackford, *Torpedoboat Sailor,* p. 84.
[103] Murnane, *Ground Swells,* pp. 393–404. Schubert, *Come on "Texas,"* p. 174.
[104] Chas. E. Gower, Chief Constable, Newport, Monmouthshire, to the Under Secretary of State, Home Office, Whitehall, London, November 23, 1917, L4-b-1917, "Discipline (On Shore)," Logistics File, 1911–27, RG 45, NA.
[105] Murnane, *Ground Swells,* p. 391.
[106] Morris, "Interview," p. 66.
[107] U.S., Congress Joint Special Committee, *Hearings: Readjustment of Service Pay* (67th Cong., 2d sess., 1921), p. 266.

C H A P T E R   E L E V E N

We Will Go Heavily Armed: The Marines' Small War On Samar, 1901-1902

BRIAN MCALLISTER LINN

FOCUS QUESTIONS

1. What effective counter-insurgency and pacification techniques had the US Army employed in the Philippines? Why were these techniques so long absent on the island of Samar?
2. What mistakes were made by Major Waller in leading the Marine Battalion on Samar?
3. What influence did the Marine Corps experience on Samar have on the subsequent development of the Corps's approach to small wars?

The actions of Major Littleton W. T. Waller and his battalion in the American conquest of Samar have provoked controversy for almost a century. In this essay Professor Linn draws on Filipino sources as well as army, navy, and marine operational records to integrate the marines' experiences into the context of the entire campaign. Challenging those scholars who have portrayed Waller as a hero and scapegoat, Linn ar-

*gues that his poor leadership contributed greatly to the uneven performance of the Marine Corps on Samar.**

On 28 September 1901 villagers and guerrillas attacked the 74 officers and men of Company C, Ninth U.S. Infantry at the town of Balangiga, Samar Island, in the Philippines. Surprising the men at breakfast, the Filipinos killed 48 soldiers, "mutilating many of their victims with a ferocity unusual even for guerrilla warfare."[1] The "massacre," which occurred when many believed the fighting between U.S. military forces and Filipino nationalists was virtually over, shocked Americans. Amidst public cries for vengeance, U.S. patrols, under orders to "make a desert of Balangiga," soon did such a thorough job that "with the exception of the stone walls of the church and a few large upright poles of some of the houses, there is today not a vestage [sic] of the town of Balangiga left."[2] Determined to crush the resistance on Samar, the army poured in troops, the navy sent gunboats, and a battalion of 300 marines was dispatched under the command of Major Littleton W. T. Waller. Some of these marines had served with the victims of Balangiga in the Boxer Rebellion a year earlier. Their attitude may have been best summarized by Private Harold Kinman: "we will go heavily armed and longing to avenge our comrades who fought side by side with us in China."[3]

Although only a small part of the total U.S. manpower on the island, the marine battalion soon became the most famous, or notorious, military force in the campaign which in turn became one of the most famous, or notorious, episodes of the Philippine War. Even college freshmen may have read of Brigadier General Jacob H. Smith orders directing Waller to take no prisoners to treat every male over ten as an enemy, to make the interior of Samar a "howling wilderness," and to "kill and burn. The more you kill and burn, the better you will please me."[4] Equally controversial are the marines' own exploits. Campaigning on Samar was such a hellish experience that for years afterwards, veterans would be greeted in mess halls with the toast, "Stand Gentlemen: He served on Samar." Yet in an early blunder, the marines lost ten men in one expedition without encountering a single enemy guerrilla. In another incident. Waller had eleven Filipino guides summarily executed, an action that President Theodore Roosevelt believed "sullied the American name" and led to Waller's court-martial for murder. Thus, both because it proved so controversial and because it represented the marines' first encounter with twentieth-century guerrilla warfare, the Samar campaign serves as an excellent starting point for a discussion of the small wars heritage of the US. Marine Corps.

Charles E. Callwell, the contemporary British expert in irregular warfare, noted that in small wars climate and terrain were often greater obstacles than the enemy forces. His observation is particularly true of Samar, where, as one saturnine marine noted there was no need for the orders to turn the interior into a "howling wilderness," because "nature had done it for us."[6] In the local di-

* Comments of editors William R. Roberts and Jack Sweetman in original publication.

alect the name "Samar" means "wounded" or "divided" an apt description for an island whose 5,200 square miles are replete with rugged mountains, jungles, tortuous rivers, razor-sharp grasses, swamps, and parasites. Because the mountains confined most of its population to a narrow coastal region, for most of its colonial history Samar was "an island of dispersed settlements only loosely bound together by a common religion, a lightly felt administrative structure, and a few ties between pueblos."[7] In the towns and barrios, authority was wielded by a few priests, merchants, land owners, and municipal officials; and in the mountains scattered groups practiced primitive slash-and-burn agriculture. The Samarenos exported abaca (Manila hemp) and coconuts from Calbayog, Catbalogan, and other ports; but they were unable to grow sufficient rice to meet their needs and suffered periodic food shortages. Although contemporary American officers described the population of the island as "savages" with a long and violent history of resistance to any authority, the Spanish praised the natives' docile acceptance of foreign rule.

Samar was untouched by the fighting between the Filipino nationalists and the Spanish in 1896; but with the declaration of Philippine independence by Emilio Aguinaldo on 12 June 1898, the Filipino revolutionaries, based predominantly on the island of Luzon, moved to secure the rest of the archipelago. On 31 December 1898, a month before the outbreak of the Philippine War between Filipino forces and the Americans, Brigadier General Vicente Lukban (or Lucban) arrived and with some 100 soldiers formally placed Samar under Aguinaldo's Philippine Republic. Although he demonstrated commendable energy, Lukban was greatly hampered in his efforts to mobilize the Samarenos by the fact that he was an outsider. Moreover, a U.S. naval blockade prevented him from obtaining reinforcements or sending the money and supplies he collected to Aguinaldo. The blockade compounded Samar's precarious food situation: "Famine appeared as early as 1899 and Lukban wrote in 1900 that his troops were close to mutiny because of it."[8]

The American infantrymen who landed on the island on 27 January 1900 had little idea of either the precariousness of the insurgents' situation or the trouble that Samar was later to give them. Their mission was to secure the islands hemp ports and prevent a cordage crisis in the United States, a task they accomplished by brushing aside Lukban's forces and garrisoning a few towns. The soldiers' rapid seizure of the ports and the apparent collapse of the revolutionaries convinced the army high command that Samar was secured. With more important islands to pacify, army leaders quickly decided Samar was of minimal value. For the next eighteen months after their arrival, the isolated companies stationed on the island would cling precariously to little more than a few ports and river towns.

The weak occupation force allowed the Filipino revolutionaries, termed *insurrectos* by the Americans, to recover and counterattack. From the beginning the *insurrectos* attempted to confine the soldiers to the Catbalogan-Calbayog area while mobilizing the inhabitants against the invaders. In some places the revolutionaries depopulated entire areas, setting fire to villages and barrios and driving civilians into the mountains. They informed the Samarenos that the U.S. Army came for the purpose of raping, pillaging, and "annihilating us later as they have the Indians of America."[9] To support their military forces, the guerrillas confiscated crops and engaged in extensive smuggling, seeking both to continue the hemp trade and to bring in rice. Filipinos who collaborated with the soldiers or lived in the towns risked kidnapping or assassination, often in the most grisly manner. One U.S. officer complained, "The Insurgents have been guilty of all kinds of cruelty to those persons friendly to us, such as burying them alive, cutting off parts of the body, killing them, etc."[10]

Although the guerrillas lacked modem weapons, they showed remarkable tactical ingenuity and ability. They made cannons out of bamboo wrapped with hemp, gunpowder from community niter pits, and cartridges from brass fittings soldered with silver taken from churches. Their primitive firearms made the guerrillas more than able both to harass the soldiers and to force compliance from civilians. Against American patrols, they relied on an ingenious variety of booby traps: covered holes filled with poisoned bamboo, spring-loaded spears set off by carefully hidden trip wires, and heavy timbers or baskets of rocks hung over trails and rivers. One soldier who painstakingly removed dozens of obstacles from a trail returned in two weeks to find dozens more in place, "and such traps one could not imagine could be made and set so cunningly."[11] The ubiquitous traps, supplemented by an extensive system of pickets and vigilantes who signaled the approach of an American patrol through bells, bamboo and carabao horns, or conch shells, effectively precluded surprise. Occasionally the *insurrectos* would go on the offensive. From carefully concealed trenches, bamboo cannon or rifles would fire on American patrols struggling along narrow trails or river beds. This sniping might be followed by a sudden "bolo rush" of machete-wielding guerrillas pouring out of the thick grass or jungle to overwhelm detachments.[12]

It was not until May 1901 that the army began to give Samar more than a cursory interest, and then only because the end of military rule on neighboring Leyte Island made the continued turmoil on Samar intolerable. With much of the Philippines pacified, the army was able to reinforce Brigadier General Robert P. Hughes on Samar and by September he had twenty-three companies of infantry stationed in some thirty-eight towns located throughout the northern and central parts of the island. Hughes established two bases deep in the interior to allow U.S. troops to operate inland and he ordered patrols to converge at Lukban's headquarters on the Gandara River, in the process crossing the island and sweeping the countryside. He expanded the army's area of operations, stationing garrisons in heretofore ignored southern towns such as Basey and Balangiga. Through the laborious process of constructing roads, building supply camps, securing boats and porters, and constant patrolling, the Americans brought the war to the interior of the island.

Frustrated because the guerrillas rarely stood and fought, Hughes became convinced that the resistance would continue as long as the enemy could secure sufficient food. He determined to cut off smuggling and to destroy the guerrilla logistical base in order to give his soldiers "a fair opportunity to kill off the bands of utter savages who have hibernated in the brush."[13] He ordered the navy to step up its blockade and closed all ports in Samar, authorizing army and naval officers to seize all boats not deemed necessary for fishing and to arrest anyone found carrying food without a pass. To increase the pressure further, he ordered U.S. expeditions in the interior and along the coast to destroy crops, houses, and fields. Although Hughes did not formally implement a policy of concentrating the population into protected zones or camps, it was common for his soldiers to deport all Filipino civilians found in the interior to the coast. The result was that the towns, often already burned by the *insurrectos*, soon filled up with destitute Filipinos with no access to food. Within two months after Hughes's policies took effect, hunger was widespread and by September the situation was so critical that he had to authorize post commanders to purchase rice for the refugees.[14]

At the town of Balangiga, the American policies provoked a violent response. Despite his alleged sympathy for the Filipinos, the post commander, Captain Thomas Connell, destroyed much of the town's livestock, fishing supplies, and crops. In addition, he confined seventy townspeople in two tents designed for sixteen men each, forcing them to work all day in the sun and refusing to pay them or give them adequate food. His men also behaved poorly, taking food without payment and probably committing at least one rape. Such abuses, coupled with weak security measures, provoked a retaliatory attack by townspeople and local guerrilla forces who slaughtered most of the garrison on 28 September.[15]

The Balangiga "massacre" provoked an equally enraged American response. In what was undoubtedly one of the worst decisions of the war, Major General Adna R. Chaffee, the commanding officer of the army in the Philippines, selected Brigadier General Jacob H. Smith to take tactical command of the pacification of Samar. A product of the army's seniority system, Smith owed his general's stars to his longevity; his physical bravery and the mistaken belief that he planned to retire. Having spent most of his life commanding little more than a company, he was bewildered by the complexity of handling the four thousand soldiers, marines, and native scouts in his Sixth Separate Brigade. To compound his problems, Smith displayed symptoms of mental instability and was subject to outbursts in which he urged the most violent and irresponsible actions.[16]

Unfortunately, among Smith's subordinates was an officer who himself was prone to rash and violent action: Major Littleton W. T. Waller, commander of the marine battalion. At first glance Waller would seem to have made an ideal commander. He was a twenty-two year veteran whose combat exploits in Egypt, Cuba, and China had shown that he possessed several characteristics vital to a counterinsurgency fighter: he had tremendous powers of endurance and was personally brave, aggressive, and charismatic. These qualities would later make him a legendary combat leader in the marines' small wars in Latin America. Nevertheless, Waller consistently relied on physical courage and endurance to make up for deficiencies in planning and judgment. In China, for example, he had engaged a vastly superior enemy force and had been driven back, losing an artillery piece and a machine gun, suffering eleven casualties, and leaving his dead behind. Prone to both braggadocio and self-pity, he was convinced that his services in the Boxer Rebellion had not been properly recognized. Moreover, he arrived in Samar under a personal cloud, having recently gone on an alcoholic binge that culminated in a ten-day suspension from duty. This disciplinary action does not appear to have cured him: one marine later remembered that on operations in the field Waller "had a bottle of liquor for his own use, and when it gave out he was in bad shape."[17] His drinking may explain his boastfulness and irritability, his willingness to blame his superiors, and his inability to accept the consequences of his actions.

It is not surprising that the marines' organizational status within the Sixth Separate Brigade is still the subject of much misunderstanding, given the confusion engendered by Smith's instability and Waller's penchant for acting rashly. Assigned to the two southern towns of Basey and Balangiga, the marines fell under both army and navy authority. Not until after the campaign did the U.S. Army's judge advocate general rule that the marines on Samar were not detached from the navy but only engaged in a "cooperative" venture with the army.[18] Equally confused was Waller's area of responsibility. From 27 October 1902 on, he apparently believed he was in charge of an independent command he referred to as "Subdistrict South Samar," consisting of all territory south of a line from Basey on the west coast to Hemani on the east coast, an area totaling some six-hundred square miles and including two army posts. A careful reading of the extensive U.S. Army operational correspondence concerning Waller makes it clear, however, that he commanded the marines at Basey and Balangiga alone and that his army superiors never considered him more than the "Commanding Officer, Basey." The actual extent of Waller's authority would later become a major issue, but at the time nearly every army garrison and navy gunboat suffered from equally tangled command relations.[19]

The organizational vagueness surrounding Waller's command was compounded by his operational orders. Upon the arrival of the marines at Balangiga and Basey, Smith ordered Waller to "kill and burn," take no prisoners, and regard every male over ten as a combatant. In spite of these grim directives, Waller's own orders to the marine battalion on 23 October conformed to army policies already current on Samar. In common with American military efforts since June 1901, Waller focused on denying food to the guerrillas and ordered his marines to confiscate all rice, allowing families only a small daily ration on which to survive. In an effort to break up the guerrillas' extensive smuggling organization in the south of the island, he ordered all hemp confiscated and all boats registered and painted red. Waller attempted to organize the population into similarly identifiable groups by allowing a short grace period for male civilians to come into the towns and register or be treated henceforth as hostile. His orders emphasized that the Samarenos were "treacherous, brave, and savage. No trust, no confidence can be placed in them." Therefore, civilians were required to perform all manual labor and Filipino guides were to walk at the head of military columns with long poles and probe for pits and traps. The area around Balangiga, garrisoned by some 159 marines under Captain David D. Porter, was to be "cleared of the treacherous enemy and the expeditions, in a way, are to be punitive." Finally, Waller stressed that the marines were to "avenge our late comrades in North China" and "must do our part of the work, and with the sure knowledge that we are not to expect quarter."[20] There were also disturbing indications that Smith's illegal orders were passed on unchanged to the men. One marine wrote home that he and his comrades were "hiking all the time killing all we come across" and another veteran remembered that "we were to shoot on sight anyone over 12 years old, armed or not, to burn everything and to make the Island of Samar a howling wilderness."[21] Captain Porter later explained that although Smith had meant that the marines were only to "kill and burn" *insurrectos*, it was "understood that everybody in Samar was an *insurrecto*, except those who had come in and taken the oath of allegiance.[22]

Under these guidelines Waller pursued the objectives of destroying *insurrecto* supplies, bringing the guerrillas to battle, and establishing a defensive cordon. His men completed the destruction of the area around Balangiga and extended the devastation—between 31 October and 10 November the marines burned 255 houses and destroyed one ton of hemp, one-half ton of rice, thirteen carabao, and thirty boats while killing thirty-nine men and capturing eighteen. Waller also learned from a Filipino who had escaped from the *insurrectos* that the insurgents had established a base about fifteen miles up the Sojoton River. The first attempt up the river on 6 November resulted in the death of two marines and the loss of fifteen rifles. A second expedition was more successful. After ten days of struggling through the jungles, the marines launched an assault on 17 November that killed thirty guerrillas and drove the rest from their entrenchments. As congratulations poured in, Waller boasted that the "operations in the Sojoton were the most important of the whole campaign as far as their effect on the insurgents were concerned."[23]

This apparent success on the Sojoton River may have led Waller to overlook some of the campaign's hard lessons. He underestimated the crucial role the navy had played in supplying and transporting his expedition. Once separated from their waterborne logistical lifeline, his marines could neither carry enough food nor live off the country. Despite their victory, they had to withdraw from the Sojoton immediately and within a month the area was again a guerrilla stronghold. Waller could take pride in the fact that his men "can and will go where mortal men can go," but he apparently disregarded the human cost inflicted on them.[24] He seems to have drawn no lesson from the fact that after its ten-day ordeal his battalion was immobilized for almost a week.

Convinced that the Sojoton Valley was cleared, Waller launched operations into the interior to destroy other reputed guerrilla strongholds. He resolved the persistent problem of supply by ignoring it; in one telegram he arbitrarily decided that six days' rations could sustain his men for nine days. Unfamiliar with all of the deleterious effects of service in the Philippines and ignoring the lessons of the Sojoton campaign, he drove both himself and his men unmercifully. The marines slogged through Samara swamps and muddy trails, climbed the razor-backed mountains, and cut their way through jungles and *congon* grass. Constant rains, inadequate maps, and poor communications dogged them and patrols often wandered lost. One marine complained that "sometimes we do not have anything to eat for 48 hours and never more than 2 meals per day. Our feet are sore, our shoes worn out and our clothes torn. It rains [and] half of the time we sleep on the ground with nothing but a rubber poncho to cover us."[25]

In December, asserting that Smith had requested him to find a route for a telegraph line. Waller decided to march from the east coast to Basey, "belting the southern end of Samar."[26] Although the planned march covered only some thirty miles in a direct line, an earlier army expedition had already determined that no route existed in the region that Waller intended to cross. Not only would the marines be marching at the height of the monsoon season, but most of their journey would be over narrow, jungle-covered valleys, necessitating the constant crossing of both mountains and rivers. Between climbing the steep hills, cutting a path through the vegetation, and fording the swollen and treacherous streams, the marines would have to display epic stamina simply to cover a few miles on the map. The local army officers, far more experienced with the treacherous interior, urged Waller not to undertake the operation without establishing a secure supply line. Another officer who recently had returned from the very area Waller planned to explore warned the marine commander immediately before he departed "of the hardships of mountain climbing, even when he had a supply camp and shelters for his men."[27]

The ensuing march of six officers, fifty marines, two Filipino scouts, and thirty-three native porters from Lanang to Basey between 28 December 1901 and 19 January 1902 has been described by Allan R. Millett as "a monument to human endurance and poor planning."[28] The trail quickly disappeared and the expedition slowed to a crawl as each foot of the way had to be cut through the sodden and steaming jungle. As Waller's men crossed and recrossed rivers and inched up hills so sheer they were almost perpendicular, their shoes and clothes became little more than torn and rotting rags. The constant immersion, parasites, razor-sharp tropical grasses, and piercing rocks literally peeled their skin off in layers.

Although the survivors' recollections of the march are vague and contradictory, it is clear that after only five days of marching, supplies ran dangerously low and the men were exhausted. On about 2 January Waller and his officers decided to abandon their objective and return to the east coast along the Suribao River. The marines cut down trees and made rafts, but the waterlogged timbers sank immediately Making a controversial decision, Waller took two officers and thirteen of his strongest men and set out in an attempt to blaze a trail to the Sojoton Valley. By 6 January they managed to cut their way through to a marine base camp. In the meantime the rest of the expedition disintegrated. Captain Porter, receiving no word from Waller, hacked his way back to Lanang with seven marines and six Filipinos. The remaining marines and Filipino porters were left on the trail under the command of Lieutenant Alexander Williams. Starving and suffering from prolonged exposure, Williams and several of his men became convinced that the porters not only had access to a large supply of food but also that they were plotting against the marines. The lieutenant later claimed that he was attacked by three of the porters, though his account of the event was somewhat confused. An army relief force, battling heavy floods, reached Williams' men on 18 January, but by that time ten marines had either died or disappeared and an eleventh was to die shortly afterwards. Starving, barefoot, and their clothes in rags, the marines who survived were literally helpless, and their rifles and ammunition had to be carried by the Filipino porters. Some of the marines were even crazed by their exertions. Although the expedition cost him over 20 percent of his command. Waller admitted: "As a military movement it was of no other value than to show that the mountains are not impenetrable to us."[29]

One result of Waller's ill-considered march was the virtual collapse of his battalion as an effective combat force. After they returned to their familiar quarters at Basey and Balangiga, the marines were incapable of further sustained operations. Instead of the large and protracted expeditions they had launched in the fall, the marines now sent between twenty and forty men out on "hikes" that seldom moved more than a day from camp. Marine patrols continued to destroy food and shelter and occasionally skirmished with guerrillas, but the real fighting of the campaign occurred elsewhere. Southern Samar returned to the backwater status it had enjoyed before Balangiga, and Waller's battalion may have been content to let the war be won elsewhere. Certainly neither Waller nor his men made any protest when the shattered battalion was withdrawn from Samar and returned to Cavite on 29 February.[30]

A second, more serious result of the march was the execution of twelve Filipinos without benefit of trial or even the rudiments of an impartial investigation. The first killing occurred on 19 January; the victim was a Filipino whom the mayor, or *presidente*, of Basey denounced as a spy. Because Waller was running a temperature of as high as 105 degrees, the camp surgeon judged him incompetent to command. As a result, authority in Basey fell to Lieutenant John H. A. Day. Through the use of "a real third degree," or torture, Day secured a confession, the specifics of which he later had trouble remembering. Acting "on the spur of the moment," he decided that the Filipino's confession warranted his immediate execution. Although Waller denied authorizing a summary execution, in a few minutes Day organized a firing squad, personally shot the suspect, and left his body in the street as a warning. Court-martialed for murder, Day was acquitted on the grounds that he was obeying Waller's orders.[31]

The following day saw an even bloodier incident. Williams and many of the survivors were in the hospital on Leyte Island; and no one at Waller's headquarters at Basey appears to have been certain of the magnitude of the disaster that had befallen their comrades. Some believed that not ten but twenty marines had died, and nearly everyone accepted the rumor that the porters had acted treacherously. Although Basey was connected by telephone with brigade headquarters on Leyte, Waller neither requested an investigation nor brought charges against the suspects. Instead, hovering between delirium and lucidity, he ordered that the surviving porters be brought over from Leyte and executed. He then apparently collapsed. When these men arrived, it fell to Private George Davis to pick out those who had been guilty of specific crimes. Davis identified three porters whom he recalled had hidden potatoes, stolen salt, failed to gather wood, and disobeyed orders. He then selected another seven men on the grounds that, as he later claimed, "they were all thieves, sir, that I know of; and they were all worth hanging, if I had anything to do with it."[32] Solely on the basis of this reasoning, ten civilians were promptly shot by Day's firing squad. At Waller's insistence, a final victim was executed later that afternoon—providing through his grim arithmetic a total of eleven Filipino victims in exchange for the eleven men he had lost on the march.

In a report written three months after the incident, Waller gave a variety of reasons for the executions: the hostility of the townspeople of Basey, an inquiry with his officers, "reports of the attempted murder of the men and other treachery by the natives," his own weakened physical condition, as well as his power of life and death as a district commander. He concluded: "It seemed, to the best of my judgment, the thing to do at that time. I have not had reason to change my mind."[33] Even after conceding him an unusual measure of moral obtuseness, it is hard to follow his reasoning. Clearly, he engaged in no procedure that either a civil or military court would recognize as an inquiry or investigation. Neither then nor since has any evidence emerged to prove that his victims were guilty of "attempted treachery" or any other action that warranted the death penalty under the laws of war. General Chaffee, who believed that Waller's actions were those of a man suffering from "mental anguish," drew attention to the fact that "no overt acts were committed by the *cagadores* [porters]; on the contrary those sent to their death continued to the last to carry the arms and ammunition after they [the marines] were no longer able to bear them, and to render in their impassive way, such service as deepens the conviction that without their assistance many of the marines who now survive would also have perished." Noting that the laws of war only justified summary executions in "certain urgent cases," Chaffee pointedly commented that after the march was over "there was no overwhelming necessity, no impending danger, no imperative interest and, on the part of the executed natives, no overt acts to justify the summary course pursued."[34] Chaffee drew attention to the fact that in executing the porters, Waller had assumed powers that both the "military laws of the United States and the customs of the service, confer only upon a commanding general in time of war and on the field on military operations." What made Waller's crime even more heinous was that he "was in telephonic communication with his Brigade Commander, but deliberately chose not to consult him regarding his contemplated action."[35] Concluding that Waller's acquittal was "a miscarriage of justice," the general chastised the major's illegal actions and publicly condemned the killings as "one of the most regrettable incidents in the annals of the military service of the United States."[36]

The subsequent court-martial of Waller for murder is almost as controversial today as it was ninety years ago. Taking place against the background of the last death throes of the Philippine War, the trials seem to embody the brutality, ambiguity, and frustration of the marines' first Asian guerrilla conflict. Waller's revelation that he had been ordered by General Smith to make the interior of Samar a "howling wilderness" and to regard every male Samareno over ten as a combatant provoked national outrage. American opponents of Philippine annexation, who had suffered a crushing defeat in the presidential election of 1900, now rallied behind the issue of atrocities to attack U.S. military policy in the Philippines.[37] Waller's acquittal did little to resolve the controversy, for both the military authorities who examined the trial transcript and the commander in chief himself, condemned Waller's actions as illegal and immoral. For years afterwards Waller was known as the "Butcher of Samar" and many attributed his being passed over for commandant to the notoriety he gained on the island.

Waller's supporters have since claimed that he was a scapegoat, a victim of politics, a Marine forced to stand trial for crimes that the US. Army committed with impunity in the Philippines. Joseph Schott entitled one of the chapters in *The Ordeal of Samar* "The Scapegoat"; Paul Melshen cites Waller's "high moral courage"; Stuart Miller praises him as an "honorable warrior" and a "sacrificial victim"; and Stanley Karnow terms Waller "a scrupulous professional" and a "scapegoat."[38] The charge that Waller was a victim of interservice rivalry is difficult to sustain. His conduct cannot be defended on the grounds that he was only following orders. In the first place, Waller claimed that as a marine he did not fall under U.S. Army authority. Moreover, he clearly understood that Smith's instructions to take no prisoners and regard all males over ten as enemies were illegal, for by Waller's own testimony he immediately told Captain Porter that despite Smith's instructions the marines had not come to make war on women and children.[39] The excuse that Waller did nothing that the U.S. Army had not been doing for years is not only morally bankrupt but factually incorrect. Although the army's operational records give ample evidence that throughout the Philippine War far too many Filipinos were indiscriminately fired on or shot "attempting to escape," the premeditated execution of prisoners was neither a common nor an accepted practice among American soldiers in the archipelago. Even on Samar, where both a thirst for vengeance and a lack of supervision led to war crimes and unnecessary cruelty, soldiers were expected to follow the laws of war. Smith, who openly advocated illegal policies, was relieved, court-martialed, found guilty and immediately retired in disgrace. Army officers on Samar suspected of atrocities were investigated, court-martialed, and, as in the case of Waller, either acquitted or given mild reprimands. Given the nature of their offenses and the lightness of their punishments, it is hard to view any of these men, soldiers or marines, as scapegoats.[40]

A third result of the marines' march and the tragic events that followed was that Waller's court martial and the charges of American brutality overshadowed Lukban's capture in February and the surrender of the last prominent guerrilla leader on 28 April. Despite Smith's attempts to turn his men into mindless butchers, the victory was due to careful planning, detailed organization, and persistence. In order to combat the guerrillas in Samar's rugged interior, the army constructed a string of supply dumps from which long-ranging columns could sweep the countryside. Through a combination of large expeditions and hundreds of small patrols that operated from towns and field camps, the soldiers demonstrated to the population that the Americans intended to stay. By recruiting Filipino volunteers, promising local autonomy, and offering generous surrender terms, the army began providing attractive alternatives to resistance. These methods, along with the destruction of most of the island's foodstuffs, eventually convinced all but the most intransigent rebels to accept American authority.

The brutality and excesses that characterized the conduct of soldiers and marines on Samar represented a radical departure from the pacification methods employed elsewhere in the Philippines. Too often lessons that had been painfully learned in the previous three years of warfare were disregarded, and only the most primitive elements were retained. Barring the first few months of American occupation, there was little attempt to found schools, build roads, or win over the population, methods that proved effective in other areas where the topography was only a little less daunting and the guerrillas better organized. Nor did the Americans on Samar later take advantage of their vastly expanded intelligence capabilities or seek to exploit the deep and bitter divisions among various sections and classes in Samareno society. With some exceptions, pacification methods remained crude and undeveloped. In part this was the result of Samar's isolation and topography which cannot be overemphasized. Yet it should not be forgotten that Samar's topography was equally harsh to the guerrillas, who, despite having little more experience of the interior than the Americans and being led by a "foreigner" from another island and culture, learned to control an unruly populace and to fight effectively with small units and with limited supplies. The marines, of course, fresh from China, could hardly be aware of this mass of tested lore; and in following their army superiors down the path of directionless retaliation, they wrote one of the most painful chapters in the history of the corps.[41]

In assessing the marines' performance in their first modern small war, it is essential to recognize that in the early twentieth century before most marines had any experience with expeditionary warfare and interventions and before the emergence of a specific doctrine for fighting "small wars," the character of the commanding officer was all important. Certainly the physical stamina and rugged endurance that the marines displayed on their disastrous attempt to march across the island may be sufficient justification for the old U.S. Marine Corps toast, "Stand Gentlemen. He served on Samar." Yet this glorification of suffering and tenacity should not obscure the fact that they did not display much expertise in their first modern guerrilla war. Inexperienced and, in the case of Waller, unwilling to learn, the marines' tactics were as physically devastating to themselves as they were punishing to their opponents.

Whether this ambiguous performance led to institutional growth or lessons learned is beyond the scope of this work. The Marine Corps took no action against Waller, and there is no indication that he displayed any remorse for his actions. He went on to become the mentor of a generation of counterinsurgency experts who emerged within the corps to fight the small wars of the Caribbean. Perhaps much of Waller's physical courage and endurance, his charismatic leadership, and his love of combat found their way into the marines' expeditionary forces. Yet it is important to note that his junior officers rejected Waller's headlong individual aggressiveness, choosing instead to discuss, disseminate, and eventually codify their experiences in the *Small Wars Manual* of the Marine Corps.

Notes

Research for this article was made possible through a U.S. Marine Corps Historical Center Research Fellowship and a research grant from Old Dominion University. The author wishes to thank V. Keith Fleming, Jack Shulimson, Patricia Morgan, and the rest of the staff of the U.S. Marine Corps Historical Center for their professionalism, their willingness to discuss Marine Corps history, and their many helpful suggestions of sources to consult. He would also like to thank Daniel P. Greene and James R. Linn for their comments on drafts. The views expressed in this paper are the author's own and should not be taken to represent those of the U.S. Marine Corps Historical Center.

[1] Richard B. Welch, Jr., *Response to Imperialism: The United States and the Philippine-American War, 1899-1902* (Chapel Hill, 1979), 41. For the Balangiga "Massacre," see Eugenio Daza y Salazar "Some Documents on the Philippine-American War in Samar," *Leyte-Samar Studies* 17 (1983): 165-87; Fred R. Brown, *History of the Ninth U.S. Infantry, 1799-1909* (Chicago, 1909), 578-96; James O. Taylor, *The Massacre of Balangiga* (Joplin, Mo., 1931); Brig. Gen. Robert P. Hughes to Adjutant General, 30 November 1901, Records of U.S. Army Overseas Operations and Commands, 1898-1942, Record Group 395, 2483, Box 39, no. 7825, National Archives, Washington, D.C. (hereafter cited as RG 395, NA); Edward C. Bumpus, *In Memoriam* (Norwood, Mass., 1902); Joseph Schott, *The Ordeal of Samar* (Indianapolis, 1964), 35-55.

[2] Quote "make a desert" from Hughes to Col. Issac D. DeRussy, 29 September 1901, RG 395, 2551, NA. Quote "with the exception" from Capt R. M. Blackford to Adjutant General, 8 October 1901, RG 395, 2571, Box 1, no. 164, NA. Capt. Edwin V. Bookmiller to Adjutant General, 1 October 1901, Annual Reports of the War Department, 1902, 1:9:625-27; DeRussy to Adjutant General,

5 October 1901, RG 395, 2552, NA. For the reaction to Balangiga, see Maj. Gen. Adna R. Chaffee to Maj. Gen. Henry C. Corbin, 25 October 1901, Henry C. Corbin Papers, Box 1, Library of Congress, Washington, D.C.; Testimony of William H. Taft, Senate Committee on the Philippines, Affairs in the Philippine Islands, 57th Cong., 1st Sess., 1902, Sen. Doc. 331, 363-64; John Morgan Gates, *Schoolbooks and Krags: The United States Army in the Philippines, 1898-1902* (Westport, Ct., 1973), 248-51.

[3] Harold Kinman to Sister, 18 October 1901, Harold Kinman Papers, U.S. Marine Corps Historical Center, Washington, D.C. (hereafter cited as USMCHC). Cf. Kinman's sentiment with Maj. Littleton W. T. Waller's 23 October 1901 orders to his command, located in typescript copies of much of the marines' official correspondence during the Samar campaign, Waller File, USMCHC (hereafter referred to as Waller Report).

[4] Records of the Office of the Judge Advocate General, Record Group 153, General Courts-Martial [G.C.M.] 30739, Brig. Gen. Jacob H. Smith, National Records Center, Suitland, Md.; Richard N. Current, T. Harry Williams, Frank Friedel, Alan Brinkley, *American History: A Survey*, 7th ed.(New York, 1987), vol. 2, Since 1865, 592.

[5] General Orders 80, Headquarters of the Army, 16 July 1902, Records of the Bureau of Insular Affairs, Record Group 350, File 3490-27, National Archives, Washington, D.C.

[6] John H. Clifford, *History of the Pioneer Marine Battalion at Guam, L.I. and the Campaign in Samar, P.I. 1901* (Portsmouth, N.H., 1914), 36; Charles E. Callwell, *Small Wars: Their Principles and Practice*, 3d ed. (London, 1906), 44.

[7] Bruce Cruikshank, *Samar 1768-1898* (Manila, 1985), 106. For Samar's topography see Anon. to Adjutant, 2d Battalion, April 1900, Records of the Adjutant General's Office, Record Group 94, 117, 43d Inf., U.S.V., Co. "G," no. 8, National Archives, Washington, D.C. (hereafter cited as RG 94, NA); Capt. Murray Baldwin to Adjutant General, Sixth Separate Brigade [6SB], 21 November 1901, RG 395, 3750, Book 1, no. 5, NA; Capt. E. R. Tilton to Commanding Officer, 1st District, February 1900, Henry T. Allen Papers, Box 32, Library of Congress, Washington. D.C.; John R. M. Taylor, *The Philippine Insurrection against the United States, 1899-1903,* galley proof (Washington, 1903), 81 HS.

[8] Holt, "Resistance on Samar: General Vicente Lukban and the Revolutionary War, 1899-1902," *Kabar Seberang Sulating Maphilindo* 10 (December 1982): 1-14; Brig. Gen. Vicente Lukban to Antonio Luna, 8 July 1899, in Taylor, *Philippine Insurrection*, Exhibit 1321, 58-59 HK.

[9] Lukban to Local Residents of the Province of Samar, 14 February 1900, Charles G. Clifton File, 43d Inf., U.S.V. Box, U.S. Army Military History Institute (USAMHI), Carlisle, Pa.; Testimony of Lt. G. A. Shields, RG 153, G.C.M. 30739, NA; Lukban to *presidente* of Catubig, 15 September 1900, Philippine Insurgent Records, Select Document 502.8, National Archives Microfilms, Microcopy 254 (hereafter cited as PIR SD); 'Copy of Lukban's Speech on his

Birthday," 1 February 1901, PIR SD 824.1; Col. Arthur Murray to Adjutant General, 4 June 1900, RG 94, 117, 43d Inf., Report No. 6, NA.

[10] Maj. John C. Gilmore to Adjutant General, 30 June 1900, RG 94, 117, 43d Inf., 2d Battalion, NA.

[11] Charles G. Clifton Diary, 10 January 1902 entry, 43d laf., U.S.V., USAMHI; Maj. R. A. Brown, "Inspection of the Post and Troops at Laguan, Samar," 31 March 1901, RG 395, 2483, Box 31, NA; Capt. William M. Swaine to Adjutant, 5 August 1901, RG 395, 3450, Box 1, no. 478, NA; Clifford, Pioneer Marine Battalion, 28-29; Brown, *Ninth Infantry*, 563; Taylor, *Philippine Insurrection*, 82-83 HS; Lukban to Local Chief of Cabalian, 3 March 1899, PIR SD 928.8; Maj. Narisco Abuke to Anon., 7 October 1900, PIR SD 846.1; Lt. Col. Francisco Rafael to Lt. Jorge Langarra, 16 July 1901, PIR SD 808.3; Hughes to Chief of Staff and Adjutant General, 3 June 1901, RG 395, 2550, Box 1, NA.

[12] "Statement of Private Luther Jessup," in Maj. John J. O'Connell to Department Commander, 30 June 1901, RG 395, 2483, Box 36, NA; Capt. John S. Fair to Gilmore, 29 March 1900, RG 94, 117, 43d Inf., Co. "B," no. 38, NA; Gilmore to Adjutant General, 18 May 1900, RG 94, 117, 43d Inf., 2d Battalion, NA; Brown, Ninth Infantry, 573, 594-95.

[13] Hughes to Smith, 15 October 1901, RG 395, 2483, Box 49, NA; Hughes Testimony, Senate, Affairs, 553.

[14] Hughes to Chief of Staff and Adjutant General, 14 May 1901, RG 395, 2483, Box 28, NA; Capt. A. B. Buffington to Capt. Leslie F. Cornish, 14 June 1901, RG 395, 3447, no. 90, NA; Hughes to Adjutant General, 10 September 1901, RG 395, 2550, Box 1, NA.

[15] Hughes to Adjutant General, 30 November 1901, RG 395, 2483, Box 39, no. 7825, NA; Schott, *Ordeal of Samar*, 16-17; Holt, "Resistance on Samar," 9; Interrogation of Joaquin Cabafies, 1 January 1902, RG 395, 2571, Box 3, no. 360, NA; Salazar, "Philippine-American War," 165-87; Richard Arens, "The Early Pulahan Movement in Samar," *Leyte-Samar Studies* 11 (1977): 59-66; Testimony of William Gibbs, Senate, *Affairs*, 2284-2310.

[16] Chaffee to Hughes, 30 September 1901, RG 94, AGO 406865, NA; Chaffee to Adjutant General, 8 October 1901, Senate, Affairs, 1599; Chaffee to Corbin, 28 November and 9 December 1901, Corbin Papers, Box 1; Manila American (7 January 1902); Lt. W. R. Shoemaker to Senior Squadron Commander, 5 November 1901, Naval Records Collection of the Office of Naval Records and Library, Record Group 45, Area File 10, National Archives, Washington, D.C. For Smith's mental instability, see Capt. William M. Swaine Testimony, RG 153, G.C.M. 30739, Brig. Gen. Jacob H. Smith, NA; Allen to Taft, 7 February 1902, Allen Papers, Box 7; Luke Wright to Taft, 13 January 1902, William H. Taft Papers, Ser. 3, Library of Congress, Washington, D.C.; Chaffee to Corbin, 5 May 1902, Cotbin Papers; David L. Fritz, "Before the 'Howling Wilderness': The Military Career of Jacob Hurd Smith, 1862-1902," *Military Affairs* 43 (1979): 186-90.

[17] Harry C. Adriance, "Diary of the Life of a Soldier in the Philippine Islands

During the Spanish-American War by a Sergeant in the U.S.M.C.," photocopy in the USMCHC. For other evidence of Waller's alcoholism, see entries of 15 November 1900 and 14-16 February 1901, Henry Clay Cochrane Diary, USMCHC; Ben H. Fuller Papers, Box 1, Folder 9, USMCHC; "Record of Waller, Littleton Waller Tazewell," USMCHC. For the incident in China, see Waller to Second in Command, U.S. Naval Force, China, 22 June 1900, and Waller to Brig. Gen. Commandant, 28 June 1900, *Annual Report of the Brigadier-General Commandant of the United States Marine Corps to the Secretary of the Navy*, 62-66. For the marines' deployment, see Brig. Gen. Robert Hall to Hughes, 19 October 1901, RG 153, G.C.M. 30313, Maj. Littleton W. T. Waller, NA; Hughes to Chaffee, 21 and 25 October 1901, Corbin Papers; *Manila American* (20 October 1901); Rear Adm. Frederick Rodgers to Commander in Chief, Asiatic Squadron, 5 November 1901, RG 45, Area File 10, NA.

[18] Brig. Gen. George Davis to Secretary of War, 27 June 1902, RG 153, G.C.M. 30313, NA.

[19] Waller Report, 8-10. Waller's defenders have perpetuated the confusion over his authority by claiming he was in charge of all of southern Samar or even the entire island. Paul Melshen, "He Served on Samar," *Proceedings* 105 (1979): 45; Stanley Karnow, *In Our Image: America's Empire in the Philippines* (New York, 1989), 191.

[20] Headquarters, Marine Battalion, Samar, 23 October 1901, Waller Report, 6-7. Quote "hiking all the time" from Harold Kinman to Sister, 23 December 1901, Kinman Papers; quote "we were to shoot" from *Modesto Bee*, 31 May 1965.

[22] Testimony of Capt. David D. Porter, RG 153, G.C.M. 30313, NA. Waller to Smith, 31 October 1901, Waller Report, 10-12; Porter to Waller, 2 November 1901, Waller Report, 15-16; Waller to Anon., 10 November 1900, Waller Report, 21.

[23] Waller to Anon., 10 November 1900, Waller Report, 25. See also ibid., 23-31; Waller to Adjutant General, 6 November 1901, RG 395, 2571, Box 1, no. 129, NA; Kinman to Sister, 23 November 1901, Kinman Papers.

[24] Waller to Adjutant General, 65B, 19 November 1901, Waller Report, 26. Clifford, *Pioneer Marine Battalion*, 34; RG 153, G.C.M. 10196, Lt. John H. A. Day, NA.

[25] Kinman to Sister, 23 December 1901, Kinman Papers; Waller to Adjutant General, 6SB, 30 November 1901, RG 395, 3451, Box 1, NA; Waller to Adjutant General, 6SB, 6, 18, and 20 December 1901, Waller Report, 43-48; Waller to Rodgers, 17 December 1901, RG 45, Area File 10, NA.

[26] Waller to Smith, 19 November 1901, RG 395, 3451, Box 1, NA. For the confusion over Waller's mission, see Waller to Smith, 31 October 1901, and Judge Advocate's Summary, RG 153, G.C.M. 30313, NA; Waller Report, 42; Schott, *Ordeal of Samar*, 104-106; Smith to Chief Signal Officer, 2 November 1901, RG 395, 3451, Box 1, NA; Adjutant General, 65B, to Adjutant General, Division of Philippines, 1 December 1901, RG 395, 2571. Box 1, no. 1188, NA;

Smith to the adjutant general, 11 December 1901, RG 395, 2573, Box 1, no. 166, NA.

[27] Waller to Adjutant General, 65B, 25 January 1901, Waller Report, 49. For the army's 1901 expedition, see War Department, 1902, 1:9:601; Brown, Ninth Infantry, 561. It should be noted that judged by the campaign conditions on Samar, Waller's march was neither over particularly difficult terrain nor of more than moderate distance.

[28] Allan R. Millett, *Semper Fidelis: The History of the U.S. Marine Corps* (New York, 1980), 154.

[29] Waller to Adjutant General, 65B, 25 January 1902, Waller Report, 58. See also Cmdr. William Swift to Smith, 20 December 1901, RG 395, 2574, Box 1, NA; Lt. Kenneth P. Williams to C.O., Lanang, 19 January 1902, *War Department*, 1902, 1:9:446; Porter to Waller, 8 February 1902, Waller Report, 60-64; Lt. A. S. Williams to Waller, 18 February 1902, Waller Report, 64-68; Schott, *Ordeal of Samar*, chap. 5.

[30] Waller Report, 68-88; Lt. Cmdr. J. M. Helms to Swift, 6 January 1902, RG 395, 2571, Box 2, no. 43, NA; Waller to Adjutant General, 8, 9, 18, and 20 February 1902, RG 395, 2573, Box 1, NA; 1902 entry, 1902, Charles G. Clifton Diary; Clifford, *Pioneer Marine Battalion.*

[31] Quotations from Testimony of Lt. John H. A. Day, RG 153, G.C.M. 10196, NA. The identity of the victim was unknown at the time of the killing, but it was later alleged that he was an *insurrecto* leader named Captain Victor.

[32] Testimony of Pvt. George Davis, RG 153, G.C.M. 30313, NA. Despite voluminous correspondence and records, the events of 19-20 January 1902 are still unclear and the evidence is inconclusive as to how many Filipinos were executed on 20 January. The above is based on the correspondence in the Waller Reports; RG 153, G.C.M. 30313 and G.C.M. 10196, NA; and General Orders 93, Headquarters, Division of the Philippines, 7 May 1902, RG 395, 2070, NA. For the confusion over the number of U.S. Marine deaths, see RG 153, G.C.M. 10196, NA; and Schott, *Ordeal of Samar*, 139, 142.

[33] Waller Report, 76-77.

[34] General Orders 93, Headquarters, Division of the Philippines, 7 May 1902, RG 395, 2070, NA.

[35] For Waller's incapacity for command, see Testimony of Dr. George A. Lin~, RG 153, G.C.M. 10196, NA. General Orders 93, Headquarters, Division of the Philippines, 7 May 1902, RG 395, 2070, NA. For the judge advocate's ruling that Waller's acts were illegal and contrary to the laws of war, see Brig. Gen. George Davis to Secretary of War, 27 June 1902, RG 153, G.C.M. 30313, NA.

[37] Millett, *Semper Fidelis*, 154; Gates, Schoolbooks and Krags, 256; Welch, *Response to Imperialism*, 138-41.

[38] Schott, *The Ordeal of Samar*, chap. 9; Melshen, "He Served on Samar," 45; Stuart C. Miller, "Benevolent Assimilation" *The American Conquest of the Philippines, 1899-1903* (New Haven, 1982), 227; Karnow, *In Our Image*, 193.

[39] RG 153, G.C.M. 30313, NA.

[40] Maj. Charles H. Watts to Adjutant General, 1 April 1902, RG 94, AGO 482616, NA; RG 153, G.C.M. 30756, Lt. Julien E. Gaujot, NA; RG 153, G.C.M. 34401, Maj. Edwin F. Glenn, NA; RG 153, G.C.M. 30757, Lt. Norman E. Cook, NA.

[41] An excellent discussion that demonstrates that the Samar campaign was an anomaly in Army pacification in the Philippine War can be found in Gates, *Schoolbooks and Krags,* chap. 9. For a study of Army pacification on Luzon, see Brian McAllister Linn, *The US. Army and Counterinsurgency in the Philippine War, 1899-1902* (Chapel Hill, N.C., 1989).

CHAPTER TWELVE

Controlling Aviation After the World War

The 1924 Special Board and the Technological Ceiling forAviation

William M. McBride

FOCUS QUESTIONS

1. What were the main issues and what was decided at the Washington Naval Conference of 1921/1922?
2. What was the significance of the *Ostfriesland* test?
3. Why did the Special Policy Board Hearings of 1924 consider the battleship superior to the airplane? Were they correct? Why or why not?
4. Why didn't naval aviators succeed in promoting airpower over the battleship paradigm during the 1920s? What had changed by the 1930s?

After the World War, the battleship's primacy was challenged on a broad front. In Britain, the battleship was attacked vigorously for having failed to prevent, and quickly win, the war. The Royal Navy actively campaigned for a new post-war building program to maintain British capital ship superiority in the face of American construction. This was an unpopular, and expensive, proposition in the wake of the "war to end all wars." Even the creator of the dreadnought battleship, Lord Fisher, publicly lashed out at the deficit spending of the British post-war plans: "It is incredible—it is uncalled for—it is a ruinous waste that the cost of the Fleet is now 40 millions a year! (In 1904 it was 34 millions!) So the whole national expenditure before the war was only a third more than the present Navy Estimates. Then a huge anti-German Fleet had to be ready to strike! Now that German Fleet is at the bottom of the sea!"[1]

In the United States, there was much less popular and professional doubt in the efficacy of the battleship. In 1920 Rear Admiral David Taylor, chief of the Bureau of Construction & Repair and a key member of the National Advisory Committee for Aeronautics, denied that any new lessons had come out of the fifty-one months of the World War. For the battleship to become obsolescent, "either in the near or distant future, it will be as a result of engineering progress and the invention and perfection of new weapons and not as a result of [technologies developed during] the World War."[2] According to Taylor, technical improvements in the design of American battleships had solved the challenge posed by the torpedo "so far as the torpedo has been developed to date."[3] Ignoring aviation's potential to concentrate torpedo power, the one commonly feared counter to the battleship, Taylor pointed out that a "torpedo from a ship in the air is no more deadly than from a submarine under the surface"[4] Taylor believed that a battleship fleet, protected by an adequate number of aircraft carriers with fighter planes, would have "no cause at all for worry against attack by bombing or torpedo planes."[5] Taylor was a key designer of naval aircraft, and his views may have comforted the technically oriented naval officers who read his comments in the *Journal of the American Society of Naval Engineers.*

Warren G. Harding's inauguration in 1921 began the Republican New Era which continued through the Coolidge and Hoover administrations. The Republicans pursued international arms control (meaning primarily control of naval armaments) to eliminate the "wastefulness" of military expenditures. Between 1922 and 1930, construction was begun on only ten of the thirty-one warships authorized—a manifestation of the Republicans' 1920 campaign for a "return to normalcy" with significant reductions in federal spending.[6]

According to Roger Dingman, Harding seized upon the issue of naval arms reductions as a means to regain the political initiative from an increasingly unruly Congress and to block renewal of the Anglo-Japanese alliance. At the time Harding invited the naval powers to Washington, the United States was challenging British naval supremacy in the same way Germany had in 1914. With the German fleet scuttled at Scapa Flow, the German threat, as far as the Royal Navy was concerned, had been replaced by an American one. By 1923–24, the United States would be close to Britain in numbers of capital ships in service or building (Britain 43, United States 35).[7] The technical superiority of the newer American superdreadnoughts reduced the quantitative difference to relative insignificance.

Harding's efforts resulted in the Washington Naval Conference and its resulting Five-Power Treaty, ratified in February 1922. The treaty measured naval power in capital ship tonnage, giving the United States parity with Britain while granting Japan a secondary status according to a 5:5:3 tonnage ratio. Battleships were limited to 35,000 tons' displacement, and a ten-year building holiday for battleships and battlecruisers went into effect. Britain was allowed to build two new battleships after the conference and the United States was allowed to retain three superdreadnoughts of the 1916 Program. Aircraft carriers were also limited by a ceiling on total tonnage, with each ship to displace no more than 27,000 tons. This was later waived to 33,000 tons as a result of U.S. pressure. Auxiliary warships—ships with gun bore not greater than 8 inches and displacement less than 10,000 tons (cruisers, destroyers, and submarines)—were not limited in any way.

U.S. naval officers generally believed that the United States had been out-negotiated by the British since Britain was allowed to maintain 580,450 tons of capital ships against 500,360 tons for the United States. Four 1916 Program battlecruisers were canceled and the remaining two were converted into the large aircraft carriers *Lexington* and *Saratoga,* which did not enter service for another five years.[8] Reduced Republican naval spending, compared to the massive outlay of Wilson's 1916 Program, promised to keep the navy well below the maximum size allowed under the treaty.

With the battleship's evolution limited by treaty, the navy came under vigorous attacks from aviation advocates, who claimed that a $10,000 airplane could sink a $10 million battleship.[9] The sensational aerial bombardments against captured German and obsolete American battleships conducted in 1921 provided aviation supporters with ammunition for their fight. The bombing trials yielded dramatic photographs of phosphorus and high-explosive bombs detonating on the huge battleships as fragile, biplane bombers flew overhead. However, the battleships that were bombed were anchored, unmanned, unarmed, and, by virtue of their age, markedly less resistant to aerial bombing than later designs.[10] The German battleship *Ostfriesland,* sunk in the tests off Cape Henry, Virginia, in July 1921, had been subjected to repeated attacks over a two-day period. During the first day, sixteen of sixty-nine bombs ranging in size from 230 to 2,000 pounds scored hits. On the second day, three out of eleven 1,000-pound bombs hit the ship, while three of the six 2,000-pound bombs exploded in the water close aboard. With most of her watertight fittings not fully repaired after her battle damage at Jutland and no damage control teams on board to fight the flooding, *Ostfriesland* sank.[11] The trials did not provide conclusive proof of the battleship's obsolescence, but a significant segment of the public believed it was vulnerable to air attack.[12]

Faced with this public relations fait accompli, the naval hierarchy worked hard to restore a common sense of the battleship's invulnerability. The navy argued that a fully manned battleship with antiaircraft guns, steaming at full speed, could thwart an attack from the air. Even if a bomb should hit, the navy claimed that the resulting damage would hardly prove fatal in light of the "superiority" of U.S. armor designs over those installed on British and German ships which had survived numerous large-caliber shell hits at Jutland.

In testimony before the House of Representatives' Joint Military and Naval Affairs Committee, Rear Admiral William A. Moffett, chief of the Bureau of

Aeronautics, maintained that the nation's "first line of defense is the main fleet . . . the second line of defense would be auxiliary vessels of the fleet [cruisers, destroyers, and submarines] and the third line of defense is our coast fortifications, augmented by the Army Air Service."[13] In a pejorative aside, Moffett doubted the ability of army flyers to defend against a seaborne attack since they have "never been to sea except as passengers."[14]

THE SPECIAL POLICY BOARD HEARINGS OF 1924

Despite the creation of the Bureau of Aeronautics, critics persisted in their claims that the navy was suppressing aviation. Amid this continuing controversy, Secretary of the Navy Curtis D. Wilbur was embroiled in a dispute with the director of the budget over what level of naval appropriations the executive branch should request from Congress.[15] Wilbur directed the General Board of the navy to consult "experienced officers from both the Army and the Navy" and to make recommendations as to "development and upkeep of the Navy in its various branches, i.e., submarines, surface ships, and aircraft" in preparation for the naval appropriations bill to be submitted to Congress early in 1925.[16] Although a Naval Academy alumnus, Wilbur wanted professional advice on the most efficient expenditure of whatever funds were allocated to the navy.[17] As a part of its study, the General Board, keeper of the battleship technological paradigm, would rule on battleship obsolescence.

During the fall of 1924 the Special Policy Board of the navy's General Board heard the testimony of seventy-six witnesses that included the chiefs of the navy bureaus, fleet commanders, junior officers from the Bureau of Aeronautics, civilian engineering representatives of the National Advisory Committee for Aeronautics (NACA), aviation industrialists, and army officers, including General Billy Mitchell.[18] In its 1925 special report, the General Board reaffirmed the supremacy of the battleship-based strategy and the battleship technological paradigm. Since the conclusions drawn by the General Board supported the status quo, it is tempting to categorize the Special Board hearings as a show trial. But with the hearings held in executive session and the minutes unpublished, the testimony was confidential and quite frank.

The General Board defined the navy's technological needs in terms of its two strategic missions: first, to gain control of disputed sea areas and sea communications; and second, to maintain control of these areas and the lines of sea communication.[19] The first strategic mission involved "fighting the battle fleet of the enemy." This required a fleet composed of "all the various types of combatant ships." Listed in order of their importance within the U.S. Battle Fleet were "battleships, light cruisers, destroyers, destroyer leaders, submarines, and airplane carriers."[20] The second strategic mission would be carried out by "attacks upon and interference with enemy commerce, the defense of our own commerce, the blockade of enemy ports, the escort of military expeditions, the repulse of invasions and, in general, the control of sea communications."[21] This mission required "less fighting strength" and would be assigned to cruisers assisted by submarines, and whatever aircraft carriers—the battlecruiser-turned-carrier *Saratoga* would not be completed until 1927—or destroyers were available.[22]

On paper, the U.S. Fleet was divided into four forces composed of various types of ships. In addition to the Battle Fleet described above were the Scouting Fleet, Control Force, and the Fleet Base Force. The Scouting Fleet was considered an auxiliary to the Battle Fleet. In principle it contained light cruisers, aircraft carriers, submarines, and destroyers. The Control Force was charged with accomplishing the navy's secondary strategic mission: maintaining control of the sea. It was to be composed of light cruisers, aircraft carriers, destroyers, submarines, minelayers, and patrol vessels. The Fleet Base Force included the Fleet Train, auxiliary vessels needed to supply the fleet, and whatever combatant vessels were assigned to protect the Fleet Train and advanced naval bases.[23]

The Board recognized the aviation threat to the battleship, but the testimony of civilian aeronautical experts indicated that the future evolution of aircraft, which were not subject to any treaty restrictions, was more limited than that of the battleship. The experts included Massachusetts Institute of Technology (MIT) President S. W. Stratton, Johns Hopkins physicist J. S. Ames, the chair of MIT's Aerodynamic Department, E. P. Warner (who later became the first assistant secretary of the navy for air in 1926), and several important NACA figures such as W. F. Durand of Stanford University, George W. Lewis, director of NACA research, and Rear Admiral David Taylor, secretary of NACA. These foremost representatives of the nation's aviation establishment all agreed that the "present maximum performance of heavier-than-air craft may be increased about thirty per cent by future developments extending over an indefinite period of years. All of them consider it most unwise to base a policy of national defense on expectation much beyond present performance."[24]

After the experts placed a technological ceiling on the future of aviation, the Board addressed the considerable agitation to create a cabinet-level Department of Aeronautics to supervise civil and military aviation. This department would include a united air service, or air force, that would absorb all army and naval aviation. The Board argued that the testimony of its witnesses supported the position that such a department would hinder the navy's ability to defend the nation. The agitation within the army and navy for a separate air service was attributed to "(1) Unsatisfactory promotion from their [aviators'] point of view. (2) A desire to be always under the command from the top down of practical flying officers. (3) A belief that there exists a lack of sympathy for them on the part of the senior officers of the Army and Navy."[25]

The Board dismissed the case for promotion as the misguided belief by pilots that an air force would be expanded so that existing officers would enter the new service with "greatly increased rank and pay." As to the command structure of naval aviation, the time was fast approaching when all the "immediate commanders of flying squadrons will be practical flying officers." However, the Board pointed out that the existing situation was no different from the fact that officers specializing in naval engineering and ordnance were not always commanded by officers of their own specialty. The lack of sympathy for aviators, if it did exist, was attributed to the fact that the "higher authorities in both Army and Navy understand the serious limitations in war operations in the air."[26] That is, they disagreed with the ardent advocates of aviation who espoused the unlimited potential of air power.

Since the push for a united air service and attacks on the battleship had grown out of the 1921 battleship bombing experiments, the Board discussed these trials at length, concluding that battleship antiaircraft guns would make the already inaccurate aerial bombing even more so. For example, when the battleship *Iowa* was attacked while being maneuvered by radio control, only two of eight bombs hit the ship from an altitude of 4,000 feet. In July 1924 the British had conducted a similar trial using the radio-controlled battleship *Agamemnon.* One hundred fourteen bombs were dropped without a single hit. Trials of antiaircraft guns had yielded 75 percent hits on small aerial targets at altitudes higher than 4,000 feet, indicating that a battleship could fend off aerial attack.[27]

The inaccuracy of the peacetime bombing trials cast doubt on the aviation argument. The navy argued that the battleship was the superior means to defeat an enemy battle fleet, since gunfire from a battleship was quicker and more accurate than aerial bombing: "The turrets of our latest battleships fire a projectile weighing 2,100 pounds to a distance of twenty sea miles [40,000 yards]. At 19,000 yards no armor afloat will withstand a normal hit from these guns. While it takes 28 seconds for an airplane bomb to reach the target, 12,000 feet beneath it, the 16-inch projectile fired from a gun traverses an equal distance in less than five seconds."

The mystique of air attack was dismissed as well: "There seems to be in the minds of most of us, the idea that there is some especially deadly quality pertaining to missiles dropped from above. This idea is probably instinctive and is kept alive by accidents which occur from time to time. The idea is not true of course, but if it were, what of the 2,100 pound [battleship] shell which, when fired at the maximum range as mounted, drops from a height of 18,700 feet?"[28]

The battleship was judged superior to aviation by what Admiral William Sims used to call "rapidity of hitting" coupled with the greater percentage of hits from battleship guns.[29] The *West Virginia* delivered a volume of carefully aimed fire which amounted to one shell every five seconds.[30] In peacetime target practice, American battleships successfully hit a relatively small target about 10 percent of the time at ranges between 19,000 and 20,000 yards. In battle, the navy estimated the rate of hits would be reduced to around 3 percent, which, according to reconstructions, was believed to be the case during the Battle of Jutland in 1916.[31] The reduction of hits during battle was attributed to "haste, smoke, nerves, et cetera." The Board concluded that such factors also would affect adversely the accuracy of bombing and torpedo fire, reducing its effectiveness from the results obtained during the "drill and experiment of peace."[32]

Battle drills indicated that a large number of projectiles, whether shells or aerial bombs, would be required to get hits on enemy ships: "If a battleship fires five hundred 2,100-pound shells in an engagement, she may count on making fifteen hits."[33] The Five-Power Treaty had set a ceiling on aircraft carrier tonnage, and even the large aircraft carriers *Lexington* and *Saratoga,* being converted from the 1916 Program battlecruisers, would each only carry seventy-two aircraft and not all of these aircraft were bombers.[34] If the navy built the maximum number of aircraft carriers allowed under the Five-Power Treaty, the total number of aircraft available at sea would be approximately three hundred.[35] If each one of these aircraft was a bomber, which was not the case, the number of bombs that could reach an undefended, motionless battleship would still be less than the number of shells fired from a single battleship's guns and the aerial bombs (based upon trials) would achieve a smaller percentage of hits. When antiaircraft fire and ship maneuvering were added to the picture, the Board argued, the success of the airborne attack would be reduced even further.

Confidential torpedo, bomb, and gunfire tests conducted in November 1924 on the uncompleted hull of the 1916 Program battleship *Washington* indicated that the three newest American superdreadnoughts could withstand eight torpedo hits. During the torpedo trials, a 14-inch shell weighing 1,400 pounds was also dropped onto the *Washington* from an altitude of 4,000 feet and failed to penetrate the thick armored deck. The members of the test board believed, however, that if the bomb had been dropped from a higher height, which was within the capabilities of contemporary aircraft, the shell would have penetrated. The Board argued that such an occurrence could be avoided by adding more horizontal armor as part of the defensive tonnage increase allowed by the treaty. *Washington* was also subjected to long-range gunfire, and the tests indicated that present U.S. battleship designs "justified expectations."[36] Additional trials were conducted to evaluate the effect of underwater explosions caused by near misses of aerial bombs. Because of their intense pressure wave, the latter were considered more dangerous than direct hits.

In developing a strategic policy for the secretary of the navy, the Special Board had to decide whether the present capabilities of naval aircraft—or rather the present capabilities increased by 30 percent—posed a credible challenge to the battleship. Both battleship advocates and aviators saw limitations in each other's artifacts, but none in their own. To ensure penetration of a reinforced armored deck, General Mitchell threatened to double the size of aerial bombs from the present maximum of 2,000 pounds to 4,000 pounds. Mitchell's plan sounded good to the public, but in reality doubling the weight of explosive (which comprised about 50 percent of the total weight in an armor-piercing bomb) only increased the pressure effect ofthe explosive charge by 50 percent rather than 100 percent.[37] While such a large bomb could penetrate the armored deck of a battleship, the navy dismissed it as too heavy to deliver based upon the testimony of the aeronautical experts. The maximum load of contemporary bombers was 4,000 pounds, which included fuel and bombs. To carry a bomb larger than 2,000 pounds would mean a significant reduction in the bomber's radius of action, even if aircraft performance improved by the predicted maximum of 30 percent. Using newly developed supercharged engines, a bomber could only reach a ceiling of 8,000 feet with a 2,000-pound bomb. A larger bomb would reduce the aircraft's ceiling, bringing the aircraft within range of ship-mounted antiaircraft guns which, as mentioned, were believed to be very effective based on live-fire exercises.[38]

The Board's focus on bombs ignored the weapon long advocated by Bradley Fiske—the torpedo plane. Although the three newest U.S. battleships of the 1916 Program had been judged capable of surviving eight torpedo hits, no mention was made of earlier designs which remained in the battle line. The definition of survival was also vague. Modern naval weaponeers speak of varying types of kills, such as mobility, mission, weapons, electronic, or total. In 1924 the Special Board's term "survival" was less sophisticated; the ship remained afloat. In May 1941 the German battleship *Bismarck* survived two hits from aerial torpedoes. The second jammed her rudder and inflicted a mobility kill, preventing *Bismarck* from reaching port.[39] Mitchell may have fared better with his antibattleship campaign if he had focused on delivering torpedoes rather than bombs. However, the torpedo was not a normal technology within the army aviation technological paradigm.

"NORMAL" STRATEGY

In their testimony before the Special Board, naval aviators reflected their philosophical identification with the normal practice of the battleship-based strategic paradigm. Rear Admiral Moffett, chief of the Bureau of Aeronautics, typified the battleship thought style, characterizing aircraft at sea as "auxiliary to the fleet—as an auxiliary arm. Its functions being, I would say, spotting [battleship] gun fire, reconnaissance, scouting, torpedo and bombing."[40] Perhaps recalling his own fondness for big-gunned battleships—he had advocated a battleship with "the largest gun" possible in 1916[41]—and his Medal of Honor-winning shelling of Mexicans at Vera Cruz, Moffett's ultimate expression was his statement to the Special Board that "Aviation is a gun; it is a form of a gun."[42] The bureau's Lieutenant Commander Marc Mitscher, who would later achieve fame as a commander of aircraft carrier task forces against the Japanese during World War II, also testified from within the battleship framework. Basing his conclusion upon bombing and gunnery exercises conducted since 1922, Mitscher told the Board that gunfire was more effective than aerial bombing.[43]

Submarine and aviation advocates were competing for reduced postwar naval funding and each claimed their technology better served the battle fleet. The submarine's future was not as a counterweapon to the battleship, as Ensign Bieg thought in 1915, but as a more stealthy and more economical scout than the rival aircraft carrier or light cruiser. Rear Admiral M. M. Taylor, commander of the Control Force, emphasized the efficiency of the submarine when he argued that a Hawaii-based, continuous naval patrol off southern Japan would only require four 2,000-ton submarines at a total cost of $16 million. The same thirty-day patrol, using highly visible and vulnerable light cruisers, would require five ships at a cost of $20 million. An aircraft carrier with its forty planes, along with four destroyers for protection, could only patrol for ten days at a cost of $22.4 million. An added consideration was the fact that the large and costly aircraft carrier would be extremely vulnerable to attack.[44]

Conversely, Rear Admiral Magruder, commander of the Light Cruiser Division of the Scouting Fleet, defended aviation as the technology that was perfectly consonant with the geographical realities of the navy's Pacific strategy.[45] The weather in the Pacific, according to Magruder, lent itself to successful air operations, and he recommended allocating a larger percentage of the shrinking naval budget to naval aviation .[46] He also argued that aviation could serve as an economical buffer against the "treacherous" Japanese until the United States reached war footing by "bring[ing] our air fleet up to . . . its proper strength," which was a quicker method of "strengthening the Fleet" and "would be cheaper also."[47]

After reviewing the extensive testimony of the special hearings, the Special Policy Board recommended a force structure in which the battleship remained "the element of ultimate force in the fleet." In a perfect expression of the battleship technological paradigm, the Board defined all "other elements" as "contributory to the fulfillment of its [battleship's] function as the final arbiter of sea warfare." The Board mimicked Rear Admiral Frank Fletcher's testimony in 1914 that "offense always beats defense":

> From time to time apparent threats to the superiority of the battleship have appeared. Each has resulted in some modifications of its design and in the methods of its employment in war, but its supremacy remains. With the invention and development of offensive weapons has always come the counter invention and development of defensive means and methods, so that in the end a fair balance is struck between them. The history of the gun and armor, and of the torpedo and interior subdivision, merely repeats the process by which offense always begets defense. . . . [Aviation's] influence on naval warfare undoubtedly will increase in the future, but the prediction that it will assume paramount importance in sea warfare will not be realized. The airplane (heavier-than-air) is inherently limited in performance by physical laws. Airplanes have demonstrated their great value to the fleet in scouting, observation, and bombing. The use of torpedo planes, [poison] gas,[48] and smoke screens still is in the process of development. Airplane carriers are necessary elements of a properly constituted fleet to carry airplanes to the scene of action."[49]

In reaffirming the battleship's dominance in *guerre d'escadre,* the Special Policy Board ignored the warning of retired Admiral William F. Fullam, whose career had spanned the battleship era and who admitted that his "whole heart was given to the biggest gun and the biggest ship that could be conceived."[50] Fullam's allegiance to the battleship ended on Armistice Day in 1918, when his flagship was anchored in San Diego harbor. The commander at Rockwell Field sent up 212 airplanes to celebrate the end of the war and they flew over the fleet for three hours "in flocks." It became perfectly clear to Fullam that if "each of those lads up there had a bomb as big as a grapefruit, that wouldn't have been the place for us, or for any collection of ships. If we started out at fifteen knots, they would have pursued us at a hundred knots."[51]

Although greatly overplaying the effect of grapefruit-sized bombs (and ignoring the potential of the torpedo plane), Fullam, like Saul on the road to Damascus, became a convert. He conceptualized a " 'Three Plane Navy' with forces on the surface, below the surface and over the surface."[52] Fullam pointed out that the most powerful battleship fleet in the world could not keep Britain from starvation and the brink of defeat in the spring of 1917. Citing German records analyzed at the Naval War College, Fullam characterized the German blockade as the epitome of efficiency, comprising only nine to fifteen submarines at any one time. He emphasized that the entire German submarine force of ten thousand men had managed to circumvent the one million men that manned the five greatest battleship navies in the worlds.[53] Using the submarine as an example, Fullam accused the navy of learning nothing from the World War since antisubmariners within the Navy Department had prevented the director of submarines from testifying before the Senate Naval Affairs Committee in February 1921 regarding the need for submarines.[54] In addition, Secretary of the Navy Josephus Daniels's appointee as chief of naval operations, Admiral Robert E. Coontz, had deleted all submarines from the naval appropriations bill.[55]

Although critical of the limited naval appropriations of the Harding and Coolidge administrations, Fullam idealistically argued that whatever funds were given to the navy should be used to develop the three-plane navy to its fullest efficiency, so that all technological factions could work together like a Nelsonian "band of brothers."[56] Rejecting the singularity of the battleship thought style, Fullam demanded the creation of a *"three idea* Navy," as it would win out over a "one idea navy every time." According to Fullam, "The nation that first does this, that first solves that very complicated problem, will win the next war."[57]

The American naval profession had no room for three disparate and roughly equal technological paradigms. Fullam's argument was for naught, and the Special Policy Board justified the retention of the battleship-based strategy for two reasons. First, the testimony of civilian aviation experts set a technological ceiling on aviation, predicting that airplanes had little potential for growth and, therefore, would never attain performance levels that would pose a threat to the battleship. Second, those charged with the advancement of naval aviation, such as Rear Admiral Moffett, were firmly rooted in the battleship thought collective and envisioned aviation as supporting the battleship rather than challenging it.

There was strong support for the development of naval aviation by senior naval officers, but only in roles that reinforced the normal battleship-based strategic philosophy. A different employment of naval aviation was only a possibility if a rival naval power should pursue a radically different aviation mission, for example, offensive operations utilizing torpedo planes, which would threaten, or in the case of hostilities, pose a serious presumptive anomaly to the existing technological paradigm.[58]

AFTER THE "AIRPHOBIA" OF 1924–1925

The Special Policy Board report was an internal navy document, and the release of its conclusions failed to end the criticism from those calling for the retirement of the battleship and the establishment of a separate air service. As a result, President Coolidge appointed a civilian panel, the Morrow Board, to study the best way to develop aviation for use in national defense.[59] The Morrow Board found no merit in a separate air force, but did recommend the adoption of a multiyear aircraft procurement program for the army and navy.[60] Believing there was merit in the contention that aviators were being suppressed, the Morrow Board recommended increased promotion opportunities and the restriction of aircraft carrier command to aviation officers. The Board also advised the president to authorize the appointment of a new assistant secretary of the navy for aviation.

Coolidge signed the appropriations act of 24 June 1926 incorporating the provisions of the Morrow Board report, including funding for a thousand new navy aircraft over a five-year period.[61] In addition, all aircraft carriers were commanded by aviators. The exclusion of nonaviators from command of the almost completed large carriers *Saratoga* and *Lexington* irked Admiral Samuel S. Robison, commander-in-chief, U.S. Fleet. He expressed his dismay to the Bureau of Aeronautics:

> The particular aircraft carriers now in mind are the largest ships we have ever built, with the greatest horsepower that has ever been installed, and to try to connect up their command with ability to fly is piffle (see Morrow Board's recommendation); and that no officers should serve on them except aviators is equally piffle and defeats the desire of the Department and of the Congress that knowledge of aviation should be disseminated as widely as possible.[62]

In the wake of the Special Board and the Morrow Board, Captain Yates Stirling captured the essence of the battleship thought style regarding the role of aviation in the navy: "The notion that the airplane is to replace that panoply of war called fleets came as a surprise to the Navy. The naval man saw in it merely a weapon to be used by the Navy for offensive and defensive action. . . . In addition to its value in scouting, the Navy's interest first was directed to the airplane for the purpose of spotting gun fire. . . . Spotting the [battleship] gun salvos from airplanes was the natural solution [to visibility problems at long range]."[63] Like, Moffett, the navy's premier aviator, Stirling also compared the airplane to a battleship shell: "Airplane carriers are to all intents and purposes battle cruisers with airplanes replacing the big guns in armored turrets. . . . The fact is that the naval airplane is merely a new sort of projectile, carried by a surface ship."[64]

Stirling compared the aviation threat to that posed by torpedo-carrying destroyers prior to the World War. The rapid-fire secondary armament of battleships was judged unable to reach attacking destroyers with sufficient accuracy to prevent a torpedo attack. The answer had been to advance the antidestroyer guns to the point of attack, that is, to place them on destroyers and use these destroyers as a protective screen around the capital ship. Stirling advocated the same course of action with antiaircraft guns: advancing them to the point of attack by carrying them in airplanes. This would ensure control of the skies, neutralization of the airplane, and protection of American capital ships. Naval air assets would cancel each other out, and war at sea would remain dependent on the battleship.[65] The airplane would join the expanding defensive rings protecting the navy's castles of steel.

The technological ceiling and pace of subsequent aviation development prevented aviation theorists from presenting a credible presumptive anomaly to the battleship technological paradigm. That would have to wait for the development and perfection of carrier air groups equipped with modern aircraft able to damage or sink a moving warship. This would not occur prior to the introduction of metal, monoplane dive bombers, torpedo bombers, and fighters at the end of the 1930s.

Naval officers tended to see conflict as intra-artifact with little, if any, crossover. In war games at the Naval War College, for example, commanders of opposing fleets regularly launched air strikes against enemy aircraft carriers, rather than against battleships, as soon as the enemy was within range.[66] Fleet exercise experience underscored the vulnerability of aircraft carriers to air attack. The consensus was that there was no effective defense against a well-mounted dive bomber attack save the destruction of the enemy carrier prior to its launching such an attack. The side whose carriers were discovered and attacked first lost its aviation force.[67] Once these preliminary bouts were completed, the ring was clear for the main event—the battleship duel. As the *Tactical Orders and Doctrine for the U.S. Fleet, 1941,* stated: "The surest and quickest means of gaining control of the air is the destruction of enemy carriers."[68] Control of the air meant freedom from destruction from above.

In justifying their existence, both submariners and aviators presented themselves as the "most effective" supporting technologies to increase the survivability of the battle fleet. Stirling typified the view that aircraft would only fight other aircraft, just as Admiral M. M. Taylor argued that submarines would primarily engage submarines.[69] Citing the confusion at Jutland, Stirling predicted a general melee in which one air fleet would be completely victorious while the other would be cleared from the air. The victorious side would then be free to use its airplanes for scouting and gunfire spotting in support of the battleships. After the battleship action had been concluded, "Bombing, gassing, and torpedoing of the enemy battle line [by aircraft] will give the *coup de grace.*"[70] It was inconceivable to Stirling and most of his colleagues that bombing, gassing, and torpedoing alone might do the trick.

THE SPECIAL BOARD AND THE STRATEGIC PARADIGM

The battleship reductions and building holidays of the Five-Power Treaty provided aviation enthusiasts with a truly "stationary" target. Technical improvements to the surviving battleships were restricted severely, while aviation technology developed at a quick rate. The Bureau ofAeronautics funded structural research at the Naval Aircraft Factory in Philadelphia and at the U.S. Bureau of Standards and NACA.[71] Wind tunnel experiments were conducted at the navy's Experimental Model Basin at the Washington Navy Yard and at the Massachusetts Institute of Technology.[72] At sea, aviators worked to improve the efficiency of aircraft carrier aviation by "speeding up operations, including takeoffs, landings, and faster handling of planes both on deck and below. Brakes and tail wheels [were] . . . now standard equipment for all carrier planes."[73] However, Admiral W. T. Mayo, commander-in-chief, U.S. Fleet, stated the reality in 1919: "The development of Naval Aviation must be governed by the development of Naval Tactics and Strategy"—the thought style which supported the battleship-based strategic paradigm.[74]

According to Rear Admiral Moffett, the biggest drawback to aviation was the failure to construct aircraft carriers, a byproduct of the limited funds for naval construction during the New Era.[75] Yet even if the carriers allowed by the Five-Power Treaty had been built, there is little to indicate that aviation's role would have been different early on. Its strategic and tactical functions were delineated by officers like Moffett, working in the intellectual mainstream of the normal strategic and technological paradigm. The lack of aircraft carriers did not strengthen the battleship's position. The battleship remained preeminent because the Special Board Hearings painted a future in which aviation technology remained weak *vis-à-vis* the battleship. The technological ceiling predicted by aviation experts relegated naval aviation to scouting, gunfire spotting, and fighting enemy aviation, assignments that endured in naval doctrine through the 1930s.[76]

Despite the dissolution of the 1924 aviation technological ceiling, naval aviation remained more presumption than anomaly and the battleship technological paradigm remained dominant. In February 1931 the chief of naval operations, Admiral William V. Pratt, reported to the House Naval Affairs Committee that the consensus of officers attending Fleet Exercise XII off western Central America was that air attacks were "of less value as a means of defense against approaching fleets" than previously believed.[77] The commander of the aviation units charged with defending the Panama Canal from attack and invasion by the battle fleet, Rear Admiral Joseph Reeves, reported that aviation alone "cannot stop the advance of battleships."[78]

The rapid improvement in aviation technology during the mid-1930s did not translate into an immediate, viable presumptive anomaly. Carrier aircraft development mirrored the often confusing coevolution of the world's armored warships during the 1870–80s. A Bureau of Aeronautics' report that considered 47 percent of aircraft in service "obsolete, obsolescent, or about to become obsolescent" was typical of a period of rapid technological advancement.[79] The addition of the New Deal carriers *Yorktown* (commissioned 1937) and *Enterprise* (commissioned 1938) required a 40 percent expansion of naval aviation.[80] A consensus existed among younger naval aviators that their day was fast approaching.

To pose an effective presumptive anomaly, naval aviation required not only more aircraft, but fighters, torpedo bombers, and dive/scout bombers that were state of the art. The acquisition of this technology began in 1936 when the navy ordered 114 all-metal torpedo bombers, the Douglas TBD-1. The TBD-1 was the first monoplane ordered for carrier use and marked a turning point in carrier aircraft.[81] The TBD entered squadron service in October 1937. Its time on the leading edge of carrier-based aviation technology was relatively brief. Unfortunately for its crews, the TBD's 105-knot cruising speed made it an easy target during the battles in the Coral Sea (May 1924) and near Midway (June 1942).[82] The first in the series of Douglas SBD dive bombers that would later play a key role in the early years of the Pacific war did not enter squadron service until December 1940.[83]

With senior aviators sprouting from the battleship thought collective and perceiving aviation as a gun, naval aviation was unable to escape the social, institutional, and technological momentum attending the battleship technological paradigm. The authorization of fast aircraft carriers in the late 1930s, to work with the post-treaty fast battleships, marked the beginning of the fast task force concept. However, American naval aviation had to wait until after Pearl Harbor for opportunities to demonstrate its abilities in war at sea.

Notes

[1]Fisher to the Editor, *The Times,* 2 September 1919, letter 552, *Fear God and Dread Nought: The Correspondence of Admiral of the Fleet Lord Fisher of Kilverstone,* vol. III: *Restoration, Abdication, and Last Years, 1914–1920,* ed. Arthur J. Marder (London: J. Cape, 1959), 590.

[2]Rear Admiral David W. Taylor, USN, "The Design of Vessels as Affected by the World War," *Journal of the American Society of Naval Engineers* 32(1920): 745.

[3]Ibid., 749.

[4]Ibid., 754. In light of the aerial torpedo's smaller size and warhead, Taylor's point was valid.

[5]Testimony of Captain Mustin before the General Board, 26 June 1922, *Hearings of the General Board of the Navy, 1917–1950,* microfilm, Nimitz Library, U.S. Naval Academy, Annapolis, Md. (hereafter *General Board Hearings*). For another view on the future of the torpedo plane, see Henry Woodhouse, "The Torpedo-plane: The New Weapon Which Promises to Revolutionize Naval Tactics," *U.S. Naval Institute Proceedings* (hereafter *USNIP*) 45(1919): 751.

[6]U.S. Senate, "Hearings: Building up the United States Navy to the Strength

Permitted by the Washington and London Naval Treaties," 72nd Congress, 1st Session (1932), cited in Robert L. O'Connell, *Sacred Vessels: The Cult of the Battleship and the Rise of the U.S. Navy* (Boulder, Col.: Westview Press, 1991), 291.

[7]Roger Dingman, *Power in the Pacific* (Chicago: University of Chicago Press, 1979), 152. Battleship numbers from Christopher Hall, *Britain, America, and Arms Control, 1921–1937* (New York: St. Martin's Press, 1987), table 1.1, 13.

[8]The Five-Power Treaty did not limit aircraft. A committee of aviation experts from Britain, Japan, Italy, France, and the United States deferred discussion of the aircraft question, believing "that it is not practicable to impose any effective limitations upon the numbers or characteristics of aircraft, either commercial or military, except in the single case of lighter-than-air craft. The committee is of the opinion that the use of aircraft in warfare should be governed by the rules of warfare as adapted to aircraft by a further conference which should be held at a later date"; *Report of Special Committee on Limitation of Aircraft in Warfare,* cited in *Tenth Annual Report of the N.A.CA. on Aviation,* 22 December 1914, reprinted in *USNIP* 51 (1925): 495.

[9]Or, as Billy Mitchell put it: "more than 1000 airplanes can be built and maintained for the outlay required for a single [$10 million] battleship"; see William Mitchell, *Winged Defense: The Development and Possibilities of Modern Air Power Economic and Military* (New York: Dover, 1988; reprint of the 1925 edition published by C. P. Putnam's Sons), 120.

[10]The older battleships that were expended in these tests had been designed to fight at relatively shorter ranges than contemporary battleships, for example, those of the U.S. 1916 Program. At shorter ranges more vertical armor was installed as the trajectory of incoming shells was relatively flat. Long-range naval guns delivered their shells at a steeper angle and as a result the later battleship designs installed heavier horizontal armor that resisted aerial bombs as well.

[11]*Report of the Special Board on Policy with Reference to the Upkeep of the Navy in its Various Branches,* 17 January 1925, in *General Board Hearings* (hereafter *1925 Special Board Report*), 23.

[12]For the aviation side of the bombing trials, see Mitchell, *Winged Defense,* chap. 3.

[13]Rear Admiral Moffett's statement before the Joint Military and Naval Affairs Committee of the House of Representatives printed in full in *Aviation* and reprinted in *USNIP* 50(1924): 1364–70.

[14]Ibid. Army flyers had recently flown across the northern Pacific from Dutch Harbor, Alaska, to Japan in April–May 1924; see "Professional Notes," *USNIP* 50 (1924): 1370.

[15]The naval officer corps deeply resented the intrusion of New Era efficiency experts, led by the administration's budget office, into naval affairs. As Admiral Rodgers told the General Board: "We are continually confronted by Treasury people who want a change, and reformers who are constantly making the point in which their business training causes them to follow a line of thought which is not in accordance with [naval] necessity. . . . [The New Era] Congress, tak-

ing over from civil life its business ideas, looks to the great corporations which have grown up by consolidation to become trusts, and says, 'Let us consolidate everything that looks alike and put them together.' They say, 'We will take those things that look alike and consolidate them in the interests of efficiency' "; Rodgers's 26 June 1922 statement to the General Board, *General Board Hearings.* For many naval officers, Republican Party New Era efficiency threatened the U.S. Navy with extinction.

[16]Secretary of the Navy Curtis D. Wilbur to General Board, 23 September 1924, reprinted in *General Board Hearings.*

[17]See *Army and Navy Register,* "The Naval Budget," 25 October 1924, reprinted in *USNIP* 51(1925): 127–28.

[18]1925 *Special Board Report,* 1–3.

[19]Ibid., 11

[20]Ibid. As yet, the navy had no aircraft carriers save the converted collier *Langley.*

[21]Ibid.

[22]Ibid.

[23]Ibid.

[24]Ibid., 43

[25]Ibid., 70.

[26]Ibid., 70–71.

[27]Ibid., 20.

[28]Ibid., 28.

[29]For accounts of Sims's experience in revamping U.S. naval gunnery practices, see Elting Morison, *Men, Machines, and Modern Times* (Cambridge, Mass.: The MIT Press, 1966), chap. 2.

[30]*1925 Special Board Report,* 20.

[31]Ibid.

[32]Ibid. For a critical assessment of the battleship, see Rodrigo Garcia y Robertson, "The Failure of the Heavy Gun at Sea, 1898–1922," *Technology and Culture* 28(1987): 539–57.

[33]*1925 Special Board Report,* 20.

[34]Testimony of Admiral Strauss, *Hearings Before the Special Board,* contained in *General Board Hearings* (hereafter *Special Board Hearings*), 132.

[35]See testimony of Rear Admiral Moffett and Captains Johnson and Land of the Bureau of Aeronautics, 30 September and 1–3 October1924, *Special Board Hearings.*

[36]Navy Secretary Curtis D. Wilbur in [Washington] *Star,* "Naval Engineers Have in View Vastly Improved Battleships," 15 January 1925, reprinted in *USNIP* 51 (1925): 501.

[37]*1925 Special Board Report,* 27.

[38]Ibid.

[39]Combat experience in World War II forced the navy to take waterborne shock from nearby explosions more seriously than before the war. See Francis Dun-

can, "Hyman C. Rickover: Technology and Naval Tradition," in *Quarterdeck and Bridge: Two Centuries ofAmerican Naval Leaders,* ed. James C. Bradford (Annapolis: Naval Institute Press, 1997), 398.

[40]Testimony of Rear Admiral Moffett, 30 September 1924, *Special Board Hearings.*

[41]Moffett had entered his "largest gun" battleship essay for the Naval Institute's Lippincott Prize. See Commander William A. Moffett, USN, to Captain William S. Sims, USN, 12 June 1916; Sims to Moffett, 16 June 1916; and Moffett to Sims, 27 June 1916, in the Papers of William S. Sims, Manuscript Division, Library of Congress, Washington, D.C. (hereafter Sims Papers), Box 47.

[42]Testimony of Rear Admiral Moffett, *Special Board Hearing;* 170. For Moffett's medal-winning in Mexico, see William F. Trimble, *Admiral William A. Moffett: Architect of Naval Aviation* (Washington, D.C.: Smithsonian Institution Press, 1994), chap. 3. Moffett was an astute politician and his use of the gun metaphor may have been to placate the battleship hierarchy. At this stage in his career at the Bureau of Aeronautics, Moffett is most likely speaking sincerely as a member of the battleship thought collective. The developments in aviation technology in the late 1920s and introduction of the large carriers *Lexington* and *Saratoga* provided the framework which allowed him to move away from this "normal" view of naval aviation.

[43]Testimony of Lieutenant Commander Mitscher, *Special Board Hearing;* 42 and 39.

[44]Testimony of Rear Admiral M. M. Taylor, *Special Board Hearings,* 310. Taylor was basing his estimate on a carrier costing $16 million; the carrier *Saratoga,* still under construction, actually cost $45 million, which would have enhanced his argument on behalf of the submarine.

[45]For an overview of the U.S. Navy's War Plan Orange against Japan, see Russell F. Weigley, *The American Way of War: A History of United States Military Strategy and Policy* (Bloomington: Indiana University Press, 1977), chap. 12.

[46]Testimony of Rear Admiral Magruder, 10 October 1924, *Special Board Hearings.*

[47]Ibid.

[48]The Board heard testimony regarding the potential use of poison-gas aerial bombs against ships. See the testimony of Rear Admiral Moffett and Lieutenant McMurrain, 30 September[?] 1924, *Special Board Hearings.*

[49]*1925 Special Board Report, 75–77.*

[50]Testimony of Admiral William F. Fullam, USN (Ret.), *Special Board Hearings,* 716.

[51]Ibid.

[52]Ibid.

[53]Ibid., 719.

[54]Ibid., 723.

[55]Coontz was a part of the what Rear Admiral Sims condemned as the reac-

tionary "Daniels Cabinet"; see Sims to John Callan O'Laughlin, 23 September 1925, Sims Papers, Box 46. Sims characterized the appointment of these admirals of the Old School as "a crime against the people of the United States"; Sims to Lieutenant Commander Dinger, 14 February 1925, Sims Papers, Box 54. For Admiral Coontz and the submarine program, see the testimony of Admiral Fullam, *Special Board Hearings,* 723.

[56]Testimony of Admiral Fullam, *Special Board Hearings,* 717.

[57]Ibid.

[58]The General Board, fearing a foreign shift in naval competition from the battleship to the air, was particularly interested in British efforts in naval aviation. Lieutenant Colonel Porte, of the Royal Flying Corps, was questioned vigorously in 1918 in order to ascertain whether the British were considering any radical employment of aircraft at sea. See the testimony of Porte in *General Board Hearings,* 18 June 1918.

[59]For the Morrow Board, see Archibald D. Turnbull and Clifford L. Lord, *History of United States Naval Aviation* (New Haven, Conn.: Yale University Press, 1949), 249–58.

[60]The Morrow Board Report was reprinted in *USNIP* 52(1926): 196–225.

[61]See Michael A. West, "Laying the Legislative Foundation: The House Naval Affairs Committee and the Construction of the Treaty Navy, 1926–1934" (Ph.D. diss., The Ohio State University, 1980), 44–47; and Turnbull and Lord, *Naval Aviation,* 257 and chap. 24.

[62]Admiral Samuel S. Robinson, commander-in-chief, U.S. Fleet, to Captain. Emory S. Land, (CC), USN, Bureau of Aeronautics, 17 May1926, Emory S. Land Papers, Manuscript Division, Library of Congress, Washington, D.C., Box 5.

[63]Captain Yates Stirling, USN, "The Place for Aviation in the Organization for War," *USNIP* 52 (1926): 1103–4.

[64]Captain Yates Stirling, USN, "Some Fundamentals of Sea Power," *USNIP* 51 (1925): 913–14. Stirling extended his gun metaphor to include the submarine, a projectile that plunges beneath the sea, but one, like the airplane, which must return to the surface; ibid., 915.

[65]Ibid., 917. Stirling's description of future aerial warfare typified the naval hierarchy's extension of its battleship worldview to this alternate technology: "(We may imagine] an air fleet . . . the great bombing planes and torpedo planes representing capital ships; scouting planes and spotting planes being the light cruisers and fighting planes the swift, agile destroyers of the air; fighting planes on each side concentrating to bring a superior force upon the enemy air fleet at a superior moment." See Stirling, "Aviation in Organization for War," 1105.

[66]Statement of Rear Admiral Williams, *Special Board Hearings,* 122.

[67]The first purpose-built aircraft carrier, *Ranger,* did not enter service until 1934. Early fleet exercises tended to pit *Lexington* against *Saratoga.* On the aviation lessons of the exercises, see Thomas Wildenberg, *Destined for Glory:*

Dive Bombing, Midway, and the Evolution of Carrier Airpower (Annapolis: Naval Institute Press, 1998), chap. 7.

[68]*Tactical Orders and Doctrine for the U.S. Fleet, 1941* quoted in Wildenberg, *Destined for Glory,* v.

[69]Rear Admiral M. M. Taylor, commander of the Control Force, *Special Board Hearings,* 263.

[70]Ibid. Other relevant articles include Hector C. Bywater, "The Battleship and Its Uses," *USNIP* 52 (1926): 407–25; Lieutenant Commander C. A. Pownall, USN, "The Airphobia of 1925," *USNIP* 52 (1926): 459–63; Lieutenant Commander O. C. Badger, USN, "History Repeats or The Application of Lessons of History on a National Problem of Today," *USNIP* 51 (1925): 707–21.

[71]For a contemporary account of the navy's Naval Aircraft Factory, see Lieutenant Commander S. J. Ziegler (CC), USN, "The Naval Aircraft Factory," *USNIP* 52 (1926): 83–94.

[72]Rear Admiral W. A. Moffett, USN, "Recent Technical Development of Naval Aviation," *USNIP* 57 (1931): 1182–83.

[73]Ibid., 1185. For the development of aviation technology during Moffett's tenure as chief of the Bureau of Aeronautics, see Trimble, *Admiral Moffett,* passim.

[74]Admiral W. T. Mayo, USN, Commander-in-Chief, U.S. Fleet, to General Board, 5 May 1919, a copy of which is contained in *General Board Hearings,* 660–71; quote on 660.

[75]Testimony of Rear Admiral Moffett, 30 September 1924, *Special Board Hearings.* At the time of his testimony, the navy had only one carrier, the converted collier *Langley;* the converted battlecruisers *Lexington* and *Saratoga* would not be ready until 1927. The effect that New Era efficiency exerted on the navy can be seen in the naval budgets from 1922 through 1932. During this period, the naval appropriations averaged $359 million per year and totaled almost $4 billion. The total naval appropriations for the dreadnought navy (1906 through 1916) was less (almost $2 billion), but on average, 27 percent of each year's appropriation went to naval expansion, that is, new ship construction and alterations to existing vessels, as opposed to an average of 15 percent ($54 million) per year during the New Era. Data drawn from West, "Laying the Legislative Foundation," table 3, 38.

[76]See, for example, Naval War College Staff Lectures: "The Employment of Aviation in Naval Warfare," serial 3429–487/9-9-37, September 1937; "Tactical Employment of the Fleet," 29 October 1937; and "The Employment of Submarines," 3 October 1938, in Record Group 14, Staff Presentations and Lectures, Naval Historical Collection, Naval War College, Newport, R.I.

[77]*New York Times,* 26 February 1931, reprinted in *USNIP* 57(1931): 538.

[78]Ibid. Also see Clark C. Reynolds, *The Fast Carriers: The Forging of an Air Navy* (Huntington, N.Y.: Robert E. Krieger, 1978), chap. 1, especially 14–21.

[79]Wildenberg, *Destined for Glory,* 156–57.

[80]Ibid., 156.
[81]Ibid.
[82]See ibid., chaps. 18 and 19; speed data on 193.
[83]Wildenberg places the initial squadron employment of the SBD-2 in December 1940 (ibid., 161). TBD squadron data from Roy A. Grossnick, *United States Naval Aviation, 1910–1945* (Washington, D.C.: Naval Historical Center, 1996), appendix 6, "Combat Aircraft Procured," 494.

CHAPTER THIRTEEN

The Amphibious Assault and How It Grew

Victor H. Krulak

FOCUS QUESTIONS

1. Why did the Marine Corps remain so uninterested in amphibious warfare until the 1920s?
2. What Marines were most instrumental to the Marine Corp's pursuit of amphibious capability between World War I and World War II? What common background did many of these men share, and how might it have influenced their beliefs about the missions the Corps should devote itself to?
3. Once the decision was made to pursue the amphibious mission, what significant obstacles were faced and how well did the Marines deal with them?
4. Considering the "Brute" Krulak was very involved in the development of amphibious doctrine and landing craft in this era, and later rose to be the Commanding General of Fleet Marine Force Pacific as a lieutenant general, how useful is his perspective in studying this subject? Are there any potential biases the reader should be on guard for?

The military world seems to be particularly prone to use cliche—thoughts and statements that do not bear the trial of proof. Classic among these is General Dwight D. Eisenhower's pronouncement in 1950 that "an amphibious landing is not a particularly difficult thing. . . . You put your men in boats and as long as you get well-trained crews to take the boats in, it is the simplest deployment in the world—the men can go nowhere else except the beach."[1] As if getting to the beach were the whole game instead of just the beginning. Another classic is General Omar Bradley's untimely rumination, "I am wondering whether we shall ever have another large-scale amphibious operation."[2] This only eleven months before the dramatic amphibious assault by the 1st Marine Division and 1st Marine Aircraft Wing at Inchon, Korea.

Also questionable is the frequently heard generalization that man has conducted amphibious attacks since the beginning of history. It is not altogether true. Man has indeed gone to war in ships, boats, or battle canoes since history began. He has undertaken innumerable expeditions overseas, using the oceans as a bridge to the enemy's homeland. From time to time, he has been able to put his forces ashore from the sea in the vicinity of the enemy's principal strength.

But a true amphibious assault against an opponent who has organized the beaches and sea approaches for defense with entrenched infantry and an array of mutually supporting arms is quite another thing. And if the enemy is on an island or a peninsula, where the attacker is limited in his choice of landing site and where the crisis is likely to occur near the beachline, then it is even more difficult. The techniques for bringing off such an undertaking are a relatively modern development, going back in concept to only the nineteenth century. Probably the earliest significant rationalization of this sort of amphibious assault was *Precis de l'Art de la Guerre* in 1838, by Antoine H. Jomini, who addressed many of the critical issues which still confront us. The *Precis has* to rank among the most visionary documents relating to amphibious war. Until the British landing at Gallipoli in 1915, the concept of an amphibious assault against determined resistance had little test, and then the British violated so many basic principles that the test was deceptive.

After Gallipoli, the amphibious assault, never taken too seriously, was largely discounted. Offshore mines, beach obstacles, heavy artillery in fortified emplacements, integrated air defense, aircraft for both observation and attack were all seen as favoring the defense—so much as to make such an assault "difficult, indeed almost impossible," according to British military historian B. H. Liddell Hart.

It is at this point that the Marine usually enters the historical scene. In truth, however, both before and after Gallipoli only a very few Marines were convinced of the feasibility of amphibious assault operations—or even interested in them. Ironically, there were visionary officers in the Navy who many years before Gallipoli—and before the Marines themselves—saw a future for the amphibious assault and, more important, identified that future with the Marine Corps. In 1861 Rear Admirals S. P. Lee and S. F. DuPont recommended that the Marines form expeditionary regiments to serve with the Union Navy in the seizure of Confederate coastal positions. The idea got nowhere, mainly because of failure by both the Navy and the Marines to grasp the wisdom of the proposal. Later, in 1896, Lieutenant Commander William F. Fullam, USN, with great vision, proposed that the Corps be organized in six battalions for expeditionary duty in support of the fleet. However, until the 1920s, there was no real institutional dedication in the Corps to the idea of an assault landing attack against organized defenses.

Probably a minority of Marines were interested in seeing the Corps involved in the establishment and defense of naval base facilities—overseas—a wholly defensive mission related to the needs of the U.S. Fleet. Many more, whose professional life had been consecrated primarily to expeditionary duty in the colonial infantry role—Haiti, China, Santo Domingo, Nicaragua—remained so oriented. Others who were convinced, before the Great War, that the Corps' future lay primarily in service aboard ship and at naval stations, favored expanding that important relationship with the Navy.

Only a few, a very few, visionaries were willing to attack the formidable conceptual, tactical and material problems associated with the modern amphibious assault landing: how to get heavy equipment and weapons ashore through surf and across reefs; how to exercise command authority during the sensitive transition period; how to communicate effectively with ships and aircraft; how to cope with mines and beach obstacles; how to provide accurate, timely, and concentrated fire support for the assault forces; how to ensure that essential supplies were delivered ashore where and when needed; how to manage the evacuation of casualties to seaward; and how to persuade the Navy to share its very limited resources in solving these problems. There was a hard core of Marines who saw a future, despite the problems, for amphibious assault. They were resolute men, true pioneers. By no means military intellectuals in the image of Sun Tzu, Frederick the Great, Jomini, or Mahan, they were nevertheless capable of seeing the close relationship between the total exercise of sea power and the narrow issue of seizing a lodgment on a hostile shore against sophisticated opposition.

Among these was John A. Lejeune, a compassionate gentleman, fearless fighter, skilled diplomat, and sensitive military thinker. As early as 1900, Lejeune, with a few other Marines and some visionary Navy colleagues, perceived the necessity of securing base facilities in the vast Pacific. He had been disappointed with the inability of Commandants Heywood (1891–1903) and Elliott (1903–10) to grasp the relationship between the global needs of the Navy and the creation and defense of overseas naval bases. Their view was that the century-old Marine Corps role of providing ships' guards and security for naval stations should still be foremost, that to commit Marine resources to advanced base force duty was an imprudent diffusion of effort. In other words, they were the proponents of a retrospective philosophy that went back a hundred years. Lejeune, in contrast, saw the Navy's need for advanced bases for coal and other logistical purposes as a cardinal factor in preparing to face the challenge of an imperialist Japan, and he was determined to get the Marines involved. He realized further that someday, somebody might have the unenviable task of capturing those logistic bases from a well-prepared enemy, and defending them, once captured. What would be a more logical organization to do the job than the Marines, with their traditional maritime orientation?

Lejeune may not have been the first to say it, but nobody of that era said it any better. With the prescience of a true pioneer, he declared, in a 1915 lecture at the Naval War College, that the ability not just to defend but to seize those bases was a logical and critical Marine function in light of the Navy's growing strategic responsibilities. He saw the Corps as

> the first to set foot on hostile soil in order to seize, fortify and hold . . . a base.

Later, after he became commandant, he stated it affirmatively and clearly,

> the maintenance, equipping and training of its expeditionary force so that it will be in instant readiness to support the Fleet in time of war, I deem to be . . . the most important Marine Corps duty in time of peace.[3]

Finally, in 1927, he procured a significant inclusion in the governing document entitled *Joint Action, Army-Navy:*

> Marines, because of their constant association with Navy units, will be given special preparation in the conduct of landing operations.

Specifically, they should be responsible for

> land operations in support of the Fleet for the initial seizure and defense of advanced bases and for such limited auxiliary land operations as are essential to prosecution of a naval campaign.[4]

Lejeune's understanding of the Navy's needs, which stemmed largely from his years at Annapolis and his continuing friendship with many prominent Navy officers, was of great value to the Corps. His views were mirrored by another Annapolis graduate, George Barnett, who preceded Lejeune as Commandant. Their views were shared by another Annapolis man, John H. Russell (later also to become commandant).

Russell, Annapolis, '92, may well have exerted greater influence in rationalizing and regularizing the amphibious assault than any other single individual in the Corps. In 1910 he made the illuminating observation that when the fleet was operating at a distance from permanent bases it should carry with it "a sufficient force and material for seizing and defending" an advanced base in the theater of operations."[5]

Later in 1916, he made, in the first edition of the *Marine Corps Gazette,* an eloquent—and almost heretical—case for both the base defense and amphibious assault tasks as Marine Corps missions. Subsequently, as assistant commandant, he persuaded Commandant Fuller and Navy leaders in Washington to accept as official his view that the amphibious assault function should be primary Marine Corps business and to adopt his conceptual creation, the Fleet Marine Force, as a Type Command of the Naval Operating Forces.

These developments, which took place over a quarter of a century, were the results of unusual and brave actions. Among those few who both understood and believed in them was one of the most extraordinary men ever to appear in a Corps that has always been generously populated with unusual personalities.

Earl H. Ellis became a Marine private in 1900 after graduating from high school. He was bright—bright enough to be commissioned within a year after his enlistment—and his unusual character surfaced almost at once. Unmarried, he quickly became devoted to the Corps and earned the reputation for studying and working long hours without rest in the Corps's behalf. As early as 1912, still a lieutenant, he began a messianic exploration of the strategic confrontation between the United States and Japan, with whom he was convinced we would eventually go to war. He predicted that the Japanese would initiate hostilities and that the United States would have to fight its way back across the Pacific in a series of hard amphibious assaults to capture the necessary bases. In some cases, the amphibious attacks of 1942–45 took place exactly as he had presaged.

Ellis's brilliance as a planner was widely recognized, both in the Navy and in the Marines. During the First World War, where he served in France as a staff officer, and the five years thereafter, he inspired great confidence on the part of his superiors despite what was already perceived to be a gravely flawed personality. He was moody, often contentious, and impatient with slow thinkers. He had a firecracker temper. He sometimes disappeared for days without explanation. And he drank. He drank a great deal—more and more as years passed. His alcoholism caused him to move in and out of hospitals continually, usually receiving such euphemistic diagnoses as "nephritis," "neurasthenia," "psychasthenia," and "exhaustion." His superiors, including the ascetic General Lejeune, always protected him because of his sheer ability and his total loyalty to the Corps. The bottle finally killed him at Koror, in the Palaus in 1923, during a secret reconnaissance of Micronesia, the area where he was convinced critical battles would be fought in the war with Japan. What he learned in his extensive exploration of the southern islands was not that the Japanese had fortified the area, as was suspected, but that they had done very little—at that time—in the way of fortification, and it was their weakness they were striving to keep secret, not evidences of strength.*

Ellis left behind a precious legacy in the form of an extraordinary thirty-thousand-word study entitled *Advanced Base Operations in Micronesia.*[6] Written in 1920–21, and based on lectures he had prepared in 1916, it was less a true study than a portrait of the future—the fruit of an incredible prescience. It turned out to be an uncannily accurate forecast of things to come. Outlining the step-by-step drive westward across the Pacific to meet the need, as he saw

*Ellis is memorialized in Ellis Hall, the instructional auditorium at the Marine Command and Staff College in Quantico, Virginia.

it, for "bases to support the Fleet, both during its projection and afterward," he traced the route through the Marshall and Caroline Islands much as it actually happened. The Ellis study was in fact the framework for the American strategy for a Pacific war, adopted by the Joint Board of the Army and Navy in 1924 as the "Orange Plan."

Even so, Ellis's essay went far beyond strategy. He addressed the full range of tactical, technical, and practical problems that would ultimately confront our forces as they drove across the Pacific from island to island. He warned of the difficulties that would be created by reefs and manmade obstacles. He foresaw the coordinated use of naval gunfire and air support; the technique of combat unit loading of equipment and supplies in specially designed transport ships; the logistical organization of landing beaches; the use of underwater demolition teams ("frogmen"); the tactical use of smoke and darkness; and the utility of amphibious reconnaissance, raids, and feints. In short, Ellis not only contributed to the philosophical "what" of the Marines' amphibious assault future, he clearly identified the more troublesome "how," opening the way for others to address the details.

Contemporary with Ellis, and one of the few Marines who foresaw the future of amphibious warfare was Dion Williams, an 1891 Naval Academy graduate who had been thinking about the amphibious problem since the turn of the century. Warm, engaging, and proud, he had a respectful relationship with the Navy that flourished when he served on the USS *Baltimore* under Admiral George Dewey at Manila Bay. Williams is credited with persuading Dewey, in 1907, to assert before the Congress that "a force of 5,000 Marines with the Fleet" would have prevented the Philippine insurrection that ensued following the Spanish defeat. Williams's concept of such a "force" was probably the first tiny beginning of the doctrinal sequence that became the "Base Defense Force," the "Expeditionary Force," and, finally, the "Fleet Marine Force."

By the 1920s Williams had become convinced that the assault function, as described by Russell, Ellis, and Lejeune was indeed the Marines' future role. Upon taking over command of the 4th Marine Brigade of the Marine Corps Expeditionary Force at the Quantico Marine Base in 1923, he aimed to prepare it to function as an assault landing force. This was at no small hazard to his own professional career. He had found that, while officially preparing for colonial infantry employment in the manner of Santo Domingo, Nicaragua, or Haiti, the unit was actually training in World War I infantry tactics, as well as reenacting Civil War battles on the nearby Virginia battlefields. This last project was especially valued by the Quantico Base commander, Major General Smedley D. Butler, because he believed its publicity value enhanced his chances of being named commandant.*

*He invited President Harding to a reenactment of the Battle of Chancellorsville in the spring of 1921. The president spent the night under canvas with the troops, the first president to do so since Lincoln.

As described by retired General Merrill B. Twining,† Williams proceeded to lecture his troops instead on the history of amphibious warfare and to exercise them in practice landings on the Potomac River. It is ironic that Williams, a vocal exponent of the landing attack, was charged, in the Fleet Exercise of 1923–24, with installing and commanding the defense of the island of Culebra in the West Indies, as a naval base. The bulk of the brigade he had trained was the assault landing force and, using the techniques he had taught them, made landings against the defense force on Culebra.

The commander of the landing force was Eli Kelley Cole, an 1887 Annapolis graduate. Although studious and dedicated, he was not highly renowned in the Corps because of an imperious, irascible personality and a lackluster World War I record.* Convinced that Russell's plea for a Marine Corps amphibious mission was valid, Cole had become intensely interested in Gallipoli—what went wrong there, and why. With the assistance of another thoughtful Marine officer, Robert Henry Dunlap, he developed a series of lectures propounding the idea that Gallipoli need not have been a disaster had it been done right.

That view, in itself, is interesting but not remarkable. What is remarkable is what Cole did with his research. He invited, but did not order, his officers to attend his Gallipoli lectures. He delivered the talks in the Post Chapel at Quantico, during the noon hour so that those leaders who still had little use for amphibious operations—led mainly by the base commander, Smedley Butler—could not criticize him for diverting his officers from their regular duties for frivolous purposes. Yet that was exactly the criticism leveled against him, giving further evidence of the deep schisms that existed among the Lejeune/Russell school of amphibious thought and those who still held, with former commandants Heywood and Elliott, that the Marines' future lay in ships' detachments and still others like Butler, who wanted an independent Marine Corps of colonial infantry, unfettered by the Navy.

Undismayed by the opposition, Cole proceeded to take his landing force, schooled under Dion Williams, into the 1924 Fleet exercises in Panama and the Caribbean. Cole's forces (some 1,781 men) landed against Williams' defenders (about 1,600 men) at Culebra. Tiny though the exercise now appears, it was accurately described by Williams as being of "a scale of magnitude never before undertaken by our country in peacetime."[7]

The maneuver was awkward to say the least. Ships were improperly

†General Twining's extensive recollections of this period contributed much to my portraits of Williams, Ellis. Generals Cole and l Lejeune. and Colonel E, B. Miller.

*He spent the bulk of the war in Haiti and Parris Island. South Carolina, arriving in France only six weeks before the armistice, His sole World War I decoration was "for his cordial cooperation with and support of the Provisional Government of Haiti and efficient efforts for improvement of the educational and social conditions of the Haitian people," (From official records. Headquarters. Marine Corps,)

loaded. Urgently needed material was inaccessibly stowed under low priority cargo. Loading of boats—such few inadequate craft as the Fleet was able to produce—was confused and badly planned. Navy personnel were uninformed and poorly trained. Boats were landed on the wrong beaches at the wrong time and in the wrong order. There was not enough naval gunfire or air support and it was directed at the wrong targets.

Despite the manifold frustrations, Cole's thoughtful and optimistic report to the commandant put the array of shortcomings into perspective and made sensitive, positive, and specific recommendations for correcting the deficiencies. After pleading for more specialized equipment, boats primarily, and for the codification of an amphibious doctrine in official policy, he ended his report with the poignant observation, "I suppose we must convince the Navy."

Lamentably, there was little progress in the next eight years. The Corps was stretched thin in order to meet its heavy expeditionary obligations in Nicaragua and China. However much they may have desired otherwise, both the Navy and the Marine proponents of amphibious warfare were denied the resources to pursue the "how" of the specialty.

In 1933, General Douglas MacArthur, who was chief of staff of the Army and openly antagonistic to the Marine Corps on the ground that the Corps constituted an economic affront to the Army, proposed to the president and to several members of the Congress that the Marines—air and ground, people and functions—be transferred to the Army. Failing in that, MacArthur proposed that at least the bulk of the Corps be transferred to the Army, leaving Marines with only base defense and seagoing detachment functions.

The substantial influence wielded by MacArthur impressed Commandant Ben H. Fuller (1930–34) with the gravity of the threat, and gave his assistant, General Russell, the opportunity he sought to drive the amphibious subject to the surface. Russell had help from wise friends on the Navy General Board who, for the first time, stated officially that the Marines' primary job should be "the seizure and defense of advanced bases." With this Navy declaration, he persuaded the commandant that a formalized, written body of amphibious doctrine was needed. It should be prepared by the Marines themselves, it should be in great detail, and should exhibit that they possessed a unique capability not shared by anybody, particularly not by the Army.

Some work had already been done on the subject as early as 1931. Russell's idea was to take these preliminary fragments, mass the total talent of the Marine Corps Schools in Quantico, Virginia*—staff and students alike—and direct them to produce, in a single volume, a full exposure of everything involved in the amphibious assault that in any way affected the landing force. Russell's proposal was carried out. Marine Corps Schools classes were halted

*In 1933 the Schools comprised a Field Officers' School for officers in the rank of major and lieutenant colonel, some fifteen students, and a Company Officers' School. thirty students, in the rank of first lieutenant and captain. The staff aggregated about thirty-five officers.

and the total resources of the institution were directed toward developing the formal doctrine.

In charge of the project was Brigadier General James C. Breckinridge, commandant of the Marines' officers' school system. But the driving force was Colonel Ellis Bell Miller, one more of the family of unusual Marine Corps personalities.

Commissioned in 1903, with service in Panama, Mexico, China, and the Philippines, Miller was intelligent, intellectual, perceptive, diligent, and thoroughly professional, with all of the essential qualifications for the pioneering job. Unfortunately, he had a few more characteristics that were not so essential. He was demanding, intolerant of any dissent, and impatient with those who could not maintain his pace. These traits, which may have kept him from advancing beyond the rank of colonel, did not keep him from producing a milestone document in the amphibious field.

The Marine officers were first thoroughly oriented on the errors of Gallipoli and given what little information there was on assault landing operations. Then each one was obliged to set down his own thoughts concerning the sequence of events in an amphibious attack, from preembarkation through completion of the landing assault. The individual submissions were organized into topical categories by an intermediate committee and further reviewed by a steering committee, headed by Miller, which, in turn, created a chapter outline for the book. After a critical review by a group of Fleet Marine Force officers, the chapter assignments were farmed out to writing committees which based the content on the meager practical experience available and, probably more so, on their own reasoning and convictions.

Miller drove the group with apostolic fervor. He set deadlines and was merciless in his criticism. When it was done—the writing took seven months—he had a respectable product. He called it *Tentative Manual for Landing Operations, 1934*. It was not too well written, it was not handsomely printed, and it was bound with shoestring but it was there, some 127,000 words of it—more hard, doctrinal pronouncement on the seizure of an objective by amphibious assault than had ever been assembled in one place in all of history. For the first time the issues of air and naval gunfire support were addressed in detail. Likewise principles of transport loading, debarkation procedures, guidance for the ship-to-shore movement and the management of logistics at the beachline were treated in what still must be regarded as great detail.

Miller was not content with the *Tentative Manual*, but it was seized enthusiastically by the Fleet Marine Force for use in training, and it was adopted immediately as a tentative text in the Marine Corps Schools for its 1934–35 term. Furthermore, it was published by the Navy Department as the *Manual for Naval Overseas Operations*.

The Corps set immediately to work to revise, update, and perfect the *Manual*. Over the next two years a series of boards at Quantico prepared revisions, notably a group headed by Lieutenant Colonel Charles D. Barrett, whose scholarly efforts and patient attention to detail resulted in a stronger and much more articulate document.

The *Tentative Manual* was ground-breaking of the purest sort, and it excited enthusiasm in the Navy, which adopted it with minor alterations in 1938 as Fleet Training Publication No. 167, *Landing Operations Doctrine, U.S. Navy*." Three years later, the Army, whose interest in amphibious operations had theretofore been minimal, copied the *Manual,* lock, stock, and barrel, and published it as *Field Manual 31–5*. The *Manual* guided the bulk of amphibious training in the immediate pre–World War II period. More important, it governed every amphibious operation during that war. And it persists today, in its essential parts, as the U.S. joint directive for amphibious operations.

It remained for the Navy and Marines, using their new doctrine, to exercise the practical details of the amphibious specialty and, not just incidentally, to provide training for those Army units which were to take part in the first Army amphibious operations of World War II. In Fleet Landing Exercises 3, 4, and 5, from 1936 to 1939, the *Tentative Manual*—not yet officially binding on the Navy—was nonetheless a powerful influence on Navy–Marine training, in the Caribbean and in Southern California.

The most significant prewar rehearsals, however, took place in 1940 and 1941 after Fleet Training Publication No. 167 had become an official Navy document. It was fortuitous that the Marines in those exercises were led by a dynamic, no-nonsense, war-oriented man, Brigadier General Holland M. Smith.

Commissioned in 1905 after graduation from Auburn and the University of Alabama Law School, Smith had followed the then-standard Marine pattern—service in the Philippines (where, incidentally, he led a company in the regiment commanded by Colonel Eli Kelley Cole), Nicaragua, Panama, China, Santo Domingo, and Cuba. Staff assignments in France in World War I were followed by a course at the Naval War College where, for the first time, the vigorous, straight-talking temperament appeared that later earned him the sobriquet "Howling Mad." He advanced his views regarding the importance of amphibious assault operations—and particularly the need for heavy naval gunfire and air support—with such logic and style as to acquire a reputation as a thinker and an eloquent speaker. Later, at the Field Officers' course at the Quantico Marine Corps Schools, he told his superiors that their curriculum was retrospective and gave them hard examples to prove his point. His renown as an outspoken pioneer was further burnished by his letters in 1935 and 1936 to Commandant Russell, whom he admired, complaining that since war with Japan was clearly approaching, too little was being done in the Marines' amphibious training to meet the inevitable challenge.

Later, in 1939, when given the responsibility for leading and training the 1st Marine Brigade, the deep resolution in Smith's character was plainly visible. While he had the appearance of a country schoolmaster—steel-rimmed glasses, thinning hair, and a slightly spreading waistline—and while he was tender and compassionate with those around him, Smith was fierce in his impatient determination that the Marines whose training was entrusted to him should want for nothing in preparation for the war he was sure was coming. Nor was he restrained in voicing his dissatisfaction with those whom he saw as deficient or derelict. I was on his staff at the time and more than once heard him quote the Chinese philosopher T'sao T'sao, "War cannot be run according to the rules of etiquette."

He took the Marines of the East Coast Fleet Marine Force—about three thousand of them, air and ground—to the Caribbean in the autumn of 1940 and drove them mercilessly in landing exercises at Culebra, grinding the rough edges off their performance. He exposed equipment and supply shortages—both in the Marines and the Navy—and was bitterly eloquent in underscoring the adverse impact on his force's combat capability resulting from these shortages. He made few friends in the Navy with his critical assessment that the landing craft and troop transport available for the 1940 exercises were wholly inadequate. The troops were carried in the demilitarized battleship *Wyoming*, a supply ship and a converted World War I destroyer and, except for a dozen experimental landing craft, they were transported ashore in standard ships' boats. The Marine Corps, it was plain, was just as impoverished as the Navy. Smith railed at his Marine superiors for widespread deficiencies—trucks, tanks, aircraft, air-ground communications, anti-aircraft weapons, ammunition, and combat uniforms. He argued that the Marine who was going to do the fighting deserved the best of everything, and he constantly called attention to the shortages, reminding us that in shortest supply of all was time.

Despite the inadequacies, everyone learned. And the next spring he did it again, this time with a much larger force—an understrength Marine Division and about half of an Army Division.* The Navy, for its part, had made much progress in a year, being able to provide four converted merchantmen as troop transports and a few more acceptable landing boats, but the shortage of floating equipment and its limited quality was still so acute as to move Smith to new heights of rhetoric in behalf of the troops who were destined to do the fighting. When he heard that the crew of the converted transport USS *Harry Lee* was bathing in fresh water while the embarked Marines were using salt water, he sent me aboard the ship to determine whether the rumor were true. "If it is," he said, "I want you to go see the commanding officer. Tell him I said we are all going to the same war and we had all better bathe in the same kind of water—fresh or salt."

The rumor turned out to be true and I made the call as directed, albeit uncomfortably as I was still only a captain. The commanding officer gave my speech a frigid reception. By the time I returned to the flagship, however, General Smith had received a message from the *Harry Lee*'s commander, "Everyone will bathe in fresh water as long as it lasts."

*Army elements included were from the 1st Infantry Division of Ft. Devens, Mass., commanded by Major General James Cubbison. The division brought its share of characters mto the Marine environment, including Brigadier General James G. Ord, who attended our first planning conference in a self-designed uniform, including cuffed trousers, spats, a cane, and pince nez.

Smith complained to his immediate superior, Fleet Commander Admiral E. J. King, both officially and privately about the state of equipment in the fleet. King was a serious man, not given to humor. He did not take kindly to criticism from anybody and, on the day Smith sent him his written bill of particulars, the general told me (at that time I was his aide) that he expected to be fired for his outspoken complaints. As it turned out, King reacted in exactly the opposite manner, exhibiting respect and trust in Smith because of his candor and his no-frills approach to his job.* His report to the chief of naval operations on the 1940–1941 winter exercises borrowed heavily from Smith's complaints. The report laid out the Navy's material problems in cold detail and concluded with the assertion

> . . . it cannot be too strongly emphasized that until this floating equipment is placed in the hands of the Fleet and brought to a suitable state of combat efficiency, *the mobility and tactical efficiency of Marine troupe will remain vitally curtailed.*[8]

Admiral King underscored the entire passage with his own pencil, double underscoring the final section on mobility and tactical efficiency.

Smith took no comfort in King's supportive letter. His simple comment to several of us on the staff was: "I hope to God it isn't too late."

Taking his force back to the United States, Smith continued to drive them unceasingly. He tasked them with perfecting the techniques of their trade, developing and codifying procedures for coordination of Marine air and ground operations, training in naval gunfire support,† and conducting schools in embarkation and transport loading. I organized the first such school, at Smith's headquarters in Quantico. Subsequent courses were conducted under Captain S. C. Tracy, USMCR, giving both Marine and Army students a complete package of all the essential embarkation and loading documents—practical standardization at the operating level for the first time.

Smith required us to commit to directive form everything involved with the landing assault, from beginning to end, to the extent that one member of the staff, Marine Major P. P. Schrider, said, "Instead of 'H. M.' his initials ought to be 'S. O. P.' (Standing Operating Procedure)."

Smith's final major effort to make his troops ready for amphibious war took place at New River, North Carolina, in August 1941. By contemporary

*King's confidence in Smith was transferred to the Marines at large. I was present at a July 1942 Navy discussion of the pros and cons of the shoestring operation at Guadalcanal and was proud to hear King concur in the enterprise at least in part because, as he put it, "Holland Smith says it will work."

†At this time Major Donald M. Weller (mentioned in the introduction to this Part) was also on General Smith's staff. The general gave him free rein in all of his efforts to formalize and codify the naval gunfire field. It must be said that Weller's sincere and engaging personality contributed greatly to his success in dealing with the Navy gunnery people upon whom we ultimately depended.

standards the exercise was large—some seventeen thousand men—the better part of two peace-strength divisions—one Marine and one Army*—a Marine Aircraft Group, some eighteen assorted transport vessels, and a sprinkling of modern landing craft. It was more complex than anything that had gone before, involving night landings, parachute operations, and heavy emphasis on close air support and on landing large quantities of equipment and supplies across the beaches.

Smith's report was detailed and direct. Sparing in praise, it underscored a multitude of shortcomings and concluded with some thirty-eight major recommendations regarding the "how" of the amphibious assault. We were finally beginning to reach bone marrow.

Even so, Smith, in his characteristic fashion, underscored "the futility of conducting a forced landing against a well-conducted defense by first-class troops" until the attacking force was not only equipped with the best in weaponry but thoroughly trained as well.[9] Smith was correct. Much did, indeed, still need to be done before we could feel fully ready for the test soon to come. In his impatience to see that state of readiness achieved, however, Smith—and those around him, too—tended to forget the long, tortuous, obstacle-strewn road the early apostles of amphibious warfare had trod. Others, in retrospect, recognized the magnitude of their innovative triumph. J. F. C. Fuller, a respected British military scholar, described the amphibious assault as perfected and practiced by the U.S. Marines as "in all probability . . . the most far reaching tactical innovation of the war."[10]

A few months after the final Smith-generated exercise in 1941, as the first Marines were wading ashore at Guadalcanal and Tulagi and as the first soldiers touched the North African beaches, the spirits of the Marine pioneers who made it all happen hovered over them. The dreams of Williams, Ellis, Russell, and other visionaries had become a reality—a major part of the strategy for World War II, a principal ingredient in the design for victory.

*The Army learned a lot under Smith's leadership after their decades of uninterest in anything related to amphibious operations. Between May 1941 and July 1942 Smith's headquarters conducted thirteen amphibious training exercises for Army troops, a total of 31,900 men. It was ironic, in this regard, to hear General Jacob Devers tell the Senate Military Affairs Committee in 1945 that "the Army received no amphibious training worthy of the name prior to World War II due to a lack of cooperation."

CHAPTER FOURTEEN

From Gallipoli to Guadalcanal

Gunther E. Rothenberg

FOCUS QUESTIONS

1. What were some of the problems that the Navy and Marine Corps addressed in perfecting its amphibious doctrine during the interwar period?
2. Did the U.S. have an "effective" amphibious doctrine at the outbreak of the war? How did it change based on combat operations during World War II?
3. How did the evolution of amphibious warfare intermesh with U.S. strategic war planning?

The end of World War One brought a speedy return of the United States to its traditional policy of political isolation and military and naval neglect. By the 1930s the army had become that of a third-rate power; the air corps had plans, but not planes, and even the U.S. Navy, which in the years 1916 to 1920 had been projected as a fleet "second to none," was in steep decline. Moreover, it was a poorly balanced fleet. "American naval policy," one writer observed, "has been guided by considerations of Atlantic and Caribbean strategy . . . very little attempt has been made [to prepare for] war in the Pacific."[1]

And yet, after 1918, the Pacific was the main area of strategic concern. The United States expected no involvement in Europe and expected only minor operations in the Caribbean, but conflicts with Japan were becoming a preoccupation with both popular writers and professional planners.[2] From the early

1920s army and navy planners in Washington prepared a series of war plans, each coded with a specific color, but only the Orange War Plan, war against Japan, was given serious consideration. After considerable debate, the navy, which had hoped to carry out early offensive operations in the western Pacific, accepted the army's contention that there were no forces available to hold the indispensable bases. The final compromise plan, therefore, envisaged a slow reconquest of the western Pacific by way of the Marshall and Gilbert islands.[3]

The necessity to project American sea power across six thousand miles of ocean made it imperative to seize, occupy, and defend advance bases. The disaster of the Gallipoli enterprise in 1915, however, had made amphibious operations against a defended shore anathema to most military and naval officers. The history of the Gallipoli debacle had become a textbook example and had convinced most staff planners that any daylight assault against a defended shore had become impossible.[4] The U.S. Marine Corps, however, realized that here was an opportunity to carve out a new and larger role for itself. From 1921 on the corps devoted itself to developing a "new body of amphibious doctrine that was to lead to one of the most far-reaching tactical innovations of the Second World War."[5]

The marine efforts were spurred by a reocurrence of intraservice rivalry: the fear that the corps might be reduced to a mere naval police force or that it might be eliminated altogether. As early as the 1880s naval officers had suggested substituting trained sailors for marines.[6] This threat, to be sure, had been defeated. In 1894 Congress assigned to the Marine Corps the mission of providing troops that could establish and defend outlying bases. By 1914 the corps had carried out this mission in Cuba, and had also fought in China, the Philippines, and in a number of small expeditions in the Caribbean. In 1913 the corps activated a permanent Advance Base Force of two regiments, one for fixed, the other for mobile, base defense. At the same time it began an elaborate doctrine for the employment of this force, the theory, if not yet the practice, of "complete tactical responsibility with a unified command." This concept struck a balance between the loose committee system, the combined operations doctrine, used by the British at Gallipoli, where command responsibility was divided between General Hamilton and Admiral de Robeck, and the army-centered marine forces then evolving in Germany and Japan. Progress, in any case, was interrupted by America's entry into World War One. The Marine Corps expanded from some ten thousand to seventy-three thousand men, but most of its strength was employed as line infantry in France, though the Advance Base Force was kept intact at full strength. From 1920 on it was based at Quantico, Virginia, and in 1921 it was redesignated the Marine Corps Expeditionary Force.[7]

Nonetheless, prior to 1921 the Marine Corps was preparing itself for the *defense* of advance bases and *not for offensive landing operations.* No serious thought was given to mounting large-scale attacks against heavily defended shores. In fact, during the early stages of the Orange Plan, naval officers once again advocated that the seizure of the necessary advance bases be accomplished by naval, and not by marine landing forces. In 1921, however, a marine officer, Major Earl H. Ellis, submitted to Major General John A. Lejeune, commandant of the Marine Corps, a set of amphibious plans, which anticipated the problems of a future Pacific war. In these plans Ellis recommended the seizure of a number of fleet bases which would require assault across well-defended beaches in daylight. He also predicted with astonishing accuracy the manpower, training, and equipment required to carry out these operations.[8] Ellis's views gained the immediate support of the commandant and other marine officers. At a critical point in its fortunes, the Marine Corps had found a new mission and from now on, except when diverted to other duties, it concentrated on developing the theory and practice of amphibious assault.

In 1922 and 1924 the corps tested some of the new doctrines in the Panama Canal Zone and at Culebra, an island in the Caribbean. The exercise at Culebra was an ambitious affair and in addition to standard landing operations and tactical beachhead problems, the marines experimented with pontoon bridging, improvised docks, and even an amphibious tractor model.[9]

Although the marines were diverted to duty in China the following year, and thereafter were kept busy with a number of small expeditions in the Caribbean, the major concepts and the preoccupation with what the corps now conceived as its main mission, were kept alive, though little active work could be done. In 1925, following exercises in the Hawaiian Islands, the Joint Board of the Army and Navy, a body in existence since 1903 to examine common problems, convinced officers of both services that the British amphibious doctrine, which continued to rely on command by committee, would not fit into projected operations against Japan.[10] Instead, the basic marine concepts, especially the doctrine of complete tactical control within a unified command, were accepted. In 1927, convinced by experience as well as by the efforts of Ellis, Lejeune, and other marine officers, the Joint Board recommended that the corps be given special training in the conduct of landing operations, thus establishing the amphibious assault role of the marines as national military policy.[11]

Even so, only after tensions had relaxed in China and in the Caribbean in 1930–31 was the corps able to begin working out the actual details of this new role.[12] In 1933 already, the secretary of the navy had implemented the Joint Board's 1927 recommendation and replaced the old expeditionary force with a Fleet Marine Force operating as an integral part of the fleet. Cooperative efforts by the Marine Corps Schools, Marine Corps Headquarters, and the Naval War College to analyze and study the lessons of Gallipoli began to bear fruit. The main burden was carried by the Marine Corps Schools, where a committee, the Landing Operations Text Board, headed by Major Charles D. Barrett, USMC, completed in 1934 the text for the *Tentative Landing Operations Manual,* published the following year. A modified version of the *Manual,* adopted by the U.S. Navy in 1938 and extensively revised in 1941 and 1942, and also adopted by the U.S. Army in 1941, became a permanent part of U.S. military doctrine during World War Two.[13]

The *Tentative Manual* outlined six major operations as being essential: (1) command relationships; (2) naval gunfire support; (3) aerial support; (4) ship-to-shore movement; (5) securing the beachhead; and (6) logistics. The command doctrine, of course, was cardinal. As used in the manual the term *command relationships* covered both organization and command. An amphibious operation was to be conducted by a naval attack force commanded by a naval flag officer. This task force was to have two main components: the landing force, composed of elements of the Fleet Marine Force, and the naval support force which would include fire support, air, transport and screening groups. The landing force commander and the commanders of each naval group were responsible directly to the commander of the attack force. The principal shortcoming of this doctrine was that it did not define when the assault phase of the landing ended and at what point the landing force commander should become free to conduct operations ashore as he saw fit, tactically independent of the naval attack force commander. During the first U.S. landing of the war, Guadalcanal in August 1942, the *Tentative Manual* was followed precisely. As a result, as late as October the landing force commander was still under the control of the attack force commander, though the latter was usually far away. Through the efforts of General Thomas Holcomb, commandant of the Marine Corps, changes were made.[14] In future amphibious operations the landing force commander assumed tactical control of his troops ashore and reported to the next higher echelon, that is, the area commander, as soon as his headquarters were established and operational.

In regard to naval gunfire support, the basic questions were the feasibility of using naval guns as artillery support and shore fire control. Naval guns with their high velocity and flat trajectory had undesirable characteristics when used against land targets. Though this problem was solved at least partially in subsequent exercises that demonstrated the capabilities of naval guns for counterbattery and reverse slope fire, there was criticism as early as the 1937 exercise that naval planners overrated the effectiveness of naval fire and that the softening-up period was too brief to reduce enemy emplacements. This criticism was repeated time and time again by Marine Corps officers during World War Two.[15]

The second critical problem of naval gunfire support was shore fire control, depending on better communications, inexperience of naval gunfire spotters assigned to the shore party, and lack of training for naval gunfire liaison officers. The first, primarily technical, proved minor; the second was resolved by having marine officers act as spotters; the third took more time, and it was not until July 1941 that twelve ensigns completed the first course in naval gunfire support.[16]

The development of close air support was even more difficult. As with gunfire support, the Marine Corps wanted longer periods of preassault bombardment, closer liaison, and more immediate air response. They claimed, especially after Guadalcanal, that the most effective close air support given to their troops was by Marine Corps aviators. At this time, however, marine pilots were not trained for carrier operations and the maintenance of fast and dependable ground-air communications also proved difficult. As a result, really close support for the infantry elements of the landing force did not materialize until late in the war.

Ship-to-shore movement remained another critical area because, until 1939, lack of funds forced the marines to rely upon the underpowered standard V-bottomed ships' boats. Moreover, these boats could not be beached high enough, nor could they back off the beach under their own power. In 1936 Andrew Higgins had designed a shallow draft boat which beached easily and retracted from the beach under its own power. Various versions of his boats, as well as craft developed by the Bureau of Ships, were tested in 1939 and 1940. In the end the Higgins model won out and became the prototype of small landing craft. At the same time, tracked amphibious vehicles (LVTs) were developed and tested by the corps.[17] Until late 1940, however, both the navy and the marines totally neglected the development of landing ships, that is ships capable of crossing a large part of the sea under their own power. This need, however, had been perceived by the British during the Dunkirk evacuation and by 1941 plans and prototypes for copying were available, though not in service.

For securing the beachhead the 1934 *Tentative Manual* recognized that there existed a critical period between full reliance on naval artillery and the employment of the landing force guns. This, in part, was resolved by better communications and by giving special attention to the complex problem of organizing the shallow supply area behind the front line. The *Tentative Manual* prescribed both a beach and a shore party. The beach party was to be commanded by a naval officer, the beachmaster, who controlled both the unloading of supplies and boat movement; the shore party was to see to the movement of supplies and equipment to the front line. Although both parties were to cooperate, the system was unwieldy: there were just not enough men available to handle supplies, and commanders were reluctant to withdraw manpower from the fighting units. In 1941 Major General Holland M. Smith, USMC, recommended that the two parties be combined, with a naval beachmaster as second in command to the shore party commander, and that special labor units be provided for the unloading.[18] These recommendations were adopted and written into the regulations in 1942, too late, however, to be implemented in time for the Guadalcanal landings where "crated equipment, boxed supplies, and drums of gasoline piled up alarmingly," and no clear lines of responsibility existed.[19]

Finally, there was the overall logistical problem of an amphibious landing operation, specifically how to ship the troops and how to load their equipment and supplies. In the first place the navy did not have the right type of transporters available; the troops were loaded on any ship available. During the 1937 exercises the navy even used battleships to carry the landing force. At the same time, the constantly varying ships made proper landing almost impossible. The *Tentative Manual* asserted that each transport should carry one assault battalion with its landing force, and also the battalion's equipment—loaded in order in which the various items would be needed. This concept of combat loading ran counter to usual naval practices. Heavy equipment often had to be stored on deck, lighter equipment in the hold. Moreover, each load was to be autonomous so that the particular combat unit aboard the particular transport would be tactically self-sufficient for the assault and landing and so that the loss of one ship would not be a crippling blow. By 1936 already, the Marine Corps had provided the necessary loading tables, but the first improvised transport ships were assigned to the corps only in 1941. These vessels, converted destroyers, did not prove satisfactory and it was not until the later years of the war that satisfactory vessels became available.[20]

In December 1941 the United States found itself at war with Japan and within a short time disaster after disaster overtook the poorly prepared U.S. and Allied forces. In the summer of 1942, when a Japanese drive threatened the security of the South Pacific area and especially communications with Australia, Admiral Ernest J. King, commander-in-chief, United States Fleet, decided on a limited offensive operation in the Pacific and gained the approval of the president and the Joint Chiefs for such an undertaking. The operation, code-named Watch Tower, was to be mounted against Guadalcanal Island in the Solomon groups.[21]

Although mounted within a short time, without adequate preparations and rehearsals, and nicknamed by some officers Operation Shoestring, the Guadalcanal landings were successfully carried out and, together with Midway, they have been considered the beginning of the end for the Japanese Empire in the Pacific. Yet, these landings also showed that much still remained to be worked out. "Most of the major problems of amphibious warfare," one analysis summarizes "had been worked out in theory, and valuable practice and experimentation had gone far to refine the doctrine, provide training for a sizeable number of Marine Corps and Navy personnel and eliminate some of the more critical 'bugs' in the procedure."[22] At the same time, however, it cannot be said that the Marine Corps, or any other branch of the armed services was, by 1942, fully prepared to carry out its amphibious assault mission. Doctrine had come a long way from Gallipoli to Guadalcanal, but it still needed improvement. Nevertheless, the Guadalcanal landings proved that the doctrine was basically sound.[23] The amphibious doctrines and techniques developed by the Marine Corps made possible the trans-Pacific advance and, in a different context, the invasions of North Africa and Europe.

Notes

I am grateful for the aid provided by BGen. E. H. Simmons, USMC (Ret.), director, Marine Corps History and Museums.

[1]Hector C. Bywater, *Sea Power in the Pacific* (Boston and New York: Houghton-Mifflin, 1921), pp. 128–29.

[2]See among others, F. McCormick, *The Menace of Japan* (Boston: Little, Brown, 1917), and Walter B. Pitkin, *Must We Fight Japan* (New York: The Century Co., 1921).

[3]Maurice Matloff, "The American Approach to War," in Michael Howard, ed., *The Theory and Practice of War* (Bloomington: Indiana University Press, 1975), pp. 220–21.

[4]Theodore Ropp, *War in the Modern World* (Durham, N.C.: Duke University Press, 1959), p. 235.

[5]Matloff, "The American Approach to War," p. 222; and Col. Robert H. Dunlap, USMC, "Lessons for Marines From the Gallipoli Campaign," *Marine Corps Gazette* 6 (September 1921): 237–52.

[6]Peter Karsten, *The Naval Aristocracy* (New York: Macmillan, Free Press, 1972), pp.82–83, 91, and 289.

[7]Col. William H. Russell, "Genesis of the FMF Doctrine," *Marine Corps Gazette* 35 (April 1951): 52–59 and (July 1951): 52–59. U.S. Navy authors on occasion have disputed the Marine Corps's preeminent role in the development of amphibious doctrine. "The Marines," Admiral Richmond K. Turner wrote, "contributed much . . . so also did the Navy, including Naval Aviation." Cited by VAdm. George P. Dyer, USN (Ret.) *Amphibians Came to Conquer. The Story of Admiral Richmond Kelly Turner,* 2 Vols. (Washington, D.C.: Government Printing Office, 1972) 1: 202–3. Dyer, however, concedes that prior to 1934 amphibious warfare was neglected by the navy. In the 1934 edition of *War Instructions, United States Navy,* the subject "amphibious warfare" was not even listed in the index, ibid., p. 223. Therefore, it appears correct to assign the Marine Corps the major role in the development of the doctrine.

[8]Major Earl H. Ellis, USMC, OPlan 712, AdvBOps, 1921. Microfilm rolls, Amphibious Warfare pertinent documents, roll 1, Marine Corps Historical Center, Washington, D.C. (hereinafter cited as Amphib. Warfare Docs.); Jeter A. Isley and Philip A. Crowl, *The U.S. Marines and Amphibious War* (Princeton: Princeton University Press, 1951), pp. 26–28.

[9]*Ibid.,* pp. 30–32; and Capt. R. Earle, USN, "Landing Operations of the Central Force, November 1921-May 1922," Amphib. Warfare Docs., roll 1.

[10]BGen. Dion Williams, USMC, "Blue Marine Corps Expeditionary Force," *Marine Corps Gazette* 10 (September 1925): 76–88; USMC, Arch. and Hist. Grp. MCDEC, Quantico, VA., Hist. Amphib. File, nos. 25–27, "Grand Joint Army and Navy Exercise, Hawaii, 1925."

[11]Isley and Crowl, *The U.S. Marines and Amphibious War,* p. 28; and Joint Board, *Joint Action of Army and Navy* (Washington, D.C.: Government Printing Office, 1927), p. 3.

[12]Navy Department GO 241, 8 December 1933.

[13]*Tentative Manual for Landing Operation,* Navy Department FTP 167; U.S. Army FM 31–5 For revisions, see Dyer, *Amphibians Came to Conquer,* 1:226–27.

[14]LtCol. Frank O. Hough, USMCR, Maj. Verle E. Ludwig, USMC, and Henry I. Shaw, Jr., *History of U.S. Marine Corps Operations in World War II* (Washington, D.C.: Government Printing Office, 1959), 1:341–42.

[15]Edward B. Potter and Chester W. Nimitz, *Seapower* (Englewood Cliffs, N.J.:

Prentice-Hall, 1960) pp. 632–33; BGen. Samuel B. Griffith II, USMC (Ret.) *The Battle for Guadalcanal* (Philadelphia and New York: Lippincott, 1963), pp. 54–55; and "Naval Gunfire Support of Landing Operations, Marine Corps Arch. and Hist. Group, MCDEC Quantico, VA., Hist. Amphib. File no. 540.

[16]Hough, Ludwig, and Shaw, *History of Marine Corps Operations in World War II,* 1:15–22.

[17]Ibid., pp.23–24; Marine Corps Arch. and Hist. Group, MCDEC, Quantico, VA., Hist. Amphib. File nos. 37, 112; and 2/LT. Arthur B. Barrows USMC, "A New Departure in Landing Boats," *Marine Corps Gazette* 23 (September 1939): 39–40. See also Dyer, *Amphibians Came to Conquer.*

[18]Hough, Ludwig, and Shaw, *History of Marine Corps Operations in World War II,* 1:21; the autobiography of LtGen. Holland M. Smith, USMC (Ret.) *Coral and Brass* (New York: Scribner's, 1949), *passim.*

[19]Griffith, *The Battle for Guadalcanal,* pp. 41–42; and Hough, Ludwig, and Shaw, *History of Marine Corps Operations in World War II,* 1:257–58.

[20]Hough Ludwig, and Shaw, *History of Marine Corps Operations in World War II,* 1:25–35.

[21]Griffith, *The Battle for Guadalcanal,* p. 25.

[22]Isely and Crowl, *The U.S. Marines and Amphibious War,* p. 58.

[23]*Ibid.,* p. 71.

CHAPTER FIFTEEN

War Plan Orange, 1897–1941: The Blue Thrust Through the Pacific

Edward S. Miller

FOCUS QUESTIONS

1. What were some of the assumptions under which U.S. naval officers worked in planning for war in the Pacific against Japan?
2. What was the difference between the "thrusters" and "cautionaries"?
3. Under War Plan Orange, what was the desired "end state" for war in the Pacific? Did the planners contemplate an invasion of Japan? Why? How did emerging technology ultimately impact this issue?

Decades before the Japanese attack upon Pearl Harbor, the U.S. Navy developed a topsecret plan to fight Japan in the event of war. Mr. Miller traces the evolution of the war plans and shows that, although the overall principles were fixed by 1914, some naval strategists urged a swift counterattack across the central Pacific while others advocated a slow, island-hopping campaign. He concludes that World War II strategists hewed to the early principles and drew selectively from campaign plans to fashion victory.

In American naval war plans against Japan created in the years before Pearl Harbor, Japan was codenamed Orange and the United States was Blue. War

Plan Orange took forty years to perfect, but its strategic principles were set long before the war in the Pacific. The focus of this essay is the Blue offensive through the central Pacific. Six periods, from the earliest years through the final days before Pearl Harbor, are discussed. In each of those periods, rivalries existed within the U.S. Navy between advocates of a quick attack and advocates of a cautious advance across the Pacific.

In 1897 the Naval War College drew up a plan to resist Japanese designs against Hawaii.[1] After 1898 and the Spanish-American War, the navy ignored Japan and planned to defend the Philippines against European encroachment; it wanted, but never got, a world-class base there.[2] The real War Plan Orange was born on 14 June 1907 when President Theodore Roosevelt asked for a strategy to fight Japan. Ironically, Roosevelt liked the Japanese; he had won the Nobel Peace Prize for his part in the Treaty of Portsmouth which settled their war with Russia. At the same time, however, he was alarmed by Japan's military strength and the tensions between the two countries over Japanese immigration to the United States.[3]

The joint Army and Navy Board drew up an analysis,[4] which over the next seven years the navy's General Board refined into the Orange Plan. Both planning boards were chaired by Admiral George Dewey. Although no strategic genius, Dewey lent his immense prestige to the process and picked brilliant subordinates.[5] The basic doctrine evolved: Orange geography determines Blue strategy.

Japan's remoteness would allow it easy victories at first, but as a resource-poor island group dependent on imports, it was vulnerable to defeat by naval blockade and bombardment. Blue's problem was how to get its navy over there.[6]

The planners were influenced by epic voyages of two battle fleets. The Russian Baltic Fleet, leaving Europe, crawled seven months to the Far East. With no Russian ports of call and its main base having fallen, the fleet arrived in a decrepit state and was annihilated at Tsushima off Japan in 1905.[7] Three years later America's Great White fleet left Virginia on a splendid peacetime cruise and circled the world in fourteen months, while serviced by a mobile train in distant ports. It returned in excellent condition and high morale.[8] An earlier voyage by the U.S. Asiatic Fleet under Admiral Robley Evans touched only at American islands from Hawaii to the Philippines.[9]

The first two cruises became symbols of a longterm debate among American naval planners. Some officers, called for convenience "thrusters," were inspired by the self-sufficiency of the Great White Fleet and championed a rapid naval offensive across the Pacific, thus seeking victory by speed and audacity. Others, the "cautionaries," called for a slow campaign with proper bases to avoid a Tsushima-style disaster. Sadly for the modern scholar, war plans were top secret and usually unsigned. The actual names of these men thus are unknown.

FIRST PERIOD, 1906–14

The early plans assumed a three-phase war. In Phase 1, Japan would strike suddenly and powerfully to the south, taking Guam and overrunning the Philippines in three to six months. The Blue Asiatic Squadron would fight briefly and then escape. To the east, Japan would raid or occupy outlying islands and possibly make nuisance raids on Alaska, the West Coast, and Panama.[10] It was feared that Hawaii would fall but, in 1908, Pearl Harbor was selected as Blue's main offshore base. Within a few years all plans assumed that it would be held, for its loss would be "an irretrievable disaster."[11] However, not even the worst pessimist believed that Japan would invade California.[12]

American naval tradition demanded victory, so the thrusters easily dominated the first plans. With Phase 2, they drew a complete blueprint to win the war. The Battle Fleet was in the Atlantic, so it would mobilize and head for the Far East. The route was via the Straits of Magellan or, after 1914, the Panama Canal.[13] The fleet would sail en masse to Manila. It would rescue the troops on the fortress island of Corregidor or, if they had perished, build an advance base in the southern Philippines and retake Luzon. It would start to blockade Japanese trade and, within the area of Guam, Manila, and Okinawa, Blue would sink the Orange battleships in a decisive gunnery battle.[14]

Planners of both schools accepted these principles. Their dispute was about getting to the Philippines quickly and strongly. The thrusters believed in speed, the cautionaries in superior strength; the debate always came down to timing and the route of the attack.

In Phase 3, U.S. forces would move northward to a base within 500 miles of Korea, like Okinawa or on the Chinese coast, and the final siege would begin. A tight blockade would be imposed by ships, mines, and submarines. Ports and industries would be smashed by naval guns and, in later plans, by air attacks. Japan, blasted and starved, then would sue for peace. Never was any invasion of Japan projected.[15]

The next important question was how Blue would cross the Pacific and where would be its bases. As there is no land mass or developed port between Hawaii and Asia, minor islands became very important. Historically, naval battles had been fought near continental shores, but now a fleet action might occur in mid-ocean.

Various attack routes were considered. The northern route, running by way of the Aleutians to Guam and Manila, was favored by Admiral Alfred T. Mahan as the shortest path. It was discarded, however, because of atrocious weather, the lack of facilities, and the dangerous leg near Japan.[16] The southern routes, from Panama and Hawaii, were the longest, but the cautionaries liked them because they were the safest from interception. The fleet could refuel at remote islands and hope their colonial masters would either not know or not care. But these routes also were rejected because of length, poor logistics, and their political complications.[17]

The south central route had distinct advantages. The fleet could steam through Micronesia, an area dense with islands and calm harbors suitable for coaling, like the atolls of Kwajalein or Eniwetok in the Marshall Islands. Admiral Dewey called the latter "the best . . . of the group."[18] The Carolines, like Mortlock and Truk, looked even better, and the group extended almost to the Philippines. The islands on this route were German, but there was a quaint belief that the kaiser would wink at the laws of neutrality.[19]

In the end, a north central route was adopted by the thrusters. It was the most direct course from Hawaii and touched only American islands. Midway was the final take-off point, and small ships might pause to coal in the lee of Wake Island. The initial target was Guam.[20] The navy often pleaded for defense forces that might hold out for the fleet, but Guam was never fortified.[21] It was hoped that Guam would be recaptured quickly, and from there the fleet could sail to Manila, perhaps consigning its train to a southern Philippine harbor safely distant from Orange's base in Formosa.[22]

The thrusters believed in speed. They called for a thundering charge across the sea, with only brief stops, a "Through Ticket to Manila." The fleet would weigh anchor the moment war broke out, head for the Pacific, and arrive off Manila one month out of Pearl Harbor.[23] The cautionaries argued for building bases en route to protect the fleet and its supply lines. Their schedule was vague, but a stepwise campaign would need months or a year to reach the Philippines. There would be no troops left to save.[24]

SECOND PERIOD, 1919–33

World War I interrupted this planning, so the next important period dates from 1919 to 1933. The cautionaries tore up the "Through Ticket" in response to new circumstances. The Battle Fleet moved to California, thus allowing a slower start for the attack. Furthermore, the Washington Naval Treaty of 1922 froze base construction in the western Pacific, making mobile advance bases a necessity. Japan had seized Germany's North Pacific islands. While naval mythology says this was a terrible blow because Orange now could block the sea-lanes to the Far East, in fact Admiral William S. Benson, the first chief of naval operations, advised President Woodrow Wilson to support a Japanese Mandate under the League of Nations. Japan then could not fortify the islands, and thus they would be easy wartime targets.[25]

The War Plans Division was formed, staffed by "capable youngsters with War College training and full of vim and vigor," some fresh from Admiral William Sims' wartime staff in England. Among them were future Fleet Commander Harry Yarnell and William S. Pye.[26] They were cautionaries who applied a sobriety test to the Orange Plan. Given larger fleets and deadly new weapons, they saw a long, bitter war with no room for bravado. They accepted the counterattack but only by the south central route with its many possible bases. By 1921 they outlined a two-step assault on the Mandates. Blue would sail into the Marshalls and seize a lagoon, preparatory to capturing the large island of Truk.

It was then on to Guam, reaching the Philippines only a month after the kick-off.[27]

The thrusters rallied. While accepting the Mandates route, they twice tried to salvage the "Through Ticket." In 1924, egged on by Generals Leonard Wood and John J. Pershing to save their troops, they contrived to reaccelerate the timetable. The fleet once again would dash immediately to the Philippines. It would occupy the Mandates, too, but implicitly the seizure of the islands would come later in the war.[28] As this plan jeopardized the supply line, the cautionaries later reinstated the island-hopping campaign. To soothe the army they did so by vague inference rather than forthrightly.[29] Several years later the thrusters tried again. The fleet would make a "Quick Movement" to Manila before the war, and the Mandates would be occupied from there when war began.[30] Wiser heads prevailed. The "Through Ticket" was dead, along with the dream of saving the Philippines.

The cautionaries stamped on the grave. Over time they did make revisions. They delayed the start of the offensive to the fourteenth day of the war, then to the thirtieth day, and then to "as soon as possible."[31] They dropped Guam from the itinerary because the Carolines' harbors were better and because bombers could not yet reach Japan from the Marianas. They definitely headed for a base in the southern Philippines. Although Luzon would be next, operations north of it were omitted, for the slower campaign left time to plan the endgame after the war.[32]

THIRD PERIOD, 1934–36

The third period extends from 1934 to 1936 when the cautionaries detailed the island-hopping offensive to the southern Philippines. They produced a study called the Royal Road, perhaps after the popular adventure book, *The Royal Road to Romance.* It was adopted as the new Orange Plan. With the main advance, the fleet would grab an anchorage at Wotje, the nearest of the Marshalls. The cautionaries hoped for a naval battle in the Marshalls where the Blue fleet would be closer to its main base than to Japan for the only time in the war. Atolls, occupied as subsidiary air bases, would extend air cover to Truk. From Wotje, the fleet would assault Truk and develop a major base there. A distant blockade of Japan would commence. Blue would take an air station west of Truk, then establish a fleet base at one of two locations in the southwestern Philippines. An aircraft pipeline over this route would replenish losses expected in the Philippines.[33]

The marines were consulted, and they wisely assumed that they would have to invade heavily defended islands, not empty beaches. There were so many islands that they recommended assaulting only a few with overwhelming force and neutralizing the rest by air and sea power.[34]

The campaign now was so prolonged that operations north of Mindanao were omitted. The thrusters had two ideas for speeding it up. The first was to attack Truk promptly, possibly before Japan could fortify it, and pick off the

Marshalls later. This idea was rejected because the Marshalls greatly improved the logistics for the Truk operation and because it was still hoped that the Imperial Navy might fight for the Marshalls where Blue aircraft would dominate the skies. The thrusters did win their second point: the Palau Islands were considered nonessential and therefore bypassed. The fleet could double back and capture them later.[35]

FOURTH PERIOD, 1937–39

As the late 1930s approached, the Philippines were promised independence; the Washington Naval Treaty expired; and Japan invaded China, grew more bellicose, and was expected to fortify the Mandates. The next planning cycle, 1937–39, was a standoff. The cautionaries further contracted the late stages of the offensive and slowed the timetable. The base at Truk did not need to be completed until a year after war began. Then they deleted specific moves beyond Truk.[36]

This time the thrusters responded realistically. Truk's location in mid-Pacific and the world-class repair and industrial facility to be established there would position the fleet to advance later to the western Pacific.[37] Objectives within range included the Marianas and Bonins, the Philippines, and perhaps even Formosa or Okinawa. It again was decided that Truk had to be taken more quickly.

A way was found serendipitously through Wake, orphan island of a doomed scheme. A special naval board under Admiral Arthur J. Hepburn had resurrected the idea of a major base on Guam to be supported by aircraft fueling stations on Midway and Wake.[38] Pan American Airways already had built flying clipper bases on the atolls with navy encouragement.[39] Isolationists in Washington vetoed Guam, but Admiral Claude Bloch and other thrusters realized that, even so, mid-Pacific air bases would greatly assist the Blue offensive.[40] Naval doctrine required that the waters ahead of an advancing fleet be scouted by flying boats, operating if necessary from tenders in remote lagoons. Planes from Wake could bring the northern Marshalls under surveillance and attack, permitting a descent on an island like Eniwetok. Such a bold move would outflank the entire Marshall group and bring Truk and even the Marianas within aerial range. Eniwetok lay 640 miles from Wake with Truk 785 miles further beyond, whereas the Royal Road's 1,115-mile gap from Wotje to Truk was too wide for most airplanes of the day without intermediate stops. The thrusters won their point. The choice of "Base One" was delegated to Pacific Fleet commander-in-chief J. O. Richardson, and in the following period he selected Eniwetok.[41]

FIFTH PERIOD, 1939–40

The next phase runs from the outbreak of war in 1939 through 1940. It was the heyday for the cautionaries. With Europe engulfed by Hitler, the American army got cold feet about fighting in Asia. It believed that the fleet should stand on the defensive and not venture beyond its air cover. Nevertheless, when the services jointly drafted five multi-colored Rainbow Plans, two were offspring of Orange, that is, transpacific wars. In Rainbow Two, the United States fought alone, while in Rainbow Three, the country had allies.[42] But in these plans the opening task of the Pacific Fleet shriveled to a mere diversionary action, in order to distract Orange forces from attacking the allied colonies in the Far East.[43] This suited Commander in Chief Richardson, a cautionary who felt unready to attack even though his fleet was poised at Pearl Harbor.[44]

What could the fleet do? Commander Forrest P. Sherman, Admiral Chester Nimitz's future wartime planner, called Truk a strategic dead end, too distant for blockade while needing continuous defense by the fleet, And if Truk were dropped, why go for the Marshalls?[45] Admiral Harold Stark, chief of naval operations, blew hot and cold. He told the fleet to act aggressively in the Mandates to save Southeast Asia but not to advance to Truk because the ships might be needed in the Atlantic. Truk was not deleted, but its schedule was in limbo.[46]

The thrusters were reduced to desperate schemes. They considered sending the navy to fight from Singapore, as urged by the British, but this was ruled "out of the question."[47] They convinced Stark to rush a carrier and reinforcements to the East Indies on Day 5, but President Franklin D. Roosevelt scratched the mission.[48] The "Through Ticket" stayed in its grave despite an eleventh-hour attempt by the army to hold the Philippines through concentrated air power.

SIXTH PERIOD, 1941

The final prewar planning period is 1941. The government adopted Rainbow Five, the plan to beat Germany first. Despite this, the year was a last hurrah for the thrusters, perhaps because cautionaries like Kelly Turner were preoccupied with the Atlantic.[49]

Admiral Husband E. Kimmel, taking charge of the fleet, was eager to distract Japan by waging offensive war in the only place still authorized, the Marshall Islands. He was captivated by the position of Wake for covering the invasion of Eniwetok. He put marines on Wake, hoping they might act as bait for a Japanese expedition and enable the United States "to get at naval forces with naval forces."[50]

Kimmel's final prewar version of Plan O-1 of Rainbow Five, updated on 26 November 1941, called for a cancellation of an earlier pet project, a cruiser sweep into the Philippine Sea to catch enemy convoys en route to take Guam or reinforce the Mandates.[51] The plan projected a four-day raid into the Marshalls. Carriers would depart from Pearl Harbor on the first day of the war, refuel at a point covered by three American islands, and then at high speed bombard and reconnoiter the Marshalls. Aircraft staging from Wake would cover and guard against intervention. (This is why no PBYs were on long-range patrol at Pearl Harbor on 7 December; they were being readied for this deployment.) The battleships would stand by at sea. The raid was to precede the invasion of Eniwetok, date unspecified, and of Truk, some day.[52] Liberation of the Philippines lay perhaps two or three years in the future.

An epilogue is needed on the prewar story of War Plan Orange. With the outbreak of war, Corregidor held out for six months, with no naval rescue attempted. The raid on Pearl Harbor canceled Plan O-1 and terminated Kimmel's career just as he tried to save Wake.[53] Nimitz took over, and his first offensive act was to raid the Marshalls.

In comparing the American counterattacks with some older plans, the advance from the Southwest Pacific resembled the southern routes rejected in the old days. General Douglas MacArthur used the Admiralties and improvised a base in the southern Philippines, at Leyte, before retaking Luzon. Admiral Ernest J. King, chief of the wartime navy and a thruster by nature, had played the Orange game at the Naval War College many years before the war. He believed in the strategy, especially the long-ago emphasis on the Marianas.[54] When the navy was ready he persuaded the Joint Chiefs to strike in the central Pacific, to the disgust of MacArthur.[55]

By examining how the war was conducted in the Pacific, it can be compared to running a film backward. The fleet did strike deep into the Marshalls, bypassing many islands. Nimitz covered the fleet with air power from the Gilberts, not from fallen Wake. Japan had a major base at Truk and, until early 1944, the navy intended to follow the Royal Road of the 1930s.[56] But success permitted Truk and later Mindanao to be neutralized and bypassed. Instead, King shifted north to the favorite target of Dewey's time, the Marianas. From there, aerial bombardment of Japan began. As predicted back at the beginning, Blue moved on to Luzon and Okinawa and drew the final noose of blockade and bombardment, including atomic, and the war ended without an invasion of Japan's home islands.

One may ponder why the services concluded late in the war that Japan must be invaded. Even granting the fanatical resistance of the enemy, the decision contradicted forty years of planning and came just when Phase 2 of the Orange Plan had been brilliantly executed. King later said that he went along because of the time needed to prepare an invasion, but in his heart he believed that sea and air power could win the war.[57] President Harry Truman said he dropped the bomb to avoid horrendous invasion casualties. No evidence has yet been found to show that he was informed of the long prewar history of the Phase 3 siege, whereas Roosevelt was familiar with the concept since his days in the Navy Department during the Wilson administration. In any event, dropping the bomb was just as consistent with the traditional strategy of blockade and bombardment as with preempting an invasion.

How, then, is War Plan Orange to be judged? It was one of the longest thought-out plans of the war and the most successful. Some critics have called it a fantasy; the army's top planner said a rapid naval offensive in the 1930s "would be literally an act of madness."[58] Other critics have seen the plan as a gimmick for the navy to justify itself and to win appropriations.[59] Neither view holds much water. The "Through Ticket" may have been wishful thinking, but the strategies of counterattack and siege were sound and the central Pacific island-hopping route was excellent. War Plan Orange persevered for forty years and eventually won the war. What more can one ask of a great plan?

Notes

[1]Ronald H. Spector "Professors of War: The Naval War College and the Modern American Navy" (Ph.D. diss., Yale University, 1967),197.

[2]Rear Admiral Henry C. Taylor, "Memorandum Read to the General Board," 10 June 1904, File 325, Record Group 225, Records of Joint Army and Navy Boards and Committees, National Archives, Washington, D.C. (hereafter RG 225, NA); William R. Braisted, *The United States Navy in the Pacific, 1897–1909* (Austin, 1958; reprinted, New York, 1969),191–239.

[3]Raymond A. Esthus, *Theodore Roosevelt and Japan* (Seattle, 1966),182.

[4]Joint Board to Secretary of Navy, 18 June 1907, File 325, RG 225, NA.

[5]Ronald H. Spector, *Admiral of the New Empire, The Life and Career of George Dewey* (Baton Rouge, 1974), 122.

[6]The principal strategic documents of the pre-World War I era are: "Naval War College to General Board, Strategic Campaign of Blue against Orange, 14 March 1911" (hereafter 1911 Plan), and "Orange War Plan, Strategic Section for War in the Pacific Ocean, Approved by the General Board, 14 March 1914" (hereafter 1914 Plan), both located in Records of the General Board, Operational Archives, Naval History Division, Washington Navy Yard, Washington, D.C. (hereafter GB, OANHD).

[7]J. N. Westwood, *The Illustrated History of the Russo-Japanese War* (London, 1973), chap. 11.

[8]Robert A. Hart, *The Great White Fleet* (Boston, 1965), passim.

[9]Edwin A. Falk, *Fighting Bob Evans* (New York, 1931), 390–92.

[10]1911 Plan; 1914 Plan.

[11]Braisted, *United States Navy, 1897–1909,* 222; 1914 Plan, App. "C," 146.

[12]Captain W. R. Shoemaker, "Strategy of the Pacific: An Exposition of the Orange Plan," lecture to Naval War College Conference, 25 August 1914, Microfilm reel #1, "Strategic Planning in the U.S. Navy, Its Evolution and Execution, 1891–1945" (Wilmington, DE, 1977), 44, 53.

[13]1914 Plan, 7. Alternative voyages through the Atlantic and Indian oceans were studied, but every Orange Plan rejected them. The Suez was too shallow for battleships and might be barred; after all, Britain and Japan were allies. The big ships might sail around Africa, but there were few major ports and perhaps no friendly ones. *Ibid.,* App. "D, 154–55.

[14]The battle locale is the author's generalization based on Orange plans from their inception to World War II and from the list of Orange war games later played at the Naval War College as cited in Michael Vlahos, *The Blue Sword: The Naval War College and the American Mission, 1919–1941* (Newport, 1980), App. 3.

[15]1911 Plan, 56–57; "Navy Basic Plan Orange, Approved by Secretary of the Navy, 1 March 1929" (hereafter 1929 Plan), Records of the Strategic Plans Division, Office of the Chief of Naval Operations, and Predecessor Organizations, 1912–47 (hereafter CNOPO Records), OA-NHD, Section 3, Miscellaneous File, 1917–47, vol. l, chap. 2, 18.
[16]Robert Seager II, *Alfred Thayer Mahan: The Man and His Letters* (Annapolis, 1977), 485–86.
[17]1914 Plan, "Transfer of Blue Naval Forces to Pacific and thence to Hostile Area," 66–67 (hereafter 1914 Plan, Transfer).
[18]1914 Plan, App. "C," Routes 1 through 3; U.S. Navy, General Board, Table of Islands, 1907, GB, OA NOD, Folder 142, OP 29, File 6.
[19]1914 Plan, Transfer, 66-67; Shoemaker, "Strategy of the Pacific," 67.
[20]1914 Plan, 27, 55–56.
[21]Earl S. Pomeroy, *Pacific Outpost American Strategy in Guam and Micronesia* (New York, 1951), chap. 2.
[22]1914 Plan, 72, 77; Shoemaker, "Strategy of the Pacific," 70.
[23]1914 Plan, 16.
[24]Louis B. Morton, "War Plan ORANGE: Evolution of a Strategy," World Politics (11 January 1959): 228.
[25]William R. Braisted, *The United States Navy in the Pacific, 1909–1922* (Austin, 1971), 446, 452–53.
[26]Told by Admiral Harry Yarnell, cited in Robert G. Albion, *Makers of Naval Policy, 1798–1947* (Annapolis, 1980), 90.
[27]Director of War Plans to General Board, 19 October 1921, GB, OA-NHD.
[28]"Joint Board to Secretary of War, Defense of the Philippines, 7 July 1923," Joint Board, No.305, Ser. 208, RG 225, NA; "Joint Planning Committee to Joint Board, Joint Army and Navy Basic War Plan Orange, 12 March 1924," Joint Board, No.325, Ser. 290, RG 225, NA.
[29]1929 Plan, chap. 2, 21–25.
[30]"Battle Problem—Special Study, BLUE vs. ORANGE, Quick Movement," Miscellaneous Subject File, 1917–47, CNOPO Records.
[31]Admiral James O. Richardson, *On the Treadmill to Pearl Harbor* (Washington, 1973), 263, 268–69.
[32]1929 Plan, The Logistics Plan, 136.
[33]Commander Cary W. Magruder, "Orange-'Royal Road'–Plan 04 Orange, U.S. Joint Asiatic Force Operating Plan Orange, 21 July 1934," File Orange-Royal Road, Box 64, CNOPO Records (hereafter Royal Road).
[34]T. Holcomb, "Memorandum for Director, War Plans Division, Denial of a Base to the Enemy in the MARSHALL-CAROLINES, 31 March 1933," monographs of attack and defense plans for specific islands by Headquarters, Fleet Marine Force for NWPD, 1934–37, boxes 56, 69, 77, CNOPO Records.
[35]Royal Road, Section 5, Course 1.
[36]WPL 13, Navy Basic War Plan Orange, vol.l (March 1939), Registered Document #22, OA-NHD.
[37]Memorandum, Chief of Naval Operations to Secretary of the Navy, 12

November 1940, 14175–15, 11, Record Group 165, NA. Known as the Plan Dog memo (hereafter Plan Dog), it was forwarded to Roosevelt and became the basis of the Rainbow Five Plan.

[38]U.S. Congress, House, Commission headed by Rear Admiral A. J. Hepburn to Secretary of the Navy, "Report on Need of Additional Naval Bases," House Doc. 65, 27 December 1938, 76th Cong., 1st sees., 1938, 26–28.

[39]Francis X. Holbrook, "United States National Defense and Trans-Pacific Commercial Air Routes, 1933–1941" (Ph.D. diss., Fordham University, 1969), chap. 3.

[40]Commander-in-Chief, United States Fleet, to Chief of Naval Operations, "Development of MIDWAY, WAKE and GUAM, 28 February 1938," Record Group 80, "General Records of the Department of the Navy," NB/ND 14, NA.

[41]Change to WPL-16, April 1938, and WPL-13 of 1939 defined "Base One" only as "a typical atoll in the Marshall Islands." Eniwetok was a possible target in "Commander Minecraft, Battle Force to CinCUS, 22 July 1939," Enclosure H BASE ONE, box 236, File A-16-1/EG 12-1, CNO Secret and Confidential Files, RG 80, NA. It was not firmly designated until Plan O-1 of Rainbow Five.

[42]Louis B. Morton, *Strategy and Command: The First Two Years,* United States Army in World War II Series, *The War in the Pacific* (Washington, 1962), 41–42, 68ff, 71–72.

[43]U.S. Navy, Rainbow Plan No. III (WPL-44), December 1940, CNOPO Records, cited on Reel #5, Scholarly Microfilm (hereafter Rainbow No. III).

[44]Richardson, *On the Treadmill,* 278–79, 288–92.

[45]Memorandum, Commander F. P. Sherman to Director, WED, CinCUS's Operating Plan O-1, 30 April 1940, Box 91, File A16-3/FF, Warfare U.S. Fleet, RG 80, NA.

[46]Commander-in-Chief to Chief of Naval Operations, 28 January 1941; Chief of Naval Operations to CinCUS, 10 February 1941, both with Rainbow No. III.

[47]Plan Dog, 16.

[48]WPL 44, Initial U.S. Strategic Deployment, Rainbow No.m; Memorandum, Chief of Staff for War Plans Division of War Department, General Staff, 17 January 1941, White House Conference of 16 January 1941, WPL 4175–18, cited in Morton, *Strategy and Command,* 85; Stark to Richardson, dispatch 212155, 22 January 1941, cited in *ibid.,* 299.

[49]Vice Admiral George Carroll Dyer, *The Amphibians Came to Conquer: The Story of Admiral Richmond Kelly Turner,* 2 vols. (Washington, 1971), l: chap. 5, passim. Admiral R. E. Ingersoll told Dyer that Turner had written Rainbow Three and the first supporting draft of Rainbow Five.

[50]Commander-in-Chief, U.S. Pacific Fleet, to Chief of Naval Operations, "WAKE ISLAND—Policy in regard to construction on and protection of, 18 April 1941," CNOPO Records, Ser. 029W, Box 91, File A16-3/FF Warfare U.S. Fleet.

[51]Commander-in-Chief, U.S. Pacific Fleet, to Chief of Naval Operations, "Initial Deployment, U.S Pacific Fleet under Plan Dog," *ibid.*

[52]U.S. Congress, Hearings before the Joint Committee on the Investigation of the Pearl Harbor Attack, Commander-in-Chief, Pacific Fleet, "Plan 0-1,

Rainbow Five," 79th Cong. (Washington, 1946), Part 17, 2578–79; Annex lI, "Marshall Reconnaissance and Raiding Plan," *ibid.,* 2595–98.
[53]Samuel Eliot Morison, *History of United States Naval Operations in World War II,* 15 vols. (Boston, 1950), 3:249.
[54]Ernest J. King and Walter Muir Whitehill, *Fleet Admiral King. A Naval Record* (New York, 1952), 239
[55]Grace Person Hayes, *The History of the Joint Chiefs of Staff in World War II: The War against Japan* (Annapolis, 1982), 431.
[56]Ibid., 546, 553–60.
[57]King and Whitehill, *Fleet Admiral King,* 605.
[58]Stanley D. Embick for Commanding General, Philippine Department, 19 April 1933, WPD 325115, cited in Ronald Schaffer, "General Stanley D. Embick: Military Dissenter," *Military Affairs* 37 (October 1973): 90.
[59]Richardson, *On the Treadmill,* 262–63, 275–77.

CHAPTER SIXTEEN

THE BATTLE OF THE ATLANTIC, 1941–1943: PEAKS AND TROUGHS

J. DAVID BROWN

FOCUS QUESTIONS

1. What was ultimately at stake for both the Allies and Germany in the Battle of the Atlantic?
2. What was the influence of each of the following factors: intelligence (code breaking), technology (ship and aircraft), experience (leadership and manpower), and strategy?
3. What role did each of these factors play in the Battle of the Atlantic from year to year?

By early 1941, three events had advanced the British assault on the German naval ciphers: the captures of the *Krebs* in the Lofotens, the *München* north of Iceland, and the submarine *U 110* to the south of Iceland. Cipher keys and the internal settings of the Enigma machine captured from the first gave the Government Code and Cipher School (GC&CS) at Bletchley Park all the February 1941 "Heimisch" traffic. The insight enabled the mathematicians there to practice their black art to such effect that they worked out for themselves the April traffic and by May the delay between interception of German signals and their decryption had been reduced to between seven and ten days.

While this was a formidable achievement, it did not approximate to the near real-time needs of the mobile war in the Atlantic—a seven-knot convoy could cover 1,100 miles in a week, while a ten-knot U-boat athwart its track could reach Iceland from the Azores in the same time. A vivid example of the effects of the lag was provided by the eastbound convoy HX 126. On 15 May, BdU (U-boat command) ordered a seven-boat wolf pack to take up a patrol line to the south of Greenland across the track of the convoy, which was escorted only by an armed merchant cruiser provided for protection against disguised surface raiders. Unaware of the U-boat deployment, the Admiralty made no attempt to divert the convoy or to reinforce its escort, for not until two days after the pack struck, on 19 May, was Bletchley Park able to pass the decrypt.

Within days, however, Bletchley Park was reading the current Enigma decrypts—usually within an hour of their transmission. Not only that, but they were reading virtually everything sent to and from the U-boats. The capture of the weather trawler *München* on 7 May, a deliberate trap made possible by the cryptanalysts' previous successes, provided June's cipher settings. At least as valuable was the acquisition of the U-boat *"Kurzsignale"* code-book and the settings for the navy's "officer only" cipher. These came from the *U 110,* briefly captured on 9 May by convoy escorts; her commanding officer, Fritz-Julius Lemp, had compounded his original gross error in sinking the *Athenia* (thereby persuading the Admiralty to institute a general convoy system from the outset of the war) with a final negligence which gave his enemies priceless advantage.

The capture of the weather ship *Lauenburg* at the end of June—a repeat of the *München* operation which provided the July 1941 keys—consolidated GC&CS's grip on the naval Enigma. Thereafter, no more captures were necessary as long as the German signals authorities did not introduce fundamental technical changes. To the in-house talent, derived from familiarity with Enigma procedures, the provision of a "bombe" computer for purely naval purposes, and sheer hard experience, were added two German contributions. The naval weather cipher was discovered to carry reports which had originally been transmitted by U-boats in Enigma cipher. Not only did this provide a useful "crib" to breaking the current keys, but it gave the reporting submarines' positions, which were carefully reenciphered for security! The other source was the seemingly unlikely *Werft* dockyards and harbor approaches hand cipher; broken originally because it was discovered that some of these signals were repetitions of deciphered Enigma signals, it was then found that some of its output was retransmitted in the Enigma cipher. *Werft* was of negligible operational value, but it brought incalculable cryptanalytical benefits. From August 1941 through May 1945, only two days' worth of the three-rotor Home Waters naval traffic was not read by Bletchley Park.

Bletchley Park's achievement was formidable, but so was the organization to which the deciphered signals were passed. The Admiralty was unique, in Britain at least, in that it provided the political and administrative direction of the navy, as well as exercising direct executive command, not only over operational headquarters but even over squadrons and individual ships at sea, and it did so not as an exceptional measure but as part of the routine of the conduct of the war. Such centralization was made possible only by the provision of a network of worldwide communications which radiated from Whitehall itself. It also required the concentration of all available intelligence, whose relevance would be assessed by the Naval Intelligence Division (NID) before it was forwarded to the Operations and Trade Divisions and, where necessary, to RAF Coastal Command operational headquarters.

Bletchley Park passed decrypts as "raw material" directly to the Operational Intelligence Centre (OIC), the NID section responsible for assessing, filtering, and channelling all forms of intelligence to the operations staffs. OIC had realized at an early stage, however, that the cryptanalysts could make valuable contributions to the assessment process, recognizing patterns and deviations in not only the content but also the form of the signals traffic; the marriage of the OIC and GC&CS talents was, in general, an extremely happy and fruitful one. Armed with information that was as up-to-date as that available to the BdU and the U-boat commanders, in the summer of 1941 the Admiralty was able to take immediate steps that were, for the first time, to weigh the balance against the submarines.

Of these, perhaps the most important were devised to minimize the boats' opportunities for sinking ships. Evasive routing, to keep convoys clear of enemy concentrations, had been attempted with varying degrees of success since the outbreak of war; the shore Direction-Finding stations, the only source of current information, were of less and less value as the "front line" moved westwards across the Atlantic, and although shipborne HF/DF equipment was under development, it did not go to sea until July 1941. Enigma decrypts of the command orders and of U-boats' sighting homing signals replaced the crystal ball with a two-way mirror, enabling the Admiralty to divert convoys to avoid the known patrol lines or to strip the escorts from unthreatened convoys to reinforce convoys which could not be rerouted in time to avoid attack.

Unrelated to the state of the communication campaign was the necessary decision to provide "end to end" anti-submarine escort. The U-boats' success against HX 126 had occurred well to the west of the radius of action of the escort vessels based in Ireland and Iceland, and it was this action that provoked the Admiralty to develop an escort force base at St. John's, Newfoundland, early in June, and to introduce convoy oilers to enable escort vessels to remain continuously with their charges. Active defense complemented passive evasive routing, for while the latter reduced the submarines' opportunities for intercepting, the presence of escorts reduced their chances of being successful when they did so.

The extension of the anti-submarine forces' reach and the availability of prompt signals intelligence produced an immediate tactical victory. In June, Bletchley Park passed a BdU order to form a patrol line to the southeast of Greenland. Two westbound convoys were routed around the line, but the eastbound HX 133 could not be diverted in time. Instead, its escort was reinforced from the two unthreatened convoys so that the ten U-boats which made contact were eventually faced with thirteen escorts. Five ships were lost during the ensuing five-day battle, but so were two of the U-boats.

The westward extension of U-boat operations had necessitated the stationing of a German tanker to the southwest of Greenland; other ships were at sea to provide middle and South Atlantic replenishment for submarines and raiders. By 25 May, the Operational Intelligence Center knew from decrypts that there were eight supply ships at sea and had exact patrol positions for half of them. The first to be eliminated was the "Greenland gas station," sunk by a pair of cruisers on 3 June; two more supply ships were intercepted and sunk on 4 June and a fourth the next day. Ten days later yet another U-boat supply tanker was sunk, as were two ships earmarked to support the *Bismarck,* victims of the Royal Navy's exploitation of Bletchley Park's success. The U-boats were now faced with an insoluble logistical problem just as the British had overcome theirs. Coinciding as it did with the reduction in sightings to the south and west of Greenland, this reverse led to an eastward move of the U-boat force, to areas within the reach of shore-based aircraft from Iceland and the United Kingdom.

The background of one of the most important decisions taken after the real break into the Enigma is obscure. On 18 June 1941, the Trade Division raised the speed limit for ships which had to be sailed independently from thirteen to fifteen knots. One of the linchpins of the journalistic approach to history is the leap to conclusions, epitomized by the formula "must have," to bridge the gaps in sequences of events or steps in reasoning which cannot be filled from available records; the equivalent for the historian teetering on the brink of legitimacy is "it is tempting to believe that."

In the absence of the missing link, however, this author is tempted to believe that, in this instance, the exploitation of decrypts did not provide the spur. Independently-sailed shipping losses had doubled from sixteen in March 1941 to thirty-two in April and had increased again to forty-three in May; twenty-eight independents had been lost in June up to the time the speed limit was raised. The reasoning behind lowering it—it had been considered that U-boats would have difficulties in locating dispersed shipping—was plainly faulty; during the second quarter of the year only thirty-nine ships had been sunk while in convoy or straggling, compared with 120 lost proceeding independently. The effect of raising it was even more dramatic for, during the second half of 1941, it nearly reversed the situation: forty-nine independents were sunk, compared with 113 convoyed ships and stragglers.

The introduction of a new concept of operations by Coastal Command's anti-submarine aircraft antedated the major cryptanalytical breakthrough but appears to have been stimulated by anticipation of success. From 9 May 1941, with Admiralty agreement, the Royal Air Force suspended routine air escort of convoys and independents: only those known to be threatened would be given protection by direct escort or sweeps. Furthermore, no night escort missions would be flown, these having proved to be particularly fruitless thus far. The emphasis on Coastal Command antisubmarine operations was to be offensive, not defensive, and aircraft would seek out the U-boats and destroy them instead of waiting for the U-boats to come to the convoys.

Offensive air anti-submarine doctrine is tailor-made for the exploitation of current signals intelligence but totally flawed in its absence. In practice it failed completely in 1941. Lack of adequate numbers of longrange aircraft—fewer than fifty could operate more than 500 miles from base—and indifferent weapons and tactics meant that many valid opportunities for offensive action were missed and little significant attrition was inflicted by the attacks that were delivered. Of twenty-five Axis submarines lost in the Atlantic during the second half of 1941, RAF Coastal Command was responsible for only one outright "kill" (captured) and two shared with surface ships, out of 139 sighted. Despite claims to the contrary, aircraft continued to serve primarily as scarecrows for many months to come.

Mention has already been made of the technical advances made by the British. The fitting of centimetric radar or of HF/DF in individual ships, or the introduction of the "snowflake" illuminant as a means of "turning night into day" around a convoy did not, of themselves, have an immediate effect at the lowest tactical level. What was needed was an adequate number of escorts with a relatively simple doctrine, consisting of standard operating procedures (to borrow a 1950s term) based on hard experience, and the experience itself.

New construction and the modification of older fleet ships met the first requirement. In June 1941, Western Approaches Command had ten numbered and "special" escort groups which, with "unallocated" ships and loans, totaled 108 ocean anti-submarine escorts; by November, the Command had nineteen numbered groups with 134 ships, with twenty-six others on loan or not allocated to groups, while a dozen others were operating from Newfoundland in parallel with the Royal Canadian Navy local forces. From 1 September, these were supplemented by the U.S. Navy's "neutrality patrol" convoy escort task groups, which the British and Americans alike believed to enjoy immunity from attack thanks to decrypts of repeated orders, emanating from Hitler himself, to avoid action with U.S. Navy units.

Doctrine was left to the Western Approaches Command—an example of the Admiralty's decentralizing policy. The curiously named "Tactical Table Unit" at Liverpool devised and played out countermeasures to meet the U-boat tactics reported by the escort commanders, improving upon them as the U-boat commanders, in turn, modified their methods; as time went by the TTU was even able to anticipate a new German tactic and have the counter in hand. Operational research analysts studied the available technical intelligence and the attack reports to work out ideal convoy and escort dispositions, depth-charge patterns, and even camouflage schemes. Between them, the tacticians and analysts provided the seagoing teeth of this organization with standard operating procedures which were subject to continuous modification.

Experience came from success, measured not only in terms of "safe and timely arrival" of the convoys but in actual scalps: by the end of the year, twelve of Western Approaches' numbered groups and thirty-two individual ships had a solo or shared "kill" under their belts from the previous six months' operations. All attacks, successful and unsuccessful, were fed back as grist to the tacticians' and analysts' mill, to be added to the mass of knowledge which was promulgated routinely, and occasionally as a matter of urgency, to all those at sea and ashore who were waging the campaign.

The U-boats moved back to the eastern Atlantic in late July 1941. The *B-Dienst* was providing details of convoy movements from its decrypts of the British ciphers, but this source of information alone was not enough to bring the boats into contact with the shipping. Three convoys were intercepted and roughly handled in July and August, but these were not transatlantic sailings but rather were on the north-south route between the United Kingdom and Gibraltar and West Africa. This route took the ships within range of the *Luftwaffes'* long-range patrol aircraft based in southwest France. Alerted by agents overlooking Gibraltar from neutral Spain, these aircraft located the convoys and homed the U-boat packs which would otherwise have been wrong-footed by the Admiralty's evasive measures. The U-boats themselves reported that the efficiency of the escorts had increased "to an astonishing degree;" in particular their ability to deal with shadowing submarines was stressed—whereas a few months previously only a single U-boat was needed for maintaining contact, now it was a task for an entire group.[1]

The improved tactics minimized losses by depriving the U-boats of firing opportunities—during the first two Gibraltar convoy operations, only one of the dozen boats making contact had been able to deliver a second attack—but it provoked BdU into ordering attacks on the escorts at every opportunity The third convoy action thus began and ended with the sinking of a British escort, but even then only one of the six U-boats which delivered a successful attack managed a re-attack.

The U-boats operating between Iceland and the United Kingdom had meanwhile been experiencing a lean time, not least because Coastal Command's new patrol policy appeared to flood that area with aircraft. In early September, with more submarines at sea than ever before (an average of thirty-six each day), BdU decided to push the groups further west once more to form mobile patrol lines which would search for convoys between Greenland and the Azores and as far afield as Newfoundland. Within three days, the redeployment had fully justified itself: a "wolf pack" found convoy SC 42 off Greenland and, although the boat which made the initial contact was promptly sunk, the seven boats which followed sank fourteen ships and damaged two others in fifty-four hours. Four made successful re-attacks but these cost the pack another of its number.

This defeat, like the attacks on three subsequent convoys, was due in part to the introduction by BdU in September of enciphered "Quadra" positions,[2] but there were other reasons for subsequent difficulties experienced by the OIC's Tracking Room during the month, not least being atmospheric conditions affecting H/F wireless reception, which also affected Dönitz's handling of his U-boat packs. This certainly hindered a U-boat concentration against SC 44 ten days later. As for the other two convoys which sustained significant loss in September 1941, both were on the north-south route and were initially sighted by submarines on passage and relocated and shadowed by aircraft.

Depressing as the figures for September 1941 may have been, with forty-five convoyed ships and an escort sunk, there were nevertheless encouraging developments. From 1 September, the U.S. Navy had begun escorting some convoys as far east as Iceland (and four days later *U 652* had fired "defensive" torpedoes at USS *Greer*), relieving the strain on the British and Canadian escort groups. Late in the month, the entry into service of the first escort carrier, the *Audacity,* at last provided a counter to the *Luftwaffe* shadowers on the Gibraltar route.

The most unlooked-for reprieve came from Hitler himself when, early in September, he ordered six of the Atlantic U-boats to the Mediterranean where the war at sea was going badly for the Axis. The numbers available for Atlantic operations were made up (including replacements for the two boats sunk during September) by new arrivals from German home waters, but this meant that the defenses faced no more submarines in October than they had in the two preceding months, while their own strength continued to increase.

After one more notable success, against SC 48 in mid-October 1941, the U-boat offensive effectively collapsed. This convoy was sighted by chance by one of a group of submarines in transit from one area to another, but although the nine CO's involved made up a "star team," so efficient and aggressive were the defenders, reinforced by a U.S. Navy group diverted from another convoy, that only four of them reached firing positions on the merchant ships, ten of which were sunk. Two British escorts were sunk and, by an act of understandable folly, the U.S. destroyer *Kearny* was damaged.

Apart from this battle, and a lesser action against a northbound convoy from Gibraltar, the OIC had the upper hand throughout October keeping the shipping out of harm's way. Only thirty merchant ships under allied control were lost in total, thirteen of them independents. The escorts were handled more roughly, for five were torpedoed and sunk: besides the two lost with SC 48, two Royal Navy vessels were sunk on the Gibraltar run and the USS *Reuben James* was lost southwest of Iceland while escorting HX 156. As in September, two U-boats and two Italian submarines were destroyed.

If October had been unprofitable for the U-boats, November was worse and December a calamity. Only eleven merchant ships were sunk in the North Atlantic during the former month, nine of them from the four convoys which were attacked. December saw sinkings reduced to ten ships (six in convoy) while Atlantic U-boat losses reached a new high, no fewer than six being sunk by convoy escorts, all on the Gibraltar route and five while attempting to get to grips with one convoy—HG 76.

Towards the end of November, the German Naval Staff had assessed a build-up of merchant shipping at Gibraltar as indicating that amphibious landings were intended in Vichy-controlled North Africa. Besides dispatching yet more boats from the Atlantic into the Mediterranean during that month and the next, the U-boats patrolling the gaps between the convoys in the mid-Atlantic and southwest of Greenland were ordered to operate in the approaches to Gibraltar. Both decisions were taken against BdU's advice and, as it transpired, better judgement.

The OIC was aware of the Mediterranean reinforcement and of the general abandonment of the Atlantic, and it took appropriate steps not merely to protect shipping but also to sink U-boats. In November, permanent surface anti-submarine patrols and night barrier air patrols[3] were instituted in the approaches to the Straits of Gibraltar to stop the U-boats heading for the Mediterranean. By the modest late-1941 standards, the results were spectacular: of twenty-six U-boats ordered between 11 November and 19 December to pass into the Mediterranean, four were sunk by mine, surface ship, and air attack, and six were damaged by air attack and forced to return to France. Arrival in the Mediterranean provided no sanctuary, for during the last five weeks of the year another four U-boats were sunk there.

The sailing of HG 76 from Gibraltar was delayed (thereby provoking the German Naval Staff's belief in an impending assault on North Africa) until mid-December, when a sufficiently strong escort could be gathered. The week-long defense of this convoy against the waiting U-boat group and against shadowing aircraft provides the classic example of the convoy as a killing ground, with the escorts as the "wolf pack"—the converse of the hunted flock of vulnerable merchant ships, as portrayed by opponents of the principle. Just two merchant ships were lost, one needlessly when it was prematurely abandoned, and two escorts: unfortunately, one of the latter was the Royal Navy's only escort carrier, the *Audacity,* which had more than proved her worth during the battle.

By any standards, the Royal Navy and its allies had achieved victory on the North Atlantic convoy routes by December 1941. The U-boats had never even closely approached the 800,000 tons-per-month sinking rate that the German Naval Staff had established as necessary for winning this campaign, and they were sustaining losses out of all proportion to their meager successes—one Atlantic submarine was lost for every three convoyed ships during the last quarter of 1941, compared with the preceding quarter's ratio of 1:8.

There can be no doubt that this trend would have been at least partly reversed without the diversion provided by the entry into the war of the United States, for in spite of losses and deployments to the Mediterranean and Arctic theaters, the number of operational U-boats leaving the Baltic training schools was increasing rapidly. Only twenty-five German submarines had undertaken North Atlantic patrols in December 1941; forty-two would do so in January 1942 and fifty in the following month.

The events of early 1942 are well known, and three statistics illustrate the grounds for criticism of U.S. anti-submarine policy and doctrine. Of nearly 50 ships sunk by U-boats during the first half of the year, only one in thirteen was in convoy; in March 1942, three U-boats were sunk by convoy escorts and the latter conceded no losses to the enemy; in the same month, of the eighty-six independently-routed merchant ships sunk, mostly in U.S. waters, fewer than a third were U.S.-flagged.

The relative immunity of the convoys owed very little to the British cryptanalysts after 1 February 1942. Certain combinations of events had led BdU's communications security branch to the conclusion that the Admiralty had foreknowledge of the movements of U-boats and their supply ships; instead of seriously considering the Enigma machine as the source of these leaks, however, BdU tightened internal security first by introducing re-enciphered positions in September 1941 then by adopting modified settings exclusive to the U-boats at the beginning of November. These GC&CS broke soon after introduction, but this success was not again possible after the addition of a fourth rotor wheel to the Enigma machine.

From 1 February 1942, Bletchley Park's Naval Section was neutralized by this one stroke, which was intended to exclude *German* personnel with no "need to know," not to deny the cryptanalysts whose success was unimagined at the time and unknown, for another thirty years. GC&CS continued to read the German Home Waters traffic and the lesser current naval ciphers, but these provided little more than indications of U-boat arrivals and departures at the bases. Even with over three years of experience, access to the peripheral ciphers, wireless traffic analysis, the "fingerprinting" of individual operators, and shorebased HF/DF, GC&CS and OIC were unable to substitute decryption of the primary U-boat communications cipher as a reliable, let alone accurate, source of U-boat movements and intentions.

The scale of shipping losses off the Americas between February and May 1942 can not be ascribed to lack of Enigma-based intelligence. As the corresponding period in 1941 bore witness, heavy independent sinkings could be expected from heavy independent traffic, which could not be given detailed instructions for evasion. The coastwise traffic off the United States concentrated the unprotected merchant ships into identifiable lanes which could be raided by the U-boats until the latter ran out of torpedoes and fuel.

The relief provided by the U-boats' concentration in American waters did not provide a sufficiently long respite for the Allied cryptanalysts, and when in late May 1942 a single group returned to the Atlantic convoy routes, the copious signals traffic remained impenetrable. On the other hand, the *B-Dienst* was currently reading the latest British "routine" convoy cipher, introduced in 1941 for Anglo-U.S.-Canadian cooperation, having completed reconstruction in February 1942 just as GC&CS "lost" Enigma.

The pendulum would have swung in completely the opposite direction when U-boat operations against the convoys resumed had the respite not granted the escort forces the opportunity to fit the latest equipment weapons, and sensors, and to become proficient in their use. This was specifically true of HF/DF and centimetric radar At the same time, the Western Approaches Tactical Unit, as the "Tactical Table Unit" had become, had been given the leisure to re-examine procedures. The result was that when, in July 1942, the U-boats began to return in force, the escorts were able to exact a toll which should have acted as a deterrent, for the dozen escorted merchant ships lost from North Atlantic convoys that month cost six U-boats, while as many more were sunk by patrols.

It was inevitable that such a favorable rate of exchange could not be sustained. "Only" seventy U-boats were on patrol in July 1942; this rose to eighty-six in August and their effectiveness was out of proportion to the small increase, for losses in convoy more than doubled. Twenty-two ships were sunk from seven ocean convoys and twenty-one from thirteen convoys intercepted in the Caribbean and Gulf of Mexico; escorts destroyed five U-boats. Independent and straggler losses rose only slightly, with fifty-two ships sunk north of the equator in August. For the first time in the war, more than half-a-million gross tons of Allied merchant shipping was lost to U-boats in a single month.

While it might have been expected that a further increase in the number of active submarines to one hundred in September would have been matched by a corresponding increase in the number of merchant ship losses this was not the case, for the U-boats managed to intercept only twelve convoys compared with the fifteen which had been sighted in August. More boats made delivered attacks, but their scale of success was much reduced. For example, in the previous month, forty-eight direct contacts had resulted in the sinking of twenty-two ships in convoy and three stragglers in mid-ocean; in September, however, the sixty contacts sank only thirteen ships in convoy and six stragglers from the ten transatlantic convoys which were actually attacked.[4] The only saving grace from BdU's point of view was that this slight success was achieved without loss and independents were still about in large numbers, fifty-one being sunk in this one month.

The last quarter of 1942 followed September's pattern, with one important difference. Six transatlantic convoys were intercepted in each month, 120 U-boats approached sufficiently close to attack or to be prevented from doing so by the escort, and these sank sixty-three ships in convoy, nine stragglers, and two escorts. The difference was that they paid dearly for these sinkings, thirteen submarines being destroyed by the escorts. Elsewhere, proportionately more was achieved by fewer U-boats at less cost: twenty-four contacts with five north-south ocean convoys resulted in eighteen sinkings for the loss of two boats. Perhaps the most important statistic of the many available was that three out of every four ocean convoys reached their destinations without loss as did ninety-seven out of every one hundred ships that sailed in these convoys.

Without doubt, chance played a hand in this long game. The North Atlantic weather was particularly severe during the winter of 1942–43, and the succession of gales affected the U-boats as badly as they did the convoy and the escorts. Thus, although as many as twenty-seven U-boats were ordered to concentrate against a single convoy in October, only eight managed to make contact and two of those were sunk before reaching an attacking position. The merchant ship masters and escort group commanders had also learned the lessons of previous winters and knew the dangers of dispersal and straggling under stress of weather: of ninety ships lost in the North Atlantic, only ten were stragglers, compared with thirty-four out of eighty-eight in the last quarter of 1940.

Although signals intelligence was of little assistance to the Allies during this phase, by the standards of the similarly Enigma-less winter of 1940–41 the convoy escorts were actually winning, for they were fending off far larger numbers of U-boats while exacting a steady toll, not simply of the Atlantic U-boat fleet as a whole but of those which were able to intercept convoys—fewer than a third of the number of boats at sea in any one month.

BdU acknowledged the increased expertise of the defenses by modifying tactics and introducing technical countermeasures of varying effectiveness. Of these, the most successful was the "Metox" UHF-band radar intercept gear, which began to enter service during the summer of 1942 and gave a useful measure of immunity against aircraft search radar and substantially reduced losses in the transit areas. Against most surface escort groups its use was limited, for the majority of Royal Navy and U.S. Navy ships were now fitted with undetectable centimetric radar sets. New anti-escort weapons, notably the acoustic homing torpedo, were under development, but these would not be ready until the summer of 1943. In the meantime, the U-boats' best defense proved to be its ability to dive deeper than the Allies imagined. The Type VIIC had a "normal" limit of 660 feet, but in an emergency it could go safely to 1,000 feet.

To extend the endurance of the U-boats operating off the Americas, BdU had in March 1942 introduced the "U-tanker," originally a modified operational boat but latterly a custom-built "Milch Cow" capable of supplying fuel oil, lubricants, provisions and even torpedoes to the fighting boats. Although the front line had moved closer to the bases in France by late 1942, the U-tankers had proved to be so successful that they were retained as a force multiplier, enabling the operational groups to be redeployed at their best sea speeds without regard to the individual boats' fuel states. Replenishment at sea in the winter Atlantic was by no means a relaxing pastime. Taken with the increasing difficulty of penetrating the convoys' defenses, BdU could not expect more than two or three active group operations—successful or unsuccessful—per U-boat sortie, even when the boats failed to make contact, because of the strain on the crew.[5]

Hindsight may be the curse of the historian but it is crucial to the analyst. A definite pattern had emerged from the renewed convoy campaign—a pattern which should have been apparent to the Allied trade divisions if not to Dönitz, who had to rely on his CO's inflated claims for his analyses. Despite increasing numbers, superior intelligence, and the Allied cryptanalysts' continuing lack of success, between July 1942 and the end of January 1943 the U-boats managed to "win" only one major convoy battle per month.

The optimistic convoy situation belied the actual state of affairs, although it reflected "what might have been" had more ships been in convoy. In October 1942 the losses again fell upon the independents, particularly in the more distant waters of the central and South Atlantic, outside the interlinking convoy system. Altogether, fifty-four independents were sunk compared with only twenty-three convoyed transatlantic ships; perhaps the worst aspect was that while the latter was compensated by the sinking of five U-boats, the independents represented completely "free hits."

November 1942 was the worst month of the war in terms of tonnage sunk, with over 720,000 tons lost worldwide, The transatlantic losses were actually marginally less than in October, with twenty-eight ships sunk in convoy and forty-seven independents lost in the Atlantic areas, of which twenty-three were off the coast of the Americas, where anti-submarine measures had been steadily improving since the bad days of the summer. The contemporary inability to read the U-boat cipher had little real effect on independent losses, but these continued to bite deep into the Allies' deep-water shipping resources. Every ship lost represented a loss of capacity either to sustain the war effort of the nations closest to the front line (and therefore fighting a campaign of survival) or to develop and sustain an offensive against the Axis. The remarkable facility with which the United States shipbuilding industry responded, first to make good losses and then to expand the Allied carrying capacity, should never blind historians to the problem of manning those ships. The merchant crews lost by policies which ignored all previous lessons were as much assets as the ships themselves and were absolute losses to the Allied cause.

December 1942 appeared to bring a ray of long-term hope. GC&CS' unremitting efforts against the four-rotor Enigma were at last making substantial progress, thanks to yet another windfall cipher material retrieved from the sinking wreck of the *U 559* off Haifa.[6] This was sufficient to lead Admiral Sir Dudley Pound, the First Sea Lord, to pass on the qualified good news to Admiral Ernest J. King. In this message, sent on 13 December,[7] Pound reemphasized the need for complete security saying that: "It would be a tragedy if we had to start all over again on what would undoubtedly be a still more difficult problem." It was a somewhat cloudy dawn. Bletchley Park's successes were spasmodic during the first three months of 1943, sometimes reading the U-boat traffic currently usually within three days, but occasionally not at all for a period of over a week.

The escorts fought on, unaware of this backroom battle. Ninety-seven U-boats were at sea during December, but the weather again favored the convoys and the escorts. Up to Christmas Day, only five transatlantic convoys were located, and fourteen contacts had resulted in just six sinkings while three of the U-boats had been destroyed. On 26 December, the weather gods smiled on BdU when the westbound convoy ONS 154, diverted far to the south to avoid storms in the Iceland area, was sighted by the southernmost boat of a patrol line. During the next five days, thirteen of the eighteen U-boats ordered to intercept made contact and sank thirteen ships from the convoy and two stragglers. Only one U-boat was lost. Even with this success, BdU could scarcely be satisfied with December's results, for besides the twenty-one ships sunk from transatlantic convoys and two sinkings from chance encounters with north-south convoys, the Allies had lost only twenty-four independents in all North Atlantic areas.

ONS 154 was, furthermore, merely a "blip on the graph." Marginally fewer U-boats were at sea (ninety-two) in January 1943, and they managed to intercept only three convoys bound for the United Kingdom, from which one convoyed ship and three stragglers were sunk with the loss of a single submarine. The *B-Dienst's* decrypts had revealed the extent of the direct traffic between the United States and the Mediterranean, and by redeploying an existing group nine hundred miles southwards and redirecting boats on passage, BdU assembled a force of a dozen submarines to intercept the first major eastbound tanker convoy, TM 1, to the west of the Canaries. Eight actually made contact and, thanks to a weak and inexperienced escort, they sank seven of the nine ships. Those U-boats which had sufficient fuel loitered in the area during the rest of the month but succeeded only in sinking four stragglers from two other U.S. Mediterranean convoys.

The most striking statistic of the month, however, was that for the first time since the outbreak of war in September 1939, independent losses in the Atlantic were fewer than those in convoy. Only nine ships were sunk in all and of those only one was in the waters of the Americas, where fifteen had been sunk in December. February proved to be even less costly, with only six independents lost, but this success was seen only in negative terms in some quarters where, the reasoning ran, that when put to the test convoy was proving to be more expensive than independent sailings. There were, of course, two underlying reasons for the trend: fewer independent ships were being sailed, reducing the opportunities for chance encounters in areas of heavy traffic, and BdU had recognition that large concentrations of ships presented the best opportunity to sink the necessary monthly tonnage.

In early February 1943, the British convoy cipher and information from a rescued merchant seaman enabled BdU to set up the first interception in force of a U.K.-bound convoy since the beginning of November. Out of twenty-one U-boats deployed, twenty made contact with the fifty-four-ship convoy in mid-Atlantic. They ran into a most determined escort (KG B.2—four old escort destroyers and four corvettes, later joined by three U.S. Coast Guard cutters and supported by Liberator aircraft from Iceland), and only five submarines managed to deliver torpedo attacks, sinking nine ships out of the main body of SC 118 and one straggler. Every U-boat was attacked, fifteen by the ships and five by aircraft, four were damaged and forced to return to base, and three were sunk.

With over one hundred U-boats at sea, BdU could call upon fresh groups to intercept the next convoys, but it was distracted from the key eastbound convoys by excellent positional information provided by the *Luftwaffe,* whose DF stations were able to intercept transmissions made by the Coastal Command aircraft escorting the convoys. This real-time intelligence coincided with a loss by GC&CS of current Enigma settings which had kept the eastbound convoys away from the waiting U-boat groups. Three successive westbound (and therefore strategically "empty") convoys were intercepted, the first by four U-boats, the next by fifteen and the last by a single boat, attempts at concentration having failed. Inevitably the largest group enjoyed the greatest success, sinking fourteen out of the eighteen merchant ships lost, but the series cost another four U-boats destroyed and several damaged. Although the U-boats had grossly overclaimed, neither the sinkings-to-contact rate nor the sinkings-to-loss ratio could be regarded as satisfactory.

From the Allied point of view, February's losses in convoy—thirty-one ships in convoy and six stragglers—were alarming, the more so as all had occurred on the transatlantic routes and had far exceeded the independent losses. The Allies could not have known that the air and sea escorts of the eleven ocean convoys intercepted or encountered had dispatched twelve U-boats out of the fifty-nine individual boats which had made contact, but it should have been evident that each major effort was followed by a lull which permitted succeeding convoys to pass either scot-free or at least without serious loss.

For this, the intermittent Bletchley Park successes can take some of the credit, providing sufficient information to the OIC for effective evasive routing. But it was noticeable that hitherto, even with several large groups at their disposal for interception and decrypts to give warning of convoy movements, the U-boat headquarters staff had seldom been able to coordinate simultaneous major operations, possibly because the sheer number of submarines at sea was growing unwieldy. They were to be more successful in March.

One hundred and sixteen U-boats operated against Atlantic shipping in March 1943, making ninety-six individual contacts with convoys, but not until the end of the first week was the first convoy sighted. SC 121 was unlucky for it had been skillfully rerouted between two waiting groups only to be sighted by a U-boat in transit. Twenty-eight submarines were redeployed to overhaul or cut off the convoy, but in indifferent weather only eleven made contact, sinking five ships from the main body and seven stragglers. The general movement of U-boat groups put another dozen boats in the path of HX 228 just as the Enigma traffic became indecipherable again, but the defending escort group kept losses down to four merchant ships and sank two U-boats.

The battle which followed four days after the last shots of HX 228 was a complete disaster for the Allies, but it should be seen in its true context. The Admiralty made a fundamental mistake in sending a "fast" convoy with a weak and indifferently led escort, HX 229, up the track of the "slow" SC 122 (the difference was, in fact a knot and a half). The official history[8] implies that lack of current decryption was behind the inability to provide effective rerouting and states that evasion on the basis of DF bearings proved ineffective. But the fact is that HX 229 was located by accident, a U-boat astern of the convoy sighting a detached escort and making the report which led to the first actual contact being made by a group which was not looking for HX 229. The two groups which were lying in wait ahead ran into SC 122, 120 miles to the east while HX 229 continued to close from astern. Eventually forty U-boats were ordered to operate against what became a confused gaggle of shipping, but of these only nineteen made attacks, resulting in the loss of twenty-three ships out of eightyseven in the two convoys.

Nearly simultaneously, twenty U-boats of three other groups made copybook interception of a U.S. Mediterranean convoy UGS 6. This convoy's track was known in detail, thanks to the efforts of the *B-Dienst,* but unfortunately for the submarines, the six U.S. Navy destroyers of the escort conducted a text book defense, and only five U-boats got within firing range to sink four of the ships. One U-boat was destroyed.

The 1943 end-of-year summary by the Naval Staff's Anti-U-boat Division stated that the heavy losses up to 20 March 1943 (i.e., from HX 229/SC 122) had led the Admiralty to believe ". . . that it appeared possible that we should not be able to continue convoy as an effective stem of defence against the enemy's pack tactics."[9] This paints a picture of an imminent change of policy, which was not the case. The intermittent failures of Bletchley Park were becoming fewer, although there was always the risk that another blow, as the introduction of the fourth rotor had been, would cause the complete loss of all U-boat intelligence derived from cryptanalysts. But just as up-to-date signal intelligence had not been wholly responsible for all the successes in the North Atlantic, so its absence was by no means the main cause of some of the worst reverses.

The Admiralty still had a number of measures which were even more imminent and which were based wholly upon the doctrine of convoy. More very-long-range aircraft were already appearing far out in the mid-Atlantic (they had supported the later stages of the passage of HX 229/SC 122), but as important were the "support groups," homogeneous squadrons of sloops or destroyers which had worked together in the anti-submarine role and which were to reinforce threatened convoys. The concept of these independent anti-submarine units dated back to the autumn of 1942, and while the lack of escorts and the demands of the North African campaign had prevented more than a brief trial, the Western Approaches staff had kept the idea alive to the extent of playing out a paper exercise on the Tactical Table as HX 228 was fighting a real battle.[10]

Two support groups, one British the other American, took the field in late March with an escort carrier attached. The USS *Bogue's* first convoy was SC 123, while the first to benefit from a Royal Navy carrier support group was HX 230. The former was not threatened, but one ship was sunk, in exchange for the U-boat responsible, from the latter. The full impact of "organic air" as a mid-ocean U-boat killer was not to be felt until after May 1943, but its defensive benefits were immediately apparent, adding an extra dimension to the U-boats' already considerable tactical problem.

Total losses for March 1943 amounted to forty-seven ships, of which ten were stragglers, from eight transatlantic convoys; four independents were also sunk in the North Atlantic. Elsewhere, on the north-south route and off the Americas, twenty-one ships were sunk from eight convoys attacked, as well as two independents; as before, the sinkings per submarine contact were higher in these areas—despite the achievements of the wolf packs which had attacked HX 229/SC 118, the U-boats had still not achieved a one-to-one rate against the east-west shipping. Over half the U-boats at sea found convoys, but seven were lost to the escorts and five were sunk by patrols. They themselves had sunk just over half a million tons of Allied shipping.

On the other hand, during the first three months of 1943, 270 more convoyed merchant ships had reached their destinations safely than during the last quarter of 1942, even though the number of convoys intercepted had increased as had the number of ships sunk. Only one convoy escort had been lost, as against three in late 1942, while the toll taken of U-boats around the convoys had risen from fourteen to twenty-four, an exchange rate of one submarine for every five ships.

Most of the U-boat losses were made good in April from new construction and by re-allocating submarines from West Africa and the South Atlantic, but although seventy U-boats were sailed from Germany, Norway, and France to operate against the convoys, bringing the total on patrol to 111 for the month, they achieved little of significance. Over fifty individual U-boats came close enough to convoys to attack or be sunk by the escorts, and they sank just twenty-four ships in convoy and six stragglers from seventy-six contacts in all areas; nine were destroyed by escort vessels and aircraft and six by patrols or mines in the transit areas.

The lack of success was not for want of opportunity. Although GC&CS had broken back into the Enigma settings after the mid-March catastrophe and could provide timely evasive routing intelligence, the *B-Dienst* was just as active and successful in decrypting the alterations of route and, in fact, the U-boats intercepted one more convoy in April than they did in March and in sufficient strength to achieve reasonable results. Weather, strong defenses, and inexperienced commanding officers were considered to be major factors, and all three were certainly present when, towards the end of the month, the twelve U-boats in contact with HX 234 managed to sink only two ships.

The U-boat command staffs appear to have taken some comfort from the fact that losses in the second half of 1942 and the first quarter of 1943 were proportionately lower than those suffered during the first twenty-seven months of the war when expressed as a percentage of the submarine force at sea on operations. In March 1943, replacements were still coming forward faster than the Allies could sink them. But what the German navy's statisticians overlooked was the *cumulative* effect of the losses and the special nature of the COs. The fifty-odd U-boats destroyed by convoy escorts during the nine most recent months represented a loss of experienced manpower needed for rapid expansion—their First and Second Watch Officers, who would have expected to get their own boats after a successful apprenticeship, were a lost generation. The boats also represented much of the potentially most effective elements of the U-boat fleet, for they were an appreciable percentage (nearly 20 percent) of the minority which actually found a convoy.

The end of March 1943 was, perhaps, not the best moment for any measured analysis by BdU's staff. Dönitz had replaced Gross-Admiral Raeder at the head of the German navy in January 1943 but was not ready to delegate the U-boat war to his capable Chief of Staff, Kapitän Godt. Instead, in the last days of March, he pulled back the operations staff from Paris (whither it had been withdrawn from Kerneval following the British Commando raid on St. Nazaire a year before) to Berlin, where it became functional on 31 March.

Quite apart from the discontinuity caused by the move, the overall commander had more than physically distanced himself and his group of talented veterans from the frontline crews. Once totally immersed in every aspect of U-boat activity, Dönitz now had the entire navy to supervise, and even the BdU staff could be regarded as "them"—the remote, rear-area warriors. Whether or not the move to Berlin reduced efficiency and morale, 31 March 1943 is a symbolic date, for it marked the beginning in the decline of the fortunes of the U-boat arm.

The Royal Navy's escort commanders certainly noticed a lack of expertise, or of determination, on the part of the U-boats during the weeks that followed HX 229/SC 122, but no great comfort was derived from the lull. As April drew to a close, initial contact was made between the escorts of convoy ONS 5 and the first of four groups, totaling sixty U-boats, which BdU had assembled for a great set-piece battle. This proved to be one of the epic encounters of the Battle of the Atlantic and has been regarded ever since as a turning point. The victory of the escorts, by six U-boats to thirteen merchant ships, was, however, a triumph for tactical and technical expertise, won mainly by the ships and aircraft involved. In this sense, it was another step on the "knock down, drag out" road shown by the defenders of HG 76, SC 118, and UGS 6.

Dönitz had held fast to a very clear aim for the past year: Britain and her allies were to be brought to their knees by the submarine blockade in the North Atlantic. He resisted every fresh initiative by the Naval Staff (the *Seekriegsleitung*) and even by Hitler himself if it appeared to lead to the weakening of the U-boat fleet in the Atlantic. One can sympathize with the *SKL,* whose only major maritime contribution to the wider war could be the submarine arm. They wished to deploy this to the Mediterranean to bolster a flagging ally, to the Indian Ocean to reassure the Japanese, and to the Arctic, where they were not only to interdict supplies to Russia but also to deter an invasion of Norway. Dönitz remained adamant and his philosophy coincided with his operational doctrine: "Strategic pressure alone is not sufficient, only sinkings count."[11] The North Atlantic convoys provided the potential numbers of victims and were, besides, the critical link in Allied strategy. Increased sinkings increased the pressure to the point where the stresses began to show at the highest level, but not, thankfully, in the commands, the groups, or the men in the line of battle.

The end finally came on 24 May 1943, after a week in which the fifty-odd U-boats had attempted two major set-piece battles only to be thwarted by evasive routing and by veteran defenders. Dönitz acknowledged a defeat which he believed to be only temporary. He would resume the campaign with new weapons and equipment, as well as with a new generation of commanding officers who would hold the ring until the new types of U-boat could enter service and achieve the victory which he believed had been so close.

Notes

[1]Gunter Hessler, *The U-Boat War in the Atlantic,* 2 vols. (London: HMSO, 1989) 1: 82. Sources consulted in the preparation of this paper include Public Record Office, ADM 119/2058–0 and ADM 234/51. Original research by Mr. R. M. Coppock of the Naval Historical Branch, MoD, and Mr. A. H. Hague, of the World Ship Society into, respectively, causes of U-boat loss and individual convoy passages, has been of the utmost value and is gratefully acknowledged.

[2]E H. Hinsley, et al., *British Intelligence in the Second World War,* 2 vols. (London: HMSO, 1981) 2:173.

[3]Radar-equipped Swordfish "stranded" by the loss of the carrier *Ark Royal* provided this patrol.

[4]Figures for U-boat sightings have been obtained from the BdU War Diaries and correlated with Jürgen Rohwer's "Die U-boot-Erfolge der Achsenmachte 1939–45," which has in turn been compared with manuscript abstracts from the "Convoy Packs" held at the Public Record Office, prepared by Arnold Hague.

[5]Hessler, *U-Boat War in the Atlantic* 2:51

[6]David Kahn, *Seizing the Enigma* (Boston: Houghton Mifflin, 1991), 223–227.

[7]Cited in Hinsley, *British Intelligence,* 233.

[8]Hinsley, *British Intelligence* 2:561–62.

[9]"Monthly Anti-Submarine Report," December 1943 (dated 15 January 1944), 3 PRO ADM 199/2060. This summary does not include Roskill's ringing phrase about "disrupting communications between the New World and Old . . ." but employs this much more mundane phraseology.

[10]Ms. notes by the late Captain H. N. Lake, RN (staff, Western Approaches, 1942–43).

[11]BdU War Diary, 13 August 1942.

CHAPTER SEVENTEEN

"Never In All My Years Had I Imagined a Battle Like That"

Ronald H. Spector

FOCUS QUESTIONS

1. Was Pearl Harbor really a turning point in the American and Japanese appreciation of the value of the aircraft carrier?
2. During the first twelve months of the war, what factors favored the rise of the carrier as the dominant naval weapon?
3. How well prepared were both sides for early carrier warfare? Consider tactics, training, technology and doctrine, and the improvements that were made in each area as time went on.
4. Was the Battle of Midway *decisive*? Why? Why did the U.S. win the battle?

In the Pacific, the Americans and Japanese were rapidly developing sea-air warfare to levels of precision and lethality far beyond anything seen in the European conflict. Both the Japanese and Americans had long expected that at the outbreak of war, Japan would attack the Philippines and the U.S. Navy would launch a drive across the Pacific from Pearl Harbor as outlined in the various Orange Plans for war with Japan, developed by the General Board of

...r College in the 1920s and 1930s. The Japanese had ... American fleet with submarines and aircraft as it ... island bases in the Central Pacific. After the ... own by these attrition attacks, the main battle ... time most favorable to Japan.

..., Admiral Husband E. Kimmel, commander of ... preparing to put the Orange Plan concept into effect ... on the Marshall Islands. This was intended to provoke ... fleet action, pitting the slightly superior American battle ... battleships of the Imperial Japanese Navy. In this scheme the ...riers would provide air reconnaissance and act as bait.[1]

... this time, the Japanese, under the prodding of the commander in ...of the Combined Fleet, Admiral Yamamoto Isoroku, had modified their ...ategy of waylaying the U.S. fleet as it sailed into the Central Pacific. Instead, the war began with a massive carrier air raid on Pearl Harbor in December 1941. Achieving complete surprise, Japanese planes sank five battleships and damaged three others as well as three cruisers and three destroyers. More than 2,100 sailors and marines lost their lives, more men than the U.S. Navy had lost in all of World War I and about as many as the Germans had lost at Jutland. Japanese losses were minimal.

In the weeks after Pearl Harbor, the Japanese moved swiftly to secure their objectives in Southeast Asia. Hong Kong, Malaya, Thailand, Burma, and the Dutch East Indies all fell to the Japanese within three months. Two days after the war began, the British battleship *Prince of Wales* and the battle cruiser *Repulse* were sunk by Japanese bombers and torpedo planes while attempting to defend Malaya. A mixed British, Dutch, American, and Australian cruiser-destroyer force was wiped out by the Japanese in the East Indies a few months later. The Philippines held out the longest, its American and Filipino defenders finally surrendering early in May after a long battle with hunger and disease as well as the Japanese.

Now only the Pacific Fleet remained to oppose the Japanese advance. All three of the fleet's carriers, *Lexington, Saratoga,* and *Enterprise,* had escaped the Pearl Harbor raid, and two additional carriers, *Yorktown* and *Hornet,* had arrived from the Atlantic. In the next twelve months these aircraft carriers would become the dominant weapons.

Even after Pearl Harbor neither the Japanese nor the American admirals had completely lost faith in the battleship. American battleships with light or moderate damage in the Japanese air attack were sent to California for repair and overhaul, while other battleships were summoned from the Atlantic. By the end of March 1942 the Pacific Fleet had seven operational battleships, six of which were more modern than the ships lost at Pearl Harbor.[2] Yet the battleships consumed more fuel than all the carrier task forces combined, and there were only a few tankers available to service the entire Pacific Fleet.

Kimmel's successor, Admiral Chester Nimitz, was loath to risk the psychological impact that would result from the loss of any additional battleships. He, and most of his principal commanders, preferred to save the old ships for the Orange Plan advance across the Central Pacific that they still hoped to put into effect eventually. The Japanese, too, preferred to hold back their battle line for a decisive battle at some future point.

So the field was left to the carriers, which could not, and did not, operate like a battle fleet. Both sides used their carriers for raiding and to support and oppose seaborne invasions. The six largest Japanese carriers, *Akagi, Kaga, Soryu, Hiryu, Shokaku,* and *Zuikoku,* which carried out the attack on Pearl Harbor, composed the First Air Fleet under Admiral Nagumo Chuichi, which operated in carrier divisions of two ships each. The planes of the two carriers in each division formed a single air group under a senior air group commander. Americans operated in "task forces" built around a single carrier screened by cruisers and destroyers.

In the weeks following Pearl Harbor, the Japanese carrier striking force supported the invasion of the U.S. Central Pacific outpost at Wake Island and the seizure of Rabaul on New Britain Island from the Australians. In mid-February, four Japanese carriers attacked the northern Australian town of Darwin. They sank more than a dozen ships in the harbor, destroyed eighteen aircraft, and sent the civilian population of the town streaming away in panic.

Many naval experts still believed that to send carriers against heavily defended land bases was too risky, except where surprise could be achieved as at Pearl Harbor. That view was emphatically not shared by the new commander of the Pacific Fleet, Admiral Chester Nimitz, nor by his boss, Admiral Ernest J. King, Chief of Naval Operations and Commander in Chief, U.S. Fleet, nor by the fiery senior carrier commander, Vice Admiral William F. Halsey. Consequently, the American carriers were even more active than the Japanese, although the two forces would not meet for more than five months. At the end of January 1942, after escorting reinforcements to Samoa, Halsey's Task Force 8, built around the carrier *Enterprise,* penetrated the northern Marshall Islands and raided Kwajalein, Wotje, and Taroa. At the same time, Task Force 17, with Rear Admiral Frank Jack Fletcher in the carrier *Yorktown,* struck targets in the southern Marshalls.

The raids did little damage, but they served to raise morale at a moment when the Allied cause in Asia seemed to be suffering nothing but defeat. "Entering Pearl Harbor after the Marshall raid was the most moving moment of the war for me," recalled a sailor in the *Enterprise.* "As we came down the channel the sunken and burned battleships along Ford Island in plain sight, the crews of the anchored ships at quarters, their white uniforms showing up against their gray ships, cheered us one after another again and again."[3]

More American raids followed. A task force under Vice Admiral Wilson Brown in the carrier *Lexington* was sent far to the southwest to strike the newly acquired Japanese base at Rabaul, while Halsey's task force carried out a raid on Wake Island, then went on to strike Marcus Island nine days later. Brown's force was spotted by Japanese search planes as it neared its launch point two hundred miles from Rabaul. Seventeen bombers from Rabaul struck the

American task force in the late afternoon. They were intercepted by the *Lexington*'s fighters almost directly over the task force.

At least thirteen Japanese bombers were shot down and two more crash-landed. Lieutenant Edward ("Butch") O'Hare became the first U.S. naval fighter ace of the Pacific War, destroying at least three, and possibly five, planes. Aboard the ships of the American task force the crews whooped, cheered, and yelled encouragement to the fighters. As planes taxied to their spots on the *Lexington*'s flight deck, pilots were mobbed by cheering sailors.[4] Admiral Brown reported, "I often had to remind some members of my staff that this was not a football game."[5]

Although Americans focused on the aerial victories and quickly made a hero of O'Hare, the tactical significance of this brief air battle was far more important. The *Lexington* had demonstrated that a carrier's fighters could successfully defend the ship against attacks by land-based aircraft—something the British had never been able to manage in the Mediterranean. Whether they could defend against attacks by other carriers remained to be seen.

Reinforced by Rear Admiral Frank Jack Fletcher in the *Yorktown*, the *Lexington* headed back for another attempt at Rabaul. But by this time, word had come of more attractive targets. Japanese forces had landed at the villages of Lae and Salamau at Huon Gulf on the Papuan Peninsula of eastern New Guinea on March 8. Learning of this development, Admiral Brown set course for New Guinea. Steaming into the Gulf of Papua on the opposite shore of the peninsula, Brown sent more than a hundred aircraft from the *Yorktown* and *Lexington* to strike the surprised Japanese invasion forces. A gunboat, two transports, and a minesweeper were sunk and three warships damaged. It was the most important American naval success to date and an unexpected shock to the Japanese. The Huon Gulf raid was also the first coordinated American air strike mounted from two different carriers.[6]

The Pacific war of raids and counterraids was fought over a vast and empty region of ocean and sky, which filled the enormous watery triangle between Japan, Australia, and Hawaii. This was a strange and remote area of the world full of names like Kwajalein, Truk, Tonga, the Solomon Sea, New Britain, New Caledonia, and the Bismarck Archipelago, which sounded exotic, strange, remote, or simply incomprehensible to both Japanese and American sailors. "Hawaii would be the first strange place," recalled marine aviator Samuel Haynes, "the edge of a world that was not like anything back home. No one I knew had ever been there . . . and it existed in my imagination as a mixture of myths."[7] Japanese sailors spoke of the "lands of eternal summer" in the romantic "Nanyo" or south seas.[8]

While the British and German battle fleets in the North Sea had gone to sea for a few days at a time, Japanese and American ships operated for weeks, crossing and recrossing the equator and the international date line, ranging from Hawaii to Japan, Australia to the Aleutians. The Americans refueled at sea from huge tankers named for rivers. The tanker would steam at the same speed and on a parallel course, twenty-five to fifty feet from the vessel it was fueling. Line handlers in life jackets passed lines and fuel hoses across the gap as the two ships rolled in the open ocean. "The waves between the ships in this operation were huge, and standing on the flight deck on the carrier you could watch the great bulk of the tanker rise up above you and then crash down."[9] The slightest brush between the two ships tore and mangled their steel superstructures "as though a head on collision had occurred. A parting manila hawser could snap back and kill a man."[10] Underway refueling enabled American fleets to remain at sea for long periods without having to reduce speed to conserve fuel.

Operating near the equator for extended periods, sailors often worked in conditions of stifling heat. "The bright sun sent out blazing rays and it was steaming hot inside the ship," wrote seaman Kuramoto Iki. "This completely dissipated my cherished illusions about the tropics."[11] Aviation Ordnanceman Alvin Kernan, who served in the *Enterprise* and *Hornet*, recalled that "heat rash tormented everyone particularly around the waist where several layers of wet clothes twisted and pulled inside the belt. A story circulated that when the heat rash . . . girdled your waist you died."[12]

Fresh water for bathing, washing, or laundering clothes was a constant concern. Aboard the *Hornet,* sailors used a single bucket of soapy water to wash both their clothes and themselves, then another bucket for rinsing, finishing up with a luxurious "five or ten seconds under the shower spray (with no time allowed to adjust the water temperature)."[13]

"The food on carriers is generally quite good for the first month," one naval aviator recalled. "Thereafter it begins to deteriorate. Fresh milk disappears almost immediately and the next to go are fresh eggs, greens, fresh vegetables and finally fresh meat. Officers and crew alike begin to live on powdered milk, powdered eggs and canned fruit and vegetables and meat."[14] A few more weeks and even the powdered milk and eggs would disappear. On one *Hornet* deployment, "beans were being ground up and called potatoes and there were beetles in the flour." Smaller ships in the task force served Spam and "a kind of artificial potato."[15] The *Saratoga,* which lacked adequate food storage space to accommodate her large wartime crew, went to sea with food stacked in the passageways.[16]

Heat, boredom, and fatigue were the staples of naval life in the Pacific. At sea, most sailors worked fourteen to sixteen hours a day. The day began for most seamen two hours before sunrise when a bugle sounded reveille followed by flight quarters and general quarters as sailors manned their battle stations and flight deck crews prepared to launch the first planes. From first light until dark, the flight deck was the scene of constant noise and activity. Although an aircraft carrier's crew of 2,000 to 3,000 men might include little more than a hundred pilots, carrier operations were a labor-intensive activity. A 1942 fighter squadron, for example, included only nineteen pilots, but 120 enlisted men.[17] Flight deck operations required a small army of mechanics, technicians, and plane handlers. Because the flight deck was invariably used to park aircraft, planes had to be pushed forward to allow room at the rear of the flight deck for landing. For takeoffs the evolution was reversed. The entire process of shifting and spotting aircraft had to be accomplished by hand with teams of plane handlers pushing aircraft back and forth at a dead run. Each team of specialists wore different-colored helmets and jerseys to aid in quick identification: "Chockmen," who handled the wooden chocks placed under a plane's wheels, wore purple. "Hookmen," who had the dangerous job of releasing the airplane's arrestor hook just before takeoff, wore green, fueling crews wore red, communications personnel wore brown, and so forth. The success of a carrier depended in large measure on how efficiently it could launch, recover, and reposition its aircraft. Aboard the *Hornet* about thirty airplanes could be shifted from forward to aft in less than six minutes.[18]

Departing planes were formed up aft as close together as possible. At the command "Start engines," dozens of engines roared to life, emitting small red and blue flames. The carrier was turned into the wind to provide maximum lift for the aircraft. The flight deck officer, the maestro conductor of the noisy concert of rumbling, thundering aircraft, held up his black-and-white-checkered flag. Following a signal from the flight deck officer, a pilot taxied his plane onto the "spot" for takeoff. With brakes set, the throttle was pushed far forward, bringing the engine to full power. When the flight deck officer waved down his flag, the brakes were released and the plane rolled down the deck and into the air.

Despite the minute precision of air operations, a carrier's flight deck remained a dangerous place even in the absence of the enemy. Accidents were far from rare. Guns in the plane's wings could go off accidentally, spraying the deck with .50-caliber bullets; lines could snap and whip across the deck, maiming or decapitating anyone in their path; busy crewmen occasionally walked into the whirring propellers of an aircraft. A plane crash on the flight deck almost always resulted in death or injuries to flight deck hands as well as to the aircrew.

Though the flight deck crews, mechanics, and ordnancemen were a critical element and hundreds of other ratings performed essential tasks, attention focused almost exclusively on the aviators, the sharp edge of the carrier's power. Mostly young men in their early twenties, with a sprinkling of older Annapolis graduates, enlisted pilots, and early graduates of the aviation cadet programs, they were members of the navy's most select caste, and they knew it.

Aviation was still romantic, dangerous, and exciting in 1942. "None of the kids I knew had ever been in a plane or expected to be in one," recalled pilot Samuel Haynes.[19] The naval aviator, in particular, constantly performed his most essential and difficult function—landing on a narrow moving deck—before a large, sometimes admiring, sometimes critical, but always attentive audience. Even in his day-to-day functions, he was a kind of star soloist.

Japanese aviators also saw themselves as the superstars of the new air-sea warfare. Survivors of the almost inhuman rigors of the Japanese flight schools, many had been flying combat missions since the beginning of the Sino-Japanese War in 1937 and had accumulated hundreds of flying hours. In the carriers *Zuikaku* and *Shokaku* nearly all fighter pilots had more than two years of flight experience.[20]

Japanese naval aircraft were technically superior to most American land-based and carrier-based planes. Fighter pilots flew the Mitsubishi A6M2 Type 00 carrier fighter, the famous "Zero." Fast, light, and exceptionally maneuverable, with a superior rate of climb and relatively long range, the Zero was the first carrier-based fighter to equal or surpass the performance of the best land-based fighters. It had dominated the skies in the China war, and several Japanese pilots had become aces. Only a few hundred Zeroes had been sufficient to maintain complete air superiority for the Japanese during their lightning conquest of Southeast Asia and the South Pacific. Losses had been very low. Fighter pilots compared their Zeroes "to master craftsmen's Japanese swords."[21] Other carrier aircraft, the Nakajima B5N2 Type 97 "Kate" torpedo plane and the Aichi D3A1 Type 99 "Val," were less spectacular but still equal or superior to their American counterparts.

Japanese aerial torpedoes were also far more reliable than similar American weapons. The Japanese Type 91 aerial torpedo could be dropped from several hundred feet by a plane traveling at more than 200 hundred miles an hour. The American Mark 13, however, suffered from numerous technical defects. It had to be dropped at the height of no more than 200 feet by an airplane traveling less than 130 miles per hour. Once in the water, the Mark 13's speed was little greater than that of a destroyer.[22] In Admiral Brown's air raid on the Japanese forces at Huon Gulf, American torpedo planes scored several hits on ships but their torpedoes failed to explode. "You could see the streaks of torpedoes going right to the side of the cruisers and nothing happened," reported one aviator. "I saw one or two go right on underneath, come out the other side, and bury itself in the bank on the other shore."[23]

American fighter pilots flew the Grumman F4F Wildcat, a rugged well-armed aircraft with pilot armor, bulletproof windscreens, and self-sealing fuel tanks, but inferior to the Zero in speed, range, maneuverability, and rate of climb. A Zero could reach 20,000 feet in just under seven and a half minutes. A Wildcat required more than ten minutes. Americans also flew the Douglas Devastator torpedo bomber, which had been a very advanced design when it was introduced in 1937. It had been the fleet's first low-wing, all metal monoplane and could carry a 22-inch torpedo. So pleased had the navy been with the Devastator that it deferred procuring a new torpedo plane, the Grumman Avenger, until 1940; the result was that no Avengers reached the carrier squadrons until months after Pearl Harbor.[24] The Devastator's low speed and lack of maneuverability made it extremely vulnerable to enemy fighters and antiaircraft guns. That slowness also made it difficult for the short-range Wildcats to provide escorts for the torpedo planes on longer missions. Of U.S. carrier aircraft, only the rugged Douglas Dauntless dive-bomber was to prove a completely effective weapon, and it remained in service aboard carriers until late 1944.

At the end of March 1942, Admiral Nagumo, with five carriers, four fast battleships, three cruisers, and nine destroyers, left the Celebes Straits near Borneo and passed through the Strait of Malacca into the Indian Ocean. Around the same time, another force under Vice Admiral Ozawa, consisting of a small aircraft carrier, six cruisers, and eight destroyers, sailed from Malaya to attack shipping in the Bay of Bengal.

For a week, Nagumo's task force roamed the Indian Ocean virtually unchallenged by the British, whose Royal Navy had held undisputed sway there for 150 years. The main British bases at Colombo and Trincomalee in Ceylon were bombed by Nagumo's carrier planes, while Ozawa's force sank almost 100,000 tons of shipping in the Bay of Bengal in just five days. The British Eastern Fleet under Admiral Sir James Somerville, which had only two modern carriers with less than a hundred aircraft, avoided a confrontation with the Japanese, but the heavy cruisers *Dorsetshire* and *Cornwall* and the small carrier *Hermes,* which were at Ceylon at the time of the air raids, were sunk by Nagumo's planes. The rest of the Eastern Fleet eventually withdrew to East Africa.

On April 18, while Nagumo's fleet was returning from its victorious foray into the Indian Ocean, the Americans pulled off a spectacular raid of their own. Sixteen Army Air Forces B-25 bombers flying from the carrier *Hornet* bombed Tokyo and a handful of other cities. The damage done was slight, but the psychological impact was enormous. "Our homeland has been air raided and we missed the enemy without firing a shot at him. This is exceedingly regrettable," reported Combined Fleet Chief of Staff Ugaki Matomi in his diary.[25]

The Tokyo raid helped resolve a long debate among the Japanese high command in favor of an offensive into the Central Pacific with the object of capturing the island of Midway and luring the American carriers into a decisive battle. Already scheduled operations in the Southwest Pacific to isolate Australia were moved forward.

The Japanese objective in the Southwest Pacific was the Australian town of Port Moresby on the south coast of the Papuan Peninsula. Once in Japanese hands, Port Moresby could serve as a base for the capture of Fiji, New Caledonia, and other points along the tenuous six-thousand-mile line of communications from the United States to Australia and New Zealand.[26] Two large carriers of Admiral Nagumo's striking force, *Shokaku* and *Zuikaku,* under Vice Admiral Takagi Takeo, were assigned to cover the invasion operations aimed at Port Moresby and the small island of Tulagi in the Solomons, which the Japanese wanted as a seaplane base. The Japanese planned to seize Tulagi first on May 3, 1942, to guard the left flank of the invasion. After that, the Port Moresby invasion force, protected by the small carrier *Shoho* and four cruisers, would sail from Rabaul.

American code breakers in Pearl Harbor, Melbourne, and Washington were by now reading large portions of the Japanese code and ciphers and alerted Nimitz to an impending Japanese offensive in the Southwest Pacific. Nimitz sent the carrier *Lexington* to join the *Yorktown,* under Admiral Fletcher, already cruising in the south Pacific. The *Lexington* task force, under Rear Admiral Aubrey Fitch, reached Fletcher on May 1 in the blue-green waters of the Coral Sea, the body of water separating Australia, the Solomons, and eastern New Guinea. *Yorktown* had been in the South Pacific for more than two months and her crew were "living on hard tack and beans."[27] Both task forces began refueling from their accompanying oilers, an extremely slow process that consumed most of the next two days.

On May 3, word reached Fletcher of Japanese landings at Tulagi and the admiral raced north with the *Yorktown* and other ships that had completed fueling to attack the invasion forces. Admiral Takagi's carrier striking force, which should have provided cover for the operations at Tulagi, was far away, having been delayed ferrying aircraft to Rabaul. Consequently, the *Yorktown's* planes were unopposed when they roared down on the Japanese destroyers' transports and landing craft off Rabaul.

The pilots returned to their carriers in a jubilant mood to report destroyers, cruisers, and transports sunk. In fact, Japanese losses were confined to three small minesweepers and minor damage to other ships. This was a small success indeed for the number of bombs and torpedoes expended, but enough to send the remnants of the Tulagi force steaming hurriedly back to Rabaul.

Fletcher's air attacks alerted the Japanese to the presence of American carriers in the region, and now U.S. Navy code breakers confirmed the presence of the *Shokaku* and *Zuikaku* in the Coral Sea area. In response, Fletcher combined his two carriers into a single task force and headed for the Jomard Passage in the Loisiade Archipelago, through which he expected the Port Moresby invasion force to pass as it rounded the eastern tip of New Guinea. While he lacked precise information about the enemy carriers, he assumed they would be covering the flanks of the invasion force. In fact, only the small carrier *Shoho* was with the invasion force. Takagi's big carriers were actually behind—that is, to the northeast of—Fletcher's force, having rounded the Solomons and entered the Coral Sea on the 6th.

The Battle of the Coral Sea was to be the first between opposing fleets of carriers, and both sides made plenty of mistakes. At one point on the 6th, the Japanese and American fleets were less than seventy miles from each other, but failed to make contact. The following day the skies over the Coral Sea were filled with search planes as the opposing forces looked for each other. Searching to the south, Takagi's planes found the American oiler *Neosho* and the destroyer *Sims* stationed by Fletcher in what he believed was a safe location. They reported them as a carrier task force. Takagi flung his entire striking force, some eighty planes, at the two hapless ships, sinking the *Sims* and crippling the *Neosho,* which sank some time later. Fletcher's carriers, however, were left unmolested.

Still expecting the Japanese to come south through the Jomard Passage, Fletcher sent search planes to the north and west, and one of these happened upon the *Shoho* and her escorting cruisers. Convinced that they had found the *Shokaku* and *Zuikaku,* Fletcher and Fitch dispatched almost a hundred planes

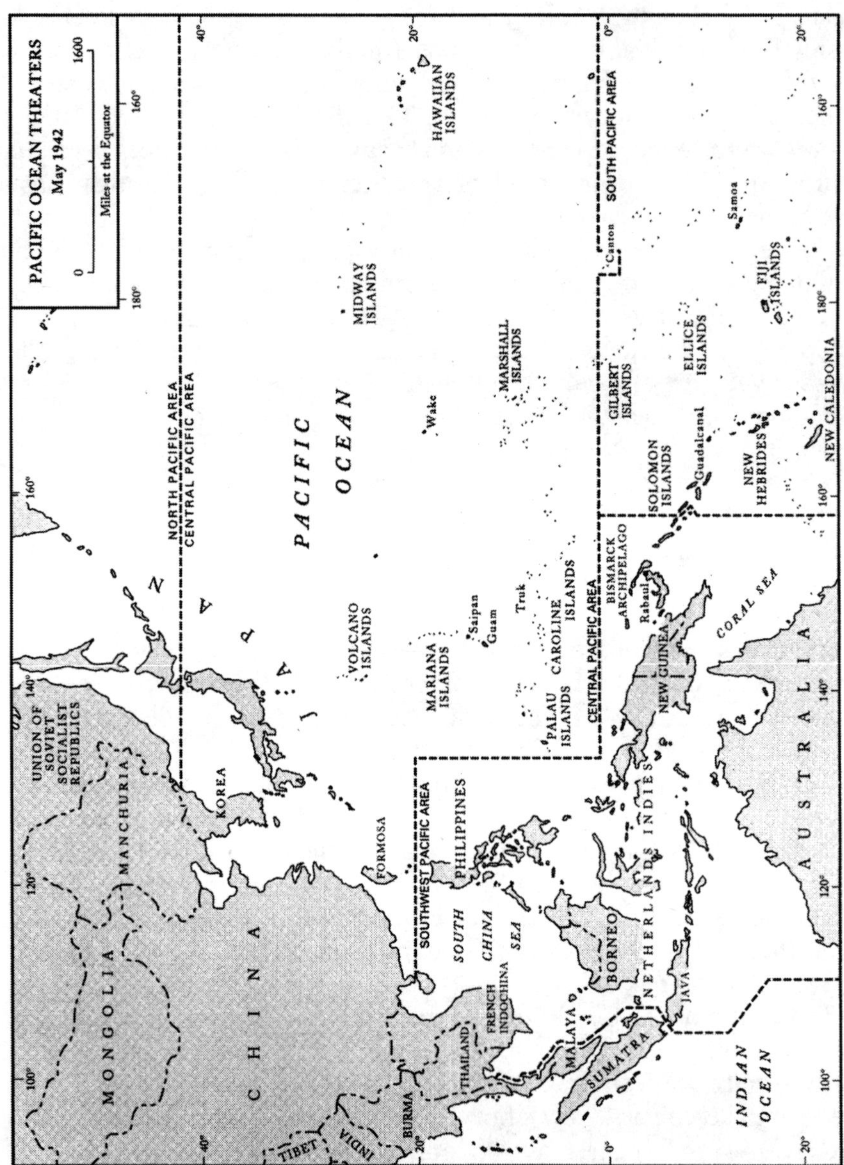

against the *Shoho,* which was soon reduced to a flaming wreck by successive waves of American bombers and torpedo planes. Thirty minutes after the *Shoho* disappeared beneath the sea, Lieutenant Commander Robert E. Dixon, leader of *Lexington's* Scouting Two, sent an electrifying message to the task force. "Scratch one flattop! signed Bob."[28]

Careful questioning of the jubilant aviators soon convinced the *Yorktown's* air staff that the carrier had not been either the *Shokoku* or *Zuikaku,* which were, therefore, still at large. Takagi had already learned that he had likewise missed the American carriers. The two opposing admirals now reached opposite decisions. Fletcher decided to keep his force concentrated and prepare for a battle the following morning. Tukagi decided to launch a late-afternoon strike even though the planes would have to make night landings on return.

Tukagi's twenty-seven bombers and torpedo planes had a harrowing ordeal. Picked up by the *Lexington's* radar, they were ambushed by American fighters, suffering eight losses. In the darkness and bad weather, several groups of Japanese planes mistook the American carriers for their own. As they approached the task force, the American cruisers and destroyers opened fire. They failed to hit any Japanese planes but came close to downing several American Wildcats preparing to land on the *Yorktown.* Ensign L. Wright, a *Yorktown* fighter pilot, was astounded to see the ship's entire starboard battery open up on him. Diving under the tracer bullets, Wright radioed the ship, "Why are you shooting at me for? What have I done now?"[29] Of Takagi's strike force, only two thirds returned safely to their carriers.

The following morning, search planes from the two fleets found the opposing carriers at almost the same time. The Americans attacked first, scoring three bomb hits on the *Shokaku,* which wrecked her flight deck but did no fatal damage. All of the torpedoes launched by the lumbering Devastators missed their targets or failed to explode. The torpedoes were so slow at long range that the Japanese ships could actually outrun them.[30]

A short time after the American attack on the *Shokaku,* Japanese bombers and torpedo planes sighted the *Lexington* and *Yorktown.* The American carriers, equipped with radar, located the attackers about seventy miles away, but this early radar could not distinguish the altitude of approaching planes and there was no way to determine which planes on the screen were friendly or hostile. Using this scanty information, the *Lexington's* fighter direction officer, an aviator, was supposed to direct her defending fighters, called the combat air patrol, to locations where they could intercept the attackers.

The *Lexington* and *Yorktown* had about twenty fighters aloft, but the fighter director had vectored them at too low an altitude and too close in to catch most of the attackers. As the Japanese planes closed on the carriers, the ships of the task force opened an intense antiaircraft fire at the attackers. "Never in all my years had I imagined a battle like that," observed Lieutenant Commander Shimazaki Shigekazu, a torpedo plane pilot. "We ran into a virtual wall of antiaircraft fire; the carriers and their supporting ships blackened the sky with exploding shells and tracers. . . . I had to fly directly above the waves to escape the enemy shells and tracers. In fact, when I turned away from the carrier I almost struck the bow of the ship for I was flying below the level of the flight deck."[31] Although it may have impressed Shimazaki, the task force's antiaircraft fire was erratic and inaccurate. The gunnery officer in the *Yorktown* claimed that the task force "started and ended our engagement by shooting at our own planes."[32]

As in the campaign off Crete, a ship's survival in the absence of other defenses depended on the captain's ability to execute violent evasive maneuvers at just the right moment. The *Yorktown*'s short turning radius enabled Captain Elliott Buckmaster to dodge all the aerial torpedoes. But several bombs barely missed the ship, and one bomb penetrated the flight deck and exploded just above a fire room.

The *Lexington,* far less handy than the *Yorktown,* was hit by three bombs and at least two torpedoes. Built as a battle cruiser, the *Lexington* had special antitorpedo protection called "bulges" so that despite the damage she was still able to steam at thirty knots. The *Yorktown,* with relatively minor damage, could make twenty-five knots. An hour after the Japanese attack ended, most of the damage aboard the *Lexington* had been temporarily repaired and fires put out, but at 12:47, gasoline released by one of the torpedo hits ignited and a violent explosion rocked the ship. Two hours later, a second internal explosion caused the fires already burning in the ship to rage out of control. Late that afternoon, the *Lexington* was abandoned; one of the escorting destroyers sank her.

The loss of the *Lexington* drastically changed the odds in the Coral Sea. Admiral Fletcher now had only a single carrier and about forty aircraft. He knew that at least one of the Japanese carriers remained in the fight, and he had received reports that an additional carrier might have joined the Japanese task force since the start of the battle.[33] Fletcher decided to withdraw, a decision confirmed by orders from Nimitz the next day. The Japanese were in no position to take advantage of Fletcher's retirement. The *Shokaku* had been damaged so badly that she had to head back to Truk and then to Japan for repairs. The *Zuikaku* was undamaged but was low on fuel and had fewer than forty operational aircraft, and there were still many Allied land-based aircraft, within range of Port Moresby. The Japanese consequently postponed the invasion of Port Moresby—as it turned out, forever.

As the first carrier battle, the encounter in the Coral Sea understandably attracted great attention. The tactics of the two sides and the quality and effectiveness of the opposing aircraft were much discussed. Yet the most serious losses on both sides were, in the end, due to defects in organization and training rather than weapons or tactics. The *Lexington* was ultimately lost because her crew were not as well trained in damage control and not as well equipped as they might have been. Firefighters lacked fog nozzles, asbestos suits, portable fire pumps, and modern breathing apparatus. The gas vapor explosion, which finally doomed the ship, was probably triggered by small fires that had not been quenched completely.[34] The presence of gas vapors was itself an indication of the lack of adequate control of aviation fuel. Over the next year, the U.S. Navy would institute enormous improvements in its damage control practices, making American ships the most survivable in history.

The Japanese carriers suffered no critical damage, but they were unable to operate for weeks after the Coral Sea because of weaknesses in the Japanese system of organization and training for naval aviation. Unlike the Americans, the Japanese had no system for advance training of replacement air groups for carriers. Thus, the pilots lost at the Coral Sea battle could not simply be replaced by another experienced air group. New aviators assigned to the *Zuikaku* and *Shokaku* had to be trained before the carriers could again be ready for combat.

By the time the damaged *Yorktown* arrived at Pearl Harbor for repairs, the rest of the Pacific Fleet was already preparing to meet the next Japanese onslaught. Since early May, intercepted Japanese messages being read by code breakers at Pearl Harbor and Melbourne pointed to a big Japanese offensive in the Central Pacific. On May 27, the day the *Yorktown* reached Pearl Harbor, code breakers definitively identified Midway as the target of the new Japanese thrust.[35] Halsey's carriers, *Enterprise* and *Hornet,* had arrived the day before the *Yorktown,* and Halsey, ill with dermatitis, turned over command of his task force to Rear Admiral Raymond Spruance.

By May 30 all three carriers were on their way to Midway. "The rumor mill began to whisper a fantastic story. The Japanese fleet, it was said, was about to attack Midway . . . and we, having broken their code, were going to lie off Midway and surprise them. . . . That deepest Navy secret—that we had broken the Japanese code and were reading their messages—was widely known among the enlisted men and the proposed strategy and tactics for the coming battle learnedly and gravely discussed by the admirals of the lower deck, who were on the whole, as always, of the opinion that the officers' plan would not work."[36]

The Midway operation involved practically the entire Japanese navy, minus the *Zuikaku* and *Shokaku,* and was intended by Yamamoto to create an opportunity for a decisive battle with the remaining American fleet. Japanese naval officers were so confident of success that they brought back aboard ship many personal belongings such as cameras, pictures, and games, which they had put ashore for safekeeping at the time of Pearl Harbor.[37]

Unaware of the American carriers lying in ambush for him northeast of Midway, Nagumo sent a strike force to attack the island on the morning of June 4. Shortly after the Japanese attack wave had been launched, Midway search planes sighted Nagumo's carriers and alerted Fletcher, who signaled Spruance, "Attack enemy carriers as soon as definitely located."[38] *Yorktown* would follow as soon as she had recovered her morning search planes. The two American carriers turned southwest toward the Japanese and Midway planes headed for the same target.

Spruance's optimum point for launching an attack was about a hundred miles from the enemy. At that distance his short-legged planes would have ample time to find the Japanese, maneuver for attack, and return. At 7:00 A.M., however, while still more than 150 miles from the reported Japanese position, Spruance decided to launch his attack, hoping to catch Nagumo while he was recovering his Midway strike. Admiral Fletcher received word of Spruance's launch, but held off for a time. Code breakers had predicted four Japanese carriers in the area and scouts had reported only two. He probably remembered how a faulty scouting report at the Battle of the Coral Sea had led him to waste his striking force on the small carrier *Shoho* while the big carriers went unmolested. Finally at 8:30 Fletcher decided to launch his dive-bombers and all of his torpedo planes, along with a few fighters, while holding back the rest of the aircraft to deal with whatever might develop.

Nagumo, already under attack by Midway-based planes, was in the midst of arming planes for a second attack on the island when, at 7:28, he received a report from one of his cruiser scout planes of enemy ships to his north. It took the scout almost an hour to determine that one of the American ships was a carrier. In the interim, more Midway-based planes attacked the Japanese fleet, but scored no hits and suffered heavy losses against the Zeroes of the carrier's combat air patrol.

Receiving word of the sighting of the American carrier, Rear Admiral Yamaguchi Tamon, commanding the *Soryu* and *Hiryu* of Carrier Division 2, signaled Nagumo, "Consider it advisable to launch attack force immediately."[39] At that point many of the Japanese strike planes lacked proper ship-killing bombs and torpedoes, having been rearmed for a second Midway strike. They would also have to make their attack without fighter escort, since almost all of the available fighters were already committed to combat air patrol or with the returning Midway strike force. Nagumo decided to wait. He would first recover the Midway attack force, then rearm and reorganize his forces for a balanced attack on the Americans.

Spruance had intended to launch a coordinated strike against the Japanese, but plane handlers aboard the *Enterprise* proved much slower than those aboard the *Hornet* in launching and respotting planes, so an impatient Spruance ordered the *Hornet*'s planes to depart together with whatever *Enterprise* aircraft had already been launched. The *Enterprise*'s fighters and torpedo planes followed fifteen minutes later.

Flying at various speeds and altitudes, and lacking information on the precise location of the enemy, Spruance's planes arrived at the estimated Japanese position to find it empty. After recovering his Midway strike, Nagumo had retired to the northeast in order to open the range between himself and the Americans while he rearmed and refueled. The *Hornet*'s fighters and dive-bombers never did find the carriers, and they had to return empty-handed when their fuel ran low. *Hornet*'s Torpedo Squadron Eight, led by Commander John C. Waldron, managed to locate the Japanese, however; it attacked alone and was destroyed. Not a single plane survived the relentless attacks of the Japanese Zeroes and the carriers' antiaircraft fire. A similar fate befell the *Enterprise*'s torpedo squadron under Lieutenant Commander Eugene E. Lindsey; it lost ten of its fourteen planes. Neither squadron scored any hits.

The *Yorktown*'s planes managed to stay together reasonably well and had less trouble finding the Japanese. Although starting later, they reached the target at about the same time as the *Enterprise*'s planes, which had had to search longer for it. Six *Yorktown* fighters led by Lieutenant Commander John S. Thach had to contend with at least thirty-five Zeroes attempting to protect the torpedo planes. "Zeroes were coming in on us on a stream from astern," Thach recalled. "Then I saw a second large group streaming right past us onto the torpedo planes. The air was like a beehive."[40] Surprisingly, the canny Thach, an expert on fighter tactics, and his five companions managed to shoot down at least six enemy fighters while losing only one of their own.[41] Yet they could not protect the *Yorktown's* torpedo squadron, which lost twelve of its fourteen planes and scored no hits.

The battle with the torpedo planes and Thach's fighters had absorbed the attention of the Japanese fighter pilots and drawn them to a fairly low altitude. The result was that they failed to notice the arrival of a new menace: the dive-bombers of the *Yorktown* as well as those of the *Enterprise* approaching at high altitude from the east. Thach "saw this glint in the sun and it just looked like a beautiful silver waterfall; the dive bombers coming down. I could see them very well because that was the direction of the Zeroes too. They weren't anywhere near the height the dive bombers were. I'd never seen such superb dive bombing."[42]

With little or no interference from the Zeroes, the dive-bombers unleashed a devastating rain of bombs on the Japanese carriers. Within minutes the *Akagi*, *Kaga*, and *Soryu* were enveloped in flames as bombs, torpedoes, and fuel on their crowded flight decks detonated in massive explosions. Only the *Hiryu*, which had become separated from the other carriers in the wild maneuvering to avoid the successive American air attacks, escaped unscathed.

For the thousands of sailors aboard the *Yorktown, Enterprise,* and *Hornet,* news of the battle was confused and fragmentary. Alvin Kernan, an ordnanceman with Torpedo Squadron Six, recalled:

> We waited for them on the deck of the *Enterprise.* Our fighters came back first intact, which seemed odd and then one, two, three, and four torpedo planes straggled in separately and that was it. The last of the planes was so badly shot up that it was deep sixed immediately after it landed. . . . The size of the loss was unimaginable and even when the crews, in a condition of shock, told us what a slaughter it had been, it was unbelievable. . . . Within a few minutes . . . the dive-bombers . . . began arriving in small clusters and singly. Shot up, some landing in the water out of gas, some crashing on deck with failing landing gear or no tailhooks and being pushed over the side instantly to make room for others coming in. But now the mood was triumphant. The bomber pilots could hardly contain themselves. They were shouting and laughing as they jumped out of the cockpit, and the ship which had been so somber a moment before when the torpedo planes returned became now hysterically excited.[43]

Lieutenant Frederick Mears watched as "the returning pilots crowded into their ready room or the pantry gulping lemonade out of paper cups, mechanically stuffing sandwiches into their mouths and at the same time yammering and gesticulating to each other about their individual adventures. . . . Their hair when they took off their helmets was matted with perspiration. Their faces were often dirty and their light cotton flying suits were streaked with sweat. They were having one hell of a good time."[44]

Before noon, the *Hiryu* launched her surviving bombers and torpedo planes in two separate waves against the Americans. Only a few survived the fighters of the *Yorktown*'s combat air patrol, but they managed to heavily damage the carrier with three bomb and two torpedo hits. The *Yorktown* was later sunk by a Japanese submarine while being towed to Pearl Harbor for repairs. By that time the *Hiryu* had also been sunk, hit by dive-bombers from the *Yorktown* and *Enterprise* late on June 4.

It has become commonplace to say that the Coral Sea and Midway established the supremacy of the aircraft carrier in naval warfare. The gunpower of the opposing fleets had proved largely irrelevant to naval battles in which the opposing ships never sighted each other. Yet if airpower advocates had been proved correct about the power of carrier-based attack, the doubters had also been right about the carrier's vulnerability and lack of staying power. Carrier admirals still had to rely on finding the enemy first in order to launch as many of their aircraft as possible in one overwhelming blow. At Coral Sea the Americans lost half of their fleet and the surviving carriers of both sides were in no condition to continue operations. At Midway the Japanese lost their entire fleet, three quarters to the single massive first blow by the opposing fleet. The aircraft carrier might be "the new queen of the seas" as journalists proclaimed, but her reign would not be secure until she could defend herself effectively.

For the Japanese, the Battle of Midway was a devastating psychological as well as tactical defeat. Accurate news of the battle was rigorously suppressed, and the surviving crews were not allowed shore leave. "All in all we can't help concluding that the main cause of the defeat was that we had become conceited because of past successes," wrote Admiral Ugaki. "This is a matter for the utmost regret. . . . This is not a natural calamity, but a result of human deeds. . . . How to rehabilitate the fleet air force is imperative at this moment."[45]

The reorganization of the Japanese fleet's airpower began almost at once. In July, a new Third Fleet, built around the surviving carriers with their supporting cruisers and destroyers, came into existence. New carriers were laid down and large commercial and support ships were taken in hand for conversion.

While some two thirds of Japanese aviators—although not their planes—were reported to have survived the Battle of Midway, many had been injured and had to return to Japan for convalescence.[46] The loss of trained mechanics, armorers, and machinists was even more serious. Unlike American air groups and squadrons, which had their own maintenance personnel, all support personnel for a Japanese air group came from the crew of a carrier. Even if replacement pilots and airplanes became available, they might still be without ground support staff. Uninjured aviators were sent to the new Third Fleet at

Kyushu to rebuild their air groups and train replacements, a task that was estimated to require two or three months.[47]

The Americans also faced the problem of rebuilding the squadrons and air groups that had fought at the Coral Sea and Midway. Nimitz reported that "new aircraft deliveries and new flight school graduates have done little more than balance operational and battle losses. . . ." Many aviators were suffering "operational fatigue due to long continued intensive operations at sea and heavy battle attrition without relief."[48]

King and Nimitz's solution to this problem was radical. The most experienced pilots, primarily those from the *Yorktown* and *Enterprise* squadrons, were sent back to the United States to train new pilots. Famous ace Butch O'Hare, for example, spent the remainder of 1942 and much of 1943 at Naval Air Station Maui training new pilots and squadrons. "Jimmy" Thach went to the United States to impart to others the secrets of the tactics that had enabled him to survive and win his encounter with three dozen enemy fighters.

To expand the pool of combat-ready pilots, King and Nimitz established "carrier replacement air groups." The nucleus of these groups was veteran pilots from the fleet who trained replacement squadrons in the latest combat aircraft. This expedient, made possible by increasing U.S. aircraft production and the personnel expansion measures introduced in 1939 and 1940, meant that squadrons could be rotated out of combat for rest and refitting and that new carriers would receive fully trained air groups.

The Japanese, too, intended to train new pilots to replace losses at Midway, but veteran aviators were not rotated away from combat duties, remaining with their air groups, which continued to provide their own advanced operational training for new pilots. Within four months, almost all of these veteran pilots would be dead.

CHAPTER EIGHTEEN

"The Haves and the Have-Nots"

Ronald H. Spector

FOCUS QUESTIONS

1. How did naval personnel differ before and after Pearl Harbor?
2. Why was the Navy able to supply so many experienced officers prior to 1944? Why was it so difficult after that point?
3. How did the Navy respond to the NAACP's complaint about discrimination in the assignment of enlisted African-Americans?
4. Why was the Navy so unresponsive to requests to establish the WAVES? Once formed, which community proved most receptive to the WAVES? What obstacles did women face in the Navy during the war?

It was June 6, 1944. As the sun rose over Majuro Atoll in the Marshall Islands, the fifteen American aircraft carriers, seven battleships, ten cruisers, and sixty destroyers anchored in the spacious blue-green waters of the lagoon were getting under way. While Allied troops in England—where it was still June 5—completed their final preparations for landing in Normandy, the massive American fleet steamed out of the lagoon. Almost all of the carriers and more than half of the battleships, cruisers, and destroyers had joined the fleet after the Battle of the Santa Cruz Islands. So vast was the assemblage of ships that it was almost five hours before the last vessel cleared the anchorage. Their destination was Saipan in the Marianas, only twelve hundred miles southeast of Japan.[1]

Only sixteen months had passed since the end of the Guadalcanal campaign. In that time the Americans had advanced more than three thousand miles through the tiny island chains of the Central Pacific, captured or destroyed the Japanese outposts in the Solomons, neutralized the Combined Fleet's major bases at Rabaul and Truk, and driven the Japanese back to the westernmost edge of New Guinea. In late 1943 the slow advance through the South Pacific toward Rabaul had been matched by an entirely new drive across the Central Pacific toward the Marshalls, Carolines, and Marianas along the lines anticipated in the old Orange Plan. Beginning haltingly with costly assaults on Tarawa and Makin in the Gilberts, the Central Pacific advance picked up speed in early 1944 with Nimitz's decision to strike boldly into the heart of the Marshalls at Kwajalein. A quick success there prompted the Pacific commanders and the Joint Chiefs of Staff to shorten their original timetable and seize the rest of the Marshalls during February rather than in May. Meanwhile, MacArthur and Halsey had isolated Rabaul and MacArthur had pushed on to the western end of New Guinea with a daring landing at Hollandia, bypassing an entire Japanese army.

Like their ships, most of the sailors were new to the Pacific and to the navy. The battles of 1942 and 1943 had been fought by men who had entered the service before Pearl Harbor. The officers mainly had been Annapolis men, reinforced by the reservists of the various aviation training programs. The sailors were volunteers who had joined the service to escape poverty and unemployment, to travel and see the world. Now, these men were reinforced by thousands of newcomers who had joined only to fight the war. "We had ex-farmers and policemen and horse trainers and salesmen, clerks and municipal employees, school teachers and deacons," one destroyer captain recalled.[2] The number of officers and enlisted men had expanded twentyfold by 1944. There had been 21,000 line officers in 1941, and by 1944 there were more than 206,000; the 3,400 aviators of 1941 had swelled to 37,000. Compared to about 250,000 enlisted men in 1941, there were now almost 3 million, including about 90,000 women.[3] The Marine Corps grew from 50,000 men in 1941 to more than 300,000 men and women in 1944.[4] While most navy recruits prior to Pearl Harbor had been youths in search of jobs and adventure, many of the wartime sailors were men with more substantial backgrounds. "We got a lot of older men from the States in their forties and fifties with big families about 3 weeks ago," wrote Seaman First Class James Fahey of the cruiser *Montpelier.* "It is a tough blow to send a man with children overseas. The new men who just came aboard would give anything to be back with their families."[5]

Every month, thousands of recruits passed through the navy's Great Lakes Naval Training Center near Chicago, where they learned basic seamanship, infantry drill, and military discipline under the attentive ministrations of perpetually angry chief petty officers. After a long train ride to the Midwest, most recruits' initial introduction to the navy was a hurried, rather rudimentary medical examination followed by a haircut "shorter than short." Recruits slept in hammocks lashed to steel rods, an experience one sailor compared to "sleeping on a tight clothesline." "When you manage to get into [a hammock] you lay there rigid like the filling of a cigar because if you moved at all you rolled out and found yourself stunned on the deck. Often at night petty officers would come around to test the tightness of the hammocks or merely to have their own kind of fun by dumping sleeping boots onto the deck. If anyone murmured the slightest protest he carried his full seabag lashed into his hammock for hours."[6] The training companies were under the command of experienced chief petty officers, usually fresh from sea duty, who subjected the "boots" to a steady barrage of verbal and sometimes physical abuse. One chief, a southerner, professed to be appalled to find himself in charge of a company of "Yankees" from the Midwest. "If I ever see a ship sailing upside down, I'll know you knuckleheaded Yankees will be on it."[7] By late 1942, however, most of the chiefs with sea experience had been recalled to the fleet and replaced by physical education teachers and other athletes co-opted by the navy from civilian life. Few recruits found them an improvement.

Boots spent long hours cleaning their barracks to standards far beyond any conventional measure of cleanliness and long hours on "the grinder," the training center's two-block concrete drill ground, baking in the summer sun or shivering in the freezing lake winds of winter. The unrelenting former phys ed teachers "ran us in formation miles wherever we had to go . . . on occasions when we merely marched, we had to sing 'Anchors Away' or 'Everybody Loves the Navy of the U.S.A.'—a very dubious proposition."[8]

A few men found the life intolerable and adopted various expedients to escape from the navy. Frank Albert encountered such a man in boot camp. "The day before graduation, our barracks was slated for a major inspection by the commanding officer. My buddy, the one that has been trying to figure a way out of the Navy, was named Captain of the Head. I was on his detail. We had those toilets shining. . . . As the captain walked in, the bugler sounded attention. That captain went through the head with a fine tooth comb . . . not a speck of dust. We passed with flying colors. Just as he turned his back to address his Marine orderly, my buddy . . . broke a Baby Ruth candy bar in half and threw it into one of the toilets. When the Captain heard the splash he yelled, 'What the hell is that?' My buddy retrieved it, took a bite and threw it back, yelling (with a snappy salute), 'That's shit sir.' He was out of the Navy the very next day with a Section 8."[9] The great majority of less imaginative sailors left boot camp after four weeks for specialized training schools or went directly to sea. After 1942, the ship in which most sailors went to sea for the first time was the one in which they went to war.

Although the navy was expanding at an exponential rate it was able to provide a cadre of experienced leaders for almost all of its new units, largely due to the slow promotion rates in the navy of the 1930s, which had created a large backlog of experienced seamen. Battleship sailors in the pre–Pearl Harbor

Navy, for example, had to sit for the same competitive examinations a dozen times or more before advancing in rate. "There were so many men and so few advancements."[10] Once war began, however, these men could be rapidly promoted to higher rank and train others in their field of expertise. Aboard the destroyer *Saufley*, commissioned in 1942, "Only 30 percent had ever been to sea before. The rest of the crew were civilians who had joined after Pearl Harbor. . . . Our regular navy crew included good officers and chiefs. The enlisted men included Asiatic Fleet survivors, men from the brigs and hard-to-control men from almost any other area in the navy. They all liked whiskey, girls and liberty. The new volunteers were ours to mold and we molded them in the same fashion we had been molded."[11] These sailors of the old navy were to provide the crucial component of leadership and experience to the fast-growing ranks of inexperienced enlisted men—as well as to thousands of inexperienced officers, for by 1944 the navy's officer corps was a far different entity from what it had been four years earlier.

While prewar navy leaders must have recognized that additional officers would be needed to man the expanded fleet, already under construction by 1940, "the Bureau of Navigation made no plans for officer procurement which did not crumble before the realities of the Second World War." As late as January 1941, the bureau's plans were based on the assumption that an additional 10,000 officers would meet the needs of a wartime navy.[12] The number of peacetime reserve officers had been kept to a bare minimum, perhaps because of fears that reserve officers on active duty might "hold up promotion for naval academy graduates."[13] In actuality more than 286,000 naval officers were added to the fleet between December 1941 and the end of 1944. Less than 1 percent were graduates of Annapolis. Unlike the army and Marine Corps, which drew the great majority of their wartime officers from experienced noncommissioned officers and enlisted men who successfully completed officer candidate school, the navy drew only 2 percent of its officer trainees from the ranks and less than 19 percent of its new officers from experienced sailors. Instead, almost 130,000 new wartime officers received direct commissions from civil life and another 84,000 were commissioned through officer training programs that they entered without having served any time as enlisted men.[14]

In both cases the key requirement was a college degree. Until 1943 almost no man or woman who failed to meet this requirement could be considered for a commission in the navy.[15] After 1943 the Bureau of Naval Personnel reluctantly agreed to consider men with only two years of college "plus 5 years of good business experience," and some men over thirty were accepted on the basis of "an outstanding business record alone."[16] So thorough was the navy's preoccupation with obtaining only college graduates for its officer corps that undergraduates still in their first or second year of college were provided the opportunity to be commissioned as officers through the so-called "V programs," which allowed them to complete college and enter the navy upon graduation. Whether either a college education or "an outstanding business record" was superior to seagoing experience or the rigors of an officer candidate school as criteria for the selection of naval officers was a question that scarcely occurred to navy leaders. The official history refers to the college-graduates-only standard as a "scantly debated decision." The rationale most frequently offered was that "the technical equipment of a naval officer justified the insistence on a good college education as a fundamental criterion."[17]

In a service so dependent on science and technology, this policy seemed eminently logical. Yet in reality, many hastily commissioned officers found little direct relationship between their academic training and their navy assignments. "The job didn't really require much knowledge," recalled one officer of his first seagoing assignment. "It turned out to be a real small ship and the guys, the most important guys on the ship, were the few enlisted men and one petty officer who knew mechanics and electricity. And we had several of those guys and they were the ones who were critical to the running of the ship."[18] Louis R. Harlan "added science courses including an entire year of physics in the expectation that its abstractions would somehow be transmogrified into useful knowledge when I became a naval officer. In fact, I never found any use whatever for physics in the Navy."[19]

An unstated but more compelling reason for the navy's insistence on college education for its officers may have been the social preferences of the career officers. If they were now compelled by necessity to share the bridge and the wardroom with non-Annapolis graduates they could at least ensure that these came from acceptable segments of society. "Officers and crew were set apart into the haves and the have-nots in different uniforms as though in the service of separate nations," recalled Louis Harlan. "Officers came from college—that was the crucial difference—and enlisted men straight out of high school or from blue-collar work. . . . In the 1940s college was only for the favored few, for those whose parents could afford to send them or help them through. To graduate from college or even to have been there, put one immediately on a higher status plateau. The Navy's hierarchical structure, its ranks and orders, challenged the democratic political credo of American society, but also reflected in high relief America's hierarchical social reality."[20]

College students and graduates who successfully passed a written test, a physical examination, and a series of interviews were assigned to midshipman's school for 90 to 120 days of training. Promptly labeled "90-Day Wonders," the graduates of the midshipman's schools often saw the ocean for the first time after they graduated and had been ordered to duty. Alfred Nisonoff, who served as an officer aboard an amphibious ship at Okinawa, trained at Plattsburgh, New York. "The only thing they used Lake Champlain for was passing the swimming test. . . . It was really a farce because we were learning gunnery and there were no guns. Learning about these parts in a gun and we didn't have a gun to play with."[21] Louis Harlan recalled that aside from a morning spent aboard a training ship his most extended seagoing experience had been aboard the Statue of Liberty ferry.[22]

With such training behind them most 90-Day Wonders felt less than total confidence when they joined their ships. "We suffered most (and this fact has been too generally ignored) from lack of confidence in ourselves and in those above and below us in rank and responsibility," recalled a sailor who served in an LST (Landing Ship Tank).[23] This problem of inexperience was exacerbated by the navy's practice of manning less imposing warships—destroyer escorts, minesweepers, subchasers, and amphibious craft—almost exclusively with reservists. When Lieutenant Commander Charles Chester took command of a new destroyer escort in 1944, he discovered that "the only officer aboard qualified to stand deck watches was the chief engineer who was not required to stand them."[24]

Many of these new types of officers went to new types of ships. As the Orange Plan had anticipated, the American advance across the Pacific soon became an island war featuring amphibious assault by heavily armed marine units backed by the guns and aircraft of the fleet. In the Southwest Pacific, MacArthur and Halsey's forces also moved mainly by sea to attack key points along the north New Guinea coast and up the chain of the central and northern Solomon islands.

By 1943 the Allies had developed a whole family of amphibious ships. The largest of the new vessels was the diesel-powered Landing Ship Tank, universally called the LST, a three-hundred-foot seagoing vessel that could carry more than two thousand tons of cargo in its cavernous interior. Its shallow draft enabled it to run right up onto or very close to a coral, sand, or mud beach, then discharge its cargo through the large doors and ramp in its bow. Its low speed and lack of maneuverability caused many sailors to declare that LST stood for "Large Stationary Target." Pacific commanders were soon busy adding extra antiaircraft guns to its original scanty armament.[25] Another seagoing amphibian was the LCI, Landing Craft Infantry, considerably smaller and faster than the LST, which discharged its troops and equipment down gangways hinged to a platform on the bow, "and lucky were the troops who got ashore in water less than shoulder high."[26] The smallest of the new beaching craft was the LCT, Landing Craft Tank, a bargelike vessel about 120 feet long, with a bow ramp that could be lowered to discharge its cargo of medium tanks or heavy vehicles. LCTs were normally transported overseas in sections and reassembled at their destination.

Leon Cannick had been out of midshipman's school less than two months when he was assigned command of an LCT. "We were supposed to have six weeks of training. When I got there . . . they told me right off there's no three [sic] weeks of training at all. Forget that. The next day they gave me my crew who were far more up on LCTs than I was. . . . I went out one day with another skipper and his crew. Then I went out the second day with my crew and another skipper on my boat. Then the third day they said 'there you are.' "[27] One of Cannick's fellow LCT skippers astounded an admiral by explaining that he could keep his ship out of the rays of the moon by zigzagging.[28]

Yet the navy's instincts in officer selection proved not wholly mistaken. The hordes of half-trained wholly inexperienced college students, professionals, and men with "an outstanding business record" quickly transformed themselves into a highly effective body of leaders and specialists. Wall Street bankers became combat intelligence officers. English majors became navigators, advertising men and lawyers became fighter director officers, mathematicians and musicians became code breakers. Overall, the ROTC graduates and 90-Day Wonders brought a breadth of experience and outlook to their jobs that was to prove invaluable in the rapidly changing arena of war. Captain Slade Cutter, a leading submarine commander, considered reservists in some ways superior to regulars. "The navy system promotes a hesitancy to do something without proper authority. . . . Academy graduates when they first got out there . . . would always say 'Captain to the bridge,' they didn't want to make a decision 'til the captain got up there. Your reserve—you never had to worry about him—he would do something. It might be wrong, but he would do it. And they didn't make too many mistakes."[29] Despite this, the navy "steadfastly denied" command of a submarine to even the most experienced and competent reservists until 1945.[30]

The navy's determination to keep the officer corps a social elite was matched by its tenacity in preserving the navy as an organization only open to white men. "Our taxes help keep up the Naval Academy where our boys may not attend," declared the NAACP magazine, *Crisis,* in 1940. "They help to maintain the numerous naval bases, navy yards and naval air bases from which we are excluded. . . . The training in numerous trades and skills which thousands of whites receive and use later in civilian life is not for us. . . . This is the price we pay for being classified as a race of mess attendants only! At the same time we are supposed to be able to appreciate what our white fellow citizens declare to be the 'vast difference' between American democracy and Hitlerism."[31]

In response to such arguments, the navy's senior officers generally took the position, as they had since the turn of the century, that crowded shipboard living conditions made it impossible to have African-Americans in rates other than messman.[32] "It is no kindness to the Negroes to thrust them upon men of the white race," declared Navy Secretary Frank Knox.[33] If integration was undesirable, segregation was impractical. The navy had neither the desire nor the resources to commission a fleet of ships crewed only by black sailors. Besides, many naval officers doubted that a sufficient number of African-Americans with the proper skills and aptitude for sea duty could ever be found, "even if you had the entire Negro population of the United States to choose from."[34] The Bureau of Naval Personnel believed that "the Negroes' relative unfamiliarity with the sea" gave them a "consequent fear of water."[35]

With the outbreak of war, the navy soon found that it was unable to maintain its traditional racial policies. Pressure from politicians, journalists, black community leaders, and the White House eventually had forced the navy and Marine Corps to begin accepting African-Americans for general service. The navy had continued to insist that only whites could serve on seagoing men-of-war. As a result, thousands of African-Americans were enlisted and later drafted into the navy to serve in harbor craft, in a few technical specialties, in the newly formed Naval Construction Battalions, or Seabees, and at naval supply and ammunition depots.

In June 1942, the navy opened a new, but segregated, boot camp for black recruits in an isolated section of Great Lakes Naval Training Center near Chicago. Named Camp Robert Smalls, after a black naval hero of the Civil War, this establishment was commanded by Lieutenant Commander Daniel Armstrong, an Annapolis graduate and son of the founder of Hampton Institute. Armstrong was a capable administrator who considered himself a genuine friend of African-Americans. But his peculiar administrative style and paternalistic philosophy caused problems for both white and black sailors at Camp Robert Smalls. White officers and petty officers complained that he was inclined to give black recruits special treatment and more lenient punishments. Aware of this reputation, company commanders were inclined to handle their disciplinary problems by "taking a recalcitrant into a closed room, where there were no witnesses and beating him."[36] For their part, black recruits resented what they considered Armstrong's patronizing attitude expressed in such policies as having recruits "learn and recite a creed . . . dealing with the advancement of the Negro race and having them sing spirituals en masse on Sunday evenings."[37]

Leaving Camp Smalls for duty, many black sailors soon discovered that navy service held many more unpleasant surprises besides compulsory singing. A small number of African-Americans did serve aboard harbor and coastal patrol vessels or in technical specialties ashore, but the majority served in less rewarding jobs. More than half of all African-American sailors worked as unskilled laborers at supply bases, air stations, and ammunition depots in the United States. Another 7,000 served overseas with the Naval Construction Battalions. Some 38,000 served in the messman branch, now grown to enormous size to accommodate the large number of new ships and additional officers in the wartime navy.[38]

In the segregated navy only the members of the steward branch could fulfill the classic sailor's role, to fight at sea. When the ship was in action, the cooks, stewards, and messmen often served as gun crews for one or more of the numerous antiaircraft guns that were rapidly installed in men-of-war after the first sea-air battles. And even before these installations had begun, Doris Miller, a steward's mate aboard the battleship *West Virginia*, had become the first African-American hero of the war when he manned a machine gun during the Pearl Harbor attack and brought down two Japanese planes.

To many whites the presence of African-Americans as fighters and not merely servants at sea must have proved disconcerting. After all, part of the argument for the exclusion of blacks from the naval service was precisely that they *could not* perform satisfactorily in these roles. Traditionalists reacted in two ways. Navy leaders praised the bravery of a handful of "boys" like Miller who had been commended or decorated for their bravery and recounted their achievements in language which was often simultaneously laudatory and condescending. One African-American hero was described in a magazine story entitled "The Messboy of Squadron X." The subject of the story was "a favorite with the whole squadron . . . as he scurried from table to table . . . his ebony face shining." His handwriting and spelling were so bad, however, that the ship's censor told him that "less'n I could write better I couldn't write mor'n two pages to my wife. . . . He said he couldn't pass my last one nohow cause he couldn't read no part of it." After the messboy, acting as ammunition passer, replaces a wounded gunner and shoots down two enemy planes, a yeoman volunteers to type his letters for him. He was reported to have written his wife that he was "mighty glad that a little colored boy from down in Texas got a chance to do his bit."[39]

Not publicized, but far more widespread in larger ships, were persistent rumors that black gun crews panicked or froze in action. How any individual behaved during the confusion and terror of naval action is difficult if not impossible to document. Officers almost invariably reported that all hands performed well, since to do otherwise might reflect poorly on their own leadership. Yet it is significant that only stories about black sailors behaving timidly were widely reported. Among white sailors such stories may have provided a means of displacing their own anxieties and fears of displaying cowardice, while reassuring themselves that those they considered unworthy to be warriors really were different.[40]

Working long hours in menial, unpleasant, monotonous, and tiring jobs, with little prospect of promotion and commanded by inexperienced, sometimes incompetent white officers, black sailors ashore felt angry and frustrated. In June 1943 a riot occurred at a naval ammunition depot in Virginia. The following month more than seven hundred African-Americans of the 80th Construction Battalion staged a protest over segregation aboard the transport that was carrying them to their duty station in the Caribbean.

These signs compelled the navy to reexamine its racial policies. Top civilians in the Navy Department, such as Under Secretary James V. Forrestal and his special assistant Adlai Stevenson, who held far more progressive views than Secretary Knox, began pressing for new initiatives to eliminate discrimination and create additional opportunities for African-Americans. They were joined by Lieutenant Commander Christopher Sargent, who, in peacetime, was a member of the powerful law firm of Covington and Burling. Sargent, whose influence in Washington far exceeded his naval rank, worked tirelessly to break down racial barriers in the navy. Yet, the admirals still refused to consider assigning African-Americans to seagoing warships except as messmen. "You couldn't dump two hundred colored boys on a crew in a battle," declared the chief of the Bureau of Naval Personnel.[41] Nevertheless, he did agree to assign all-black crews to serve under white officers and petty officers aboard a newly commissioned destroyer escort and a subchaser as a test of the ability of black sailors to serve at sea. The destroyer escort *Mason* was commissioned in March 1944 and served on convoy duty in the Atlantic until the end of the war. As time passed her white petty officers and some of her junior officers were gradually replaced by African-Americans.

Although the U-boat threat had largely abated by the time the *Mason* went to sea, her sailors found the sea itself as formidable an opponent as ever. "In the North Atlantic when the water hits the steel deck it turns to ice," recalled Radioman Benjamin Garrison. "If a line was two inches thick, by the time it hit it got four times as big, and difficult to handle. . . . You can't walk upright. . . . The ship is rolling and pitching. . . . The handrails were only waist high. If the deck was slanting and you lost your grip you were gone. . . . It's rough, it's dark, total darkness. It's slippery. The ship is bucking up and down, right and left."[42]

In the end the North Atlantic weather provided the men of the *Mason* with their greatest challenge. In October 1944, NY119, a slow convoy that included tugs towing barges and car floats, escorted by *Mason* and four other destroyer escorts, encountered a massive Atlantic gale with forty-foot seas and wind gusts of ninety miles an hour. In the heavy weather the unwieldy barges quickly became unmanageable. Two tugs capsized as the barges to which they were attached plunged beneath the towering sea. The *Mason* was sent ahead with the faster ships of the convoy to make for Falmouth and then return with additional ships to bring in the tugs and barges, now almost stationary in the face of the winds and mountainous seas.[43]

At 6:00 P.M. that same day the *Mason* brought all twenty of her charges safely into Falmouth Harbor. Two hours later she was again under way headed back toward the slower elements of the convoy, still scattered about in the storm. Two Royal Navy sloops, ordered to accompany *Mason,* reported that they could make no headway in the forty-foot seas and turned back. The *Mason*, although damaged by the storm, continued on alone, making four knots while her engines made revolutions for twelve. Over the next two days, as the storm gradually abated, the *Mason* rejoined the remainder of the convoy and shepherded the surviving small craft to safety. It was an outstanding display of seamanship and determination that earned the ship special praise in the convoy commodore's report. After the *Mason* no one could doubt how blacks would perform at sea.[44]

Although blacks and whites served aboard the *Mason* with little friction, ashore and in port black sailors were constantly reminded that they still belonged to a segregated navy. "We had four ships tied up together and we were on the outer most side. To get back to the pier we had to cross every one of those ships," recalled Radioman James W. Graham. "There would be off-duty sailors on the ships and they would say some derogatory remarks as we passed. 'He's from the nigger ship' or 'Here come the coons.' "[45] In Charleston, a crowd of white shipyard workers, angered by the sight of white USO girls performing aboard the *Mason,* attempted to board the ship. "The Captain had us man our battle stations and we trained the guns on them. That stopped it. Really though we didn't need the guns. We could have taken them on one by one."[46]

A month after the *Mason* was commissioned, Navy Secretary Frank Knox died and was succeeded by Forrestal. A former naval aviator and Wall Street investment banker, the new secretary had been a member of the Urban League, a moderate civil rights organization. Forrestal believed that a segregated fleet, along the lines of the Mason experiment, was both impractical and undesirable. Instead, Forrestal began to take the first steps toward dismantling the whites-only navy. A handful of black officers, "the golden thirteen," had already been commissioned, and Forrestal pressed for more. With the support of Admiral King, he began the assignment of black sailors to "general service" (non-messman) duties at sea aboard fleet oilers, repair ships, and other auxiliaries. Black women were also admitted to the Waves, the navy's female branch. Specialized training schools were desegregated, and Lester Granger, a former head of the Urban League, joined the Navy Department as the secretary's special adviser on racial policy in 1944.[47]

All of this came too late to make much difference in the lives of most African-American sailors. The great majority of black sailors never went to sea except as waiters, cooks, or bakers. The rest continued as construction workers, warehousemen, and stevedores. In 1944 there were more racial incidents. At Port Chicago, at Mare Island Navy Yard, California, two ammunition ships exploded, killing more than three hundred people including about two hundred African-Americans serving in cargo-handling battalions at the ammunition depot. Those who survived, not surprisingly, concluded that the conditions were too hazardous to continue working. Refusing to return to work, they were charged with mutiny, and fifty sailors were convicted on this charge and sent to prison, although they were later granted clemency after strenuous efforts by Lester Granger and the NAACP, represented by future Supreme Court justice Thurgood Marshall.

A few months later, racial tensions exploded on the newly captured island of Guam in the Marianas, which was being rapidly converted into a major headquarters and supply base. The trouble grew out of fights between white marines and black sailors of the naval supply depot over relations with local women in the town of Agana. While fights between marines and sailors were far from rare, the trouble on Guam soon took on racial overtones. Marines in trucks or jeeps roared by the supply company camps, yelling racial insults and threats; they were met with showers of rocks from the sailors.[48] The situation was made worse by a lack of experienced leaders and effective discipline. All of the supply depot company's officers were inexperienced young white ensigns and lieutenants junior grade, some of the men with "an outstanding business record" to whom the navy had given direct commissions. The units also lacked experienced petty officers of either race.[49] The military police and shore patrol on the island was exclusively white.

In the face of repeated threats from white marines, the sailors began to arm themselves illicitly with rifles and knives. The marines, of course, had ready access to weapons. The spark that touched off the final explosion was the shooting of a black sailor by a white sailor in Agana on the night of December

24. That same night, shots were fired into one of the supply camps. Groups of black sailors commandeered trucks and attempted to drive to Agana but were stopped by military police. A riot and more shootings followed.

A navy court of inquiry was appointed to investigate the incident. The president of the court was an amiable officer, chiefly noted for his ability to ingest 190-proof torpedo alcohol. "He was just a nice guy with a little too much rank for his capability," recalled one sailor. "He wasn't the kind of officer to put in charge of an inquiry if you were really trying to find out anything, so he was probably perfect for the job."[50] Most of the African-Americans involved in the riot refused to testify before the all-white court of inquiry. Even a visit by the executive secretary of the NAACP, Walter White, failed to persuade them to come forward.[51]

The court found that while there was "an unfortunate tendency on the part of comparatively very few white service personnel to indulge in the use of slighting and insulting terms and acts of personal aggression applied to individuals of the Negro race on the Island . . . there is no organized or concerted racial prejudice or discrimination existing in the armed forces on the island of Guam." The court also deplored what it believed to be "a comparatively much more widespread tendency among a high percentage of Negro troops to magnify and accentuate the racial prejudice of a few white service individuals, to seek personal and unlawful redress, to foster groundless rumors of racial discrimination."[52] Given the navy's racial attitudes and assumptions, the court's conclusions were hardly surprising.

While the court thus found the status quo satisfactory, Admiral Nimitz, who had just moved his headquarters to Guam, was infuriated and, with King and Forrestal, was determined to move toward a deliberate policy of integration in the navy. This was finally achieved in February 1946 when the Bureau of Naval Personnel issued a circular letter notifying commanders that "effective immediately all restrictions governing types of assignments for which Negro personnel are eligible are hereby lifted. Henceforth they shall be eligible for all types of assignments in all ratings in all activities in all ships of the Naval Service." By the close of the war, the U.S. Navy had become, in policy, the most racially integrated of all the services. In practice it remained the least. Following V-J Day, the regular Navy had 7,000 black officers and sailors, just more than 2 percent of the total naval force, and nine out of ten of these black sailors were in the steward branch.[53]

While the idea of black sailors was unwelcome to many naval professionals, even more agreed with Senator David Walsh, the Naval Affairs Committee chairman, that women sailors would lead "to the decline of civilization." Rear Admiral John Towers, the chief of the Bureau of Aeronautics, saw it differently. Since the days of Admiral Moffett, aviation had been the most dynamic element in the navy, and Towers and his associates were long accustomed to looking outside the traditional navy organization for ideas and talented people. Just as aviation had been the first to welcome large numbers of reservists, so it now took the lead in incorporating women.

Towers had learned from Captain Ralph Ofstie, an aviator who had served as naval attaché in London, about the work of women in the Royal Navy, which had begun to recruit them even before the outbreak of World War II.[54] Originally assigned to replace male sailors as secretaries, cooks, telegraphists, code clerks, telephone operators, and drivers, the Women's Royal Naval Service, universally called the WRENS, quickly expanded into other occupations and specialties. "This is in praise of the WRENS," wrote an unknown bard in *Punch*:

> *Boat WRENS, coder WRENS, steward WRENS.*
> *Quarters WRENS, general duties WRENS*
> *WRENS ashore and afloat*
> *Rolling off signals—"TOP SECRET" "IMPORTANT"*
> *WRENS in the dock yard*
> *WRENS on an MTV's deck*
> *With greasy small wrists and a spanner*
> *Plotting WRENS, messengers, sparkers*
> *Torpedo WRENS, ordnance WRENS, cooks*
> *Trim bright staunch overworked*
> *And, let it be gladly proclaimed,*
> *Utterly indispensable.*[55]

Wrens also composed part of the crew of HMS *Philante*, the anti-submarine school training ship at Derry.[56] By 1944 there were more than 90,000 Wrens in the Royal Navy. Joy Hancock, the civilian head of public relations in the Bureau of Aeronautics (BUAER) returned from Canada with similar reports of women in the Royal Canadian Navy and Air Force.[57] At the same time, Captain Arthur Radford, head of the training section of the BUAER, was aware that dozens of new schools and airfields would soon be commissioned for the large-scale pilot training programs then getting under way. Radford began planning to employ women as instructors, technicians, machinists, and metalsmiths and in other essential duties in the training effort.[58]

Women's advocates, led by Eleanor Roosevelt and Congresswoman Edith Nourse Rogers, had succeeded in pressing the army into establishing a Women's Army Auxiliary Corps in late 1941, but the navy had remained unresponsive. When the chief of the Bureau of Naval Personnel queried navy bureaus and headquarters on positions that women could fill, most replied that they had few or none. Even while the Bureau of Naval Personnel was concluding that women were not needed, Towers and BUAER were working behind the scenes to push legislation through the House and Senate allowing women to serve in the navy. Congressman Melvin Maas, a Marine Corps Reserve aviator, was persuaded by a woman friend to introduce a bill, an amendment to the Naval Reserve Act of 1938, providing for a women's reserve. At the same time, Lieutenant Commander George Anderson of BUAER, who was related to Senator Walsh's legislative assistant, plied the senator with food and drink until

Walsh, after several scotches, agreed to withdraw his opposition on condition "that the morals of these girls will be protected and never will anybody propose that they be sent to ships."[59] Legislation creating a women's division of the Naval Reserve, soon labeled "the Waves," passed Congress at the end of July 1942. Mildred McAfee, president of Wellesley College, was appointed director of the Waves with the rank of lieutenant commander. BUAER immediately requested 23,000 Wave officers and sailors.

McAfee's first challenge was to squelch a proposal that the Waves be fitted with a comic-opera red-white-and-blue-striped uniform.[60] Instead, Mrs. James B. Forrestal, wife of the Navy Under Secretary, arranged for a well-known fashion designer, Mainbocher of New York, to design a dignified but stylish set of uniforms that proved so successful they remained standard for more than twenty years.[61]

Before the new uniforms had even been issued, the first classes of Waves had already reported for training at Hunter College in New York, which the recruits immediately dubbed USS Hunter. Here they were subjected to much the same regimen of physical training, compulsive cleaning, and drill as boots at Great Lakes. In the early days, marine drill instructors were employed to teach close-order drill to the 6,000 women who passed through Hunter every few weeks. "We have two drill masters," wrote one young woman to her parents. "One has red hair and the other is handsome. . . . The one with red hair swears at us although we're not really sure what he is saying. . . ."[62] Another Wave recalled a dress parade at Hunter for a group of visiting VIPs:

> The morning of the review dawned dark and sleeting. The parade ground bordered a huge frozen reservoir and the chilly wind caused instant freezing as the sleet hit the paving. Our platoon, dressed smartly in havelocks, raincoats, gloves and rubbers, stood shivering at parade rest for over an hour. At last the reviewing party came into view. . . . The sergeant called "Attention!" whereupon we dutifully snapped our feet together leaving our rubbers solidly frozen to the paving. Instant reflex action sent us all stooping to retrieve our errant rubbers and dissolved the formation into chaos. With a wretched cry of agony the Marine [drill sergeant] snatched off his hat, threw it on the ground and stalked off the field.[63]

Entering the navy with hopes of adventure, travel, and new experiences, many Waves found themselves serving alongside other women in traditional "female" occupations: secretaries, stenographers, receptionists, waitresses, dispersing clerks, mail sorters, and performers of various auxiliary medical services. "Women would join expecting that they would get to the Pacific and they would see sights they had never seen," recalled Captain Jean Palmer, "and they ended up doing mess duty or something in Bainbridge, Maryland."[64] So many Waves were employed at headquarters and installations in the Washington, D.C., area that a popular Wave song proclaimed.

We joined the Navy to see the sea
And what did we see?
We saw D.C.

Among those in the most critical and most demanding occupations were the several hundred Waves assigned to the Office of the Chief of Naval Operations. By 1944, 70 percent of all decoders and 80 percent of all communicators in the Washington area were women.[65] Captain Wyman H. Packard, a veteran intelligence officer, who was in charge of a watch in the Navy Department code room, recalled, "The typing pool had the toughest task. They had to type up the ditto masters for all incoming messages and make additions to some outgoing messages. By the end of the watch they would have the blue ditto coloring all over their hands and sometimes on their faces. After eight hours of pressure trying to catch up with the backlog they would be exhausted."[66]

Not all Waves found the navy a happy experience. "Many of the patients we got at Bethesda [Hospital] were from communications," recalled a navy psychologist. "They had come into the navy expecting to work with men. They found the swarms of women at boot camp, then in their quarters, disillusioning and wanted out at any cost. The strain of secrecy at work was also a major problem."[67] Captain Jean Palmer agreed: "There were those who really cracked up. By far the majority just looked around their little cell, hung up their curtains and made themselves at home and had a wonderful time. We had a wonderful time. I've never worked such hours, never felt so much frustration, but you felt part of something."[68]

During the course of the war, Waves were never "sent to ships," but airplanes were another matter. As naval aviation expanded, women moved into more and more nontraditional occupations. By late 1942, women gunnery instructors were learning to fire service pistols, shotguns, and machine guns, to disassemble and repair all types of ordnance, and to qualify in aerial gunnery. By May 1943, Waves were being trained as aviation machinist's mates, aviation metalsmiths, parachute riggers, aerographers, aircraft gunnery instructors, and air traffic controllers.[69] Instruction in the new Link navigation trainer, introduced by Captain Luis de Flores, a brilliant engineer whose imagination and inventiveness gave birth to a family of realistic training devices that revolutionized flight instruction, was largely in the hands of Waves.[70] After 1943, no aviator was sent to the Pacific who had not received part of his training from a Wave.[71]

By the spring of 1944 this new wartime navy, built around the slender framework of the old, trained and supported on an unprecedented scale by outsiders—women, African-Americans, and civilians—and manned in large part by determined but inexperienced amateurs, was on its way to the two last and greatest naval battles of the twentieth century.

One thousand miles from Majuro lay the island of Saipan, one of three large islands in the Marianas that the Americans intended to use as advance naval and air bases. From airfields on Saipan and the nearby island of Tinian a new Army Air Forces superbomber, the B-29, could attack cities in the heart of Japan. The assault on the Marianas was entrusted to Admiral Raymond A. Spruance, as commander of the Fifth Fleet. Under him were more than 127,000 troops in the transports and landing craft of Vice Admiral Richmond Kelly Turner's Joint Expeditionary Force. They were divided into two segments. The Northern Attack Force, made up of two marine divisions with an army division in reserve, was to assault Saipan and after that Tinian. The Southern Attack Force comprised the 3rd Marine Division and the 1st Provisional Marine Brigade, the latter earmarked for Guam after the assault on Saipan.[72]

The fast carriers of Task Force 58 under Vice Admiral Mark Mitscher supported the landings. The fast carrier task forces had demonstrated their power and effectiveness already with attacks against Rabaul and Kwajalein in the fall of 1943. To support the invasion of the western Marshalls, Mitscher's carriers had attacked and crippled the major Japanese Central Pacific base at Truk, delivering thirty air strikes in two days, each of them more powerful than either of the two Japanese attack waves at Pearl Harbor. This was a vast improvement over the Guadalcanal campaign, when the Americans had never had more than three operational carriers. In the Marianas invasion, Mitscher would have fifteen fast carriers. Only the *Enterprise* remained from 1942, but there were six new *Essex*-class carriers. Large fast ships of 27,000 tons, they carried a crew of more than 3,000 men and could accommodate about ninety planes: thirty-six fighters, thirty-six dive-bombers, and eighteen torpedo planes. The first *Essex*-class carrier was commissioned on the last day of 1942, fifteen months ahead of schedule. The next ship of the class, *Yorktown,* was completed seventeen months early, a testimony to the extraordinary capabilities of American industry, labor, and technology, which, by late 1943, was to provide the United States with an enormous edge in the tools of war.[73]

Mitscher also had eight light fleet carriers of the *Independence* class, constructed on cruiser hulls. They were considerably smaller than the Essex class and embarked twenty-four fighters and nine torpedo planes. In all, Task Force 58 embarked more than 900 airplanes in its fast carriers. The "battle line," Task Group 58.7 under Rear Admiral Willis A. Lee, included four new fast battleships of the *North Carolina* and *South Dakota* classes, which had fought at Guadalcanal, and three new even larger and faster 45,000-ton *Iowa*-class battleships.

The carriers now operated in groups of three or four, a concentration made possible by much-improved radar, fighter direction, and communications developed after the bitter lessons of Santa Cruz. The *Essex*- and *Independence*-class carriers carried more than a hundred of the new deadly 40mm Bofors and 20mm Oerlikon cannons that had proved so effective against aircraft. Cruisers and destroyers carried so many of these new weapons in sponsors and gun tubs protruding from their sides and deck that one admiral declared that "they looked like the hanging gardens of Babylon."

The heaviest guns in the carriers, the 5-inch, .38-caliber, fired a new type of projectile, a shell equipped with a variable time or proximity fuse. Because even a near miss by a 5-inch projectile was usually enough to destroy a plane, a tiny radio transmitter and receiver built into the war-head detonated the shell when it came close to an aircraft. The *Essex*-class carriers were armed with eight 5-inch guns, the cruisers and battleships with as many as twenty. The new high-performance aircraft that the Bureau of Aeronautics had promised the frustrated fighter jocks in 1942 had arrived in the form of the F6F Hellcat, a single-seat plane that could outclimb and outdive the Zero. It was also thirty miles per hour faster, more heavily armed, and much better protected.[74]

Supporting the fast carriers was a mobile logistical fleet composed of supply ships, oil tankers, ammunition ships, hospital ships, tugs, floating dry docks, lighters, and cranes. "Every three to four days the carriers would steam away from the battle zone during the night and meet the tankers in the morning. After each carrier had taken on oil and aviation gas it would move on to the ammunition ships for bombs and shells and the provision ships for food. Battle ships and cruisers, waiting their turn with the tankers, would refuel the task force's destroyers, and escort carriers, with the logistics squadron, would fly replacement planes and pilots to the fast carriers. In this fashion the fast carrier task force could and did keep operating at sea for three months without respite . . . 4,000 miles from Pearl Harbor."[75] For maintenance and repairs the ships of the fast carrier force put into a protected lagoon where the floating docks, cranes, repair ships, tenders, and tugs would be safe from submarine attacks and usually were out of range of air strikes. This mobile logistical force, which followed the fast carriers through the Central Pacific, made it possible for Task Force 58 to range the seas for far longer periods than had ever been possible since the age of sail.

On June 15, after three days of air strikes by Mitscher's carriers and bombardments by the older battleships of Admiral Turner's invasion force, marines of the 2nd and 4th Marine Divisions landed on Saipan. By nightfall almost 20,000 men were dug in on a beachhead a thousand yards deep. Casualties were heavy, but the marines succeeded in repulsing three large Japanese counterattacks against the 2nd Marine Division during the night.

As the marines were digging in on Saipan, Lieutenant Commander Robert Risser, captain of the submarine *Flying Fish,* was peering through his periscope at a parade of Japanese battleships and carriers silhouetted against the coastline of San Bernardino Strait in the central Philippines about nine hundred miles from Saipan. It was the biggest group of targets Risser had ever seen, but he knew that his first priority was to get word of this fleet to Spruance and Nimitz. When darkness fell the *Flying Fish* surfaced and sent out her message: "The Japanese fleet is headed for the Marianas."[76]

The Japanese fleet, about to challenge the American invasion of the Marianas, was more than twice as strong as the fleets that had fought at Midway and Guadalcanal. Like the Americans, the Japanese carriers operated in task forces or "divisions" of three ships each. The most formidable ships were in Carrier Division 1, comprising the veteran *Zuikaku* and *Shokaku* and the brand-new 29,000-ton carrier *Taiho* under the command of Vice Admiral Ozawa Jisaburo. Ozawa was also overall commander of the new First Mobile Fleet, organized that March. Beside Carrier Division 1, the mobile carrier fleet included six more aircraft carriers that had been converted from fleet auxiliaries or fast passenger liners, seven battleships, and ten heavy cruisers. The mobile fleet's carriers embarked just over 400 planes, compared to more than 900 in Task Force 58. Yet the greatest disparity between the two fleets was not in ships or planes but in pilots. By the end of the Guadalcanal campaign, the Japanese were already beginning to suffer from critical shortages of experienced aviators. "Veteran pilots were killed leaving us like a comb with missing teeth. The development of planes fell behind and the training of pilots lagged."[77]

For many months after Guadalcanal, the Japanese navy's carrier-based air units had been dispersed to defend scattered island bases and had suffered heavy losses in the air battles over Rabaul and the central Solomons. "Not for a moment did the Americans ease their relentless pressure," recalled one Japanese aviator. "Day and night the bombers came to pound Rabaul, to smash at the airfields and shipping in the harbor while the fighters screamed low on daring strafing passes shooting up anything they considered a worthwhile target. . . . As the months went by we watched the qualitative superiority of the Zero fade before the increased performance of new American fighter planes which by now not only outfought but also outnumbered the Zeros. There existed a growing feeling of helplessness before this rising tide of American might. Our men felt keenly the great difference between American industrial and military strength and the limited resources of their own country."[78]

Yet it was not entirely American industrial superiority that underlay the dangerous manpower situation of the Japanese in late 1943. For one thing, the Japanese navy took very poor care of its pilots. Men flying from island bases in the Pacific, like those aboard carriers, were rarely rotated home except in the case of severe illness or injury. Moreover, the navy made little attempt to locate and recover downed pilots. "Any man who was shot down and managed to survive by inflating his life raft realized that his chance for continued survival lay entirely within his own hands." In contrast, "the Americans sent out flying boats to the areas in which their planes had fought, searching for and rescuing air crews. . . . Our pilots could not fail to be impressed with these daring search missions."[79]

Food and medical care at the advanced air bases was also poor, often inadequate. The noncommissioned officers, who made up the great majority of aircrews, resented the special privileges afforded to the small minority of commissioned officers. "If they had the gold stripe or two stars of a lieutenant, well, they were 'honorable lieutenant, honorable officer.' [The rest of us] were billeted out in the drafty common room while the nation put them into their own individual rooms. . . . They were young kids . . . fresh from the homeland who'd never be able to get themselves or their Zeros back if they went into action. . . . Meals were completely different too. Veteran aces were fed with food and provisions best fit for horses, while those who hadn't done anything were given restaurant meals. . . . When we were at the airfield our ready room and the officers' ready rooms were separate. When were we going to consult? When were the leaders, the officers and the non-coms in the 2nd and 3rd planes to get to know each other. . . to develop the unspoken understanding needed for combat?"[80]

In Ozawa's fleet steaming toward the Marianas, most of the pilots had less than six months of experience. Some had as little as two months. By contrast, even the newest American aviator assigned to a carrier had at least 525 hours of flying time. Senior Japanese air group commanders with Ozawa were on the average ten years younger and ten years less experienced than those who had sailed with Admiral Nagumo at Midway. In practice bombing operations against an old battleship moving at sixteen knots (half the speed of a modern warship), some of the Japanese dive-bomber squadrons had failed to score a single hit.[81]

The Imperial Japanese Navy's plan for meeting the American advance across the Pacific, Operation A-Go, anticipated that a decisive sea battle would be fought in the area of the Palaus or the western Carolinas. In those regions the Japanese counted upon using their land-based airpower to compensate for their inferiority in carriers. Despite the plan, the invasion of the Marianas was too serious to be ignored. By stretching their fuel supplies and using unprocessed Borneo petroleum (good but highly flammable), the fleet could give battle near the Marianas. On June 15, Ozawa received orders to activate Operation A-Go.[82]

Although outnumbered almost two to one in aircraft, Ozawa was confident he could handle the Americans. His planes, owing to lack of armor and self sealing fuel tanks, had a greater range than those of his opponents. Japanese planes could search as far out as 560 miles and attack at 300 miles, whereas Mitscher's could search only to about 350 miles and attack at 200. Ozawa was counting heavily on land-based planes at Guam, Rota, and Yap to whittle down the American fleet; in actuality these forces had done no damage to Task Force 58 but had instead already been well worked over by Mitscher's planes. Vice Admiral Kakuta Kakuji, who commanded the land-based planes, had so misled Ozawa about his strength that Ozawa steamed into battle expecting substantial help from Guam and Tinian.[83] Ozawa also expected to use Guam to rearm and refuel his own aircraft after striking the Americans.

When he learned of the approach of the Japanese, Spruance sailed from Saipan in his flagship, the cruiser *Indianapolis,* accompanied by seven other cruisers and twenty-one destroyers to join Task Force 58. He left behind the older battleships and a few cruisers and destroyers to support the beachhead.

Around midnight on the 17th, the U.S. submarine *Cavalla* reported a Japanese task force eight hundred miles west southwest of Saipan and closing. In the morning the *Cavalla* radioed again that the Japanese fleet was still on course and a hundred miles closer to Saipan. Mitscher wanted to steam southwest at high speed to close on the *Cavalla's* contact, but Spruance wanted to keep Task Force 58 in position to cover Saipan against all eventualities. He feared that the Japanese might divide their forces, using one portion as a decoy and the other to make an end run around Task Force 58 to get at the transports. Additional intelligence from high-frequency direction finders, which pinpointed Ozawa's position during the night of the 18th, failed to dissuade him. Mitscher again asked to head for the area of contact so as to be in position to launch an attack in the morning, but Spruance actually ordered the fleet to double back toward Saipan to prevent any Japanese force from passing them in the darkness.[84]

Thanks to the greater range of his search planes, Ozawa had already located the American fleet late on the afternoon of the 18th, and on the morning of the 19th he launched four massive strikes against Mitscher's carriers. Spruance and Mitscher were still in ignorance of Ozawa's exact whereabouts when the first Japanese raid of about seventy planes showed up on American radar screens about a hundred miles distant.[85] "Over the ship's bull horn every few minutes came announcements of the bearing and distance of incoming raids. 'Raid I now 232.86 miles. Raid II now, 238.78 miles.' These announcements were punctuated by the air officers' exhortations to flight deck crews . . . who were engaged in pushing the planes aft."[86]

The key role in defense of the task forces now fell to a handful of reserve officers and enlisted men, the fighter directors in each of the task groups. They had the responsibility for detecting and identifying enemy raids, for allocating the right number of fighters to intercept them, and for directing the fighters to the best possible position and altitude for an interception. The fighter director officers were young reservists in their twenties, most of whom had been in the navy less than two years. Aboard the carrier *Langley* the fighter direction team included an advertising executive, a lawyer, a college instructor, and "an Atlanta architect who specialized in the design of Methodist Churches."[87] The fighter director and his team worked in a small dimly lit compartment surrounded by radar screens, plotting boards, and radios. "CIC was not a happy place to be," recalled one fighter direction officer. "Here you sat around these radar screens and watched these things happen with young seamen who were 18 or 19 years old, just off the farm or out of the shoestore or what have you, and their reactions were, for the most part, wonderful. . . . We had a few who lost control of themselves and started weeping, crying, praying and things like that. Nobody minds people praying but it's not a happy circumstance for men at their battlestations."[88]

This was the system that had been attempted with indifferent results at Santa Cruz, but on this occasion it worked superbly. And all four Japanese raids were intercepted at fifty or sixty miles from the task force. The veteran American pilots, flying superior aircraft, made it a very uneven contest. Only one U.S. plane was lost to this first wave of attackers. Those Japanese who survived the onslaught of the Hellcats ran into a blizzard of fire from the fast battleships accompanying Mitscher's carriers. Using proximity fuses, the battleships and their escorts downed a dozen more Japanese planes. Only one enemy plane scored a hit, which did minor damage to the battleship *South Dakota.* The second raid, more than 125 aircraft, suffered even heavier losses. Only a handful survived the gauntlet of fighters and fire from the battle line to attack Mitscher's carrier; none did any damage. The third group of attackers eluded the battle line by circling around to the north; it attacked one of the carrier task groups after fighting its way through intercepting Hellcats. Again no carriers were hit. The final wave of attackers became separated and attacked piecemeal during the early afternoon. Many failed to find the American task force at all and were intercepted and shot down while trying to land on Guam. In all fewer than a hundred of the 373 planes which had attacked Task Force 58 in the four mass attacks managed to return to their carriers. The Americans lost only twenty-nine planes in the one-sided action, which one of Mitscher's pilots in *Lexington* labeled "the Great Marianas Turkey Shoot."

Some of the returning Japanese fliers found no carrier to land on. U.S. submarines *Albacore* and *Cavalla* made contact with Ozawa's fleet and sank the carriers *Shokaku* and *Taiho,* obliging Admiral Ozawa to transfer his flag to a destroyer and then to the carrier *Zuikaku.*

In Task Force 58 there was elation at the day's results, combined with frustration over inability to find the Japanese. As darkness fell the Americans knew no more about the whereabouts of Ozawa's fleet than they had known that morning—and because the U.S. carriers had been obliged to steam east into the wind to launch and recover their planes they were still no closer to the enemy. It was not until 8:00 P.M. on the 19th that Mitscher completed recovering all his planes and detached one carrier group under Rear Admiral W. K. Harrill to fuel and keep Japanese air bases on Guam and Roda under attack. There were a handful of night-fighting Hellcats and Avengers that could have conducted night searches, but, as in the case of radar, most admirals were uninformed and skeptical about night fighters. In addition, most night fighter pilots had been trained for short-range interceptions, not long-range searches. There were no searches that night.[89]

The next day the sky was filled with American search planes, flying boats from Saipan, heavy bombers from Manus and the Admiralties, bombers and torpedo planes from the carriers. One group of Hellcats from the *Lexington,* with belly tanks, flew out as far as 475 miles but found nothing. Afternoon came; nerves were on edge and tempers grew short aboard the carriers. Then around 4:00 P.M. a plane from the *Enterprise* sighted Ozawa's fleet about 275 miles from Task Force 58.

That was a very long range. But with only three hours of daylight remaining, Mitscher could delay no longer in launching his warplanes. Attacking at that distance, some planes would probably have insufficient fuel to return. The rest would have to land on their carriers after dark, something for which they had not been trained. Mitscher consulted his operations officer, Commander

W. J. Widhelm. "It's going to be tight," was Widhelm's reply.[90] At 4:10, pilots and crews who had been on alert all afternoon received the order: "Man aircraft." Boldly chalked on the ready rooms' blackboards were Mitscher's final instructions: "Get the Carriers."[91]

Working at a frenzied pace, deck crews launched more than 200 planes in under twelve minutes. As the planes left their carriers, additional reports and calculations by Mitscher's staff revealed that the Japanese were sixty miles farther west than had been first anticipated. This unhappy news was relayed to the pilots and crews already headed for Ozawa's fleet. Aviators made quick worried calculations. It was clear that even under the best circumstances the chances of having sufficient fuel to return from this longer trip were slim indeed. "The intercom chatter, today quite subdued, died away to almost nothing as the pilots realized the import of the new position report."[92]

Only twenty minutes before dark, Mitscher's tired pilots finally found the Japanese fleet. The attackers sank the carrier *Hiyo,* badly damaged three other carriers, and sank two of the accompanying oilers. Three other Japanese carriers escaped unhurt, and the damaged ships returned to Japan for repairs.

It was pitch dark, with no moon and only occasional flashes of lightning from an approaching thunderstorm, by the time the first American planes finally returned to their carriers. "I turned on my lights dim," recalled Lieutenant James D. Ramage, "ate an apple which I brought along and then readjusted my oxygen mask as I was feeling tired and my eyes were seeing things that weren't there. . . . Apparently there were many of our pilots that day who hadn't used their fuel economically. The results began to show. . . . I heard one pilot tell his rear seat man to get ready for a water landing. . . . I saw a group of lights to my right getting lower and lower, then there weren't any more. Apparently a whole section of planes had been low on gas and decided to go in together, thus giving a greater chance of being picked up. I heard some pilot, apparentry lost, calling desperately for a carrier. His base was too far away to pick him up. Finally he called again, he was out of gas, bailing out, then silence."[93]

Mitscher's carriers sighted the first returning planes at 8:30. As the carriers reversed course from west to east to come into the wind, Mitscher ordered the task groups to turn on their lights. Standard flight operating procedure provided for carriers to display their deck landing and ramp lights for night landings even though this might reveal the ship to lurking submarines.[94] Mitscher went much further, ordering the carriers to flash their signal lights and point a searchlight beam straight into the sky. Cruisers and destroyers illuminated the area with star shells and turned on all of their navigating lights. To one night fighter pilot sent aloft to guide the planes home, the scene seemed like "a Hollywood premier, Chinese New Year and the Fourth of July all rolled into one."[95]

Chaos reigned as groups of planes, almost out of fuel, attempted to land on the closest visible carrier deck. "By the time we arrived there was bedlam," reported one *Enterprise* pilot. "It was too pitiful to be disgusting. Planes made passes at everything afloat."[96] Carrier decks periodically "closed" as crews cleared away the wreckage of planes that had ignored wave-offs and crash-landed aboard. The carrier *Bunker Hill* experienced a double disaster when a dive-bomber disregarded frantic warnings and hit the crash barrier, toppling onto its nose. While flight deck crews struggled to dislodge the bomber an Avenger torpedo plane, likewise ignoring wave-offs, crashed on the deck and careened into the wrecked dive-bomber, killing four men and wounding others.[97]

As the planes were forced down in the water, cruisers and destroyers left formation to search for crews. Radios crackled with reports, orders, and questions as dozens of ships maneuvered at over twenty knots in the darkness.

LZT MESSAGE 20 June 1944

2045 TG 58.3 V CTG 58.3.	Execute to follow. Turn 090. ComDesRon 50 acknowledge, over.
(Ack'd for).	
TG 58.3 V CTG 58.3.	Standby . . . Execute, Turn 090.
2103 CTG 58.3 V KNAPP.	Am dropping out to pick up plane, over.
KNAPP V COMDESRON 50.	After completion your recovery, trail approximately 3000 yards astern, over.
COMDESRON 50 V KNAPP.	Wilco, out.
2105 CTG 58.3 V KNAPP.	We are going after one on our port side. How about the flare, over.
(Ack'd for).	
2106 HEALY V COMDESRON 50.	Drop astern and find that man in area astern then trail 2000 yards astern, acknowledge, over.
(Ack'dfor).	
2107 CTG 58.3 V KNAPP.	Request permission to turn off searchlight, over.
V CTG 58.3. Affirmative.	COMDESRON 50 assign another of your boys to searchlight duty, over.
2108 BRAINE V CTG 58.3.	Did you see plane just outside screen to port about abreast of LEXINGTON, over.
2109 BRAINE V COMDESRON 50.	Leave screen abeam of LEXINGTON for man in water acknowledge, over.

2110 COMDESRON 50 V CTG 58.3.	Where do you have ANTHONY now, over.
CTG 58.3 V COMDESRON 50.	ANTHONY is astern of LEXINGTON as plane guard. COGSWELL is on other side. Have directed HEALY to drop back and pick up pilot on starboard side of KNAPP.
2113 CTG 58.3 V PRINCETON.	Am ready to pancake two or three if desired, over.
CTG 58.3 V SAN JACINTO.	Our two planes are trying to come aboard, may we take them, over.
TG 58.1 V CTG 58.1.	My course 110, speed 28, out.
CTG 58.3 V SAN JACINTO.	Answer please my last request, over.
CTG 58.3 V PRINCETON.	Did you receive my last transmission, over.
V CTG 58.3.	Negative, Say again, over.
V PRINCETON.	I can take 2 or 3 if desired, over.
V CTG 58.3.	Roger, out.
2117 PRINCETON V CTG 58.3.	If any come around you and wanting to come aboard take them aboard, over.
(Acknowledged for).	
TG 58.3 V CTG 58.3.	One in water on port bow of ENTERPRISE.
COMDESRON 50	Acknowledge, over.
V COMDESRON 50.	Wilco.[98]

Well over a third of the planes that had begun the return flight from Ozawa's fleet were lost in ditching or deck crashes. More than 160 pilots and crewmen were pulled from the water during the night of the 21st and over the next few days, however. Only forty-nine aviators were lost.

"The enemy had escaped," concluded Mitscher's chief of staff, Captain Arleigh Burke, in the action report he drafted for Mitscher. It was a succinct expression of the feeling of frustration and disappointment among many of Spruance's commanders. "We could have gotten the whole outfit!" declared Burke many years later. "Nobody could have gotten away if we had done what we wanted."[99] Spruance's decision on the night of the 18-19th to turn back toward Saipan rather than continue west to place Mitscher's search planes within range of the Japanese fleet by morning immediately became the subject of controversy and has remained so until the present. Spruance's defenders argue that his decision—although based on the faulty premise that the Japanese had divided their forces—in the end worked out for the best. The last of Japan's carrier-based planes and pilots were virtually annihilated at small cost to the United States. Spruance's critics, on the other hand, have gone so far as to suggest that he and his battleship-oriented staff, trained at the Naval War College to refight the Battle of Jutland, did just that, allowing the Japanese to slip away exactly as Admiral Jellicoe had allowed the Germans to rush by him in 1916.[100]

While the strategy of the Japanese and Americans has remained a subject of debate, the operational results were clear and striking. The aircraft carrier, when organized in task forces and equipped with radar, high-performance aircraft, and powerful antiaircraft guns firing proximity-fused shells, was more than capable of holding its own against any size surface or air attack. The extreme vulnerability of warships to mass air attack, so graphically demonstrated at Crete, had been almost completely reversed. Warships were now not only highly survivable, they were capable of destroying large land-based air forces, as the Pacific carriers demonstrated at Rabaul and Kwajalein in the fall of 1943 and at Truk in 1944. Warships once again ruled the waves, but the contest between ships and planes had not ended. The final round would not begin until some nine months after Saipan.

Whatever Japan's losses in the Marianas, the foundation of her defeat had already been laid. The root of this defeat lay in Japan's inability to protect the shipping upon which her war economy depended. By the end of 1944, U.S. submarines operating from bases in Australia, New Guinea, and Hawaii had sunk more than half of Japan's merchant fleet, including about two thirds of her tankers. Japanese industries, almost totally dependent on imported oil and raw materials, had been dealt a devastating blow.[101] This defeat came as a complete surprise to both the Japanese and U.S. navies. Before Pearl Harbor neither navy had expected to imitate the German submarine war against merchant shipping. Instead Japanese and American submarines were expected to play a role in the fleet actions that both sides had confidently expected.

The Japanese navy, obsessed with the need to reduce the odds in an encounter with the superior U.S. battle fleet, gave its submarines the mission of observing and blockading enemy ports and bases. Once the enemy fleet put to sea, the submarines would keep it under surveillance and make repeated attacks to sink or cripple the American battleships and carriers.[102] In U.S. Navy thinking, the submarines were to act as an advance scouting line for the battle fleet, attacking the enemy's battleships and carriers in a coordinated underwater attack. Of thirty-six submarine exercises conducted by the Pacific Fleet during 1940–41, twenty-one were directed against battleships and aircraft carriers, eight were against cruisers and destroyers, and only one was against a convoy of cargo ships.[103] One submarine tactical publication noted that, "in battle the primary objectives of submarines are enemy heavy ships. A heavy ship is defined as a battleship, a battlecruiser or an aircraft carrier. Attacks on secondary objectives while an opportunity for attack on primary objectives remains possible or which would in any manner prejudice the success of the main attack should not be made."[104]

The personnel of both the Japanese and American submarine service were a specially selected elite comparable to naval aviators. American candidates for submarine duty, all volunteers, were carefully screened through tests and personal interviews to determine whether they held "any unfounded objections to undersea service, probably instilled by their mothers. To belong [a submariner] *must be a man* regardless of age or background."[105] Since the 1920s, both officers and enlisted men assigned to U.S. Navy submarines had been required to "qualify" by demonstrating that they had mastered the skills and knowledge required to perform the duties in their area of responsibility. This knowledge could only be acquired through service in an operational submarine. An officer, besides mastering the technical knowledge about the submarine and its weapons, had to direct ten practice dives and mock attacks successfully before being permitted to wear the distinctive dolphin badge of a qualified submariner.

Far more completely than the captain of a surface ship, the captain of a submarine and his key subordinates could, in effect, set their own rules and standards for their crew and reject any individual who failed to measure up. Like the German U-boat men, American and Japanese submariners lived in a claustrophobic world of machinery, stale air, and unpleasant smells. Japanese I-class long-range submarines carried provisions for more than three months so that "the entire deck space except for the diesel engine room was covered with bags of rice, boxes of dried food and tins of provisions to a depth of two feet. It looked like our crewmen were living in a circular food warehouse." In the torpedo room men had to squeeze between "the two foot floor of food and the 'steel fish' in order to get needed rest."[106] An American submariner described the unique odor of a submarine as a by-product of diesel fumes plus the "three Fs—feet, farts and fannies—of eighty-one souls living in close quarters with limited bathing and laundry facilities."[107] American submariners did have one great advantage over their counterparts in the Japanese, German, and British navies. U.S. submarines built since the mid-1930s were air-conditioned—more for the welfare of the machinery than of the sailors. Though air-conditioning equipment took up additional space inside the cramped hull, it made submarines far more livable, especially in tropical waters. Condensate from the air-conditioning units also provided an additional supply of water, which could be used for a kind of primitive laundering.[108]

Both the Japanese and U.S. navies held a high opinion of their own submariners and a correspondingly low opinion of their likely opponents. Japanese submariners were popularly believed to possess "almost supernatural skill" while Americans were considered too soft and luxury-loving to cope with the austerity of submarine duty.[109] Ikezaki Chuko, a popular writer on naval affairs, assured readers of his book, *Nippon Sensuikan* ("Japanese Submarines"), that Japan's inferiority in capital ships would be more than compensated for by the superior design of Japanese submarines and the high quality, morale, and offensive spirit of their crews.[110] The Americans disagreed. An intelligence report, endorsed by the commander in chief of the Pacific Fleet as "a shrewd analysis," observed that though the Japanese had "quick lively minds" they were woefully lacking in initiative. "This mental sluggishness in reacting to new situations appears to be the basic reason for indifferent results the Japanese have attained in submarine and air operations."[111] German technical experts working with submarines in Japan told an American diplomat that "the Japanese make poor submarine personnel. . . . They do not react quickly enough in emergencies. They react only per instruction not by instinct." Japanese submarines reportedly "rarely dive to depths greater than 70 feet." The Germans believed "they are afraid to dive to greater depths. . . ."[112]

Yet World War II had opened with resounding failures by both the U.S. and Japanese submarine forces. Americans were shocked by the failure of their submarines to interfere seriously with the Japanese invasion of the Philippines. "We had the greatest concentration of submarines in the world there," recalled correspondent Hansen W. Baldwin, "but we didn't do a thing."[113] Japanese submarines did almost as poorly at Pearl Harbor. Specially designed midget submarines, attacking shortly before the carrier planes, failed to do any damage, and their activities almost alerted the base. Larger Japanese submarines lurking in Hawaiian waters failed to sink or even sight an American warship, while I-70 was sunk by planes from USS *Enterprise.*

During 1942, U.S. submarines sank 180 Japanese ships, for a total of about 725,000 tons. Japan was able to replace all but 90,000 tons by new construction, and she actually increased her tonnage in tankers. Imports of raw materials from Southeast Asia remained unimpaired. U.S. submarine operations were handicapped by faulty torpedoes, which suffered from defects in their depth mechanisms and their warhead exploders. The last of these imperfections was not corrected until well into 1943.[114]

During 1942, almost 30 percent of all U.S. submarine commanders were relieved for unfitness or lack of results. About 14 percent were removed for these reasons during 1943 and 1944.[115] Prewar submarine commands had generally gone "principally on the basis of seniority, to men who had not tried to force new ideas on their seniors, who had behaved themselves ashore, had kept their submarines clean and their sailors out of trouble," recalled a wartime submarine officer. What was required was "a good man with a tough mind—one who did not have an oversupply of imagination. There were enough real problems . . . to leave no place for a man who saw shadows. A sort of dogged, imperturbable stolidity was preferable to brilliance and imagination. But there had to be at least some of the latter, combined sometimes with an almost reckless aggressiveness, to get the best results."[116]

Prewar submarine doctrine had not emphasized reckless aggressiveness.

Experience in prewar maneuvers and exercises also had given naval officers an exaggerated idea of the effectiveness of aircraft and destroyers in locating and sinking submarines. Submarine commanders had been cautioned against making attacks from periscope depth if the sea was calm or the target was screened by destroyers. In prewar years, it was generally believed that a depth charge exploding anywhere closer than a half mile from a submarine would prove fatal, while actual war experience demonstrated that boats could survive explosions as close as fifteen or twenty feet. Given the supposed vulnerability of the submarines, attacks by periscope had been considered generally too dangerous. Commanders had been encouraged to attack from one hundred feet or more, using sonar to locate the target. Such a "sound attack was considered far safer than one utilizing the periscope. It was also, as war experience would demonstrate, completely impractical."[117]

By mid-1943 a number of favorable developments vastly increased the effectiveness of the U.S. submarine war. Reliable torpedoes were finally available and more aggressive skippers had replaced many of the overly cautious commanders of the early war. Code breakers at Pearl Harbor were reading the Japanese code and transmitted the schedule and routing of convoys so that American submarines could be sent directly into the path of slow-moving Japanese shipping, eliminating the need for long, fuel-consuming searches in the vast Pacific. Beginning in late 1943, submarine admirals at Pearl Harbor and Australia began to direct coordinated attacks against enemy convoys. In addition, substantial numbers of new submarines began to arrive in the Pacific. By July 1944 there were about one hundred U.S. submarines operating from Pearl Harbor and forty more from Australia.[118]

The Japanese were singularly unprepared to deal with the deadly onslaught. Prewar Japanese plans had concluded that transport of petroleum and food supplies to the home islands would not be much of a problem.[119] Japanese strategists expected to lose about 800,000 tons of shipping the first year of the war but then expected a sharp drop in the rate of losses.[120] The indifferent success of the U.S. submarine effort during the early months of the war, together with evidence of American torpedo failures, served to reinforce this false sense of security.[121]

Japanese complacency rapidly dissipated as sinkings by U.S. submarines mounted. By the end of 1943, these losses were already twice the expected total, and by the end of 1944 more than four times the prewar estimate. For every ton of shipping Japan could build, she lost three tons to submarines.[122] In addition, many Japanese submarines also fell victim to American men-of-war coached on to their locations by code intercepts. The Japanese were slow to react to this growing crisis. At the beginning of the war the Imperial Japanese Navy had no units assigned exclusively to antisubmarine warfare. Combined Fleet admirals demanded the best destroyers for duty with the combat forces. The first two escort groups, formed in April 1942 to protect communications to Singapore and Truk, had only a handful of old destroyers. In November 1943 a Grand Escort Command Headquarters was established to coordinate and direct protection of all overseas shipping, but the Combined Fleet continued to get the best escort vessels while the Grand Escort Command received only older ships.[123]

Japanese submarines might have mounted a counteroffensive but failed to do so. They had been trained in the same supercautious mode of "sound attacks" and self-preservation as the prewar U.S. sailors, and unlike the Americans they seem never to have entirely abandoned it.[124] Japanese strategists reasoned that a submarine blockade of the entire United States West Coast was impractical and also unnecessary since the Pacific war was expected to be short. In addition, they decided to divert more and more submarines to carry supplies to beleaguered Japanese garrisons in the Pacific. Japanese submarine commanders protested this dangerous and unrewarding assignment, but the navy high command, unimpressed by the I-boats' performance in the first year of the war, were more willing to assign subs than the more highly valued destroyers to supply and reinforcement duties. The navy even laid down a new type of cargo-carrying submarine.

The U.S. submarine offensive against Japan was one of the decisive elements in ensuring the empire's defeat. A force comprising less than 2 percent of U.S. Navy personnel accounted for 55 percent of Japan's losses at sea. U.S. submarines sank more than 1,300 Japanese ships, including a battleship, eight aircraft carriers, and eleven cruisers, in the course of the war."[125] Yet, the cost was high. About 22 percent of U.S. submariners who made war patrols in World War II failed to return—the highest casualty rate for any branch of service. For the Japanese, the cost in lives was higher still. About 16,000 merchant seamen were killed as a result of submarine attacks and some 53,000 were wounded. The number of civilians, including women and children, who lost their lives in merchant and passenger ship sinkings has not been calculated.

CHAPTER NINETEEN

The Battle Off Samar

Wilfred P. Deac

FOCUS QUESTIONS

1. What was the Japanese strategic rationale in pursuing Plan Sho-1?
2. What was the U.S. Navy's strategic focus at Leyte Gulf? How did Admiral Halsey's operational decisions relate to operations both at Leyte Gulf and to the larger context of the Pacific naval war?
3. What factors contributed to Admiral Kurita's decision to break off his attack?
4. A common perception is that Pearl Harbor marked the clear ascendancy of naval aviation over surface forces. If this is true, how can one explain the Battle off Samar?
5. It took several days to mount a rescue mission to retrieve American sailors who survived the sinking of their ships off Samar. Large numbers died in the interim because of exposure or wounds. Compare that with current American military operations. What reasons might explain any differences?

Wednesday, October 25, 1944—a gloomy overcast punctuated by rain squalls gave the predawn sky a dirty yellow-gray hue. Six small United States carriers and seven escort ships moved through the somber seas east of the Philippine Island of Samar. From the gently swaying flight decks of the carriers, white-starred planes took off on routine early-morning missions.

On the bridge of the flagship, U.S.S. *Fanshaw Bay,* Rear Admiral Clifton

A. F. Sprague watched the Grumman aircraft rise into the northeasterly wind toward the broken ceiling of clouds. The day had all the earmarks of being another long, tiresome succession of reconnaissance, anti-submarine, and ground-support missions. Sprague, a forty-eight-year-old veteran, scanned his little fleet, called Taffy 3 (its radio call sign). Merchant-ship hulls turned into baby flattops to meet wartime needs, the thin-skinned escort carriers—designated CVEs—were not even half the size of conventional aircraft carriers. Old hands claimed the CVE stood for "Combustible, Vulnerable, Expendable." Three destroyers and four destroyer escorts ringed the flotilla of CVEs like watchful guard dogs. Somewhere to the south, Sprague knew, two other carrier groups, Taffies 1 and 2, were on similar missions in support of the American G.I.s who had gone ashore at Leyte Gulf five days earlier. Together the three Taffies made up Escort Carrier Task Group 77.4 of the United States Seventh Fleet.

The first warning of a break in the morning routine came shortly after six thirty as the strips' crews sat down to breakfast. Radio equipment in the *Fanshaw Bay's* Combat Information Center picked up Japanese voices. Since the nearest enemy ships were supposedly over a hundred miles away, the American radiomen reasoned that the enemy chatter must be coming from one of the nearby Japanese-held islands. With the exception of the beachhead on Leyte and a few islands in the adjacent gulf, all of the Philippine archipelago was in Japanese hands.

Eleven minutes later, a message flashed in from an American scout plane. The unbelievable words were hurriedly relayed to the bridge: "Enemy surface force . . . twenty miles northwest of your task group and closing at 30 knots."

Admiral Sprague, at this moment, was trying to make sense of two other odd reports. His lookouts had just seen anti-aircraft fire on the northern horizon, and his radar had picked up an unidentified something in the same direction. Surely, Sprague was thinking, the cause of all the unexpected commotion must be Admiral William Halsey's Third Fleet, the closest large naval unit to Taffy 3. The pilot's message stopped him short.

"Check that identification!" ordered Sprague, hoping with a growing feeling of doubt that some innocent mistake had been made by the scout plane. But confirmation came from another source—a lookout on one of Sprague's other carriers, the *Kitkun Bay.* Scanning the horizon beneath the gradually clearing cumulus cloud canopy, the seaman could make out pagoda-like masts: Japanese battleships and cruisers.

Admiral Sprague's voice boomed into the squawk box: "Come to course 090 degrees . . . launch all planes as soon as possible . . . speed 16."

The little carriers swung due east, far enough into the wind to launch aircraft without bringing them closer to the enemy. Planes were soon soaring into the damp sky armed with whatever bombs and bullets they had when the alarm sounded. Gun crews steeled expectantly behind the breeches of the carriers' 5-inch guns—the biggest they had.

At 6:58 A.M., bright flashes lit the horizon seventeen miles north of the flotilla. Sixty seconds later, Japanese range-marker shells rattled into the sea to throw towering geysers of colored water into the air behind the American carriers. The Battle off Samar had begun.

The Battle off Samar was a direct result of Japanese High Command plans. As the American forces advanced relentlessly across the Southern Pacific during the final months of World War II, four *Sho* (Conquer) plans were devised to blunt U.S. thrusts against the Empire's inner defenses. At best, these were little more than delaying tactics which might postpone the end of the war and give Japan a better bargaining position at the peace table. *Sho* No. 1 was designed to counter any United States move against the Philippine Islands, and by the fall of 1944, with the Americans moving northwestward, it appeared that the time for putting it into effect had arrived.

In mid-October the Imperial Japanese Navy began to move. Powerful naval forces steamed eastward from the Lingga Archipelago near Singapore, and southward from the home islands. On October 18, when the Japanese fleets were still at sea, the word flashed from Combined Fleet commander Admiral Soemu Toyoda in Tokyo: "Execute Sho Plan No.1!" American landings had begun in Leyte Gulf, in the east-central Philippines.

Two U.S. fleets were covering the invasion beaches—the Third Fleet, under Admiral William F. Halsey, composed mainly of fast new battleships and big carriers; and the Seventh Fleet, commanded by Vice Admiral Thomas C. Kinkaid, made up mostly of pre-Pearl Harbor battlewagons and cruisers. The Third Fleet was acting the role of roving watchdog, while the Seventh was directly overseeing the landing of Sixth Army G.I.s on Leyte Island.

Sho No. 1 was to be a three-pronged maneuver supported by land-based aircraft. A Northern Force under Vice Admiral Jisaburo Ozawa would steam southward from Japan and attempt to decoy away the protecting American Third Fleet. This Japanese force was made up of four regular carriers, two converted battleship-carriers, and smaller screening vessels. The battleship-carriers—the *Ise* and the *Hyunga*—were merely old battleships with their two main aft turrets replaced by small flight decks. Designed to compensate for Japan's shortage of aircraft carriers, the hybrid ships would never have a chance to prove themselves. There were not enough airplanes available in the fall of 1944 to give the *Ise* and the *Hyunga* even one of the twenty-four each was supposed to carry; and Ozawa's other carriers were decidedly short of planes, too.

The second prong of *Sho* No. 1 was to swing in against the Americans in Leyte Gulf from the southwest, through Surigao Strait. The melange of battleships, cruisers, and destroyers in this Southern Force—seventeen ships in all—were commanded by Vice Admirals Kiyohide Shima and Shoji Nishimura.

The third prong, the Center Force, was the most potent of the Nipponese units, and was to deliver the knockout blow. Salting from Lingga Roads during the early morning hours of October 18, it would stop at North Borneo for refueling and final preparations. Then, following a devious path through the Sibuyan Sea and San Bernardino Strait north of Leyte, it would swing around and enter Leyte Gulf through "the back door"—from the east. In this key

Center Force, under Vice Admiral Takeo Kurita, were the world's two largest warships, the *Yamato* and the *Musashi.* Each displaced 68,000 tons and carried 18.1-inch guns, as compared to 45,000 tons and 16-inch guns for the largest U.S. warship. Also in this formidable fleet were the battleships *Haruna, Kongo,* and *Nagato,* twelve cruisers, and fifteen destroyers.

Once inside Leyte Gulf, Shima's and Nishimura's Southern Force and Kurita's Center Force were to pool their firepower to disrupt the American invasion. Whatever lay in the gulf or blocked its approaches, warships and cargo vessels alike, was to be wiped out. The importance of Ozawa's Northern Force as a decoy to draw off the powerful U.S. Third Fleet was emphasized by the marked Japanese inferiority in aircraft and by the total number of fleet units involved—64 Nipponese vessels against 216 American and 2 Australian warships.

In undertaking *Sho* Plan No.l, the Japanese were placed in the unenviable position of the frantic poker player who, reduced to a few chips after a losing streak, plays his hand all or nothing. Admiral Kurita said to his officers before the battle: "I know many of you are strongly opposed to this assignment. But the war situation is far more critical than any of you can possibly know. Would it not be a shame to have the fleet remain intact while our nation perishes? . . . You must all remember there are such things as miracles. What man can say there is no chance for our fleet to turn the tide of war in a decisive battle?"

First blow in the Battle for Leyte Gulf was struck by the U.S. submarine *Darter* against the Center Force as Kurita's ships steamed northeast along Palawan, the dagger-like island jutting southwest from the middle of the Philippine archipelago. The sub's torpedoes slammed into two of the enemy cruisers just as the first light of October 23 was streaking the eastern sky. The force flagship, the heavy cruiser *Atago,* shuddered and sank in less than twenty minutes, sending Admiral Kurita and his staff for an unscheduled swim before they were rescued by a destroyer. The cruiser *Takao,* also hit, belched fire and smoke. The task force swung to starboard into the path of a second U.S. submarine. Torpedoes from the *Dace* scrubbed the cruiser *Maya* from the scene in four minutes. Kurita, shifting his command post to the huge *Yamato,* was badly shaken up. The enemy hadn't even been sighted, and already five valuable warships (counting two destroyers detached to escort the damaged *Takao* to Borneo) were eliminated from the battle to come.

The sun shone down from clear skies on white-capped water and mountainous islands as the Center Force moved into the Sibuyan Sea northwest of Leyte on Tuesday, October 24. Within twenty four hours, if all went well, Kurita's ships would be steaming into Leyte Gulf from the east. But their bad luck had not left them yet. Their anti-aircraft batteries, nervously anticipating American air strikes, cut loose at a flight of fighter planes soon after dawn. It was a mistake, and a costly one for the Center Force. The planes were land-based Japanese Zeros ordered to provide air cover for Kurita. Faced with heavy anti-aircraft fire from the very warships they were to protect, the fighters understandably returned to their island base.

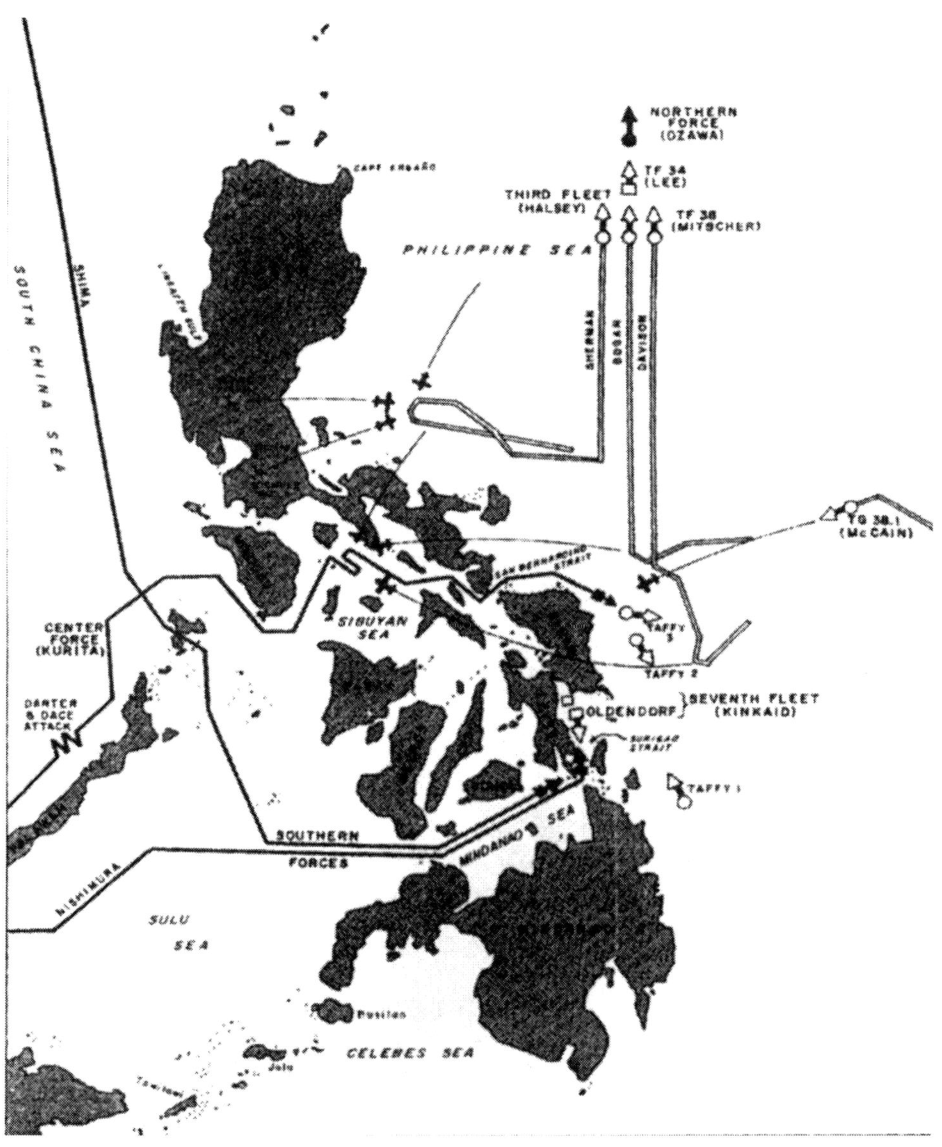

Then, at 8:10 that morning, an American scout plane sighted the Japanese armada. Two hours and sixteen minutes later, single-engined bombers and fighters from the carriers of Admiral Halsey's Third Fleet pounced on the Center Force. Dodging the pink and purple bursts of anti-aircraft fire, American Helldivers and Avengers pressed one attack after another against the wildly weaving ships. At the cost of eighteen dive bombers and torpedo planes, they sank the gargantuan *Musashi,* badly damaged a heavy cruiser, and slightly hurt the other battleships. Kurita wavered—he actually had his fleet reverse course for several hours—but in the end he rallied and carried on toward San Bernardino Strait.

Admiral Halsey was very much pleased by his carrier pilots' reports of their successes over the Sibuyan Sea. Unfortunately, the reports were somewhat exaggerated, and led him to the optimistic conclusion that Kurita's Center Force "could no longer be considered a serious menace." Meanwhile Admiral Ozawa's decoy Northern Force had been cruising the waters of the Philippine Sea off Luzon, hoping to be spotted by Halsey's search planes. About 4 P.M. on October 24, one of the searchers made the contact, and by 8:30 that evening the whole U.S. Third Fleet was off in enthusiastic pursuit of the Japanese bait—sixty-five warships against seventeen.

It was a questionable action, and led to one of the hottest controversies about naval tactics in World War II. Halsey had enough ships and planes to handle both Ozawa and Kurita; but as it was, nobody was left to guard the exit of the San Bernardino Strait. Through that exit Kurita's still very menacing force was steadily plowing in order to turn southward off the eastern coast of Sarnar and come in to Leyte Gulf on October 25—its role in *Sho* No. 1.

Steaming at twenty knots through the narrow strait between Luzon and Samar islands, Kurita's Center Force debauched into the Philippine Sea at thirty-five minutes past midnight. In addition to the battleships *Yamato, Haruna, Kongo,* and *Nagato,* there were the heavy cruisers *Chikuma, Chokai, Haguro, Kumano, Suzuya,* and *Tone,* the smaller-gunned light cruisers *Noshiro* and *Yahagi,* and eleven destroyers.

Prepared to have to fight their way through to Leyte Gulf, the Japanese sailors were pleasantly surprised when dawn revealed nothing on the southern horizon but open water. Well beyond that horizon, below Leyte Gulf, Admiral Kinkaid's Seventh Fleet had turned southward to encounter the Japanese Southern Force under Admirals Shima and Nishimura in a triumphant fight, later to be known as the Battle of Surigao Strait. Nothing but the three light Taffy forces now stood between the U.S. invasion troops on Leyte and possible disaster. Of the three, only Taffy 3 lay directly in Kurita's path as his Center Force swept south.

This was the astonishing situation when, just after dawn on October 25, Admiral Kurita's twenty-three warships, three hours north of Leyte Gulf, ran into Admiral Clifton Sprague's small group—the 10,000-ton black-and-gray camouflaged escort carriers *Fanshaw Bay, St. Lo, White Plains, Kalinin Bay, Kitkun Bay,* and *Gambier Bay;* the 2,050-ton destroyers *Heermann, Hoel,* and *Johnston;* and the 1,275-ton destroyer escorts *Dennis, John C. Butler, Raymond,* and *Samuel B. Roberts.*

Kurita, thinking he must have stumbled onto Halsey's Third Fleet, abruptly ordered his ships into pursuit formation. Since the Center had been in the process of switching over from its tight night formation to a dispersed daytime deployment, the new order spread confusion through the Japanese fleet. The result was a fierce but surprisingly uncoordinated attack on the American ships.

At 6:58 A.M., a salvo of 3,200-pound shells, each some fifty percent heavier than the largest U.S. warship projectile, spun out of the *Yamato's* huge gun barrels. It was the first time the superbattleship had fired its 18. 1-inch batteries at another ship. The *Haruna's* 14-inch guns joined in three minutes later.

At 7:01 A.M. Admiral Sprague ordered the transmission of an urgent plea for help. The request was immediately picked up, and planes from Taffies 1 and 2 were ordered to the assistance of Taffy 3. Glancing away from the enemy, Sprague noted with pride that his little fleet was following orders with the precision of a well-trained team. Straddled by the red, yellow, blue, and green splashes of marker shells, Taffy 3 was laying heavy smoke screens, the white clouds pouring from chemical generators contrasting sharply with the oily black smoke from the strips' funnels.

Launching her planes as rapidly as possible, the *White Plains* trembled violently as the mere concussion of the big enemy shells caused minor damage. Water spray from a shellburst that threw a geyser high above the carrier rained over the ship's bridge. One plane preparing to take off from the flight deck was bounced forward by the concussion of explosions pummeling the sea. Its spinning propeller bit a chunk out of the wing of another fighter. The *St. Lo,* ebony clouds pouring from her four small exhaust stacks, was also buffeted by the Japanese barrage.

Although the enemy ships had closed to within fifteen miles of their prey, they were still beyond the range of the puny U.S. 5-inch guns. If only he could keep his ships swinging in a wide circle around to the southwest without being overtaken or cut off, Sprague thought, he could hope to lead the Japanese fleet into the guns of the now-altered battleships of the Seventh Fleet. Then, even though Kinkaid's ships were not in top shape for battle after their heavy night action in Surigao Strait against the Japanese Southern Force, the Americans would have some chance of stopping the enemy.

Deployed in a formation of two concentric circles—the six carriers forming the inner circle—the U.S. flotilla was rapidly being overtaken by the speedier enemy ships. Then, at 7:06 A.M., Taffy 3 dipped its nose into a welcome rain squall. Hindered by ineffective radar, enemy fire fell off in volume and accuracy. During the fifteen-minute respite afforded by the rain, Sprague made a decision. He would order a torpedo attack by his destroyers.

In the meantime, the first desperate strikes by the U.S. carrier planes had been made on the pursuing enemy. Dropping the small bombs and depth charges with which they had been loaded in expectation of routine missions, the Navy planes harassed the Japanese ships for twenty minutes. Bombs soon gone, they strafed with machine-gun fire. And even when their ammunition was exhausted, the pilots continued to buzz the enemy, hoping to bluff the Nipponese ships off course and give Taffy 3 a chance to escape. Only when their fuel ran low did they leave. Unable to land on their own carriers because the ships were heading downwind, the Taffy 3 planes were forced to rearm and refuel at an air-strip on the Leyte beachhead to the west, and on the flattops of

Taffy 2 to the southeast. Joined by other Wildcat fighters and Avenger torpedo bombers from Taffy 2, they soon returned to the attack.

First for the airmen was drawn when a bomb pierced the deck of the heavy cruiser *Suzuya.* Shuddering under the detonation, the 14,000-ton warship slowed to twenty knots and fell behind the Japanese formation. The bold American planes, delaying the pursuers by forcing them into time-consuming evasive maneuvers, also inflicted minor damage on a few of the other Japanese ships.

The two-funneled *Johnston,* which had already opened fire with her five 5-inch guns, was the first destroyer to respond to Sprague's order for a torpedo attack. As the helmsman swung the wheel hard to port, the outgunned *Johnston* sliced bravely through the gray sea at twenty-five knots toward the Japanese heavy cruiser *Kumano.* At 9,000 yards the destroyer heeled steeply over, her ten torpedoes splashing into the sea. One of the missiles reached the sleek cruiser, blowing off its bow in a thunderous eruption of flame, smoke, and debris. Its blunted nose dipping deep into the low swells, the limping *Kumano* dropped astern and joined its damaged sister ship *Suzuya.* The battle was already over for the two badly hit cruisers.

Then luck ran out for the plucky *Johnston.* As she turned about, three 14-inch and three 6-inch shells slammed into her thin hull. "Like a puppy being smacked by a truck," as one of her officers put it, the ship dipped into the boiling sea and bobbed back up, her steering gear severely damaged, and many men dead and wounded both above and below decks. Commander Ernest E. Evans, who had a very short time to live, emerged from the salvo with half of his clothes blown off and minus two fingers of his left hand.

The destroyers *Heermann* and *Hoel* swept past the stricken ship toward the enemy. Although smoking and slowed to sixteen or seventeen knots, the *Johnston* swung awkwardly in behind the other destroyers to support them with her guns. Further back, the slower destroyer escorts formed a second attack wave. It was the story of David and Goliath in a terrifying modern context.

With guns banging and torpedoes knifing toward the Japanese ships, the *Heermann* and the *Hoel* won much-needed time for the fleeing escort carriers. But while the *Heermann* received reparable damage as she darted nimbly in and out of the Japanese salvos, the *Hoel* was less fortunate.

The first hit smashed high on the *Hoel's* forward superstructure, sending hot pieces of steel whistling through her radar antennas and falling on her decks. Seeking out her target through blotting rain and clouds of black and white smoke, the destroyer dashed to within 9,000 yards of the giant *Kongo* and released a spread of five torpedoes. Not sixty seconds later, one of the battleship's 14-inch projectiles screeched into the *Hoel's* side behind the funnels. Detonating in the aft engine room, it hammered one of the ship's two engines into junk. A second 14-incher plowed into the ship's tail, knocking out guns, damaging the electric steering gear, and bouncing men limply off bulkheads.

Steaming on one engine and maneuvering on emergency steering apparatus, with three of her 5-inch cannons out of commission, the *Hoel* made another run on the enemy. The target this time was the heavy cruiser *Haguro.* The destroyer's five remaining torpedoes swooshed from their tubes. Then, as one of her officers later stated, the *Hoel* tried to "get the hell out of there." But this was easier said than done.

Barely able to keep ahead of the onrushing enemy, much less get out of the line of fire, the *Hoel* absorbed over forty hits as she fought back with her two remaining guns. The big battleships passing to port and the heavy cruisers steaming by to starboard deluged the quivering destroyer with heavy shells. Flames erupted from the *Hoel's* aft section, explosions shredded her superstructure, and an inferno raged inside her hull. And still the dying ship's remaining guns fired stubbornly at the thundering enemy. Then, punched full of holes, the ship finally gave up the uneven struggle. She was dead in the water, her stern almost submerged and her forward magazine ablaze, when the "abandon ship" order was given. Only a handful of the warship's crew was able to respond. At 8:55 A.M., an hour and a half after she was first hit, the *Hoel* rolled over and sank to the bottom of the Philippine Sea. Of her crew of more than 300, 253 went down with her. Fifteen of her wounded later died.

The first torpedo run was over. Despite the destruction of the *Hoel,* the skipper of the shell-peppered *Heermann* calmly radioed a modest report to Admiral Sprague: "Exercise completed."

At a quarter of eight, meanwhile, the destroyer escorts had sailed in under the cover of rain and smoke. Intended primarily for anti-submarine patrols, the lightweight escorts were no match for some of the world's most powerful ships. Yet, running to within 4,000 yards of the enemy with their 5-inch guns blazing, the American escorts managed to throw the Japanese off stride.

Dashing ahead of the pack, the little *Roberts* traded blows with the enemy heavies for forty-five minutes before she was hit. At 8:51, a heavy shell thumped into the water alongside the veering ship and plowed into her side, opening a hole below the waterline. One hit followed another, turning her into a shambles. That the heroic escort managed to go on fighting for three-quarters of an hour is an amazing tribute to her captain and crew. Answering the 14- and 8-inch shells of the Japanese cruisers with her inadequate 5-inchers, the *Roberts* was raked at point-blank range.

At approximately 9 A.M., minutes after the *Hoel* went down, two or three 14-inch shells from the *Kongo* slammed into the *Roberts'* port side. Like some gigantic can opener, the monstrous explosion tore a jagged hole over thirty feet long and seven to ten feet high in the escort's hull. The area aft of the tossing ship's funnel became what one survivor called an "inert mass of battered metal."

One gun crew, courageously ignoring flame and smoke, continued firing its weapon by hand after the ammunition hoist went out of action. Suddenly, one of the charges ignited in the hot breech before the 5-inch gun could be fired. Demolishing the cannon, the blast sent the gun crew tumbling in all directions like so many rag dolls. The first man to enter the gun mount after the shattering detonation found the gun captain, his body blown open, holding a cannon shell in his scorched hands. He was begging for help to get the fifty-four-pound projectile into the cannon. Minutes later, he was dead.

In all, the *Roberts*—the runt that fought like a champion—fired 608 shells from its 5-inch guns before the end came. She had inflicted serious damage on an enemy cruiser and had incurred almost two dozen Japanese hits. Five minutes after ten that morning, the second of the "little boys" went down off Samar. Killed in the action were 3 of her 8 officers and 86 of her 170 men.

Their torpedoes expended, the surviving escort ships fought their way back to cover the carriers. To the manmade maelstrom nature added her own effects, giving the scene an eerie quality. One moment the sun's rays would clearly illuminate the opposing forces. A few seconds later, the whole tableau would be obscured by a curtain of rain or drifting smoke. And between the clouds and the sea was the incessant lightning and thunder of gunfire. Narrowly avoiding collisions as they zigzagged to escape the enemy shells, Admiral Sprague's flotilla churned southward.

The Japanese pursuit had by now assumed a rough pattern. In an attempt to box in the carriers, which could barely reach eighteen knots, the swift Nipponese heavy cruisers raced across the wakes of the Americans to close in from the east at almost thirty knots. The Japanese destroyers and light cruisers, kept to the rear until now, pushed down along the starboard side of the baby flattops. And, at a greater distance, the *Nagato* and the huge *Yamato* were doing their best to aim straight down the back of the U.S. formation. In the meantime, the battleships *Haruna* and *Kongo* swung wide to outcruise the cruisers to the east.

For almost two and a half-hours—between 6:58 and approximately 9:20—the little American carriers were under constant fire from Kurita's Center Force. Only the *Yamato* and the *Nagato,* badgered by the U.S. destroyers into performing wild, evasive maneuvers that ultimately steered them out of range, were denied the honor of remaining in the slugfest. Admiral Kurita, aboard the *Yamato,* was thus out of touch with the action, a development that was to produce unhappy consequences for the Japanese.

As the battle unfolded, Admiral Sprague saw that the greatest immediate danger to his group were the four enemy heavy cruisers *Chikuma, Chokai, Haguro,* and *Tone.* Closer than the other Japanese ships, they were rapidly moving in from the northeast—their 8-inch shells striking into, and in many cases through, the thin-hulled carriers. Sprague told his planes and ships to concentrate on them.

Although smoke screens and maneuvering threw Japanese marksmanship off, Admiral Sprague's flagship, the *Fanshaw Bay,* received four direct hits and two near misses which killed three of her crew and wounded others. The *White Plains,* the *Kitkun Bay,* and the *St. Lo* got off lightly; but the *Kalinin Bay* took more than a dozen heavy projectiles, miraculously remaining afloat.

Shrewd guesswork and clever steering by her skipper saved the *Gambier Bay,* steaming on the exposed left rear corner of the U.S. formation, for a full twenty-five minutes. Then, at 8:10 A.M., a shell from a Japanese cruiser hit the aft end of the carrier's flight deck. Fire broke out in the ship's hangar as the projectile sheared through the upper deck. More heavy-caliber shots slashed in. A gaping hole was torn in the *Gambier Bay's* forward port engine room, flooding it with cascading water. Less than half an hour after first being struck, the escort carrier slowed to eleven knots and dropped back. The heavy cruisers *Chikuma, Chokai,* and *Haguro,* the light cruiser *Noshiro,* and a Nipponese destroyer poured salvo after salvo into the blazing carrier's hull. Steering and power aboard the *Gambier Bay* were shot out, the aft engine room was flooded, and men cursed and died at their posts. Efforts by the destroyers *Johnston* and *Heermann* to draw attention away from the dying CVE failed.

By 8:45 A.M., the carrier was entirely without headway and was settling. Five minutes later, the 750 living of the *Gambier Bay's* 854-man crew began going over the side. Still the enemy shells came, killing some men in the water. Seven minutes after 9 A.M., their ship turned turtle and sank. Fighting the suction of the plunging 10,000-ton flattop, the survivors struggled to keep afloat until help came. It would come—almost forty hours later.

Meanwhile Taffy 3 aircraft pounced like hawks on the enemy cruisers. Bomb bursts erupted on the ships as the Japanese paid for their lack of air power. The *Chokai,* mortally wounded by the sea and air blows it received, turned away. Moments later, struck by a torpedo dropped by one of the American bombers, the *Chikuma* also pulled out of the battle. But the *Haguro* and the *Tone,* the remaining enemy heavy cruisers on the port side of the American formation, pressed closer.

Pounding in behind the cruisers for the kill, the closest of the Japanese battleships—the *Haruna*—suddenly veered to the southeast. The big ship's observers could see, about twenty miles away, the northernmost ships of Admiral Felix B. Stump's Taffy 2. With the Imperial Navy's penchant for dividing its forces, the *Haruna* swung her heavy two-gun turrets toward the new target. Although the 29,300-ton leviathan lobbed 14-inch shells at the Taffy 2 ships for almost half an hour, it failed to score a hit.

Nipponese destroyers were now also closing in on Taffy 3. Led by the light cruiser *Yahagi,* four of them streaked in from the west for a torpedo attack on the crippled *Johnston.* Her decks littered with wreckage tinted by blood and the dye of enemy marker shells, the *Johnston* challenged the Japanese attack with her two operational guns. Trading blows with five undamaged ships, the limping destroyer scored a number of hits on the 6,000-ton *Yahagi.* A U.S. plane joined the fray with chattering 50-caliber machine guns. Twenty minutes after starting their attack, the enemy ships released their torpedoes and turned about. But the Japanese had been tricked into releasing their missiles prematurely. Losing their aim and speed because of the extreme range, the torpedoes failed to score.

Now the cruisers *Haguro* and *Tone* swept by on the opposite side of the *Johnston.* The American destroyer rolled under the rain of shells for another thirty minutes. Fires raged through the beaten ship, cremating the wounded and dead huddled in the wreckage, trapping the living in the steel coffin of her hull. Her ammunition blew up in a series of blasts, adding to the carnage. Her engines gone, her communication system obliterated, the wallowing destroyer still barked pugnaciously at the enemy with her remaining cannon. Then, at 9:45 A.M., Commander Evans ordered the surviving crewmen off the doomed ship.

Like Indians in a western movie, the Japanese destroyers steamed around the settling *Johnston* in a circle until the riddled vessel turned over and sank at 10:10 A.M.

The survivors in the water watched their blazing ship disappear. One of them reported that as it went down a Japanese destroyer captain saluted. Most, swimming or clinging to life rafts and debris, were numbed and shocked. One moment they had been going about their daily routine; the next they were racing to their battle stations. And then, after hours of brain-pounding battle that demanded automatic response, they had been cast into a tropical sea shadowed by the haze of gunsmoke and burning ships. There was now only the slapping of waves and the gasping of hoarse voices. A torpedo-man, with a casualness produced by shock, remarked to a fellow survivor that they gotten off all torpedoes.

In a sea alive with activity, the fate of the *Johnston's* crew was to be a harsh one. Only 141 of her crew of 327 would be saved—49 were killed during the action, 45 died of their wounds after abandoning ship, and 92 (including Commander Evans) perished while awaiting rescue. Sharks got at least one man; the others succumbed to exposure.

As the battle raged, the ultimate weaknesses of the Japanese attack finally made themselves felt. Hampered by a combination of rain squalls, screens, stubborn American resistance, poor communications, lack of coordination, and, above all, the lack of air strength, the enemy attack fell apart. The *Yamato* and the *Nagato* had let themselves wander off; the *Haruna* was in pursuit of Taffy 2.

Expecting at any moment to be swimming for his life, Clifton Sprague had been grimly sizing up the situation as the enemy salvos boomed into the midst of Taffy 3. His ships had arced into their southwesterly course as ordered. Ahead and a bit to the right he could make out the dark outline of Samar some thirty miles away. Then, at 9:25, as he concentrated on evading the torpedoes launched minutes before by the *Yahagi* and her destroyers, the skipper of Taffy 3 was treated to the sweetest words he could ever hope to hear.

"Goddamn boys, they're getting away!" called out a signalman on the bridge of the *Fanshaw Bay*.

Unable to keep in touch with his fleet because of bad radio communication, Admiral Kurita had launched the *Yamato's* two reconnaissance planes less than an hour apart to survey the situation. Both were shot down some fifteen minutes after they were catapulted from the stern of the battleship. Unaware that his ships were finally closing in on their prey—with victory off Samar still possible—the confused Japanese admiral had decided to regroup his fleet before a fuel shortage and the relentless American air attacks put it out of action. At 9:11 A.M. Kurita had ordered all his units to take a northerly course.

Despite the blows dealt to Kurita's ships, there was precious little to keep his fleet from blasting its way through Taffy 3 to Leyte Gulf. Far to the north, off Cape Engaño, too distant to do any good, Halsey's Third Fleet was only now reluctantly giving up its chase of Ozawa's Northern Force and turning about in answer to urgent messages from Admiral Kinkaid and Pacific Fleet Headquarters at Pearl Harbor. To the south, Kinkaid's Seventh Fleet was on the other side of Leyte Gulf. Its ships, low on fuel and ammunition, were still busy with mopping up what remained of the Japanese southern thrust.

Yet it takes no great stretch of the imagination to understand the indecision and uncertainty that marked Takeo Kurita's actions at this point in the battle. He had been forced to swim for his life when the *Atago* was sunk on the twenty-third. The Center Force had been under repeated air assault since it first entered the Sibuyan Sea. He had received no news of Ozawa's success in decoying Halsey, and was still under the impression that Taffy 3 was part of the U.S. Third Fleet. Discouraged by reports of the Surigao Strait action, he felt his ships were alone. Fatigued, his nerves strained, Kurita decided to disregard the order that called for his charging into Leyte Gulf. Instead, as a face-saving gesture, the Center Force would shift to a new target.

Earlier in the day, an American task force had been reported in the Philippine Sea to the northeast. Kurita would attack it. Several hours spent in search of the phantom U.S. force proved fruitless. Assisted in his decision by the nagging persuasion of U.S. Navy planes that continued to peck at his ships, the Center Force commander finally called off the hunt and ordered his fleet to head back where it came from.

Suffering the final indignity of being mistakenly attacked by two Japanese land-based aircraft, the Center Force slipped westward through San Bernardino Strait a few hours later. Fast warships from Halsey's Third Fleet reached the strait soon afterward, too late to catch Kurita but in time to bag one lagging Japanese destroyer.

But despite Kurita's departure, the ordeal of Taffy 3 was not quite over.

At 10:50 A.M., soon after Admiral Sprague ordered Taffy 3's pilots to return to their carriers, five Japanese planes had roared in just over the wave-tops. Soaring upward, they climbed a mile above the carriers and suddenly dived down. The Divine Wind—the newly organized Kamikaze suicide corps—was about to wreak its vengeance on Taffy 3.

A single-engined Zero fighter crashed on the port side of the *Kitkun Bay* and bounced into the sea. Its bomb, however, exploded and damaged the carrier. Tensely watching from the *Fanshaw Bay,* Clifton Sprague saw the ship's 40- and 20-millimeter antiaircraft fire chew apart two of the diving suicide planes. They fell into the ocean. The *White Plains* sent screams of tracer bullets into the remaining Kamikazes. One of the enemy exploded a few yards behind the flattop, injuring eleven Americans and spraying the deck with debris and pieces of the pilot. The other plane, its engine sputtering, swerved toward the *St. Lo.* With a grinding of metal and a shower of sparks, the Zero tore into the carrier. A ball of fire sent clouds of smoke boiling heavenward. One explosion followed the other as bombs and torpedoes stored inside the *St. Lo* were set off. Torn apart and burning from stem to stern, the little ship that had survived the *Yamato's* great shells sank in less than twenty minutes. She was the first major victim of the Divine Wind. Of her more than 800 men, 734 were saved by Taffy 3.

There was more to come. At 11:10 A.M. Admiral Sprague's little fleet was attacked by enemy torpedo planes. Two were immediately shot down by U.S. interceptors near the *Kitkun Bay.* A third exploded almost on top of the carrier and showered the ship with flaming aircraft parts. The *Kalinin Bay* was severely damaged by planes making suicide runs. One smashed into her flight deck, the other caught her on the starboard side in the aft exhaust pipe. Only the *Fanshaw Bay* escaped unscathed.

By 11:30 A.M. the attacks had ended. Admiral Sprague's battered flotilla headed into Leyte Gulf for a much-needed reset In an over-all battle where American naval forces far outnumbered the Japanese, Taffy 3 had been overwhelmed by almost 2-to-1 odds and immeasurably greater fire power—yet Clifton Sprague and his men had made a fighting retreat and convinced Admiral Kurita that he was engaged with a full-fledged fleet.

Having dispatched the surviving Taffy 3 escort ships to pick up crewmen of the stricken *St. Lo,* Admiral Sprague asked Seventh Fleet Headquarters to handle the rescue of the survivors of the *Gambier Bay, Johnston, Roberts,* and *Hoel.* Unfortunately, poor coordination, a sudden flurry of Japanese suicide plane attacks, and erroneous position reports radioed in by aircraft delayed the rescue operations for almost two days.

Finally, at 10:29 on the night of October 26, a seven-ship detail personally ordered out by Admiral Kinkaid obtained results. Guided by flares fired high above the rough black sea, the vessels under Lieutenant Commander J. A. Baxter picked up more than 700 survivors from the *Gambier Bay.* Suffering from exposure, hunger, and fatigue, the carrier survivors had clung to life rafts for some thirty-nine hours and drifted almost to the coast of Samar before being sighted. Many had drowned. With the dawn, survivors from the *Johnston, Roberts,* and *Hoel* were found.

The last raft, containing fifteen men from the *Johnston,* was spotted at 9:30 A.M. on the twenty-seventh, forty-eight hours after the sinking of the destroyer. By early the following morning, the 1,150 survivors of the Taffy 3 ships sunk by the Center Force had been transferred from Baxter's seven vessels to hospital ships and transports in Leyte Gulf.

The over-all Battle for Leyte Gulf, spread across a total area twice the size of Texas, was the greatest sea fight in history. Every element of naval warfare, from submarine to aircraft, was involved. And when it was over, the Imperial Japanese Navy had ceased to exist as a fighting unit. The United States and her allies had undisputed control of the Pacific Ocean.

Between October 23 and 26, Japan's *Sho* Plan No.1 cost her three battleships, four carriers, ten cruisers, and almost a dozen other fighting ships. Scores of aircraft and some l 0,000 Japanese seamen were also lost by the Empire. The U.S. losses added up to 2,800 lives, about two hundred aircraft, and six warships. Taffy 3, bearing the brunt of the punishment, had lost the escort carriers *Gambier Bay* and *St. Lo,* the destroyers *Johnston* and *Hoel,* the destroyer escort *Samuel B. Roberts,* 128 planes, and 1,583 men killed and missing.

"In no engagement of its entire history;" Samuel Eliot Morison has written, "has the United States Navy shown more gallantry; guts and gumption than in those two morning hours between 0730 and 0930 off Samar."

Rear Admiral Clifton Sprague had his own observation on the battle: "The failure of the enemy . . . to completely wipe out all vessels of this task unit can be attributed to our successful smoke screen, our torpedo counterattack, continuous harassment of enemy by bomb, torpedo and strafing air attacks, timely maneuvers, and the definite partiality of Almighty God!"

December 1966

CHAPTER TWENTY

THE "REVOLT OF THE ADMIRALS" RECONSIDERED

JEFFREY G. BARLOW

FOCUS QUESTIONS

1. What were the issues facing the military services in the period immediately following World War II?
2. What were the most important issues affecting the Navy's future that emerged in the "Revolt?"
3. What was the Air Force's position regarding the use of air power? How did this differ from the Navy's position?
4. A central issue raised, but not addressed, by the article is: Who has control over military policy? How did the "revolt" reveal the problems in civil-military relations following the reorganization of the armed forces in 1947?

The House Armed Services Committee's 1949 hearings on the B-36 program and on unification and strategy, and the events which led up to them, had a pivotal influence on the navy. At a time when naval aviation was dangerously close to enforced obsolescence, the hearings provided a forum which allowed the navy's grievances and concerns to be publicly expressed. Many of the records from 1949 have been declassified in the last decade, and in this essay, Mr. Barlow examines this important chapter in the history of the modern U.S. Navy in light of this new material.

INTRODUCTION

Four decades have passed since the navy fought for its life in hearings before the House Armed Services Committee. The events of the summer and fall of 1949 are remembered, if at all, as "The Revolt of the Admirals"—a pejorative phrase that is as inaccurate as it is sensational. It was never a revolt, and naval officers of almost every rank were actively involved in the effort. The phrase quickly stuck not only because of its eye-catching headline but also because of the assiduousness of anti-navy propagandists.

The events that are grouped as the "Revolt of the Admirals" occurred from May to November 1949. The new secretary of defense, Louis Johnson, directed on 23 April that construction of the navy's newly-laid flushdeck aircraft carrier, the *United States,* be discontinued.[1] Three days later, Secretary of the Navy John L. Sullivan tendered his resignation in protest of the way this action was taken. He was replaced by Francis P. Matthews, a man of no military or government experience, who saw himself as a servant of the defense secretary's policies.

In early May, several members of Congress received an "anonymous" document, subsequently revealed to have been written by Cedric Worth, special assistant to Undersecretary of the Navy Dan A. Kimball. Alleging that serious improprieties had taken place in the air force's procurement of the B-36 bomber, this document implied that Secretary of the Air Force Stuart Symington and Secretary Johnson had a financial stake in the program's outcome. The allegations contained in this document eventually led to the House Armed Services Committee's hearings on the B-36 bomber program and later hearings on unification and strategy. At those hearings the navy put forth the case that the secretary of defense was stripping away its naval aviation because of a dangerous overemphasis on the war-deterring and war-fighting properties of strategic bombing as propounded by the air force. In the aftermath of these hearings, the secretary of defense fired Chief of Naval Operations Admiral Louis E. Denfeld and punished other naval officers in an effort to bring the service into line behind his policies.

Since 1949 a sizeable number of books and articles of varying pretensions to significance have touched on the navy's fight. To date, however, the navy's actual role has been inadequately analyzed. In a paper of this length, events in all their historical complexity cannot be described. Nevertheless, an outline can put the events into better perspective.

The most significant work to deal with the incident remains Paul Hammond's 1963 study, "Super Carriers and B-36 Bombers."[2] It is a well-written study, being thorough and judicious in tone, and has become the standard account of the events. Several aspects, however, have diminished its final accuracy. For one thing, it is too dependent upon newspaper accounts for its facts.

For another, its version of the incident is affected by a pro-air force perspective on the events—one no doubt influenced by air force briefing materials.[3] Other accounts which have followed in the wake of Hammond's study, even those by authors partial to the navy, have used many of his basic judgments uncritically.

Largely as a result of historians continuing to rely on press stories and dated or biased information, we have little more insight into the actual circumstances behind the so-called "Revolt of the Admirals" than did contemporary observers. This no longer needs to be the case. Most of the navy's classified files relating to the events are free of security restrictions, and the U.S. Naval Institute released a large oral history (the first of several projected volumes) in 1983, giving a detailed account of Op-23, the pivotal organization behind the preparation of the navy's case.[4] This oral history, which includes a substantial written text, was the product of a dedicated effort from 1979 to 1983 by Admiral Arleigh Burke, who had headed Op-23 during that organization's fateful ten-month existence.

"REVOLT OF THE ADMIRALS": IMPRESSIONS AND REALITY

A review of the writings on "The Revolt of the Admirals" shows that all suffer from certain misconceptions about the navy's involvement and, more specifically, the role that Op-23 played in organizing the navy's presentation before the House Armed Services Committee. One reason for this is that the authors lacked sufficient detailed background on the navy-air force fight to enable them to explain why certain things happened as they did. It is necessary to fill in a bit of that background before examining a few of the major misconceptions about the navy's role.

Background

The first point to understand is that, from 1946 to 1949, the air force was highly effective in putting its view of a proper defense posture before Congress and the press and in propagandizing against the navy's view. Much of the initial focus of this effort was on establishing its status as a separate service. Nonetheless, from the first, air force publicity was designed to accentuate the positive aspects of its doctrine of air power (even to the extent of distorting the record on occasion) and to minimize the positive aspects of the doctrines espoused by the other services.

From the beginning of its postwar drive for separate service status, the air force was aware that a strong public relations organization was a necessity. As retired Major General Follett Bradley wrote to General Carl Spaatz, then acting commander of the army air forces, in early 1946:

> In my view, the Army Air Forces will never be successful in your organizational objective until you can control your own publicity. . . .
>
> If our objectives are to be attained, it will be necessary for one or

> more of the civilian organizations who back us to put on a publicity campaign employing all media, movies, newspapers, radio, etc., to convince the American public of the necessity for action now by Congress. Such a publicity campaign would be little different from marketing a new toothpaste or fountain pen.[5]

By 1948, the air force's Directorate of Public Relations had developed into a highly effective, centralized organ for controlling every aspect of air force public relations.[6] The message that the air force was selling was that only the strategic air power provided by the air force could attack effectively a continental land power such as the Soviet Union. However, since sufficient air power to accomplish the task would require a larger (70-group) air force, it was time for the Congress to decide that it could no longer allow competing and duplicative (air force/navy) air forces to squander available resources.

In contrast to the air force's information program, the navy's public relations effort was dismal. The navy seemed to view public relations as something of a necessary evil. The service's senior leadership had little understanding of the importance of getting their message across to the public until it was far too late to do much about it. One man who saw this deficiency all too well was Captain Walter Karig, who was serving as a special advisor for public relations on the staff of the chief of naval operations (CNO). He attempted to educate Admiral Louis Denfeld, the CNO, on the important nature of the navy's public relations effort throughout 1948 and 1949. Whatever success he had in educating Denfeld, it did not seem to have much of an effect on the state of navy public relations which, as an organizational entity, remained under the secretary of the navy's cognizance. In June 1948, Karig wrote to Denfeld:

> Vice Admiral Radford said at DCNO meeting Friday that the fate of the Navy will be determined in the next two years. I think the time is shorter than that, in a public relations sense. The effort must be to utilize every outlet of public expression to build up public appreciation for the Navy as a continuing component of the national defense, by abandoning our defensive and explanatory role and adopting a policy of vigorous, sustained coordinated propaganda (in the true, and best, meaning of the word).[7]

Karig campaigned unsuccessfully for an integrated navy public relations outfit headed by a professionally-qualified officer who would stay in the job long enough to make a difference. In November 1948, he wrote to Harold Brayman, a civilian who headed a committee making an inspection of public relations for the secretary, giving him a detailed look at his own thinking on the issue.

> The Navy prides itself on precision in gunnery, precision in bombing, precision in courts martial and real estate procurement, but in public

> relations it still uses the technique of the manure spreader (But it isn't spreading awfully good fertilizer). The output as a whole is dull, uninspired, tardy. The element of zeal, esprit de corps, all the devotion to a cause that the Air Force exhibits, is lacking. (I don't know how it can be acquired, either).[8]

In June and July 1949, even as the navy was finding itself becoming involved with the events that were to lead to the B-36 and the unification and strategy hearings, Captain Karig was pressing the CNO to obtain the transfer of the Office of Public Relations (OPR) from the secretary's shop to the CNO's. He also cautioned the CNO that the navy's attitude about the value of public relations would have to change if the organization was going to work as it should. He explained:

> One of the handicaps OPR has always suffered from is the attitude within the Navy itself that Public Relations is somehow on a par with garbage collecting. Too many senior officers hold the "feather merchant" concept of Public Relations, and then wonder why in hell naval aviation is on the way out, the fleet is shrinking to a ferry service, and Admirals are called "brass hats" and cartooned as pompous nitwits—all products of anti-Navy press agentry, unopposed.

However, by July 1949, nothing the navy could have done about its public relations organization would have had a significant impact on the struggle that summer and fall.

Another important point concerns the navy's view of the strategic air offensive as set forth by the air force. Because the overwhelming number of studies on "The Revolt of the Admirals" fail to delve into the nature of navy thinking on strategic air warfare before the events of 1949, they imply that the navy's opposition to the B-36 and to the air force's idea of strategic bombing in mid-1949 was in direct response to Secretary Johnson's cancellation of the navy's flush-deck aircraft carrier. Since this was the gist of contemporary anti-navy news stories (many inspired by the air force and its supporters), there is the overall impression that the navy's opposition was unprincipled—largely designed to strike back at the air force for what had been done to the navy. This was not the case.

The navy's concern about the likely success of the force's proposed strategic air offensive in case of war with the Soviet Union can be traced to the early postwar period. Naval aviators, in particular, remained unconvinced that the results of strategic bombing in World War II (as analyzed in the many reports of the United States Strategic Bombing Survey and those of its British counterpart) had validated the inherent decisiveness of strategic bombing in warfare. And as navy strategic planners working on the preparation of the Joint War Plans began to compare the air force's projected strategic air offensive with its assumptions about available overseas bases, the ability to penetrate Soviet air defenses, and many other issues, they began to express serious concerns about the viability of the air offensive. The navy shared these concerns with appropriate outside agencies. It made some of its reservations clear in October 1948 in its presentation before the Eberstadt Committee, which was looking into national security organization and planning. The CNO made a blunt presentation of his concerns about the success of the strategic air offensive to Secretary of Defense James Forrestal and the Joint Chiefs of Staff (JCS) during meetings on the 1950 budget in early October 1948. Thus, by 1949, the navy's questions about the air force's capability of carrying out the strategic air offensive were well known within the national military establishment and in other appropriate quarters.

With the above information supplied to provide a bit of background to the events of mid-1949, one can now analyze several of the major misconceptions about Op-23 and the navy's actual role in the hearings that are present in writings about "The Revolt of the Admirals." Two have to do with Op-23 itself, while the last concerns the longer term effects of the unification and strategy hearings.

Op-23: A Dirty Business?

Paul Hammond asserted that the navy treated Op-23 like a "dirty business. He wrote:

> Set up for a normal and wholly legitimate purpose—to study Navy organization, and formulate Navy policy towards the organizational problems incident to unification—Op 23 was treated by the Navy from the beginning like a dirty business; and the press had soon drawn the same conclusion. Upon its establishment it was located next to the Office of Naval Intelligence, and its activities from the beginning were subject to an unusual degree of secrecy. The press was soon aware of its existence, but could obtain no satisfactory explanations from the Navy.

This same negative appraisal of Op-23 (though without it being directly named) comes through in other accounts of the navy's fight, such as that by Paolo Coletta.

This is a point that needs clarification. From the first, Op-23 was designed to be a regular division in the office of the CNO. It was neither devised to do "dirty business" (however Hammond might define it), nor was it an *ad hoc* organization, as its predecessor organizations, SCOROR and UNICOM, had been. It was created because the secretary of the navy and the CNO believed the navy was in need of a permanent organization that could provide advice on the complex issues involving unification of the services. Brigadier General Samuel Shaw recalled what was said by Marine Corps Commandant General Clifton B. Cates:

> He said he'd spent several conferences with the Secretary of the Navy and [Admiral] Denfeld, his Chief of Naval Operations. And they were determined that something had to be done to get the Navy back into believing in itself. That was the . . . principal thread of the problem—[to] get the Navy to believe in itself.

At first, it was thought that the new organization could be just a re-established SCOROR—a committee under the cognizance of the secretary. Eventually, however, Secretary Sullivan, Admiral Denfeld, and General Cates decided that it would have to be set up under the CNO. General Shaw remarked:

> First, . . . [SCOROR] was the Secretary's organ and that wouldn't necessarily get all the uniformed Navy to think they ought to get up and follow whoever happened to be the Secretary of the Navy. And furthermore, SCOROR had not endeared itself to lots of Navy people. So, . . . if I remember what Cates was saying correctly, they'd decided it [the head of the new organization] had to be a guy—a uniformed Navy guy—who when he was announced, everybody [would believe] . . . "let's go with that guy." So apparently . . . [in] one of the last conversations they had they decided it was going to be Arleigh Burke . . .

When Captain Arleigh Burke reported to his new boss, Rear Admiral Charles Wellborn, Jr., the deputy chief of naval operations for administration (Op-02), he found that his new organization had been assigned a tough and demanding job and one that was still in the process of being defined by the navy's senior leadership. When Admiral Denfeld briefed Burke the following day, he asked the CNO for concrete ideas on what Op-23 could do to help. As Admiral Burke recounted:

> He [Denfeld] replied to my query by saying the charter included the best guidance he could give me: OP-23 was to familiarize itself on all matters pertaining to unification; advise him and keep him and other senior officers involved and informed on all unification matters; keep other navy commands informed of the situations; and be the clearing house within the navy for unification matters. . . . He said it was our job to do what was necessary and proper to be able to advise navy groups on unification matters. The navy was being castigated for the stands it had taken, and we had not been very successful in persuading either the other services or the administration and the Congress of the correctness of our stands.

Within the first few hours of his taking over, Arleigh Burke realized that he had been put on a spot.

> I realized that what I was to do was to do a job that nobody else would do or could do . . . which is [to] fight what we thought was [going] to be an effort to consolidate [the navy and the other services] into a single Service. . . .
>
> People were very fearful They were very much afraid . . . of their own personal careers. And . . . everybody . . . felt that if you opposed . . . what the powers-that-be wanted—what we thought the powers-that-be wanted—you were very likely to be in a bad way in the future, because you probably wouldn't be able to win it [the fight to avoid consolidation] and if you didn't win it, why you would be labeled, correctly so, as antagonistic to the ideas of the people who were in charge. . . . Nobody wanted the job. I don't blame them. I didn't want it either.

Burke also realized that in order to retain its success in the face of opposition, whether from within or without, Op-23 would have to be entirely above board in its activities. He noted:

> The biggest thing—the biggest trouble—is people want you to do things quietly, confidentially, . . . without a lot of other people knowing about it. It can't be done. . . . That's one thing I had learned . . . before the Op-23 thing that . . . not only did God know everything you did but so did everybody else—eventually.22

To ensure that Op-23 would be effective and yet be permitted to continue to operate, Captain Burke established a set of rules for the staff to follow. These included: avoiding involvement in secret activities or anything that the rest of the navy could not know about; remaining scrupulously ethical in everything Op-23 did (even if people in other services were not operating that way); distributing Op-23's products through regular navy channels to all sections that could use them so that they all were aware of what the organization was doing; and making sure that facts stated by Op-23 were indeed facts and not opinions. In regard to this last rule, General Shaw recalled:

> [I]n the B-36 query, . . . we did a lot of research. We were made available to anybody who wanted the stuff written for 'em. Burke had one requirement there—that if we put our hand to the thing and we said this is not true or this is not accurate or this is illogical, they had to accept it or quit using us at all, you see.

Probably the one aspect that most links Op-23 to "dirty business" in the eyes of authors such as Hammond is the unlikely coincidence of the actions by Cedric Worth and Captain John Crommelin which began the B-36 investigation and then helped to keep the House Armed Services Committee hearings going long enough for the navy to present its case. They remain convinced that these actions were part of an organized navy plan, and since Op-23 was the focal point of the navy's fight, they assume that Op-23 was involved in Worth's and Crommelin's activities.

This was not the case. Cedric Worth's plans to release the "anonymous document" on the B-36 were known to no one in Op-23 (and likely no one else in the Navy Department) until the day he released it. Op-23 staff member Commander Thomas Davies, who acknowledged during the navy court of inquiry that he had supplied technical information on the B-36 bomber to Worth at his request, was not informed of Worth's planned use of the material until just before the "anonymous document" was turned over to members of Congress. As Davies later recalled:

> I had no idea what Cedric was going to do with the information, and, as a matter of fact, I was completely taken aback when he showed me the document that he had written, which had all kinds of stuff in it which I hadn't told him. . . . [H]e showed it to me just—oh—a few hours before he handed it to [Congressman James] Van Zandt. . . . So I didn't really see it until it was essentially in Van Zandt's hands. . . .
>
> I knew that Cedric Worth was doing something, but on the other hand, he had done about fifteen other things. . . . And I didn't really know what the hell he was gonna do with it, because it never occurred to me in a million years that he would give it to a Congressman to make a speech on the Hill. . . .

Similarly, General Shaw recalled that the first time that he and Arleigh Burke learned that Cedric Worth was suspected of writing the "anonymous document" was in mid-July 1949, some two months after it had first been given to several members of Congress.

As with Cedric Worth, Captain John Crommelin's surreptitious activities were neither sponsored nor condoned by Op-23 or the senior naval officers involved in the navy's presentation. Admiral Burke remembered:

> [W]hen the situation became more critical and when it appeared that the hearings might be called off before the Navy could be heard on [Committee Agenda] items 3 to 8, . . . [Crommelin] had grown very tense. He deplored the inaction of the SecNav and CNO. He thought that OP-23 should take more positive action and insist that the Navy take a very strong stand. . . . My arguments [against this] did not convince John who wanted to take the controversy public and who felt OP-23 was not doing its duty properly because we insisted that our cause was just and that if we presented our case clearly, logically and forcefully we would eventuall [sic] win.

This account is enriched by additional comments by Rear Admiral J. L. Howard, another former Op-23 staff member, who noted:

> I . . . was the only other person present at one of the conversations between Captain Burke and Captain Crommelin (in Burke's office) and in capsule form, Crommelin's view was that we should (as he had been doing) leak anything we deemed appropriate to the press to make the Navy's points, make a big public "splash," call curbstone interviews, go on the stump nationwide, and "martyr" ourselves if necessary to get our message to the world. This was apparently Crommelin's opinion of the "courageous" way to go.
>
> Burke, on the other hand, argued that we should operate completely within the system, using proper channels and forums, and conduct ourselves in a wholly correct manner . . . [ellipsis in text] and let the full force of our effective arguments influence the decisionmakers in both the Executive and Legislative branches. Several senior naval officers also did their best to convince Crommelin not to speak out and thereby jeopardize the navy's case. In early September 1949, several days before Crommelin first spoke out, Admiral Radford sent Burke a message asking him "to convey the following message . . . to John Crommelin. . . . In particular the Admiral would appreciate it if John will hold his horses and not jeapordize [sic] the Navy's presentation and the selection of witnesses now being arranged by the Task Force." Vice Admiral Felix Stump, Commander Air Force, Atlantic Fleet, was similarly moved to caution Crommelin about taking unilateral action which might endanger "results you are patriotically endeavoring to accomplish." However, these appeals, too, failed to sway John Crommelin from his course of public protest.

Op-23 Poorly Prepared for the Hearings?

Another charge that is commonly made about Op-23 is that it was inadequately prepared for the unification and strategy hearings in October. For example, Paul Hammond stated:

> The major avoidable handicap for the Navy was its lack of thorough preparation. . . . The results of their preparation indicated their inadequacies. What the witnesses said showed that their preparatory work had not been carefully coordinated, for the statements were sometimes unfounded, often exaggerated, and not always consistent;. . . . In short, irrespective of its inherent merits, the Navy's case was inadequately prepared and poorly coordinated.

Interestingly, Hammond contrasted what he thought to be the navy's poor presentation with the air force's highly effective one. Despite the strength of the assertion, however, it lacks merit.

Where Hammond apparently went wrong in his assessment of navy preparation was in attempting to judge the navy and air force presentations according to the same set of criteria. The air force's testimony during the B-36 hearings, masterminded by Harvard Law School Professor W. Barton Leach, was designed to follow the lines of a legal presentation before a court. In their prepared remarks, the air force witnesses, for the most part, denied out-of-hand the allegations contained in the "anonymous document," presumably because to admit that aspects of the document might have some validity could have undermined the air force case. And when air force witnesses such as Stuart Symington and General Hoyt Vandenberg returned to answer the navy's charges during the unification and strategy hearings, they stuck to the air force testimony previously given in order to avoid lending credence to the navy's positions.

The navy's case, on the other hand, was fashioned like a military-style briefing—one presented to acquaint the members of the committee with the navy's differing conception of strategic air warfare and the role which it desired to play in the country's national security. The case's preparation stressed interlocking presentations, a certain amount of repetition for effect, and the use of expert testimony delivered by relatively junior officers. While the navy's case may have proven difficult for the members to follow at times, it showed that there existed important divergences in navy and air force thinking. While in some senses it may have seemed less polished than the air force presentation, in most regards it was just as professionally handled.

The Results of the Hearings

Most of the works that touch on "The Revolt of the Admirals" appear to conclude that the navy either lost its case before the committee or that its testimony had only a very modest influence on congressional thinking. For example, Hammond noted that "the Navy appeal was not so successful as to make the House Armed Services Committee an ally of the Navy. At best, it secured a slight shift in committee sympathies." And Paolo Coletta claimed that the navy presentation had little positive influence.

Did the navy's hard-fought campaign really have only a minor impact on the House Armed Services Committee's view of the navy? The answer to that question is in an understanding of how far the navy had to go in attempting to change the view which the committee, and particularly its chairman, Carl Vinson, then held about the navy's role in the atomic age.

To fully grasp the magnitude of the navy's task, one must turn back to mid-January 1949 when newspaper columnist Stewart Alsop had a riveting interview with Vinson. He recounted the important aspects of this conversation a few days later, in a letter to an editor at *The Saturday Evening Post.*

> I talked with Carl Vinson the other day. His long love affair with the Navy is now definitely at an end—if he talks to the Admirals the way he talked to me they must be muttering about the sharpness of serpents' teeth. His line is—and it seems to me a sensible line—that our only potential enemy is Russia, that we can't touch Russia with a navy,

> that we can't hope to equal Russia in ground forces, and that the only way we can really and immediately bring our superiority to bear is by air.

Thus, it can be seen that at least six months before Cedric Worth's "anonymous document" helped to trigger the B-36 hearings, Carl Vinson, the powerful chairman of the House Armed Services Committee and a longtime friend of the navy, had accepted, apparently without reservation, the air force's assertion that against a continental power such as the Soviet Union, the U.S. Navy was useless. This shows the difficulty of the task which the navy had to face in convincing the committee that it had a significant role to play in the country's defense.

That it had achieved its goal of changing the committee's thinking regarding the navy's usefulness was demonstrated finally in March 1950, when the Armed Services Committee released its report on the unification and strategy hearings. On most of the significant issues raised by the navy witnesses, the committee sided with the navy. Among the most gratifying conclusions for the proponents of naval aviation were its statements that:

> 6. Intercontinental strategic bombing is not synonymous with air power. The Air Force is not synonymous with the Nation's military air power. Military air power consists of Air Force, Navy and Marine Corps air power, and of this, strategic bombing is but one phase.

and

> 9. Difficulties between the Air Force and the naval air arm will continue because of fundamental professional disagreements on the art of warfare. Service prejudices, jealousies and thirst for power and recognition have had only a bare minimum of influence on this controversy.

Some historians, viewing these events from a vantage point of perfect hindsight, have argued that even if the navy fight had not taken place, the eruption of the Korean conflict in June 1950 would have pulled naval aviation out of its doldrums. Yet, it can be argued with even more plausibility that if the navy had not made known its case for modern carrier aviation during the unification and strategy hearings, the Korean War-generated Congressional funding for naval aviation would have gone merely for keeping the existing types of naval aircraft and carriers in commission. Under the circumstances then likely to be obtaining, the U.S. Navy would not have gotten congressional approval for the *Forrestal*-class super carriers and the long-range attack aircraft that provided the navy with its primary offensive striking power during the bulk of the 1950s and 1960s.

Whatever the second guessing on the outcome of the hearings, the senior officers who put their careers on the line to fight the navy's fight evidently believed that it had been a successful effort. For example, Rear Admiral Ralph Ofstie wrote to Captain Fitzhugh Lee:

"Personally, Fitz, I feel that we are now well over the hump, or rather the low point, in the fortunes of the post-war Navy. . . . I think things are looking up very definitely and in good measure this is a result of the fracas of last fall." Similarly, Admiral Radford wrote to Captain Roy L. Johnson, then on staff of Second Task Fleet:

> I am very optimistic about the long range effects of the recent Hearings in Washington, and see no reason why any intelligent naval officer should feel otherwise. Naturally, I have no illusions as to the difficulties we face in the immediate future, but what is particularly gratifying to me is to feel that for the first time we are on the offensive. You can quote me to any individual in the Navy as saying that it behooves all naval officers to thoroughly acquaint themselves with what went on in Washington, and to make an effort to understand what was behind it all. Also tell them, before they arrive at any conclusions, to estimate what the situation would have been if the Hearings had not taken place. The Navy is not in a horrible mess, but just coming up out of a deep pit, and we have good times ahead.

And in a letter of Christmas greetings to Admiral Richard Conolly, commanding naval forces in the Eastern Atlantic and Mediterranean, Radford expressed his optimism about the future. "I look back on the last twelve months with mixed feelings, but arrive at the conclusion that, if I had to do it all over again, I would not change one thing I did or said. I sincerely hope that you feel the same way in spite of the developments of the last two months."

CONCLUSION

The events of the summer and fall of 1949 were pivotal for naval aviation and, in a larger sense, for the navy's future as a component of the country's armed forces. But for far too long, this navy fight for survival has been seen only in a highly distorted fashion.

Now that the documentation is available to analyze the true dimensions of the fight over the B-36 and over unification and strategy, the task of historians must now be to re-examine the standard interpretations of the navy's role. The naval and marine officers who took an active part in preparing and presenting the case for naval aviation when it appeared to many that all had been lost deserve to be known for what they accomplished on the navy's behalf.

Notes

The author would like to thank Admiral Arleigh Burke, Admiral Charles Griffin, Vice Admiral Fitzhugh Lee, Rear Admiral Thomas Davies, Rear Admiral

A.B. Metsger, Brigadier General Samuel Shaw, and colleagues Bernard Cavalcante and Wes Pryce of the Naval Historical Center's Operational Archives, for help with this article. The views expressed are those of the author alone and do not necessarily represent those of the Department of the Navy or the Department of Defense.

[1]For a brief background review of the *United States,* see Arleigh Burke to the Judge Advocate General, 11 May 1949, "History of the 6A Carrier Project," "A21/1-1/1 Carrier" folder, Section 11, Op-23 Records, Operational Archives, Naval Historical Center (hereafter OA), Washington Navy Yard, Washington, D.C.

[2]Paul Y. Hammond, "Super Carriers and B-36 Bombers: Appropriations, Strategy and Politics," in *American Civil-Military Decisions: A Book of Case Studies,* ed. Harold Stein (Birmingham, 1963), 465–564.

[3]See Hammond's acknowledgement that W. Barton Leach, the Harvard Law School professor (and air force reservist) who headed the air force team preparing for the B-36 hearings, "made available . . . a portion of his personal file covering the B-36 investigation." *Ibid.,* 555.

[4]Admiral Arleigh Burke, USN (Ret.), "A Study of Op-23 and its role in the Unification debates of 1949, Special Series: Volume IV," Naval Institute Oral History Project, 1983.

[5]Follett Bradley to Carl Spaatz, 21 February 1946, "Diary, 1946-Feb" folder, Box 25, Papers of General Carl A. Spaatz, Manuscript Division, Library of Congress (hereafter MD-LC), Washington, D.C. In his reply, Spaatz noted that "I am doing everything possible to put into my organizational objectives a set-up along just the lines you suggested." Spaatz to Bradley, 28 February 1946, *ibid.*

[6]On the organization of the air force's Directorate of Public Relations as of mid-1949, see Vice Admiral J.W. Reeves, Jr., to Admiral Arthur W. Radford, 16 September 1949, and the enclosed excerpt from *Air Force Public Relations Letter,* 29 July 1949, "J.W. Reeves" folder, Box 36, Papers of Admiral Arthur W. Radford, OA.

[7]Memorandum from Captain Walter Karig (Op-004) to the CNO, 21 June 1948, Public Relations" folder, Box 4, Double Zero Files 1948, OA. This and several later memos by Karig on the state of navy public relations were copied and sent to Secretary of the Navy Sullivan by Denfeld in July 1948. See "Personal and Confidential" memorandum from Denfeld to Sullivan, 10 July 1948; "ADM DENFELD FILE CONF-SEC Jan–Dec 48" folder, Box 3, Double Zero Files 1947–1950, Admiral Louis E. Denfeld Papers (hereafter Denfeld Papers), OA.

[8]Karig to Brayman, 8 November 1948, "ADM DENFELD PERS FILE Nov & Dec '48" folder, Box 3, Denfeld Papers, OA. At the end of this letter, Karig commented: Admiral Denfeld, his Vice Chief of Naval Operations, Admiral Radford, and Under Secretary Kenney are all very much worried over the Navy's public relations operation. . . . The concern of these men would be useful, if public relations were under their jurisdiction, which it is not. But it's good to know that the top men in the Navy are aware that there is a problem that is damn near a crisis.

CHAPTER TWENTY-ONE

ERRORS OF THE KOREAN WAR

COMMANDER MALCOLM W. CAGLE, USN

FOCUS QUESTIONS

1. What were the major errors of the Korean War and why does the author believe they were mistakes?
   What lessons have contemporary relevance?
2. Do you agree with the author that the Wonson landing was a mistake? Why or why not?

The strangest and most unusual war the United States ever fought was the Korean War. It certainly was the most frustrating. It was the war (and it *was* a war, not a police action or a mere "conflict") which many Americans chose to ignore while it was being fought and would prefer to forget now. But, as the chief of naval operations has said, the Korean War was the first limited war the U.S. ever fought. He also made the point—since repeated by many American military leaders—that limited wars are more likely to occur than global wars in our thermonuclear age. It is important, therefore, to absorb Korea's errors and avoid its mistakes.

For there were mistakes in that 37-month war, and we would be exceedingly foolish to say there were not. It would be equally foolish to attempt to conceal our errors and choke off constructive discussion of them, believing that in so doing we give aid and comfort to the enemy. If the Communists make any study of Korea, the mistakes we made will be as obvious to them as theirs are to us. Likewise, it is foolish to believe that the Korean War was an anachronism that cannot happen again and that it has no significance, lessons, or meaning . . .

The first major military error of the Korean War was the Wonsan landing in October, 1950. It was unnecessary and it should never have been made.

The Inchon assault, a month earlier, had been vastly successful. As General MacArthur predicted, it was the anvil on which the North Korean People's Army would be pounded to pieces; the successful amphibious assault would sever the Communist's supply routes; and it would send that army scurrying north of the 38th Parallel, broken and beaten.

So it had. As early as September 29, when the commanding general first proposed the amphibious assault at Wonsan, evidence was growing that the disorganized Reds could scarcely make a solid stand except in the rugged mountains of North Korea. On the east coast, the north-bound Republic of Korea First Corps was meeting only spotty resistance, and since its break-out from the Pusan perimeter, it had averaged more than ten miles per day. At this rate of advance, the ROKs would soon capture Wonsan. (In fact, the advancing First Corps did capture the city on October 10 with only minor resistance, a full ten days before the Marines finally got ashore.)

The U.S. Navy opposed the landing for several reasons. Loading Marines and their equipment for a Wonsan assault would tie up the small port of Inchon, whose capacity was already fully needed for unloading. Second, there was not enough logistic shipping in the Far East Theater to supply an advancing Eighth Army on the west coast and simultaneously carry and support a large amphibious effort on the east coast. Finally, there was gathering evidence and many more suspicions that Wonsan's harbor and approaches were mined, and clearing a path to the nearby beaches would be time-consuming and difficult with the skimpy mine warfare forces available. Vice Admiral C. Turner Joy summarized the Navy's opposition when he said, "None of us at NAVFE could see the necessity for such an operation, since the Tenth Corps could have marched overland to Wonsan and with much less effort than it would take to get the Corps around to Wonsan by sea."

The U. S. Marines also opposed the Wonsan operation. First, they still had a job to finish; the Leathernecks had their hands full on the western front. On October 2, in fact, the First Marine Division suffered sixteen killed and 81 wounded in fighting north of the capital city of Seoul. Second, the Marines were of the opinion that the ROKs would soon and easily capture Wonsan and make the roundabout sea-assault unnecessary.

Many Army commanders agreed with the Navy and Marines that the proposed operation was unnecessary. The general consensus was that the Tenth Corps need only climb in their tanks and trucks and drive overland to Wonsan—150 miles by land in contrast to 800 by sea.

Why, then, was the operation not cancelled?

First, because the Wonsan assault would physically separate the Tenth Corps from the Eighth Army and give the former independent status. The decision had been reached earlier that the Korean peninsula would be divided—with Lieutenant General Walton H. Walker's Eighth Army holding the western half and Lieutenant General Edward M. Almond's Tenth Corps (Almond was concurrently MacArthur's chief of staff) responsible for the eastern half. An amphibious landing would hasten the separation and guarantee the division of command.

Primarily, however, the Wonsan operation was not revised or cancelled because the objections and alternatives to Wonsan were never presented to the one man who could have revised or cancelled it. "I was never apprised of any Navy objection to the seaborne landing at Wonsan," General MacArthur said.

The second error of the Korean War followed and was a result of the intervention of the Red Chinese armies. When the Chinese Communists attacked the U.S. Eighth Army in late November 1950, and the Tenth Corps in early December, UN forces commenced falling back. The First Marine Division found itself surrounded by six divisions near the Chosin reservoir and so commenced its historic attack "in another direction."

In Far East headquarters at this time, a degree of panic and inertia reigned. Many believed (and so stated) that the Red Chinese Army had both the capability and the intention to drive the UN forces into the sea and overrun the entire Korean peninsula. Command uncertainty was underlaid by a genuine apprehension that the entry of the Red Chinese into the war might also be a prelude to further Soviet adventures elsewhere—perhaps even the start of World War III.

Accordingly, the UN retreat was made in an overanxious mood. On Korea's west coast, the North Korean capital city of Pyongyang and the seaports of Chinnampo and Inchon were evacuated and abandoned to the enemy. The South Korean capital, Seoul, was also abandoned. In fact, contact with the enemy in the western zone was completely lost. On the east coast the U.S. Marines succeeded in fighting their way out of the Communist trap, fracturing five Red divisions in the process. The Leathernecks were lifted from Hungnam to South Korea. Wonsan was now abandoned. A new line, far to the south of the 38th Parallel, was ordered established to staunch the Red Chinese.

Retreating was not the mistake (for the UN forces were scarcely positioned or prepared for the heavy Red assault). The error lay in the distance or amount of the retreat. A defensible new line could have been held in the vicinity of Korea's narrow waist (no further south, certainly, than the truce line which was finally agreed upon two and one half years later). Both Lieutenant General James Van Fleet and Rear Admiral James H. Doyle felt such a line could have been held. It follows, of course, that had this been done, a great amount of the costly fighting which occurred later might have been avoided.

The third mistake of the Korean War was the failure to coordinate the aerial interdiction program on the theater level. The UN effort to "isolate the battlefield" with airpower was a lengthy and expensive effort. From early 1951 through 1952, almost 100% of the offensive efforts of the carrier task force,

60% of the offensive effort of Marine Air, 70% of the offensive effort of the U.S. Fifth Air Force, and 70% of the blockading effort of the blockade force (Task Force 95) was devoted to "interdiction." At no time during the course of the war did Far East headquarters assign areas of responsibility, coordinate targets, or establish priorities or interdiction criteria. As time went on, an agreement of sorts grew to be accepted—the Air Force would take the western half, the Navy the eastern half of Korea. (Within its own area, the Navy coordinated the interdiction effort of surface forces and naval air.) This lack of coordination was undoubtedly a responsible factor in the over-all failure of interdiction to "isolate the battlefield."

In the writers opinion, the Navy made a mistake in the Korean War by failing to use and operate night carriers. Another of the principal reasons why the long, costly, and intensive effort to sever the enemy's supply lines failed was the inability of the UN air forces to locate, identify, and destroy at night the thousands of trucks and trains which operated from dusk to dawn and which brought ample supplies and munitions from Manchuria to the front. A single carrier, operating at night, could scarcely have staunched the Red's heavy nighttime supply flow, but it would have done far more damage than the same carrier by day. Moreover, its use would have added knowledge and experience in the night-flying, night-operation art.

Another error of the Korean War was the UN failure to adopt and use the close air support system and doctrine of the U.S. Navy and Marine Corps, which, by every yardstick and in every demonstration, was proved far superior and more productive than the system which came to be used. On three occasions, the defense of the Pusan perimeter, the invasion at Inchon, and the redeployment at Hungnam, the Navy-Marine system functioned flawlessly and efficiently, proving ideal for the rugged North Korean terrain. To the soldiers in the battleline foxholes who had a chance to observe both systems, whether ROK, U.S. Army, UN trooper or U.S. Marine, it was obvious that the Navy-Marine system was superior and the one which hurt the enemy the most. The Navy-Marine system made both the task of defense and offense easier; it killed more enemy soldiers; it boosted morale.

Another and major error of the early days of the Korean War lay in the area of command. Vital military questions and problems could often not be debated or even presented to higher authority because of an insulating command ring. Inchon is a classic example. Undeniably, Inchon was a brilliant maneuver in conception as well as execution, one which reflects lasting credit on the fertile brain wherein it was conceived, and upon the Navy-Marine experts who made it successful. However, Inchon was first chosen, almost arbitrarily, and then reasons were found to justify it. Whereupon, the military means were assembled to carry out the plan.

The normal practice, of course, calls for a commander, with the assistance and advice of his principal subordinates, to decide that an amphibious assault is needed. The next step requires that the amphibious warfare experts select one or more areas where the commander's objective can be achieved; then the forces and hardware are assembled The Inchon decision was a reverse of this time-honored procedure. The mistake lay not so much in the selection or designation of Inchon but in the method and manner by which it was designated. The same command insulation led to the debacle of Wonsan.

Furthermore, had a sound and approachable command structure existed in the Far East in the early months of the war, many of the aforementioned errors might have been avoided. A hearing for the close air support dispute might have been held. Less real estate might have been surrendered to the Reds following their November–December, 1950 assault. Interdiction might have been coordinated on a theater-wide basis; and the early division of the Korean peninsula into east and west zones might have been avoided.

But the gravest error of the Korean War can be summed in one word: timidity. Timidity kept the free world from winning the Korean War. Had the will to do so existed and the decision made quickly and pressed resolutely after the Red Chinese intervened, the Korean War could unquestionably have been won by the UN—and won without widening the area of conflict, bringing the Soviets themselves into Korea, or inviting a third world war in Europe. By limiting our objectives and limiting our means (as well as the geographic arena) but fully using the forces at hand, a decisive military victory could have been won in Korea. As General Van Fleet pointed out we had superior firepower, we had control of the air and control of the seas; we had abundant resources; we enjoyed the advantages (had we chosen to use them) of flexibility, surprise, and mobility. We denied ourselves "hot pursuit"; we refused to strike legitimate military targets (in Korea, not outside) for fear we would prejudice the truce-talks or perhaps even rile the Soviets. (North Korea's hydroelectric system was one such target; others were Rashin and military targets in the city of Pyongyang.)

The sentinel mistake of the Korean war, then, lay in not recognizing the need to win the war and in not having the fortitude to do so—all the while keeping it limited. In both previous and subsequent limited conflicts the free world succeeded in doing so—the Berlin blockade, the Greek Civil War are examples. A more recent and striking example of limiting both force and objectives is the Jordanian crisis. Each of these successes lay in the realm of "short-of-total-war" actions where the right amount of force of the right kind in the right place brought us the goals we were seeking. In fact, since 1945, whenever and wherever the Communists have been faced with resolute, determined, and superior force, they have retreated. But in Korea, during a shooting and major war, we were frustrated by the curious American notion of total war and total victory.

The lesson of Korea, therefore, is to prepare for and win the limited wars of the future. If we do, we may yet learn to deter the small war and defeat piecemeal aggression.

CHAPTER TWENTY-TWO

The Black Sailor

Chambermaid to the Braid and Nothing More

JOHN DARRELL SHERWOOD

FOCUS QUESTIONS

1. Why did the service of African-Americans in the Navy change prior to 1900, specifically what decisions affected their service in 1798, 1842, 1861, and 1896?
2. What type of service did African-American sailors perform during World War 2?
3. What was the 1944 Port Chicago Mutiny?
4. What role did Secretary of the Navy James Forrestal play in increasing opportunities for African-American sailors?
5. What steps did the Navy take to implement Executive Order 9981 of 1948? What did the Navy do to recruit African-American officers and sailors?
6. Why were African-American sailors still forced into narrow areas of service after the Korean War?

During the early 1970s, most black sailors viewed the Navy's record on race relations with a profound sense of skepticism. As of March 1971, blacks accounted for only 5.3 percent of the Navy's enlisted personnel and a mere 0.7 percent of officers. By contrast, their representation in the other services was much more substantial. "The figures made it clear,"Admiral Elmo Zumwalt wrote in his memoir *On Watch,* "that as far as breaking down racial barriers was concerned, the Navy was marching in the rear rank of the military services."[1] The reasons for this disparity were deeply rooted in the history of the service and the nation at large.

The history of African Americans in the U.S. Navy can be traced all the way back to the nation's colonial roots. Black seaman often served on Royal Navy ships and privateers well before the onset of the War for Independence. During that subsequent war, African Americans continued to serve the British cause, especially after the royal governor of Virginia, John Murray, issued a proclamation promising freedom to slaves who fought with the loyalists. Hundreds of slaves used small boats and watercraft to escape slavery and volunteer their services to Royal Navy vessels in the Chesapeake Bay.[2]

But African Americans also joined the fledgling American cause. It is impossible to know how many African Americans served in the various American navies during the American Revolution. Some historians have suggested that the number could be as high as 10 percent of the sea services. Whatever the case, black sailors fought not only in the Continental Navy but also in the eleven state navies and privateer forces as well. Local black watermen from the Chesapeake Bay area were so valued as pilots for American ships that George Washington offered warrants of as much as $100 to these men. In several cases, blacks working for privateers received generous land grants for their service. Still others received pensions for service in the Continental Navy. For most, however, the most valuable compensation was freedom. Even the Virginia state legislature passed an ordinance that freed all slaves who served in their master's place in the Virginia State Navy.[3]

TABLE 1

Black Participation in Armed Forces, 1971

Service	*% Black Enlisted*	*% Black Officers*
Navy	5.3	0.7
Marines	11.2	1.3
Air Force	11.9	1.7
Army	13.7	3.5

SOURCE: Office of the Deputy Assistant Secretary of Defense, Equal Opportunity table, as cited in Morris J. MacGregor and Bernard C. Nalty, eds., *Blacks in the United States Armed Forces: Basic Documents,* vol. 13 (Wilmington, DE: Scholarly Resources, 1977), 439.

Despite their contributions to the cause of American independence, Secretary of the Navy Benjamin Stoddert decided to ban "negroes and mulatoes" from the service in 1798.[4] The reasons behind this decision are still unclear.

Stoddert, the son of a Maryland tobacco farmer, may have viewed blacks as inferior beings.[5] Stoddert's fear that the French Navy might export the recent slave revolt in Haiti to the American south may also have played a role.[6] According to historian Michael Palmer, the prevention of an invasion from the Caribbean "became the first task of the United States Navy," and as a consequence, Stoddert may not have wanted to man his ships with crewmen who might show sympathy toward the ex-slaves of Haiti.[7]

The manpower demands of the Quasi War with France caused some of Stoddert's captains to disregard this directive and recruit blacks any way. During the War of 1812, the Navy officially ended its ban on African American recruitment, and by the end of the conflict, blacks represented 15 to 20 percent of the enlisted force. Black sailors manned guns, served in boarding parties, and took part in forays ashore. They also cooked, cleaned, caulked, and handled the sails. During the age of sail, the sea provided blacks with an alternative to slavery because the Navy, with its harsh discipline, dangerous work aloft, long periods at sea, low pay, and bad food, was so unattractive that the service had to accept any stable, sober volunteer, whatever his skin color. Still, some officers protested about recruiting blacks. In an 1813 letter to Commodore Isaac Chauncey, Master Commandant Oliver H. Perry, the hero of the Navy's Lake Erie campaign, complained that some of the men sent to him were a "motley set, blacks, Soldiers and boys, I cannot think you saw them after they were selected—I am however pleased to see any thing in the shape of a man." Chauncey, in response to this prejudiced note, wrote, "I have yet to learn that the Color of the skin, or cut and trimmings of the coat, can affect a man's qualifications or usefulness."[8]

Despite the strides made by black sailors during the War of 1812, the political situation between the northern and southern states led the Department of the Navy to impose quotas on black recruits during much of the early nineteenth century. To appease powerful, pro-slavery southern politicians like John C. Calhoun of South Carolina, Secretary of the Navy Abel P. Upshur promised in 1842 that African Americans would make up no more than "one-twentieth part of the crew of any vessel." This quota succeeded in reducing the percentage of blacks in the Navy to 4.2 percent by 1850.[9]

The situation changed dramatically once the Civil War began in 1861. While blacks could not serve in the Union Army until 1862, they could serve in the Navy throughout the conflict, albeit at lower wages. Overall, blacks represented 10 to 24 percent of the warship crews, depending on time and place, during the Civil War. The proportion rose even higher on service craft and sailing vessels. Most served as cooks and stewards, but a small number became captains of the hold, captains of the foretop, carpenter's mates, coxswains, and even gunner's mates and quartermasters.[10]

As early as 1861, Secretary of the Navy Gideon Welles authorized the recruitment of escaped or liberated slaves in the Atlantic Blockading Squadron. The Navy found escaped slaves easy to assimilate, and the racial policies on ships of the Atlantic Blockading Squadron had no impact on Union loyalists in

Kentucky or Missouri who owned slaves.[11] Initially, these "contrabands"could only serve as apprentice sailors or "boys," but by 1862, they could enlist as landsmen (adults with no maritime experience). Landsmen received twelve dollars a month, about four dollars less than ordinary seamen, and "boys," eight to ten dollars a month. The recruitment of former slaves significantly increased the numbers of blacks serving in the Navy during the Civil War. As of 2007, researchers have identified 20,000 Union black sailors from this war.[12]

After the Civil War, the percentage of African Americans in the Navy dropped from a wartime high of more than 20 percent to 13.1 percent in 1870, as segregation began to take hold in the United States. In the "Jim Crow" Navy, blacks mainly served as cooks, stewards, and landsmen, but some also worked as firemen, storekeepers, carpenters, water tenders, oilers, and in other specialized billets, and they messed and berthed with their white shipmates. A few even rose to the rank of third class petty officer.[13]

The 1896 *Plessy v. Ferguson* decision by the Supreme Court legitimized segregation in the United States and ushered in the beginning of a new era for blacks in the Navy. Beginning in 1905, the Navy began creating separate messes for these sailors, and recruitment decreased. By World War I, blacks constituted less than 3 percent of enlisted men, and almost all served in the galleys or engineering spaces. The Navy stopped enlisting blacks altogether in 1919 because officers thought Filipinos made better messmen. Commander (later rear admiral) Robert R. M. Emmett, the head of enlisted training in 1932, explained the nature of this bias in a letter to the Bureau of Navigation director of training, arguing that Filipinos "are cleaner, more efficient, and eat much less than negroes."[14] When Germany invaded France in 1940, only 4,007 African Americans served in the Navy, most as mess attendants, officers' cooks, and stewards.[15] It would take the Navy more than thirty years to erase this negative image of the sea service as a place where blacks were excluded from all occupations except that of domestic servants.

The prominent role white sailors played in the race riots of the summer of 1919 also tarnished the image of the service in the eyes of the nation's African American community. In Charleston, South Carolina, an altercation between a black man and two white sailors in May 1919 ended with the black man being shot and killed. Shortly afterward, a series of running skirmishes erupted between sailors and members of the local black community. Eventually, Marines and police managed to quell the riot and compel the hundreds of sailors involved to return to the Charleston Navy Yard, but not before white sailors managed to inflict extensive property damage on black-owned stores.[16]

In Washington, D.C., an even more ugly confrontation occurred. Shortly after 10:00 P.M. on 18 July, a young white woman was jostled by two black men on Twelfth Street in the southwest quadrant of the city. The woman screamed and the men fled. The next day, the *Washington Post* and *Washington Evening Star* carried sensationalized accounts of the episode, claiming that this "wife of a naval aviator" was "attacked" by black men.[17] The next day, a group of several hundred white sailors, soldiers, and Marines set out for the predominantly black section of the city near the Washington Navy Yard intent on lynching the suspects involved in the incident. This mob beat two black citizens with clubs and lead pipes and injured several more. On the 20th, a white mob beat two blacks in front of the White House. Shortly thereafter, soldiers attacked a group of blacks near the American League Baseball Park. On Monday, 21 July, four black men in a speeding car fired eight shots at a white sentry and several patients at the naval hospital in Georgetown.[18] Another black man stabbed a white Marine near the White House, and a black woman shot and killed a white detective who had entered her home to investigate a shooting in the area. That night, a group of black men and women in a car sped through the streets of Washington, firing at various white pedestrians. This group wounded a policeman, a soldier, and several others before police managed to stop the car and kill the driver. On Tuesday, a mob of 2,000 whites attempted to attack a black section of the city but were dispersed by mounted troops aided by a heavy downpour of rain. More than 800 Federal troops and numerous police finally quelled the disturbance on the 23d. In all, six people lost their lives in the incident, and more than 70 others were injured. It was the worst riot in Washington to date, and the first 1919 riot to receive national attention by the press.[19]

By the end of the summer, rioting had spread to more than twenty-five American cities. In Chicago, 23 blacks and 15 whites died, and more than 290 people of both races were wounded in a conflagration on 27 July, which began as a stone-throwing fight between black and white youths at a local whites-only beach. During the unrest that followed, white sailors stationed at the Great Lakes Naval Training Center participated in the beating and killing of black citizens caught in the downtown "Loop" area of the city. Significantly, the role of white sailors in the riot received much publicity in the *Chicago Defender,* one of the most widely read black papers in the country.[20]

As in Charleston and Washington, the causes of unrest in Chicago were complex. Massive troop demobilizations, competition for jobs between whites and blacks, urban overcrowding, and a local media prone to sensationalism were major reasons. However, it is significant for this book that white sailors helped provoke the riots and that all three events occurred near major naval shore facilities: the Navy connection to the riots of 1919 left an indelible impression on African Americans.

Relations between the "white" Navy and the black community improved little during the course of years leading to World War II. In 1932, blacks constituted just over one-half of 1 percent of the enlisted force (441 out of a force of 81,120), and 1 out of every 4 blacks in the Navy served as messmen.[21] One year later, the Navy again opened the steward branch to blacks, but blacks did not begin to enter the Navy in significant numbers until after America's entry into World War II. Illustrating the complete absurdity of these policies was a black mess attendant named Doris Miller. During the attack on Pearl Harbor, Miller was collecting laundry when he heard the call for general quarters. He headed for his battle station, the antiaircraft battery magazine amidship, only to discover that torpedo damage had wrecked it, so he went on deck, where he was assigned to carry the wounded to places of greater safety. An officer then ordered him to the bridge to aid the mortally wounded captain of the ship. He subsequently manned an antiaircraft machine gun until he ran out of ammunition and was ordered to abandon ship. For his heroism, the Navy awarded Miller the Navy Cross, the nation's second-highest award for gallantry.[22] Miller's deed proved that blacks were just as capable as whites in performing all the duties required of a sailor.

The manpower demands created by that war necessitated a change in racial policies, but the Navy initially resisted the pressures. In March 1942, President Roosevelt finally ordered Secretary of the Navy Frank Knox to begin accepting more blacks; Knox responded by enlisting more blacks for general service, but only in segregated units. By 1945, some 166,915 blacks were serving in the Navy (5.5 percent of the total enlisted force). Half of these men still served as cooks and stewards, and a third, as unrated seamen in black labor and base companies. Only 64 blacks received an officer's or warrant officer's commission—.02 percent of the total Navy officer corps.[23] Among the first African Americans to receive officer commissions were the "Golden Thirteen."[24] In January 1944, the Navy selected a group of 16 black sailors to attend the V-12 officer training program, a college commissioning program similar in some respects to the modern Naval Reserve Officers Training Corps (NROTC) system.[25] Of this number, 12 graduated with commissions and 1 became a warrant officer, apparently because he lacked a college education. The subject became a cover story in *Life* magazine and inspired many African Americans throughout the nation, but it did not end segregation in the Navy.[26]

During the war, the *Pittsburgh Courier,* the nation's leading black newspaper, waged a "Double V" campaign to defeat fascism abroad and discrimination at home, but as the numbers reveal, discrimination ended up being a more insidious enemy. The Port Chicago mutiny epitomized this struggle. Located thirty-five miles north of San Francisco, Port Chicago served as a munitions transshipment facility. It was staffed mainly by poorly trained black sailors organized into ordnance battalions. These men worked around the clock loading explosives onto ships under extremely dangerous conditions. On the evening of 17 July 1944, munitions exploded on a pier, detonating the contents of the merchant ship *E. A. Bryan* and spinning another empty merchant vessel, *Quinalt Victory,* into the air. The seismic shock of the explosion could be felt as far away as Las Vegas, Nevada, and the blast caused damage forty-eight miles across the bay in San Francisco. All 320 men on loading duty that evening died. Of this number, 220 were black, and these deaths represented 15 percent of all black Navy casualties of World War II.[27]

A month later, 258 black sailors refused to load ammunition at Mare Island, a large naval shipyard located in northern California, to protest the appalling conditions under which they worked. The Navy drummed 208 of these men out of the service with bad conduct discharges and sentenced another 50 to prison terms of between eight and fifteen years. After the war in 1946, President Harry Truman commuted the sentences of the men but did not offer them clemency or honorable discharges.[28]

In 1944, black sailors again lashed out against the oppressive conditions they confronted in the service. At Guam, whites of the Third Marine Division attempted to prevent blacks, most of whom were sailors, from visiting native women who lived in the capital, Agana. White Marines sought to intimidate blacks by hurling insults, rocks, and occasionally smoke grenades at a cantonment area for black sailors of the Guam Naval Supply Depot. The situation turned violent in mid-December after an off-duty white military policeman fired at some blacks in Agana, hitting no one; a white sailor shot to death a black Marine in a quarrel over a woman; and a Marine guard reacted to harassment by fatally wounding his tormentor, a white Marine.[29] Rumors soon started to fly about these incidents among the black sailors of the naval supply depot, and on Christmas night, forty-three black sailors armed themselves with knives and clubs and invaded a camp that housed white Marines. The ensuing riot resulted in the arrest and imprisonment of the forty-three black sailors who carried out the attack.[30]

Three months later, a Mississippi-born, white battalion commander sparked a two-day hunger strike by 1,000 black Seabees at Port Hueneme, California, by displaying racial bias in promotions and quarters assignments. The black Seabees, all veterans of overseas tours, reacted to the discrimination in a peaceful manner by continuing to perform their duties but without food. This thoughtful response prevented the Navy from charging the Seabees with mutiny. Furthermore, an official investigation ultimately recommended that the battalion commander in question be replaced.[31]

The events in Guam and California did not go unnoticed in Washington. When Secretary Frank Knox died in April 1944, Roosevelt elevated Under Secretary of the Navy James V. Forrestal to the post. Before the war, this former investment banker had worked with the National Urban League on civil rights issues, and upon assuming the position of secretary of the Navy he became a strong advocate for black sailors. He told Admiral King, the CNO, during the summer of 1944, "I don't think that our Navy negro personnel are getting a square break. I want to do something about it."[32] Forrestal proposed integrating blacks into the crew of auxiliaries, not to exceed 10 percent. He argued that such a move would boost morale and break up large concentrations of blacks in shore facilities. In February 1945, he published the *Guide to Command of Negro Naval Personnel,* which declared, "The Navy accepts no theories of racial differences in inborn ability, but expects that every man wearing its uniform be trained and used in accordance with his maximum individual capacity determined on the basis of individual performance."[33] In short, the Navy rejected segregation but stopped short of advocating policies aimed at making minority representation in all ranks proportional to black representation in society.[34] It instead asserted that merit would be the sole determinant for career placement throughout the service.

The highlight of the early cold war period for African Americans in the military was the signing of Executive Order 9981 in 1948 by President Harry S. Truman. This order established a policy of "equality of treatment and opportunity for all persons in the armed services without regard to race, color, religion, or national origin." In theory at least, it paved the way for greater opportunities for blacks in the Navy. In practice, the Navy's emphasis on qualitative recruitment and merit promotion meant that blacks actually lost ground during most of this period.

Despite Forrestal's strong commitment to civil rights, the number of black officers in the Navy declined from a wartime peak of sixty to just three reserve officers on extended active duty by 1946. In the enlisted grades, 62 percent of all blacks in the Navy still served as stewards on the eve of Truman's desegregation order in 1948. The situatton was so bad that Forrestal's successor, John L. Sullivan, commented that the service had "slipped back into its comfortable prewar ways, with enlisted blacks waiting on white officers."[35]

Black officers commissioned during World War II tended to be older than newly commissioned ensigns and therefore not as easy to promote. Moreover, the NROTC commissioned only sixteen new black officers tetween 1946 and 1948. One reason that NROTC failed to produce more black officer material was that it did not establish any programs at black colleges. Civil rights leaders did not press to change this situation because they feared that black schools would attract the best and brightest black officer candidates, thus demonstrating that "separate but equal" facilities were the best solution to the military's minority recruitment problems. Another problem had to do with the poor image of the service in the eyes of America's black community. Lieutenant Dennis D. Nelson, one of the Navy's few black officers in the 1940s, learned just how deeply African Americans resented the U.S. Navy during a recruitment tour in the 1948–1949 school year. After addressing 17,000 black high school seniors, this World War II veteran managed to persuade just 90 students to take the NROTC examination.[36]

The Naval Academy could have helped the service to solve the officer recruitment problem, but it too failed miserably in this regard. It did not graduate a single black officer until 1949, the year Ensign Wesley Brown finally broke the color barrier. According to Brown's biographer Robert Schneller, "Pressure along the entire chain of command—from fellow plebes, upperclassmen, midshipmen officers, Executive Department officers, the Secretary of the Navy, and congressmen—crushed the effort to run Brown out and ensured him a level playing field." It would take three more years, however, until a second black graduated from the academy. In all, the classes of 1950 through 1968 produced fewer than three dozen black graduates. Schneller blames this shortfall on institutional racism in the Navy and the Navy's policy of racial neglect. The black community's perception of the Navy as a racist institution discouraged its brightest youth from seeking admission to the Naval Academy, and the "policy of racial neglect prevented the establishment of a permanent minority affairs organization or program charged with recruiting blacks for the Academy."[37]

Problems in the area of minority recruitment not only plagued the Navy's efforts to increase black participation in the officer corps but also extended down to the lowest ranks. In 1948, just 4.3 percent of the enlisted force was black, and most were still concentrated in the steward's branch. President Truman's Committee on Equality of Treatment and Opportunity in the Armed Forces attempted to understand why the Navy's progress was so slow. Headed by George Fahy, a white Georgia lawyer with a liberal attitude toward issues of race, the committee asked Chief of Naval Personnel Vice Admiral William Fechteler, why so few blacks served in the Navy. Fechteler's response was that blacks were "not a seafaring people."[38] Captain J. H. Schultz, the assistant chief of naval personnel for the Naval Reserve, had a more plausible rationale. "We make no special effort to get any race, creed, or color," he explained.[39] Lieutenant Nelson confirmed this observation by testifying that the Navy had no programs to recruit or commission blacks.[40]

The Navy reacted to the Fahy Committee's concern over its dearth of minorities by stepping up efforts to recruit African Americans. During the next several months, the Navy activated five black reserve officers for recruiting service and sent three of these men on a tour through seventeen southern cities to recruit black NROTC candidates. The trip yielded only one suitable candidate for NROTC. Although 2,700 blacks in those cities submitted applications to NROTC, only 250 actually took the entrance exam, and out of this number, the Navy found only 1 candidate mentally and physically eligible for the program.[41]

On the eve of the Korean War, the overall number of black personnel in the Navy had declined from 17,518 in 1949 to 14,842 in 1950—just 3.4 percent of the total Navy force.[42] By comparison, the Army had nearly four times as many blacks in uniform: 56,446 enlisted men and 1,317 officers. Although most blacks still served in support units, the Army had a higher percentage of black soldiers in 1950 than it had at the end of World War II: 9.8 percent compared with 8.5 percent in 1945.[43]

Despite their small numbers, black sailors and officers demonstrated their competence in a variety of military occupations in which they had never served previously. A handful distinguished themselves as naval aviators. Lieutenant Frank E. Petersen, the first black Marine to become a naval aviator, flew sixty-four combat missions over Korea in the F_4U Corsair. Petersen ultimately retired from Marines as a lieutenant general.[44] Others served as surface warfare officers. In the enlisted ranks, blacks found new opportunities serving as clerks and even became medical and dental aides.[45]

Still, the picture was bleak. During the Korean War, 65 percent of the steward branch was still black. Low test scores among many black recruits precluded them from being assigned to more skilled positions. The Navy also tended to assign blacks to the branch in large numbers because these positions, according to historian Richard E. Miller, were "undesirable for whites."[46] Furthermore, following Philippine independence in 1946, the United States stopped recruiting Filipinos for naval service until 1952, when a "direct procurement" agreement between the two countries allowed the Navy to enlist up to 1,000 Filipinos a year for service as stewards. As a consequence, the branch still offered some of the best opportunities for advancement and promotion for black sailors.[47]

Following the Korean War, black representation in the Navy continued to slide. African Americans represented 9.5 percent of Navy enlistees in 1956 but then slid to just 3.1 percent during the next six years.[48] The reason for this decrease had much to do with the Navy's emphasis on qualitative recruitment. The Navy rejected so many blacks in the 1950s and 1960s because of their low scores on the Armed Forces Qualification Test (AFQT). The AFQT classified all recruits into five categories based on scores. Those who scored in the 93 through 100 percentile were classified as category I; 65 through 92 percentile, category II; 31 through 64, category III; 10 through 30, category IV; and 0 through 9, category V. A percentile score of 10 was considered the equivalent of a fifth-grade education. A 1963 Bureau of Personnel study found that approximately 80 percent of draft-aged black males scored in the two lowest categories of the test, compared with 25 percent of white males.[49] It should be noted that Navy-sponsored studies in the early 1970s later determined that the AFQT and other Navy entrance exams of the period were culturally biased against blacks.

During the Korean War, the Department of Defense (DOD) had allowed the services to accept up to 24 percent of their recruits from category IV. When the buildup ended in the midfifties, the Navy reverted to qualitative recruiting. Between 1957 and 1959, the Navy drastically reduced the percentages of recruits it accepted from category IV and the lower part of category III, in order to reduce training costs and to obtain the maximum effectiveness and permanency of personnel.[50] Hence, by 1962, only 5.1 percent of the Navy was black, even though blacks represented 11 percent of the U.S. population at the time. In the officer ranks, the situation was even worse: only 0.2 percent of the Navy's officer corps was African American in 1962, and most were concentrated in the lower grades (O-1 through O-3). By comparison, blacks constituted 12.2 percent of the Army's enlisted force and 3.2 percent of its officer corps.[51] The Army's high demand for low-skilled recruits allowed it to more easily meet minority recruitment targets during this period than the Navy.

The Army's emphasis on recruiting men of all skill levels and abilities versus the Navy's emphasis on qualitative recruitment partially explains this disparity, but so too does the Army's unique experience with black troops during the Korean War. The poor performance of the all-black 24th Infantry Regiment early in the war convinced that service's leadership that segregation undermined military effectiveness. After the war, the service strove for a 10 percent quota of black troops in all its units—roughly the same proportion of blacks in the general United States. By the early 1960s, the Army could boast not only of having achieved proportional representation but also that integrated units functioned better and were more combat effective than previously segregated forces.[52]

In addition to falling short of the other armed services in the area of recruitment, the Navy also lagged behind the other branches when it came to assignments for black personnel. Although more black enlisted men began entering technical fields in the early 1960s, one in five still worked in food services—a factor that perpetuated the image of the black sailor as a menial servant.[53] De facto segregation also existed at many enlisted clubs on Navy bases (the other services all suffered from this problem), and blacks continued to suffer discrimination off base. Civilian communities near naval bases often prevented black service personnel from living in white neighborhoods and sending their children to white schools. These segregation practices even extended to public swimming pools, movie theaters, bowling alleys, churches, and libraries.[54]

Ensign Louis Ivey's career typifies in many respects the segregation experienced daily by black naval personnel in late 1950s and early 1960s. Ivey graduated from the Penn State NROTC program and became the first black officer to ever serve on the battleship *New Jersey* (BB-62) in 1954.[55] His first roommate, a higher-ranking white officer, ordered him to find other quarters, but he eventually formed friendships with other white officers. At various ports of call abroad, such as Cherbourg, France, he found he could move freely without feeling any discrimination, but American ports were a different story. At Norfolk, Virginia, he could not eat at local restaurants or watch movies at theaters with his shipmates, and he was compelled to spend his entire leave on base or on the ship.[56]

To improve black participation in the Navy as well as the other services, President John F. Kennedy in 1963 formed the Advisory Committee on Equal Opportunity in the Armed Forces and appointed a Washington attorney, Gerhard A. Gesell, as its chair. The Gesell Committee found that Navy was "falling behind the other services" in the area of equal opportunity and suggested "expanding the recruiting teams in black communities, developing special training programs and methods for recruiting African Americans, and setting up recruiting stations on the campuses of black colleges."[57]

While the Navy leadership recognized its problems with respect to black recruiting as early as 1963, the situation did not begin to change until the end of the Vietnam War. With the war in full swing, Navy leaders confronted a unique dilemma. On the one hand, large numbers of highly qualified whites eager to avoid being drafted into the Army flocked to recruiting stations; on the other, the Kennedy and Johnson administrations petitioned the service to recruit more blacks, even those with lower AFQT scores.[58] Throughout the war, Navy leaders, anxious to recruit the best possible sailors to fight the war, chose to ignore demands to fill racial quotas and instead continued the trend of qualitative recruitment. This situation would not change until Nixon began scaling back the draft in the early 1970s—a move that ultimately compelled the Navy to begin actively recruiting low test category persons of all races into the Navy.

Notes

[1]Elmo R. Zumwalt Jr., *On Watch: A Memoir* (New York: Quadrangle,1976), 198.

[2]James Barker Farr, *Black Odyssey: Seafaring Traditions of Afro-Americans* (New York: Peter Lang, 1989), 106.

[3]Ibid., 111–113.

[4]Letter from Benjamin Stoddert to LT Henry Kenyon, Navy Department, 8 August 1898, in Morris J. MacGregor and Bernard C. Nalty, eds., *Blacks in the United States Armed Forces: Basic Documents,* vol. 1 (Wilmington, DE: Scholarly Resources, 1977), 192.

[5]For more on Stoddert's biography, see S. Charles Bolton, "Stoddert, Benjamin," in John A. Garraty and Mark C. Carnes, eds., *American National Biography,* vol. 20 (New York: Oxford University Press, 1999), 825–826.

[6]See Farr, *Black Odyssey,* 114.

[7]Michael A. Palmer, *Stoddert's War: Naval Operations during the Quasi War with France, 1798–1801* (Columbia: University of South Carolina Press, 1987), 18

[8]For the full text of these letters, see William S. Dudley and Michael J. Crawford, eds., *The Naval War of 1812: A Documentary History,* vol. 2, 1813 (Washington, DC: U.S. Naval Historical Center, 1992), 529–531.

[9]Bernard C. Nalty, *Long Passage to Korea: Black Sailors and the Integration of the U.S. Navy* (Washington, DC: U.S. Naval Historical Center, 2003), 6.

[10]Robert J. Schneller, *Blue, Gold, and Black: Racial Integration of the United States Naval Academy* (College Station: Texas A&M University Press, forthcoming).

[11]Bernard C. Nalty, *Strength for the Fight: A History of Black Americans in the Military* (New York: Free Press, 1989), 33.

[12]A partnership of researchers from the U.S. Naval Historical Center, the National Park Service, and Howard University is currently involved in this identification process. See Nalty, *Long Passage to Korea,* 9–10.

[13]Schneller, *Blue, Gold, and Black;* Nalty, *Long Passage to Korea,* 12–13.

[14]CDR Robert R. M. Emmett, letter to CAPT Leigh Noyes, 19 October 1932, quoted in Richard E. Miller, *The Messman Chronicles: African Americans in the U.,S. Navy, 1932–1943* (Annapolis, MD: Naval Institute Press, 2004), 8.

[15]Nalty, *Long Passage to Korea,* 15.

[16]Chester A. Wright, "The U.S. Navy's Human Resource Management Programs in the Aftermath of the USS *Kitty Hawk/Constellation* Racial Incidents" (paper presented at the Thirty-fifth Military Operations Research Symposium at the United States Naval Academy, 2 July 1975), AR, 17–19.

[17]Actually, her husband worked as a civilian employee in the Naval Aviation Department. See Lloyd M. Abernethy, "The Washington Race War of July 1919," *Maryland Historical Magazine* 58 (December 1963): 315n22.

[18]They did not hit anyone. See ibid.

[19]Ibid., 309–322; Constance McLaughlin Green, *Washington: Capital City, 1879–1950* (Princeton, NJ: Princeton University Press, 1963), 266–267; "Capital Clashes Increase," *New York Times,* 22 July 1919, 1; Wright, "The U.S. Navy's Human Resource Management Programs," 17; Terry Ann Knopf, "Race, Riots, and Reporting," *Journal of Black Studies* 4 (March 1974): 303–313.

[20]Wright, "The U.S. Navy's Human Resource Management Programs," 17.

[21]See Miller, *The Messman Chronicles,* 6.

[22]For more on the Doris Miller story, see ibid., 285–319; and Naval Historical Center, "Ship's Cook Third Class Doris Miller, USN," www.history.navy.mil/faqs/faq57-4.htm, accessed 20 August 2006.
[23]Schneller, *Blue, Gold, and Black.*
[24]The Navy accidentally commissioned Harvard medical student Bernard Whitfield Brown on 8 June 1942 because the recruiter, who had not seen Brown before the commissioning, thought he was white. On 28 September 1942, the Navy commissioned Oscar Wayman Holmes in the Civil Aeronautics Administration-War Training Program before learning that Holmes, a light-skinned person, was black. Holmes was also the first African American to earn the naval aviator designation. For more on Holmes, see Robert J. Schneller, "Oscar Holmes: A Place in Naval Aviation," *Naval Aviation News,* January-February 1998, 26–27. See also Robert J. Schneller, *Breaking the Color Barrier: The U.S. Naval Academy's First Black Midshipmen and the Struggle for Racial Equality* (New York: New York University Press, 2005), 155.
[25]The V-12 program sent 120,000 men to civilian colleges to receive up to seven semesters of education. These selectees attended school in uniform and received commissions upon successful completion of the program. Many returned to college after the war to complete undergraduate or graduate degrees. For more details, see U.S. Navy Memorial Foundation, The Navy V-12 Program, www.lonesailor.org/v12history.php, accessed 20 September 2006.
[26]For more on the Golden Thirteen, see Paul Stillwell, ed., *The Golden Thirteen: Reflections of the First Black Naval Officers* (Annapolis, MD: Naval Institute Press, 1993).
[27]For more on the Port Chicago explosion, see Robert L. Allen, *The Port Chicago Mutiny* (New York: Warner Books, 1989).
[28]U.S. Naval Historical Center, Port Chicago Naval Magazine Explosion, 1944, www.history.navy.mil/faqs/faq80-1.htm, accessed 20 September 2006.
[29]Courts-martial eventually convicted the men who fired the fatal shots of voluntary manslaughter. See Nalty, *Strength for the Fight,* 195–196.
[30]Ibid.
[31]Ibid., 196.
[32]Forrestal quoted in Schneller, *Breaking the Color Barrier,* 158.
[33]Bureau of Personnel, U.S. Navy Department, *Guide to Command of Negro Naval Personnel,* 12 February 1945, vol. 6., 275–293.
[34]"Affirmative action" did not come into effect in the general society until the 1960s.
[35]Nalty, *Long Passage to Korea,* 26.
[36]Ibid., 27.
[37]Schneller, *Blue, Gold, and Black.*
[38]Nalty, *Long Passage to Korea,* 30.
[39]Schneller, *Blue, Gold, and Black.*
[40]Nalty, *Long Passage to Korea,* 30.
[41]Schneller, *Blue, Gold, and Black.*

[42]Dennis D. Nelson, *The Integration of the Negro into the U.S. Navy* (New York: Farrar, Straus and Young, 1951), 227.
[43]William T. Bowers, William M. Hammond, and George L. MacGarrigle, *Black Soldier, White Army: The 24th Infantry Regiment in Korea* (Washington, DC: U.S. Army Center of Military History, 1996), 27.
[44]Nalty, *Strength for the Fight,* 263.
[45]Ibid., 265.
[46]Author interview, Richard E. Miller, the author of *The Messman Chronicles,* 20 August 2006.
[47]The policy of recruiting Philippine nationals into the U.S. Navy exclusively as stewards was modified in 1971 by State Department agreement with the Philippine government to allow Filipinos entering the Navy to strike for any enlisted rating they were considered qualified for by means of education, prior experience, and security qualifications. In 1992, the Navy stopped recruiting Filipinos. See Bureau of Naval Personnel, Filipinos in the United States Navy, October 1976, www.history.navy.mil/library/online/filipinos.htm, accessed 18 August 2006.
[48]Schneller, *Blue, Gold, and Black.*
[49]MacGregor and Nalty, *Basic Documents,* vol. 12, "Memorandum on Recruitment Trends," 16 July 1963, 527–559.
[50]Schneller, *Blue, Gold, and Black.*
[51]Gerhard A. Gesell, The President's Committee on Equal Opportunity in the Armed Forces Report, AR, 6–8.
[52]For more on the Army's experiences with integration, see Morris J. MacGregor, *Integration of the Armed Forces, 1940–1965* (Washington, DC: U.S. Army Center of Military History, 1981); and Bowers, Hammond, and MacGarrigle, *Black Soldier, White Army.*
[53]Gesell Committee Report, 43.
[54]Ibid., 45.
[55]While Ivey was the first black officer to serve on *New Jersey,* other blacks had served on battleships before him. For example, Samuel Gravely served on *Iowa* (BB 61) in 1953 as a communications officers and in various capacities, including assistant operations officer. See Samuel L. Gravely bio file, AR.
[56]Nalty, *Long Passage to Korea,* 45.
[57]Schneller, *Blue, Gold, and Black;* Gesell Committee Report, 43.
[58]A DOD survey in 1964, for example, found that 75 percent of Naval Reserve enlistments were draft related. George Q. Flynn, *The Draft, 1940–1973* (Lawrence: University Press of Kansas, 1993), 209.

CHAPTER TWENTY-THREE

A New Kind of War

Victor H. Krulak

FOCUS QUESTIONS

1. According to Krulak, what qualities should the U. S. Marine Corps foster in its personnel? Why are these qualities important?
2. How does Krulak think the U. S. Marines should have been used to fight the Vietnam War?
3. Krulak asserts that Secretary of Defense MacNamara's strategy to win the Vietnam War was fundamentally flawed. What is Krulak's view on how the United States should have waged war in Vietnam?
4. What is Sun Tzu's philosophy of insurgent warfare as discussed by Krulak? How does the "ink blot" formula counter the ability of the insurgents to emerge victoriously?

When Daniel Ellsberg was on trial for stealing the Pentagon Papers, his defense lawyers, to confuse the issue, introduced the claim that U.S. participation in the Vietnam conflict was premeditated, that the Tonkin Gulf incident was a contrived excuse for our intervention. I was one of the witnesses for the federal government. On cross-examination, Ellsberg's attorney, Leonard Weinglass, wanted me to admit that well before we went to Vietnam the Marines were preparing for combat there. I surprised him by confessing. Yes, I said, we were indeed preparing for the eventuality of having to fight in Vietnam. Even more important I told him, we were preparing to fight in a lot of other places, too.

Unwittingly, Mr. Weinglass had underscored one of the characteristics that has distinguished the Corps—a standing determination to be ready for combat wherever and however it may arise. Total readiness is, nevertheless, more an objective than a reality, because of the enemy—his strengths, his aims, and his resolve. We have learned, to our regret, that while you are certainly the better for preparing, the war you prepare for is rarely the war you get.

Thus, we come to an unusual, and generally unheralded, aspect of the Marines' quality as fighters. Adaptability, initiative, and improvisation are the true fabric of obedience, the ultimate in soldierly conduct, going further than sheer heroism to make the Marines what they are. "The battle is what it's all about," Marines say. "Try as hard as you can to be ready for it but be willing to adapt and improvise when it turns out to be a different battle than the one you expected, because adaptability is where victory will be found." This virtue of adaptability has found expression many times in the Marines' combat history, especially since the beginning of the twentieth century.

In 1916, for example, Marines went to Santo Domingo on short notice with the simple mission of protecting the American Legation in Santo Domingo City. They were still there eight years later, involved in the far broader tasks of both pacifying and governing the country, to which they had adapted readily. In 1950, they went to Korea intending to make a decisive amphibious assault at Inchon to sever the North Korean supply line. Ten weeks later they were still in Korea, fighting quite a different kind of war—a protracted land campaign in the subzero ice and snow of the Chosin Reservoir. And three years later they were still there, fighting an attritional war of position. They stood up to these varied combat challenges because of an instinctive determination to adapt.

The sternest fighting test of all, where the need for adaptability was greatest, came in Vietnam. The onset of that conflict found the Corps in an advanced state of training oriented primarily toward its traditional amphibious mission but with some attention given to counterinsurgency situations. Since 1962, when President Kennedy required all of the services to emphasize counterinsurgency training, the Marines had been preparing to operate in a counterinsurgency environment, not just in Southeast Asia but anywhere in the world.

Serving in the Joint Staff as the focal point in counterinsurgency operations and training, I went to Vietnam eight times between 1962 and 1964. In those early years, I learned something of the complex nature of the conflict there. The problem of seeking out and destroying guerrillas was easy enough to comprehend but winning the loyalty of the people, why it was so important and how to do it, took longer to understand. Several meetings with Sir Robert Thompson, who contributed so much to the British victory over the guerrillas in Malaya, established a set of basic counterinsurgency principles in my mind. Thompson said, "The peoples' trust is primary. It will come hard because they are fearful and suspicious. Protection is the most important thing you can bring them. After that comes health. And, after that, many things—land, prosperity, education and privacy to name a few." The more I saw of the situation facing the Vietnamese government and the Vietnamese Army, the more convinced I became—along with many other Americans—that our success in the counterinsurgency conflict would depend on a complete and intimate understanding by all ranks from top to bottom of the principles Thompson had articulated.

In 1964, I assumed command of Fleet Marine Force, Pacific, embracing all the Marines in the Pacific Ocean area. Following the experience of Thompson and based on what I had learned in the preceding two years, we set about orienting our training toward combat in a counterinsurgency environment. The training culminated in early 1965 in a major series of exercises called Silver Lance, patterned as closely as possible upon the emerging situation in Vietnam. All counterinsurgency issues were explored: fighting both large units and small bands of guerrillas; handling situations involving the local civilian population; supporting training and cooperating with the indigenous military; dealing with our own diplomatic representatives; and meeting the challenge of a privileged sanctuary, where a bordering, ostensibly neutral country is used as a base and a route of approach by the enemy. We added realism to the exercise by having Marines, carefully rehearsed for their roles, take the parts of friendly and hostile native forces as well as of our own political and diplomatic personnel. Everyone, from the high command to the individual Marine, was tested, and we all learned from the experience.

The exercise could not have been more timely. About a third of the Silver Lance forces—the air/ground 1st Marine Brigade—were at sea off the California coast when the decision was made to land at Danang. The brigade was turned westward immediately and directed to sail toward the anticipated battle. It was actually disembarked in Okinawa, but it ultimately ended up in Vietnam, as did all the other participants in the exercise. And the 3d Battalion 9th Marines from Okinawa, the first unit to be committed, actually war-gamed a landing at Danang only two weeks before the landing took place.

So the Marines, from colonels to privates, were mentally prepared and reasonably ready for a counterinsurgency conflict. However, it turned out that the mission of the initial force to land at Danang was greatly different from what they had been practicing. The unit was restricted to protecting the Danang air base from enemy incursion, nothing more. It was not permitted to "engage in day-to-day actions against the Vietcong," nor were the Marines allowed to leave the air base or to be involved directly with the local population—which is what counterinsurgency is all about. Soon the force was enlarged to include the whole of the 9th Marine Expeditionary Brigade of five thousand men, but it remained confined to the air base area, tied to what the senior U.S. command, "COMUSMACV" termed "protection of the Danang air base from enemy attack."

This was never going to work. We were not going to win any counterinsurgency battles sitting in foxholes around a runway, separated from the very people we wanted to protect. Furthermore, the air base was overlooked by hills to the west and northwest, giving the enemy a clear view of the field. On two sides, the airfield complex was cheek-by-jowl with the city of Danang, only a wire fence separating the base from two hundred thousand people—most of them suspicious of us, some of them hostile. Despite all this, General Nguyen Chan Thi, the Vietnamese commander of the area, termed the I Corps Tactical Zone, agreed with General Westmoreland. He did not want the Marines moving outside the airfield area either. Thi, an intense, mercurial personality, had had no experience with Americans. He had, however, been involved with the French—not altogether favorably—and was determined, at the outset, not to allow the Americans to infringe his authority. Ultimately, Thi became totally confident in the Marines, willing to do just about anything they asked.

As commanding general, Fleet Marine Force, Pacific, I was responsible for the training of all the Marines in the Pacific, for their equipment, their supply of Marine Corps items, and their readiness, but I had no authority whatever over their operational employment in Vietnam. That was General Westmoreland's business, and he answered to the commander of the Pacific Theater, Admiral U.S. Grant Sharp.

Nevertheless, I felt strongly that American lives, as well as many valuable aircraft, were going to be hazarded if we could not patrol the hills around the Danang field. Furthermore, I believed that we could do little to help the people if we were obliged to shun them. I went, with Brigadier General Frederick Karch, the Marine brigade commander, to remonstrate with Thi. Thi listened. After we were finished, he just said, patiently, "You are not ready." We repeatedly pleaded with him, and he relented slightly. By 20 April 1965, the Marines were patrolling the hills about two miles west of the airfield and the countryside about four miles north of the field. I suspect, in both cases, that General Thi felt safe—there were few Vietcong in those areas but, as we were to learn there were many not far distant.

These tiny moves into the hinterland turned out to be the first steps in a massive expansion responding to the siren calls of seeking more favorable terrain and engaging the enemy. The eight-square-mile enclave around the Danang airfield grew, in six months, to more than eight hundred square miles. Another enclave of some one hundred square miles was created fifty miles to the south at Chu Lai to accommodate construction of a second airstrip. A third enclave of some sixty square miles was established at Phu Bai, fifty miles north of Danang, at the direction of General Westmoreland, to protect a communications unit there. The creation and growth of the three enclaves brought a great opportunity to work among the native population, to seek out the Vietcong guerrillas in each area, and to bring a little stability to rich and populous areas, some of which had been under enemy control for a decade.

By mid-1965 the five-thousand-man force had grown to over eighteen thousand, and there was still a crying hunger for more Marines. This was so because the Marines' concept, from the start, involved fighting the Vietnam battle as a multi-pronged effort. They aimed to bring peace and security to the people in the highly populated coastal regions by conducting aggressive operations against the guerrillas and expanding the pacified areas as rapidly as they were totally secured. At the same time, they planned to train the local militia and to support the Vietnamese Armed Forces in their fight against the Vietcong. Finally, the Marines were determined to go after the larger organized units whenever they could be definitely located and fixed. They set about this balanced strategy with a will, showing persistence and no small degree of innovative genius.

The Marines' first experience of protecting the people began in May 1965. It was a challenging test of the lessons practiced earlier in the year in exercise Silver Lance. To secure the Danang air base from guerrilla attack from the northwest, it was necessary to cover the broad valley of the Cue De River. They learned quickly that Le My, a village of about seven hundred people, comprising eight hamlets,[2] only six miles from the main airstrip, was truly enemy country. Two guerrilla platoons—about forty men—lived in the village where they had constructed an extensive cave and tunnel system. They moved in and out at will, extorting the people's rice and money, coercing their youth to join the insurgency, and threatening the village officials. Because of the Vietcong oppression, Le My was sick unto death. There was little government, little agriculture, little commerce, no security, no public services, and no schools. The Vietnamese Army and regional troops had made a few feeble passes at chasing the Vietcong away, but the enemy retained control of the area, its resources, and its people. Further complicating the situation was the fact that some of the active guerrillas had relatives in the village, from whom they received food, sanctuary, and information. Nevertheless, the people at large were despondent and terrified. Even the village chief spent many of his nights in Danang because of his fear of assassination or capture.

In early May, after every patrol in the area reported receiving sniper fire, the Marines decided to clean the guerrillas out of Le My. They launched a two-company operation and found they had undertaken a time-consuming and enervating job. The Vietcong reacted to the American threat strongly—by fire ambush and booby trap, giving the Marines a foretaste of the bitter anti-guerrilla war that was to absorb them for the next six years.

Eventually, however, the insurgents were rooted out of their caves and tunnels, and killed, captured, or driven away. The people's confidence was slowly restored by the security provided by the Marine units as well as by local militia, which resurfaced as the Marine influence grew. By ministering to the villagers' health, by supporting them in construction projects, and by helping them to dig wells and reestablish schools and markets, the Marines brought the villagers a level of stability unseen in a decade. Concurrently, the Marines encouraged and assisted the local militia, training them, repairing their weapons, and helping them construct strong defensive positions around the village.[3]

The Marines tried to put into effect in the village of Le My exactly what they had practiced before coming to Vietnam. Although lacking in the polish that comes with experience, the effort turned out to be classic—actually a good pattern for their subsequent actions, in scores of other villages, to deliver the people from terror. Among other things, it illustrated that the pacification process demanded the combined efforts of both Americans and Vietnamese. To this end, Lieutenant General Lewis Walt, the senior Marine commander, created a "Joint Coordinating Council," which included representatives from all organizations involved with the pacification process.

I learned a lasting lesson at Le My. In late May 1965, I went there with Lieutenant Colonel David A. Clement, whose battalion had done the entire Le My project. We met the district (county) chief and the village chief, who showed us with much pride and gratitude the rejuvenation of the village—the whitewashed dispensary with two shy nurses wearing white; the one-room schoolhouse filled with serious-faced little children; the thriving marketplace; and, more seriously, the newly constructed outposts and security installations around the village perimeter. Neither of the two officials could speak English, but the district chief could speak French, and, amid all the smiles, bows, thanks, and congratulations, he said to me in a very sober way, "One thing. All of this has meaning only if you are going to stay. Are you going to stay?"

It was a hard question, but basic. The villagers could not risk giving us their trust if we were going to go off and leave them unprotected in the vain belief that the Vietcong, once driven off, would not come back. They had already had the experience of being encouraged and then abandoned by the French, and by their own army, too. So I said, "These same Marines will not stay here, but others will never be far away, and your own militia will be here all the time." He made it clear that this was not exactly what he wanted to hear but it was better than nothing. It turned out to be good enough to encourage one hundred fifty people from two Vietcong-dominated hamlets some ten miles distant to leave their homes and their precious land and move to Le My just to be under the umbrella of American protection.

Le My had its ups and downs in the next five years—minor forays by guerrillas, assassination of one of its mayors—but the Vietcong never took over the area again. Le My was a microcosm of the entire war at this period, reflecting on a small scale the perspective of ten million rural Vietnamese in fourteen thousand hamlets. They always feared, and sometimes hated, the Vietcong for their extortion, taxation, brutality and designs on the local youth. They wanted and welcomed our protection but were terrified at the prospect of getting it and then losing it. The nearer we were to them and the more thorough our efforts, the better the system worked. This painstaking, exhausting, and sometimes bloody process of bringing peace, prosperity, and health to a gradually expanding area came to be known as the "spreading ink blot" formula. In the effort to free and then protect the people, it should have been at the heart of the battle for freedom in Indochina. Many people applauded the idea, among them Army generals Maxwell Taylor and James Gavin. General Westmoreland told me, however, that while the ink blot idea seemed to be effective, we just didn't have time to do it that way. I suggested to him that we didn't have time to do it any other way; if we left the people to the enemy, glorious victories in the hinterland would be little more than blows in the air—and we would end up losing the war. But Defense Secretary Robert S. McNamara expressed the same view as Westmoreland to me in the winter of 1965—"A good idea," he said about the ink blot formula, "but too slow." I had told him in a letter dated 11 November

1965, "In the highly populous areas the battle ground is in the peoples' minds. We have to separate the enemy from the people, and clean up the area a bit at a time."

With the tiny experience of Le My to encourage them, the Marines moved assertively into more Le Mys, as well as on to other combatant efforts aimed at breaking the guerrillas' hold on the people. One such endeavor was called "County Fair." It began as a simple U.S.-Vietnamese program for rooting out Vietcong military and political cells from the villages. Under cover of darkness a Marine unit would surround a village believed to be infiltrated by Vietcong. Then a Vietnamese Army unit would enter the village, search for tunnels and caves, and flush out any hiding guerrillas. Concurrently, they would screen the residents for identity cards and take into custody any suspicious persons.

The idea was sound in principle and sometimes effective in execution. But often it went aground on either of two circumstances. First, the Vietnamese Army was never enthusiastic about working among the people, and they were not particularly good at it. Second, the Marines were sometimes anxious to do too much for the same people.

Some County Fairs were immensely complicated. While the Vietnamese Army troops were busy digging out guerrillas, there might be a Marine band concert in progress, a soup kitchen, a medical program, a dental program, a population census, some native entertainment, possibly a film, and even some political speeches—all going on at once. I never saw a County Fair where I did not wonder whether the villagers were absolutely sure of what we were doing. And I wondered how long it would take the Vietcong to percolate back after the Marines and Vietnamese Army had packed up and left.

A more effective project was called "Combined Action," a scheme which brought together a squad of Marines and a platoon of the Vietnamese Popular Forces. The Popular Forces were at the very bottom of the pecking order in the Vietnamese military. They were recruited from and served in their own hamlet and, as soldiers, they were pitiable. Poorly equipped, poorly trained, poorly led, and given only half the pay of the Vietnamese Army, they fought indifferently, if at all, and were notorious for their desertion rate. They were literally afraid of the dark; they were quite unwilling to fight at night when the Vietcong were at large. It is not remarkable that they inspired little confidence among the villagers.

My first experience with the Popular Forces was on a trip I made to Vietnam in 1962 with Defense Secretary McNamara. In a hamlet outside the town of Nha Trang, we saw a Popular Force unit of about twenty-five thin, grave-faced little men, drawn up as a sort of ceremonial honor guard. No two in the same uniform, armed with an assortment of battered rifles, carbines, and shotguns, they were monumentally unimpressive to look at. As we walked down the ragged front rank, McNamara pointed to one rifle and asked me, "Do you think those things will shoot?" I took one from a soldier, had trouble getting the bolt open and, when I did, could not see daylight through the gun barrel. The ammunition in the youngster's belt was green with corrosion.

When I told McNamara, he said, "We are going to have to do something about this. These may well be the most important military people in Vietnam. They have something real to fight for—their own hamlet, their own family." And he was right. Unfortunately, little was done on their behalf between 1962 and 1965, when the Marines hit upon the possibilities inherent in combining the loyalty and local knowledge of the Popular Forces with our own professional skill. It is hard to say just where the idea for Combined Action originated, but Captains Paul R. Ek and John J. Mullen, Jr., and Major Cullen C. Zimmerman are prominently mentioned as the architects and Lieutenant General Lewis Walt, the overall Marine commander, lent his energetic support.

A Marine squad composed of carefully screened volunteers who already had some combat experience, was given basic instruction in Vietnamese culture and customs and then combined with a Popular Forces platoon. The Marine squad leader—a sergeant or corporal—commanded the combined force in tactical operations, and the Popular Forces platoon leader was his operational assistant. The remaining Marines were distributed through the unit in subordinate leadership positions.

The initial effort, organized as a "Combined Action Company,"[4] involved four such units. In the summer of 1965, the 3d Battalion, 4th Marines, launched the program at Phu Bai. The combined platoons lived together in the hamlets. The Vietnamese taught the Marines the language, customs, and habits of the people and the local geography The Marines conducted training in weapons and tactics. Together, they fought the Vietcong, gradually acquiring the respect and confidence of the villagers. Living conditions were humble—or less. One platoon I visited was living in two squalid native huts—dirt floor, no doors or windows, a blanket of flies. At the moment the Marines and Vietnamese were busy cooking, sharing their food, and chattering in a mixture of English and Vietnamese. With much pride, they were anxious to tell me that only the night before they had conducted a successful ambush outside the village, killing one Vietcong and capturing another—a triumph, considering that only weeks before the Popular Forces troops could not be induced to go forth at night. Together the two components were effective in often bloody operations against the Vietcong, bringing a measure of peace to localities that had not known it for years.

The Combined Action program spread quickly to all three of the Marine enclaves. By early 1966, there were nineteen Combined Action units; by the end of 1967, there were seventy-nine. All were engaged in offensive operations against the Vietcong to protect their own home village. As they fought their little engagements they were reminding us of the wisdom of the ancient Chinese military scholar Sun Tzu, to which Mao Tze-tung adhered, who declared that in an insurgent war the revolutionaries are the fish and the people are the medium in which they swim. If the medium is hospitable, you are likely to win; if inhospitable you are sure to lose. North Vietnamese General Vo Nguyen Giap had his own way of saying it, "Protracted war requires a whole ideological struggle among the people. Without the people we have no information. . . . They hide us, protect us, feed us, and tend our wounded."

The Vietcong had enjoyed a free ride in the Vietnamese hamlets because of the general incompetence of the Popular Forces and the consequent uncertainty of the people. The Combined Action idea was an effective answer to the problem, helping to free the people to act, speak, and live without fear. It was a multiplier, where the final product had combatant value many times the sum of its individual components. There were hundreds of skirmishes and many casualties, but two extraordinary statistics reveal that the unique organizational arrangement paid off: no village protected by a Combined Action unit was ever repossessed by the Vietcong; and 60 percent of the Marines serving the Combined Action units volunteered to stay on with their Marine and Vietnamese companions for an additional six months when they could have returned to the United States.

Senior Marine officers and those who had an interest in Marine Corps history knew that the Combined Action idea had been applied with success before—in Haiti (1915–34), in Nicaragua (1926–33) and, probably most effectively, in Santo Domingo (1916–22). There the Marines organized, trained, and directed, a new national police force, the Guardia National, later to become the Policia National. Formal training schools imbued the Policia rank and file with a sense of discipline. Under Marine leadership, the Policia exercised their new knowledge of weapons and tactics in hundreds of antiguerrilla patrols. But even more important, the Marines got to the heart of security in the Dominican villages by organizing, equipping, and training "Home Guard" units composed of residents who were willing to defend their own homes and families. Led by a Marine officer and including ten to fifteen Dominicans and two or three Marine enlisted men, these mixed groups successfully brought a measure of peace to their small communities. In Vietnam, half a century later, similar combined formations again validated the concept, proving that their effectiveness far exceeded what might have been expected from their small numbers.[5]

Even guerrillas have to eat and the Vietcong had no fields of their own. They depended on the farmers for their sustenance, about 1½ pounds of rice per man per day. At harvest time it was their habit to come down to the coastal plain and extort food from the people who had put in six, hard months planting, cultivating, harvesting, and collecting the grain. The Vietcong extortion (called rice taxation) not only drove up the price of rice but, for many poor peasants, dangerously narrowed the margin between survival and starvation, a fact that did not seem to dissuade the guerrillas at all.

Beginning with the autumn rice crop of 1965, the Marines in the Danang and Chu Lai areas moved to free the peasants from the Vietcong rice tax collector. Using intelligence supplied by the villagers themselves, they launched attacks against Vietcong units massing to commence their rice-collecting operations. The Marines also deployed into the fields to protect the harvesters and then helped transport the rice to central storage areas.

The formula, called Golden Fleece, was a success, assembling in the first harvest season some 870,000 pounds of rice for local use that in other years would have been vulnerable to Vietcong seizure. Put in other terms, the

Marines' offensive actions disrupted Vietcong units and, in addition, kept sufficient rice out of the enemy's hands to supply an estimated thirty-fve hundred guerrillas for an entire growing season. Subsistence, always a serious problem for the Vietcong, became a crisis.

Another step in winning the battle among the people was to prepare the individual Marine for the contacts he would have with the local residents as he moved about in the densely populated areas. We set about it in a methodical manner, developing a *Unit Leaders Personal Response Handbook.* The idea began back in Exercise Silver Lance at Camp Pendleton in early 1965. Its principal architects were three chaplains—John Craven of my staff, Robert Mole, and Richard McGonigle. Craven persuaded me, in preparing for Silver Lance, that we would never be effective in counterinsurgency unless our troops had not only an understanding of, but a respect for, the local people, their habits, and customs. The idea grew slowly, as both commanders and troops had to be convinced of its importance. The *Handbook* took a practical, case-example approach, explaining to Marines the simple rights and wrongs of dealing with the shy and sensitive Vietnamese people. It became a standard weapon in our arsenal to deal with the complex problem.

The final prong of the Marines' multipronged strategy was to confront enemy units whenever they could be located. The first such large operation, Starlite in late 1965, was marked by two noteworthy characteristics. First, it was based on good intelligence. Intercepted Vietcong communications plus the report of a Vietcong deserter pinpointed an enemy regiment. There was little doubt what the target was or where it was, which was often not the case as the war wore on. Second, Starlite was conducted under conditions of complete secrecy. It was one of the few large operations planned and launched without the knowledge of the Vietnamese Army. Because of these two factors, the enemy force, holed up on the Batangan Peninsula, twelve miles south of the Marine Chu Lai enclave, was taken by surprise.

The Marine approach to the battle—their planning, tactics, and task organization exhibited the very best of their combatant stock in trade. Once the intelligence was in hand they did not hesitate. Stripping the defenses of the Chu Lai base and securing the permission of commander-in-chief, Pacific, to use a carrier-based Marine battalion from the U.S. 7th Fleet, they planned in two furious days a combined amphibious and helicopter-borne operation. Heavily supported by Marine fighter and attack aircraft from Danang, as well as by naval gunfire from three ships of the 7th Fleet and by Marine heavy artillery at Chu Lai, the Marine force struck the 1st Vietcong Regiment from three sides. In two days of bitter hedgerow and bunker fighting, the Marines killed 614 of the enemy, rendering the 1st VC Regiment ineffective for six months.

The successful operation showed the power and flexibility that fixed wing and helicopter air support gives to well-trained ground forces. Indeed, a major factor in the procession of Marine ground operations which followed against the growing North Vietnamese strength, from Quang Ngai province in central South Vietnam to the Demilitarized Zone, was the immense power of the

Marine aviation component and the extraordinary tactical momentum and flexibility with which it endowed our ground operations. Nobody else in Vietnam had it, and it was the justified envy of others.

The great combatant quality that marine aviation brought to Vietnam was adaptability. They came—fixed-wing and helicopters—prepared to cope with the demands of the operational environment and thus enjoyed a great advantage over other aviation formations. Apart from the professionalism of pilots and crews, they were truly organized and equipped as expeditionary forces. Their ability to supply and maintain themselves in the field and their expeditionary hardware—bulk fuel systems, mobile arresting gear, air-transportable airfield operations systems, and unique aluminum planking "Short Airfield for Tactical Support" (SATS)—all gave marine aviation formations an enviable flexibility.

SATS was not taken seriously by anyone but the Marines until it was decided that a second field was needed to supplement the overworked field at Danang. At a meeting in Honolulu in late April 1966, attended by the secretary of state, the secretary of defense, the U.S. ambassador to Vietnam, and the principal military commanders, we discussed how long it would take to build a field at Chu Lai, some fifty-five miles south of Danang. The conservative figure for a reinforced concrete installation was eleven months. I stated that the Marines already had the ability to construct an articulated aluminum runway and taxiway in far less time and that we already had the material available in the Far East.

The secretary of defense, Robert McNamara, had heard of the aluminum field concept but was not acquainted with its characteristics. He asked questions concerning its components and design and then asked how long it would take to build such a field at Chu Lai. In Marine Corps Schools problems in Quantico we had been talking of building a three thousand-foot strip and essential taxiways in five days. In this case we were considering an eight thousand-foot installation, so I said twenty-five days, thinking that would give us an adequate cushion. McNamara said, "Go ahead. Keep me informed of how you are doing." A few minutes later, Admiral Sharp (CINCPAC) said to me, "You know your neck is out a mile." Which turned out to be true.

Problems with tropical summer heat, where tractor operators could work only in thirty minute shifts; equipment breakdowns caused by the fine sand; and difficulty in stabilizing the sand sub-grade ate up the days all too quickly. Even so, on the twenty-fifth day, we had a four thousand foot strip from which four 1st Marine Aircraft Wing planes were able to fly eight bombing sorties before sundown. I asked Admiral Sharp to send a message to the secretary of defense, "Chu Lai Expeditionary Airfield operational this date." A few days later I received a longhand note from McNamara, "Brute: I thought you were dreaming. Nice going."

Well and good. The real significance of this small incident, however, is that it illustrates that the air Marine, like his ground counterpart, had been thinking in terms of the realities of combat, even in times of peace.

All together, the first Marines in Vietnam created an innovative strategy that was well attuned to the problems. It recognized that the people themselves were both the battlefield and the objective and that the usual tactical objectives—hills, bridges, rivers—meant little and the usual battlefield statistics—enemy killed and wounded—meant even less.

Between 1962 and 1968, I went to Vietnam fifty-four times for periods of five to twenty days. I saw a lot of the country, from the DMZ in the north to the Ca Mau Peninsula in the south. And I saw a lot of the people, from French-speaking dilettantes in Saigon to Moslems at Phan Rang on the seacoast to Montagnards in the hills near the Laos border. As far back as 1963, I went on operations with the Vietnamese Army and the Vietnamese Marines and saw how easily sizable enemy forces could melt into a countryside willing to support, or at least to tolerate, them. Everything I saw kept bringing me back to the basic proposition that the war could only be won when the people were protected. If the people were for you, you would triumph in the end. If they were against you, the war would bleed you dry and you would be defeated.

Sound and logical as it appeared, the Marines' strategy had two defects: General Westmoreland did not agree with it; and it was unable to address the reality that the enemy enjoyed a privileged sanctuary in the ports of North Vietnam and in Laos, through which a growing cascade of deadly munitions was flowing.

A CONFLICT OF STRATEGIES

In June 1966 the Marines' multiple approach, hardly begun, was altered by a new philosophy announced by General Westmoreland. His strategy was to turn over the liberation and protection of the heavily populated coastal regions to the Vietnamese and to launch American units into the hinterland to seek out and destroy the larger enemy forces. As he described it later, he proposed to ". . . forget about the enclaves and take the war to the enemy."

General Westmoreland knew that the North Vietnamese regular units were moving southward down the Ho Chi Minh Trail in growing numbers. They were carrying increasingly sophisticated equipment through Laos, a privileged sanctuary, and then into the central provinces of South Vietnam. He had a reasonable apprehension that their purpose was to drive to the seacoast and cut the country in two. His thinking, generally shared in Washington, was that under these circumstances the North Vietnamese regular forces, with their Soviet artillery, rockets, and mortars, were too much for the Vietnamese Army. The correct action, as they saw it, was to send large U.S. units into the backcountry to face the North Vietnamese formations—in other words, to pit our manpower against theirs. Wiping out the guerrillas and giving the people day-to-day protection would be left to the Vietnamese military, who really had little stomach for the task.

This approach worried a lot of people. Marine Commandant General Wallace M. Greene, for example, believed that the concept was defective in its "failure to make the population secure." Much later, an American observer illuminated the weakness of Westmoreland's strategy: "Force without reform, finally fails."

It became plain that the United States faced a problem that had three distinct parts: one part concerned the geography of the country; another the movement of material on the enemy's side; and, the third, the political implications of any move to deal with the first two elements. Geographically, it was significant that 80 percent of the people in South Vietnam lived in 10 percent of the country, within a few miles of the seacoast. These heavily populated areas—as many as one thousand persons per square mile—are where the rice, salt, and fish are. Indeed, fully 70 percent of the people outside the cities were involved in raising rice. Rice culture requires land and whoever could guarantee the peasants their land—the Vietnamese government, the Vietcong, or the North Vietnamese—would have their loyalty. Vietnamese President Ngo Dinh Diem, who had been assassinated in 1963, had recognized this fact and had instituted a policy of modest land redistribution to put more of the countryside in the hands of the peasants. By the early 1960s, however, it was less a matter of ownership than of protection, and the Vietnamese Army was not enthusiastic about providing the protection the people required.

Outside the rich coastal plain, South Vietnam is generally unproductive, especially in the heavily forested, inhospitable western half, where mountains rise to altitudes of seven thousand feet. There the population is only two people per square mile, and the mountain tribesmen want nothing more than to be left alone. They had little loyalty to the Vietnamese government and no loyalty whatever to the Vietcong or North Vietnamese. Any North Vietnamese forces based in these mountains would either have to be provided food from outside South Vietnam or they would have to come down to the coastal lowlands and take their food away from the rice-growing peasants—or require the Vietcong guerrillas to take it for them.

The North Vietnamese units had to bring all combat material with them—weapons, gasoline, ammunition, medical supplies—from North Vietnam, perhaps four hundred miles. But, beyond that, the critical hardware of war—artillery, antiaircraft mortars, rockets, radios, transport—had to come from sources outside North Vietnam, a little from Red China by rail, but primarily in ships from the Soviet Union and Bloc countries. The North Vietnamese could not produce sophisticated arms themselves.

If these indispensable warlike things could be prevented from entering North Vietnam, then their fighting forces in the south would soon begin to suffer. The only way to stifle the importation of weapons, however, was to bomb and mine the North Vietnamese ports and to destroy their key airfields. Of course, such action was not without risk. It could introduce a political problem—the possible effect on relations with the Soviet Union of overt American military operations against the North Vietnam ports and logistic centers where Soviet ships or aircraft might be found.

Our national policy assumed that all-out American air and sea operations against the North Vietnam ports, airfields, and transportation systems would risk galvanizing the Russians—and perhaps the Chinese, too—into participation in the conflict. The flow of sophisticated material, so the rationale went, must therefore be dealt with primarily in South Vietnam, with a limited and carefully controlled aerial counterpoint against communication routes in North Vietnam. The ports, harbors, and docks would be left untouched. It was also decided that Americans would take the lead in the ground campaign against the large North Vietnamese units, with the South Vietnamese assigned the role of destroying the guerrillas and providing local security.

As a consequence of this fundamental decision, the Marines were urged in 1965–66 to launch out from their enclaves, to seek out and bring to battle the North Vietnamese regular units that were moving into the northern provinces of South Vietnam in growing strength. Implicitly, because of our limited personnel strength, this so-called search and destroy concept would have to take priority over the spreading ink blot of pactfication and stabilization.

This represented a divergence in strategic concept, and it was not just between the Marines and General Westmoreland's Military Advisory Command (MACV). Others—General Maxwell Taylor and General James Gavin, for example—had expressed views similar to those held by the Marines. Their idea was to take advantage of a base on the seacoast, exploit our supporting arms, and bring peace and security to an ever-growing number of people—the spreading ink blot. Marine Commandant Green summarized this philosophy, clearly pointing out that "I Corps is ideally situated geographically to undertake security operations from the sea against key points on the coast."

The Marines' view of how to fight the war, shared by everyone from General Greene on down, could be articulated in three convergent declarations:

> (1) Put the primary emphasis on pacifying the highly populated South Vietnamese coastal plain. In conjunction with South Vietnamese forces, protect the people from the guerrillas so that they will not be forced to provide the enemy with rice, intelligence, and sanctuary. Expand the pacified areas as rapidly as possible, but only as fast as they are secure, tranquil, and effectively policed by Vietnamese military and paramilitary forces.
>
> (2) Degrade the North Vietnamese ability to fight by cutting off their military substance before it ever leaves the North Vietnam ports of entry.
>
> (3) In coordination with South Vietnamese forces, move out of our protected and sanitized areas when a clear opportunity exists to engage the V.C. Main Force or North Vietnamese units on terms favorable to ourselves.

The MACV concept would make the third point the primary undertaking, even while deemphasizing the need for clearly favorable conditions before engaging the enemy. General Westmoreland was determined to pursue the enemy relentlessly, bring him to battle and destroy him, a unit at a time. He placed constant urging on the Marine commander, Lieutenant General Lewis Walt, to "get out of the enclaves" and go after the enemy in the hinterland. Furthermore, there was little pressure—and I could never understand why—to organize a campaign to stop the flow of supplies through the port of Haiphong.

The Marines saw the MACV idea as flawed. It would leave the population and the wealth of the land largely uncovered, it would engage the enemy in the hinterland where circumstances favored him, and it would generate very large U.S. manpower requirements. And something else—the Americans' conduct of search and destroy operations would be hampered by the fact that more often than not the enemy would know in advance what we were going to do. This was exhibited to be true time and again. Almost all of the American ground operations were known to the Vietnamese Army, at least in some degree, before being launched. Because North Vietnamese or Vietcong agents had infiltrated the Vietnamese Army, there was always a possibility that the enemy would be forewarned. This was certainly true of Vietnamese Army operations, many of which were obviously compromised.

I saw what was happening as waste of American lives, promising a protracted strength-sapping battle with small likelihood of a successful outcome. I made my views known to General Westmoreland, but, for reasons of his own, he did not concur. So I did what I could. I put my convictions on paper in a seventeen-page strategic appraisal of the situation in Vietnam and set about getting it to people who could take some effective action.

The appraisal began by condemning the current strategy, characterizing it as aiming to do no more than "attrit the enemy to a degree which makes him incapable of prosecuting the war, or unwilling to pay the cost of so doing. . . . If this is indeed the basis for our strategy it has to be regarded as inadequate. . . ."

The study continued with an evaluation of the critical importance of loyalty and support of the people, ". . . it is these simple, provincial people who are the battlefield on which the war must be fought. Their provincialism is exploited by the V.C. at every turn. Not enough is being done to give the people a feel for a strong central government." I wrote, "A key point is this: the conflict between the North Vietnamese/hard core Vietcong, on the one hand, and the U.S. on the other, could move to another planet today and we would not have won the war. On the other hand, if the subversion and guerrilla efforts were to disappear, the war would soon collapse, as the enemy would be denied food, sanctuary and intelligence."

I also included some sobering statistics on attrition. Calculating it at the then-current rate, about 2.5 enemy killed for one American, it would "cost something like 175,000 lives to reduce the enemy manpower pool by a modest 20 percent." An altogether unacceptable prospect, yet it fit North Vietnamese General Nguyen Giap's own prediction, "It will be . . . a protracted war of attrition." And war of attrition it turned out to be. At its end, in 1972, we had managed to reduce the enemy manpower pool by perhaps 25 percent at a cost of over 220,000 U.S. and South Vietnamese dead. Of these, 59,000 were Americans; 59,000 coffins over which American families grieved without knowing exactly how or why it happened.

The study concluded with four recommendations:

- "Shift the thrust of our effort to the task of delivering the people from guerrilla oppression, and to protecting them thereafter; meanwhile seeking out and attacking the main force elements when the odds can be made overwhelmingly in our favor."
- "Address our attritional efforts primarily to the source of North Vietnamese material introduction, fabrication and distribution;—destroy the port areas, mine the ports, destroy the rail lines, destroy power, fuel and heavy industry. . . ."
- "Put the full weight of our effort into bringing all applicable resources—U.S. and Vietnamese—into the pacification process. . . . Increase the level of medical assistance. . . . Increase the level of Popular Forces training. . . . Direct the conduct of comprehensive military civic action programs."
- "Press the Vietnamese Government to move immediately into a major land reform program. . . ."

I took the completed appraisal to Admiral Sharp, commander-in-chief, Pacific. He liked it, and I asked his permission to pass it on to Marine Commandant Greene in Washington. General Greene liked it, too, and encouraged me to show it to Defense Secretary McNamara, with whom I had had extensive contact during the 1962-64 period, when I served in the Joint Staff as the focal point for the military counterinsurgency effort.[6] My relationship with McNamara had been good, and he saw me immediately. I gave him the study and explained its content in detail.

McNamara made only brief comment. He rationalized his own alternative of a slowly intensifying air campaign, "the tightening screw," he called it, designed to persuade the North Vietnamese that they could not win. He suggested, "Why don't you talk to Governor Harriman?" Averill Harriman, then serving as assistant secretary of state for Far Eastern Affairs, agreed to see me. We had lunch at his Georgetown house, just the two of us.

Over the soup, I spoke of the ineffectiveness of the air campaign as it was being waged and of the impressive quantities of artillery, rockets, mortars, and anti-aircraft guns pouring down the Ho Chi Minh Trail. Finally I got to the explicit proposal for action—"destroy the port areas, mine the ports, destroy the rail lines, destroy power, fuel and heavy industry." At that point Harriman stopped me. His forehead wrinkled, his heavy eyebrows bristled. Waving his soup spoon in my direction, he demanded, "Do you want a war with the Soviet Union or the Chinese?" I replied that I did not, that I was sure the Russians were not about to start a war with the United States over a fight in Indochina and that if put to the test, the North Vietnamese would probably prefer having Americans in their country to Chinese, whom they hate.

Harriman shook his head; he did not agree. Mining the harbor at Haiphong, he said, would probably bring on hostilities with the Soviets. Conversation flagged and the luncheon moved quickly to a cool conclusion. It was plain he had little enthusiasm for attacking the ports and logistic bases in North Vietnam, and I winced when I thought about the kind of advice he was giving President Johnson and Secretary of State Rusk.

I have not recited this incident of the strategic estimate to illuminate any prescience on my own part or even on the part of Commandant Greene, General Walt, or the many other Marines who believed as I did. Rather, my purpose is to bring to the surface two qualities that the Marines have always possessed in abundance, two indispensable qualities that our government failed to exhibit in the Vietnam crisis: courage and flexibility. As Governor Harriman made clear—and as our subsequent national conduct verified—we did not have the Washington-level courage to take the war directly to the North Vietnamese ports where every weapon, every bullet, truck, and gallon of fuel that was prevented from entering the country would ultimately contribute to the success of our arms and the preservation of our lives in South Vietnam. I believed then, and still do, that mining Haiphong harbor would have generated Soviet protests but that they would have done nothing more—and the indispensable pipeline to North Vietnam would have been interrupted.

For the next five years nothing happened to alter this appraisal. Until that moment in 1972 when President Nixon ordered the mining of Haiphong harbor and intensified attacks on logistic installations—by which time it was far too late—we were fighting the war the wrong way. A sort of one-sided Marquis of Queensberry situation prevailed, where we voluntarily focused our operations on the geography called South Vietnam while the enemy was free to use neutral Laos, the 17th Parallel Demilitarized Zone, and the material support of their Soviet and Chinese allies. Despite our aerial interdiction of communication routes, four thousand artillery pieces, twenty-five thousand heavy rockets, eight thousand anti-aircraft guns, six thousand trucks; a hundred tanks—these and the other sinews of modern war were able to find their way into North Vietnam and into battle in South Vietnam, and their effect was decisive.

The Marines never gave up on their multipronged concept for victory. To the very end, and within the limits of the forces available, they strove to protect and emancipate the people. They never ceased pleading for decisive action against the North Vietnam port and logistic system. And they went into the hinterland after the large enemy units—far more than they really wanted to—but in response to the strong pressures from MACV Headquarters.

This last challenge greatly drained the Marines, as it did the other U.S. and South Vietnamese forces. As Soviet supplies and equipment continued to flow into the ports of Haiphong and Vinh, the North Vietnamese units became more effective and more formidable. More of their operating forces could be supported in the South,[7] which, in turn, generated a demand for even greater numbers of U.S. troops to pursue General Westmoreland's search-and-destroy strategy. Those battles were fought too often on the enemy's terms, where close-quarters combat in the fog-shrouded hills, forests, and vine-thick jungles, with which he was familiar, stretched our logistic system and diminished the effectiveness of U.S. supporting arms, particularly air. Although we claimed a statistical victory in almost every battle, by our own calculations we were killing only about two and a half North Vietnamese for each U.S. fighting man who lost his life. Under those terms the attritional battle had to be more costly than we could prudently endure. Obviously we had become involved in a self-punishing, self-defeating cycle brought on by a faulty attritional strategy. Thus, our self-declared victories in the search-and-destroy operations were not relevant to the total outcome of the war. Things were bad and bound to get worse unless our strategy was altered.

On one of my visits to Washington immediately after a Vietnam trip in mid-1966, the commandant arranged for me to see President Johnson. His first question was, "What is it going to take to win?"

I spoke of the need for improvements in the quality of the South Vietnamese government and for acceleration in the training of South Vietnamese forces. But, most of all, I told him we faced a self-defeating attritional cycle involving engagement with large and increasingly sophisticated North Vietnamese units. We had to stop the flow of war materials to those forces. The president asked if I were implying that the air campaign against communication routes in North Vietnam was ineffective, noting that it amounted to as many as four hundred to five hundred sorties a day. That was what I meant, I said, that for the most part we were attacking the wrong targets. I told him that the only real answer was to stop the supplies, not when they were dispersed in the North Vietnam road system or when they got to the Ho Chi Minh Trail in Laos, but before they ever crossed the dock in Haiphong. Then I voiced the critical words, urging that we "mine the ports, destroy the Haiphong dock area."

That was it. As soon as he heard me speak of mining and unrestrained bombing of the ports, Mr. Johnson got to his feet, put his arm around my shoulder, and propelled me firmly toward the door. It was plain to me then that the Washington civilian leadership was taking counsel with its fears. They were willing to spend $30 billion a year on the Vietnam enterprise but they were unwilling to accept the timeless philosophy of John Paul Jones: "It seems to be a truth, inflexible and inexorable, that he who will not risk cannot win."

That was the last time I saw Mr. Johnson. A month or so later I read a speech that he made to the Tennessee legislature. He described our strategy, among other things, as aiming "to limit the flow or substantially increase the cost of infiltrating men and supplies into South Vietnam." Here, I realized, was a losing strategy.

Under the considerable pressure from MACV Headquarters, and at the expense of their efforts among the people, the Marines gave a good account of themselves in bringing to battle the Vietcong Main Force units and the North Vietnamese formations which, by mid-1966 were appearing in regimental and even division size. There was a general sentiment, however, in both Saigon and in Washington, that the Marines were wedded to their enclaves. The common talk was that they were absorbed in caring for the people and in training the native militia, and preferred to leave the unhappy task of going after the large enemy units to others.

Twice during the summer of 1966, by Defense Secretary McNamara in May and by Navy Secretary Nitze in July, I was questioned directly as to why the Marines were not doing their share in meeting and defeating the major North Vietnamese forces. I responded to them both in writing, in the hope that what the Marines were trying to do would percolate into the Washington sensibility. To McNamara I said,

> In the past there seems to have been some question as to the matter of the intensity [of the Marine operations against the large units] although I am hard put to perceive why. Last year they conducted 88 air/ground team operations of battalion and larger size, aggregating 301 battalion days of operation. Every one involved helicopter envelopment and 14 of them involved an amphibious attack too. They were calculated to strike the enemy where the likelihood of doing him substantial hurt was great, not just to trade manpower with him. . . . The Marines are not just addressing one part of the problem, they are covering all the bases. They are not bemused with handing out soap or bushwhacking guerrillas at the expense of attacking the Main Force units. They are treating the whole patient.

To Nitze I said,

> The Marines, comprising 21 percent of U.S. and Free World ground forces troops in Vietnam have, since 1 January 1966, participated in 39 percent of all U.S. battalion or larger operations, in 35 percent of all major operations and have been responsible for 28 percent of the total enemy killed in those operations. So, in the precise area where Marines are sometimes alleged not to be carrying their share, they have exceeded the contribution which might have been expected of them.

Although the pursuit of large enemy formations was not the Marines' preferred formula for winning, they continued to seek them out and attack them with skill and aggressiveness throughout the 10,000 square miles of their tactical zone. Their air/ground team performed effectively and certainly visited destruction and confusion on the enemy. But, victories notwithstanding, we were pitting American bodies against North Vietnamese bodies in a backcountry war of attrition, while the enemy was free to make political speeches in the hamlets and villages of the populous coastal littoral.

Some false comfort was taken in the statistics deriving from the air campaign in North Vietnam. Reported destroyed in 1966 were the following: eighty-two hundred buildings; forty-eight hundred motor vehicles; eighteen hundred railroad cars; eighty-nine hundred boats and barges; and twenty-two bridges. The impressive statistics lost their impact when measured against what was actually going on in South Vietnam. There, as everyone had to agree, more and more North Vietnamese units were turning up, equipped with more, bigger, and better weapons.

The truth was that, even at considerable hazard to their lives, our pilots were not allowed to attack the targets that really counted. General William W. Momyer, commander of the 7th Air Force, put it bluntly in 1966: "Our air operations are nowhere near enough. With the current limitations on targets North Vietnamese air defense will become more effective and our losses will grow." And, in January 1967, I told Defense Secretary McNamara that what was needed was "constant bombardment from the sea of every sensitive point on the enemy communications, transportation and air defense system within naval gun range; greatly increased . . . aerial destruction of North Vietnamese transportation, military logistic support and power resources."

However valiant, however skillful were the Army and Marine operations against the large formations, however impressive were the tonnages of bombs dropped on North Vietnamese communication systems or on the Ho Chi Minh Trail, it was plain that the strategy was futile—analogous to pushing a wet noodle. In the end, in terms of doing what we came to Vietnam to do, the costly, blood-sapping, grinding battles were blows in the air.

The worst of them all was Khe Sanh. There, the Marine air/ground team, with much help from the Air Force and the Navy's 7th Fleet, caused as many as ten thousand enemy casualties[8] and destroyed large quantities of enemy material. But when it was over nothing had changed—nothing.

Notes

[1]Commander, U.S. Military Advisory Command, Vietnam," commanded, since 1962, by General William C. Westmoreland, U.S. Army.

[2]The Vietnamese hamlet is the equivalent of our small village. Their village equates to our township, their district to our county, and their province to our state.

[3]Le My, and its hundreds of successors, was quite different from President Ngo Dinh Diem's Strategic Hamlet program of 1962. In that program, a fortified hamlet was created in a Vietcong-dominated area. People were moved into it without regard for their personal wishes and were required to stay there except for organized and protected trips to and from the fields. They did not like it and it failed.

[4]The title, initially the "Joint Action Company," was changed from "Joint" to "Combined" to signify that the forces of more than one nation were involved.

[5]Marine Corps experience in stabilizing governments and combatting guerrilla forces was distilled in lecture form at the Marine Corps Schools in Quantico, Virginia, beginning in 1920. Eventually, the lectures were compiled in a book, *Small Wars Manual, 1930,* which after revision, was adopted as an official publication in 1940—a fifteen-chapter compendium of everything the Corps had learned in its Caribbean experience. Although now largely outdated because of advanced technology, *Small Wars Manual,* like similar prospective writings in

the amphibious and helicopter fields, shows the Marines' determination always to record what they have learned and, just incidentally, to make it available to all who want to use it.

[6]My title was "special assistant for counterinsurgency and special activities." The "special activities" part meant anything that the JCS chairman, the secretary of defense, or, on occasion, the president, wanted me to do.

[7]During the first six months of 1966 at least 50,000 additional North Vietnamese were deployed in the South.

[8]As estimated in Joint Chiefs of Staff Fact Sheet on Khe Sanh, 26 April 1968.

CHAPTER TWENTY-FOUR

HIGH-LOW

ADMIRAL ELMO R. ZUMWALT, JR., U.S. NAVY (RETIRED)

FOCUS QUESTIONS

1. How did the Vietnam War shape Zumwalt's perception of the state of the Navy and its future development?
2. What personnel policies did Zumwalt implement, and why?
3. What was Zumwalt's thinking behind the ships that he proposed in Project 60 and High-Low?
4. To what or whom did Zumwalt point to for the failure of High-Low? How might Zumwalt himself have been responsible for his plan's demise?

The accelerating obsolescence of the U. S. Navy since the end of World War II as opposed to the impressive growth and modernization of the Soviet Navy during the same period was a contrast I emphasized and dwelt upon in the long interview I had with Secretary of the Navy John Chafee in 1970 when he was searching for a new CNO. Since he chose me I assume he agreed with what I said then on that subject, and I shall summarize it here. I said that, given the Nixon administration's determination to reduce military budgets, the only way I could see for the Navy to free funds for developing up-to-date ships and weapon systems that could cope with the new Russian armaments was to retire immediately large numbers of old ships and aircraft. That meant that the price the nation would have to pay for sufficient and appropriate naval capability in the 1980s would be a seriously reduced naval capability during at least the early Seventies, while the new systems were being designed, built, and deployed.

I said that this was true of both general-purpose (conventional) forces and strategic (nuclear-missile) forces. In the former case, some of our carriers and their escorts had seen service in World War II; in the latter case, the oldest Polaris-Poseidon submarines would, by 1980, reach the end of the 20-year life for which they had been built. I said that three sets of delicate decisions would have to be made. One was how far to reduce current capability so as to get the most money possible for modernization without becoming so weak as to tempt the Soviets into rash action. A second was how to bring the Navy into balance by supplementing the high-performance ships it was building in small numbers, because they were so expensive that small numbers were all it could afford, with new types of ships that had adequate capability for many missions and at the same time were inexpensive enough to build in the larger number required for an American naval presence in many parts of the oceans. The third was how to allocate resources between general-purpose and strategic forces so that the enormously important and enormously expensive strategic forces would neither starve nor consume so much as to reduce conventional capability to a point at which a major conventional threat could be countered only by a threat to escalate to nuclear war.

My colleagues and I made our decisions in those three areas against a background of asymmetrical U. S. and Soviet maritime development, which in turn had resulted from the great dissimilarity of the maritime situations of the two nations. To begin at the beginning, the Soviet Union is a land power in both an economic and a political-military sense, while the United States is, as I like to put it, a "world island" whose every activity is bound up with use of the seas. If it had to, the Soviet Union could feed itself and keep its industry going without ever sending a ship beyond its coastal waters. In addition, all the Soviet Union's most important political relationships, except the one with the United States, are with nations that also are situated on the Eurasian land mass. Russia can protect all her client states or attack all but one of her most likely enemies without going to sea. By contrast, the industry and trade of the United States depend on ocean traffic in both directions and most of her important allies are on the far side of broad oceans as well. The economy of the United States requires that she have a large maritime capability. The political interests and commitments of the United States require that she be capable of having a large military influence overseas. Both of those exigencies, in turn, make a powerful U.S. Navy imperative. Even more to the point, they define the double mission of the U. S. Navy: to keep the seas open for commercial and military traffic of all kinds, which we call "sea control," and to make it possible to apply military power overseas, which we call "projection." In World War II the U. S. Navy was called upon to perform both missions and at the end of that war it was the best balanced, most powerful Navy the world has ever seen. The Soviets on the other hand had virtually no Navy at all; they never had had much of one, and most of it had been destroyed or captured during the fighting.

In the late Forties and early Fifties, when the Cold War and their aspirations to become a world power led the Soviets to begin a naval buildup, they found that having to start from scratch was in one way a great advantage, for it allowed them to "optimize," that is build a Navy to precisely the specifications that would make it most capable of showing strongly against the only likely opponent, the United States. That meant a Navy that could challenge U. S. sea control—for it is obvious that without sea control the projection mission is impossible to carry out. In choosing this as their top priority mission, the Soviets gave themselves a second advantage. Denying sea control to an enemy is a far easier task than maintaining sea control oneself. Denying sea control means cutting lines of communication, which requires fewer ships, less sophisticated equipment and smaller risks than maintaining lines of communication, since a line of communication has to be maintained throughout its length, but can be cut anywhere.

In the war in Southeast Asia, as in the Korean War, the enemy could not dispute U. S. control of the seas and so the Navy's main business became projection: amphibious landings, air strikes, and occasional episodes of naval shore bombardment. Not only did the Navy's share of the budget shrink during those wars because the Army and the Air Force underwent greater attrition of equipment, but under the circumstances the Navy had to put a disproportionate share of the money it did receive into maintaining its capability for projection—its carriers and attack planes, its amphibious vessels, its ships with the weapons for bombardment. Sea-control forces—antisubmarine planes and their carriers and ships suitable for patrol and escort duty—were allowed to obsolesce and, finally, retire without replacement. More damaging yet, work on future sea-control requirements—new types of ships from which planes or helicopters could operate, new techniques for combating submarines, new vessels to escort convoys, new kinds of weapons with which to fight on the surface was postponed for many years. The one exception was nuclear-powered attack submarines, which through Admiral Hyman Rickover's special influence on Capitol Hill, got built in ample numbers.

Internal forces in the Navy had contributed to unbalancing it in the 1960s. I no more intend to suggest that George Anderson, David McDonald, or Tom Moorer, the three aviators who preceded me as CNO, deliberately allowed the surface Navy to deteriorate than I would welcome a suggestion by them that I deliberately neglected air during my watch. The point is that for the last quarter-century or more there have been three powerful "unions" in the Navy—the aviators, the submariners, and the surface sailors—and their rivalry has played a large part in the way the Navy has been directed. (The submariners have not had a CNO in recent times, but they have had the aforesaid Admiral Rickover, who most of the time is more than a match for most CNOs.)

The intense competition for resources and recognition among the three unions—for there is never enough of either to satisfy everybody, or even satisfy anybody—has had both constructive and destructive consequences. It tends to lead the Navy's civilian masters, who presumably are not parochial, to examine alternatives far more rigorously than they would if there were no push-and-shove. It develops a pride in service that is invaluable not only in combat situations, but as an antidote for the routine hardships of peacetime naval duty. It stimulates professional expertise. On the other hand it almost inevitably breeds a set of mind that tends to skew the work of even the fairest, broadest-gauged commander if he is given enough time. Whichever union such a commander comes from, it is hard for him not to favor fellow members, the men he has worked with most closely, when he constructs a staff or passes out choice assignments. It is hard for him not to think first of the needs of his branch, the needs he feels most deeply, when he works up a budget. It is hard for him not to stress the capability of his arm, for he has tested it himself, when he plans an action. I am not the person to evaluate the extent of my own bias, but I think it fair to point out that following three air CNOs in a row, as I did, I was bound to have some redressing to do. Regular rotation of the top jobs among delegates from the respective unions seems to me to be a prerequisite for institutional stability.

The union system has one other curious side effect. Certain crucial activities are outside the jurisdiction of all the unions and therefore tend not to concern them very deeply. No union has a vested interest in mines, which have no bridges for captains to pace. No union has a vested interest in the increasingly great variety of electronic surveillance instruments that operate independently of ships or planes. All the unions should have a vested interest in secure, high-speed communications but somehow they too have been in no-man's-land. Such adjuncts to fighting, important as they are, receive no automatic institutional protection. Thus, the Navy was far behind the U.S.S.R. and our own Air Force and NASA with regard to use of satellites, computers, and modern communication management techniques. I resolved to do my best to protect the nonunion shops from the indifference of the unions.

A final malady that afflicted—and continues to afflict—the whole Navy, though the surface Navy was and is the greatest sufferer, can be described in one word, a word I have used already: Rickover. By virtue of the force of his personality, his apparent permanence in office, his intimate relations with key members of Congress and his statutory independence of the Navy as Director, Division of Naval Reactors, Energy Research and Development Administration (formerly the Atomic Energy Commission), Admiral Rickover for years had been able to tilt the Navy toward relying exclusively on nuclear propulsion. If nuclear power is not the earthly paradise that "Rick" makes it out to be, it is surely an excellent way to propel warships, chiefly because a nuclear-powered ship can steam at high speed without refueling for ten or 12 years. Thus nuclear power is particularly appropriate in strategic submarines, and advantageous in attack submarines and a limited number of big carriers and their escorts.

However it has a vice that outweighs its virtues in many kinds of vessels. Nuclear-propulsion systems are so big and heavy that making some types of ships nuclear means making them much bigger and hence much more expensive than conventionally powered ships that fight almost as well, as much as five times as expensive in the case of certain types. The sea-control mission, as I have just explained, requires a large number of platforms from which weapons can be fired and planes launched, a large number of ships. In most cases seven or five or even three ships of moderate capability would contribute far more to the success of this mission than one supership, as a series of analyses ordered by Robert McNamara, when he was secretary of defense, decisively demonstrated. For 20 years Rickover has been working successfully toward a supership Navy, and so it is partly his doing that for 20 years the Navy has been getting smaller except of course in the item of nuclear-propelled submarines. Occasionally, someone outside the Navy has made the obvious case for numbers of lower cost ships. One of them during my watch was U. Alexis Johnson, an entirely professional foreign service officer, who at the time was under secretary of state for political affairs. Twenty-seven days after I became CNO Alex wrote a letter to Deputy Secretary of Defense David Packard expressing his concern that the Navy was not adequately addressing the cost-numbers tradeoff in going for fewer large expensive systems rather than large numbers of lower cost systems.

I was no stranger to problems of the kind I had to solve in order to "reoptimize" the U. S. Navy to meet the Soviet threat. As soon as President Nixon announced my appointment, in mid-April 1970, a month before I was relieved as commander, U. S. Naval Forces, Vietnam, I began to create machinery to produce a long-term plan that I hoped would reconcile the dilemmas I had discussed with Secretary Chafee. The first thing I did was to persuade the commander of the Seventh Fleet to lend me Rear Admiral Worth Bagley, then commanding Cruiser-Destroyer Flotilla Seven, to serve as my principal assistant in this project.

I picked Worth for his brains, but it was no accident that I picked a brainy destroyerman rather than a brainy aviator or a brainy submariner. The first imperative as far as I was concerned was for the program to be conceptually ready in the shortest possible time. I had been around Washington long enough to have a clear idea of what was involved in bringing a program from concept to reality through the competitive officeholders in the Department of Defense, through the cheeseparers in the White House budget apparatus, through the political parochialists on four congressional committees and the political opportunists in two houses of Congress—and I had only four years. I named what Worth and I were starting to do "Project 60," to signify my determination to have something to put before John Chafee and Secretary of Defense Mel Laird by the time I had been in office no more than 60 days. Actually there was a lot more to Project 60 than the modernization program that this article deals with. Project 60 was nothing less than a comprehensive plan for my four years as CNO, and included a variety of programs for meeting the two other principal issues the Navy confronted in 1970: how to maintain a high-quality all-volunteer force when the draft expired, which it clearly was about to, and how to maintain sufficient capability during the modernization process for the Navy to continue to perform its assigned missions.

Worth was Project 60's full-time man. From the middle of April to the middle of May, I still had my wartime command responsibilities in Vietnam. Then I took a long trip home, visiting many Navy commands in various parts of the world. The trip made an important contribution to Project 60 because it gave me an opportunity to exchange ideas about it with most of the Navy's top commanders. Worth could not join me in Washington immediately; he was unable to leave his flotilla until August. However another destroyer officer of high intellect was available during the interim period, Captain Stansfield Turner, Secretary Chafee's executive assistant. Stan, a Rhodes Scholar, had just been selected for flag rank, but his new command would not be ready for him until Worth was ready for me, and the secretary graciously relinquished him to me for six weeks or so. Stan, incidentally, got his fourth star not long ago as commander-in-chief of NATO's Southern Forces—CinCSouth. First Stan, then Worth, drew into the work on Project 60 on an ad hoc basis whichever other staff members they needed. I estimate I spent an average of two hours a day on it myself. At the time I also was spending about two hours a day on my new personnel program, about two hours a day on Joint Chiefs' work and about two hours a day making myself known on Capitol Hill. That left the other eight hours of my working day for running the Navy.

There is an inherent difficulty or reluctance of a democracy, absent a crisis, to keep its attention on military possibilities and contingencies. Another of its effects is to preclude the kind of comprehensive planning and optimal use of assets that occur routinely in the Soviet Union. To speak only of the Soviet Navy, its chief, Admiral Sergei G. Gorshkov, has control of land-based long-range aircraft that can attack our naval platforms with bombs and cruise missiles; in lay terms, he has a piece of the Air Force. Every Soviet merchant ship serves as a surveillance and intelligence collection platform for the Soviet Navy. Many Russian merchant ships are configured so as to be readily useful as naval auxiliaries in the event of war. Even in crises short of war, these ships can be promptly diverted from commercial to military activity. Every Soviet fishing vessel, every space support ship, every oceanographic and survey ship contributes to the Soviet naval mission. From time to time over the years the U. S. Navy has tried to persuade the government to acquire similar assets in order to enhance the total power it might bring to bear in a crisis. However, under our system, with the co-equal Congress and its associated lobbies working outside the Defense Department, and with each agency of the executive branch applying parochial pressure on Congress, it has not been possible to achieve the total maritime strength of which this country is capable. But, this field of effort is potentially so fruitful that I decided during our Project 60 evaluation to see what I could do to make available the resources of outside agencies.

We examined the use of Army helicopters on merchant ships and on escorts on the theory that unless the Navy could control the seas, the Army could not be deployed anyway. This effort did not emerge from the bureaucratic jungle. We asked the Air Force to broaden its contingency plans to include the use of its strategic bombers for mining important waters. That was approved in 1971. We asked the Air Force to install our new Harpoon cruise missiles in its bombers so that it could give the Navy long range support of sea lines, similar to the assistance Admiral Gorshkov was getting. This initiative got nowhere.

I personally believed that the Defense Department was making a great mistake by not requiring some, if not all, of the Air Force's tactical air wings to be carrier capable so that the United States could have optimal air power to use in a typical crisis. In three of the four crises during my watch—Jordan, September 1970; Indo-Pakistan, December 1971; Yom Kippur War, October 1973—the U. S. Air Force was totally incapable of playing a role due to lack of access to airfields, and only carrier aviation could be brought to bear. I brought this up personally with General Jack Ryan, chief of staff of the air force. After studying the problem, he declined to take it on. I gave the secretary of the navy a copy of a proposed directive for the secretary of defense to forward to the secretary of the air force and the secretary of the navy on the subject of "employment of Air Force aircraft on carriers," that "died on the field of honor." I then went to Melvin Laird and his deputy David Packard and urged that they get it done. Both of them thought it was a good idea, yet both declined to touch it. Their reason was probably a good one, that the Congress and its lobbies would not permit it, and a jurisdictional wrangle would hurt the Defense budget. On the other hand, General Leonard Chapman, Commandant of the Marine Corps, readily agreed to use Marine aircraft to help augment carrier wings as necessary, recognizing that the Marines must be able "to get there" and had better help the Navy to do so, given our dramatic reduction in power.

We tried using merchant ships for refueling at sea and found they could do it. But we never could get the leverage within the executive branch to get the merchant ships being built in this country properly configured during construction so that they would be most efficient in that role. We examined the feasibility of using commercial container ships for replenishment of ammunition and other logistics in conjunction with a heavy lift helicopter. This proved practicable but no program was approved. We examined the feasibility of giving super tankers the capability to handle vertical-short takeoff or landing (V/STOL) aircraft and antisubmarine helicopters during wartime, together with the necessary shipboard equipment so that they could provide their own fighter, antimissile, and antisubmarine capability. The answer was that it was technically but not politically feasible to bridge the jurisdictional differences between DoD and the Maritime Administration.

As I have said, the underlying theory of that segment of the project dealing with modernization was to accelerate the retirement of obsolete ships in order to free as much money as possible for new development and construction. We then worked out a concept we called "high-low." I first advanced this concept in a November 1962 *Proceedings* article entitled "A Course for Destroyers," in which I had used the terms "the complex mainstream" for certain kinds of destroyers (including frigates) and "the simplified mainstream" for others. Obviously "high" and "low" expressed the idea more clearly. "High" was short for high-performance ships and weapon systems that also were so high-cost that the country could afford to build only a few of them at a time; there are some missions the Navy cannot perform without the great flexibility and versatility of such ships. "Low" was short for moderate-cost, moderate-performance ships and systems that could be turned out in relatively large numbers; they would ensure that the Navy could be in enough places at the same time to get its job done. In sum, an all-high Navy would be so expensive that it would not have enough ships to control the seas. An all-low Navy would not have the capability to meet certain kinds of threats or perform certain kinds of missions. In order to have both enough ships and good enough ships there had to be a mix of high and low.

The innovative part of this program was the low. In contrast with the Soviet Navy, which always has operated on the principle that "better is the enemy of good enough," the U. S. Navy has traditionally insisted on traveling first class. There was more than enough high, more than enough too high, already under construction or under contract when I began Project 60, and almost no low at all. This was true especially in the case of ships. A new group of too sophisticated, too expensive attack submarines, the USS *Los Angeles* (SSN 688) class, was being built at what would soon approach $300 million a copy. I knew something about that submarine because the concept for it had been sprung upon me as a fait accompli when I was director of the Division of Systems Analysis in the late sixties. That was the office where all concepts for new weapon systems were supposed to be worked up first. Somehow Admiral Rickover had gotten the work done elsewhere and without my knowledge. I protested, but my immediate boss, a submariner himself, approved the concept anyway.

Similarly, the Marines were in the process of getting something they had long wanted, a big modern amphibious ship, the LHA, which also was too expensive at $133 million a copy in 1973 dollars, but at least had the virtue that each one could carry as many troops as the several smaller landing vessels it replaced. (We used 1973 dollars in all Project 60's low calculations because the fiscal year 1973 budget would be the first in which low projects were funded.)

The day before I took command, but with my assent, the Navy signed a contract for 30 8,000-ton $100 million 30-knot destroyers of the new *Spruance* (DD-963) class to replace the almost obsolete 2,100- and 2,200-ton World War II destroyers that were still serving as escort vessels for carriers and convoys. At that time the Navy had in operation or under construction only 150 of the 250 escorts its studies showed were needed for the future. The *Spruances* would raise that figure to 180. The genesis of DD-963 is a story of some interest because it typified the Navy's institutional resistance to modest programs. When Paul Nitze was secretary of the navy in the mid-1960s he pushed vigorously for the development of a new class of inexpensive escorts to succeed the

Knox (DE-1052), an escort that would begin to join the fleet in the late Sixties. The DE-1052 had been a breakthrough for advocates of low. It was a modestly equipped single-screw vessel that many sailors of the old school predicted would be unable to keep up with fast carriers, and in any case would forever be under tow because one propeller, one engine, and one boiler were obviously not enough for a warship. These forecasts proved to be almost entirely wrong. DE-1052 was no star, but she performed adequately and since her cost was low, the Navy could afford probably twice as many of her as of a more brilliant performer. It was a ship of this character, with somewhat improved performance, that Nitze wanted as the next class of escorts. However, the admiral he put in charge of the project, together with the engineering duty officers on the development staff, found a host of technical reasons to recommend a larger, more expensive ship. Paul fired that admiral and got a new one to manage the project. The new admiral came up with the same findings. My guess is that both of them thought they were speaking for the CNO. Anyway, three project managers later, when the new escort finally got designed, it was the far too expensive DD-963.

There were two other very high programs under way. One involved nuclear-powered aircraft carriers (CVANs), the most expensive ships there are. The *Nimitz* (CVAN-68) was under construction. The *Dwight D. Eisenhower* (CVAN-69) was being developed; that is, work was going forward on her long-lead-time components, the reactors particularly. The *Carl Vinson* (CVAN-70), was on the drawing board, but no money had yet been authorized. The second program involved DLGNs, nuclear powered guided missile frigates, used to escort the nuclear carriers. A class of five was being planned by Admiral Rickover.

Most of those high ships, SSN-688, LHA, DD-963, CVANs, DLGNs were given. Congress had authorized them and appropriated funds for them and the Navy had signed contracts for them. Moreover there was no question about their quality. The trouble with them was that they were too good in the sense that the Navy had given up too much to get them. They came within the purview of Project 60 only to the limited extent that we could increase or decrease the construction tempo, or the total number of each ship delivered. And that narrow option was narrowed further by the absence from even a drawing board of any low types. We would have to start on low from scratch. That meant that for at least two years, while preliminary design work was proceeding, practically all the Navy's construction money, that which had been provided by my predecessor and that which we hoped to add by early retirement, would of necessity go into the high. Another of Project 60's theoretical underpinnings, to correct as rapidly as possible the tilt toward projection and away from sea control that the Korean and Vietnam wars had produced, dictated how the high money should be spent. We cut back the LHA program (projection) from nine ships to five, as the contract allowed us to, a decision made easier by the cost overruns and construction delays that were occurring at the Litton Shipyard in Pascagoula, Mississippi, where the *Spruance* class also was to be built. Since we wanted to get an inexpensive escort into the fleet as part of our low, we resolved not to expedite DD-963. However, escort vessels are a critical component of sea-control forces, so we resolved not to slow down DD-963 either but simply to proceed with the program as it had been planned. We put DLGN in the same category. We decided we would try to expedite work on the fourth nuclear carrier since for reasons of both obsolescence and operating costs the carrier forces were dwindling fast. As for the SSN 688, like everything in which Rickover has a hand, it had complications leading to ramifications resulting in shenanigans.

Project 60 visualized starting work on four new classes of ships, all of them designed primarily for sea-control duty. Three of them were inexpensive and well within the means of existing technology, and one was a long-range research and development project. The simplest and cheapest was a high-speed 170-ton hydrofoil patrol boat, PHM, armed with a new weapon I shall describe later in this chapter, the Harpoon cruise missile. Its purpose is mainly as a strike vessel against enemy surface craft. It will patrol narrow or coastal waters like the Gulf of Tonkin or the Mediterranean or the Red Sea, or serve as a low-value trailer of high-value Soviet ships in such waters. We found this concept so attractive in Project 60 that we made a decision immediately to deploy two gunboats (PGs) with 3-inch guns to act as interim trailers in the Mediterranean. PHM'S advantage to the Navy is that in those places where it can operate, it will replace on a one-to-one basis much larger ships, with much larger fuel consumption and big payrolls, thus freeing those ships for essential deepwater duties, and more important, making it possible for the larger and more valuable ships to be outside the range of surprise Soviet cruise missile attack.

Second there was the patrol frigate, PF (now FFG-7), another attempt to get that modest escort vessel that Paul Nitze had seen miraculously metamorphosed into DD-963. Like the *Knox* class, the FFG-7 is a single-screw ship of about 28 knots and, at 3,400 tons, about half the tonnage of DD-963, with a somewhat smaller crew, and about half as costly to build. We insisted on a top limit of 50 million 1973 dollars. Yet it is almost as heavily armed as DD-963, since Harpoon is the basic weapon in each and each carries two helicopters. The FFG-7 may have some limitations as an escort for carriers, particularly nuclear carriers. Part of its low cost comes from foregoing some speed and range and part from using certain less sophisticated kinds of sensing and communications equipment. However, it is quite adequate as a patrol vessel or as an escort for convoys of merchantmen or naval auxiliaries and, like the *Knox,* can serve as an escort for carriers in a pinch. The surface union was at first no more enamored of the PF than it had been of the DE-1052. That the program is on track and has turned out so well is a tribute to Vice Admiral Frank Price, the deputy charged with preventing a repetition of the DD-963 growth problem.

The third "low" component, and the one nearest my heart, was an extremely austere carrier we first called the "air capable ship," then the "sea control ship." She was to be a 17,000-ton, 25-knot ship with endurance of 7,500 nautical miles at 20 knots. She was to be capable of carrying 14 helicopters and three Harrier V/STOL planes. She could handle only such aircraft because she would have no launching catapults or arresting gear for landings. Her price was to be 100 million 1973 dollars, about one-eighth the cost of a nuclear carrier. Her principal peacetime purpose was to show the flag in dangerous waters, especially the Mediterranean and the Western Pacific where the Sixth and Seventh Fleets operate, so that the big carriers that are the Navy's most important ships could withdraw from the front lines and deploy out of reach of an enemy first strike, thus putting themselves in a favorable position to respond to such a strike—and therefore to deter it. To use the undoubted vulnerability of carriers to Soviet missiles as an argument for getting rid of carriers, as some Defense critics do, seems to me a classic example of throwing out baby with the bathwater. The solution to the problem is to deploy big carriers out of reach of cruise missiles and replace them with low-value ships that at the same time have some defensive capability, to wit sea control ships.

In a wartime situation the positions of the two kinds of carriers would be reversed: the big, powerful ones would fight their way into the most dangerous waters, destroying opposition beyond cruise missile range with their planes, and the sea control ships would serve in mid-ocean. The Navy's 12 or at best 15 big carriers would be needed in wartime for the large, complicated tasks of conducting air strikes against enemy vessels or shore installations, searching out and destroying submarines over long distances and at high speeds, providing air support for the land battle, interdicting land- or sea-based enemy air and cruise-missile attack against ships and ports. They had far too much offensive capability to waste on convoy duty. Yet in any real war situation there might be at sea as many as 20 convoys of merchantmen, troop transports, and naval auxiliaries in need of air protection from the time they left the reach of land-based air until they entered areas where the deployed carriers were operating. Providing this protection would be the chief wartime mission of the sea control ships. Eight vessels capable of that mid-ocean job could be built for the price of one full-fledged carrier, which in any case, if it was assigned to convoy duty, could protect only one convoy instead of eight. Moreover the SCS would be fast and easy to build because all of her systems—propulsion, weapons, sensing communications—had already been proved out in other vessels and needed minimal modifications. Clearly SCS was a good investment. Unfortunately it was seen as a good investment when it was first proposed by no union but my own. Both the nuclear folk and the aviators saw it as infringing on their turf. Later the aviators got behind it.

Finally, for the future, there was the "surface-effect ship." This would be a 4,000–5,000-ton vessel that could skim just above the surface of the ocean at 80 to 100 knots. Such a ship, which could cross the Atlantic, say, in not much more than a day, virtually immune from underwater or surface attack, could revolutionize naval warfare. At that speed, it need not be equipped with a launching catapult and arresting gear; it could carry four or five carrier planes, even the big F-14s, and turn them virtually into V/STOLs. Thirty-five such ships, a member of my staff once calculated, could carry two divisions of troops to Europe in three days. The ramifications of such capability in anti-submarine, anti-aircraft, and other kinds of warfare are endless. We put the development of this ship—for which the basic propulsion technology already was in existence—in a ten-to-15-year time frame. As of this writing two promising 100-ton prototypes have been built. I have ridden on one. It's quite a thrill.

In addition to these measures for increasing sea-control capability in the future, we hit upon one expedient for increasing it overnight, as it were. This idea, suggested by then Rear Admiral James L. Holloway, III, was to make all carriers, which customarily had been designated either as attack carriers (CVAs) or anti-submarine carriers (CVSs) into dual-purpose vessels. This increased sea-control capability because CVAs outnumbered CVSs by almost two to one. All that this involved was modifying the deck loadings so that each ship carried both attack and anti-submarine planes instead of one or the other, adding some minor command-and-control apparatus and, of course, installing the spare parts and the maintenance equipment that such change in deck loading necessitated. The cost of thus changing a carrier over was $975,000, a sum so miniscule by comparison with what almost anything else in Defense costs nowadays that even Senator William Proxmire might not bother to pick it up if he saw it lying in a Pentagon corridor, but just leave it for the sweepers. Of course, modifying carriers in such a way dissatisfied some people. They pointed out (correctly) that making a carrier capable of two dissimilar missions made it less capable than it had been of either one. They also pointed out (again correctly) that on the record of recent wars and crises a carrier was more likely to be called on for projection than for sea control. However, a 12-carrier Navy with as much water to cover as the U. S. Navy has would simply be incapable of keeping the sea lines of communication open in a major war if those carriers had no sea-control capability, and I thought that was too big a risk to run. Fortunately, the majority of my colleagues, including the most important sachems in the aviators' union, agreed with me.

As might be expected in a Navy that aviators had presided over for a decade, we were in good shape as far as types of planes were concerned. During the latter years of the Southeast Asia war, CVAs had carried two types of modern attack plane, the workhorse A-7, a light, relatively inexpensive machine that performed most strike and ground support missions, and the heavier, costlier A-6, which had similar armament but was built and equipped to operate effectively in bad weather and at night. Both were recent additions to the fleet. Both planes had proved their value in Vietnam. Both, with technical modifications, would be serviceable for another decade at least. The aviation admirals were content with them. There was no reason for me not to be.

On the sea-control side a new antisubmarine plane, the S-3 was about to go into production at Lockheed. It contained up-to-the-minute equipment that enabled it to drop sonar buoys over large areas, monitor the signals of those buoys and fire Mark 46 torpedoes at whatever enemy submarines the buoys—or other localizing sensing devices—find. There was every reason to believe that this plane would be serviceable for many years. The problem it presented was that at $13 million a copy it was not inexpensive, to use a cautious double negative, and Congress was showing some reluctance to buy as many as the Navy needed. The S-3 came into Project 60, therefore, as an action item for the Navy's legislative liaison people.

Somewhat further from production than the S-3, though already contracted out to Grumman, was the plane most of us thought of as the new star of the Navy's air arm, a fighter, the F-14. It was to replace the F-4, which had been designed in 1954 and had proved itself a superb one-on-one machine in fighting MiGs over Vietnam. However, with the massive deployment of cruise missiles by the Soviets, the day of the one-on-one fighter was ending; it was not capable of defending ships against a massive cruise missile attack. The F-14 was. In addition to excellent flight characteristics, it had a new missile system, the Phoenix, able to intercept Russian Foxbat aircraft at altitudes above 80,000 feet. And it had an extraordinary fire-control system that could track 24 targets simultaneously, automatically choose the six most threatening and fire at them simultaneously. Such equipment comes high. The F-14 is a very expensive plane, to use a well-justified double positive, even when you consider that the multiplied capability it gives a carrier makes operating with a reduced number of carriers feasible. The precise price of a single plane is harder to state than that of a ship, since planes are bought by the hundreds rather than by the fives or tens, and the unit price goes down sharply as the size of the buy goes up. However, it is pretty hard to find a way of stating F-14's price that makes it less than $14 million in 1973 dollars, and pretty easy to kind a way of stating it that makes it a lot more.

I had become convinced that the F-14 was the world's best fighter plane long before becoming CNO. In 1966, when I came back to Washington from San Diego (after a year as a new rear admiral in command of Cruiser Destroyer Flotilla Seven) to set up the Navy's Systems Analysis Division, my first assignment from Secretary of the Navy Paul Nitze was to study the cost effectiveness of the F-l l lB plane in comparison with all competition. The reader may recall that there had been quite a controversy in the Pentagon several years earlier when Robert McNamara had ordered that there be as much commonality as possible between the new land-based fighter plane the Air Force needed and the new carrier-based fighter plane the Navy needed. Thus was born the swing-wing plane that first was called the TFX, then the F-111, the Air Force's version being F-111A and the Navy's F-111B. Despite heroic efforts by the secretary of defense and secretary of the navy to make F-111B successful, the compromises that had to be made to develop an airframe capable of performing two different missions led over time to greater and greater weight, and it presently became a close question as to whether the plane could land on and take off from a carrier.

It was while this weight question was still in doubt that Secretary McNamara asked the Navy to examine again the cost effectiveness of the plane, assuming for the purpose of the study that it *could* land on and take off from a carrier. I soon learned that an earlier generation of analysts had done their work well. The fire control and missile system had been brilliantly designed to deal with the Navy's special problem—to crowd into a small airfield at sea a few fighter planes with the capability to search the air surrounding a carrier task force for hundreds of miles and provide a very long range capability to kill many airplanes and cruise missiles coming from several directions simultaneously. The study concluded that if the F-111B could use a carrier, it was by all odds the most cost effective aircraft for fleet air defense and other fighter roles.

However, by the following year it had become almost certain that the F-111B would not be able to use a carrier. Meanwhile, four companies had sent in bids to produce a fighter that put the F-111B's engine, fire control system, and missile in a new airframe. I did another study that showed that this new airplane, subsequently known as F-14A, was probably the way to go. The Navy decided to go that way. By March of 1973, to get ahead of myself, I was able to report to Congress that our calculations showed that when we compare a 13-carrier force carrying 301 F-14s with a 16-carrier force carrying 903 of the old F-4s, we found the smaller force to be militarily more effective; $2.5 billion cheaper in procurement costs; $500 million a year cheaper in operating costs; and requiring 17,000 fewer sailors.

Helicopters are coming into increasing use in naval warfare. They have been used for many years as rescue craft on board carriers, and for some time troop-carrying helicopters have been an important element in the amphibious forces. Project 60 demonstrated that we could achieve high payoff if escort vessels carried one or two helos on their decks to use as aids in detecting incoming aircraft, cruise missiles, and submarines. We had available in inventory over 100 SH-2s, a sort of all-purpose helo that was not highly satisfactory for the new mission, being too light to load with all the equipment the mission calls for, but it was adequate and inexpensive and available, so we decided to adapt the SH-2 for the near term and at the same time begin R&D on a more advanced machine. We called the new helo, together with its embarked detection and kill equipment, LAMPS, for light airborne multi-purpose system, a combination of sensors to find submarines and equipment to fire Mark 46 torpedoes at them. Expediting LAMPS, which was already in the design stage, was one of the high priority items in Project 60. The SH-3, the carrier rescue helo, which is bigger than the SH-2, is the one we planned to put on the sea control ship. The third important component in Project 60 that involved helicopters was to economize on and modernize minesweeping techniques by retiring almost all our surface minesweeping vessels and adapting the big CH-53 helicopters the Marines were using for amphibious operations for minesweeping. In the mid-Sixties, helicopters had successfully demonstrated a modest capability to sweep moored mines and a study had recommended they be used for this task. By 1970, helos had doubled their rates of sweeping mechanical mines and had demonstrated a significant potential to sweep magnetic mines. Our cost analyses showed that shifting the emphasis to helos for minesweeping could achieve significant savings on both operation and maintenance costs. In addition helicopters had the operational advantage over ships of being able to deploy rapidly to any location in the world. Developing the equipment and techniques took time and money, and meant going almost entirely without minesweeping capability for more than two years, which was a pretty big risk. Fortunately we got away with it. The new system was in operation by 1973, when the Navy was called upon to sweep the mines out of Haiphong harbor as part of the Vietnam cease-fire agreement, and the force that did that job proceeded almost immediately thereafter to repeat its performance in the Suez Canal. In these operations the ability of the helicopters to sweep areas much faster than surface ships and with less manpower demonstrated that this concept was a winner.

When it came to weapons, all of us who worked up Project 60 felt strongly that the most urgent task by far was to develop and deploy a proper cruise missile as rapidly as possible, in surface vessels, particularly escorts, first, then as soon thereafter as possible in planes and submarines. To my mind the Navy's dropping in the 1950s of a promising program for a cruise missile called "Regulus" was the single worst decision about weapons it made during my years of service. That decision was based on the theory that our carriers were so effective that we did not need cruise missiles, though I always have suspected that the reluctance of the aviators' union to give up any portion of its jurisdiction played a large part in the decision. In any case, without cruise missiles practically all our long-range offensive capability was crowded onto the decks of a few carriers. Even those pets of Rickover's, the enormously expensive nuclear-propelled guided-missile frigates (DLGNs) remained almost purely defensive ships without cruise missiles. It was another case of numbers being more to the point than quality.

Fortunately, while I was heading the Division of Systems Analysis, the secretary of the navy had in effect rescinded the Regulus decision by directing my office to do a study that would lead to a program for a new cruise missile, Harpoon. The most significant string attached to this order was the verbal message relayed to me through the aide system that the missile was to have a range of no more than 50 miles if it was to be acceptable to the CNO, Admiral Moorer. Evidently the aviators' union was still nervous about its prerogatives. We did the study, it was accepted, and a development program got under way, in the course of which Harpoon's range increased a few miles. However, the program was not proceeding at a rapid enough pace to suit the needs of a Navy that was in the process of divesting itself of much of its other offensive capability. Expediting Harpoon to the maximum extent possible was one of Project 60's most urgent proposals. And to fill the gap until Harpoon became operational, we directed interim programs adapting various surface-to-air missiles into a short range surface role temporarily.

One other weapon whose development we proposed to accelerate was Captor, a rather spooky mine that, when it detects an approaching submarine, releases a Mark 46 torpedo to make a run against it. This was one of the cases of a program proceeding slowly for no other reason than that no union was pushing it; it clearly was a weapon that could be of great importance in fulfilling the mission of denying straits to the Soviets.

Finally, to round out only the most important of Project 60's 52 separate points, there were several kinds of "non-union" electronic systems that badly needed strengthening. These had been heavily on my mind since 1965–66, when I commanded a cruiser-destroyer flotilla in the First Fleet, and took part in four fleet exercises designed to test, among other things, communications, detection, and deception systems. Those exercises showed serious deficiencies in at least four areas where the Soviets were known to be extremely effective. The most important was in battle-condition communications within the fleet. In order to fight a modern battle successfully it is necessary to transmit and receive rapidly and securely—in other words without deciphering or jamming by the enemy—a staggeringly large volume of data about the rapidly changing speeds, courses and ranges of hundreds of ships, planes, and missiles, and about changes in the intentions of our own forces and in the estimated intentions of the enemy. Otherwise ships will not perform the correct maneuvers, planes will not go where they're supposed to, missiles will not hit their targets. Technological development in electronics has been so rapid that it is almost impossible to keep up with. When the World War II battleship *New Jersey* (BB-62) was recommissioned for shore bombardment duty during the Southeast Asia war, it turned out that her communications systems, the finest that could be produced when she was built, were so far out of date that she was virtually out of communication with the fleet. The communications systems in a modern front-line ship are probably a hundred times more effective and complicated—and expensive—than the *New Jersey's* yet they still have a hard time handling the amount of work they are given to do, reliant as they still are on high frequency transmission with manual transmission methodology. We proposed to increase our investment in this critical field by almost three-quarters. It is a large sum if you do not compare it with the cost, say, of one SSN-688-class submarine.

Besides this general problem in communications, a special, particularly difficult one was communicating reliably with submerged submarines. Historically, submarines in naval engagements have operated almost entirely on their own because there was no way to control their activities, minute by minute, and fit them into a battle plan. But of course their effectiveness would be greatly enhanced if such coordination were possible. We wanted to work harder on this problem. A similar, and perhaps even more critical, problem is maintaining communications with strategic submarines without, of course, giving away their positions. The most persuasive criticism made of the effectiveness of the Polaris-Poseidon system is that sometimes it is difficult to stay in touch with the boats and that in a nuclear exchange situation a breakdown in communications would have major consequences indeed. This was an aspect of communications in which there was intense union interest; the reason progress was slow was the inherent difficulty problem.

In sensing and detection, acoustic and electronics, our equipment was quite good, but this is a field in which there always is need for improvement, especially in the electronics field where the Soviets were clearly ahead of us. We needed higher probabilities of detection in order to reduce the losses we would take in wartime from the undetected platforms which would get through. Much of the newest sensing and detection equipment operates out of buoys or satellites or other kinds of devices that no union cares much about, so it always is necessary for top management to take special care that work in this area is not neglected. The same can be said about the deception devices designed to frustrate the enemy sensing and detection system, with the addition that this is one of the several places where the Russians are well ahead of us. One of Project 60's most potentially worthwhile innovations was to call for a central office with the responsibility for overseeing and coordinating all electronic warfare and command-and-control projects, instead of leaving them to the mercy of individual project managers as in the past. High-energy laser development was accelerated as a result of Project 60.

I hope it is clear from this perhaps too discursive account of the main features of Project 60 that it had a central theme: to reoptimize the Navy so that it was equipped to meet the specific threats that the Soviet Navy posed. While we had been engaged in Vietnam, the Soviets, driven by the lesson of the Cuban Missile Crisis, had built a force that came close to being able to challenge our control of the seas. They had two-and-a-half times as many attack submarines as we. They had cruise missiles in many of these submarines and in many ships in their rapidly growing surface fleet and in their land-based naval aircraft. They had superior electronics. Meanwhile Korea and Vietnam had tilted the U.S. Navy dangerously away from sea control. Project 60 was an effort to begin to redress the balance. It was completed almost on schedule. I briefed the secretary of defense on it on 10 September, 72 days after I had been sworn in. The secretary of the navy had approved it earlier. Laird appeared to be pleased with it. My own attitude probably is reflected best in some comments I made to the very first meeting of my CNO's Executive Panel on 24 October 1970.

> "I haven't really met my original objective. I had hoped that we could get going very quickly with Project 60 as a pilot effort toward changing direction, and by the end of that period we would have this group [the CEP] up to speed so that we could pass the baton without any significant missteps. As is so often the case we were just not able to get it set up that quickly. The Project 60 effort has been completed, and it expresses some changes of direction, but not as many as I would have liked. However, it represents the best we could do with a reasonable degree of consensus. This was also all we could manage in time to have much impact on this year's budget."
>
> I find myself with a great sense of impatience in that I have been in the job for four months (and that represents 8 percent of my time) and as yet I have only gotten the rudder over about 10 degrees. I am really looking forward to the fruit of this effort. I advised all flag officers in distributing the presentation to them on 16 September 1970 [that] I considered that [it] set forth 'the direction in which we direct the Navy to move in the next few years.' "

CHAPTER TWENTY-FIVE

The 600-Ship Navy

JOHN F. LEHMAN, JR.

FOCUS QUESTIONS

1. According to former Secretary of the Navy John Lehman, what are the three "enduring elements" which post-1945 maritime force planners have had to consider?
2. Why was the 1960s and 1970s "swing strategy" deficient in dealing with the 1980s Soviet maritime threat?
3. How did Lehman see the relationship between American naval strategy and the Navy's force structure?

Clemenceau once declared that war was too important to be left to the generals. But if war is too important to be left to the generals, it is also too important to be left to the civilian experts. In the United States, with our constitutionally mandated civilian control of the armed forces, we forget sometimes that hard-earned military experience must leaven the theories of civilians if our system is to work.

We would do well to keep this in mind as we near our goal of a 600-ship Navy. Media-anointed experts have raised questions about the size, character, and complexity of the Navy: Do we really need so many ships? Are the Navy and Marine Corps effective in helping to deter Soviet aggression—across the full spectrum of violence, from terrorism to nuclear war? Do we have a strategy that guides the planning and training of our forces? Is it the correct strategy? If it is, are we building the right types and numbers of ships to execute it? Finally, can this nation afford to sustain a 600-ship fleet—not only well-equipped but properly manned—for the long term? When defense restrictions become law in the zero-growth 1986 budget, and retrenchment is the theme of the hour, the answers to these questions take on added significance.

WHY 600 SHIPS?

To understand how we arrived at the size of our planned fleet of ships, we must begin by discarding the idea that this number has sprung, full blown, from the brow of some would-be Napoleon of the high seas.

Since World War II, maritime force planners have found themselves at the mercy of three enduring elements. First is geography. Water covers three quarters of the world; and the United States is an "island continent" washed by the Atlantic and Pacific oceans.

Second are the vital interests of the United States, expressed in the web of more than 40 treaty relationships that bind us to mutual defense coalitions around the world. These relationships shape our national security requirements—together with the energy and commercial dependencies that support our economy in peace and in war.

The third element is the Soviet threat. Whatever its original rationale, the Soviet Navy's postwar expansion has created an offense-oriented blue water force, a major element in the Soviet Union's global military reach that supports expanding Soviet influence from Nicaragua to Vietnam to Ethiopia. From the Baltic to the Caribbean to the South China Sea, our ships and men pass within yards of Soviet naval forces every day. But familiarity, in this case, is breeding a well-deserved respect.

The Navy's recently updated *Understanding Soviet Naval Developments* provides the facts about the Soviet Navy. Every American should be aware, for example, that Soviet nuclear submarines operate continuously off our coasts. "Victor"-class nuclear attack submarines are routinely found lurking near many of our principal naval ports. Soviet surface units are now making regular deployments to the contentious and vulnerable chokepoints of the Caribbean Sea and Gulf of Mexico. Worldwide, we find the Soviet Navy astride the vital sea-lanes and navigational chokepoints, through which most of the Western world's international trade must pass.

This is the new reality. The pattern of Soviet naval deployments has revealed itself in only the last several years. These deployments constitute a post-World War II change in the global military balance of power that has been surpassed only by the advent of thermonuclear weapons. No planner, civilian or military, can ignore the growing dimensions of Soviet maritime power.

Geography, alliances, and the Soviet threat combine to dictate the actual numbers of ships—the "size of the Navy"—required to fulfill our commitments in each of our maritime theaters. Before reviewing in detail the forces we need in each theater, some observations are in order:

- Any view of the global disposition of the U.S. Navy reveals that we often deploy in peacetime very much in the same manner as we would operate in wartime. For purposes of deterrence, crisis management, and diplomacy, we must be present in the areas where we would have to fight if war broke out. Of course, the operational tempo is different—a roughly three-to-one ratio in wartime, as compared with peacetime.

  We also train as we intend to fight. A full-scale general war at sea would rarely find a carrier battle group operating alone. So we train often in multiple carrier battle forces in such exercises as FLEETEX, READEX, and NATO exercises, like Northern Wedding, which we conduct in the North Atlantic and the Norwegian Sea.
- Our maritime security depends on significant assistance from allies in executing our missions. Fortunately, we count among our friends all of the world's great navies, save one. Clearly, in areas such as diesel submarines, frigates, coastal patrol craft, minesweepers, and maritime patrol aircraft, allies of the United States have assets absolutely essential to us for sea control in war and peace. In some regions, such as the Eastern Atlantic and the waters surrounding the United Kingdom, our allies supply a significant portion of the antisubmarine capability to counter the Soviet threat. In fact, if we could not count on our allies, we would require a U.S. fleet much larger than 600 ships, to deal with the 1,700 ships and submarines that the Soviets can deploy against us. But the world's greatest navies are on our side, and this gives a tremendous advantage to the U.S. Navy and a significant cost savings to the U.S. taxpayer.
- America's increasing commercial and energy interdependence with Asia, and the growth of the Soviet Pacific Fleet—now the largest of the four Soviet fleets—have negated the so-called "swing strategy" of the Sixties and Seventies, which planned to reinforce the Atlantic Fleet with combatants from the Pacific in time of crisis. Today, the United States has an Asian orientation at least equal to its historic engagement in Europe. Existing treaty relationships in the Pacific have been augmented by growing commercial connections. For example, in 1980, the value of U.S. trade with the Pacific rim nations was roughly equal to trade with the country's Atlantic partners. Four years later, Pacific trade exceeded that with Western Europe by $26 billion.

Similarly, oil dependencies have shifted tremendously in the last five years. This forces America to reconsider the priorities of naval deployments in the Northern Pacific and Caribbean regions. The reorientation of U.S. sources for crude oil—on a hemispheric axis—is a long-term geopolitical reality that has gone largely unnoticed. Western dependency on Middle Eastern oil is still debated at length, for its impact on our military thinking and force planning. But we must also take into account that, in 1985, the United States imported eight times as much oil by sea from the Western Hemisphere as it received from the entire Middle East. Oil from Mexico has increased to almost 25% of our imports, while oil from Saudi Arabia had dropped to only 2.6% of the U.S. import market. We no longer depend primarily on the Middle East and Persian Gulf supply for our vital energy needs. Instead, the locus of our oil trade is in the Western Hemisphere: Alaska, Canada, Mexico, Venezuela, and the Caribbean area.

With these observations as background, let us review our forces in the main geographic areas: the Atlantic, the Mediterranean, the Pacific, and Indian Ocean-Persian Gulf. The numbers used are "notional." They illustrate force packages constructed for peacetime tasks now assigned to our naval forces. But they are capable of expansion or contraction, should war break out—a flexibility characteristic of naval power.

The Atlantic: The large Atlantic theater encompasses the North Atlantic, the Norwegian Sea, the Northern Flank of NATO including the Baltic throat, the South Atlantic, the Caribbean, and the Gulf of Mexico. It includes the coasts of South America and the west coast of Africa, all vital sea-lanes of communications. And it involves the Mediterranean and the Middle East.

The U.S. Navy operates in the Atlantic theater with two fleets, the Sixth and the Second. The Sixth Fleet in the Mediterranean is the principal fighting force of the NATO Southern Europe Command and provides strike, antiair superiority, antisubmarine, and close air support for the entire Southern Flank of NATO—a principal makeweight in the balance in the Central Front.

In addition, the Sixth Fleet is the principal naval force that supports our friends and allies in the Middle East. The threat there is significant. The Soviets maintain a fleet in the Black Sea and a deployed squadron in the Mediterranean. In wartime, we expect to see also Soviet naval strike aircraft, aircraft carriers, a formidable number of diesel and nuclear submarines, and a full range of strike cruisers, destroyers, and other smaller combatants.

To deal with this threat, as we do in all our planning, we start with a base of allied forces in the areas under consideration. The navies of our allies are good. For example, we count on them to provide about 140 diesel submarines, which are effective for coastal and area defense, for establishing and maintaining barriers, and for certain other useful missions.

In wartime, purely U.S. forces in the Sixth Fleet would have to include three or four carrier battle groups, operating to meet NATO commitments. We would also need to deploy a battleship surface action group and two underway replenishment groups. In peacetime, we average over the year one and one-third carrier battle groups deployed in the Mediterranean.

The Second Fleet is the heart of the Atlantic strike fleet for NATO. It is responsible for naval operations in the North Atlantic, the Eastern Atlantic, Iceland, the Norwegian Sea, the defense of Norway, and the entire Northern Flank including the North Sea and Baltic throat. It must simultaneously accomplish any naval missions required in the Caribbean, where we now face a very large Soviet and Cuban naval presence; in the South Atlantic, where we have vital sea-lanes; and along the West African sea-lanes, where the Soviets now deploy naval forces continuously.

For the Second Fleet, in wartime, we must plan to have four or five carrier battle groups, one battleship surface action group, and three underway replenishment groups. This is the equivalent firepower of 40 World War II carriers and can deliver accurate strike ordnance on target equal to 800 B-17s every day. In peacetime, we generally run higher than this, because most of our principal training occurs in the Second Fleet's operating areas.

Today, we have six carrier battle groups cycling in the Second Fleet at one time or another. We have exercises underway with our NATO allies, with our South American and Central American allies, and with other nations, on an ad hoc basis, in every season of the year.

The Pacific: Clearly, our increasing commercial interests and historic security ties in the Pacific impact on our naval planning for the area. If we are to protect our vital interests, we must have forces available to deploy—not only to the Atlantic theaters and the Sixth and the Second fleets—but also to the Pacific simultaneously, to the Seventh and Third fleets in the Middle East Force of the Central Command. We cannot abandon one theater in order to deal with the other. The great paradox of the 1970s was the reduction of the fleet's size so that it could only be employed in a swing strategy—just as that strategy was being rendered obsolete by trade, geopolitics, and the growth of the Soviet Navy.

The Seventh Fleet is our forward Western Pacific fleet, which meets our commitments to Japan, Korea, the Philippines, Australia, New Zealand, and Thailand, and in the critical straits of Southeast Asia, as well as the Indian Ocean. In wartime, we would need to deploy five carrier battle groups to the Seventh Fleet, two battleship surface action groups, and four underway replenishment groups. In peacetime, we average over the year the equivalent of one and one-third carrier battle groups in the Western Pacific. That, of course, helps us maintain a peacetime fleet-wide operational tempo that provides for a least 50% time in home port for our people and their families.

We do not have a separate fleet in the critical area of Southwest Asia, the Indian Ocean, and the Persian Gulf, although some have proposed the re-creation of the Fifth Fleet for that purpose. In peacetime, we have the Middle East Force of the Central Command and elements of the Seventh Fleet, normally a carrier battle group.

In wartime, we plan for two of the Seventh Fleet carrier battle groups to meet our commitments in the Indian Ocean, Southwest Asia, East Africa, the Persian Gulf area, and Southeast Asia. Notionally, a Seventh Fleet battleship surface action group and one underway replenishment group would also be assigned to operate in these areas.

The Third Fleet has responsibility for operations off Alaska, the Bering Sea, the Aleutians, the Eastern Pacific, and the Mid-Pacific region. In wartime, there would be considerable overlapping and trading back and forth between the Seventh and Third fleets. This happened in the Pacific during World War II. To cover that vast area, we must assign two carrier battle groups and one underway replenishment group.

These requirements compel us to deploy a 600-ship Navy as outlined in Table 1. In peacetime, we deploy in the same way to the same places we must control in war, but at one-third the tempo of operations. This allows a bearable peacetime burden of six-month deployment lengths and 50% time in home ports. Looked at either way, we require the same size fleet to meet peacetime deployments as we do to fight a war. Taken together, they add up to the following:

- Fifteen carrier battle groups
- Four battleship surface action groups
- One-hundred attack submarines
- An adequate number of ballistic missile submarines
- Lift for the assault echelons of a Marine amphibious force and a Marine amphibious brigade

When escort, mine warfare, auxiliary, and replenishment units are considered, about 600 ships emerge from this accounting—a force that can be described as prudent, reflecting geographic realities, alliance commitments and dependencies, and the Soviet fleet that threatens them. Unless Congress reduces our commitments or the Soviet threat weakens, there is no way to reduce the required size of the U.S. Fleet and still carry out the missions assigned to the Navy.

TABLE 1 *Current Navy Force Requirements*

	Peacetime Maritime Strategy	*Wartime Maritime Strategy*
	Sixth Fleet	
CVBG	1.3	4
BBSAG	.3	1
URG	1	2
	*Second Fleet**	
CVBG	6.7	4
BBSAG	1.7	1
URG	4	3
	*Seventh Fleet***	
CVBG	2	5
BBSAG	.5	2
URG	1	4

	*Third Fleet**	
CVBG	5	2
BBSAG	1.5	—
URG	4	1

*Includes forces in overhaul
**Includes Indian Ocean Forces
Note: CVBG = carrier battle group; BBSAG = battleship surface action group; URG = underway replenishment group.

DOES THE NAVY HAVE A ROLE IN THE NATIONAL STRATEGY?

While the Carter administration questioned whether the Navy could influence a "short war" in Central Europe, such a proposition is indefensible today. The coalition of free nations bound together in NATO must have maritime superiority as a prerequisite for any defense strategy. Maritime superiority alone may not assure victory but the loss of it will certainly assure defeat—and sooner rather than later. The chronicles of warfare from the classical era forward are a consistent testament to the influence of sea power upon history, in which great continental powers do not long prevail against an opponent with mastery of the seas. Today, continental defense in NATO rests on early achievement of mari-time superiority. The Soviet Union, as evidenced by its ongoing naval expansion, understands the experience of history far better than our trendier military reformists.

DOES THE NAVY HAVE A STRATEGY? IS IT THE RIGHT ONE?

Now, consider the charge leveled by some parlor room Pershings that our current naval buildup lacks an underlying strategy.

Not since the days of Theodore Roosevelt have the Navy and Marine Corps exhibited such a strong consensus on the comprehensive strategy which now forms our naval planning. Briefly stated, our strategic objectives are the following:

- To prevent the seas from becoming a hostile medium of attack against the United States and its allies
- To ensure that we have unimpeded use of our ocean lifelines to our allies, our forward-deployed forces, our energy and mineral resources, and our trading partners
- To be able to project force in support of national security objectives and to support combat ashore, should deterrence fail

To achieve these objectives, we need a strategy at once *global, forward deployed*, and *superior* to our probable opponents. Global, because our interests, allies, and opponents are global; forward deployed, because to protect those interests and allies, and to deter those opponents, we must be where they are; superior, because if deterrence fails it is better to win than lose.

But do we have the correct strategy? Today's debates would benefit from a more precise understanding of the role of strategy. Strategy is not a formula for fighting each ship and deploying each tank in the battles that may take place around the world. That is not the function of the military establishment inside the Washington Beltway. Such is the proper function only of the theater commander who is given the responsibility to carry out the defense objectives set by the national command authorities.

Beyond the central concept of global, forward-deployed, and superior naval forces, strategy's role is to give coherence and direction to the process of allocating money among competing types of ships and aircraft and different accounts for spare parts, missile systems, defense planning, and the training of forces. It provides guidelines to aid us in allocating both resources and shortages.

Title 10 of the U.S. Code charges the Secretary of the Navy with ensuring the highest level of training appropriate to the responsibilities placed upon both the Marine Corps and the Navy. That is what strategy provides to us—a framework within which to train. For example, U.S. naval forces recently conducted a major training exercise, "Ocean Safari 85," with our NATO allies and the U.S. Coast Guard and Air Force. The "Safari" assembled off the East Coast of the United States and fought its way across the Atlantic, moved north of England and east of Iceland, and ended up in the Norwegian Sea. Approximately155 ships and 280 fixed-wing aircraft and helicopters operated for four weeks in this environment, against 19 real Soviet ships and submarines and 96 Soviet aircraft sorties.

That is very effective training, and it is being carried out as part of a coherent training operational plan—linked to the way that the theater commanders intend to fight a war. One will search in vain, however, for a Navy cookbook that tells those on-scene commanders when to move aircraft carriers, or how or where to move attack submarines or Aegis cruisers at any given point after a conflict commences. There should never be any such cookbook and certainly it should never come from Washington. Those who criticize our strategy for being the wrong cookbook or for not having a cookbook do not understand strategy.

Other critics argue that our Navy should be less global, less forward-deployed, or less superior, with the resources saved to be poured into a stronger continental defense. To be less global means to abandon some area of our vital interests. To believe that in the case of the Northern Flank of NATO, for example, a "passive" defense line thrown across the Greenland-Iceland-United Kingdom Gap will somehow protect our sea-lanes or defer an engagement with Soviet forces demonstrates a lack of understanding of the fundamental mechanics of war at sea and the workings of NATO and the Soviets' own operational requirements. No coalition of free nations can survive a strategy which begins by sacrificing its more exposed allies to a dubious military expediency. To suggest that naval support of Norway or Turkey is too dangerous because it must be done close to the Soviet Union is defeatist. To suggest that such a strategy is provocative of the Soviets just indicates the lengths to which some critics will go, in order to portray Soviet intentions as solely defensive.

As for strengthening our continental defenses, we and our allies are also doing just that. To discard maritime superiority in an attempt to match the larger Soviet ground forces, however, would give us neither conventional deterrence on land nor secure access by sea unless the Western democracies are prepared to militarize their societies to an unprecedented, and unwise, degree.

ARE WE BUYING THE 'RIGHT' NAVY FOR THE STRATEGY?

Because research and development projects span decades, and ships take many years to build, the makeup of our fleet can not change radically with each administration. Instead, the fleet evolves over time with policy and technology. The fleet today reflects the wisdom of the deck plates, the labs, and lessons learned from our exercises. The size and design of our ships and weapons reflect the inputs of sailors in contact with Soviet "Victor" submarines, *Kiev*-class carriers, and "Bear" aircraft. The wisdom of common sense and the highest available technology are tremendous advantages, brought to the design of today's Navy and Marine Corps.

Of course, there are many kinds of ships not in the fleet today that could do very well. The British *Invincible*-class vertical or short take-off and landing (VSTOL) carriers are quite capable antisubmarine warfare ships. It would be nice to have some of them in the U.S. Navy. There are many attractive European frigate designs, and we could make good use of them. There are also diesel submarines in our European alliance navies that fulfill very effective roles.

If the taxpayers of our allies around the world were not buying these vessels, the burden would fall upon us. But happily, they are carrying a considerable share of the cost of naval defense and American taxpayers do not have to fund a Navy greater than about 600 ships.

Perhaps the most debated issue on newspapers' front pages and television talk shows is whether our aircraft carriers should be large or small. There is no absolute answer to this question, but in my view, the evidence still seems overwhelmingly in favor of the *Nimitz* (CVN-68)-class carrier of 90,000 tons as the optimum size and design for putting air capability at sea.

Could we gainfully employ more mid-size carriers like our 64,000-ton *Midway* (CV-41) and *Coral Sea* (CV-43)? Yes, indeed. They would be very useful. The Navy would like to have five more of them if we could afford to buy them. At least, we will keep these two smaller carriers steaming in the force for a long time to come.

Similarly, with our nuclear attack submarines, we could buy more of them if we compromised on their capabilities. But our tremendous edge in technology is a permanent potential built into the nature of our culture and our economic system compared with the Soviets. We must build to this advantage, and not trade it away for cheaper, smaller, less capable ships built in greater numbers, which is the forte of a totalitarian, centralized, Gosplan economy.

It would be a great mistake for us to adopt a defense strategy at sea—any more than on land—that attempts to match totalitarian regimes in sheer numbers of cheap reproducible items. Time and again, the high-tech solution has proved to be the wisest investment, and by far the most advantageous one for the United States and its allies. This is true of our missiles, our aircraft, and our ships. We have the world's finest fighting equipment.

So we are getting the "right" Navy. Although there are plenty of other kinds of ships we would like to have, and we could certainly use the larger Navy long advocated by the Joint Chiefs, we have stayed consistently with the 600-ship fleet because we are prepared to bet that our allies will continue to maintain modern, effective navies and air forces. We are prepared to accept the risk that our nation will make the right decisions to prevent losses of forces early in a conflict, and we think that that is a prudent risk to run in order to have an affordable Navy.

CAN WE AFFORD THE NAVY THIS NATION NEEDS?

Numerous studies and surveys, among them a tome by the Congressional Budget Office, suggest that we cannot afford to sustain, or properly man, a 600-ship Navy. Just the reverse is true. Consider the facts. We have now, under construction and fully funded, *all* of the ships necessary to attain a 600-ship Navy centered on 15 carrier battle groups, four battleship surface action groups, and 100 nuclear-powered attack submarines.

Our long-term plans in a "zero growth" budget for fiscal year 1986 now reflect reductions in our shipbuilding and aircraft procurement programs. These reductions will be to levels we call the sustaining rate for the 600-ship Navy, an average 20 ships a year in new construction. The actual number will be higher or lower in a given year, depending on the block obsolescence of various types of ships.

The 20-ship average is a sound basis for planning, in part because of improved maintenance and the corresponding increase in longevity. Instead of the average 26 years of life that we realized from our ships in the 1960s and the 1970s, we are now getting 30 years' service from our ships, because of better maintenance, the absence of a big backlog of overhauls, and the higher technology that we are putting into our ships.

This "good news" should not blind us to the requirements of the future. A steady 20-new-ships-a-year average will require a 3% budget growth. A future of zero-growth budgets would mean that we will be unable to sustain a 600-ship Navy—or for that matter, a capable defense. We know from painful experience in the 1970s that the damage done by no-growth funding is far greater than the mere percentage budget loss would indicate. With zero- or negative-growth budgets, the industrial infrastructure vital to fleet construction and support shrinks dramatically. The result is a loss in competitive bidding and a return to sole-sourced monopolies. Rates of production must then be cut, individual unit costs increase dramatically, productivity falls, and, in the final accounting, the American taxpayer gets much less "bang for the buck." Even worse is the decline in the quality and morale of the people who man the fleet, as we saw in the late 1970s.

Is 3% real growth beyond our means? Throughout the past two decades, many commentators favoring a reduced defense effort have repeatedly predicted that the American people will not support sustained defense growth. That refrain is now put forward by some, including the Congressional Budget Office, as a fact of life. While it may express their hopes, it is not supported by history. That view takes as its norm the flat or even declining figures of the immediate post-Vietnam War period. In fact, except for those years, post-World War II naval budgets maintained growth commensurate with our national economy.

The middle and late Seventies, by contrast, are now being seen as an anomaly in U.S. history. It is not apparent, the Congressional Budget Office notwithstanding, that the American people wish to "restore" that aberrant pattern of declining numbers of ships, morale, and readiness.

In procurement, we should not assume that Congress will refuse to make the necessary legislative changes in the way we in the Department of the Navy are permitted to conduct our business. Indeed, I suggest that, in the current aura of public concern over budget deficits and government spending, there would be a few more cost-effective and money-saving moves that Congress could undertake than the removal of excessive regulations and red tape that characterize the environment in which the Navy operates today. For example, there repose in the Library of Congress today no less than 1,152 linear feet of statutory and regulatory law governing procurement alone! That is the *real* Washington Monument!

Along with over-regulation, we are faced with excessive, layered bureaucracies, and the accretion of authority without concomitant responsibility into a confusing labyrinth of congressional oversight committees and federal agencies without end, creating tremendous inefficiencies.

The Congressional Budget Office staffers and others who look at the Navy's future costs assume that just because this bloated, inefficient congressional-executive system has been in place it will *remain* in place. I do not accept that. Moreover, we have shown in the Navy a historic reversal of the trend of inevitable cost increases.

Today, for example, the last contract that we signed for a follow-on Aegis cruiser was $900 million. Four years ago, these cruisers cost more that $1.2 billion each, and were projected to reach $1.6 billion by the end of 1985. It did not happen, though, because we brought competition into the program. Both producing yards brought in new efficiencies and instituted strict cost discipline, while we in the Navy applied a new asceticism to our gold-plating lusts. All of our shipbuilding programs show the same pattern. We have gone from only 24% competition in 1981 to 90% competition in 1985, producing an average of $1 billlion in cost *under*runs for each of the last four years.

Contrary to what the nay-sayers predicted, the costs of Navy aircraft have been going down, not up. This is a sea change, a break with 30 years of uninterrupted cost escalation in the naval aircraft procurement. During 1976–1981, growth in aircraft unit prices averaged about 10% in constant fiscal year 1980 dollars. In 1981, we implemented vigorous cost management programs which emphasized competition, no design changes, and firm fixed-price contracts. These efforts have paid off in reduced aircraft prices every year since 1982.

For example, we reached agreement with McDonnell Douglas on a fiscal year 1985 fly-away price of $18.7 million for the F/A-18 strike fighter. In terms of fiscal year 1982 dollars, this is a price 32% below that paid in 1982. Purchases in 1985 represent a savings to the taxpayer of $126 million for that year alone.

So, there is nothing inevitable about escalating costs and overruns in defense procurement. During the last four years we proved that it can be just as consistent to have underruns. And so if we just make prudent assumptions, not even optimistic assumptions, there is no question that we can maintain the size and the current mix of our force through the rest of this century with a 3% growth budget.

Just as significant, we can also maintain the tremendous turn-around in readiness that we have achieved with President Ronald Reagan's 7% growth budgets. During the past four years, the readiness of our ships and aircraft has increased nearly 40%. Even these statistics do not do justice to the palpable difference in the fleet itself, in morale, in readiness, and in safety—i.e., uncrashed airplanes and unbroken equipment and reduction of tragic accidents.

We know what we have accomplished during the past five years. Furthermore, we know we can maintain this record of success with the size budgets that are currently envisioned by the President.

The German military philosopher Clausewitz once observed that in the balance of power among nations, battle is to deterrence as cash is to credit in the world of commerce. One may live entirely by paper transactions *only* when there is no doubt about one's ability to settle accounts with hard currency when challenged.

Similarly, there must be no doubt in the minds of the Soviet leaders that the United States and its allies can and will settle accounts, on both land and sea, if challenged. The 600-ship Navy is an essential element in this credibility. We *can,* and *must,* afford the naval power that will sustain the defense of this country's allies and interests around the world.

COPYRIGHTS AND ACKNOWLEDGMENTS

This page constitutes an extension of the copyright page. Grateful acknowledgment is made to the following authors, publishers, and agents for permission to use the articles. Every effort has been made to seek and secure permission from copyright holders. We respectfully acknowledge the material represented and will make changes to the attributions in future printings should any questions arise.

Archibald, Roger. "Six Ships that Shook the World." Invention and Technology, Fall 1997: 24-37. Reprinted by permission of American Heritage, Inc. 1997.

Barlow, Jeffrey G. "The Revolt of the Admirals Reconsidered." New Interpretations in Naval History: Selected Papers from the Eighth Naval History Symposium, 1989. Copyright © 1989 Naval Institute Press. Reprinted by permission.

Beach, Edward L. "Mutiny?" The United States Navy: 200 Years, 1986, pp. 177-195. Reprinted by permission of SLL/Sterling Lord Literistic, Inc. Copyright by Edward L. Beach.

Brooke, George M., Jr. "The Role of the United States Navy in the Suppression of the African Slave Trade." American Neptune article courtesy of Peabody Essex Museum, Salem, MA © 1961.

Brown, David J. "The Battle of the Atlantic, 1941-1943: Peaks and Troughs." From TO DIE GALLANTLY by TIMOTHY RUNYAN and JAN COPES. Copyright © 1994 by Westview Press. Reprinted by permission of Westview Press, a member of Perseus Books, L.L.C.

Cagle, Malcolm W., Commander (USN). "Errors of the Korean War." Reprinted from *Proceedings* with permission; Copyright © 1958 U.S. Naval Institute/www.usni.org.

Conrad, Dennis. "John Paul Jones, the Ranger, and the Value of the Continental Navy." Sea History 100, pp. 9-13. Copyright © National Maritime Historical Society, Spring 2002. Reprinted by permission.

Deac, Wilfred P. “The Battle off Samar.” American Heritage Magazine, December 1966. Reprinted by permission of American Heritage, Inc. 1966.

Felker, Craig C. Testing American Sea Power: U.S. Navy Strategic Exercise, 1923-1940, Chapter Two, Texas A&M University Press, 2007. Reprinted by permission.

Frederick S. Harrod, MANNING THE NEW NAVY: THE DEVELOPMENT OF A MODERN ENLISTED FORCE, 1899-1940 (Westport, Conn: Greenwood, 1978), Chap 10 "Life of a Sailor," pp.140-65. Reproduced with permission of ABC-CLIO, LLC.

Krulak, Victor H. “A New Kind of War.” First to Fight: An Inside View of the U.S. Marine Corps, 1984. Copyright © 1984 Naval Institute Press. Reprinted by permission.

Krulak, Victor H. “The Amphibious Assault and How it Grew.” First to Fight: An Inside View of the U.S. Marine Corps, 1984. Copyright © 1984 Naval Institute Press. Reprinted by permission.

Lehman, John. “The 600-Ship Navy”, Reprinted from *Proceedings* with permission, Copyright © Jan. 1986, pp. 30 – 40, US Naval Institute/www.usni.org.

Linn, Brian McAllister. “We Will Go Heavily Armed: The Marines Small War on Samar.” *New Interpretations in Naval History: Selected Papers From the Ninth Naval History Symposium*. Edited by William R. Roberts and Jack Seetman. U.S. Naval Institute Press, 1991. Reprinted by permission.

McBride, William M. “Technological Change and the United States Navy, 1865-1945. pp. 139-156. Copyright © 2000 The Johns Hopkins University Press. Reprinted with permission of The Johns Hopkins University Press.

Miller, Edward S. “War Plan Orange, 1897-1941: The Blue Thrust Through the Pacific.” Naval History: The Seventh Symposium of the U.S. Naval Academy edited by William Cogar, pp. 239-248. Copyright © 1988 by Scholarly Resources. Reprinted by permission of Copyright Clearance Center.

Morison, Samuel Eliot. "The Somers Mutiny." From OLD BRUIN by Samuel Eliot Morison. Copyright © 1967 by Emily Beck, Elizabeth Spingarn and Catherine Morison Cooper. By permission of Little, Brown and Company, (Inc.)

Prothero, Ernest. "Life in the Age of Sail." The British Navy: Its Making and its Meaning by Ernest Prothero. Copyright © 1914 by E.P. Dutton and Company.

Rothenberg, Gunther E. and Merrill Bartlett. "From Gallipoli to Guadalcanal." Assault from the Sea, 1983. Copyright © 1983 Naval Institute Press. Reprinted by permission.

Sherwood, John Darrell. BLACK SAILOR, WHITE NAVY: RACIAL UNREST IN THE FLEET DURING THE VIETNAM WAR ERA (New York: New York University Press, 2007), Chap 1 "The Black Sailor," pp. 1-15.

Spector, Ronald H. "The Haves and the Have-Nots", "Never in All MyYears Had I Imagined a Battle Like That:, from AT WAR AT SEA: SAILORS AND NAVAL COMBAT IN THE 20TH CENTURY by Ronald H. Spector, copyright © 2001 Ronald H. Spector. Used by permission of Viking Penguin, a division of Penguin Group (USA) Inc.

Still, William N., Jr. "A Naval Sieve: The Union Blockade in the Civil War." Naval War College Review, May/June 1983.

Symonds, Craig L. "The Anti-Navalists: The Opponents of Naval Expansion in the Early National Period." American Neptune article courtesy of Peabody Essex Museum, Salem, MA © 1961.

Zumwalt, Elmo R., Jr. Admiral U.S. Navy. "High-Low." On Watch: A Memoir, 1976. Copyright © 1976 Adm. Elmo R. Zumwalt, Jr.